SURVIV
THE FA

C000070266

An alternative review of the
'96-97 football season

Compiled and edited by

David Jenkins

&

Judi Holly

Red Card
Publishing

Survival of the Fattest 3
An alternative review of the '96-97 football season

Front cover illustration by
David Banks

First published in 1997 by
RED CARD PUBLISHING LIMITED
4 Bowater Place
Blackheath
London
SE3 8ST

British Library Cataloguing in Publication Data.
A catalogue record for this book is available from the British Library

ISBN 0 9526610 20

Printed and bound in Great Britain by
Mackays of Chatham Plc

CONTENTS

Contents

CHEAT'S LIST (Contents in order of club)

CHEAT'S LIST, CONT.

CHEAT'S LIST, CONT.

ROLL OF HONOUR

Our thanks go to this book's contributors who managed to send in the articles which appear in these pages. To all of you who risk health, wealth and happiness in the pursuit of your obsession: thanks for making the sometimes frustrating and heart-breaking business of supporting our teams more enjoyable.

This year, the constraints of space and budget (we're from the Barry Fry school of astute financial management) do not allow us room for individual *Fanzine Facts* following each article. However we couldn't publish *Survival of the Fattest* without giving credit where it's due: to the people who help to write, produce and sell the fanzines. Below is a 'roll of honour' of the main people, as far as we know, who edit the mags included in this book. In each case, the articles' authors (where known) are listed first. Apologies to those we've forgotten or missed, and also to the thousands of other un-named contributors; it's not much consolation, but *you* know who you are!

Fanzine	Author/editor/s
The 2nd Of May	Hazel Potter, Ian Marriott
The 69er	Anna Merriman, Craig Jack
A Large Scotch	Kevin, Gary Bright, Adrian Plimmer, Rob Palmer
A Load Of Bull	Charles Ross
A Lot 2 Answer 4	Dominic Daley
A Love Supreme	Tom Lynn, Martin McFadden
A Slice of Kilner Pie	Phil Humphreys
The Abbey Rabbit	Steve Jillings
The Adams Family	Andy Dickinson, Jon Dickinson, Dave Chapman
All Quiet On The Western Ave	Peter Doherty, Adam 'Kebab' Wheeler
Another View From The Tower	The ed
Another Vintage Liverpool Performance	Andy Hampson, Roy Gilfoyle
Are You Blue Or Are You Blind?	Francis Fowles
Bamber's Right Foot	Hayden Jones
Beyond The Boundary	Pete Mason
The Blue And Wight	Colin Farmery, Chris Hougham
The Blue Eagle	Jason Skinner, Robert Searle
Brian Moore's Head	Simon Baker, Chris Lynham, Eddy Alcorn, Professor Tarquin Zoological-Garden
Cheat!	Chris Hogg
Cheep Shot	Martin Betts, Julie Carmichael
The Chelsea Independent	Mark Meehan, Andrew Wrench

City Gent .... Richard Halfpenny, John Watmough,
David Pendleton

Clap Your Hands, Stamp Your
Feet .... Matthew Bentote, Ron Manager,
Vic A Rage

The Claret Flag .... Matthew Pasiewicz

Cock A Doodle Doo .... Martin Cloake

The Crooked Spireite .... Craig Thomas

Cumberland Sausage .... Roger Lytollis

Deranged Ferret .... Gary Parle, Kevin Stow

Eastern Eagles .... Trevor Edwards

Exceedingly Good Pies .... Mark Wilbrahim, Matthew Smith,
S Elvidge

Exiled! .... Andy Burton, Gordon Buchan,
Adrian Smith

Ferry Across The Wensum .... Jim Emerson

Flashing Blade .... Matthew Bell

Fly Me To The Moon .... Robert Nichols, Sharon Caddell,
Bob Fisher

Follow The Yellow Brick Road ...... Keith Parnill

Forest Forever .... Richard Fisher

Give Us An R .... David Goat

The Gooner .... Mike Francis

Grorty Dick .... Glynis Wright

Gull's Eye .... Eldrich, Billy Watson, Lenny Rider

Gwladys Sings The Blues .... James Corbett, David Pearson

Hanging On The Telephone .... Mick , Mini, Wights

The Hanging Sheep .... Chris Stringer

The Hatchet .... Chris Bainbridge, Jeff Hoyle,
Tony Dallas

Heaven 11 .... Simon Blackburn, Jonnie Blackburn,
Peter Stevens

Heroes And Villains .... Dave Woodhall

Hey Big Spender .... Mark Aldridge, The Shadow,
Simon Evans

Highbury High .... Tony Madden, Ian Trevett

The Holy Trinity .... Steve Whitehouse, Steve Hood,
Rob Rodway

In Dublin's Fair City .... Paul Wheeler

Into the O's Zone .... Andy Campbell

Iron Filings .... Andy Skeels

January 3rd, '88 .... Steve Bone, Michael Whitcombe

Keegan Was Crap Really .... Phil Martin, Alan Caldwell,
Karen Wright

Kicker Conspiracy .... 'Ed Lines'

King Of The Kippax .... Ged Isaacs
The Latic Fanatic .... Andrew Werrill
Leyton Orientear .... Jamie Stripe, Tom Davies,
                                  Stephen Harris
The Lion Roars .... Carl Prosser, Paul Casella
Liverpool Are On The Tele Again Ian 'Duke' Lindsay, Martin Betts
Loadsamoney .... Paul Loftus
The Mighty Shrew .... Mark Fielden
Mission Impossible .... Steve Harland, Steve Raine,
                                  Dave Sowerby
Monkey Business .... Paul Mullen
Moulin Rouge .... Matt Norcliffe, Hugh Vaughan
Moving Swiftly On .... Andrew Poole
No More Pie In The Sky .... Ivan 'Bart' Bainbridge, 'The Band'
No-One Likes Us .... The Albatross, The Jocko, Alex Hall
Not The 8502 .... Gavin Meadon, Mick Cunningham
The Number Nine .... Steve Wraith, Rob Wraith, John Wraith
The Oatcake .... Martin Smith
On The Terraces .... Marc Williams
One More Point .... Cris Lehmann, Wags, Safety,
                                  Tony Dobson
One Nil Down Two One Up .... Mike Collins, Tony Willis
One Team In Bristol .... Andrew Jefferson, Rob Humphries
The Onion Bag .... Jon Wainwright
Over Land And Sea .... Gary Firmager
The Peterborough Effect .... Andy Groome
The Pie .... Electric Steve & Sue Westby,
                                  Neil McGowan
Pie Muncher .... Steve Brennan
Rage On .... Beavis, Boris, Mr G Love
Randy Robin .... Matthew Arnold
Red All Over The Land .... John Pearman
Red Card .... Alan Collis
Roots Hall Roar .... Bob Sills, Mark Withers
Rub Of The Greens .... David Pay, Steve Nicholson,
                                  Tony Scowcroft
The Seadog Bites Back .... James Hunter
Seaside Saga .... Marc Twibill, Paul Libel, Jackie Mooney
The Sheeping Giant .... Richard 'Dai Shovett' Sympson,
                                  Gavin Evans, Bryn & Tom Law
The Silence Of The Lamb .... Sheridan Monks
Sing When We're Fishing .... Steve Plowes, Jim Connor
Son Of A Referee .... Paul Singleton
Sour Grapes .... Jane Hart, Richard Crabtree

South Riding	Cuthbert Blasphemy, Iggy Stallybrass, Fatboy
Speke From The Harbour	Mark Staniford
Spitting Feathers	Graham Lightfoot
The Sunderland Fanatic	Robert Stein
Super Dario Land	Jules Hornbrook
Talk Of The Tyne	Michael Swan, Kev Fletcher
Talking Bull	Chris Jones, Nigel Preece, Elaine Harrison
The Tea Party	Martin Frost, David Espley
There's a good time coming (be it ever so far away)	Alan Crockford, Andrew Dye, Dave Peters
There's Only One F In Fulham	David Lloyd, John Gordon
The Thin Blue Line	Andrew Turton
Those Were The Days	Philip Ham, Steven Mellen
Tiger Rag	Geoff Bradley, Andy Medcalf
Till The World Stops	Pete Vale
The Tommy Cook Report	Matthew Griffin, David Jarvis
The Tricky Tree	Andy Lowe, Neil Shaw
Tripe 'N' Trotters	Chris 'n' Dave, Gary Parkinson
Two Together	John Cosgrove, Hugh Godwin
The Ugly Inside	Clive Foley, Nick Illingworth
United We Stand	Steve Black, Andy Mitten
Voice Of The Beehive	Rob Bartram
Voice Of The Valley	Rick Everitt
Wake Up Blue	Steve Caffrey, Dave Branwood
We Are Leeds	Steve Abbott
What A Load Of Cobblers	Rob Marshall
What's The Story, Southend Glory!	Harry the Hat, Dave, Tony Hall
When Skies Are Grey	Phil Redmond, Graham Ennis, Dave Swaffield
When You're Smiling	Geoff, Tom, Jock Lobster
Where Were You At The Shay?	Craig Clarkson
Where's The Money Gone?	'Buckets', John Regan
Where's The Money Gone?	Daniel King
White Love	Dick Smiley, Ray Burke, Paul Hanley
Wot! No Quarters?	The Eternal Optimist, Mr Angry
Yidaho!	Colin Leonard, Peter Jones, Jamie Johnson
Zulu	Dave Small

INTRODUCTION

Survival of the Fattest 3 is a compilation of articles from fanzines throughout England and Wales, reviewing the on and off-field goings-on at the clubs in the Carling Premiership and the Nationwide League Divisions One, Two and Three.

Although the articles within these pages have been edited, the theme, often passionate and heartfelt, and the content, sometimes raw and controversial, remain as the author(s) intended. We may not agree with some of the sentiments expressed in these pages but very little gets taken out.

RANTING FROM THE EDS

Welcome to the third and probably the best edition of *Survival of the Fattest* yet. Whether you're a regular reader or whether this is your first experience of SOTF *(back issues are still available!)*, we'd sincerely like to thank you for stumping up the cash to buy the book and for allowing us to complete this third tome.

You might think that the two of us relish the opportunity to say our bit here, having read and edited nearly 250,000 words of other people's writings, but the truth is, there is very little we can add that isn't already said within these pages. We're both pretty emotionally drained anyway, as one of us is a follower of a certain homeless, expulsion-threatened South Coast club, and the other is a euphorically exhausted East Midlander eternally grateful for the efforts of Martin O'Neill and the boys. However, we would like to wish this country's first Football League community club Bournemouth success over the next few months. The animals, as some club directors in unguarded moments might describe fans, have well and truly taken over the asylum (to mix a metaphor or two), and it'll be interesting to see how they get on. Congratulations also go to Hull City who, since *Tiger Rag* penned their article, look like they've finally sorted out their problems. Wonder if Tim Henman's any good up front...

Finally, good luck to Hereford in the Conference; hopefully no other group of fans will ever have to suffer the blood-curdling agonies that 8,500-odd of us witnessed at Edgar Street on May 3rd 1997.

Enjoy the book!

David Jenkins & Judi Holly

SPECIAL THANKS

Thanks are due again to the unstinting efforts of our typist Mags and the sterling job done by cartoonist David Banks, who we think has outdone himself this year and produced the best cover so far. Also warranting a special mention this year are Pete Bro (no pun intended, Pete) and Rich and family in the States.

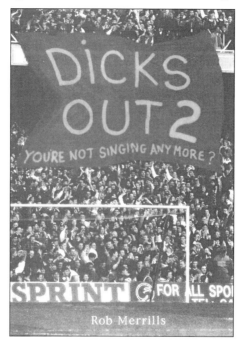

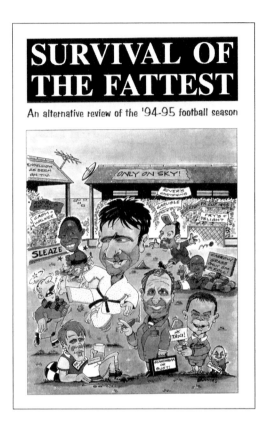

Limited numbers of both books are available from the publishers.

To order your copies, send a cheque/PO for £9.99 per book (includes P&P) made payable to Red Card Publishing Ltd to: Red Card Publishing, 4 Bowater Place, Blackheath, London SE3 8ST.

Bookseller's note: ISBN SOTF1: 0952661004; SOTF2: 0952661012

THE 2ND OF MAY

Bristol Rovers

Gasheads began the season with their usual (and almost always misplaced) optimism. After all, the prodigal son had returned in the shape of Ian Holloway, and Rovers were back in Bristol at the Memorial Ground, only a short distance from their spiritual home of Eastville. Holloway, a Gashead from birth, would surely get the whole team playing with his customary enthusiasm - not to mention instill in them the belief that they were playing for the greatest team in the world.

It didn't quite go to plan. On August 17th we found ourselves not in Bristol but back in Bath for our first home game. The Memorial Ground had failed to meet the

THE SECOND OF MAY
An independent view of Bristol Rovers F.C.   £1

CICA Prototype Revealed

standards required by the ever-pedantic and surely City-supporting Bristol City Council, so instead of a homecoming we had another farewell to Twerton Park. We also had a new kit - with the rest of the country introducing quarters, we had managed to abandon ours in favour of something resembling a Tesco carrier bag! The visitors were Peterborough, themselves looking forward to the new leadership of Barry Fry. Fry himself spent the afternoon resembling a beached whale on the touchline, wearing just a pair of shorts. In retrospect, getting a suntan was probably the best thing the afternoon could offer. A very poor Peterborough were beaten 1-0 by a Rovers side who weren't much better, in a display that was not so much the beautiful game but one of the ugly sisters.

After a tedious 0-0 draw with newly-promoted Preston, who seemed more comatose than sleeping giants, it really was our homecoming. Players past were paraded and balloons galore launched at the Memorial as Rovers finally made it back to the city they had left over ten years earlier. Our suspicions about the leanings of the council were confirmed as the Mayoress appeared dressed in red, and for the first time at our new home the heart-warming chant of "Shithead, shithead" made itself heard. The game itself, a 1-1 draw with Stockport, was less important than the event itself. To be back home was incredibly significant for Gasheads. Not least because City could no longer taunt us with "One team in Bristol" chants. OK, so it was a rugby pitch and the grass was way too long, not to mention one goal was higher than the other, but it was Bristol and in the end that's what mattered. The homecoming celebrations lasted well into the night as groups of Rovers fans staggered down Gloucester Road on the seemingly endless pub-crawl towards town.

Rovers enjoyed their first home-town win against Bournemouth. Unfortunately, the rollercoaster nature of the season was already becoming apparent, our unbeaten run at home lasting just four days when old boy Devon White returned to score the only goal for relegated Watford. It was to be the first of 17 games we were to lose by the odd goal.

They say that there are two certainties in life - death and taxes. For Rovers fans, add midweek defeat at Wrexham. On a more serious note, at a time when Bosman is threatening the very existence of smaller clubs, does it really make economic sense for the Football League computer to come up with midweek trips to Wrexham, York and Rotherham?

Anyway, we then travelled to Plymouth. It's always one of those strange games at Home Park. Plymouth see it as a local derby, not having anyone nearer, but all we can muster is a mild dislike. Inevitably Plymouth fans try and scale the double fence to the Rovers end, inevitably they fail (you'd have thought they'd have learnt by now) and inevitably you get kept in for hours and then have to clamber through the seats along the stand to get out. This time, however, we didn't mind the wait much. A Lee Archer strike gave Rovers our first away win of the season and we'd have savoured it a bit more if we'd known how long the next one was going to be in coming... It was also a promising debut for new signing Jamie Cureton who was to show his worth with four goals in the next three games.

The Plymouth game, along with Cureton's arrival, marked the beginning of a seven match unbeaten spell for The Gas. Soon afterwards we faced high-flying Brentford. The 5,163 there that night were treated to an excellent performance by both the Rovers team and an unexpected source - the Phantom Whistle Blower. As Brentford 'keeper Dearden looked around for a non-existent fourth official, Marcus Browning nipped in to score Rovers' second goal! Such was the enormity of the gaffe, it made both *News at Ten* and *A Question of Sport* - probably the first time we've featured on the latter since Barry Daines' infamous moment of madness for Spurs back at Eastville in the 1970's.

It wasn't the only time we made the telly, the FA Cup usually sees to that. It has often been said that Rovers' road to Wembley tends to mean breaking down on the M32, but hopes were high this year following a pairing with lowly Exeter City. Surely we couldn't lose at home to the Third Division strugglers, and even if we did, we wouldn't receive the same exposure on *Match of the Day* as we had the year before following our pathetic exit at the hands of Hitchin Town. Such was the anticipation that two cardboard FA Cups - complete with silver foil - appeared in the pub prior to the match. Yes, you've got it. We had 25 corners, they got two goals, and to rub it in, the lack of other giant-killing acts (if you can call any Rovers cup defeat an upset) ensured that our annual appearance on *Match of the Day* was secured yet again.

Following the Exeter fiasco and a couple of 2-1 defeats, the murmurings were starting on the terraces. And so to December, the season of 'goodwill', a term which can be interpreted in different ways, as Gasheads were to find out... December 16th, away at Trashton Gate, home of our not-so-friendly rivals Bristol City, live on *Sky*. It looked as though we were heading for defeat until Peter Beadle, hero of last year's Ashton derby, scored an equaliser in the last minute. What happened next has been well documented, and led to the *Sky* presenters uttering the phrase 'disgraceful scenes' on at least ten occasions! As a couple of Rovers fans spilled onto the pitch in the celebrations that followed the goal, hundreds of City fans ran on and over to the Rovers end. To Gasheads it wasn't a great surprise - for as long as we can remember City fans have tried to storm the pitch from the same area, usually resorting to tearing up their own ground in frustration. Granted, we didn't expect them to attack our players after the pitch had been cleared once, nor that they may be allowed to get to the away end after the game had finished and chuck missiles at families, but their general behaviour was sadly predictable. We're usually thankful to get out of the place in one piece - a point or more is a bonus.

Goodwill of a more conventional kind was forthcoming the following week with the visit of bottom-placed Wycombe. With 20 minutes to go, we were 3-1 up and Wanderers looked happy just to avoid a cricket score. Just imagine how much happier they were when Man Mountain/Freak Terry Evans headed in their fourth with just a couple of minutes to go. The Boxing Day fixture was Bournemouth away - and there are very few Gasheads who can remember a win at Dean Court. '96-97 was no different, with a 1-0 defeat. Rovers had now slumped to 15th in the table and still only had one away win under their belts.

1997 and we all had renewed hopes, but it wasn't to be. The weather and our lack of involvement in the cup meant only three fixtures in January - and we went into February still without a win! However, this was probably our most successful month of the season - only one defeat, away to Gillingham, and good home wins against Shrewsbury, Luton and Plymouth (our first double of the campaign!). Many Gasheads had hoped that the midweek victory over Plymouth would signal the end of our flirtation with the relegation zone. But disappointment was to follow, with the 2-0 defeat at Wycombe widely seen as the lowest point of the season so far. Talk of relegation was now rife on the terraces and the prickly question of whether you should clap your team after a shameful performance resulted in a couple of minor scuffles amongst Gasheads on the way out. Surely we couldn't go down - Rovers were the only side never to have been in the highest or lowest divisions - and we were desperate to keep our record!

It was a pity that the fans' passion didn't transmit itself to the team, as were treated to one of the most lacklustre home derby performances in living memory, going down 2-1. To make matters worse, the game had seen us awarded what was to be our only penalty of the season. Unfortunately, Peter Beadle hit it so feebly that visiting 'keeper Naylor probably had time to visit his mother in West Bromwich before retrieving it from the edge of the six yard box. Ah well, at least we didn't feel the need to imitate our neighbours and attack the City players afterwards.

By now, the R-word was being mentioned regularly. Something had to be done. Thankfully, it was. Out went youth team coach Tony Gill and first team coach Terry Connor - both rumoured to be unpopular amongst the players - and in came ex-Rovers' favourite Phil Bater. The backroom staff was now true blue, and a couple of astute tactical changes resulted in a much more effective team. A 1-0 defeat of Preston - which left their manager Gary Peters whining about having to play on a 'cowfield' - was greeted with a final whistle cheer that suggested we'd just won the cup. The subsequent arrivals of the vastly experienced Brian Gayle and Jamie Clapham on loan, together with February signing Julian 'Demolition Man' Alsop reaching full match fitness meant that Rovers were, somewhat belatedly, getting away from danger. The Preston game was followed by maximum points over Easter, including our second away win of the season at Peterborough. Six months is a long time in football, and Barry Fry's opening day jollity was now nowhere to be seen. Instead, he was reduced to effing and blinding on national television. The 2-0 home defeat of Wrexham on Easter Monday just about guaranteed our survival and ensured a carnival atmosphere. Even Wrexham's Joey Jones joined in the spirit of the occasion by volleying a half-eaten pasty which had somehow found its way out of the nearby terrace!

It was somewhat fitting that our last away game of the season was at Blackpool - the home of the rollercoaster - and it can only be described as one of the most surreal games ever. First of all, there was the sight of 1,500 Gasheads enjoying a beach party in the rain, with ex-Shithead Mickey Mellon being bombarded with beach balls, rubber dinghies and even an inflatable woman every time he took a corner! Then there was the game. With Blackpool one place behind City in the play-off race, there was the bizarre case of the away fans actually cheering the home end. Hence, each of the five goals in a thrilling 3-2 home win was greeted with ecstatic jumping around from the travelling Gasheads.

After that, the final game was a bit of an anti-climax. It should have been a nice easy victory, but hating to conform, we managed to lose to Rotherham. However, our season wasn't quite over. Bristol City had managed to make the play-offs under the leadership of former Rovers boss John Ward, and we were quite understandably tense. Sadly, City scored twice. What a shame then that Brentford got four!

THE 69'ER

Swindon Town

In his first full managerial term at Swindon, Steve McMahon guided us to the Second Division Championship - a season of only four defeats and a record-breaking 13 away wins - but as we entered the '96-97 campaign, most Swindon supporters recognised that the challenge was to establish a comfortable foothold in the First Division. While it may have been too much to hope for involvement in the Premiership shake-up, we certainly didn't expect to struggle against relegation.

There was a dearth of new faces during the close season: Mark Walters, Kevin Watson and Peter Holcroft all arrived on frees and Scott Leitch lightened our purse by

Issue 23
February 1997

80P

The 69er

In Control?

£80,000. Lack of money was already a problem. In fact, only two more money signings were made during the entire season: Gary Elkins from Wimbledon for £110,000 - supposedly to solve our age-old left-back problem - and Darren Bullock from Huddersfield in March for somewhere around £400,000. The one truly excellent signing of the season - Marlon Broomes from Blackburn - was unfortunately nothing more than a loaner. I mean, why would they have wanted to sell a 19 year old who might play for England - and could we have afforded him anyway?

We were still singing 'Ciampioni, Ciampioni' when Norwich brought us down to earth with a bump on the very first day. With the 'pace' in our defence we were left hoping there weren't many more forwards as fleet-footed as Darren Eadie in the First.

As early as August, McMahon made his first mistake. Team captain and Player of the Year Shaun Taylor was dropped and sold a week later to local rivals Bristol City for £100,000 amid rumours of a dustup with the boss. "A good deal for Shaun and for the Town" said the club. Oh yeah - not when the replacement Mark Seagraves was slower, less talented with his feet and less able with his head than Taylor. McMahon immediately gave him the captain's armband and in so doing made Seagraves the least popular Town skipper in most people's memories.

In October, the Crystal Palace game at Selhurst Park provided us with another sign of things to come when a multi-player scuffle produced six Swindon yellow cards and one sending off. And this just as we were running a feature in *The 69er* on the fact that we'd not had a red since the end of the '94-95 season. Mark Walters broke the run with a second bookable offence, but his was only the first of six other early baths during the course of the season. So much activity in the ref's notebook inevitably meant key players missing through suspension, but when questioned about the team's poor disciplinary record, McMahon somewhat curiously said that he expected players to "look after each other." This presumably explained why during the mass brawl against Manchester City at the County Ground in November, players ran 20 yards to get involved, and why in February Peter Holcroft - 'the new Kevin Sheedy' - got sent off on his debut for elbowing Paul Dickov.

Frank Talia then felt the McMahon backlash after a dreadful goalkeeping display at home to West Brom in October left him dropped for the rest of the season. Still, with McMahon not averse to the odd knee-jerk reaction he shouldn't have been surprised. This gave another of McMahon's least favourite players Fraser Digby the chance to show the boss what he'd been missing and he didn't disappoint, playing brilliantly and justifiably winning the Player of the Season award. No doubt he'll be on his way soon!

Over Christmas and New Year league results were mediocre to say the least. Home draws against relegation-haunted Bradford and Grimsby were of little comfort, and three away defeats including a third round FA Cup knock-out by Everton made things worse. Ian Culverhouse's cup interlude was short-lived in the extreme. Adjudged to have handled the ball on the goal-line in the first minute, he was already off down the tunnel as we settled in our seats, and in the end we were happy enough to get off with a 3-0 defeat.

The 69er spouted gloom and despair in February as the team spiralled downwards, only for McMahon himself to turn out at home to Sheffield United and completely control the midfield, inspiring the team to an impressive 2-1 victory. We then hit something of a purple patch, with belting wins at West Brom and at home to Birmingham. Happy as we were to witness the upturn, our pessimism-laced editorial drew predictable responses from some: "Give McMahon a chance, he's doing a good job on a shoestring budget."

OK, so what sort of job did Steve do? Well, of his playing staff only Digby and Broomes really deserved a mention. On the pitch itself a few individual games and incidents stood out like the 6-0 demolition of a sorry Huddersfield team and away victories at Palace and West Brom. There was also the unexpected delight of dumping QPR out of the Coca Cola in September: 2-1 down from the home leg we travelled to Loftus Road more out of duty than hope, only to come away with an extra-time 3-1 win. But there was little of the flair or consistency we'd become used to, partly due to the ever-changing line up and some curious tactical moves by McMahon. The best example was his decision to throw on 18 year old reserve team 'keeper Steve Mildenhall as a makeshift centre forward at Tranmere when the team was 2-1 down.

The last ten games were a nightmare - one win, two draws, seven defeats, goals conceded 24, goals scored two. You really couldn't have got much worse. The 7-0 drubbing at the hands of almost-Champions Bolton was the low point. Or was it the 5-1 defeat at almost-relegated Oldham, or the 2-0 defeat at bitter rivals Oxford? Despite these abysmal showings McMahon continued to roll out his usual post-match blabberings: "I've told the players what I think of them; I'm really at a loss... I'll get players in who really want to play for this club." He seemed to have forgotten that in the final line-ups of the season, there were only two or three players turning out who he hadn't signed himself and even those he *had* signed didn't seem to want to play for him.

So we finished sixth from bottom on 54 points, eight points off the last relegation place. Despite this, supporters were still calling a radio phone-in held during May and congratulating McMahon on a great job. Look, we'll admit that Steve McMahon was an excellent player in his day; a player full of passion and commitment. But managing is different to playing. Bullying players in the dressing room might get the best out of a few, but won't work for everyone. The way in which he offloaded youth team boss John Trollope and assistant manager Andy Rowland, both long-term servants of the club, also left something to be desired.

However, his loyalty cannot be questioned and he has shaken up youth team development and got the wage bill under control; all he really needs is a bit of proper financial backing so that he isn't forced to sell players like Kevin Horlock to Manchester City.

Yet, the dire conclusion to the season and continuing lack of cash doesn't fill this set of Swindon fans with overwhelming optimism. And with the club offering a cash back scheme if we don't make the top six next time around, we can almost see the queues forming already.

A KICK UP THE R'S

Queens Park Rangers

Ray Wilkins MBE, ex-England captain, occasional TV pundit, all-round super bloke and, at that precise moment, but not for too much longer as things transpired, current player-manager of Queens Park Rangers, fixed me a steely glare and asserted: "The guys at Crystal Palace tell me we would beat ninety per cent of the teams in the First Division." Then, after a pause for effect - wasted on me, I'm afraid, such was my desire to scoff openly and loudly by way of immediate response, he added: "If we do go down, we'll come straight back up."

Seeing as the fortunes or otherwise of my beloved club are of supreme indifference to anyone but we chosen few (and even fewer

A KICK UP THE R's
AN ALTERNATIVE VIEW OF QUEENS PARK RANGERS FOOTBALL CLUB

Q. NAME THE ODD MAN OUT...

A. BASIL BRUSH
(The others are all muppets...)

INSIDE: THAT GOAL; THAT DRAW; AND THAT SENDING OFF...

| Issue 82 | £1.00 | February 1997 |

as the season progressed), those predictions didn't quite attract the sort of nationwide ridicule as, say, Michael Fish's infamous hurricane denial, even though it was to prove every inch as wayward.

Nonetheless, being a conscientious, meticulous sort of an editor, and a complete and utter bastard when the mood takes, I made sure my readers were reminded of Ray's words time and time and time again over the next twelve months. Getting my retaliation in, I think the phrase is.

To understand why I, talentless non-entity of the first order, should wish to rabble-rouse a literary lynch-mob against a man whose public persona is even cleaner than that of the Leicester Lug-holes, it's necessary to start this essay not at the beginning of the season under review here, but at the back-end of the season before that.

Long before even the last chocolate bunny of the year had had its brains smashed in and been devoured, all but the most optimistic of QPR fans had accepted relegation out of the Premier League as inevitable. Only three years before, we had finished fifth and were but a shrewd signing or two away from being Championship material. Now we languished in the bottom three, a position we'd occupied most of the season, had a side that was clueless, patternless and everything else-less when it came to style, shape and ability; and we were already hard at work trying to find Port Vale on the map.

Beyond the team, there was a malaise about the club as a whole, an insidious cancer eating away from inside: the phone call that gets answered abruptly and unhelpfully; poor communication and non-existent public relations; the lack of any official response to letters; the 'them and us' attitude - all typifying the gulf existing between boardroom and terrace, and in their own way equally as damaging as the frustrations engendered by a policy whereby any player worth a seven-figure cheque would be sold off to the highest bidder. And, of course, those responsible, the Thompsons, one of Britain's richest families and about as interested in football as I am in schoolgirl hockey (sorry, bad analogy, that one), were incapable of seeing that this particular part of their vast empire was crumbling around their ears.

"Too emotive, too dramatic," cried Chairman Peter Ellis in response to our pointing out to him the situation-as-it-was, at least amongst the QPR fans at large. "Why," he exclaimed in 'tish and nonsense' manner, "everyone who comes to Loftus Road tells me it's the friendliest ground in the country to visit. Only the other day, the Jamaican Ambassador was saying..."

I won't go on - you'll have got the picture by now.

It wasn't exactly anarchy on the Loftus Road terraces, but there was a great deal of anger and frustration at the way the club was being run. If football was a game of cards, we'd been dealt three jokers: a calculating owner (miscalculating as it turned out), a puppet chairman (a label he absolutely hated, but a widely-held view) and a manager who had conspired to turn a decent, attractive side into one who would struggle to beat ninety per cent of the Vauxhall Conference, let alone the 24 teams battling to swap places with us at that very moment, and whose disastrous activities in the transfer market brought about mutterings of toilet seats and sitting the right way.

Despite, or perhaps because of, the unrest, myself and two of my oppos on the fanzine were asked if we'd like to have a meeting with Ray Wilkins, along with our regular meeting with the chairman. Would we? Are bears Catholic? Does the Pope sh....

Of course we would! For a few seconds, fantasy took over. It was obvious: We'd meet. I'd furnish Ray with my wisdom on team selection and pattern of play. My two colleagues would shoot impressed glances at each other and whisper "He's dead right, you know." Ray would nod in agreement, saying "Well, if you really think..." And then he'd hurry off to put my master tactical plan into place... "Yes, we'd love to," I replied, snapping back into the real world.

Ray made it perfectly clear from the off that if one of us was pleased to be at this meeting, it wasn't him. He greeted us that post-match Saturday evening wearing the sort of scowl you might reserve for some bastard who's just nicked the last space in the car park. He opened by attacking the fanzine for being too negative - perhaps he and Peter Ellis had been talking beforehand - rounded on us for slagging off Karl Ready (he should hear what they saying around where *we* sit) and then accused us of making vast sums of money out of the fanzine (not as much as he suggested; more than we let on).

This was the other side of Ray Wilkins. The side only jumped-up fan-zine editors and South American ball-boys ever get to see or hear.

Our objective from the meeting was to find out why, in the face of all the available evidence, he (Ray Wilkins) was still manager of QPR; what, in other words, had he said to the chairman that had convinced him (Peter Ellis) that he was still the right man for the job. Convince us, too, we offered.

Ray, without a game-plan, short- or long-term, and visibly squirming at our analogy of QPR being a one-time successful greenhouse manufacturer but now ailing and at its lowest standing for many years (don't scoff, it was brilliant, honest), didn't know why he was still manager. You'll have to ask that man there, he replied pointing at the chairman. Peter Ellis fixed us a steely glare - they *had* been talking beforehand - and proceeded to give Ray a glowing character reference. "Much respected..." "Great diplomat..." "Honest as the day is long..." and so on and so forth. Nothing about strategy or structure.

Ray Wilkins MBE, ex-England captain, occasional TV pundit, all-round super bloke and, at that precise moment, sitting opposite me harbouring a deep desire to jump up and punch my lights out, was, in the face of all the available evidence, still manager of QPR because... because... well, we never did get the real reason. Because he was a good bloke, presumably.

A coup took place at QPR over the summer. The Thompsons, like rats deserting a sinking ship, scurried off to Leeds, leaving us to pick up the pieces in the First Division. They readily accepted a proposal put to them by two of the directors, by which they would assume control of the club and negotiate its sale. Peter Ellis stood down as chairman and a change of ownership duly took place.

Our knight in shining armour turned out, as many QPR fans hoped it would, to be Chris Wright, founder of Chrysalis Records, the man who discovered Jethro Tull and Blondie, and still a hippy at heart but with a shrewd and successful business brain. More importantly, he had been a season ticket holder at QPR for 20 years.

There was a condition, though, to his taking over. It was dependent on QPR joining forces with Wasps Rugby Union Club and ground-sharing Loftus Road, with the two clubs, sooner rather than later, combining to form one named company, which would be floated publicly.

For a set of fans who over the years have spent more time on the Loftus Road pitch, protesting, than some of the players, and who were the first to form their own independent supporters' association, the LSA, there was, and remains, surprisingly little, if any, dissention to the deal. The Thompsons had brought the club so far down to its knees, and were so loathed and despised, that QPR fans would probably have welcomed Ken Bates' long lost brother if it meant getting rid of them.

And so spectators at Loftus Road were treated to a game where the objective seemed to be either to kick the ball into touch or hoof it the length of the field; where everyone ended up falling over all the time and play got concentrated down one touchline. And of course - yes, you're way ahead of me - some of them came back the following day for the rugby. Boom, boom.

Any fears that Chris Wright might not know the difference between a decent QPR team and a small piece of Wensleydale cheese were dispelled when, five games into the season, he summonsed Ray for a convivial chat and to make the suggestion that perhaps it was time he hung up his boots and concentrated solely on the management side of his, until then, dual role. Ray, who felt he still had a lot to offer, and indeed did, given that he was still one of our most accomplished players by his own default, couldn't have taken it more to heart than if the edict had been personally delivered by some scruffy fanzine editor. He got his coat and handed over the reins to Rangers' resident caretaker manager, Frank Sibley, for his 104th spell in charge of QPR.

"Rangers're coming home," we sang loudly on a sunny afternoon in Barnsley as we watched Rangers playing, in the first half at least, the sort of football that made nonsense of the "Just like watching Brazil" song that Barnsley took with them all the way to promotion. And at that time we truly believed it, just as we'd done on leaving Fratton Park three weeks earlier, with maximum points from our two opening games; and just as we'd done at Wolves next up, when not only did we head home with a hard-earned point, we did so still buzzing about our equaliser which, eight months on, won the Sky award for Nationwide Goal of the Season. It was scored by Daniele 'Danny' Dichio, dubbed the 'Italian Stallion' by the more starry-eyed amongst the QPR support, and the 'Hammersmith Horse' by the more cynical, and a player for whom there never seems to be any middle ground about his game - he's either brilliant or useless, and most often the latter. If you haven't seen it, describing his goal would be pointless because, as good as it was, it wasn't within a hundred miles of the one which walked away with the Goal of the Season as voted for by *Match of the Day* viewers - Trevor Sinclair's stunning scissors-kick in an FA Cup tie, inevitably against Barnsley. That goal, truly brilliant in execution and breath-taking in style, rightly exhausted the supply of superlatives, although as always you had to be there to really appreciate it. Dichio's was superb, Sinclair's even better, and their respective awards fully deserved. And there's us moaning we never win anything...

Like a teenage boy on his first successful foray south of a female waistline, Rangers peaked too soon. Barnsley proved the highlight of the playing season in terms of both performance and result, a comfortable 3-0 win at Man City eight months down the line notwithstanding. In between times, ninety per cent of the teams in the First Division were rubbing their hands in glee at the prospects of taking at least one and, if it was at Loftus Road, more often than not three points from QPR.

The 'guys' at Crystal Palace had a lot to answer for.

Frank Sibley stood down straight after the win at Barnsley, and into his shoes stepped Stewart Houston, previously assistant to Bruce Rioch at Arsenal. It wasn't just that Houston wore the gaunt look of someone in the latter stages of terminal cancer that worried QPR fans - or the prospect of the millions of 'Houston, we have a problem' headlines about to be typeset. The worry concerned ... concerned ... well, no-one could really put their finger on exactly what it did concern. It's just that Houston was ... well, from Arsenal, for heaven's sake.

Perhaps Ray Wilkins hadn't really made such a fist of things after all, and maybe if...

There was another twist: days after Stewart Houston had been appointed manager, it was announced his number two would be ... Bruce Rioch, not as joint-manager, but as Houston's assistant - a role-reversal to their time at Highbury. Both, they were at pains to point out, were entirely comfortable with this arrangement. And aware of Rioch's reputation as a strict disciplinarian and mindful of what he achieved at Bolton, so too were the QPR fans.

Under Stewart Houston, the name of the game was entertainment. Sure, the team were still as shit as they were under Ray Wilkins, but Houston himself kept the crowd amused with his touchline antics. He seemed, and to this day still seems, to think he's taking part in One Man and His Dog. He would stand there doing the arm-waving equivalent of John Cleese's silly walks, while occasionally letting out ear-piercing whistles in coded form. The whistles may mean something to a Welsh border collie, but yer average footballer can't match that breed for intelligence, and so merely spend the game doing passable impressions of sheep, rather than the sheepdog.

After a while, though, the joke began to wear thin, and as yet another home defeat to a side the guys at Crystal Palace hadn't given a prayer to, pressure on Houston began to mount. God knows, QPR fans weren't expecting any miracles - but improvements in shape and style wouldn't have gone amiss for starters. Any one of ten thousand managers around Loftus Road would have happily pointed out where the problems lay. Houston did, eventually, cotton on - but it would take him months rather than a couple of games to spot what was blindingly obvious to the rest of the Saturday afternoon gathering.

One of the major problems was a tendency for our forwards not to trouble the opposition goalkeeper unduly. The one QPR forward capable of doing that had his leg in plaster, and had been laid up ever since the second game of the season, at Portsmouth. Eventually the penny dropped and Houston made a double swoop down the road at Bates Motel for John Spencer and a former free transfer out of Loftus Road, Gavin Peacock. It was an inspired bit of transfer business, even if there wasn't much change out of £4m for the pair. They brought with them not just Premiership quality, but a breath of fresh air with their attitude and commitment. "I'm yer fucking man" Spencer shouted at QPR fans after scoring on his debut at Reading. And so he was - being voted Player of the Year, despite only coming to the club in November.

There was one more memorable moment in Rangers' largely forgettable season. Not the bout of fisticuffs on the field, involving Barnsley, yet again, and Andy Impey throwing one punch too many, thus sealing his summer transfer out of Loftus Road; nor the bout of fisticuffs off it, as Portsmouth fans turned the clock back ten years one unpleasant afternoon in West London. It certainly wasn't the streaker at Fratton Park either; nor the sight of thicko here trying to put up a banner at that same ground in the teeth of a force 12 gale and nearly succeeding in becoming the first man ever to hang-glide to the Isle of Wight. And nor, though it could very well have been, was it the FA Cup fifth round tie at

Wimbledon, to which Rangers took a following of 14,000 and for once when backed by a massive support didn't let us down, in terms of performance, if not result.

No, the third of the three truly memorable highspots of the season came, unsuspectingly, at Port Vale. Only about twelve hundred QPR fans had bothered to travel up to the Potteries that Sunday for a one o'clock kick-off, the rest presumably having still not managed to find it on their maps. In years to come of course, I will meet five thousand QPR fans who were there that afternoon, but by a quarter to two, like most of the QPR support, I was thinking longingly about comfy armchairs and Sunday afternoon naps, as Rangers trailed 4-0.

The only thing half-way amusing during that surreal first half (apart from a large black dog which wandered on the pitch, walked nonchalantly around the touchline, back on to the terrace on the other side of the ground and disappeared to goodness knows where) was a pigeon which decided to risk life and limb to take up residency in front of Rangers goalkeeper Tony Roberts. Had it opted for the other goalmouth, it would have been able to peck away to its heart's content completely undisturbed.

The only time any of us could remember being four down at half-time had been against a rampant Chris Waddle-inspired Newcastle in the mid-eighties. That day we had fought back to gain an improbable 5-5 draw. Lightning couldn't strike twice, could it? Could it? It bloody well could - and it did.

Even then, we left it late. What looked like a consolation own goal from a Port Vale defender ("One number thirteen, there's only one number thirteen" and "Sign him on, sign him on, sign him on" we sang) was made to look a little more respectable by a tasty volley from Andy Impey ("Two number thirteens, there's only two number...") with just three minutes on the clock. Unbelievably, a minute later it was 4-3, an exquisite little chip from Paul Murray. Cometh the hour, cometh our "fucking man" - John Spencer, shooting low and hard from three yards out and bringing it back to an unbelievable 4-4. The pitch invasion which followed was inevitable. From 4-1 down to level terms in the time it takes to play an average chart single. Incredible.

Not as incredible though as the fact it's Barnsley and not us who line up in the Premier League this season. Three wins and nine goals meant we held something of an indian sign over them. No wonder we asked if we could play them every week. Still, if they only but knew the performance at Oakwell was a one-off, at least until they came to our place where we repeated the punishment, and Trevor Sinclair's goal was about the only thing he did all season, they might not be quite so incredulous as to why QPR aren't at the very least joining them in the Premiership. We're not, because as a club we were too long in the hands of people like Richard Thompson and Peter Ellis, and the team for long periods, when it really mattered, were as inept and clueless as the manager who prepared them for their First Division campaign. If only Ray Wilkins had listened to us instead and reserved his contempt for the great bunch of guys at Crystal Palace and their over-estimation of his team's ability, then, it might have been a very different story altogether...

A LARGE SCOTCH

Shrewsbury Town

When our season kicked off a day late because of the Shrewsbury Flower Show (!), many of us were still receiving counselling for post-traumatic stress disorder after losing our first ever Wembley final in the AutoWindscreens.

The majority of Town fans just wanted manager Fred Davies sacked; the rest demanded a public flogging. Even watching England do so well in the European Championships did little to boost our enthusiasm for the coming season. Optimism was, to say the least, lacking.

We did however have two new Danes in our side to add an international flavour. Goalkeeper and Peter Schmiechel look-a-like Benny Gall and defender and long throw expert Thomas Neilson were both revelling in their new surroundings and contributed well to an OK start; a draw with Wycombe and two good away victories at Burnley and Rotherham (it's too late beating them now!) was fair enough. The victory at Burnley was particularly pleasing. Surrounded by thousands of partisan home fans in a good stadium, against a team costing a hell of a lot more than our own, we beat them 3-1 playing on the break. Lovely!

The Coca Cola Cup soon lost its fizz (sorry) and we were able to 'concentrate on the league'. The only things that stuck in the memory about the two Tranmere games were that a squirrel ran onto the pitch in the first leg, and that we saw Ron Dixon from Brookside outside their ground. Exciting stuff! It was a bit like that in the league as well; plodding along quite nicely, nothing too adventurous, nothing too attacking. Not scoring many but not conceding many either.

Mind you, a Paul Evans wonder goal did give us victory over draw-specialists Watford, which prompted excited talk from the club about a top ten finish at least. This happens year after year. We build our hopes up, and just when we start saying "a win today and we'll be in the play-off zone," that's it, we drop like a stone. You'd think we'd have learned by now. Six defeats on the trot later and everything was back to normal. (Told you so). Attendances

ISSUE 18   ONLY 50p

∴ A LARGE SCOTCH ∴

" Is there light at the end of the tunnel ? "

" I can't see where our next win is the coming from ? "

THE ORIGINAL & BEST SHREWSBURY TOWN FANZINE

plummeted, and if our midweek games happened to clash with televised footy, then the chap on our PA was able to announce crowd changes!

November summed up Town completely. Three wins, including one of the best matches seen at the Meadow, a 3-2 victory over Stockport, with another goal of the season contender from Paul Evans, a 5-1 defeat at Crewe (bloody local derbies!) and elimination from the FA Cup by Scarborough in a replay. Ironically, Boro's match winner was John Keay, who'd played for us somewhat controversially (got the nod in front of a host of local lads and loyal club servants) at Wembley during a brief loan spell. It was getting harder and harder to forget that tragic day out at the Twin Towers.

We signed a couple of players on loan ourselves: Frankie Bennett from Southampton and Junior Bent from Bristol City. Bennett scored a few goals and Town were keen to sign him, but despite a fee being agreed between the clubs, Bristol Rovers stole in, offered better terms and off he went. Er, sadly (!), Frankie got injured as soon as he signed for Rovers and didn't play for months - yesss, there is a God. We'd seen Junior Bent on telly, and he looked the business. As it turned out he *was* good, had lightning pace, and was going cheap... something had to go wrong. Instead of signing Junior, Town opted for Mickey Brown from Preston. The same Mickey Brown who'd walked out of the club previously. The same Mickey Brown our former chairman had said "would never play for this club again." This was Mickey's third spell with us and he got an extremely mixed reception on his return. Junior on the other hand went back to Bristol City, regained his first team place and did well.

After losing on Boxing Day to a Bristol City side fielding the aforementioned Mr Bent, we had a home match with York City, which was probably the funniest match I've ever been to. The visitors had former Town 'keeper Tim Clarke in goal, who'd been released the previous season following several dodgy performances. The York fans we talked to before the match were saying what good a signing he'd been, at which point we felt sure that sod's law would guarantee he'd have a blinder.

The chants of "dodgy 'keeper" were ringing out from the terraces long before Trev dropped a cross for our first goal, and when the ball went through his legs for the second the Meadow faithful erupted in a mixture of cheering and laughing. Great stuff - cruel but funny. "Can we play you every week?" "Dodgy 'keeper, dodgy 'keeper."

In our next game the only joke was that the game was actually played. Snow covered the pitch, and fans and players alike assumed the match would be off and went out to celebrate the new year. Unbelievably the referee gave the go-ahead against Blackpool even though the only bit of green visible was where the lines had been swept over. Opposition manager Gary Megson pleaded with the referee not to go ahead with the match, then praised him to the hilt for a brave decision after they'd won.

Despite this set back, the side were still accumulating enough points to stay in a comfortable mid-table position. "If only we could get a run of three straight wins, we could get into the play-off zone," said our ever-optimistic manager Fred Davies. Well the players certainly responded with an extended run for their manager - ten straight defeats! Half way through this scintillating spell the club were staying calm. Relegation was not an issue; we still had two home games against fellow strugglers Plymouth and Rotherham - if we won both of those games we'd be all right. Shite. We lost both and the safety net had gone.

Despite our dire plight we could still take advantage of transfer deadline day. Who would we sign to help us in the fight? How would we use our remaining loan player options? It didn't take long to find out that nobody would be joining the club. Instead the chairman did his best to sell anything that wasn't screwed down. Both our first choice strikers were said to be leaving: big Steve Anthrobus to Crewe and top scorer Ian Stevens to Plymouth. Skilful winger Darren Currie was also linked with Stoke. What the hell were the club doing - did they *want* us to go down? As it happened Stevens' and Currie's deals both fell through at the last minute which gave our depleted morale a bit of a lift. Maybe there was still a chance for us.

It was off to relegation-threatened Wycombe next. They'd spent the last few days signing players in a bid to revive their faltering season and they saw us off with a 3-0 win, and of course stayed up. We needed a miracle now - it was time for the lucky pants.

With charmed undergarments in situ, Burnley and their large following never stood a chance. Despite going behind to a goal totally against the run of play, the lads rolled up their sleeves and with the help of a crowd that just got louder and louder, stormed to victory with a goal from Dean Spink in the dying minutes. The feeling was unbelievable and going to work was for once at least, a joy - no mickey-taking from mates today!

Time was running out as a noisy Town following travelled to Brentford desperately hoping our luck was going to stay. In the end we got a creditable draw, but should have won. Never mind though, two more wins would do us, and with bitter rivals Wrexham next up at the Meadow we anticipated a larger than usual crowd singing us to victory.

That was the plan anyway. But after ten minutes our hearts sank after skipper Dean Spink was sent for an early bath after belting a Wrexham player. Yet, our remaining ten played well and it looked like a draw would be a fair result. The problem was that Wrexham had in their side *the* player we all love to hate - Gary Bennett. He is disliked so much because of his inability to stay on his feet when he's anywhere near our penalty area. True to form he received some merciless none-stop stick from the Meadow faithful. So guess who scored in the very last minute to virtually send us down? The git even celebrated by running the length of the home terrace, just to endear himself to us a tad more.

It had now got to the stage where looking at others' results was more important than our own. If York were to win at Rotherham and we lost at home to Preston then it would be curtains! Preston, who had nothing to play for and one of the worst away records in the league, brought another large following. As the drama unfolded Town hit the post twice and went close on numerous occasions. With our game goalless at half time, news filtered through that York were winning 1-0. In the second half Preston scored a 30 yard scream-er, and this time there was to be no famous comeback. York scored another goal, so did Preston, and that was that. We slowly trooped off home to sulk. The club who had not even considered relegation were down. We rounded off the season with a 2-0 defeat at Gillingham, which meant we had won only once in the last 15 league games.

Manager Fred Davies naturally took most of the blame for our relega-tion but he was adamant that he would not resign, especially as he had almost two years of a contract to run. Could the club afford to sack him, they asked? At the end of the day could they afford not to? A few days after the final game, Fred and his two coaches were shown the door, and all the money we'd re-ceived from selling our two main strikers went on paying contracts off.

So what of the future? Well, there have been some positive moves. Former player Jake King has been appointed boss, after doing well during his managerial apprenticeship in non-league football, and there actually seems to be a glimmer of hope and optimism for the coming season. But hey, isn't there always? We'll have to wait and see. Long live the King.

WE HATE WREXHAM !!

A LOAD OF BULL

Wolverhampton Wanderers

"There will be absolutely no excuses if we don't win promotion next year." Thus spake Mark McGhee at a fans' forum back in April 1996. Another hostage to fortune come the eventual defeat in the play-offs in May 1997.

Wolves had finished the '95-96 season in a truly dismal 20th place and the masses were not happy. Not least because they suspected that the squad inherited by McGhee was deeply infected with a culture of fat cat complacency. Here were any number of players, bought at a cost of over £1 million each, many of them on contracts which grossed

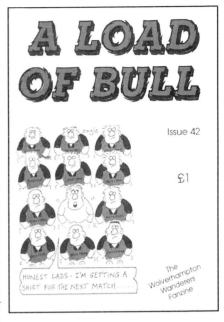

Issue 42

£1

The Wolverhampton Wanderers Fanzine

HONEST LADS - I'M GETTING A SHIRT FOR THE NEXT MATCH......

them over £250,000 per annum, who were unable to regularly beat the likes of the (financially) impoverished Port Vale and Grimsby. Some seemed to assume that promotion would come naturally and left it to others to get on with it; others seemed scared of going up lest it cost them their cushy existence. McGhee had warned that attitudes had to improve or many would be on their bikes at the start of pre-season training. Some responded by over-indulging on a May stag break in Cyprus: cue a publicly apoplectic manager and a thoroughly disillusioned set of supporters.

Come the start of the season, McGhee had started to reshape his squad. Simon Osborn and Steve Corica, both of whom had played for McGhee before, had joined Wolves the previous winter. Over the summer he went back to both Reading and Leicester, but only figuratively and with a chequebook in hand (safer that way), to recruit Iwan Roberts and Adrian Williams. Williams was shortly diagnosed as having damaged a cruciate knee ligament, so Keith Curle swelled the ranks of Molineux internationals. He too failed to make it through pre-season in one piece and it was to be January before either he or Williams started a game for their new club. By August McGhee had got through £5 million in eight months and the expectancy and pressure were right back again.

By Christmas Day the season had taken on an almost surreal, lopsided hue. Twenty three games into the league programme - the halfway mark - and Wolves had only won three out of their 12 home games. Away from home and the reverse applied: six wins and only a solitary 1-0 defeat at Norwich in 11 trips. Away from Molineux we'd learned how to play a compact, defensive holding game, getting plenty of bodies behind the ball and relying on the work rate and pace of Bully at the other end to snatch a goal.

Nowhere did our away game work better than on one glorious Sunday lunchtime in Smethwick in the Black Country derby against Sandwell Town (sometimes known as West Brom). Half an hour gone and we were 3-0 up; ecstasy of a far purer quality than any taken the night before. Albion were eventually slaughtered 4-2 and Alan Buckley made an early claim for the season's BAFTAS (Buckley Award For Talking Absolute Shite) by explaining how his team had "battered" Wolves in the second half. Ho hum.

On the road, goals from Bully alone secured wins at Grimsby, Portsmouth and Manchester City. Others chipped in to bring wins at Swindon, Tranmere and Crystal Palace, where Geoff Thomas' fairytale comeback from injury was celebrated with the winner.

But those who only saw Wolves at Molineux formed a different impression. Here, the wingback system we were using was nowhere near as effective, as Wolves were unable to break down visiting sides of limited ambition. Passing was aimless, penetration minimal. Play was prone to become nervy and desperate, errors were legion and games were gifted both to decent visiting sides (Bolton and Sheffield), to adequate ones (Birmingham and Port Vale) and to abject ones (Oldham and Reading). Already out of the Coca Cola Cup (Swindon, first round), we duly exited the FA Cup too, again at home, to Portsmouth. Free to concentrate on the league at the earliest possible opportunity, then. Not that an average gate of 25,000 quite saw things that way.

All of this meant that the return Black Country derby took on massive significance. Defeat, and the roof would have come crashing down on the season. Fortunately, Wolves played like a team possessed and crushed the visitors, the 2-0 scoreline a kindness to Albion who were lucky to get nil! It was to prove the final nail in Buckley's coffin, and there were plenty of Wolves fans volunteering to hammer it in.

The next game brought a rare but significant away defeat, a 3-0 January thumping at Bolton which left our hosts 12 points clear of us and headed for the title. It was also the end of Dean Richards' season - twelve months on from an M1 car crash, his knee which had been troubling him all season was finally operated on. Question then was, were Wolves good enough to claim the second automatic promotion spot or was it to be the lottery of the play-offs again?

Six days later we went to second placed Sheffield, for whom a win would mean a nine point advantage over us. That night, Steve Bull took to the pitch after failing to score in the previous five games and with, unbelievably, some siren voices suggesting he be dropped. In the 89th minute and with the score at 2-2 Adrian Williams hoofed a ball 40 yards downfield. Bull was onto it in a flash. Facing possibly the division's best 'keeper in Alan Kelly, he didn't bother with the niceties of a controlling first touch. From just outside the box, at full tilt, he drilled it first time into the bottom corner in front of the travelling Wolves fans. Had we finally laid our old, old bogey of being unable to win the really big games to rest? For a while, it seemed like it. With players like Emblen, Williams and Curle variously returning to fitness and form Wolves won their next three games, Bull scoring four of the team's five goals as none were conceded. Sadly, that was to be our longest and best winning sequence of the season as the twin disasters of home defeats (a 0-3 horror show versus Crystal Palace) and injured centre-halves (Williams, again) returned to haunt us.

A month after the apparent turning point at Bramall Lane, the result of another trip to South Yorkshire seemed at the time likely to prove pivotal to both sides. And so to Oakwell, where second-placed Barnsley were three points ahead of us with a game in hand. Bull scored after 99 seconds and the convincing 3-1 win that ensued would surely break Barnsley's resolve and in turn see Wolves gain inexorable momentum. If only...

A freak of the fixture list meant that Wolves faced three away matches in the space of eight days in mid-March. Given both our fantastic away record at this stage and the fact that two of our opponents were in the bottom three, a neutral would never have forecast our eventual return: three straight defeats. *We had blown it.* The crucial moment came at Ice Station Boundary Park. Oldham had taken an early lead, but Bully, with his tenth goal in as many games, had brought us level. We were looking at our watches and anticipating the warming effect of half-time's hot drinks when, running back upfield after a tangle with their skipper Craig Fleming, Bull appeared to wave a dismissive hand in Fleming's direction. Only one person on the field, Fleming included, took any notice. Out came a red card. To his credit, the Oldham skipper protested immediately that no offence had occurred (he later confirmed that there had been neither contact nor malice intended from Bull) but the ref, who had lost control long since, wasn't the listening type. Mr Pearson, from Peterlee, coming to a club near you soon. If you're really unlucky. Oldham went on to win the game 3-2 and we were faced with a three game ban for our talisman.

Before that took effect there were trips to Stoke and struggling Bradford from which to steal a march on Barnsley. We lost both. Only by the odd goal, and in tight contests, but that counted for nought. Whether the team still had their collective minds on Bull's impending ban and were suffering a sense of injustice was hard to tell. Maybe they simply bottled it; maybe the luck just ran out. Either way, the feeling at the time was that we had just chucked away our best hope of automatic promotion in over a decade. 'Useless, spineless bastards let us all down again' was the general sentiment.

And so it proved. Barnsley wrapped up automatic promotion on the penultimate weekend after Wolves had gone ten consecutive games without a clean sheet. No Daz in our defence. Winning our final away game of the regular season at Port Vale had been rendered academic by Barnsley 24 hours earlier, although it did have the somewhat unusual effect of ensuring that Wolves won more points away from home over the course of the season than they did at Molineux, the best stadium in the division. All those home defeats before Christmas had duly caught up with us, compounded as they subsequently were by those three desperate away defeats in one week in March.

Looking back over the 46 games and the statistics tell a few inescapable truths. Bully had been magnificent: 23 League goals, all in open play. But we were still hopelessly over-dependent on him: Roberts's contribution was 12 goals, Goodman six, and the others added very little. It was hard to refute the charge of one Bolton fan: "you're a one-man team if ever there were one."

Injuries had played their seemingly inevitable part. In theory we were blessed with a surfeit of talented centre-halves. In practice, Richards started 19 League games, Curle 20 and Williams a mere six: i.e. one full season between the lot of them. Our midfield powerhouses, Thomas and Emblen, began 15 and 27 League matches respectively. Our creative fulcrum, Simon Osborn, also missed a quarter of the season. On the flanks, 27 starts from Froggatt and none at all from Tony Daley. Given only one regular goalscorer and considering the amount of games missed by key personnel then perhaps automatic promotion was too much to hope for. And yet... Given the injury records of some of our big names prior to their joining Wolves, was it really just a case of 'bad luck'? And besides, the entire Barnsley squad cost less to assemble than Tony Daley alone. They pipped us to second spot on merit, playing the very kind of football to which we aspire.

And so to the play-offs and a two-legged rematch with Crystal Palace. Shorn of so many key players, most would have settled for a 1-0 defeat as we entered the 89th minute at Selhurst. When Freedman then made it 2-0 that seemed to be that. But this is Wolves we're talking about; seconds later, Jamie Smith's first ever goal for the club made it 2-1 and we had an away goal to take back to Molineux. But this is Wolves we're talking about; seconds later, Freedman made it 3-1 as we tried to play offside and the inappropriately named linesman Mr Joy failed (correctly, as the videos later proved) to raise his flag. Three goals in 90 mad seconds. An ashen-faced, interminable journey home unnecessarily elongated by the fact that they keep the train doors locked these days. I was all for throwing myself out.

Molineux for the return was a cauldron, and Atkins' goal gave a frenetic crowd real hope. But legs tired as the second half wore on, Hopkin scored on the break and although a Williams goal five minutes from the end reduced it to 3-4 on aggregate, it was not enough. The crowd stayed behind to cheer a stupendous effort. Two years previously Steve Bull had to be dragged from the pitch in tears after the play-off defeat at Bolton. Weeks later, Taylor tried to sell him to Coventry, but he stayed "because of the fans." Now aged 32 and with his best years behind him, it was heartbreaking to watch him slowly tear himself away. Before doing so, he came down towards the South Bank who broke into a deafening chorus of our anthem:

> Oh, Stevie Bull's a tatter; He wears an England cap;He plays for Wolverhampton; He is a lovely chap... etc.

The key words here are "plays for Wolverhampton," i.e. rather than for himself. However much defeat hurts us, the fans can wait for promotion. But for this guy, the sands of time are running out; he has sacrificed his personal career ambitions on the altar of getting us up. Many on the South Bank that day were in tears; not so much for ourselves, but for Steve Bull.

A LOT 2 ANSWER 4

Swansea City

After a summer getting over relegation we were the bookies' favourites for an immediate return, so the hardy souls full of blind optimism (otherwise know as the 'more money than sense' brigade) trooped down to Mecca Vetch for the 'on loan to Division 3' season.

People began to believe the hype after the opening day win over Rochdale. We anticipated a slaying of all in our path and wondered how early it would be before we were confirmed as Champions. Such dreams lasted approximately three weeks, at which point we hit the proverbial wall and slumped to 91st in the entire league. In the meantime the club's on/off ownership saga continued; a buy-out appeared imminent and all sorts of space-age plans for a sports city were doing the rounds. We hit rock bottom when ten-man Torquay beat us 2-0 at Plainmoor. Molby was now slating the team and squad and rightly having a pop at the chairman too for putting every single player, Molby included, up for sale. Forgive me for saying this but who in God's name was going to fork out for any of our duffers languishing at football's basement? Anyway, I began to feel like St Peter - you know, denying your allegiance three times before the cock crowed - but before it got to that the team played a blinder and beat table-topping Wigan on a cold winter's night. When the winner went in, a mate of mine went berserk and whipped another friend's trousers and kegs down to his ankles who like a trooper carried on celebrating as if nothing had happened. It was quite surreal...

To use a football cliché, the Torquay debacle seemed to be the spring-board for the rest of our season. As if by magic our fortunes reversed; win followed win and we shot up the table, stopping at fourth. Looking back, two matches stand out during this time, each for different reasons. The first was our FA Cup exit at the hands of Drizzle City. After a good 1-1 draw we headed off to Ashton Gate 1,500-strong. The game itself was settled after 30 seconds courtesy of a very poor back-pass by our very own Steve Jones, but my abiding memory is of the after-match confrontation in the car park, when all hell broke loose. In the near pitch dark the police arrived to break up the trouble and when one Bristol City fan was collared, he tried to get out of it by saying, "But officer, I'm Bristol." The amazed look on his face was a picture, especially when he complained he'd lost one of his expensive shoes. At this, the policeman pinned him half inside the van whilst his other shoe was removed and tossed away. No doubt he was then rushed off to the nearest cop shop and charged. Whoever said football was a funny old game? How true!

The second highlight was our trip to Sand Park, home of our beloved countrymen Cardiff Shitty. Now I don't know if you're aware of this, but both sets of fans are now banned from visiting the away fixture, but if you are daft/clever enough (delete as applicable) you can obtain a ticket, although you have to sit with the natives and listen to their conversations - always an eye-opener. Anyway, what a night! We cruised to a 3-1 win, and I can tell you it's nearly impossible trying to hide your total delight whilst remembering where you actually are. Some just couldn't handle it as they rashly leapt out of their seats in the grandstand, but luckily I was sitting behind the goal where Dai Thomas scored. It soon resembled a zoo - after he netted he celebrated with arms aloft slowly marching towards us. I didn't need to conceal my smiles since everybody else was too busy trying to climb the fence and rearrange his features. What made it all the more enjoyable was the fact that Thomas used to follow Cardiff as a lad, and had just humiliated them to the delight of his secret admirers dotted around the ground. My award-winning performance disguising my 'disappointment' was almost on a par with that of my team.

The 'on loan to Div Three' tag seemed less ridiculous as we secured our place in the play-offs. Chester were our opponents and after a niggly 0-0, Ratcliffe let rip in the Cardiff-based *Wales on Sunday* saying how Swansea didn't have a chance and his club Chester and Northampton were the teams sure to make it. Isn't it funny how such gobby predictions from managers always come back to haunt them? In the second leg we played our best football of the season, hammering Ratcliffe's lot 3-0 in a very one-sided game. Funnily enough he wasn't quoted in any papers after the game, poor sod. So it was off to Wembley for a date with destiny (and Northampton).

We started up the M4 at 6am, heading for a nice pub in Harrow just up the road from the Twin Towers. Myself and eight other happy jacks drank ourselves closer to 3pm whilst entertaining the Cobblers (strange name!) with our card school and footy facts, chanting, "Cobblers, Cobblers, you're a load of cobblers." And it was true - despite being outnumbered 2:1 on the day, we were the real fans as we didn't find anyone in the pub who'd actually seen their team play all season.

On arrival at the ground we gave the Cobblers a lesson in passion as we sang our Welsh National Anthem like there was 100,000 of us, drowning out *God Save The Queen*. It was quite amusing to hear "Football's coming home" with our own little twist: "England's full of shit, it's full of shit" reverberating around the old stadium. However, 93 minutes later my world caved in when Northampton were awarded a dubious free kick that was at first missed, then re-taken and then cracked into the net. One half of the stadium erupted, the other half just sloped off home. How true it is that Wembley is only a place for winners - after totally dominating the match, to lose in such a fashion was hard to take. What a sucker punch. And after the day had begun so well, too. What with five lads dressed as the Spice Girls, men in boiler suits and back-packs doing a spot of ghost-busting and the coach-load of flares and afro-wigs parading as the Jackson 50. I couldn't laugh any more. When I got home in the early hours I went to the video to exorcise a few ghosts and watch the match taped off *Sky*. I rewound the tape only to be greeted by the poxy Scot-tish Cup final! I'd taped the wrong channel, which just about summed up my day. No, it summed up my season! So close, yet so far. Until next time...

Source: *Flashing Blade*

A LOVE SUPREME

Sunderland

What a difference a year makes! After cheering Sunderland fans up by winning the First Division title in '95-96, Peter Reid proved he was a mere mortal by overseeing a relegation from the Premiership that was described in the local evening newspaper as "like seeing a car crash in slow motion... you can see what's happening but you can do little to stop it."

In truth there was plenty that could have been done to stop it, primarily the signing of players of genuine quality to replace too many honest journeyman who were just not good enough for the weekly high standards of the Premier League. The bottom line is that any football team could take eleven out of their crowd who would try hard but still never be good enough!

Pre-season correspondence sent to fans by the club secretary promised that "with your support in purchasing a season ticket, Peter Reid will be at the forefront of the queue to sign international stars." Fed on hype and broken promises for decades, 18,000 fans clearly thought "oh, what the hell's another year, I'll buy my ticket," but by the time the season kicked off against Leicester City the influx of new talent numbered striker Niall Quinn and 'keeper Tony Coton of the reserve sides of Manchesters City and United respectively. International stars eh? Mmmm...

I won't bore you with every minor detail of our season, so let's take a general overview. After a bright start that included a 4-1 win at Forest and a gutsy 0-0 draw at Liverpool, Reidy committed a cardinal sin which was to prove the first in a succession of questionable and controversial team selections - even allowing for the fact that football is a game of opinions. In September he broke up the defence which had been the cornerstone of the team's rapid success under the scouser's stewardship by replacing the excellent 40 cap Polish right back Darius Kubicki with the tubby Gareth Hall (who'd been voted the worst ever Chelsea player by Blues supporters). Kubicki would have equalled a club post-war record of 124 consecutive appearances that day, so the decision seemed spiteful as well as uncalled for. After this decision (which he has refused to explain to this day), we saw players Reid had signed such as £1m Alex Rae and Swedish international Jan Eriksson ignored, others like striker David Kelly played out of position and young local lads such as the previous season's top scorer Craig Russell and England U21 winger Martin Smith mystifyingly ignored for months on end, even during injury crises.

After the aforementioned early season shut-out at Anfield, Reid jokingly commented to the media that "I know nothing about tactics" and then justified his words on many subsequent occasions. Even vital home matches against fellow strugglers at the end of the season saw the unsuccessful ploy of operating with a lone striker flop badly, but still he persisted with these tactics of mindnumbing negativity, to the horror of the crowd. Stubbornness was the order of the day. "I'll do it may way or not at all," bellowed Reid to the Press. It has to be said that because of Reidy's success the previous year coupled with his aggressive no-nonsense nature, the local media and supporters alike were very wary of showing outward criticism, despite clear evidence on the field that Sunderland would struggle to retain their Premiership status.

We took some notable scalps at home including Man United, Arsenal, Villa and Chelsea, but it was not enough overall. We were perceived as being strong defensively but ended up with a 'goals against' column worse than most; we were called a fighting side but whenever we conceded a goal first we'd be finished, and we lacked foresight and ambition in the transfer market. Thus relegation.

The supporters had had their hopes falsely built up by the directors who promised the mistakes of '90-91, when we'd been immediately relegated on the back of a fortuitous promotion (thanks to Swindon's financial irregularities), would not be repeated. We were told there was £10m in the transfer kitty plus cash raised from the club's stock market flotation at the beginning of 1997. Arguments raged as to whether it was really there, whether the club would pay the wages of top players and so forth. But until Sunderland go out and buy big, fans will err on the side of cynicism. We noted with interest just how much money certain club officials, including the directors, manager and company secretary made from the flotation.

The *Daily Telegraph* writer Mihir Bose related the story of Sunderland's directors authorising pink slips to be given to club staff, including players. These slips allegedly allowed the holder to purchase huge amounts of shares, but they were not offered outside the club (say, to any long-standing supporters) who might've liked to buy a substantial amount. Many people who had been at the club five minutes were allowed privileges ahead of fans who had given a lifetime's devotion to the red and white cause. Without the fans' support through 40 years of hurt (Sunderland have not finished in the upper echelons of the top-flight since the mid 1950's) the club would not exist, but then who are we in these commercially-orientated days where many involved in running the people's game genuflect at the altar of the great god Money? Did I say 'the people's game'? Well, it used to be, didn't it?

Season '96-97 was our last at Roker Park, which was always going to be an emotional affair. Only on Wearside could it coincide with relegation. Ironically we played a farewell match against the first ever visitors, Liverpool, two days after we were relegated on 15th May. The crowd was the biggest of the season - a full capacity of 22,657 with people locked out. There you see part of the problem: the fans are arguably TOO loyal! The directors probably expected a backlash from relegation but no, a full house! They must have been laughing into their gin and tonics. The post-match displays at the farewell game epitomised just why Sunderland's general standards serve to frustrate their followers. A 'spectacular laser show' consisted of two blokes with illuminated torches from Woolworth's, a brass band you couldn't hear because there was no amplification and a girl who didn't know the lyrics for a supposed crowd singalong to *You'll never walk alone*. What a mess. The only highlight was when SAFC 'Player of the Century' Charlie Hurley dug up the centre circle and then told the club to "get your act together for these wonderful people."

The new stadium on the banks of the River Wear in the heart of the city is an imposing structure destined to be the catalyst of brighter times ahead, according to club propaganda. However, another relegation has been a bitter pill to swallow for many supporters. It seems fairly obvious that if the club want to fill the majority of a 42,000 European super-stadium (the FA have already earmarked it for their 2006 World Cup bid) when our opponents will include the likes of Crewe, Stockport and Bury, they are going to have to buy big and make money talk to attract decent players to perform for even one season in the comparative backwaters of the Nationwide First Division.

The Premier League was a big tease. It was there, but just as quickly it was gone. Just like Chris Waddle. After 18 months of being linked with the ex-England genius, he came just before the transfer deadline and played seven matches. Thirty six or not, he was superb and in the seven goals we scored after his arrival, he made six and scored our Goal of the Season, a free kick at home to Everton. Waddle, who fancies becoming a manager and who was very popular in the dressing room, has been released. Was it because Reid saw him as a threat to his own job if things didn't go well? Any other reasonable explanation is hard to find. Logic said the Waddler played very well and was a massive influence on the team; his dead-ball expertise has no better exponent in the current international side. Having to accept decisions like these without explanation from the club is par for the course of being a Sunderland supporter.

With the new stadium opening in the summer with a match against Ajax lined up, next season really is the 'last chance saloon' for many Sunderland fans desperate to see their club reciprocate their desire to see us up there with the Premiership elite. Potential is a word bandied around for too long and at the moment the only two big things about the club are the supporters and the excellent new ground. Only a great team will fill it.

A SLICE OF KILNER PIE

Huddersfield Town

The giant slept heavily

And so we were locked in combat in the return fixture at Valley Parade. Once again a textbook derby battle ensued: numerous bookings, fighting between players, handbags between the managers (amateur dramatics from Chris Kamasutra) and more ill feeling than an episode of *Emmerdale*. And if Kamara was Kim Tate, then Gordon Watson surely filled the part of Chris Tate, confined as he was to a wheelchair with a broken leg after an admittedly viscous 'challenge' from Kevin Gray. The threat of legal action still lingers, but to be honest Watson dug his own grave when

BRADFORD SH*TTY FC
Friday 8th November

FRESH — THE INDEPENDENT TOWN REVIEW

he elbowed Paul Reid in the face moments earlier. Apart from that, the game proceeded quietly and without incident.

Between the two derby fixtures came the first round FA Cup tie at QPR. This was another marvellous away trip, with the team for once putting in a performance which justified their salaries and the massive Town following behind the goal. They played with tremendous spirit and fought like their first team places depended on it. . On top of this, 'Top Cat' Cowan dispelled a certain myth concerning Scottish goalkeepers. Regular No.2 Tony Norman was forced out of the action early on after stretching for a back-pass that simply wasn't there (it happens at his age), and with Horton gambling on three outfield subs our plucky left back Cowan gleefully accepted responsibility between the sticks. More than that, he further adhered himself to the Town faithful. And not just the blokes either.

"Ooooh he's got a lovely arse," said one woman in the first row. Yes luv, but what about his sliding tackle? Oh stop it this instant!

Town spent most of the game upstream without a paddle (and a hope), but did manage to sneak a goal through that man Gary Crosby early in the second half. Cue inane celebrations in the School End Lower. Perhaps something similar was going on in the upper tier, but to be honest a bomb could have gone off up there and us downstairs would still have been none the wiser.

There's a chance they didn't even see it go in, such is the reported level of restricted viewing. I don't know, you pay to watch a game of footy and miss a goal from Gary Crosby. Funnily enough the club had been paying to see nothing from him all season as well. Maybe something similar pissed off the Pompey fans?

For Town though the final whistle brought a mixture of relief and frustration. Big Mark Hateley, the man the Rangers' fans love to despise, had slammed in an equaliser with two minutes left to deny us the victory we richly deserved. "Score when you're cheating, you only score when you're cheating..." rang out from the School End, in reference to a disputed goal they got away with at our place in the league. Now no-one expects Lady Luck to play on their side every week, but it would been nice if she didn't always score in the last minute for the opposition.

Having thrown away the replay 1-2, the season began its long annual drift towards an inevitably dull conclusion. Not quite bad enough to go down, certainly not good enough to go up. And yet in between the boredom there were little moments of magic to justify renewing the season tickets: the Stewart hat-trick against Wrexham; the routing of Birmingham and last-minute equaliser and winner v Oldham; the hero-worshipping of the Stoke City goalkeeper on his return to the scene of the crime (see last year's entry), and the bombardment of the Town No.1 with snowballs by the aggrieved Potters faithful. Even the dullest of dull trips to Port Vale was made enjoyable by the Town fan who mercilessly taunted a Vale midfielder with cries of "He's a baby!" and "What's the scores George Dawes!"

However, although it would be an exaggeration to say the season was over before it ever started, we never really recovered from early knocks, and even by September the "injuries, such appalling injuries" grumbling noises were being made. I think the problems started earlier than that when we sold Booth and Jepson, the strike-force which scored more often than an Essex girl in Turkey. If you take 40+ goals a season out of a team, then even with £2.7 million and forty grand (the pittance Bury gave us for Jeppo) you're going to struggle to win matches. And we certainly did that.

The moronic chant received by the few hundred Town fans at Swindon back in November just about summed up our whole season. A few Southerners from a crappy Mid-Westcountry town belting out "Hud-ders-field, Hud-ders-field, can we play you every week?" I mean, this was Swindon not bloody Old Trafford! Nothing more than an enlarged Welcome Break Service Station on the M4, famous only for financial irregularities and a Norwegian named Jan Aage, and here were their supporters mercilessly ripping the piss out of us. Farmer Jack with a piece of straw up his arse and a few of his mates from the country, slagging off the famous blue and white shirts of Huddersfield. The season had plumbed to new depths.

OK, so we *were* 6-0 down at the time with half an hour still to play. Things had gone a bit pear-shaped either side of the interval, and our back four let six goals in over an 18 minute period. Not so much makeshift as make-believe. Still, not to worry eh? We'd bounce back from this one...

We were hammered 5-1 the following week in the CCC at Middlesbrough! And with Juninho, Emerson, Beck and Ravioli all on the scoresheet, what else were the 5,500 Town following left to sing except "In-ger-land, In-ger-land, In-ger-land!" The foreign legion could stuff us out of sight on the pitch but the war of songs in the stands was ours. And by golly we made it a night to remember.

There is always something special about travelling to a Premier League ground knowing you're about to receive a stuffing but not caring one way or another. How nice it is to poke fun at the spoilt little rich-boys, with their fancy foreign imports; how bemused they become when you fail to look concerned if they score a goal. Or two. Or five. For example Boro took the lead and rows D and E broke into a merry song - the only one they have it seems: "Come on Boro! Come on Boro!" In response, ironic cheers and incessant arm-waving broke out in the away end. This was a complete laugh. Then Ravioli scored and the blue and white shirts were pulled over our heads and the 'tosser' gestures made, etc, etc. Then Rigatoni went down in the box for a penalty (not given) and the shirts were pulled over our heads, etc, etc. Fusilli farted downwind (it's all that pasta) and the shirts, etc etc. We were on a roll.

To cap a brilliant night on Teeside, Andy 'haircut like a Legoman' Payton scored with three minutes left to send the Town following into raptures. He'd done it against his old club and now we had something to really go mental about. One bloke sat in front of us took it slightly too far and lamped a steward trying to stop him invading the pitch. I suppose he had asked for it in a steward-ish sort of way.

We danced out of the stadium and into the streets, happy that we'd been not altogether disgraced against the crappest team in the Premier League, a team we'd be playing again next season on level terms (although we didn't know it at the time). In truth the prospects were awful if we won promotion. Fortunately the chances of winning promotion were even worse. And we can always take comfort in the knowledge that Boro voted Town the biggest and best travelling support to visit the Riverside in 1996. So even if our current team would die on its feet in the top flight we could be sure that Town fans would more than hold their own.

The next game of any note on our epic quest to fulfil the '96-97 fixture calendar came at home against Sadford Sh*tty in November. And true to current form we were three goals down inside half an hour, and all this in front of the *Sky* cameras. The first goal did, though, bring an element of satisfaction if only because some sad Sh*tty w*nkers (sitting proud and cheering all too loud) were literally booted out of the front of the Kilner Bank stand with their tails between their fat little legs. The same thing happened in a later game against Bolton in February. I suppose some people never learn. It was a special atmosphere and match inside the 'Alf' that night, though, especially the way we came from behind to draw and almost snatch a winner in stoppage time. If only Payton could score from eight yards out on a consistent basis (i.e. more than once a month). Special mention is due to a superb Paul Dalton curler for our first and a rather nice bullet header from young Ian Lawson for the second. The ultimate honours, though, were destined to remain even.

Having Marcus Stewart on the treatment table all season did us no favours however. Nobody realised that we were paying a lot of money for a pair of ankles more brittle than an IRA peace treaty, and when they finally collapsed during the Birmingham game in October, Stewart was left to join club captain Andy Morrison on the sidelines. We dispensed with the services of big gun Darren Bullock in February for nutting too many nightclub bouncers, and with the backbone and spearhead removed, the team limped onwards like a Tory shadow cabinet. If only Town could vote on whether to go into Europe.

In the end the romanticists of Huddersfield would be left to dream of once more joining the big boys in the promised land. Many still believe that this club will rise again before it falls anywhere. In truth spineless performances like those at Junction 17 (Swindon) will have to be eradicated if that is to be the case.

Oh, and by the way, the Swindon taunts didn't go unheeded during that spectacular six-nothing roasting. "We are Bradford in disguise..." came the witty riposte from the Town faithful. Well yes, this season we probably were.

THE ABBEY RABBIT

Cambridge United

'Board' with Success?

First, a quick recap for regular readers. The end of the '95-96 season saw the Mighty U's having suffered a run of form that had seen them not only blow an automatic play-off, but also left them looking worryingly over their shoulders at the fortunes of Torquay. We finally settled for mid-table anonymity. The term 'underachievement', so often and quite rightly associated with our north county cousins, could for once be directed at the Abbey Stadium's finest...

However, the board of Cambridge United obviously felt that supporters and more importantly (in their eyes anyway) shareholders, should have been impressed with the previous season's debacle. With the action no sooner done and dusted, they attempted to extract some £300k from shareholders to ensure "the future of Cambridge United." They even offered a carrot in the form of a 'guaranteed' 27% return on any investment. Not surprisingly, given that, (a) this sort of financial offer is normally associated with dodgy and unscrupulous businesses, (b) those with any rudimentary grasp of mathematics would have noticed that this sum would at best only keep us afloat for another season at best, and (c) our own board were proving very reluctant to put their hands in their pockets, this opportunity was dismissed out of hand.

Meanwhile our underachieving neighbours (see how easy it is!), shocked the world by announcing that loveable fat cockney Barry Fry was buying their lame pup. At the same time our very own loveable fat cockney Tommy Taylor shocked U's fans by announcing a major transfer coup - no, not the signing of yet another free transfer utility player (our stable fare of late) - but the signing of ex-Derby and Luton midfield-maestro David Preece, as player-coach. Unfortunately, some of this warm glow wore off when we discovered he was injured.

And so as the season kicked off in bright August sunshine, United comprehensively turned over Barnet, er... 1-0. Actually this match could be held up as a microcosm of our season. United huffed and puffed but seemed reluctant to convert pressure and chances into goals, whilst our defence often seemed in quite charitable mood. In the end it took a hired gun, this time in the shape of geriatric pensioner Gary Brazil, to finally stop looking at the proverbial gift-horse's gob.

However, students of the basement division will know that any grasp or semblance of footballing nuance isn't really necessary at this level (fans of Wigan and Carlisle can ignore this statement, whilst those of Fulham and Northampton can be thankful that a somewhat 'robust' approach often reaps dividends). No, what is needed is a huge dollop of luck.

Now luck was something that the Mighty U's appeared to have by the bucket-full. The emergence of David Preece and new hired help, on-loan P*sh reject Scott McGleish, saw us embark on a run of 21 points from a possible 24 and a place in the heady, nose-bleed-inducing heights of second in the division... And then, out of the blue, our traditionally cash-strapped directors (or three of them at least) managed to find the funds to purchase a derelict warehouse in front of the ground. This turned out to be the sole reason that the club were so hungry for 300 grand to secure our future. Hmmm, seemed more like an opportunity to indulge in a bit of property speculation. Still, they managed to persuade shareholders to back a move where the club picked up the mortgage payments, whilst they worked out what to do with it. Some of us were concerned that if the board were prepared to be *economical with the actualité* with shareholders, could they be trusted to tell fans the truth? The jury is still out on this one...

Nevertheless, riding high in the league - despite a severe tonking at Fulham, predominately due to that other variable in the lower division equation, totally inept and incomprehensible match officials - the U's still appeared to be on course for automatic promotion... What could possibly stop us?

Er, step-forward our erstwhile board of directors (again). In a shock move they surprised fans by announcing that the club was officially up for sale (even taking out a box ad in the *Financial Times* to prove that they were serious this time!). Did I say 'shock'? The only shock and surprise was the fact that they announced it. We'd assumed all along that the club had been for sale for years! To no great surprise though, negotiations with 'interested parties' foundered - usually because the board would claim that all any prospective suitor wanted to do was build houses on the football pitch. Funny really; that's our chairman's avowed aim!

A more sinister development however, was the protracted contract negotiations between board and manager which were soon to fall under the gaze of the local media. In the summer, Tommy Taylor had been making noises about the fact that his contract expired mid-season. At this stage you could perhaps understand the directors' reluctance to pursue matters. Only a few months previously fans had been calling for the manager's head. Now though, with praise being heaped upon both manager and team, the fans began calling for our chairman's head (a regular occurrence in these parts). Stung into action, no doubt influenced by workman-like East London club Leyton Ointment's decision to part company with their manager, the board acted decisively and offered TT an extension until... the end of the season. Did we say decisively? Actually we meant dividedly, for rumours began circulating that some directors, who saw the manager as a stop-gap measure, were rather keen to ditch TT. Problem was that after a somewhat rocky first season, he'd begun at last to deliver the goods despite being handicapped by the financial strait-jacket imposed by the people upstairs. They insisted that Taylor had verbally agreed to a new contract, a rolling-one at that, subject to normal employment legislation. This left us with the bizarre impression that if he'd signed it, Taylor effectively couldn't be sacked. Indeed the directors had termed it a 'job for life' (funnily enough, the last manager - incidentally TT's immediate predecessor - who'd been offered such glowing terms had been, er, sacked). Unsurprisingly then, given the overtures from Brisbane Road, after much soul-searching (OK about five minutes) Taylor decamped down the M11 and straight into the clutches of diamond-geeza Barry Hearn.

Feigning surprise, our board insisted that they would offer the job to Taylor's number two Paul Clark, despite it being common knowledge that (a) Clark would follow Taylor to Orient and (b) the board appeared to already have a replacement lined-up in Brian 'Biffer' Laws. Indeed, when news of this surprise announcement was leaked on local radio, the club, instead of blandly denying that such an announcement was afoot, immediately expressed outrage as if their secret had been blown. With the fear that the situation could get out of hand, this fanzine editor was informed that "in order to not inflame events further, and reluctantly acting on Police advice" the *Rabbit* was banned from being sold prior to a potentially inflammatory fixture against Swansea. However-er, with the Police's football liaison officer - a legend in his own fertile imagina-tion - collapsing with laughter at this suggestion and with Brian Laws strutting around the ground prior to the game... what were we saying earlier about directors being less than honest with fans?

Clarky did resign and was followed promptly by McGleish who bug-gered off to Orient muttering darkly about a lack of ambition (guaranteed to give the chairman apoplexy). With fans quite rightly fearing that our season was about to come to a premature end (and all this before Christmas - a record for all our underwhelming efforts of the past few seasons), a rabbit (so to speak) was pulled out of the hat as the club announced a new manager... Roy McFar-land. Was this the master stroke to pull our fortunes out of the fire? Despite rumours that the helping and bejewelled hand of Coventry's director of foot-ball was involved, and that according to fans of McFarland's previous clubs here was a man in much need of managerial rehabilitation, a faint chink of light appeared to be breaking through the thick pall of smoke that rose above the ashes of our season.

Afraid not. With a horrible recurrence of a particularly vivid case of *déjà-vu*, the Mighty U's season went into a tail-spin. McFarland's period at the tiller saw United win only seven out of 31, including a truly horrible home defeat at the hands of non-league Woking in the FA Cup; the U's were, it has to be said, comprehensively out-fought and out-thought. The fact that until the last three weeks of the season we clung to a play-off berth says more about the turgid state of Third Division football than anything else.

It would be all too easy to lay the blame at McFarland's door. Most fans though gave him the benefit of the doubt. Indeed, as the man himself said, "six months is far to early a time period to judge me." For the time being we'll even overlook some of his more bizarre tactical changes - after all he was the ex-England centre-half, but it's hard to see the tactical wisdom of playing your recognised centre-half at right-back, and your five-foot-and-a-teeny-bit wing-back in the in his place...

At the halfway stage the Mighty U's had been second in the division. So any self-respecting U's fan observing the annual play-off jamboree could be justified in screaming from the highest mountain (a somewhat difficult task in vertically-challenged East Anglia), "It should have been us!" Especially as we had to endure the cheesy grin and grating brummie whine of Ian Atkins revelling in glee as the Cobblers battered their way to play-off success. He pointed out to all and sundry (OK then, *Anglia TV*, whose own hopes of a successful Anglian triumvirate foundered as both Ipsh*t and Looting fell at the final hurdle) that at one stage his team were some 16 points behind United. So he still obviously bears a grudge after we sacked him a few years back. But what really stuck in the back of the throat was the fact that the truth sometimes hurts.

Mind you, after our bright start just reaching the play-offs would have been considered a disappointment. Indeed the play-off finals should have allowed our fans to concentrate on other things - gardening, DIY... anything to pass those bleak mid-summer weekends between May and August.

In the end we failed by a mere handful of points. But what the hell, hope still springs eternal. In fact that final pain was somewhat dulled by the administration (nearly literally) of our loveable north county cousins' shot of Novocain. At least poor old fat Barry Fry, relieved that indeed he didn't own the pile of horse manure that is P*sh, succeeded in half his objective of leading them to Wembley and out of the Second Division. Still, we're not convinced that relegation was what he had in mind! So that's six points in the bag next season then...

THE ADAMS FAMILY

Wycombe Wanderers

First there was eighties pop icon Howard Jones, who threw off his mental chains (whatever they were) to put our beloved town on the map. Now there is crusty eco-warrior Swampy, flying the flag for Wycombe with his burrowing antics; that is, when he's not residing in his parents' rather sumptuous abode in one of the posher districts of town. In between these two, the flag was carried by Wycombe Wanderers, until Alan Smith put an end to that with his 'style' of play. But after a season and a half of expensive shame under South London's finest, new gaffer John Gregory's efforts, combined with Howard's deserved demise and Swampy's

one-trick show, will soon see the Wanderers back where they belong as the town's finest export (outside Bryant & May Matches and the Isaac Lord hardware store).

Many people have claimed that the fateful day that Wanderers capitulated to Peterborough 6-3 after being 3-1 up was the worst of the season. Nonsense! Admittedly, at the time I was reduced to giving Boro's mouldy shed a few well hearty bootings on the way out, but at the end of the day the result got rid of Smithy. Personally, I think all of our players on duty that day deserve a decoration, for choosing temporary humiliation over personal pride; all for the good of the club.

But you probably know all about Smith (and be *very* scared if he gets appointed at your club), and how he makes Alan Ball look like Alex Ferguson; you must know that Wycombe escaped relegation thanks to Johnnie Gregory's fine budget signings and superior football tactics; and you *definitely* know that Wycombe Wanderers are going to whip your arse next season! So let's discuss what you may not know, and what made us at *TAF* weep with laughter or despair.

Our main campaign last year involved trying to secure the release from the nick of former striker Simon Garner, who had been outrageously incarcerated for failing to pay his ex-wife's maintenance! Our special no-expense-spared insert gave supporters a pre-written letter to send to the Queen and a message of cheer to send to HMP Kirkham (and you wouldn't believe how suspicious they were when we asked for the address!). Joyfully for Simon, if not so much for us, he was released on appeal a few days before our issue came out, which meant we had to suffer all manner of smug bastards pointing out the obvious. Note to punters: fanzines are *not* printed on the day of the game using black paint and a carved out potato!

The season began with the opening of our new stand. Admittedly it was a few weeks late, but what do you expect with brickies, eh? The fine summer should have aided construction, but in reality it just helped to top up suntans and the length of the average lunch hour. Anyway, once opened it afforded a fine view of some quite monstrous football, and all for the reasonable price of eight quid. Of course the club quickly realised that it had broken the unwritten law that a football club must fleece its fans at every opportunity, and for the coming season prices have been amended dramatically upwards.

Unfortunately, as many of you will already know, seats bring problems too, such as "Help, I've bought a season ticket and I'm sitting next to Fred West incarnate." Also, you tend to find annoying regulars sitting nearby who have voices that could only have been created by the grabbing hands of Mad Frankie Fraser. We at *TAF* were plagued all year by 'The Steptoe Family', who screamed like Wilfred Bramble's rag and bone man, offering such pearls as, "Shoot!," "Tackle!," and "Run!." Without this wisdom, Wanderers would have surely been relegated...

Another grave annoyance was an all-new brass band, 'Adams Apple'. The band leader had constant run-ins with this fanzine, claiming that we should support their efforts. Utter Arse! As one of our writers put it, would you be happy if you went to see Acker Bilk in concert (probably not, but bear with me), and a bunch of crap footballers appeared in the middle of 'Strangers on the Shore' with bags for posts? I think not. Maybe we could have put up with them if they'd occasionally moved about the ground and annoyed someone else, but like gypsies to a scrap metal yard, they moved in and stayed put. Thankfully, they have now split up, which will save us the trouble of the barrage of 'accidentally' spilt Fanta and live wasp-nests we were planning from the upper tier this coming season!

Also, this was the first season in ages that Wanderers went out to battle wearing a kit that looked like a painter had been testing his brushes on it. Worse still was the away shirt that made most, nay *all*, pub team kits look classy. Thankfully a spirited campaign could see our classic 'quarters' returning soon. Even John Gregory is on record asking if the kit was designed by Stevie Wonder. However the club has stacks of fabric left over, so if anyone's organising a carnival or thinking of opening a blue stripe theme pub, just give them a call.

Player-wise, off the pitch at least, it was a quiet year. The only real incident involved injured midfielder Keith Ryan being assaulted at dubious new 'slapperspot', Club Eden. The press coverage of this event was very cagey, but made it clear that Keith was not at fault. We at *TAF* believe this whole-heartedly, as Keith is your original lovely man. However we can't help but cast our minds back a few years to an occasion when Keith held one of our contributors in a steely headlock outside a late night boozer. At the time, there was a rival fanzine called *Rhubarb Rhubarb* which had been slagging Keith off big-time, and as we bumped into the player we'd thought it would be a laugh to point out our contributor Doug Peters as the editor of said tome. Only after desperate squealing and pleading did the combative midfielder release his grip, and we have long since laughed away the unpleasant affair, and are all now close friends. Well, he says hello every now and then. Probably the saddest aspect of the 'Eden Incident' was that on the same night Club Eden hosted a live PA by a male strip troupe (we think), in which shamed Gladiator Shadow whipped his kecks off for the lasses (and lads).

Other off-pitch amusement was provided by financial director Graham Peart who seems to think he's the new head of M15, with his sinister missives in Wanderers' newspaper *Blues News*. Peter Mandelson couldn't hold a candle to this master of propaganda and spin-doctory, who in one extraordinary outburst claimed that sending letters to the press marked 'Name and address supplied' was the tactic of the terrorist! So now, every time we get one of these we pass it on to New Scotland Yard. You'd be surprised how many timid teenagers or old grannies are active members of the IRA!

On the pitch, fans were shocked by the return of the Mack. No, not stun-gun wielding soul machine Mark Morrison, but lardy Steve Mc-Gavin, who, *à* la Howard Jones, threw off his mental chains (so *that's* what it means) after Smith's departure and became the catalyst for Wycombe's revival. Once he was a figure of derision, but now Wycombe don't look the full ticket without him - and he even scores the odd goal. Flying wing-back Mickey Bell won just about every award going, and at the time of writing he's holding back his signature on a new contract. Perhaps he's hurt his hand, but somehow it seems likely that Sir Mick the second (Nuttell was the first) could be elsewhere soon.

Wycombe were joined by some decent players who played their part in keeping us up, and a mixed bag left the club, including skipper Terry Evans, who will still do someone a damn fine job next season. Joining Terry on the way out were three of the costly signings of the Smith era, John Williams, Dave Farrellalong and Jason 'Lord Lucan' Rowbotham (who simply disappeared). These 'three kings' cost in the region of 300 grand, and within two years were released for nothing; a scandalous waste of money. So next time you see Alan Smith babbling on about the £20 million worth of talent he has created, remember the shit he lumbered us with here.

So, on to the biggest outrage of the season, which was undoubtedly Wycombe at home to Peterborough. After playing a series of crap games on skating rinks, it was nice to see Wanderers go two up on an improved surface against Fatty Fry's Posh, especially as they were relegation rivals. We then witnessed the Peterborough jessies in the second half, falling around like the bastard sons of Norman Wisdom, eventually persuading learned official Fraser Stretton to call the whole thing off with 25 minutes to go, citing a frozen pitch. After the game, deprived of the chance to harangue the referee, who'd sneaked out the back door, a mob of supporters ensured that Fry and his bunch of fairies would not make a quick getaway from their crime. Hilariously, the fans walked slowly in front of the Posh team coach, forcing one player who was clearly incensed at the possibility of missing *Casualty* to fly off the bus for a ruck. Only the soothing tones of Barry Fry (!) placated him. And we beat 'em 2-0 in the re-match - tossers!

But all this is mere trivia. The real reason Wycombe stayed up had nothing to do with players, management, directors or fans. It was all down to Elvis. Travelling to away games, we worked out that we never lost when the King's *American Trilogy* was played. It's true! Shrewsbury, Walsall, Blackpool, Brentford, Luton, and Notts County; it worked every time. And at home, Terry Evans' insistence on playing Guns N Roses' appalling version of *Live and Let Die* to intimidate the oppo did the same trick, ridiculous as it seems. So mock it if you dare, and next season watch out: Axl and Elvis are taking us higher!

TERRY AND MIQUEL SHOW THE LENGTHS PLAYERS ARE GOING TO JUST TO AVOID THE FINES DISHED OUT BY THE NEW BOSS. CLEAN SHAVEN HAS TAKEN ON A WHOLE NEW MEANING.

ALL QUIET ON THE WESTERN AVENUE

Queens Park Rangers

All Quiet On The Western Avenue.
Issue Five   £1

The Notting Hill Situationists had been active in the gent's bogs at the Loft End. The whirling, untidy handwriting in smudged blue biro on a plain white sticker caught my eye, and ignoring the strange mumbling and rustling from the elderly fellow stood at the next urinal I read the words quietly to myself: *Queens Park Rangers Football Club is not dead, but it would appear that our balls have burst.*

Like the Paris students of the 60's, various South American Marxists, and a stained rain-coated ex-policeman in Salford, these here Notting Hill Situationists are clearly fully alert to the impact slogans can have. I know this because assistant editor Adam 'Kebab' Wheeler explained it to me when I returned to my seat. It was half-time in the FA Cup third round and we were soon to be one-nil down to Huddersfield Town: "The revolution, innit," he said, his eyes darting from side to side, "Say no more." I begged him to elucidate. "Well, it's obvious that we're heading towards the margins, you can't ignore it. Look around - what have we lost over the past few years? Everything: players, terraces, our rightful place in the top flight. All hope. It's 'The Man'. And that bloke with the beard comes in with the money and brings his rugby team with him and his sponsorship deals..." He tailed off. I insisted that nothing should be said against Chris Wright, the new multi-millionaire chairman; he winced, strangely: "I'm not saying he's 'The Man', though he is one of that type. All I'm saying is that nothing will really change. If this club is going to be great, to reach its potential, the whole system needs to be destroyed and a new one built on new foundations. Mediocrity - is that what you want?"

It was after this rant that he explained about the Notting Hill Situationists, with a tone of seriousness in his voice not heard since his appearance on camera before the game against Bolton in September (you know how *Sky* have those Vox Pops clips of fans outside the ground talking about the game beforehand? Well, he was on it - although his lengthy dialogue which encompassed his seething hatred of Mark Hateley and a quite startling disgust of Andy Gray was cut to a three second "Er... I think it'll be two-nil" shot). I tried to lighten the mood, but to no avail, and not even Mark Hateley's equaliser could cheer him up - it merely confused matters since five minutes before the powerful 25 yard strike had kept us in the cup, he'd begun another of his remorseless cold-blooded attacks upon the gangly forward. It had started with sly mutterings about excessive wages for talentless, fat-arsed good-for-nothings, and just as he'd reached a crescendo with a full-throated scream of "Hateley - You Baboon Wanker Tart," the said baboon scored a blinder.

We went our separate ways after the game, but his revolutionary talk and bitter Hateley-related outbursts lingered with me. Indeed, it was as I was assessing his theory of disestablishing the current regime in favour of one founded on a communal, non-profit based surge for play-off glory, that I worked my way through the crowd on the east-bound platform at White City and came face to face with the chewing gum and chocolate bar machine. A sticker was emblazoned across the 'Change Given' screen and on it the smudged biro appeared again: *The Hoops are burning - move the goalposts and nutmeg the Ellerslie Road Stand Bourgeoisie.*

Looking back now over the previous nine months, it's all very simple: new chairman... cash... Wilkins the goon goes, Houston the gooner comes... he brings the gang, and by the end of May has snapped up some of his old mates... and sold Hateley... Gallen injured... Sinclair going (?)... other various schemes and whispers... no promotion, no cup glory... faint glimmers of hope made things worse... looking forward to the new season, new signings, new dawns...

But at the time? Confusion and a tickling nausea.

Last season began to ram home all the unspoken fears, all the dark dreams. The effect was like a knee-high Rufus Brevett lunge. The Situationists (who by this time had been to work on a grander scale, with spray paint on the side of a White City estate tenement block), asked all my questions for me: *What is QPR? The sick man of Nationwide? If only because he knows well his heavy history.*

I was less impressed with the answers, and I was increasingly distressed by the Kebab's metamorphosis into some kind of latter-day West London Proudhon, with paranoid anarcho-syndicalist outrage forming the foundation of all his criticisms of Houston's team selection. His usually good-natured slag-offs became nasty and bitter, and his celebrations when things picked up were manic and unnatural. I remember the epic 4-4 draw at Port Vale, where we all justifiably went berserk when the last-gasp equaliser went in. He wrestled an advertising hoarding to the ground and beat the hell out of it for taking the game away from its roots, for being a symbol of capitalist terror, and, inexplicably, for selling Les Ferdinand. I wish he hadn't mentioned Les Ferdinand.

Something had to give, but unless the FA was prepared to hand over the control of English Football to the mysterious Loft Boy Soviets of Liberty that the Situationist slogans had begun to cite in late March as the Playmakers of the Revolution, then it would be my sanity. Everything became unreal. I tried to merge the ideals of *Match of the Day*, Immanuel Kant and the *Shepherds*

Bush Gazette into some coherent socio-shinpad philosophy, only for my research to be turned upside down by a bloke behind me during the Charlton home game. I'd been considering Kant's refusal to accept that the existence and nature of objects in space and time is entirely independent of our knowledge of them (possibly meaning that there's no such thing as anything) when the aforesaid bloke bellowed "Referee you dozy Kant!" I spun around, excitedly questioning his meaning, wondering if all the transcendental realism had thus been defined. The bloke, a stout shaven-headed guru with mystical paintings on his burly forearm and a scar on his cheek that must have been a symbol of wisdom, wasn't too concerned with my questions and simply re-emphasised what appears to be the final, eternal, truth. "I can't believe that Kant. Never offside. Kant!" Everything was upside down for a while.

Even the token bouts of violence and hooliganism that occurred from time to time seemed strangely unworldly. As we stood up at the back of the away stand at West Brom at Christmas for example, watching the First Battle of the Hawthorns, and adding our tuppence worth with well aimed gestures in the general direction of thousands of rabid young Black Country men, growling and gnashing, I remember having to rub my eyes as a giant Andy Impey stepped behind the goal and trampled on the marauding hoards. Naturally reality hit home hard at full time, not just because we were hammered on the pitch (4-1), but in observing assorted skirmishes in the sidestreets around the ground I realised for the first time what a terrible thing it all is. On the same day the Kebab atoned somewhat for his wanton behaviour at Coventry the previous season (Oh! The Premiership! The Premiership!), by cursing the quarrellers and urging them to stop the fighting, join forces, and attack 'The Man'. This 'Man' is an elusive character, all I can be certain of, from what the Kebab and the Situationists have told me, is that:

a) he's a capitalist, with connections in the *Sky TV* hierarchy and the media at large, various multinational organisations, the Criminal Justice system, Oxbridge and the new Stamford Bridge Hotel and Leisure complex, and b) he is a man.

General existential angst prevailed, and in early April, before the Grimsby game, I took out all my metaphysical torments on the people in the Supporters Club office (though I was provoked). My perfectly calm and amiable request for a fixtures card was followed by a farcical exchange of Pythonesque proportions, involving the old lady at the ticket counter and two other members of staff. There was lots of shouting and confusion, and eventually a row with the whole queue behind me. The fracas ended with one bloke telling me that he'd read my fanzine and that it was the "biggest pile of shit" he'd ever read. By the sight and sound of him he didn't seem to be the most discerning of literary critics, so I told him as much and thanked him for his words which might well be twisted into a compliment, in the right hands. He asked me what I meant, so I explained, and he mistook my honest observations about his general character and intelligence to be a request for a punch in the face and made a lunge at me, only my nimble toes and his intervening girlfriend preventing me from receiving a pained head.

I am dissembling. I am shaking at the memories, the horrors. The order is chaos and perhaps a brief summary is now needed: QPR might stagnate, and the thought of eternal nothingness is already breeding despair. Last season John Spencer led the way out, and without his help this entire piece may simply have read: 'Tied, bound, gagged and rogered with a rolled up programme by a balaclavered thug. On the left breast of his black bomber jacket was a small white sticker with a smudged biro message:- *mediocrity*'.

Morrissey, Martin Amis and Zoë Ball all bought copies of the fanzine last season. Along with about, oooh, at least 70 others. The Notting Hill Situationists left their last known mark on the wall outside the South Africa Road Stand in early June. In white paint, it simply read: *St. Jude - don't leave us*. It's all a bit weird if you ask me.

HAVE FUN WITH THE PROGRAMME

READER'S VOICE: WOT, THIS PHOTO AGAIN!

ALL YOU NEED IS:

A) A COPY OF THE BARNSLEY FA CUP PROGRAMME
B) A PAIR OF SCISSORS
C) SOME GLUE
D) A DEVELOPED SENSE OF CYNICISM ABOUT TONY ROBERTS

SIMPLY CUT AROUND THE BOTTOM LEFT HAND CORNER OF THIS PAGE AND GLUE IT TO THE BOTTOM LEFT HAND CORNER OF YOUR BARNSLEY PROGRAMME.

THE RESULT? AN INSTANT VERDICT ON BARNSLEY'S FIRST GOAL....

ALTERNATIVELY, YOU CAN CUT ROUND THE DOTTED LINES OF THE SHAPE OPPOSITE AND SELLOTAPE THE FLAPS (FNARR, FNARR) TO THE BACK OF THE BOTTOM LEFT HAND CORNER OF THAT SAME BARNSLEY PROGRAMME. HEY PRESTO! A NEW WORD MOST ASSOCIATED WITH TONY...

CAN ALSO BE USED TO ILLUSTRATE BLUNDERS v NORWICH, v PORT VALE, v HUDDERSFIELD, ETC. (FOR FULL LIST, SEND SAE TO USUAL ADDRESS...)

Source: *A Kick Up The R's*

ANOTHER VIEW FROM THE TOWER

Blackpool

Another Roller Coaster Season (but sadly - again - not The Big One)

So why, you may wonder, was there not the slightest whiff of anything Tangerine in *Survival of the Fattest 2*? The answer for anyone with the merest trace of a brain (so this naturally excludes Preston and Burnley fans) was there for all to see. The '95-96 season saw Blackpool blow the Second Division title, promotion and then the play-offs, when even Keith Gillespie would've put his shirt on us going up. Like Manchester City, our chairman performed disgracefully and eventually went down, and our manager, fresh from

another......
VIEW FROM THE TOWER

The Blackpool FC Fanzine
Issue 4
Season 96-97

VICKI AND GARY TO TAKE OVER FROM RICHARD AND JUDY

AFTER 'POOL'S PERFORMANCES IN '96, PRODUCERS CHANGE THE NAME OF THE PROGRAMME TO 'IN MOURNING'

YES, IT'S STILL A QUID!

collecting the Manager of the Month award in March and April, went on to pick up his P45 following his sacking in May. In case you still haven't worked it out, the reason SOTF2 received no contribution from Blackpool fans was because we'd all chucked ourselves off the North Pier in a desperate state of depression and didn't resurface till August.

When we did eventually draw breath, Blackpool had a new manager in Gary Megson, a new assistant in Mike Phelan and a new Chairman/woman/ person (or whatever is deemed as politically correct) in Vicki Oyston. We'd brought in a few new faces - Tony Butler and Gary Brabin - and seen the departure of our captain Andy Morrison, who took all of his 36 stone over to Huddersfield Town. Things hadn't changed very much at Bloomfield Road for the opening fixture against Chesterfield. Our man on the PA hadn't bought any records over summer, so we were still enduring The Nolans singing *Blackpool, Blackpool* and still had the worst shirt sponsors in the league: Rebecca's Jewellers (only the name 'Rebecca' had become even bigger on the new shirts just to add insult to injury). When the players came out of the tunnel they were lead by Scooby Doo and Fred Flintstone (sadly not inspired summer signings, but there to promote cable TV) and so began some cartoon capers by the Seasiders. We lost 1-0 to the most boring team in the country (I can only presume they got to the FA Cup semi final by sending their opponents to sleep) and having ended the season in the 'heady heights' of the top three, we started our new campaign in 17th place!

There then followed an indifferent spell where we won a few and lost a few more (including a dreadful night at Turd Moor, home of our beloved Burnley neighbours where we lost 2-0. Not even a chorus of "He's sh*t, he's scouse, he'd rob your f**king house, David Eyres, David Eyres" cheered the proceedings up). The next highlight was Chelsea's visit to the seaside for the Coca Cola Cup. Zola, Gullit and Vialli packed up their bucket and spade and headed for a night at the coast, stopping only to buy a 'kiss me quick' hat and a bag of Harry Ramsden's chips. Within 55 seconds we'd taken the lead, I danced up and down like a headless chicken before feeling a damp patch down my right leg (I was quite relieved when a man next to me with a half empty cup of tea apologised for chucking it all over me!). Andy Gray and Martin Tyler were positioned a hundred feet up above the West Stand covering the game for *Sky* (I asked the club if I could I have that seat for the next game, but they told me unless I had a few hundred yards of scaffolding, I could forget it!). As is always the case when *Sky* follow Blackpool our lead crumbled like a Tory majority and very soon we'd conceded four goals. Revenge was sweet some two weeks later when we went to Stamford Bridge and beat the boys in blue 3-1. With a victory like that under our belt, the fans felt the 'Pool could go all the way, and they did - all the way down the table.

After the debacle of the previous season, it was reasonable to hope that the bad times were behind us, but the final three months of the year were to show that football's not a 'funny game' at all. We had Gary Brabin arrested after Brentford's captain Jamie Bates was daft enough to put his face in front of Brabin's fist; we let a 3-0 home lead slip against Wrexham (final score 3-3); we were robbed at Millwall (two unbelievable penalties awarded against us) and again at Stockport (three goals disallowed and a player sent off during one of the most incompetent spells of refereeing I've ever witnessed) and Nob End beat us 3-0 at Deepdung (once again in front of *Sky* bloody TV). Even worse was to follow. December 6th - the FA Cup second round - Blackpool had a plum home tie against piddling little Hednesford Town. Unfortunately, just like Gillian Taylforth, we blew it. In a moment of utter madness, a man from the crowd wearing tangerine (I refrain from calling him a Blackpool fan) ran on to the pitch and went to deck Gary Megson (as you can see fighting is prevalent at Bloomfield Road, so much so it'll be available on *Sky TV*'s *Box Office* next year) and so was written another rather appalling chapter in the Blackpool saga. After that distasteful event, I honestly believed that Megson (who hadn't been received too well by the fans) would go and Blackpool would be on the slippery slope to relegation.

Then, just before Christmas, things changed. Against our one time bogey team York City, we won 3-0. Not a great victory in the scheme of things, but from this acorn an oak flourished to such an extent that the play-offs almost beckoned. The new year started at Gay Meadow on a pitch that looked more like a picture from a St Moritz holiday brochure. A tangerine ball was used on a surface Torvill and Dean would have been lucky to score points on, and 'Pool secured a valuable away win.

On the playing front, Chris Malkin had arrived from Millwall at the end of '96, but an injury was to rule him out for most of the season, and then in March Phil Clarkson, a local lad who'd supported the Seasiders as a youngster, 'came home' (guess which Skinner and Baddiel song we adopted for him!).

We'd had another derby defeat at the hands of the claret and blue scum, so when it came to our home game against PNE, we were almost resigned to the loss of another three points. Wrong! 'Pool won 2-0 and Phil Clarkson became an overnight hero by scoring both goals. Thanks Scunthorpe for letting us have him, hope the bruises heal after you've kicked yourselves!

Amazingly the end of season party which we all thought would be held in March, started to be put back as the 'top' teams in Division Two started leaking points left, right and centre. So much so that after victories against the eventual top two, Stockport and Bury (how they did it I'll never know) we were within reach of the play-offs. It all came down to the last day of the season against Wrexham. Crewe had to lose at York and we had to beat the sheep-ish ones. 'Pool took about 4,500 fans to the Racecourse Ground, to prove once again we are a 'sleeping giant' (I just wish we'd wake up!) and both the team and the fans outclassed the Welsh. As is often the case though, chances count for nothing and we were to eventually lose 2-1 (we did win 1-0 on the streakers front, but the less said about that the better). After the game the Blackpool team came back on to the pitch to a standing ovation, and for the first time in twelve months optimism had returned to the hearts and minds of the 'Pool faithful.

Before I leave events of '96-97, a word about one of Blackpool's most loyal and ardent followers. Graham Berry was known to everyone at Blackpool and regularly brought a smile to the faces of his fellow 'Pool fans. He sadly died towards the end of the season, and to illustrate how much he was thought of by all at the club, a minute's silence was observed by fans before a game. The Blackpool Independent Supporters Association have ensured his name will always be remembered by naming their Player of the Year award the Graham Berry shield.

So who received my end of season bouquets? Goalkeeper Steve Banks is a player of international class (who had thankfully signed for two more seasons) and has been many fans player of the year. Tony Ellis once again showed the class and skill that will hopefully give him (and 'Pool) the rightful chance to play in a higher division. Our Northern Ireland international James Quinn has matured into a fine player. Andy Preece's end of season form has seen him at his best for a long time and new signings Tony Butler and Phil Clarkson have proved invaluable. But my biggest plaudit of all goes to a man who was criticised by the Norwich fans in *SOTF2*. After falling foul of the faithful early on, Gary Megson proved what a great manager he is. He had to be released from the shackles of Billy Bingham (a director and interfering old sod who thankfully walked out of the club in March, which coincided with an upturn in our results!) and now has the full confidence and support of the majority of Blackpool fans.

So what of the new season? Well, when Billy Bingham left, he took Rebecca's Jewellers sponsorship with him, so we'll get a new backer and we'll be able to wear our shirts without folding our arms across the sponsor's name. Owen's served a year of his stretch and should be out fairly soon, and plans for our new stadium are finally moving along nicely. Hopefully, additions to the side in the summer should strengthen the team and we'll finally be looking at getting out of this wretched division next year. And so I head off into the summer with a smile on my face; maybe football *is* a funny old game after all.

THE 1997 BURNLEY CALENDAR

YES HERE IT IS THE MOMENT YOU HAVEN'T BEEN WAITING FOR THE OFFICIAL 1997 BURNLEY F C CALENDAR - AND IT'S FREE COURTESY OF AVFTT.

JANUARY

1	2	3	4	5	6	7
8	9	10	11	12	13	14
15	16	17				

(Just like Burnley's season it finishes half way through January !!!!)

ANOTHER VINTAGE LIVERPOOL PERFORMANCE

Liverpool

When players with the talent to win the Championship dip their toes in the waters of success but whip them out again upon finding the temperature too hot for their liking, then the only possible outcome was going to be a season of immense disappointment to most Reds. Up until February or thereabouts the team flattered to deceive. On certain days they gave the fans real hope that this year the Championship really could be coming home, but on others, when the going got tough, our lads went modelling.

What really annoyed us about this season was that players with undoubted potential didn't

> ## ANOTHER VINTAGE LIVERPOOL PERFORMANCE
> *A Liverpool Fanzine   Issue 4   Price £1*
> ## EVANS SPICES UP MIDFIELD
> **Pop sensation in shock Kop move**
>
> ROY EVANS has rocked the football world by completing an unprecedented transfer.
>
> Evans, who has been looking to spice up the midfield for the Championship run-in, has signed Mel C from the Spice Girls in a deal worth £3m.
>
> The deal, which also sees Jamie Redknapp join the all female pop sensations in part exchange, is thought to suit all parties.
>
> Redknapp has been looking to move somewhere where his talents will be better appreciated and Mel C would fill the tough-tackling midfield role at Anfield perfectly.
>
> Redknapp, who has vast experience of pouting and appearing in pop videos said of the deal: "It came out of the blue, but I'm happy."
>
> A delighted Mel C said: "It has always been my dream to play for Liverpool, but I had it written into my contract that I didn't want to wear shorts."
>
> Geri Halliwell, the Spice Girl keen to get her kit off for Playboy readers, said of the move: "Mel C wanted to go and Jamie will fit perfectly in to the group. I've heard he likes to hog the bathroom though!"
>
>
> *Jamie with his new teammates yesterday*

seem to have their minds on the job. Or if they did, 'the job' wasn't playing football. Essentially, our lads stopped being serious footballers and became media darlings instead; you couldn't switch on the TV without some bimbo claiming to have bedded one of our stars. Nope, it saddens us to say it but this year Liverpool footballers became the Spice Boys.

Stan and Babb appeared on *TFI Friday* and made right prats of themselves (the latter is said to have gone out with Mastermind contender (!) Jo Guest). Macca started the season having to deal with the stigma of being involved in *that* boozing session with Gazza; Jamie confirmed his status as the catwalk king and in the process got himself a relationship with the gorgeous Louise, and Robbie got himself a real Spice Girl of his own.

Then there was David James. Fresh from modelling for Armani, he had a good first half to the campaign before falling foul of the Mario Brothers. No, not some latest Italian imports to Middlesbrough, but the Nintendo plumbing partnership. After his dodgy performance in our twice in a lifetime 4-3 beating of Newcastle, he claimed that he'd been playing on the GameBoy for eight hours the previous day. Is this really the life modern footballers have? Do they concentrate so little on their game that they're able to spend the best part of a day on such mind-numbing activity?

At least being addicted to computer games isn't as bad as being an alcoholic. This was the accusation levelled at Mark Kennedy by the *News of the World*. Admittedly everything written by this paper has to be taken with a bucket-load of salt, but was there anything in it? Then came the fiasco when Neil Ruddock's Porsche was written off by a mysterious friend. Has Razor got so much cash that he can loan his treasured car to someone who can't drive? So many questions!

It wasn't all bad news though; our loveable neighbours from across Stanley Park always see to that and invariably help us to put our own problems in perspective. They started the season as 'possible title contenders' and ended it as they usually do, battling against the drop which they have more than earned the right to in the last few years. So far have they now fallen that they're reduced to chanting the name of their messiah, Eric 'Le finished' Cantona to try and get on our nerves. Their form on the pitch wasn't that good either, but if you're going to go out of the cups, I suppose it might as well be to potential winners like York City and Bradford.

All of this culminated in the departure of BJ (Big Joe) which of course turned around their league form - they actually won a game during the run in... heady stuff. As bad as they were, I couldn't hide my embarrassment at the postponement of the Anfield derby. Sure there was plenty of rain, but it was hardly unexpected, and if Tranmere can play at home on the same night we must be doing something wrong.

The big pluses were the emergence of three new potential stars in David Thompson, Jamie Carragher and Michael Owen. Owen has generally been described as "Robbie Fowler but faster." Now if that isn't enough to frighten the Premiership in the coming years I don't know what is. I've seen this lad in the youth team and the reserves and he is going to be a real hit. Carragher was given his home debut against Villa but unfortunately for him he tackled too much and scored a goal from midfield, so he was promptly relegated to the bench.

Like David James, the first half of the season was quite impressive. We'd beaten Arsenal twice, including a 4-2 win in the Fizzy Pop Cup which was probably our best performance of the year, and we'd also competently disposed of tricky opposition in the Cup Losers Cup. The 6-3 second leg victory over Sion was heart-stopping at times, but sensational by the end. By Christmas we were still in every competition and top of the league so you couldn't really ask for much more. Who would have guessed then that we would end the season trophyless, putting the fans into what seems like terminal depression?

Our league campaign was solid rather than spectacular. What helped was that no-one seemed to want to challenge us, and we kept on picking up points. Hell, there was even a blue moon after we won at Coventry away. As I stared out of the window and spotted a four leaf clover I realised that it was Phil Babb who had scored the goal. A case for Mulder and Scully I think. Even Stig had got on the scoresheet a few times and if you're a Liverpool fan you'd realise that this was truly the work of a higher being.

The only blot on the copybook at this stage was our home form. Fortress Anfield had turned into Mothercare. Taking points from us was like taking candy from a baby, and with Evans' stubbornness not to change the formation to bring a little variety, home draws looked frighteningly predictable. The days of marking down Liverpool as a definite home win seemed to have gone.

The atmosphere inside the ground didn't help things much either. *AVLP* rippled onto the scene with issue two in August; an illustrated jibe at the deadpan Main Standers was used to try and inject some life into their lungs. We failed miserably. But undeterred we tried again, and it was great to hear the odd murmur when Stan spared our blushes against Leicester on Boxing Day. The festive season came and went and we childishly raised a glass or two to Dave Beasant for his belated gift to John Barnes at the Dell. We've since grown up and realised the mistakes of goalkeepers are no laughing matter (hem hem).

The Championship charge failed to gather its expected momentum despite the Carragher-inspired win over Villa, but at least through the cups we were given some temporary respite. 'Temporary' was of course the operative word as we allowed Ruud Gullit and his men to turn us inside out and brutally pull us apart at the Bridge. People said that *Escape to Victory* was a crap film, but if this had been a movie it would have been the Tory Party equivalent of Hollywood. No-one would plausibly believe the action (although it would probably gross billions at the box office, so well does complete over-the-topness sell these days). The punters would love it for its excitement, and Michael Caine would make a great Mark Hughes, but they'd say it could never happen in real life because Liverpool capitulated like Liverpool never do. True, it was one of the great cup comebacks of all time, but the words 'lacking' and 'bottle' still sprang to mind. Still, I was pleased for the BBC though. At last, here was a decent, good-footballing, London-based team they could heap adoration on. Arsenal of course never fitted the bill and for years they tried with Spurs but never succeeded because Spurs are just Spurs. They were clearly loving it and, with ITV ready to take over, you can even forgive them for over-doing it (*Cup Final Grandstand* back to 11am, A-Z of Chelsea and not Middlesbrough, interviews with Mellor, Lovey-Darling Dickie...).

In fact lessons were not learnt from the '96 Cup Final defeat by the Mancs. The aforementioned Chelsea fixture restored the appallingly unsuccessful midfield pairing of Redknapp and Barnes, and things didn't change either as points were dropped like Melinda Messinger's bras during the run-in. All bar the men in charge had realised the partnership of one player camped in the centre circle with a head that drops as soon as an opponent makes a tackle, and another who works tirelessly for the cause but unfortunately has his best days behind him just didn't work. But still, change was resisted, not in the hope of things coming right, but rather to protect some rather over-inflated egos.

And so, many Collymore sulks later, as the finishing line approached, the boys did their best to make sure we'd endure another season of Martin

Edwards' big-headed gloating. That might be OK for those who knew that come September they'd be chewing the green green grass of pastures new at Villa Park, but for the poor folk who pay their wages it is not an attractive proposition.

However with England's new number one unlikely even to catch a cold, and the national team's new number nine booking himself a seat in the stand for the final few games on a night that humiliatingly saw a third season pass without a win over Everton, then another year in the shadow of the Mancs started to look inevitable. How damn annoying that Paddy Crerand was right.

Thank heavens for Andy Cole though. Without him and his international-standard finishing, the Anfield faithful, and their not so faithful glory-hunting colleagues, would have had nothing to smile about on that fateful day. It was an absolutely dire performance, but sadly there'd been worse only nine days earlier in Paris. Ah well, empty-handed again.

The final push against PSG was a great spectacle, but it came too late. That one fixture saw Liverpool's best and worst of the season. Things petered out rather shamefully after that. Not even the prize of a runners-up spot and Champions League place could spur them to push hard until the end. The last act at Hillsborough was a heart-stopping affair, and the Reds fell by the width of a post, a substitute 'keeper's bootlace and a centre-forward's knee hair away from coming out of the season with something. But yet again, it was too little too late. Time to eat the hat and hand out the tenners.

ARE YOU BLUE OR ARE YOU BLIND?

Manchester City

La Tristesse Durera
(scream to a sigh)

Well, the previous season's relegation didn't exactly come out of the blue with Alan "I've got a World Cup winner's medal" Ball at the helm. Absurdly and against our better judgement, chairman Lee had decided to retain the services of The Squeaky One. We also surprisingly managed to keep the mercurial talent that is Gio Kinkladze, whilst the team's strengthening consisted of selling Keith Curle and Niall Quinn. Quietly confident was the general mood throughout the club, especially as we were the bookies' favourites for the title, and they rarely get it wrong...

Anyway, relegation and the prospect of trips to Grimsby *et al* didn't seem too... erm, well, grim; especially after having had a season to think about it. Previous encounters with the nation's Second Division had brought us 10-1 wins, the inflatable banana army, and while we were down here I could tick some more grounds off the list. Actually going into games expecting victory was going to be another novel experience, whilst the prospect of some (any!) silverware had us positively salivating. In fact by the time the fixtures were announced, the newly-named Nationwide Football League was going to be *the* league to win, not some poxy Carling Premierboat/ship/thing.

The season opened up early with Murdoch's millions forcing us to play Ipswich Town at home, on a Friday night. They were going to be the first of many lambs to the slaughter - we would win convincingly, go top of the table and stay there from the beginning to the end of the season.

Or so we thought.

We did go top, but only courtesy of a shaky 1-0 win. This was to be the highlight of the season; the peak, the pinnacle, the zenith.

In the next two away games we were kicked off the park at Bolton and well beaten by Stoke. For most of the Stoke game, 21,116 fans were calling for Squeaky's head. Yes, that was both sets of fans at both ends of the ground singing in unison. The following day, there was dancing in the streets when he resigned. OK, *I* was dancing in the streets when he resigned. It was one of those teletext moments. You flick the text on to see what's happening in the football world, and bingo! Your team has finally got round to buying that multi-million pound striker you've always dreamed of, or the chairman who has brought your club to its knees has suddenly been killed in a freak car accident.

Getting back to that little ginger twat, when I say 'resigned' what I really mean is 'sacked'. Now Chairman Mao had an opportunity to gain a morsel of respect from the fans by admitting that he'd made a mistake by appointing Ball, and was now rectifying this by sacking him; instead a charade took place whereby Lee paid Ball a big wedge of cash to keep his mouth shut. Within minutes of the announcement about Ball's 'resignation' the rumour-mill ground into operation about who was going to take up the hot-seat. George Graham expressed an interest in taking over, but was told by Francis Lee that he should apply like everyone else. He was the fans' choice but was scared off by either the lack of money, or the chairman's lack of ambition.

The search for a new manager continued and Asa Hartford took charge as caretaker. During this time I saw probably the luckiest win ever (Charlton at home), the best individual performance ever (Gio Kinkladze at Port Vale) and the most spineless performance ever (Lincoln in the League Cup).

September was deeply depressing. Not only did we have the ignominy of a 5-1 aggregate defeat by Lincoln, but we also had to endure Dave Bassett rejecting us. Then out of the blue in early October, Steve Coppell was declared to be the man to lead us out of the wilderness. Initial thoughts were "Can he be trusted, being a rag?" but these were tempered by his reasonable record at Palace and a general feeling of, "Thank God, we've finally got a manager."

A mere 33 days later and we were back again as the laughing stock of British football. Maine Road press conferences were turning into productions of which Shakespeare would have been proud. Questions were asked of Steve Coppell's mental health, his physical welfare, his sexuality and his interest in young boys and prostitutes. His physical condition might well have deteriorated had he visited some of the pubs I frequent. Once a red bastard, always a red bastard was the conclusion and it's a lesson we won't be forgetting in a hurry.

The prospect of losing Steve Coppell and inheriting Phil Neal (despite only being caretaker) was like losing a fiver and then being kicked in the bollocks. Within a week of his tenure we fell to third from bottom and the lowest league position in the club's 105 year history. After a particularly galling midweek defeat against Oxford United, the prospect of relegation entered my head. It also seemed to enter the minds of fellow supporters/sufferers/masochists as a demonstration outside the main entrance of the ground followed the game. We managed to keep our sense of humour as a chant of "Dig him up! Dig him up! Dig him up!" was raised (oooff!), referring to Franny Lee's deceased predecessor Peter Swales.

The press had decided that Howard Wilkinson was to be the next man to be offered the poisoned chalice, having been deposed at Elland Road by

George Graham. This was about as appealing as having Alan Ball back. I hoped and prayed that Wilkinson wasn't offered the job. Then suddenly on the horizon, there was light. A man with a silly moustache and the right credentials became available. Frank Clark resigned as manager of Nottingham Forest, a team which on the December 19th was rooted to the bottom of the Premiership and without a win in the league since the season started.

Three straight defeats over the festive period persuaded Clarky to be City's FIFTH manager in as many months. Frank Clark's arrival instantly instilled a confidence in the team that hadn't been seen for over two years! This led us to a nine game unbeaten run in the league which included a televised 4-1 mauling of Oxford. Chants of "What the fuck is going on?" were heard yet again by Oxford fans, but this time after the Blues had taken a two goal lead.

By mid-February, FA Cup fever hit Maine Road. The fifth round had been reached after stuttering performances against Brentford and Watford in rounds three and four respectively. We were pitted against Middlesbrough in what was looking like a relatively easy cup to win, with a lot of the 'big' teams already knocked out. After all the season ticket holders had gained seats, the rest of the tickets went on sale with an estimated 10,000 fans in the queue, some having been there all night. Obviously on the day the tickets became available, it rained. Solidly! Well, for the eight hours I queued anyway. Compare this to the fact that nearly half of Middlesbrough's 7,000 allocation were returned. I bet the 'other' Yorkshire Boro (Scarborough) would've brought more. The fever ended up being no more than a cold after a disappointing 1-0 defeat, where we were quite frankly robbed.

The rest of the season was a bit dull really. We threatened to make a last-ditch bid for the play-offs but it just didn't materialise. Safety was mathematically secured with four games to go and the real question which was being asked in the final 16 games was whether our Georgian genius would still be with us at the start of the following season. Luckily the answer to that question is yes. Gio has shown some real loyalty, unlike that Brazilian dwarf up on Teesside.

I look forward to next season with the same wide-eyed anticipation that I always do - expecting everything and nothing.

BAMBER'S RIGHT FOOT

Torquay United

When the editor of this esteemed organ contacted me in the close season to ask if I was going to be lending my considerable, weighty cynicism and current angst to the third edition of this continuing footballing saga, I flippantly suggested that he could in fact simply re-run last year's contribution a far as TUFC were concerned, or perhaps even dig out the original copy from *SOTF1*, such is the continuing plight of the loyal and hardy at Plainmoor. Many a true word was said in jest!

The brief is to write about the alternative things that happened at your club; to discuss the lighter, perhaps funnier moments that occurred, and it's all supposed to be done in an up-beat and humorous manner. So I'll apologise right now to all readers of the book who alight on this particular page, and especially to all Torquay United supporters, for being so negative and offering nothing in the way of a cheery message to warm your sagging hopes for the new season.

You see, I find it hard to discover even the slightest chink in the armour of this relentless disappointment. It's not just because we had a bad season, but because this was yet another in a series of bad seasons. What's more we've come to expect it; we're no longer surprised by how pitiful our team can be, and that's desperately sad and worrying. As a club we've done little to change things, to ensure we don't struggle again; we've been neglected by those upstairs and we continue to be neglected as the decline gathers momentum.

Déjà-vu, more of the same, seconds, repeats, action replay; use what term you will, the fact is that we continue to skirt the very edges of the Football League. As the rot spreads, it seems to many that it is only a matter of time before we are inextricably drawn under that dreaded dotted line and into the vortex that spins and churns and deposits you in the Vauxhall Conference.

Last season we finished bottom of the entire Football League; this year we hauled ourselves to a pathetic fourth from bottom. What an accomplishment for all those who are satisfied with complacency and under-achievement! Once again the huge irony of it all was that we were fooled by yet another positive start; the rarefied atmosphere at the higher echelons of the table lulled us into a tremendous sense of well-being.

The new triumvirate of Kevin Hodges, Garry Nelson and Steve McCall, the men charged with the task of navigating the good ship Torquay to some distant, undiscovered island of achievement, steered their way admirably through stormy seas in the early part of the season. Little did they know that their fate was already sealed, like so many captains before them, by the squabbling sharks in the boardroom. Nothing will ever come to fruition when you've got two groups of people pulling in different directions. The managerial trio believed, somewhat naïvely, that their masters would back them all the way and worked extremely hard to bring some dignity to the club, but in the end it all came to nothing.

A few things spiced up the proceedings, including the early-season form of Paul Baker, who bagged goals like a man gone mad, only to be sold at for a pittance. Another cause for celebration was the end of nepotism at the club via the departure of a very unpopular striker who had allegedly assaulted a certain Torquay United supporter in a chip shop during the summer break. A battering indeed! Rumours were also rife concerning further fisticuffs on the training ground and conflict in the dressing room. This could have been seen as a sign of spirit, but unfortunately too many players just seemed to be going through the motions again

I'm no businessman, but I do realise the importance of investment in anything that you want to improve; you only get out what you're prepared to blah, blah ... The irony of our situation is that we do have a successful businessman at the helm, who was more than willing to invest in the early days of his ownership. When the novelty was exactly that, all manner of plans were vaunted and often carried through; we got new stands, an excellent club/pub facility, and we even got promoted! But the momentum soon slowed. We never want to pay for talent, we virtually *give away* our better players in order to save on a wage - there never appears to be any negotiation, we just seem to bite their hand off with whatever it is they're offering - and the saved money remains just that. And this is at a club that was so merrily announcing its profitable status only a few seasons ago.

Now of course I realise that the climate in football has changed, and that the purse strings of clubs outside the Premiership are being squeezed ever tighter as the march toward a financial monopoly continues. So wouldn't it make logical sense to look at some alternatives to give the club some sort of fighting chance? With nurturing local talent being so important to other clubs, shouldn't we set out a business plan to reinstate our reserve team? We could play in the regional leagues to sniff out local talent, our injured first-teamers would have the opportunity to regain fitness after lay-offs, it could foster good community relations and it might even promote competition!

Garry Nelson, famed for his nice-guy image and best selling football diatribe *Left Foot Forward*, was given the opportunity to do a weekly column in *The Guardian*, charting the ups and downs of life on the edge of the Third

Division. Now for those of you who read these articles, you will undoubtedly have noticed how over a period of time the attitude of the man changed; how the cynicism enveloped him as he fought against the ever-prevalent restraints put on him and his fellow coaches at Plainmoor. Now we must have restraints, particularly at this level, and I think the guys drew up their campaign plans fully aware of what the binds on them were. Nevertheless, reading between Garry's lines, it would seem that these restraints were not set in stone. In other words and to coin a much-loved football cliché: someone kept moving the goalposts.

His early columns merely reported the day-to-day goings on at lowly Torquay United, but as time went on these reports hinted at a little more frustration creeping in, until finally Garry realised that he was banging his head against a brick wall, and that everything he attempted for the good of the club would somehow be sabotaged from above. It was no great surprise then when he bode us farewell just after the season's close.

And our chairman told us that he too would be leaving Plainmoor just as soon as he could find someone to take the club off his hands. Not as much of a shock as finding out that he sponsored Peter Fox's playing kit last year (yes, that's right, Exeter's boss and sometime goalkeeper!) but a surprise nonetheless when it was confirmed. And if you're interested, the price is falling all the time.

BRF has supported the chairman in the past, most notably when we encouraged him to fight on during a boardroom power struggle a few years ago, but it's now time for a change. All we hope is that someone gets behind the wheel soon, before it's too late.

So if there are any multi-millionaires out there wondering what to buy themselves for Christmas, what better present could you find than a football club with huge potential in the right hands, in a beautiful part of the world and with some of the most loyal supporters you could find anywhere. Go on, get your wallet out and come on down!

And finally to all those really loyal fans who've attended no matter what; that happy dwindling band who've maintained the faith, stayed ultra-loyal and shown a love for their club like few others in the country: take a bow. You know who you are...

BEYOND THE BOUNDARY

Oldham Athletic

As the kick-off to the new term got closer, those who were looking on the bright side may had begun to feel somewhat less sanguine about the club's prospects. The failure to invest in experience to go alongside the undoubted promise of youth, coupled with the departure of yet more senior players, left the first team squad looking thinner than Kate Moss. Leaving Boundary Park during the summer were Darren Beckford, Neil Pointon, Paul Gerrard and Chris Makin. The sole arrival, that of John Morrow on a free transfer from Rangers, seemed unlikely to offset the outflow, regardless of the promise of youth.

No. 49
(April/May '97)

INSIDE: THE LATICS REPORT
DUFFLECOAT DAN
THE FALL OF JOE ROYLE
GREAT LATICS MATCHES
MEMORABLE PRE-MATCH PINTS
LETTERS, MATCH REPORTS AND
MUCH MORE............

VOTE NEIL WARNOCK! VOTE NEIL WARNOCK!

As election fever mounts, the fans make their voice heard. New Latics, new football, new success, new Warnock, new Ritchie, new team, new now, new now............

80p

So on August in a mood of somewhat tempered optimism, the season got underway with a home fixture against Stoke City. As the side took to the field, the assembled throng got their first glimpse of the garish dog's dinner of a playing outfit that new sponsors Pony had come up with. Pink and blue hoops were claimed to have a connection with the club's heritage but the fact that the side had apparently played in such garb for a single season shortly after the Second World War was lost on most.

More substantial versions of the shirt are more commonly seen on the rugby field where the theory runs that the horizontal hoops add bulk to a player's appearance, giving an impression of solidity. On the Latics' players the outfits just made them look slow and fat; not I suspect the message that they were designed to convey to the opposition!

The 90 minutes against Stoke encapsulated the entire season rather neatly, as the game was lost to a couple of sucker blows before a brief revival raised the hopes, only for a long drawn out denouement to end in eventual disappointment. If we'd known then how things were going to pan out, then perhaps we'd have called it a day there and then. It would have saved an awful lot of time, money and heartache, and we could all have taken up something rather more productive; basket weaving maybe.

Regardless of prospects, perceived or otherwise, there was no doubt that we had a tough start with a succession of games against sides who had either featured in the play-offs or had been promoted during the previous term. Selhurst Park for example, a venue where Latics' haven't tasted victory in my lifetime. (We actually led there 2-1 in the late 80's but eventually lost 3-2 thanks to a first league goal scored by a certain Ian Wright.) This year was no different and we were pasted 3-0.

Two games, two defeats, but no need to panic. Oh dear, another 1-0 reverse in the next one at Swindon and the seeds of doubt started to germinate. It was the manner of our beating which caused the most anxiety; we played a 10-0-0 formation and lost in the last minute to a very limited side. Principal among our problems was an obvious lack of power, a situation exasperated by Darren Beckford's departure and our failure to hold onto the on-loan Gerry Creaney. The 3-3 draw at home to Ipswich therefore came as something of a comfort as goals from Redmond, Banger and Rickers bagged Latics their first point of the year. That draw sent us to our highest league placing of the entire season: a remarkable 20th place!

Previous failings also meant that we faced the prospect of the first round of the League Cup for the first time in a decade. Our desperate start persuaded just 2,975 hardy souls to turn out and see Latics go down 1-0 at home to Grimsby. Yet this competition was to prove our only bright spot during the first part of season as a McCarthy goal levelled the aggregate score to prompt the first penalty shoot-out involving the club since an Anglo-Scottish tie in the early 70's. Our lack of practice wasn't a problem as all five Latics penalties hit the back of the net to secure a second round tie against Tranmere. A victory at Prenton Park allied to a home draw saw Latics through to a potentially terrifying visit to Newcastle's St James' Park to play the Magpies only a few days after they had smashed five past Man United.

Hell, on our form a trip to St James' Park Exeter would've been scary enough, but in the event we actually did ourselves proud, losing only to a highly debatable penalty. In the meantime the struggle continued mercilessly and it was of little surprise that after three months Latics were rock bottom without a single credit in the win column. Still, for a little while it appeared that salvation may have arrived in the highly unlikely shape (literally!) of the crane-like Ian Ormondroyd, picked up on a free transfer from Bradford. We were to be pleasantly surprised as our stilt-like apparition suddenly began banging in the goals with staggering regularity. In his second game he got the opener against West Brom and buried two more at home to Port Vale to finally get our season up and running. At one point we actually strung together an eight game unbeaten run, but it still wasn't enough to lift us off the bottom of the pile.

We beat Wolves at Molineux (who didn't?) with Ormondroyd scoring again, and then recorded the undoubted highlight of the whole nine months by beating neighbours Man City in front of a near capacity 13,000 Boundary Park crowd. Out of the bottom three at last!

Just as we seemed to be getting up a head of steam, the bloody weather intervened. A creditable point at Bramall Lane was all we gleaned from the festive period and Barnsley ended our interest in the FA Cup. By the time the league action restarted in earnest the momentum had gone and we began the headlong slide to relegation with a vengeance. When Huddersfield came to Boundary Park at the end of January they were the first in a sequence of five games against fellow relegation strugglers. Quite simply if we were to stand a reasonable chance of retaining our First Division status we had to put one over these teams. We lost all five!

The die was cast. We were now reduced to performing wild calculations in an attempt to prolong our tenure in the upper reaches of the Nationwide. And to our credit we managed to keep 'mathematically certain' at bay until very nearly the last day. But in all reality, apart from the occasional shaft of light, we never really looked like making the escape.

Another 3-0 defeat by Grimsby marked the defining moment in the Oldham careers of Graeme Sharpe and Colin Harvey as they decided enough was enough and headed for the exit. The directors then moved with commendable rapidity in securing the services of Neil Warnock and Andy Ritchie. Ritchie's appointment as assistant was a neat way of deflecting criticism for denying him the opportunity to take over when Joe Royle left, and in Neil Warnock we acquired a dynamic manager well used to the struggles common to so many smaller clubs.

Even at this late stage, could Latics turn it around? Well, we weren't going to throw in the towel without a fight. We beat QPR at Loftus Road, did the unexpected double over Wolves and thumped Swindon 5-1 on Easter Monday. But it was too little too late especially with Bolton and Barnsley (our successors as carriers of the small town club torch) to come. And so to the final two games. A tame defeat at Reading rather summed things up, especially when Andy Ritchie's scuffed penalty barely reached the goalkeeper; it was a sad postscript to the great man's Latics playing career. But incredibly escape was still technically possible, as the anorak tendency tried to convince themselves that we could score eight on the final day. Needless to say it never came to that as a midweek Bradford win confirmed what we'd known all along... Welcome to Division 2!

There can be no excuses, no hard luck stories. Latics were one of the worst three teams in an average division, and at no point during a long and wearing journey did they do anything to persuade all but the maniacally blinkered that they would have been worthy of First Division status in '97-98.

BLUE AND WIGHT

Portsmouth

Every so often a season comes along which makes supporting a club seem all the more worthwhile. And although Pompey missed out on both promotion and cup glory there is little doubt that the outcome of the '96-97 season fell into that category, partly because it started so disastrously.

The post-Euro '96 euphoria seemed to have largely passed Pompey by as the players reported back for pre-season training. Optimism that the previous May's brush with relegation was a one-off had dissipated as the loathed Gregory family - fronted at Fratton by father Jim's son Martin - had failed to invest a bean in new players. Even the conversion of Fratton into an all-seater stadium was something of a joke, with just 4,500 seats being installed, reducing the capacity to just over 11,000.

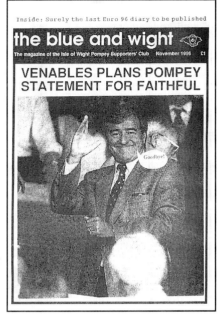

Inside: Surely the last Euro 96 diary to be published

the blue and wight

The magazine of the Isle of Wight Pompey Supporters' Club   November 1996   £1

VENABLES PLANS POMPEY STATEMENT FOR FAITHFUL

Goodbye!

But as July turned to August rumours emerged that Terry Venables - architect of much of that Euro '96 euphoria - was poised to seal a deal with the Gregorys to take Pompey over. Before their substance was confirmed though, fans loyal to a consortium of Northern businessmen who had been rebuffed by Gregory the previous season staged one last protest - at a pre-season friendly in France against Le Havre.

Unfortunately their 'sit-down' pitch protest was hijacked by the less than sensible end of Pompey's support and the match had to be abandoned at half time. Trouble on the ferry home only added to the club's embarrassment - and led to inevitable headlines about hooligans.

Against this backdrop though, Venables expressed his 'interest' and on the eve of the season struck a deal whereby he would act as Pompey's football 'consultant' with an option to buy the club for a nominal sum - £1 was the figure usually cited - within three years.

The more cynical of us (the *Blue and Wight* included - see our chosen cover!) saw this as Venners' chance to fleece the club for a few quid, with no risk, until something more lucrative turned up. And although the team's tactics undoubtedly changed to a more passing game that suited the diminutive stature of most of the squad, results hardly improved and by the end of October we were stuck in the relegation zone again.

And then things began to happen... First, Spurs reserve winger Andy Turner arrived in September - they actually stumped up money to sign him. Then the club - by now effectively run by Venables' long-time business partner Eddie Ashby - heeded the fans' desperate pleas to add seating to the ground to make it look like a football stadium again.

A 4-0 thrashing of West Bromwich Albion in early November - all four goals coming in the first half, prompting half time memories of a 4-4 draw with Fulham among 90% of our notoriously pessimistic following - suggested better things on the field. By the end of the month Stoke and Manchester City had been seen off at Fratton and at the same time a defender, Adrian Whitbread, a midfielder, Arsenal's David Hillier, and a striker, a young Swede called Mathias Svensson, had all been signed for money. Inevitably the words 'play' and 'offs' entered the fans' vocabulary for the first time, though not necessarily in that order.

Throughout the Autumn Venables was being linked with every half decent job that came up - Blackburn and Manchester City most notably - and as he wasn't exactly turning them down, it meant most of us still didn't expect him to be around for FA Cup third round day, let alone three years. So when TV confirmed speculation he was to be the new Australian national coach, the words "We told you..." stuck in our throats, as at the same time he added he'd just become Pompey chairman too. Not exactly a multi-million pound investment, but enough for most fans to give his commitment the benefit of the doubt for the first time.

Pompey's progress on the field was hampered by a lack of consistency over Christmas, summed up by our new Swedish striking sensation Svensson - to overuse the alliterative art - who netted twice on his home debut against Huddersfield, only to be sent off in the next game. When Pompey travelled to Wolverhampton for our third round cup game, few of the 2,900 fans expected much. The last time Pompey had won at Molineux was 1951 and Wolves were short-priced favourites for promotion, despite some dodgy home form. So when Alan McLaughlin put us 1-0 up with just over 20 minutes to go, the first thing we expected to happen was Wolves to go straight up the other end and equalise. Which they did. Less expected was for Paul Hall to nudge home from close range with time running out and seal a memorable day out.

But typically, the following week, Bolton came to a foggy Fratton and won with embarrassing ease, a result which apparently caused some soul-searching in the home dressing room afterwards. The players and manager didn't think they were relegation material, whereas most of the fans, backed up by the league table, did. And then they went and won at promotion-chasing Crystal Palace, at Selhurst Park of all places, scene of three promotion debacles for Pompey in '85, '86 and '97. And a 5-1 thumping in 1993. And a last minute cup defeat in 1990... the list goes on. Scorer of the equaliser was Lee Bradbury, plucked from army obscurity by manager Terry Fenwick 18 months previously. Scorer of the winner was Andy Thomson, snapped up by Fenwick from Swindon's reserves twelve months before. Perhaps the bloke hadn't been bullshitting about the potential of this lot after all...

Three home wins later - including a 3-0 stuffing of Reading in the cup - and Fenwick was, admittedly for the first time in his managerial career, trying desperately to play down the fans' expectations of his emerging team. The words 'play' and 'off' were now frequently used together, not to mention 'Wembley' and 'two times this season'.

After Pompey's 3-2 victory at Premiership Leeds in the FA Cup fifth round he could forget keeping the lid on the fans' hopes. Backed by almost 4,000 newly-recruited 'Blue Army' members - if there's a money-spinning bandwagon, you can guarantee a football club will jump on it - Pompey simply outclassed Leeds, both on the pitch and in the stands. Fickle they may be, but when Pompey's fans have a team worth supporting, few can match their passion...

At last Fenwick had exorcised the ghosts of his predecessor Jim Smith - he even now had his own 'Corporal Punishment' in Bradbury - and could be judged on his merits.

In the league, points continued to be gathered as if a play-off spot was considered a right rather than the rash bet it had seemed in mid-January. Even a goal deficit and a man short at Huddersfield proved no barrier to a Sammy Igoe-inspired 3-1 win! But in the cup, our Premiership pretensions were somewhat exposed by Mark Hughes, Gianfranco Zola and Co, who dismantled Pompey 4-1 in front of a 15,800 full house at Fratton for the benefit of the watching nation on *Sky*. Thanks for that.

Our eight match unbeaten run in the league was ended by QPR in a game held up by fighting in the stands, an event which was blown somewhat out of proportion by the fact that BBC TV Centre is 500 yards down the road. Friends of mine in Italy even saw it on their TV news! Wouldn't have made a paragraph in the 'good old days' (i.e. the late 1960's) grumbled my mate Chris... Hmmm.

The play-offs were still there for the taking however, provided games in hand were won. Six of our last nine matches were also at home, and two of them soon provided six more points as Reading and Bradford were firmly put in their place. With another three points there for the taking on Easter Monday at bottom of the table Southend, the season had been turned on its head and now Pompey were favourites to claim a play-off place. And then, it all went wrong. An inspired second half display by Southend 'keeper Simon Royce after a catastrophic first half defensive trauma had gifted our opponents a 2-0 lead, sowed the first seed of doubt that perhaps getting into the Premiership might not be such a good idea after all. Twelve days later a highly ordinary but well organised Tranmere side stuffed us 3-1 at Fratton and the following week lowly Charlton were good value for a 2-1 win, effectively leaving our play-off dream in tatters.

To be fair the team rallied, giving Barnsley a 4-2 pasting at Fratton as they looked for three points to go up. Star that night was Bradbury, who bagged an impressive hat-trick and sealed his well deserved call-up for the England U21 side. Although Ipswich finally ended our mathematical possibility of the play-offs three nights later, the season ended on a high note as Paul Hall repeated his Molineux late show to secure an unprecedented second win at Wolves. Typical. You don't have one for 46 years, then two come along at once...

Pompey fans still regard our club as potentially one of the biggest in the land. On the face of it that's a ridiculous notion, as our only trophies since the First Division title was lifted (in 1949 and 1950) have been two Third Division titles in 1962 and 1983. Oh, and don't forget the Southern Professional Floodlit Cup in 1957. The last time we reached Wembley was for the London War Cup in 1942... even Darlington have reached the twin towers more recently than that!

But it seems as if the well respected Terry Venables has been seduced by the dream of restoring Pompey to 'greatness'. Shortly before the Leeds game he stumped up his quid and Pompey now belongs to him. Under TV's guidance Terry Fenwick is almost looking like a tactically astute manager, and what little money he has had to spend has been, by and large, spent wisely. Within four months of taking over, the Fratton End - truncated since 1986 - is now actually being rebuilt, and we have a membership scheme with more than 10,000 members.

Time will tell if 'Tel spent his money wisely. There is still concern that there doesn't seem to be an investor behind the scenes with several million pounds burning a hole in his (or her) pocket and the willingness to back Venables' judgement. But at the moment Pompey seem to be moving in the right direction again. Talk among the fans this summer is of a promotion bid rather than a relegation struggle next season. Cautious optimism prevails. Wembley may not exactly be beckoning again just yet... but it's better than contemplating the AutoWindscreens Shield.

THE BLUE EAGLE

Colchester United

We like it down here - honest!

Welcome to another season characterised by one word: inconsistency. Readers of the first two editions of *Survival of the Fattest* will know that this is a term well known to supporters of Colchester United, and basically we're getting fed up using it. In recent times we've promised much, never more so than this year, and failed to deliver every time. Impatience is growing!

Having made the play-offs last year, we set our sights on achieving at least the same this time around. An opening day home defeat at the hands of Hartlepool

> **The Blue Eagle**
>
> The Colchester United Fanzine
> Written By Supporters For Supporters
>
> We're All Going To Wembley.
>
> Your guide to life, football and everything. Essential reading for all CUFC supporters and still you can own a copy for only....
>
> **Issue 22**   **£1.00**

wasn't the ideal start, although a 2-1 defeat at home by West Brom in the League Cup (can't get used to all that sponsorship lark) wasn't exactly unexpected; we've only won one game in this competition in donkey's years (see SOTF2 for full details). So imagine our astonishment when we went to West Brom in the away leg and won 3-1. Phewee, into the second round; it was like Man Utd winning a European Cup leg! Needless to say we progressed no further, but it was still mighty encouraging, and lulled us poor souls into believing that great things lay ahead for the U's.

Meanwhile, back in the league we were fast becoming the pools punters' favourites as we racked up the draws at a phenomenal rate. All told we would record 17 of the little buggers over the course of the season, 12 of which were scoring draws worth three points. If only! Orient certainly gifted us one of those draws courtesy of the most pathetic penalty kick I've ever seen. What was even funnier was that it was a retaken effort after they'd already scored; we pissed ourselves.

We also got to the second round of the AutoThingy and were drawn to play Millwall at the New Den. Mmmm, nice! Mind you it's a great looking stadium with good facilities, decent catering (including beer inside th hurrah) and an excellent view. The Lions were actually going w played them on a bloody freezing Autumn evening, and wha game of footy it was too, with the U's staging a great fight-back to draw 2-2 at the end of normal time. Into Golden Goals time and we only had to wait a couple of minutes for new boy Paul Buckle to score the instant winner. There wasn't even any trouble afterwards, although there were a few mouthy sprogs on the train back to London Bridge. Into the third round of the WashWipe and Brentford were the next team from the upper reaches of the second to succumb to the rampaging U's; our winning goal came from Paul Abrahams who'd just started his second spell at Colchester after being released by... Brentford. Wey hey!

The fourth round, or regional semi-finals as they were billed, saw us finally get a home tie to fellow Third Division hopefuls Northampton Town. Gulp, another 2-1 victory and suddenly everyone started to take the highly prestigious AutoWindscreens Shield (to give it its full and rather splendid title) seriously. We were now only two legs away from Wembley and only Barry 'cor blimey guvna' Fry's Peterborough stood in our way. The first leg was a disaster and we gave a lacklustre display, losing 2-0 at London Road, but never fear, the U's pulled out a magnificent performance in the return and we trounced the Posh 3-0. (Why oh why couldn't we play like that in the league?)

Unfortunately, the evening was marred by trouble after the game, caused by visiting supporters. Any club where one of the supporters' coaches stops and spills its fans onto the street enabling them to lay into 14 and 15-year-olds has a real problem. I'd have preferred if they'd stayed in the Second Division, because I don't want them anywhere near our place again. Anyway, we won, so ha, and up yours!

The final against Carlisle was actually a pretty dour affair, and it was no real surprise when it remained goalless after 120 minutes of football. Having gone out of the season's other cup competitions on penalties, things didn't bode well for the U's, and sure enough this game was no different. After fleeting encouragement when Carl Emberson saved the third Carlisle penalty to put us 2-1 ahead, fate then realised what was going on and threw a bloody great spanner in the works to ensure that our last two penalties were saved. So Carlisle became the holders of The Dodgy Wheelbalance Cup or whatever the Mickey Mouse thing's called... no sour grapes here!

And so it was back to the league. Since our home win over Exeter back in October we'd had an amazing run which in which we'd been unbeaten for 18 league games, not to mention all those Autowotsit matches. Unfortunately, nine of these were draws, which, coupled with our seven draws from the previous 15 matches, cost us dear at the end of the season. We did have some highlights along the way, including a 7-1 win over Lincoln and a 3-0 away win at old friends (not) Exeter. But then, of course, it all turned sour.

It used to be that the U's would play really well until Christmas. Then we stretched the winning streaks into January and February, and this year we even reached March. But due to some crap time-tabling by the Football League, he season carried on for another two months, which was our downfall. Sod ¬x Ferguson wanting to lengthen the season - I want it shortened! Two or three games a week, every week, finishing in February. Premiershit here we come...

Anyway, back to planet Earth, and a trip to Scunthorpe which for some of us turned into a bit of an epic trek. A few hardy souls figured that the 45 minutes' planned coach stop at a service station outside Grantham would be ample time to jump into a cab, knock back a pint (or two) of real ale in a decent hostelry in town, return to the coach and continue our journey to Scunny. One market-day traffic jam, an explanatory phone call to the service station and a couple of pints later, we resisted the (strong) temptation to forget the game in favour of a decent drinking session, and made a cardiac-inducing run to the station for the next train. We should have stayed in the pub. A 2-1 defeat brought our winning streak to a shuddering halt, with Cambridge and Scarborough to follow suit, followed soon after by a run that saw us lose to Hartlepool, Darlington and Hereford in a fortnight (I bet the Brighton fans were cursing us). We'd thrown it away.

I'd also like to pose a question at this point: where do Wigan get their stewards? As the end of the season approached, being ever-optimistic of reaching the play-offs, several of us travelled north on a cold Tuesday night to watch our game with the big-spending Latics. Since the away end was devoid of any catering facilities, we ventured into the home stand at half time (as directed by the stewards). Spotting the Colchester players trudging off the pitch (we were losing at this stage), a quick cheer from one U's fan saw his quick ejection on the grounds of crowd incitement! Once outside, he spent the second half chatting to Wigan fans who'd also been ejected, this time for over-zealously cheering their own goal! Where the hell are these stewards from? Scarborough, home of the school of "that pasty is a dangerous weapon" crowd control, perhaps? Thank God we won't be going there next season.

By the time our final game came along we needed four points in order to wrench seventh spot away from Cardiff, and no matter how hard we looked down the back of the sofa for those missing points carelessly mislaid by Brighton and Middlesbrough, they were nowhere to be found. I reckon Souness found them and hid them in a cupboard at Southampton just in case they needed them; who knows?

So we finished eighth, one poxy point off the play-offs. I can't stop thinking that just one goal in any of the 17 drawn games could have meant we'd be playing in the Second Division next season, but never mind. So what will next season bring? Internal strife has seen the departures of Player of the Year Chris Fry to Exeter and the respected Adam Locke to newly-promoted Northampton, both of course for our usual fee - nothing! We have a strange (that's 'unique and revolutionary' according to the club) sponsorship deal which will see different company's names emblazoned on home and away kits, and we have buckets of anticipation. And of course Notts County is a new ' most of us. See you next year...

BRIAN MOORE'S HEAD

Gillingham

It was a season of two halves (Brian). The first was disappointing in terms of league results, but contained a memorable cup run. The second saw Gillingham produce the best football seen at Priestfield for years. But exactly how do you follow the first promotion-winning season for over 20 years (if not with another one?). Read on...

As you would expect from a set of supporters who'd witnessed promotion not four months earlier, optimism abounded amongst the Priestfield faithful at the season's commencement. The team had been strengthened with the signing of Andy Hessenthaler from Watford for a club record of £235,000 while other new faces included the allegedly highly rated teenager Lennie Piper from Wimbledon, Ian Chapman on a free from Brighton (who had just been voted their Player of the Year, which is right up there with being recognised as Norway's most popular beat combo), defender Matt Bryant from Bristol City for £65,000 and an injury-prone winger called Iffy Onuora from Mansfield for £25,000 (more of him later).

Opening day opponents were Bristol City, foes of old who we'd not met since relegation in '89. The result was a hugely satisfying 3-2 win courtesy of a last minute debut goal from the lad Piper, and pre-season optimism remained intact. Well, for a couple of more games at least. At Griffin Park the Gills were utterly outclassed by Brentford, leaving us in no doubt that the class divide between the bottom two divisions was a yawning chasm.

Chesterfield won 1-0 at Priestfield four days later, something they have done with monotonous regularity since we beat them 10 (ten) - 0 in 1987, and any lingering expectation was well and truly buried by mid-September, when consecutive away defeats at Luton and Walsall saw the team slip to a less than comfortable 18th position. To make matters worse, top scorer Leo Fortune-West broke his ankle against the Saddlers, effectively ending his season.

Although we didn't realise it at the time, Leo's injury was to prove a turning point. The previously lumbering and ineffective Onuora was shifted from the wing to centre forward and responded immediately by scoring a last minute goal in the League Cup game at Barnsley... in his own net! Despite this we returned home with a highly creditable 1-1 draw at the First Division high flyers, Iffy's late *faux pas* cancelling out Simon Radcliffe's 35 yard wonder goal.

The iffy Iffy came good in the next game though, rounding several Rotherham defenders (OK, probably no great shakes) and beating the 'keeper at the near post for his first Gills goal. He followed that with an even better second, a stonking 25 yard volley, which caused me to comment to my fellow Rainham Ender that I was beginning to warm to him a little bit now. By the time Iffy lamped in his hat-trick my temperature gauge was rising even further.

Barnsley were removed from the League Cup to set up a third round meeting with Coventry, while Iffy continued his one-man Goal of the Season contest against Notts County a week later. Apparently, boss Tony Pulis noted that the County 'keeper was coming a long way off his line, and let his players know. Iffy needed no second invite, running deep from his own half before chipping the 'keeper from 30 yards for a quite stunning goal.

The now decidedly un-iffy Iffy got us back on track after a bit of a wobble with another snorter at Gay Meadow, but hopes for the Coventry game were dampened when we lost at home to Millwall, exhibiting the kind of defending that would have seen steam coming out of Alan Hansen's ears had he witnessed it. Thankfully, Tony Pulis had already recognised the need to strengthen the back line, and the signing of Guy Butters from Portsmouth for £225,000 didn't come a moment too soon.

And so to Coventry. At half time and 2-0 down it was all over for the plucky lower division minnows. Or was it? Iffy pulled a goal back soon after the break and the Premiership outfit showed exactly why they were struggling so badly by totally bottling it thereafter. Simon Radcliffe's 25 yarder levelled matters, and by the end the Sky Blues were hanging on for dear life.

At this stage it became clear that some of the players had things other than the winning of league points on their minds. A grim no-score draw at Bristol Rovers (where Andy Hessenthaler had a paddy because a section of the Gills support allegedly shouted nasty things at him - ah, didums) was sandwiched between defeats by Plymouth and at Wrexham where a ludicrous display of refereeing by Fraser Stretton culminated in an increasingly frustrated Onuora being red-carded for kicking out at some Welshie defender.

Not the best of preparation for the Coventry replay then, but over 3,000 Gills travelled to Highfield Road in party mood. What followed will go down as one of the greatest nights in the club's history as the massed ranks of blue and white watched in raptures as our team outplayed the Premier League big boys. We controlled the game for long periods, while so-called stars Gary McAllister, John Salako and, erm, Noel Whelan, gave every indication that they just didn't fancy it. In the 72nd minute Steve Butler escaped down the wing and sent over a cross, Liam Daish half-cleared and the ball ran across goal to the club's longest serving player Neil Smith. Goal-a-season-Smudger slotted joyously home and the Gills contingent went totally mental. I still get goose bumps thinking about it now. Make no mistake, we deserved to win: the papers said so, their manager said so, their players said so and we *knew* so.

Back to the bread and butter of league football. A Tuesday night at Peterborough wouldn't usually warrant a mention but on this evening 'keeper Jim Stannard's increasingly dodgy hamstring finally went ping. Caught out at not having a proper second choice 'keeper, centre half Mark Harris had to don the gloves. Boro, sensing their chance, responded by peppering the stands, corner flag and floodlights (you might have seen fatty Fry going ballistic on TV). The profligate Posh managed a solitary shot on target, and even that went straight at our part-time custodian. Much to our amusement Gills' only two efforts on goal saw Butler smack the bar and Iffy bury the rebound.

While league results continued to be patchy, over 5,000 followed the team to Ipswich for the League Cup fourth round. The performance matched that at Coventry in all but one respect; we failed to find the killer touch in front of goal, and were unlucky to lose 1-0. We all now hoped that we could concentrate on improving on our steadily declining league placing.

Christmas was a disaster. Luton accepted our gift of a last minute penalty miss on Boxing Day and Yo-Ho-Hoed all the way back home. Two days later we collapsed 5-1 at Burnley and had Iffy sent off for lobbing the ball at the linesman (well, it was *never* their throw-in!). These two results saw us slip into the dreaded bottom four for the first time.

Once again, cup football intervened. The visit of Derby proved something of an unwelcome distraction, especially when the ref was named as Paul Alcock. Last year he'd managed to stitch us up in the cup at Reading and this time he annoyed us further by abandoning the goalless game after 66 minutes due to a frozen pitch, even though the players didn't appear to mind playing on the surface.

In the new year we signed striker Ade Akinbiyi from Norwich for a new club record of £250,000. But he could do little to help in the rearranged Derby game. Once again Alcock proved a factor in the 2-0 defeat by failing to send off Derby's Sean Flynn after he blatantly elbowed Simon Radcliffe (still, to be fair to Mr Alcock, he didn't have an ideal view from his position *six* feet away looking *directly* at the incident!).

January's home game with Plymouth saw more strange weather conditions and the threat of further unwelcome abandonments. After racing into a 3-0 lead we were in a state of panic as banks of fog rolled across Priestfield. By the time Akinbiyi's excellent first goal for the club had all but sealed a 4-1 win we still had to get through a final ten minutes played in a worsening eerie gloom.

With goals and entertainment starting to flow again, fears of relegation were finally banished. One of the best moments of the season came at Ashton Gate, scene of so many dodgy penalties, sendings off and defeats in the 80's, where we clinched a 1-0 victory with, oh sweet irony, a penalty. In fact, Gillingham were now the form team in the division, and continued to climb up the table as the campaign drew to a close.

At the end of the day (Brian) we were treated to cup glory, great goals and good football. And with a tally of 40 points from our last 20 games there is realistic hope of a better finish next time out. On the debit side our disciplinary record was poor again and we had some bad luck with injuries (none more so than the bizarre accidents which saw Matt Bryant accidentally shoot himself in the leg while out hunting and Glen Thomas almost lose his sight in one eye when he ran into a tree during training - no, really). But all in all it was an enjoyable nine months. I doubt if there are many supporters of mid-table sides happier with their lot.

THINGS TO DO DURING THE CLOSE SEASON

a little light reading

hang around in downtown Chatham

construct a giant model of Jimmy Hill's head

start the Toyah revival (you know it's gonna happen)

staple yourself to the floor

CHEAT

Sheffield Wednesday

We changed our name mid-season to The Hard To Beat Sheffield Wednesday. We would have of course much preferred to be The Incredibly Brilliant Sheffield Wednesday, but it would do for now; after all it was an improvement on last season's The Crap Sheffield Wednesday by a long chalk.

In fact we'd been so dire for much of '95-96 that we really weren't expecting much at all this year. Apart from the on-off, on-off, on-off Lombardo fiasco, summer activity in the transfer market was hardly inspiring either; no Ravanellis, Viallis or Emersons for us, just an untried youngster from

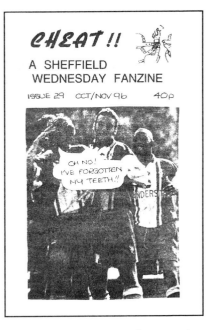

CHEAT !!

A SHEFFIELD
WEDNESDAY FANZINE

ISSUE 29   OCT/NOV 96   40p

Huddersfield in Andy Booth. And he wasn't cheap either. Mind you, neither did he continually bleat to the Italian press about how crap we were, want out every time he was dropped or keep running off to Brazil. Other arrivals were Scott Oakes (he of FA Cup hat-trick against West Ham a few years back), Wayne Collins (utility player from Crewe) and Matt Clarke (a promising young 'keeper from neighbours Rotherham, for a ludicrously low fee). The major outgoings were Belgian Marc Degryse who'd promised much during his first season, but presumably couldn't take to Yorkshire puddings and Henderson's relish and tripe, and Darko Kovacevic whom we hadn't really made our minds up about yet anyway. Waddle was still with us, but in name only and he clearly wasn't going to pull on the blue and white again - more of him later.

We greeted August with dread rather than anticipation; so when after three weeks we were sitting pretty at the top of the tree with four wins out of four, we just couldn't believe it - and I bet neither could the rest of you! Ritchie Humphreys was the big news; only in the side due to yet another Hirst injury, he'd hit three goals already and looked set to be the sensation of the season. On Wednesday's pre-season tour of Holland the great Marco Van Basten had apparently remarked what a prospect he looked, the best he'd seen, no less! There was also rumour of a £3m bid by new Leeds boss George Graham.

So it was something of a surprise when by May's close, Humphreys had only started 14 games, many of those in midfield with even a couple as a stand-in left back. Sensible handling of a young talent by an experienced manager?

Maybe, but then again I can't help thinking that if Beckham had come through Wednesday's ranks he'd still be plugging away in the reserves. The other early season sensation was Yugoslavian defender Dejan Stefanovic. Pleat had splashed out £2m on him the year before and it looked a complete, unequivocal waste of money. Signed as a left back, he started the new season at centre half, and if he was a revelation, it was nothing compared to our discovery that his Wednesday debut had been his first ever at left back! The rush for foreign talent has surely to be rationalised when a manager renowned for his knowledge of the game pays big money for a player he clearly knows very little about.

A 2-0 home defeat at the hands of media darlings Chelsea (who were - and are - nothing special) brought us back down to earth a bit, but if we could win down at Highbury then this really would be our season. We've not won at the Arse since Harold MacMillan was PM; drawing's a major cause for celebration. With us 1-0 up and well in charge at half time, it looked like that elusive win was finally on its way, but a disastrous second half including a Des Walker sending off meant we went down 4-1 (even the truly-awful David Platt managed a goal). That, incidentally, is a rule of football: all useless gits do well against us. Cole and Poborsky also found our net, and Kitson, who is definitely nowhere near good enough to ever get a top flight hat-trick, did just that against us. In case anyone is still not up to speed on this, even Jason Lee scored against us the previous season, though it must be said that we were not quite bad enough to let Kevin Campbell get one.

That second half Highbury collapse heralded the start of a relegation-type form slump. When Southampton left at the beginning of November with a point, albeit from a very dubious penalty, our sorry record read eight league games against generally mediocre opposition without a win. Waddle had finally left during this period, to Falkirk of all places (no offence). Now don't get me wrong, Waddle was a hero at Hillsborough, but during the tail-end of his time with us he certainly knew how to play silly buggers. We'd previously had to endure his *MOTD* interviews in which leaving Wednesday was always his favourite topic. On second thoughts, it was his only topic. For those of us with blue and white blood this blatant disloyalty was hard to take. Since Pleat's appointment he'd seemingly bent over backwards to please Waddle. Literally his first act had been to offer him a player/coach role, a post that you'd have expected him to jump at given his wish to progress into management, but one that he turned down without explanation then or since. He was often in the team when he shouldn't have been, and yet after he left he had the audacity to say that he was never made to feel part of Pleat's plans. That's bollocks, Chris. Narked at not being offered the boss' job when Francis was sacked if you ask me. At least he did nothing against us for Bradford, even if *Sky* did manage to make him their Man of the Match; well, why let the facts get in the way of a good story?

The win-less run came to an end with a 2-0 success over bottom-placed Forest, and was wrapped up by a classic strike from Carbone. Our recent record-signing Italian was quickly christened Sonic the Hedgehog by my youngest son on account of his red boots (we've also had blue, green and even black occasionally). We then embarked on a 13 game unbeaten run, ended only by two ridiculous pens against abysmal Middlesbrough (Beck's a better actor than footballer). Why were we so susceptible to crap teams and players?

A predictable Old Trafford defeat and a disappointing FA Cup quarter final exit at the hands of Wimbledon aside, we had a very successful couple of months following our embarrassment at The Riverside. We enjoyed a satisfying win over England (aka Spurs). How can such an average side provide so many England internationals? Just about every one of their English born players is in the England set up. Mark my words: last year in these pages I got it right with my 'Boro to be relegated' tip, and with Sheringham looking for the exit (their one player who deserves an England shirt) don't be too surprised if they're in the bottom three come May 1998. The other highlight of the run-in would have to be the 2-2 home draw with Leeds, who amazed everyone, not least their own fans, by attacking from the off and playing a full part in an end-to-end classic.

We were well on course for a European spot, but after only having lost twice in 25 league games, we preceded to lose three on the trot. A rip-roaring finale against Liverpool wasn't enough, but what a game to finish the season with. It was football as it should be: blood and thunder passion, dodgy reffing (I'm never happier than when I'm abusing the officials, and this one deserved everything he got for sending off young 'keeper Matt Clarke after just nine minutes of his enforced debut) and the perverse joy of watching the total dejection on the Liverpool players' faces when they realised they'd not qualified for the Champions Cup.

You might say at least they qualified for something. OK, but so what? At least we'd given it everything, and against the odds stopped them reaching their goal; they'd finished fourth and trooped of heads bowed, while we went on a jubilant lap of honour after finishing seventh. Weird.

I slagged Pleat off this time last year but I'm happy to say I was wrong. I'm still far from 100% behind him though. He packed my all-time Wednesday hero John Sheridan off to Bolton, he under-used Regi Blinker to the point where he'll probably leave this summer, he played Whittingham and Nicol too often, and he insisted on converting Atherton to a battling midfielder, a position where we're already overstaffed. But there were plenty of successes too: the tactical masterstroke that saw Liverpool beaten at Anfield, likewise at Stamford Bridge where we came from 2-0 down to draw 2-2, and his inspirational half-time substitutions at The Dell, the first time we'd come from two behind to win since the early 80's. And not forgetting his signing of a very special diminutive Italian. It'll be back to the usual pre-season optimism for us, especially with a reputed £17m available to spend.

Oh, just one last thing, I can't not mention Grimsby's tremendous supporters who sang, danced and waved their inflatable haddocks all through their side's 7-1 defeat in the third round of the FA Cup - fans as they should be.

CHEEP SHOT

Norwich City

Average was good

The season before last was, by any stretch of the imagination, an absolute bloody nightmare. We lost Martin O'Neill to Leicester City, we nearly finished in Division Two and we were buried up to our nostrils in the financial excrement which former chairman Robert Chase had dumped on us.

All was not well in the city of Norwich: children wept, grown men tearfully refused to renew their season tickets and women screamed for the return of the Messiah. And lo, he came...

Swooping down from football heaven on a giant cloud, with god-like white hair majestically

ISSUE 6   50p

CHEEP SHOT

" ISSUE 6 " FEB.– APR. 1996 " THE FANZINE THAT SELLS TO SURVIVE "

INSIDE - *The Boxer Short Incident,Smeggy Meggy's Message,The Big Posties Sack,Fly On The Wall and a lot of pages full of abusive material...*

blowing in the wind, Saint Mike Walker returned. Ahem. Okay, I got a bit carried away there, but June 21st 1996 was a momentous occasion at Norwich City. It was something every Canary fan had dreamed of.

The new board had shown itself to be more progressive in thought than Chase had been in ten years. They told Walker that they would try and remedy club problems by not selling players if they could possibly help it. "Yeah, bollocks," most of us thought, but it was nice to hear as we revelled in the post-Euro '96 new-era-at-Carrow Road-feelgood factor. We looked forward, with hope, to a bloody good season.

August 17th trundled along and Mike Walker's brave new world faced its first test against Swindon Town. Not very scary-sounding I know, but I'm trying my best! Thanks to massive club debts, no new players had been brought in and so Mike was forced to persevere with the players who had tried their best to get us relegated the season before. By half-time it was 2-0 and Norwich were playing out of their skins, the only nagging problem was that I didn't want City to score too many more. "What?" I hear you cry. Because I thought this would lead to complacency in the squad and distract them from the tough work ahead of them this season? No, it was a sweltering day and the excitement and plastic seats were making my bum sweat profusely, leaving an unsightly patch on my undercarriage. A Norwich game filled with such trivial, if uncomfortable, worries; we'd be up by Christmas at this rate!

Nobody would have put it past us to get promoted after our 'early doors' form. After a 3-1 defeat at Bolton, where Bryan Gunn handled the ball like a hot potato (he also mis-kicked a back-pass to let Nathan Blake score; *déjř vu* Gunny?), Norwich went ten matches unbeaten, eight of them wins.

It would be rude at this point not to labour over one of the streak's better wins, funnily enough, against Ipswich. I couldn't get to Carrow Road for this one, so I decided to visit my mates in Nottingham and have a bloody good night on the drink during (and after) the match, which was live on *Sky*. Mind you, isn't everything? After a few beers we settled down in a sports bar called *RKO*, which had the mother of all giant screens. Amazingly, the place was absolutely crawling with Ipswich Town fans.

As you may or may not know, the first half became a classic example of attacking football, with City going two up by half time. You can imagine how 'touchy' the Ipswich fans were becoming. In fact, as I innocently made my way to the toilet through the 'scum' at half-time, one of them threatened to stub a cigarette out on my head. How dreadfully unsporting of him; all I did was cast a shadow of doubt over John Wark's parentage.

Ipswich struck back quickly in the second half and things looked a bit dodgy. But City defended resolutely and ended up grabbing a third to cap a top display. Cue ridiculous David Pleat-like dancing around the room which annoyed the Town fans a smidgen! If the 3-1 result made them angry, me standing on my seat and boozily dropping my trousers to reveal my shapely buttocks made them ballistic! And not content with pointing my twin globes at the Ipswich fans, I proceeded to slap them while shouting a mixture of drunken obscenities. If this was the aperitif, the main course was when I parted my cheeks, revealing my 'nought'. It was at this point the Ipswich fans erupted like a volcano and I made a tactical retreat to another pub. Marvellous entertainment!

Mind you, things didn't really get much better after that, as a long slump in form began.

November was probably the last month of smiles. First, Delia Smith and husband Michael Wynn Jones joined the big cheeses at City as part of a major boardroom reorganisation. Suddenly the chant was "Ooh, aah, Delia" as the TV cook was elevated to Mike Walker status among the City fans. Even her culinary literature began to sell at record rates in Norwich... I still can't get that bloody soufflé right, though. Second, Bryan Gunn, the huge shaven-headed shot-stopper, was having his testimonial season and his benefit match was against Manchester United. For ten years Gunny had been the personification of the Norwich City team: hard-working, unsung and always trying to do things with a touch of style and humour. Even though his form, like his hair, had been non-existent recently, Gunny is the ultimate professional, and deserved his moment on the centre stage.

Despite losing 3-0, it was a good night for everyone, with Manchester United fielding Eric Cantona, Paul Scholes and Brian McClair (even Steve Bruce made an appearance). I may not be the biggest fan of Gunn but it was a pleasure to see him honoured with a match against the Champions in front of a full house.

No wins from November until the end of December however, and the smiles were turning to frowns. City were playing without style, pattern, heart or pride. In each match the players looked increasingly clueless, especially away from home. Coupled with the fact that Norwich players had as much discipline as a gang of wild juvenile delinquents, the form was absolutely disgraceful.

It was hardly Walker's fault though. Without any financial muscle, he was forced to use players who'd failed him again and again. Injuries to Eadie and O'Neill left City desperately short of fire-power, and injuries to Polston and Milligan left them weak at the back (seen graphically when we were mauled away at Port Vale and West Brom). All he could do was bring in Everton's Matt Jackson for peanuts and borrow David Rocastle and Kevin Scott. Mike's hands were firmly tied.

Despite the decent performances of some players, it was pure luck that helped City get through the FA Cup third round tie against Sheffield United. After taking the lead in the first half, Norwich had to survive a bizarre goal-mouth scramble in which the ball hit the post, the bar twice, the post and the bar again before falling into Gunn's hands. Quite literally one of the luckiest escapes I've ever witnessed... and I've seen more than a few. It was a pity we went out to Martin O'Neill's (if only he had stayed...) Leicester next round. For a silly moment I thought City's name was on the cup. I know, I know...

So, more a short stroll than a run in the Cup, and Norwich went back to patchy form. It was consistently ordinary. A win, a couple of draws and a defeat was the pattern until the end of the season. Impressive victories at Sheffield United and Swindon were followed by suicidal performances, such as those against Charlton and Oldham. All of this meant our play-off hopes disappeared into the ether like a Matt Jackson shot. And with the beer in the Barclay End still tasting like a mixture of dirty water and urine, Norwich fans could have been forgiven for feeling a bit disappointed with the season.

It was just so bloody *average*. There had been some decent football, some amazing matches and some downright mundane ones too. And in the end we didn't finish much higher than we did last season. On that showing, Mike Walker is going to have to do better. Mind you, compared to the games under Gary Megson's management, it was a 1000% improvement. I would have willingly sold my soul to the devil and let him remove my finger nails with pliers while simultaneously shoving a hot poker up my arse rather than let Megson back in.

What Walker's done, with the help of the new board, is to stabilise the club and give it a fighting chance of promotion next season. Anyone who says differently deserves the same outraged reaction from Norwich fans as a father might give a bloke who mentions he would like to have anal sex with his daughter. Those who moan fail to remember that less than twelve months ago we were nearly bankrupt and close to relegation to Division 2. Be in no doubt, average was good this season...

CHELSEA INDEPENDENT

Chelsea

Every season with Chelsea Football Club is like an episode of *Only Fools and Horses* with every fan telling themselves that "this time next year..." How ironic it was then that the same year that Del Boy, Rodney and Uncle Albert finally found gold at the end of their rainbow we too won something for the first time since you could get eight blackjacks for a penny.

The season started with the Ruud Revolution and the arrival of Gianluca Vialli, Roberto Di Matteo and Frank LeBouef. As someone said at the time we had signed a maestro, an assassin and a cultured defender. But it was Vialli we all wanted to see. We seeked

CHELSEA independent

ISSUE 79   DECEMBER 1996   PRICE £1

FAREWELL TO WEE MAN NUMBER TWO

When they said "Do you want to join Rangers?" I thought they meant Glasgow Rangers

INSIDE: JOHN SPENCER INTERVIEW, WHAT IS IN A NAME RON HARRIS INTERVIEW; UNITED THEY STAND, DIVIDED THEY FALL, NEVER LET CHELSEA BE MAN UNITED, THE PENSIONERS, HILLSBOROUGH, CALL ME OLD FASHIONED COLLIESPONDENCE AND MUCH MUCH MORE

him here, we seeked him there, we seeked that Vialli everywhere. After his non-appearance in the five pre-season friendlies the bookies' money was on the Italian finally showing up in the prestigious Umbro trophy being held at the City Ground Nottingham, with our good selves, Forest, Man Utd and Ajax making up the numbers. The first day saw Chelsea beat Forest 4-3 on penalties with Dmitri Kharine saving from Gemmell and Pearce to set up a final with Ajax. The following day we had perfect sunshine, a Vialli second half appearance (hurrah!), a 2-0 victory with goals from Wise and Petrescu and Chelsea's first trophy of the season. 'Is it to be joined in the cabinet by any others?', we wondered.

Two weeks later the serious stuff started. Away to Southampton, home to the Smog Monsters of Middlesbrough and Big Fat Ron's Sky Blue Army were our opening fixtures. How well would we do? Well after three games gone, three goals, three clean sheets, seven points and second place in the table. Now who would not have settled for that at the start of the season? After the disappointing 0-0 draw at The Dell on the opening day it was encouraging to hear Ruud Gullit say: "The good thing was that everyone was disappointed by the result." If the players had that attitude for the next few months we were going to be in for a good season.

It might as well rain until September. Well, if this was how it was going to be for the rest of the season, it could rain all year as far as I was concerned.

Early September saw us visit the Highbury library and produce a first 45 minutes of football that was as good as I have seen for many a year. The new 'Kaiser' Frank LeBouef opened the scoring from the penalty spot and Luca made it 2-0 after half an hour. We held on until the half time whistle when tragically a drug-free (and Chelsea fan) Paul Merson pulled one back for the Arse. We lost the plot in the second half and went 3-2 down, only for Spenny to come on late in the game and save the day with a delightful through ball for Wise to slip past Lukic in injury time.

Buoyant from getting a point we duly went to Hillsborough and beat the league leaders for the first time since 1969, when Peter Osgood had the most fashionable sideburns in London and John Dempsey still had some hair on his head. The only down-side was losing Dmitri Kharine for the rest of the season through injury. Sadly the wheels came tumbling off with a vengeance when in the space of a week we got thumped 5-1 at Anfield, surprisingly lost at home to Blackpool in the Fizzy Pop Cup and laughingly conceded a pineapple - sorry peach - of a goal in the last minute to a newly-shorn Jason Lee and Nottingham Forest. In between, Ruud once again delved into the transfer market to sign Frode Grodas from Lillestrom. At least October could not end as bleakly as September, we told ourselves.

How wrong we were. How *very* wrong. Things started well enough with a win at Leicester when an inspired substitution in the second half saw Luca come on and turn a one goal deficit into a comfortable 3-1 victory. The following week our bogey team came, saw and duly conquered and gave Frank LeBouef a battering in the process in a 4-2 victory for the Dons. I dare say I don't think Mr LeBouef would forget that game in a hurry, finishing the game with a lump on the side of his head so big Tiger Woods would be looking to hit it onto the nearest fairway.

Three days later the team headed north to a rampant Bolton who were riding high at the top of the Nationwide League, scoring goals left, right and centre and many a Chelsea fan - myself included - were not surprised when we got turfed out of the competition. The many who thought this was disastrous soon had that put into perspective the following morning when the tragic news filtered through that Matthew Harding had been killed in a helicopter crash returning from Burnden Park. Also tragically losing their lives were Matthew's close friends Ray Deane and Tony Burridge, pilot Mick Goss and Bob Dylan fan and Q journalist John Bauldie.

Tributes poured in from England manager Glenn Hoddle, ex-Chelsea midfielder Vinnie Jones, Virgin Supremo Richard Branson, the then Prime Minister John Major and his eventual successor Tony Blair. The list was endless, but perhaps Wimbledon chairman Sam Hamman summed it up when he said "It's only the good who die young." His floral tribute read 'A football tragedy. A Chelsea catastrophe. You were full of life my good friend'.

Matthew Harding's contribution to the club will always be remembered by all Chelsea supporters. Without Matthew, we would not now have a North Stand bearing his name. Without Matthew Harding, we would not have Ruud

Gullit. Without Ruud Gullit we would not have Gianluca Vialli, Roberto Di Matteo, Frank LeBouef, Gianfranco Zola. The man was unique and since that tragic October day "There's Only One Matthew Harding" becomes more and more apt each time Chelsea fans sing it.

For days after Matthew's death, Stamford Bridge became a shrine for Chelsea fans to visit and mourn his loss. The week culminated in the home game against Tottenham Hotspur and Chelsea's biggest crowd of the season witnessed emotional scenes when the players laid wreaths at both ends of the stadium, a pint of Matthew's favourite was left in the centre of the pitch and the minute's silence was only interrupted by the ironic sound of a distant helicopter.

If there ever was to be a day when Chelsea just had to win this was it, and who better to open the scoring than player/coach Ruud Gullit. Subsequent goals from David Lee and Roberto Di Matteo set the seal on an unforgettable day and no doubt Matthew was up above with his oysters and his Guinness and a smile across his face.

The Matthew Harding wave of emotion swept forward the following week to Old Trafford. Hot on the heels of United's defeat by Fenerbache, Chelsea fans serenaded the Stretford End with such memorable tunes as "One Team in Turkey" with Turkish flags in tow just to rub a bit more salt in the Berkshire and Devon – oops, sorry Mancunian - wounds. The 3,000 fans there that day plus one above in heaven inspired "Matthew Harding's Blue and White Army" on to a memorable victory over the Premier League Champions with goals from Doobs and Luca shattering Man Utd's long-standing unbeaten run at home.

The following week Ruud persuaded Gianfranco Zola that he could add to his medal collection by joining his Blue revolution at the Bridge. The £4.5 million paid for the diminutive man from Parma would later prove to be the transfer bargain of the season. He was probably the best free kick and dead ball specialist in Italian football and we had not seen anyone score from free kicks with regularity since the Wee Man left us many moons back. Talking of Wee Men, Wee Man Number Two departed through the back door shortly after Zola's arrival when he joined our West London neighbours QPR. Spenny was very popular with Chelsea fans; his 100% commitment, bubbly personality and ability to score special goals will live long in many Chelsea fans' memories. Who will ever forget that goal in Vienna?

A third of the season in, we were fifth in the table. Despite chances to improve on this we only managed disappointing draws away to Leeds and then Everton. And just as we thought things could not get any worse, the Blues travelled to Roker Park for the last time to face a Sunderland side peering through the relegation trapdoor. An easy away win, a comfortable three points. Forget it. We got caned 3-0 and the *Sky* match statistics told our sorry story of only one shot on target during the 90 minute debacle. The players' day was made complete when they had to watch *Toy Story* on the way home. Reach for the fast forward button someone please, and don't let Scott Minto bring any videos on the team bus ever again!

West Ham were next and we were back on track. Zola twisted and turned Julian Dicks inside-out for our first goal and Mark Hughes chipped in with a brace as we ran out 3-1 winners. There was just time to tuck into the roast turkey and all the trimmings before we broke Villa's unbeaten run at home with two goals from the new king of Stamford Bridge, and although we then dropped two points by failing to beat an ever-improving Sheffield Wednesday we had West Brom at home in the FA Cup to look forward to.

We overcame the Baggies, the highlight of which was Frank Skinner being serenaded "He's going home, he's going home, Skinner's going home" by the West Stand. My one wish for next season: no more songs sung to the *Three Lions* tune... PLEASE!

The month ended with probably the game of the season, your lifetime, my lifetime, this century, when we somehow managed to turn around a two goal deficit against the Scousers to win through to the fifth round of the FA Cup. With Hughes surprisingly left on the bench we were going nowhere fast and the Scousers had one foot in the next round when the half-time whistle went. Enter the Welsh anti-Christ who to put it bluntly for the next 45 minutes scared the shit out of the Spice Boys and Co. He scored the first, set up Zola for a typical outside-the-area top corner blast for the second, played his part in the third when Luca was on the end of a brilliant move and was instrumental in winning the free kick that led to Luca's second and our fourth goal. I can safely say I have never seen such scenes at Stamford Bridge as on that day. After the game you just felt we were invincible and that Matthew's dream would be realised come May 17th at Wembley.

There was the small matter of Leicester City away in the fifth round when the BBC once again decided to send their cameras along to see that man Di Matteo (again) score a tremendous goal, Hughes chipped in with a second and surely we were in the hat for the Quarter Finals. Oops! In true Chelsea fashion we took the foot off the accelerator and that dreaded word 'inconsistency' reared its head again as Leicester scored two goals including a last minute own-goal from Eddie Newton to bring us back to the Bridge for a replay.

As for the replay, well, with no apologies to any Leicester fans reading this, you made no attempt to win the game and then had the audacity to moan about that penalty. Who cares if Erland Johnsen fell over or was struck by an invisible bolt of lightening? I bet if Steve Claridge had fallen over to win a penalty in the Coca Cola Cup Final against the Smog Monsters there would have been thousands of Leicester fans saying "No, no, no that was *never* a penalty. Get up Mr Claridge, you unsporting chap you, besmirching the good Leicester name." Get real! The free kick in the first game that led to Eddie Newton's goal should never have been awarded against Steve Clarke as BBC cameras showed it was never a foul. No foul, no free kick, no own-goal, no replay, no penalty dispute. Here endeth the lesson.

By now with half an eye cocked at Wembley we were losing interest in the league and chucking away silly points. That will be one thing for next season, Ruud. Stop losing to rubbish teams. As you said yourself, "the team that wins the league is the one that beats all the sides in the bottom half of the table."

We snuffed out the Pompey chimes in the quarter finals, so it was Highbury and a London derby against the Crazy Gang. Frank LeBouef brought his golf clubs just in case they were needed but Gayle and Ekoku's attempts to rough up our defence proved groundless as the Kaiser, Frankie and the recalled Moonman Erland Johnsen stood firm and gave as good as they got. Hughes opened the scoring in the first half and with time ticking on Zola once again added another candidate to his ever-growing list of Goals of the Season when he somehow managed to back-heel the ball, turn and shoot in one amazing movement. Cue mass celebration not seen at Highbury since they opened the library at the North Bank end a few years ago. Just to make the score look respectable Man of the Match Mark Hughes scored a third goal in injury time.

So onto Wembley and with our bums just barely touching our seats that man Di Matteo (again) scored the fastest goal in a modern FA Cup Final and the Smog Monsters' jaws hit the floor never to recover. When you've lost a Cup Final already, been relegated and all your top players are set to leave, the last thing you would want to happen is to concede a goal in the first minute of a Cup Final. Well, happen it did and Chelsea then spent the rest of the game trying to score the crucial second. We had to wait until eight minutes from time but it was worth it. When Wise went up to lift the FA Cup we were there and then 30,000+ Chelsea fans embarked on the longest celebration Wembley had ever seen with the victorious team doing more laps of honours than Boro had points deducted, before the party that lasted till Monday morning began. But I hope the last person to leave Wembley Stadium remembered to turn out the lights and leave a note for the milkman saying "we'll back in August." Yes Rodney, this time next year...

Oh, I nearly forgot. For any Arsenal and West Ham fans reading this, all I can say is:

Silverware, silverware, we've gone and won some silverware,
From Stamford Bridge to everywhere,
We've gone and won some silverware

CITY GENT

Bradford City

When the usual suspects who assist in the production of *City Gent* got Dave Jenkins' letter inviting our contribution to *SOTF3* we had a bit of a chuckle. We'd been asked to avoid blow-by-blow accounts of every game - there was no chance of that! The amount of alcohol we'd consumed to alleviate the pre-match tension and (usually) post-match gloom rendered recollection uncertain to say the least. Of the matches attended sober, the horrors of the City performance has induced hysterical amnesia. Dave had also asked us to provide the sort of information which didn't reach the papers, insights and off-field traumas. This gave us the biggest laugh; he clearly

THE

CITY GENT

The Voice of Bantam Progressivism

ISSUE 67　　APRIL/MAY 1997

BRADFORD CITY
LONDON SUPPORTERS' F.C. **100**
UNVEIL THEIR LATEST
SIGNING　　pence

ANOTHER 100 PAGE ISSUE

doesn't realise that BRADFORD IS THE BIGGEST VILLAGE IN THE WORLD. The whole place absolutely thrives on gossip, rumour, information from people who know people, speculation, hearsay, scandal and busybodying. If we were to write up all the information we'd received about the club during the season we'd fill the entire book.

Even by Bradford City standards this season has been a classic for behind-the-scenes goings-on as reported to the good denizens of *City Gent* Towers. We have used 43 players in the first team alone, plus many more who trained with us or had trials in the reserves. This is a record for Bradford City (outside the World War Two seasons when guest players were allowed). And had we signed and/or played others about whom there was speculation, we would have had double that number and a squad size that would have made Barry Fry green with envy. Having said that, even with Chris Kamara playing his cards very close to his chest, we did get to hear about most of the arrivals. One of the exceptions was a Finnish player called (if I remember correctly) Valhala. He appeared on the bench for one match, made his debut as sub amid a gabble of City fans asking who the fuck he was and was back in Finland on the day the local paper wrote up his career prior to coming to City.

Mind you, we were a bit naughty on the rumour front ourselves. Just as an experiment, to see how quickly stories travel, we started one off stating that a certain experienced Premiership striker was about to sign for City to play and also to coach the other club forwards. It was back to us as absolute gospel within a week. Strangely enough, City at the time of writing are now actually trying to sign Brian McLair to this very end. Spooky isn't it?

If the comings weren't bad enough, the goings and goings-on reached epic proportions. There was always somebody who knew a player's mum, who worked with a player's wife or who'd installed the player's new plumbing to provide chapter and verse as to why players were dropped, farmed out on loan or ultimately transferred out. Very rarely was this because they were crap; it was always because they'd had an argument with Kamara or even a fight (or so we believe in the case of one of our transient Portuguese), or they were critical of City playing the wing back system (a point of view which would have endeared them to the majority of City fans, who would have preferred some stoical defending and plenty of dull draws than the excitement of playing with style and losing to the odd goal in the last ten minutes, as happened so often this season).

Having said this, some of the players arrived and went so quickly that most fans wouldn't recognise them in the street, let alone assume any sort of inside confidence with them. Then we had to rely on the 'somebody who knows somebody' within the club to get our information. Our favourites of these stories concerns an overseas forward who City tried to sign on reputation alone, the lad having never been near Bradford. When he turned up, Kamara must have scratched his head and wondered if he'd got the wrong page of the *European Players Handbook*. The so-called 5'10" striker turned out to be 5'4" on his tippy-toes and was dispatched back home promptly. Hey, ho.

Well, enough of this sort of stuff and onto a *City Gent* view of the season. It's hard to know how to pitch this stuff - we don't imagine that this book would be attractive to the type of fan who is more interested in the statistics of the season (you know the sort, they can tell you that 67% of their club's conceded goals came in the first 15 minutes of the second half and from corners when attacking the home end). More likely it's bought by exiles who cannot get to their club's games, and fans who want to hear how clubs for whom they have a soft spot got on that season. So here goes: a compete set of statistics about Bradford City's season. Only joking!

So what were the feelings about City's season down at Valley Parade? (We refuse to call the place The Pulse Stadium at Valley Parade.) Last time we were faced with impending relegation from Division Two (we refuse to call it Nationwide Division One) there was a very ugly mood amongst fans. The majority were calling for the manager's sacking, the resignation of the board, the head of the chairman and the castration of a number of the playing squad. *City Gent* was criticised by some for not being critical enough (and we *were* pretty critical), and a publication called *Relegation Times* was produced. But this season, despite spending most of it languishing in the danger-zone, there curiously hasn't been much anger; it seems that fans have reacted on the basis of their personalities. Optimists have remained optimistic; pessimists who predicted our relegation from the first match of the season have remained, until the last match anyway, firm in their views; the critics have remained critical; the 'my club right or wrong' brigade have been loyal throughout. And so on.

However, overall, the majority of fans have stuck by Chris Kamara and Geoffrey Richmond who made money available later in the season for players. Many also have praise for the way Richmond kept the profile of the club as high as possible given our league position. For example, getting the Queen to officially open the new Midland Road Stand was an incredible piece of publicity. It's rare enough for a reigning monarch to set foot in a football stadium, but to open a stand must be a first. Geoffrey is also a man who has not missed an opportunity to generate money for the club. That he has done so without putting up season ticket prices for '97-98 and without ripping fans off for club merchandise has also earned him praise.

Onto the squad. Whilst one or two players have become a target for the boo people (not a bad name for a band, eh?) most of the regular squad have been seen as good players, and transfers out have been greeted with moans rather than cheers. Even the Bradford City Liberation Front, who are normally calling for the chairman and players to come and live next to the ground on Cornwall Terrace, or threatening assassination for missing penalties, have been quiet.

No *City Gent* fans' questionnaire this season, so the awards for this piece are the more obvious ones. Not bestowed by the usual suspects this time, but by my good self and a bunch of North Bradford's loyal City fans I now drink with (or 'with whom I drink' if I want to avoid the ire of any English teachers reading this!).

Player of the Season: Wayne Jacobs; always gave 100% even when being played out of role.

Signing of the Season: Edinho, rapidly becoming a Bradford City cult figure. I am sure opposing fans hate his guts but we love him for his enthusiasm, goalscoring, celebrations and, er, his ability to get fouled.

Goal of the Season: Whilst Chris Waddle's brilliant effort against Everton in the FA Cup is the obvious winner, a vocal minority reckon Robert Steiner's goal in the same match is just as good. The obligatory lone voice voted for "all of them" as they kept us up...

Most Improved Player of the Season: Some reckoned it was Shaun Murray after taking over Chris Waddle's No.7 shirt, but this was overruled as he was only playing to the standard of which he is capable. As a consequence the award goes to 'young' Andrew O'Brien who got better and better in defence as the season went on.

Miss of the Season: Forget the attempts to computer-analyse Carlos Alberto's wonder free-kick goal for Brazil against France. Get IBM to tell us how Ole Bjorn Sundgot missed that goal away at Barnsley. We reckon there must have been some sort of rent in the space time continuum or a dimension shift, or something. It was just not possible to have missed.

Wildlife Moment of the Season: Fans in the Sunwin Stand peering into the rafters trying to see the squirrel spotted by Les which turned out to be a magpie.

CLAP YOUR HANDS STAMP YOUR FEET!

Watford

The new season promised much for the Golden Boys. Despite relegation, the form at the end of last year made most fans confident that this was to be our season. I wasn't so sure...

Kenny Jackett was appointed manager (it was all we could afford), and Graham Taylor went about his work getting the right structure in place. Towards the end of the summer we managed to sign some players: Steve Talboys came from Wimbledon on a free transfer, and subsequently managed to outdo Houdini by disappearing up his own arse. Richard Flash was signed from Wolves, and there are no prizes for guessing how much he cost. (I'll give you a clue: it begins with F and ends with ree).

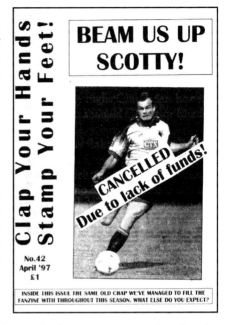

Alec Chamberlain completed the hat-trick of signings, joining for what the papers would call 'a nominal fee'. In his quest for First Division football, last season's captain Andy Hessenthaler joined Gillingham (!). They probably think he was a bargain at £235,000 but we're still chortling at getting that much! As it turned out, none of our summer signings played much and as Graham Taylor was to say throughout the season, "What you see is what we've got."

We opened at a sweltering Dean Court. Despite Watford advising them that 4,000 fans were going, Bournemouth in their wisdom decided not to make the game all-ticket. When the match finally kicked off at 3.15, our fans were still queuing halfway round the ground. Bournemouth had very cleverly opened only three turnstiles - and one of those was for OAPs only! No wonder they're in the shit. Expectation was certainly high; one group of fans sported 'Championship Tour 1996-97' T-shirts (which were never seen again). We won 2-1.

Now, in all my years of following Watford, successful seasons have always begun with an away win followed by a complete f***-up at the next home game. Hurrah! Along came Millwall, and f*** up we did - 0-2. However, screwing up again at home to Plymouth was not in the script. This awful performance was followed by the inevitable demonstration against owner Jack Petchey. The bloke doesn't seem to have much stomach for a fight, having already quit as chairman following a supporters' boardroom raid in 1994, and he obligingly quit as a director. He then announced that there would be no money to spend.

September was a successful month. We even started to win at home, and managed four out of four on our travels, finishing with three points at Bristol Rovers, who should be up for a Dressing Room of the Year award for their two-tier barn effort. But Barry Fry seems to have an Indian sign over us, and we could only draw 0-0 against his team of Barnet, Southend and Birmingham rejects. We even managed to finish the game with only ten men as we had three players stretchered off. Sunderland knocked us out of the Coke Cup and then our all-time jinx team, Shrewsbury Town, won 1-0 at Gay Meadow with a shot from somewhere in Wales. We didn't know it then but it was to be our last league defeat until March.

October for all Nationwide paupers was a busy month, starting for us with Preston at home. Here's a poser: why does Bobby Mimms always play like a Keystone Cop against every other side in the country - except Watford? I swear there are Watford fans who can't understand why he never won an England Cap! Despite 33 goal attempts including 16 on target, all we could manage was one goal, and that was deep into injury time. And even then no-one was quite sure whether it was Steve Palmer or Devon White, although I was too busy going ape-shit to actually care. It was York away next, and if Watford fans needed proof that the refereeing standard in this division is abysmal then Mr Peake of Darwen offered conclusive evidence. When we finally won a free-kick in the 85th minute, the away end celebrated as if we'd scored a last minute winner against Luton in the play-off final. The punchline is that we won 2-1. We didn't know it then (this is fast becoming a catchphrase) but it was the last time we scored twice in an away match. DDDD might be a hugely impressive bra size, but unfortunately it was also Watford's next four results.

Next up was Luton. It was nine and a half years since we last beat them, but everyone had a good feeling about this one. Just a few minutes into the second half, Mitchell Thomas blatantly handled a cross a clear two yards inside the box. "Penalty!" Nope. The myopic ref gave a free-kick just outside the area. It took about five minutes to sort it all out, but those wasted minutes were to prove vital. Luton scored a lucky shinner from 18 yards from Showler. (It was actually quite a good goal but saying that makes me feel better about it.) The dread curse had struck again, but deep, deep, deep, *deep* into injury time Darren Bazeley's goalbound effort was knocked in by Steve Davis. Bedlam ensued at the Vicarage Road end. Nigel Gibbs was seen being chaired off to the half-way line by a couple of supporters; Bazeley and others were buried under a mass of delirious fans. It felt like a win but at the end of the day it was only a point. D'oh!!

Brentford, rivals from an ancient age, were beaten 2-0. At this point I must warn fans travelling to Rotherham: avoid the bogs at all costs. I'll leave it at that! Northampton were beaten in the FA Cup with a Darren 'Cup King' Bazeley wonder goal (I still insist it was a cross, and the fact that he's failed to repeat the feat in every game since, only succeeding in threatening the corner flag, only serves to strengthen my argument).

DDDDDDD - sounds like the *Match of the Day* theme tune I know, but it's nothing more than Watford's next seven league results. But amongst these monotonous draws came a highlight of the season in the game at Preston. For some unknown reason, they have a duckling as a mascot, and as mascots do, it made one or two gestures in front of the Watford fans. For one gentleman this was too much, and he reported the duckling for inciting a riot!

We were fast falling behind the pack when we clinched the signing that changed our season. Keith Scott was a player I said we should have nabbed 18 months ago. So when he arrived on loan from Norwich with a view to a permanent transfer I was in 'told you so' heaven. He scored on his debut at Brentford and was instrumental in helping up beat Bristol City in the AutoW-hatsit. That was also the game which saw us come from behind to win for the first time in two years! Bristol City also saw the return of Kevin Phillips to first team action, and it seemed to herald a partnership that would take us up. The midget Phillips is superb at playing off a big man, and when Bristol City returned two weeks later in the league, Super Kev notched a hat-trick. The unbeaten league run was now 22 games, until the Barry Fry jinx struck again.

Then, the bombshell. It transpired that Scottie was not to join our 'enterprise' (ahem) as Norwich wanted at least £150k for him; Watford couldn't afford a penny of it! This certainly put a dampener on things, but with ten games to go, we were still joint top. Transfer deadline day was approaching and Jackett had the opportunity to get one more player on loan. He tried to get Scott back; Norwich said "buy or forget it," and Wycombe got their man. He then tried to get Jason Lee from Forest. "Not available." Funny - a day later he joined Grimsby on loan! The deadline passed, and then the final nail in the coffin. On *Sky*, Glenn Roeder, between all the er's and um's that are his trademark, said that the title was ours. Double d'oh!!

The one possible saving grace was that Watford always have a good finish to the season. We did our sums and reckoned that seven wins out of the last ten would be enough. Bournemouth came to Vicarage Road on Easter Saturday and the equation immediately changed to seven from nine. Plymouth on the Monday was 0-0, and that sums it up apart from their PA who'd obviously been affected by the unusually hot weather. He decided to announce the half-time scores in the First Division by managers and the Second Division by shirt sponsors. Bizarre!

So, promotion hopes were downgraded to play-off hopes, but a defeat at Crewe and a draw at Chesterfield didn't help matters. The new equation was four wins out of six for the play-offs. A 4-0 victory over York was the first, and also our biggest home win for six and a half years. But then it all went pear-shaped: Stockport, Wrexham and Chesterfield made sure of that. Bury at home on the penultimate Saturday had been pencilled in as a promotion party. And so it was. Trouble is, no-one had told us it was going to be theirs. With play-off hopes also gone, there was some consolation when at 2.45 that Saturday, Graham Taylor came onto the pitch and announced that Elton John, who'd put together a consortium to buy out Petchey, was coming back. A thrashing at Burnley on the last day of the season summed up our miserable finish, and to make matters worse it meant that we ended up in the bottom half of the table.

This summer will see many changes: Graham Taylor is now in charge of team affairs, Jackett remains as first team coach, and it appears that there *is* money to spend. Yet Taylor has inherited a very young side that needs experience. My fear is that sides will look at Watford next season and think we are the team to beat, the team to get one over, and I'm not sure we have the stomach for that. Goalscoring has to improve and we must start turning draws into victories. Expectations are high like last season, perhaps even more so, but perhaps not going up first time around may be the blessing in disguise we have waited a long time for.

How to do it like a Hornet Lesson 2
Passing
featuring
Richard Johnson

1. Receive Ball

2. Spot Porno on the wing

3. Lay off an inch perfect pass....

.... to the roof of the stand

THE CLARET FLAG

Burnley

I'm struggling here... really struggling. There's very little to say about a season which started with a whiff of the obligatory optimism but ended with barely a whimper.

I suppose that the pre-season form was good in Ireland, plus we beat Man City at the Turf, but our signings left a lot to be desired. Damien Matthew, a powder-puff midfielder, and Stoke rejects Nigel Gleghorn and Vince 'oops is that another injury' Overson joined the club. The Potteries two were particularly disappointing; Overson, who missed almost the entire season, must be the most injury-prone footballer in the country and you have to wonder why his fragility

wasn't spotted at his medical. On the other hand Gleghorn was ineffective in a battling midfield role, which at his age might have been expected; he was bound to run out of puff by half time. No, for me there were other players, some bought and others who were products of our burgeoning youth system, who provided the bright spots.

Paul Barnes was signed in September from Birmingham City, for what now seems a bargain £350,000. You know, the same Paul Barnes who scored those goals against Man Utd a year or two go. He repaid manager Adrian Heath's faith in him by netting 23 goals, including one of five against Stockport - the team who consider us as rivals, but who we don't care about. It wasn't half funny to see them trying to slink away just after half time. He also cracked in two other hat-tricks against Blackpool at Bloomfield Road and Peterborough.

There was a positive aspect to come out of our comparative lack of good signings, though. The emergence of our younger players was very heartening. Chris Brass, our Player of the Season and mainstay of the defence, was a revelation and is now worth around a million quid if press reports are to be believed. Paul Smith, a winger or wing-back, was always a threat to opposition defenders, and striker Andy Cooke joined from non-league Newtown for a bargain £35,000 which as we all know is chicken feed in today's transfer market. Paul Weller, another product of the youth team, also came of age this season after getting some stick from the boo boys. He's proved them all wrong with some fine displays in the Clarets' midfield.

It's been all change behind the scenes as well. Adrian Heath lost the experience of assistant John Ward to Bristol City at a vital time, but wasn't too proud to seek advice from Howard Kendall, and found himself a good replacement for Wardy in the shape of Colin Harvey (spot the ex-Everton mafia). Nope, this season has been one of learning for our novice boss and it should stand him in good stead.

He also introduced the trendy wing-back system, which the team seemed to enjoy. Unfortunately, Gary Parkinson, who's just had his best campaign in years, left shortly after the last game, which is a real pity because he was one of a few players to have really gained their form and confidence playing the quick counter-attacking passing game favoured by Heath. In fact both of our wing-backs, Parkinson and Eyres, were selected in the PFA Second Division select eleven. If only our central defence had been up to it, or Overson had been fit for more than a handful of games, then the final outcome could have been a lot different. Let's face it, there wasn't a lot wrong with our 'goals for' column!

So, in no particular order, here are my five top memories of the '96-97 footie season:

1. Beating Luton on the opening day at their place. We looked world beaters... if only it'd lasted!

2. Paul Barnes bagging five against Stockport 'it was a flock' County. All bloody good goals they were too. Doubt if we'll see something like that again in a hurry.

3. Going to Liverpool for the third round of the cup, after the famous floodlight failure fiasco. Walsall whined and we won. Poor Walsall? I don't think so.

4. Playing the Saddlers, again this time on *Sky*. "Brazil, it's just like watching Brazil!" And it was, especially with David Eyres' spectacular free kick in the first half. That was us at our imperious best.

5. The way that the fans rallied around crisis clubs Bournemouth and Brighton. I couldn't make the 'Fans United' day, but got down to Bournemouth and was proud to see Burnley fans digging deep to put cash in the Cherries' buckets. In my opinion football should look after the interests of supporters of clubs like Torquay and Lincoln far more than the glory-hunting armchair fans who seem to be the priority at the moment.

Overall we had a pretty ordinary nine months. But I'm not down, because the pre-season activity has already started and we've steamed in to sign a player called Gentile from Holland - Bosman ruling and all that. So onwards and upwards to the First Division... The future's bright, the future's... CLARET.

COCK-A-DOODLE-DOO

Tottenham Hotspur

"It is difficult to relate any part of Tottenham's recent history without a deep sigh, the ensuing pause acting as a warning that here begins a tale of self-inflicted woe and lost opportunities. A season of transition, it would appear, is the permanent status quo at White Hart Lane. By default."

So wrote Alex Fynn and my fanzine colleague H Davidson at the start of the season in *Dream On*.

Now the season is over, it's clear Spurs have made the transition, turning in membership of the Big Five to become just another club. This was the season Spurs became the Coventry City of London - but without the expenditure; Wimbledon with fans - but without the ambition; when Spurs became the new Chelsea - trading on the glories of an increasingly distant past - while Chelsea began to look a little like the old Tottenham. Most painfully of all, this was the season Spurs became the new Arsenal - boring and negative, but without the effectiveness.

What follows are snapshots of what, for Tottenham fans, was the season that got away.

White Hart Lane, 21 August 96, v Derby

Huge blocks of empty seats greeted the teams for the first home game of the season. The departure of promising youngsters Steve Slade and Chris Day to First Division teams in the close season spoke volumes about the club's ability or willingness to retain a squad and added to the sense of aimless drifting which pervaded. Gary Mabbutt's broken leg, sustained at Ewood Park on day one, put further pressure on our threadbare squad and introduced this season's key word - injury. Other markers laid down this day: the football was awful, Darren Anderton was unfit, Ruel Fox was rubbish, there was no midfield, and a bizarre late substitution by Gerry Francis helped the opposition to an injury time equaliser.

Selhurst Park, 4 September 96, v Wimbledon

Allan Nielson's first game. His signing summed up the new Spurs way. Gerry found an obscure and, most importantly, cheap Scandinavian who he secured in the face of fierce competition from football giants Wolves. The deal was signed, but Nielson wouldn't be joining us until a few games into the season.

Sheringham and Armstrong were crocked, so we played Rosenthal and Fox - seriously, we did - up front. The game was, again, awful with Ruel Fox the most awful. Nielson was substituted at half time, Wimbledon were reduced to ten men, but we still lost 1-0.

WHL, 16 October 96, v Aston Villa

Mark Bosnich made his infamous Nazi salute - part of his banter with the crowd, he said in a stumbling apology afterwards. Many Spurs fans were outraged and upset, but the consensus in the sports press was that we were a bunch of politically-correct killjoys. Wonder how those same writers would have reacted to a section of a club's support 'humorously' directing straight arm salutes at a Jewish or black player. Fans, it would appear, have a responsibility to set a good example, but only rarely do players.

Highbury Stadium, 24 November 96, v Arsenal

This game is too important for Spurs fans these days. While most Gooners see us as only a mild irritant to be dealt with twice a year, many Spurs fans work themselves into a lather of twisted hatred. Instead of the passion of a local derby infused with humour and underwritten with a sense of proportion, something more disturbing is breeding, something which surfaces in the split-seconds of snarling confrontation outside Arsenal tube.

This was a hellish day. It was dark, sheets of rain soaking the uncovered Spurs support. Arsenal played good, passing football like Spurs used to play, chiefly through the use of Bergkamp and Viera, the sort of players Spurs used to buy. We were humiliatingly defeated, and the vast bulk of the Spurs section was empty well before the end.

The match report in fanzine *Cock-a-Doodle-Doo* indicated that Gerry's now familiar litany of post-match excuses was beginning to grate: "The players weren't used to wearing white for away games. None of their players were injured. We had a full strength team out - it was a strange situation and bound to unsettle the team. We chose the wrong studs. It's not nice playing in wet shirts. Changing ends at half time was disorientating. We badly miss Klinsmann, Barmby, Popescu and Darren Caskey. And Ruddock and Gough and Sidney Wale and Irving Scholar and The Beatles and Herman's Hermits. The referee blew for time before we could score another three."

Burnden Park, 27 November 96, v Bolton

Gerry pronounced the Coca Cola Cup our best route into Europe, and we had a full strength team out, so the long journey north to stand on an open terrace on a cold night with half the pitch obscured by a supermarket seemed worth it.

Before the game we witnessed the bizarre antics of Bolton mascot Lofty the Lion, who engaged in a complex routine of jumps, roars and hand signals with a delirious home support. During the game we witnessed the bizarre antics of a Tottenham team who apparently didn't give a toss. Bolton were excellent, but they could have been awful and still caned us. To cap it all, we were standing next to two of the most irritating, cliché-recycling bores ever to attend a game. Their stream of comments during the game made even the thought of a Bob Wilson post-match analysis seem attractive.

We left at 4-1. As we walked across the car park we heard the roar that greeted goal number five. We switched the radio on in the car just in time to hear the sixth. A fellow season ticket holder who couldn't make the game phoned on the mobile to say "What the fuck's going on?" He couldn't believe what he was hearing; we couldn't believe what we'd seen.

Only an inspired Danny Baker show cut through the gloom on the drive home. But listening to the stream of season ticket holders vowing never to attend another game provoked wry smiles. The club has the money, so what do they care if we turn up or not? And Spurs fans have threatened boycotts but rarely delivered too many times before to be taken seriously now. We act like mugs, so we'll be treated like mugs.

WHL, 2 December 96, v Liverpool

Good football returned to London N17, but it was Liverpool who played it. They were superb; we were outclassed - with the exception of the excellent Sol Campbell, who marked Robbie Fowler out of the game. But a freak goal - a shot hitting a divot and flipping up and over a diving Ian Walker - provided Gerry with another excuse to obscure the decay at the club, plus the usual injuries of course.

Highfield Road, 7 December 96, v Coventry

Apparently exciting, and Scandinavian, Steffan Iversen made his Spurs debut. True to form, we'd actually signed him months ago, but a clause in the deal allowed him to stay at his former club Rosenberg until they completed their Champions League group matches. Rumours circulated that Gerry had signed Ronaldo, but that he wouldn't be joining us until after he retires. Oh, and Spurs won.

Rome, 30 December 96, on holiday

The bargain break to Rome for New Year was too good to miss, but I still had to go in search of a British newspaper to check the scores. Having paid £1.20 for a two-day-old *Daily Mail* from a stall outside the Colosseum I startled the other tourists milling around with a loud, Victor Meldrew-esque "I don't fucking believe it." We'd lost 7-1 to Newcastle. I spent the next hour or so thinking of what Gerry's excuses would be, perhaps "I've never conceded seven goals to a north-eastern team in striped shirts during the holiday period before."

Ian Walker said this defeat didn't hurt as much as Bolton, because it was "only three points." Something was badly wrong. Fact - If Allan Nielson hadn't scored for us, this would have been Tottenham's worst defeat in 115 years.

Old Trafford, 5 January 97, v Manchester United

We knew we were going to get thrashed, but like the supporters of a non-league side drawn against the Champions, we were determined to enjoy our day out. Our season would be over after today, so it was worth one last effort. Injuries and the lack of a squad had wiped the team out, but still 6,500 Spurs fans dominated the stadium with noise, balloons and ticker tape. The support was magnificent and, surprisingly, so was the spirit of those who played. The youngsters drafted in - inexperienced because Gerry doesn't like to pick them - did well, particularly Neale Fenn who played so well he was destined never to be picked again. This was a revelation: a Spurs team playing the ball on the floor, to feet.

Of course, United's greater strength and experience - together with the obligatory dodgy refereeing decisions - finally told and Spurs were beaten. But we'd retained some honour, and Ian Walker's sprint the length of the pitch to throw his shirt, gloves and towel into the crowd was appreciated.

It was only afterwards that the dreadful reality struck home. We were happy with not losing by too much. Had it really come to this?

WHL, 11 January 97, v Manchester United

Exciting, and not Scandinavian, new signing Ramon Vega made his debut, but went off injured before the end. He would be injured for most of our remaining games. Spurs lost 2-1. The high point was a rousing half-time singsong in the bar at the back of The Shelf.

WHL, 11 May 96, v Coventry

At last the end was in sight. A spoof Gerry Francis column in *Cock-a-Doodle-Do* said: 'On a seasonally-adjusted basis, we are actually doing much better than one would have thought when looking at the league table. A true picture is given if you cross out all the teams who have spent more money than us, have better players or win trophies - we then come out close to the top.'

According to the same article, the injury list looked like this: Dave Mackay (broken leg), Darren Anderton, (itchy teeth), Gary Stevens (sawdust in head), John Scales (split ends), Ramon Vega (bruised shinpad), Allan Nielsen (burnt tongue testing baby food), Ronny Rosenthal (tripped over settee doing housework), Martin Peters (dandruff), Colin Calderwood (Scottish), Clive Wilson (ingrowing nasal hairs), Dean Austin (lost contact lens), Justin Edinburgh (hiccups), Jason Dozzell (German measles), Ruel Fox (hairy back) and Steffan Iversen (combination skin).

Coventry's fans became the latest to out-sing us at home, and the latest to be allowed to stand and dance and shout throughout the game while stewards did their best to kill off the atmosphere in the Spurs' sections. The noise I will remember most from this season is that of stewards whining, "Can you sit down please" every time excitement threatened to take hold. For the second time this season there was a mass exodus to the bar for a half time singsong.

Coventry, almost certain to go down before the game, of course won and so stayed up, prompting joy and celebration in at least part of the ground for almost the first time this year. The Spurs team looked nervous about doing a lap of honour, and when they finally got round to it the Spurs sections were all but empty. Enough said, really.

THE CROOKED SPIREITE

Chesterfield

Two years ago (for it was CS stalwart Dave Radford not I who wrote the Chesterfield spiel last year) I fretted my way through an article which was supposed to celebrate our promotion out of the basement, the club's first success since 1985. Exhausted by the emotional turmoil of slagging off manager John Duncan in the pages of the fanzine while trying to dig beneath the surface of events so CFC fans could know what actually was happening (to whit, Duncan being threatened with a spell on the rock and roll because of his commitment to all that's dull and dreadful in modern football, etc), I could barely muster a post-

Wembley hoot on my party whistle. I finished the article with a pompous quote from the Bible: 'he who increases knowledge increases sorrow', bemoaning my inability to just lay back and enjoy the ride to Division 2. Twenty-four months, a goatee beard, more hair loss and a lurch over the cliff towards my fifties on, I'm going to whinge my ass off again.

Thought you'd be pleased. Surely, you're saying, this is the club which took on the recent history of British football - the development of the footer club as grasping multi-national corporation trampling the game's traditions underfoot, no less - and nearly got all the way to Wembley! Must be the most successful season in the club's history, you're thinking! Away with moaning Jeremiahs and slice their nuts off with a rusty army knife, yes?

Certainly a lot of Chesterfield fans would be lining up to whip off the first gonad. Whatever else, this was an instructive season for those of us who like making an occasional study of fan psychology. This, for me, was the season of North East Derbyshire McCarthyism. We scorched our way into the semi-finals of the FA Cup this season, in case you'd just spent the past decade stranded in the tropical jungle of New Guinea and were wondering what the hell was going on in the lower divisions of the Endsleigh League (it's OK, I'll explain what all that's about later when you've had a shave). It was a fantastic event; a wonderful three months for fans weaned on FA Cup defeat and raised on a traditional empty first Saturday in December. Instead of sniffing the opportunity of giant-killing and making shit-loads of cup cash, the average fan among us - and that means practically everyone - normally says something like, "Oh shit, not that again!" For the town of Chesterfield it was a truly transformational event. Folk who thought football was as relevant to their lives as Morris dancing is to Bill Clinton's were hanging out blue flags, flying streamers from their car aerials, whistling on their way to work, shagging more often, and - look out! - buying cup tickets.

But it wasn't fantastic for everyone. Plenty of regulars had their noses splattered all over their metaphorical faces by the generosity of CFC chairman, one J. Norton Lee (ex-Mansfield director). 'Good ol' Norton' as he was regularly and nauseatingly referred to by one particularly brainless sycophant, thought that everyone should have a fair shout for a ticket for the big ones - Forest, Wrexham, and Middlesbrough 1 & 2. Never mind that you'd gone to 50 games a season for 20 years; unless you had a season ticket you had to take your chances in the queue with no-timers, never mind part-timers.

In the midst of the cup run some geezer from the *Independent*, nice bloke, came up for an interview. He asked me if Chesterfield was a football town. Mmmmm... Bearing in mind that I've stood in a heaving, swaying mass of, ooh, 1,600 Spireites spread all around Saltergate, I chewed it over for a while before nodding sagely. But was I ever right (for a change)! When we made the semi-final, 20,000 tickets went in a flash. Staggering really when you think we were barely attracting 4,500 for league games. Come the 3-3 with the Boro, I confidently predicted easy availability for the replay: people would go on a community outing once, but all those fair-weather folk wouldn't fork out twice, and anyway, the kids would have to be in bed for school the next morning. Besides, Boro would return about 10,000 of their tickets and we'd get those, I was sure. When I went up to the club to get my two as a privileged season ticket holder the afternoon before 18,000 went on general sale, people were already queuing down St Margaret's Drive. "Mad! Must need something to fill their empty lives," said I, the cocky amateur sociologist. Next morning I discovered that on police advice the club had started selling tickets at about 10pm and within six hours, not long before the spring dawn, the whole lot had been swallowed up by a desperate Chesterfield public. Shows what I know!

The free availability of tickets got Lee into a lot of trouble with fans who abused him by letter, by phone and by going up to him and shouting. Never a popular chairman at the best of times for his remote, heavy-handed management style, often contemptuous of fans' concerns (now *there's* a rarity among chairmen), his stock sunk to an all time low, and rightly so. This, together with a cock-up in issuing vouchers for the Forest tie, left grown men in tears through Lee's doctrinaire *laissez-faire* approach (*Oxbridge Dictionary*: Laissez-faire: (Fr) not having a fucking clue how to organise anything), but we were well on board the gravy train by now so what did he care? Despite an hilarious programme page before the Wrexham quarter final game where he all but suggested that the cup run was actually costing the club money, most of us fans were greedily licking our lips at the first prospect of serious moula in the club's history. Until we woke up, that is, and realised that much/most/all of it would disappear into the new ground fund as opposed to boosting the fans' choice: an all-out attempt in the near future of doing a Bury/Stockport/Crewe and getting (back) into the old Division 2.

By the time the cup run was over in the replay at Hillsborough where Juninho, Ravanelli and Emerson ran amok - we were as shite as we'd been heroic at Old Trafford - we calculated that we must have made a million from the cup run easy, plus the inevitable cash input from transfers (we've the worst record for selling players in the last 15-20 years among league clubs). This latter pot stands at an alleged £750,000 for the sale of Kevin Davies to Southampton. A bit on the low side, and a suspicious figure when you consider that the Saints had a £1.2 million bid for Davies turned down shortly before deadline day. With captain and all-round hero Sean Dyche expected to go to Coventry for another million and perhaps more cashing-in to follow, a netting of three million pounds in one season is, all in all, pretty good going. And we've played in two cup semi-finals and scored three goals! And we're only a Division 2 side! Oh, and I was so moved as the teams came out at Old Trafford that I was on the verge of sobbing like a baby and only just held on. But was I ecstatic like seemingly everyone else who's ever claimed allegiance to CFC and was around to witness the record-busting cup run? Afraid not.

Before the cup run had really started I was involved as editor of *The Spireite* in an on-going dispute with some of the readership/ex-readership over the magazine's treatment of Johnny D, and was also getting some personal abuse from chappies on the internet. Around Christmas we were in a healthy league position, just off the play-off places, by virtue of some luck and gritty, determined and mind-numbingly boring displays away. We won our first four games on our travels, as they say (what else is there but this God-awful cliché as we wended our way around the footballing bus-stops of England? Oh the travails of the struggling writer), 1-0 with barely more than a handful of efforts on goal in 360 minutes. In December we were shocking at York (0-0) and lowly Wycombe (1-1), and Mr D. was on the receiving end of a lot of stick. We weren't up to much, I was arguing, because as usual, the manager was playing crude, lump-it football, and our best attacking player and top scorer Tony Lormor was out of favour and had been dropped for having a spat with the boss. As usual we weren't slow at CS mansions to point out that things could be better. By the time we hit, ooh, round five, we were guilty according to some of un-Chesterfieldian activities for our lack of unswerving loyalty. By the time we got to Old Trafford John Duncan was suddenly a god in the eyes of 98% of Town fans, despite the fact that long-ball disasters and the negative affects of the cup run - injuries, tiredness - had put us out of the promotion race by the end of March. Of course, you couldn't put forward the former case for fear of being branded not a true fan. Indeed, in the close season it got worse. For rightly criticising the chairman concerning the cup tickets fiasco, one disabled supporter was told by Lee to his face that his support wasn't welcome and that he should bugger off and get a season ticket for Notts County. Worse, the guy was pilloried in the local press for his candour by fellow fans.

It was easily forgotten, probably not even noticed by many, that during our five month cup run, we won only six of our 26 league games. It was even worse after the third round - two from 15. But it wasn't the bare facts that annoyed me. Any team can have a bad spell, but what stuck in my throat was that Duncan still sent the side out in the league playing the long-ball stuff and it was a complete waste of time. And as cup fever temperatures ran ever higher, it was clear that no-one was interested in true debate any more. The propaganda poured out of the club lauding the management to the skies, when the truth is, we only best Forest through ditching the long-ball (Duncan's tactical genius? If so, why wouldn't the passing game work on Division 2 sides?) and beat Bolton through the unexpected brilliance of Kevin Davies.

So, a great season? Yes, for the overwhelming majority. For me, no. Call me old-fashioned, but I still think keeping your brain in place instead of letting your emotions swamp every thought process in sight is the way to go when you're having a discussion about football. Call me an old scrote too, but I want my team to play the game as the Big Cheese intended (he'd have put grass in the sky, etc.), not the crude reductionist aberration currently in vogue at Saltergate. I suppose you can say I want too much, or that I want the wrong thing; that I'm a hopeless purist. But no, it's not that. If Duncan playing long-ball gets us to Division 1, I'll doff my hat and say "fair play." But this year's winners, Crewe and Stockport, got there by playing football and scoring goals. Bury, the other promoted club, although admittedly direct at times, at least scored over 60 goals and passed it at times. By the end we'd only scored 42 in the league and by the involuntary cringe when I think now of all the league home games I watched, it bloody feels like it.

By Survival of the Fattest IV we'll likely as not be on our way to a new ground, something I'm dead set against, so for the 1998 volume I'll have to give way to a colleague once again. After all, I won't want to find myself guilty of writing the second longest suicide note in history, now, will I?

CUMBERLAND SAUSAGE

Carlisle United

Aliens! UFOs! Close Encounters of the Third Division Kind!

Well, it wouldn't be possible to write about Carlisle United's '96-97 season without mentioning all that bollocks, would it? But first things first...

The previous campaign had ended in bitter disappointment with relegation back to the basement after one whole season in Division Two, the club's only respite from eight seasons in the bottom division. But some of the doom and gloom was dispelled by manager Mervyn Day's two main summer signings. Former Celtic winger Owen Archdeacon arrived from Barnsley to play at left wing-back. His attacking forays contributed to a huge proportion of the team's goals and Archie bagged 14 himself to become the world's first combination of left back and leading scorer, as well as Player of the Year. But the man who really captured Cumbria's imagination was a giant French central defender by the name of Stephane Pounewatchy - a nightmare for opposition strikers and public address announcers alike. Pounewatchy (pronounced poon-e-vach-ee) was valued at £500,000 in France, where he had played at the top level for several years, but he was snapped up on a free transfer under the Bosman ruling to become Carlisle's cult hero.

The league campaign began in the most depressing way possible, with a trip to Doncaster Rovers' Belle Vue ground. What a shit-hole! But at least we won, as we did so often during the first half of the season. September saw Carlisle renew acquaintances with Mick Wadsworth, the manager who'd walked out on us during our relegation struggle last year for an ill-fated stint as Norwich coach. He was now in charge at Scarborough, where a section of the 1,500 United fans gave their former hero the 'Judas' treatment for much of the match. When Scarborough scored a last-minute equaliser, Wadsworth turned to them and responded with a V-sign. I suppose there may have been better ways to restore his tarnished image, but at least he didn't try a Cantona karate kick...

Carlisle were a sophisticated side playing excellent football which was enough to see off the vast majority of teams in a mediocre division. We looked forward to an immediate return to the Second. While this was satisfying to Cumbrians, there seemed little reason for Carlisle United to figure prominently in the national media. But that all changed in the most bizarre circumstances imaginable.

KNIGHTON: "ALIENS SPOKE TO ME."

So read the headline in the Carlisle *News and Star* on Saturday November 16th, 1996. This signalled the start of an incredible media frenzy; not since the heady days (all seven of them) in August 1974 when the club were top of the old First Division had we been so much in the nation's mind.

The story (for anyone who was on another planet at the time - excuse the pun) concerned comments made by chairman Michael Knighton about an alien encounter he claimed to have experienced on a motorway near Manchester in the 1970s. He described seeing a UFO and hearing a voice saying: "Michael, don't be afraid."

Knighton appeared on local news the following day to announce his resignation in protest at the manner in which his UFO comments had been reported. The *News and Star* had apparently printed the story following an off-the-record chat with its reporter, who had also upset him by mentioning his friendship with David Icke (they were apprentices at Coventry together). Knighton thought the paper was implying that he was some sort of space cadet...

The UFO story made the national press on Monday with coverage along the lines of 'Knighton Is A Nutter.' While fans of any Third Division club would usually give their right back for such extensive coverage, we were torn between savouring the publicity and cringing at the rest of the country taking the piss out of us.

Monday's *News and Star* pleaded with Knighton to stay and invited readers' opinions. The verdict: over 70% of respondents didn't want him to go. Knighton said he'd stay until the end of the season, due to popular demand, before considering his future over the summer.

Explanations for these strange events ranged from acceptance of Knighton's story to theories that he had engineered the whole thing as an excuse to get out or to gain publicity. He certainly achieved the latter, but it's strange how quickly things returned to normal. Within days there seemed nothing unusual about having a chairman with a direct line to E.T.

On the pitch the team remained on course for promotion, entering the top three in December and staying there for the rest of the campaign. Christmas was most notable for goalkeeper Tony Caig spending the early hours of December 25th in a police cell after being caught up in a street brawl which had to be broken up with CS gas. The ordeal didn't prevent him keeping a Boxing Day clean sheet against Hartlepool, although Terry Waite could probably have managed that on his first day of freedom too.

The New Year brought more controversy as midfielder Warren Aspinall was involved in a 4am punch-up over a game of cards. That's Warren for you - nice feet, shame about the brain!

A third round FA Cup victory over Tranmere was the only time that we've ever knocked a team from more than one division above us out of any cup competition. We were rewarded with a home fixture against Premiership opposition and our first fourth round tie for 11 years. Sadly it was an anti-climax as Sheffield Wednesday turned us over easily.

The game at Cambridge in February was broadcast on *Sky* - our first ever nationally televised live match - and not a bad time for the team to produce some of their best moments in a superb second half. But it was also one of the last occasions when United's flowing football shone a beacon through the basement. Loss of form, injuries and suspensions all took their toll on Mervyn's attempts to play the beautiful game, as well as highlighting the need for more players. Dealings in the transfer market had netted us nearly £1million, and as the squad began to look a little threadbare, speculation was rife that those aliens had buggered off with the chairman's wallet.

Another factor for the decline was fixture congestion in a season which saw Carlisle play 61 games. Six of those came on the road to Wembley via the AutoWindscreens Shield, the northern final of which produced the most difficult opponents possible - Stockport County, who had beaten four Premiership sides in other cup competitions. But United won the home leg 2-0, leaving a second Wembley visit in three seasons just 90 minutes away.

In the moments leading up to the second leg, the thoughts of Carlisle's travelling supporters were of Hillsborough rather than Wembley. The match had not been made all-ticket and when 4,500 Cumbrians turned up, this decision looked like proving tragically negligent. After being herded onto the overcrowded away terrace, a potential disaster was only averted when several hundred supporters escaped to an empty home stand. Someone should carry the can for allowing such a dangerous situation to arise.

The match itself was a backs-to-the-wall job in which Carlisle held out for a goalless draw and a return to the twin towers. But the distraction of Wembley led to a dreadful league run of two points from six matches. By this time, Fulham and Wigan had made the Championship a two horse race. Despite our hiccup in form we were virtual certainties for promotion, although we took a long time to make it official. Confirmation finally came in a dull televised goalless draw at Mansfield. Mission accomplished.

The next game was at Wembley, and it certainly had a lot to live up to. Carlisle's only previous appearance there was in the 1995 AWS final against Birmingham City - a match which boasted an attendance of over 76,000. There were concerns that an inevitably smaller crowd against Colchester would lead to a muted atmosphere. And OK, it wasn't *quite* the same, but 25,000 Cumbrians in an attendance of 45,000 is better then a poke in the eye or a trip to Doncaster. The atmosphere was still moving in its intensity, even though the match was no classic, but it was still far better than the average FA Cup Final!

After the agony of losing the Birmingham game to a golden goal, there was a desperate will to win amongst the Carlisle fans. And with the Championship out of reach we wanted silverware. We still saw ourselves as the best footballing side in the division and here was our last chance to prove it.

Normal time was a tense stalemate. Sudden-death extra time was frighteningly familiar. Then came penalties. Colchester took a 3-1 lead. They think it's all over... but Tony Caig had other ideas. Two superb saves gave captain Steve Hayward the chance to win it. His penalty kissed the net - and Carlisle United had won at Wembley.

In those moments of ecstatic madness, nothing else mattered. The tournament's name was irrelevant. The victory and the venue were everything.

There was controversy after the game when our goalkeeping hero said he wouldn't commit his future to the club unless the chairman learned from past mistakes by investing in the squad for next season. Knighton was furious, but Caig was merely articulating the wider view that no-one wanted to see another immediate return to the basement.

United finished in third place, 12 points clear of the play-offs. Even with our end of season slump we were still far too accomplished for Division Three. But as we know too well, being too good for the Third Division is no guarantee of being good enough for the Second. So it's imperative that Knighton makes the signings necessary to continue the momentum. If he does, there's no reason why Carlisle fans shouldn't continue to follow the example set by their chairman - as they go soaring over the moon.

SAUSAGES
FOR THE LADS!

The definitive player rating system that positively outweighs the tabloid reviews of United's squad.

Not only does it give unrequited praise for quality performances and calls of beheading for atrocious gaffs, it offers the ultimate prize for the player who accumulates the highest total each month.

The prize is none other than... *A POUND OF CUMBERLAND SAUSAGE!* kindly provided by...

Ernest Wrightson
(Purveyors of Quality Meat)
CARLISLE COVERED MARKET

This prestigious award, so we at TCS reckon, will provide an incentive for the lads and result in us attaining mid-table respectability. See our next edition for full details on our first winner and pray to God that they aren't a vegitarian...

DERANGED FERRET

Lincoln City

'96-97 was to be "a season of consolidation" for Lincoln City according to manager John Beck. At the end of it we were left wondering what his definition of 'a season of progress' must be! True, we didn't win anything and we didn't even make the play-offs but we made national headlines several times, had a mini cup run and kept the whole thing alive until the very last game... all feats that seldom happen at 'little old Lincoln' (© John Beck 1996).

It all started when the fans were asked to raise the money to buy Kevin Austin from Leyton Orient. O's fans may be amazed to hear it but JB considered Big Kev

DERANGED FERRET! £1

ISSUE 32   Feb.97/Mar.'97

A LINCOLN CITY FANZINE

LINCOLN CITY GOALSCORER CURSE

HAS THIS MAN FINALLY LIFTED IT?

SPONSORS OF GARETH AINSWORTH AND SHANE WESTLEY

to be a "vital cog" for City. £30,000 was the asking price - us fans came up with, give or take a few grand, £1,000! We still bought him (and very well he played all season) but suddenly the price of admission to our pre-season matches with Derby and Aston Villa went up from £5 to £8. Many boycotted the two games.

No-one lucky enough to have a ticket missed our final pre-season match. As part of the deal that took Darren Huckerby to St James' Park the previous season, Kevin Keegan had said he would bring a full strength side to Lincoln for a match. Given that the game was scheduled 48 hours before the Charity Shield, many City fans expected to see a reserve side with the star names playing for a few minutes here and there. To Keegan and Newcastle's eternal credit not only did he field a full strength side for all 90 minutes (only Ferdinand who had flu didn't appear) but he also gave Alan Shearer his first game. £15 million Al up against £30k Kev!! In the lead-up, the national press had a bonanza making out City to be a bunch of thugs who would spoil the big day. In the event the game passed off peacefully, no doubt much to the dismay of the massed newsmen, but it was a superb occasion for the packed house. Al duly scored his first goal as Newcastle won 2-0, but the real winners were the Lincoln public. Relations between the clubs were perhaps soured later in the season when chairman John Reames tried to get some more money off Newcastle when they sold Huckerby to Coventry. His pathetic attempt to claim that

Huckerby hadn't been given enough time to make a certain number of appearances thus generating a further fee was laughed off both by Newcastle and eventually an FA tribunal.

After the pre-season glamour games came reality... Torquay away. Seven hours it took to get there. People in caravans should be banned! To cap it all we lost to an injury time goal to give Torquay the start they were praying for and the one we were dreading. Still, it only took us five hours to get home. Welcome to the season.

The media spotlight fell on us again on the second Saturday when JB failed to witness our 1-1 draw with Leyton Orient. He was helping HM Customs & Excise with enquiries into a VAT fraud concerning own brand whiskey that wasn't going to Poland as planned but Huddersfield amongst other places. And we all thought something serious had happened like him getting the sack! (All charges against JB were subsequently dropped.) Mind you, if he had been present he may well have been facing charges of GBH as the first crap ref of many (Leake of Darwen) turned up and awarded the O's a dodgy free kick deep into injury time from which they equalised. He made a very quick exit at full time pursued by an irate City 'keeper Barry Richardson. Before the Premiership start moaning about the Polls, Dansons and Reids of this world they ought to see who the replacements are likely to be! Leake, Baines, West and Taylor (more of him later) are names that will probably send shivers down the spines of us Nationwide League unfortunates.

Our first league win occurred at the Swansea's Vetch Field, after which a flashing blue light police escort took us through numerous red lights and halfway up the M4 before it was deemed safe to abandon us. It was just one of eight league successes prior to the new year. Interspersed were wallopings at Colchester in which despite the 7-1 scoreline the Man of the Match was their centre half, and against Chester (4-1), although the wins at Brighton and Fulham were sweet. Funny how the friendly Cottagers didn't want to speak to us afterwards - before the game they couldn't wait to tell us how much we were going to lose by. How we'll miss taking our regular six points off them!

Just before setting off to the Goldstone (a mere 180 or so miles on a Tuesday night) Teletext informed the world that the match was in doubt as demonstrations were planned against their board and the police were advising the club to call the game off. A quick call to Brighton was met with assurances that the game would be played and would be finished so off we set. It was obvious on arrival that something was going to happen, a feeling confirmed by talking to locals in the pub beforehand. Fifty-six minutes (to coincide with the amount their chairman Bill Archer paid for the club) was the favoured time for an invasion. In the ground the atmosphere was tense. A few City fans earned applause by starting an "Archer Out" and "Sack the Board" chant but all most of us wanted to do was get three points and get home. Our first goal was the signal for the invasion. It was peaceful and lasted for about 15 minutes. A second invasion began after City scored again but only a handful came onto the pitch and the majority of Brighton fans booed them off. The game ended in a 3-1 win for City. We gratefully left with the three points and left them to it. In the return match a minority of City fans took pleasure in antagonising the Brighton fans with chants of "Archer In." Of course many people had sympathy for the situation the Brighton fans found themselves in, but the overwhelming press coverage their plight received and the fawning support they got from the media irked a few. And let's face it, no-one would have given a toss if it was Lincoln, Rochdale, Hartlepool or any other smaller club in the same situation.

During this indifferent league form City once again made national headlines by knocking out Manchester City in the Coca Cola Cup. One down after 41 seconds we feared the worst, but it was to be one of those nights which only supporters of the 'small clubs' can truly appreciate. Four Lincoln goals hit the City net. 4-1. Four-bloody-one! The pubs hadn't had it so good on a Tuesday night since God knows when. Of course once the hangovers had gone reality set in and the second leg loomed. Surely we couldn't blow it? Being Lincoln supporters means you suffer from a severe case of terminal pessimism, but we needn't have worried as 1,500 + travelled to Maine Road and saw us win 1-0. According to Blues fans they had never been beaten in both legs of a cup tie before - not even in Europe! We went mental doing the Dambuster in the stand whilst the players did it on the pitch!

The third round took us to Southampton and the Dell. Considering the improvements at many grounds in Division 3, theirs was a disgrace; a wooden stand with limited access - it's an accident waiting to happen. Poor organisation meant many were locked out (at a Lincoln game!) whilst those who got in saw Lincoln take the lead, go behind and then equalise in the last five minutes. Cue the Dambuster. Cue Souness whinging about our style. Cue a money-making replay. Three days before the rematch admission prices went up by a quid. The reason for this was that JB (and the fans) desperately wanted to get the signature of Jae Martin, an on-loan winger from Birmingham. Fine, said the chairman, we'll stick a quid on admission to pay for him. He then refused YTV permission to show extended highlights of the replay because they wouldn't pay what he considered a reasonable fee. 10,523 packed the Bank and most were soon orgasmic with delight as we took the lead. Both 'keepers were having blinders as the game ebbed and flowed until 15 minutes from the end. Enter referee Helibron. Ostenstad turned in the box and fell over. No City player was within six feet of him. It was the most blatant dive since Greg Louganis in the Olympics. The ref gave the penalty. Stunned silence. It gave them a lifeline, and two further goals earned them an undeserved 3-1 victory. Souness again spouted crap, claiming his side were always in control. At least they lost to Stockport, but you couldn't help feeling it should have been us knocking them out.

After losing three games to the weather, we began 1997 in mid-table, but only two defeats in the first nine games of the new year saw us rise steadily. One was another thrashing (5-2 at Darlington) whilst the other saw media spotlight number four fall on the Imps.

During the 3-1 home defeat by Wigan, City player Terry Fleming was booked by ref Taylor for a foul. Six minutes later Tezza went to take one of his long throws but for some strange reason decided to leap feet first at a Wigan player. The ref went over and brandished a... nother yellow card (!) No-one could believe it. Taylor was the only man (apart from his assistants it seemed) who hadn't realised he'd booked the same player twice. Afterwards it emerged that for the second booking cheeky chappy Tez had given team mate Tony Dennis' name to the ref. Fleming got a hefty fine from the club and a lenient three match ban from the FA, while the ref got his wrist slapped. This little incident even made *News at Ten*. I bet John Reames charged them for using the footage!

What he did do just prior to transfer deadline day was announce that unless the fans could raise £125,000 in seven days the club would have no option but to sell top scorer and all-round hero Gareth Ainsworth in order to survive. Ever generous, the City fans put their hands in their pockets, and only fell short of the asking sum - by a mere £122,000! Ainsworth stayed at the club however, but for how much longer remains to be seen.

More reffing madness occurred at Carlisle where thanks to the wind, the ball appeared to defy the laws of physics by first going out of and then coming back into play. Thus our last minute equaliser was ruled out, and after a home defeat by Torquay on Easter Saturday (their first win in 17 games) the season appeared dead. However, a 3-1 win at Cambridge heralded a storming finish: Swansea were despatched 4-0, Scunthorpe 2-0 (sadly ending any hopes they had of reaching the play-offs!) and Scarborough 2-0, which together with a 3-3 draw at Exeter meant we went into the final game needing a win, with a defeat for either Northampton or Cardiff to see us in the play-offs for the first time.

Now, most clubs faced with a home game against a side with nothing to play for would be confident. And if that club were Rochdale (no disrespect), then a win would definitely be expected. Unfortunately, of all the clubs Lincoln have as a bogey team, Rochdale is probably top of the heap. We haven't won a league game against them at home since 1988. Of course we bombarded them, and of course our goalscoring heroes Stant and Ainsworth missed chances that they'd been burying all season, and of course Cardiff lost. And of course, so did we.

So, at the end of the day, Brian, we ended up in ninth place. But things look promising for the future if we can keep the squad intact, add a couple of new faces and get some decent refereeing decisions. Oh, and of course, it's also going to cost us more, as admission goes up (again) to £10!

EASTERN EAGLES

Crystal Palace

Many questions were asked of Palace at the start of the season following our heart-rending loss in the last minute of the '95-96 play-off final. Certainly the bookies didn't think we'd be able to pick ourselves off the floor and make another challenge, and the first few games of the season seemed to confirm this. A televised loss on the opening day away to Birmingham was followed by one win and four draws; hardly Championship form. Truth was, Palace were still trying to complete their passing game revolution. It simply took a few matches to get into their stride.

A 3-1 win over struggling

The Eastern Eagles Fanzine

ISSUE **19** £1

THE NEW MESSIAH?

WILL WE AGAIN BE LED TO THE PROMISED LAND?

THE FAREWELL ISSUE - BYE!

Manchester City was followed by an amazing burst of goals. In the League Cup, Bury were sent packing with a seven goal aggregate score, whilst in the league Reading and Southend were both stuffed 6-1 (22 goals in a fortnight!). The early form of strikers Dyer and Freedman was phenomenal, as were midfielders Hopkin and Veart, and the goals kept coming.

All this despite losing our manager Dave Bassett, for a few hours anyway, when he changed his mind about joining Manchester City (our ex-manager and technical director Steve Coppell agreeing to take the job instead). Deep suspicions remained about the manager and his motives for almost going, but the mistrust was put to the back of our minds as we basked in the early season form.

And then it happened. A touch of tinkering, Keegan/Asprilla style, in order to make the team perform better, only succeeded in making them worse. The day in question was November 10th and following a 3-0 televised win against pre-season favourites QPR, Bassett decided to break up the successful back four by re-introducing an unfit Dean Gordon to left back following a lengthy lay-off. A few games earlier he had done the same to the forward line by purchasing Neil Shipperley from Southampton. Up to and including QPR, Palace had played 17 games, winning nine, drawing six and losing just two (including a travesty of justice on the opening day at Birmingham). In this time we'd scored 39 goals, conceding only 13.

The changes to the side in November transformed the club's fortunes alarmingly. Successive defeats saw more drastic chopping and changing, and confidence drained away. Players displayed a marked loss of form and the style of football became more hurried and 'long-ball'. Bassett preferred to use the strength of target man Shipperley to the cultured, attractive, passing game that we had grown to love. In one home game Gordon and Roberts came to blows over a goal conceded, hardly boosting team morale.

Over the winter period the overused Selhurst pitch had cut up badly and that passing game was proving impossible. In January, an effort was made to shore up the defence when Andy Linighan was drafted in, and Carlo Nash replaced the faltering Day in goal a month later. We were flirting with the play-offs, but a bad Easter period saw us slump to 10th place following a 3-0 defeat at promotion rivals Sheffield United. In the 24 games since that QPR fixture, Palace had managed only seven wins, six draws and had suffered 11 defeats, scoring only 30 goals (10 of these in three games) and conceding 31 goals. What a marked contrast to our earlier performances! We were all but out of it.

Whilst all this was going on Dave Bassett decided to leave us in the mire, this time with no second thoughts, as he upped and left for Nottingham Forest. Whatever his personal motives, his attitude to the club and its fans, especially following his earlier dithering, smacked of betrayal. Steve Coppell, who had returned as a scout following his unhappy month at Manchester City, took over as caretaker manager. At least he was a Palace man, and the fans were behind him.

At first the Coppell magic failed to sparkle, but with the reintroduction of Simon Rodger to midfield and Shipperley in rampant form, our fortunes changed. Over the remaining five games we won three and drew two, whilst our rivals faltered, and Palace dragged themselves into the last play-off place. At least now we had a chance.

One point of irony which we can now look back on with a wry smile was the 'third kit fiasco'. This yellow and red 'Romanian' effort, different to our normal blue and white away kit, had been worn on several occasions and we'd always failed to win in it. The jinxed outfit was mistrusted by both players and fans and it was eventually dropped. But when Birmingham came to visit, there was a clash of shirts and they had to wear it. The Romanian hex struck again and they beat us 1-0!

The home play-off semi-final against Wolves was a tense affair but Palace were clearly the better side and in a frantic last couple of minutes we secured a 3-1 advantage to take to Molineux. The away leg was war, to say the least. The atmosphere was intimidating, not least because the Palace contingent were totally surrounded by the home hoards. We showed all our battling qualities (on the pitch, that is), having a good percentage of the game, and though we lost on the night we came through on aggregate. It's a pity that some of the Wolves supporters couldn't take their frustrations out on their team as opposed to the visiting fans. Roaming gangs ensured that at least two

Palace fans had an unscheduled stop-over in the West Midlands, care of the local hospital. When will they ever learn?

And so to Wembley. A tide of emotion engulfed us. A trip to North London for a second successive year - would luck be on our side this time? Would we perform this year? Surely we couldn't fall *twice* at the final hurdle... And if we did, would we ever recover?

Palace tore into the Blades from the off. The team seemed more focused on what lay ahead and had real purpose, but only our poor finishing kept the scores level. In the second period the opposition pushed hard to make an impression and forced a succession of corners. Our defence remained rock solid and Sheff U failed to trouble Carlo Nash's goal. The last ten minutes or so and Palace seemed to find new strength and surged forward looking for a winner. Screamed on by a crescendo of noise, wave after wave of attacking play ensued as Sheffield wilted in the sun. Then, with the ref's lips pursed around his whistle (oo-er!), Hopkin curled a blinding shot into the top corner. Justice had been done and the memory of the Steve Claridge's fatal blow last year was instantly eradicated.

Our sympathies went out to United - God knows, we'd been there before. The pundits had written us off but we'd shown great resolve in coming back from such a disaster. It says a lot about the team's character. Let's hope that we can now emulate Leicester in more ways than one, and with a will to succeed and a few sensible buys learn to survive, and survive comfortably.

Source: *The Abbey Rabbit*

EXCEEDINGLY GOOD PIES

Rochdale

OK, I'll get it over with now! Rochdale are still the longest serving members of the Football League's basement division, extending their position to an unflinching 23 years! No other club outside the Premiership can boast such a record, so we Dale fans should be proud of the club's achievements! Indeed due to Hereford's relegation to the Vauxhall Conference, we are now the only club in our division to have *not* experienced a promotion of any kind in the last 15 years - yes, even Doncaster, Scunthorpe and Torquay have achieved more than us.

So why do we do it? That's the question most of us

THE ALTERNATIVE VOICE OF ROCHDALE A.F.C.

EXCEEDINGLY GOOD PIES

AS MENTIONED ON
RADIO 5 LIVE and in
"90 MINUTES" and in
Scunthorpe's Programme
and on TELETEXT subtitles
and on "COUNTDOWN"

Burnley fans prepare themselves for second Cup replay against Walsall

Issue 21 March 1997   Later than advertised, but still **£1**

were probably asking last July when we set off for our first pre-season friendly at Great Harwood, a little place near to Blackburn. This was our first chance to see how our new manager's team would shape up and around 200 hardy souls made the short trip. Ah, yes, the new manager. Graham Barrow was appointed by huge public demand back in May, after the '95-96 season had ended. In *EGP*'s end of season questionnaire, he was the most popular choice for boss should Mick Docherty have been relieved of his duties. Barrow won promotion with Chester and was surprisingly sacked by Wigan, so he had earned a good reputation in his short managerial career. But this was Rochdale where previous bosses had tried and failed to change our fortunes, although Graham Barrow's appointment was seen by many as the second coming of Christ! Only time would tell...

Back at Great Harwood we made an inauspicious start and ground-out a 0-0 draw. Only the presence of a home supporter who was the spitting image of Paul Calf made it bearable. Further prestigious friendlies at Morecambe, Halifax, Southport, Chorley and Ashton United were 'enjoyed' before we made the long trip to Swansea for the season's opener.

Dale took to the field wearing a much vaunted new strip: made out of the same cloth as the Italy Euro '96 shirt, we were informed. Great! The Italians went out in round one and our start to the season was about to follow a similar pattern. We said "Ciao" to the Coca Cola Cup despite out-playing

Barnsley over two legs, which by the season's end were revealed as an even more remarkable couple of performances. Quite how their rickety, wooden disgrace of a stand will cope with Premiership crowds is anyone's guess. We then had to wait until September 14th for our first league win, but the events of that day made the wait worthwhile. By half time Dale were down to nine men, and with 20 minutes to go we were trailing 1-0. At that point (you know how it is) we really did think that it was all over; but then, from somewhere, we conjured up a two goal salvo in a five minute spell that almost raised the roof at Spotland! We toasted our victory by sinking numerous pints that evening!

As usual we failed to build on this win and lost 3-0 at Hereford the week after, before Leyton Orient arrived at Spotland at the end of the month. This was your standard tedious game that burst into life when we were awarded a late penalty. Steve Whitehall duly converted the kick and minutes later was on the receiving end of a punch from Orient's Andy Arnott after another collision in the box brought another pen. Old war-horse (or should that be cart-horse?) Alvin Martin completely lost the plot and insisted on hitting anyone wearing blue as a mass brawl developed. This was some fight and lasted much longer than any Prince Naseem walk-over! Arnott was sent off, but Martin escaped the red, only to be reported to the FA by the police for various other incidents during and after the bundle. Oh, and Whitehall's spot kick was saved by Les Sealey.

Into October and a new signing was made. Robbie Painter arrived on loan from Darlington and scored in each of his first three games, prompting Dale fans at Darlington to blast out a version of the 1970's Boney M classic *Painter Man*. On the last Saturday of the month we drew 2-2 at Scunthorpe, our third result by that scoreline on successive Saturdays. Unfortunately the sight of a bloke wearing a Burnley coat in the car park afterwards thoroughly spoilt our homeward journey... Ughh.

Two home wins followed and we extended our unbeaten run to eight games. The first of these was 3-0 against a Brighton side that included ex-Dale midfielder Jason Peake. He'd refused a new contract at Spotland the previous summer and so was a 'Judas' in our eyes. And didn't the Sandy Lane end let him know it! Despite our animosity towards Peakey there was a remarkable incident involving Dale and Brighton fans towards the end of the game. The Brighton supporters had been singing about their directors' lack of parentage throughout the game and then decided to climb out of their section and headed for our end. This prompted quite a few Dale fans to do the same and when we met there was much back-slapping and shaking of hands as we wished them well in their fight. Unfortunately, incidents like that don't make good copy and never make the news.

Off the field events were starting to attract interest by now. The club had eventually got the funds to build a new stand at the Pearl Street end, which in itself provides a saga for later, and a book was released about Dale's fortunes in '95-96 entitled *Kicking in the Wind*. This 'fly on the wall' look at football club life was well received by the fans, but upset many of the club's employees with its candid, embarrassing and sometimes hurtful portrayal of everyday goings-on at Spotland.

Back on the field there were a couple of good performances to report: a thoroughly professional 2-0 cup win over Conference-Champions-elect Macclesfield and a 1-0 win at high-flying Wigan. Then we had our mid-winter break as the frost and snow took a grip. Upon our return to action after nearly a month off, results and performances were more erratic than Australia's First Test batting and we won only one of the next 11 fixtures. Alarmingly, Dale were now within shouting distance of the dreaded bottom spot.

In stark contrast, Dale's reserves were storming ahead at the top of Pontins' League Division Three with a 100% record. The mixture of youngsters and first team fringe players ultimately got them some silverware and a much-deserved promotion come the season's end. A really good sign.

March was a frustrating month as far as the first team were concerned. We won the first three games, defeating Wigan on the way yet again, but then went on to lose the next three. What's the word we don't know? Well it's spelt C-o-n-s-i-s...! Easter Monday saw us frustrate Fulham to a 1-1 draw at Craven Cottage, and a conversation with *Radio 5 Live*'s Alan Green on the train home rounded off a good day.

Around this time the club's commercial department launched a newly designed scarf which, for some inexplicable reason, had a Scottish flag at each end. Of course the rumours that the manufacturer thought Dale played at Scotland are totally untrue! Unfortunately, the commercial manager didn't appreciate the criticism of his merchandise and decided to launch a broadside at all and sundry in the match programme. This strained relations with the fans (aka *customers*!), and yet more bad feeling surfaced when it was announced that next season away supporters would be using Sandy Lane.

How could they do it? Sandy Lane is our Kop, our Stretford End, so leave well alone. Demonstrations were planned, leaflets and petitions were distributed as supporters voiced their anger over the lack of discussion and consultation. Fortunately, the board did listen to our cries of derision and a meeting was hastily arranged to thrash out the problem. This meeting was meant to be a small affair, featuring influential parties such as *EGP* and the Supporters' Club. Unfortunately the *Rochdale Observer* got its facts wrong (yet again) and invited all interested parties to attend. Still, the meeting was successful and fan power won the day when Sandy Lane was handed back to us along with a promise that home supporters would get use of the new stand if and when it was completed.

The league season finished with three wins in the last four games, including a 2-0 success at Lincoln on the final day. That victory stopped the home side getting into the play-offs and sparked the customary pitch invasion by disgruntled Red Imps' fans. It also meant that we had lost just two of the last 20 league games against Lincoln.

So Dale finished in 14th, one place better off than last year. An improvement? Hard to say really because many of us were expecting better things, but on reflection we'll call this season the new manager's bedding-in period. Next year should be different though, as players like Alex Russell and Alan Johnson, who both enjoyed excellent seasons, become the rocks on which Barrow builds his squad for '97-98. Let's hope that in *SOTF4* I'm not writing about Dale going into their 25th consecutive season of basement division stability!

EXILED

AFC Bournemouth

There will always be a Bournemouth

In all the 27 years I have supported AFC Bournemouth, I have never experienced one quite like this. It had everything: the highs, the lows, important fixtures and clashes with the big boys. And that was just what went on off the park!

We should have realised from day one that the new season was going to be anything but normal as we set about creating a new club record of five straight home league defeats. But away from home we were picking up points at places like York, Stockport and Preston where we don't usually win

EXILED

SAVE AFC BMTH

THE OFFICIAL NEWSLETTER OF AFC BOURNEMOUTH EXILES CLUB

THE CRUNCH HAD TO COME - WILL THE WINTER GARDENS MEETING GO DOWN AS THE FIRST DAY OF THE REST OF AFC BOURNEMOUTH'S HISTORY ?

CAN FAN POWER (AND MONEY) WIN THE DAY ?

FEB '97 ISSUE   £2·00 NON-MEMBERS

for love nor money. We had to wait until October 12th for our first home points, when dear old Wycombe gave us a run for our money in a five goal thriller. Then three days later we bloody well went and did it again against bogey side Plymouth!

However, the upturn in form didn't last. For a club reportedly £2.5m in the red, we were busting for a decent cup run, but, you guessed it, we crashed out of all the cups in the first round. No surprise really, especially when the draw pitted us against the highest placed teams in the main competitions: Ipswich (CCC), Brentford (FAC), and our bogey mob Plymouth in the AWS. Millwall's song 'No-one like us' sprang to mind.

Then, just before Christmas, the shit hit the fan (no not us on the terraces - Steve Fletcher isn't *that* bad please) as his Royal Pipeness chairman Ken Gardner - aka King of Bullshit - resigned (ha!) upon his return from a holiday. Was pushed, more like after owner Norman Hayward 'checked the books' after a 2˝ year absence to reveal that we were really £3m in debt! Rumours concerning the appointment of Administrators were strongly denied and the team did nothing to lift the festive spirits of the Dean Court faithful, winning only one game in eight (thanks to our perennial home win over Bristol Rovers).

With the club in turmoil we needed some steady hands to steer the ship into the New Year. What actually happened was that three directors jumped overboard days before another visit to the High Court. Nice one guys - there's nothing like a bit of solidarity when the going gets tough - and this was nothing like (blah blah)..! Fortunately the visit to the courts ensured another stay of execution thanks to our promise to put the club into Administration which ultimately failed when Lloyds Bank froze our bank account. HELLLLPPP!! The League then slapped a transfer embargo on us for monies owing to the PFA, and war broke out between Gardner and Hayward. Unity is what we needed, and that's exactly what we *didn't* get.

Then on January 24th our most feared scenario started to be played out: Lloyds called in the receivers after disclosing that the debt was in fact a massive £4.4m. Shiiittt!!!!

Gloom and doom shrouded Dean Court as the end looked likely. The end? NOT BLOODY LIKLEY! With the League's permission we played at Bristol City and the first team lead by example, playing for nothing and still winning in what was a hugely moving afternoon for the away support. Three days later inside the Bournemouth Winter Gardens a public meeting was held by the newly formed Trust Fund whose initial intention was to get the club through to the end of the season. The first of many emotional evenings, Mel Machin was virtually in tears, along with most of us in the 2,000 strong audience, as he paid tribute to the fans and those who had lost their jobs at the club during the day in a bid to save money. That evening saw £50,000 raised, along with the news that the League had given permission for us to continue for the time being.

Further High Court adjournments came and went as Hayward (plus henchmen Roy Pack) gradually decided that their knee jerk reactions to everything would probably guarantee our closure and lose him everything he'd invested, whereas if he helped keep the club alive he just might get something back. This line of argument seemed to sink in.

Meanwhile the Trust, realising that there was no millionaire white knight ready to ride in, decided on the brave decision to go it alone, proposing to turn AFC Bournemouth into Europe's first community-owned club, but it needed £1.5m in bundles of £10,000 to do so. OUCH!

Despite support from the Town, the fans and local business, both the League and Lloyds rejected the initial proposal as the creditors had not had their interests satisfied. Unsurprisingly the bank were slated locally and a mass boycott began to take shape. I know that fans bombarded Lloyds from all corners of the globe on e-mail and at one point they were getting over 200 mail items per day from those of us hooked up to the internet. Still, the pressure seemed to have the desired effect as they started to give the necessary backing and even some support. Could it have had anything to do with bad press and closed accounts I wonder?

Back on the pitch the team were producing their best run of results. After the City game they played a further 17 league fixtures of which only three were lost with a mere 11 goals conceded and 10 clean sheets in all. Not bad given that they weren't being paid!

D-Day arrived (again) on March 20th with another visit to the High Court. With arse cheeks squeaking all morning, news finally filtered through that one last chance has been granted. Relief for the time being. Then a miracle happened. Hayward and Gardner went off to settle their differences behind closed doors; Lloyds had separate talks with Hayward about his loan guarantees, and best of all Lloyds agreed (in principle) with the Trust's financial plans for a community club. This just left the League to decide which way they were going to go.

At the time of writing even the Inland Revenue look to have agreed in principle to the deal they've been offered and a further High Court adjournment has been granted. This leaves us a deadline of June 12th to have everything settled in time for the League AGM 24 hours later which will pave the way for the dream to be kept alive.

At this point I'd like to publicly thank (although I usually don't like doing so) Southampton for bringing their full first team down for a money-raising friendly. They were the only Pretentioushit club to do so when we needed it most. Needless to say we beat them (but then, who didn't last season??).

What have the *Exiles* done? Well, along with our friends on the internet we have raised over £12,000 for the community club so we can be part of the future at Dean Court. Personally I am very proud of what we have achieved in the last three months and other clubs' fans should take note of what can be done without resorting to violence.

Above all we will at least be there in '97-98. It's now up to those with the acumen to get on and secure our long-term future.

Stop Press..

For most of you the season finished weeks ago. But for us it concluded on June 18th 1997. Having got the Creditors Voluntary Agreement signed and High Court action dropped, it only left the Football League to grant its blessing on the deal. Understandably they said that we'd have to be out of receivership by the time the new season kicks off again in August.

So at 4pm on said date the club's assets (such as they are) were transferred over to the Trust Fund, thus securing the future of AFC Bournemouth both for the next generation of supporters and for those of us who have aged considerably in the last few months!

UP THE CHERRIES!!

FERRY 'CROSS THE WENSUM

Norwich City

Phew - what a relief, as all the best managers say at the end of a season when their club has neither gone up nor dropped down. And after the turbulent last couple of seasons, when football was last on many peoples' agendas, '96-97 was a period of consolidation and a refreshing change. We all had to learn to enjoy football again and, by and large, we did.

It wasn't all sweetness and light, chocolate cake and roses, though. Two members of the old board somehow managed to cling on to their posts (one actually becoming chairman, although fortunately this doesn't give him any extra powers nowadays) and more

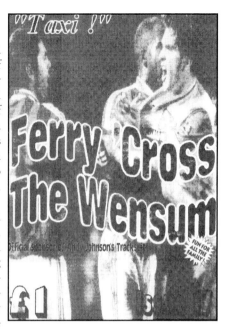

muck was dug up about the previous regime, making it very difficult for the new board to forget about the past. Most importantly, one fat bastard's crimes ensured we were in the shit financially all season which kept Mike Walker's hands totally tied behind his back as far as transfers went (although he still managed to pull off a few minor miracles, more of which later).

The season started with great expectations from all except the manager, who stated that he would be happy with a top ten finish. After the first game even he must have thought that perhaps he'd been a bit conservative, as we totally outclassed newly-promoted Swindon in front of one of the most passionate crowds seen at Carra Rud for a long time. The city was buzzing that night about what might lay ahead. Unfortunately what came next was a defeat, 3-1 away at Bolton. We were actually the better team, but the first of many costly Bryan Gunn mistakes threw it away. A sign of things to come?

Despite this setback City hung around the top two places until around November time, superb wins against Wolves, Birmingham and of course the trouncing of the binmen from Suffolk/Essex were countered by poor performances and results against the likes of Charlton, Man City and Barnsley. It was around this time though that our poor disciplinary record caught up with us (we'd had three players sent off in two games against Oxford alone), and this combined with injuries to key players caused a slide of Tory proportions. Ten games without a win, including seven losses, meant that by Boxing Day we were down just above the relegation zone. What was Walker's resolution, bearing in mind the threadbare nature of the squad he'd inherited and the debt the football club was in? He brought in a few internationals - easy when you know how!

Matt Jackson and Kevin Scott were nabbed for a pittance (considering today's market) to shore up the seriously leaking defence, David Rocastle came in on loan to fill the midfield berth of the constantly injured Andy Johnson and the Swede Ulf Ottoson was flown in to try and score the goals Robert Fleck wasn't able to. Immediately we embarked on a five game winning run which included the 1-0 over Sheff Utd and the FA Cup third round that set up a mouth-watering clash between Martin O'Neill's Leicester and Mike Walker's Norwich.

With our 3,000 official tickets gone within a couple of hours it was left to the City boys to try and fill up the home areas at Filbert Street. We did our best, but repeated warnings from Leicester City and Norwich police about the game being sold out meant that it was only hundreds rather than thousands who travelled without tickets. The crowd? 16,703, about 5,000 below capacity, and the police wonder why no-one believes them when they say that there's no point travelling without a ticket. The game itself resulted in a highly honourable 2-1 defeat, with half our youth team playing.

Back to 'concentrate on the league' then, although with the injuries and suspensions still coming thick and fast and with neither Rocastle or Ulf (ulf, ulf, ulf, ulf) really doing the business, the remainder of the campaign was always likely to be a struggle. And so it was. A win was followed by a loss which was followed by a draw which was followed by a loss... Not really promotion form! Amazingly though we continued to figure amongst the play-off positions right until the third from last game, away at Essex Man Town. The less said about that one the better, other than we were crap, Ipswich police were worse and I hate them more than ever. Not a very satisfactory state of affairs, and not a very pleasing way for our season to finish. So it was good to bring down the curtain with a good ol' fashioned sing-song at Carra Rud and an encouraging display by a very youthful side. A meaningless defeat at already relegated Oldham left us in a disappointing 13th place.

So, what's the verdict on this first post-Chase year? Personally, I reckon we have a very bright future. NCFC is a football club now, a *real* football club. The board and management are doing absolutely everything they can to try and win back the supporters' confidence after years of taking the piss out of us. If anything they may be over-compensating in some ways, but bloody hell, you can't moan when your views are genuinely wanted, valued and acted upon. This 'new broom' mentality has extended to the stands as well; there's been a new type of atmosphere at Carra Rud this season. Very little moaning, patience with the players and management, and full-blooded and full-throated support at virtually every match. Attendances kept up well; we averaged nearly 15,000 for home games (compare this to our supposed rivals for 'biggest club in East Anglia', who struggled to get to five figures for the vast majority of the season) and our away support continues to be amongst the best in the division. Even the old hooligans started coming regularly again after many years of hibernation. NCFC is a broad church nowadays!

On the pitch things are looking good too. All our young starlets stayed loyal to the club; even if Andy Johnson has personal problems and may have to be allowed to leave, it will be the club's choice and not his. Keith O'Neill looked class when not injured and Matt Jackson has to have been the bargain of the season. Andy Marshall has at last replaced the ageing Bryan Gunn between the posts and Darren Eadie was just a class apart, fully deserving of his recent England call-up. Aside from these, the youth team ran away with their league and looks set to provide the first team with a sound base for many years to come. Four or five of them have already made their debuts, including Wales' youngest ever U21 international at 16, Craig Bellamy. Look out for them next year!

The club has a new national image also, thanks to the efforts in particular of director Delia Smith. This shone through over the summer with the launch of the new kit, a very smart and well designed (by Bruce Oldfield no less) combination of the practical, comfortable and, yes, sexy. Boy, are we going to look good this season - let's just hope that with record season ticket sales the players are looking good in the Premiership this time next year.

DELIA SMITH'S RECIPE FOR SUCCESS

Source: *Liverpool are on the tele again!*

FLASHING BLADE

Sheffield United

The Last Minute Winner

We'll begin at the end. And I mean the very end. The final minute of the final game of the '96-97 football season. Spring Bank Holiday Monday 1997, Wembley Stadium, 4:48 pm.

Picture the scene: the Nationwide First Division play-off final is heading for what seems to be an inevitably goalless stalemate. For a dire 89 minutes and 36 seconds Sheffield United and Crystal Palace have cancelled each other out. Then Palace win a corner. The ball is half-cleared but is swung back in. Carl Tiler heads it out. This time it drops straight

HANGING IN THERE!

Despite a plague of injuries and illness that has deprived United of Ward, Short, Whitehouse, Vonk, Nilsen, Sandford, Hodgson, Taylor, Hutchison and White, against the odds the Blades are still hard on the heels of Barnsley and Bolton in the race for promotion

No.52 January 1997

to David Hopkin. What the hell, thinks Mary's lad, I might as well have a pop. Bang! He curls the ball an inch under the crossbar, an inch inside the post. It's a goal totally out of context with the rest of the game. After nine months' hard slog, there are 24 seconds to go. South London goes mad, South Yorkshire drops to its knees.

Sheffield United have got a thing about the 90th minute: *we don't like it.* When Petr Katchouro scored a last minute winner at Wolves in September 1996 it was the first time we'd done so for five and a half years, in fact not since Brian Marwood beat Neville Southall at Goodison Park in February 1991. But during those same six seasons we saw Chris Price, Robert Fleck, Ian Wright, Steve Whitton, Kevin Scott, Mark Stein, Richard Cadette, Neil Emblen, Craig Russell, Bruce Dyer, Ian Moore, Paul Mortimer, Jimmy Quinn and Steve Bull *all* deny United points with injury-time goals.

And for David Hopkin, Wembley '97, read Mark Stein, Stamford Bridge '94. It was the final day of this particular season, and an unlikely combination of four different results had to occur for United to go down. They all did! Wimbledon handed (sold?) Everton a 3-2 win after being two up, Ipswich bored their way to a 0-0 draw at Blackburn and Southampton won 1-0. Meanwhile, we were clinging on for a 2-2 draw at Chelsea, when Stein decided he needed to convince Glenn Hoddle that he was worth a place in the Cup Final team, so he smacked in an injury time winner to send the Blades down.

When Hopkin did the same at Wembley, Simon Tracey, Mitch Ward and Dane Whitehouse felt it more than most, for they had also played in that game at the Bridge three years earlier. Tracey was only playing because Alan Kelly was injured, but as he lay prostrate on the Wembley turf he must have been wondering how this could happen to him - twice. Ward and Whitehouse, both Sheffield-born and Blades fans since childhood, wept uncontrollably, like thousands of their compatriots in the Wembley stands.

Is there anything that can generate such contrasting emotions as a last-minute winner in a vital game of football? Pleasure or pain is usually a personal thing, but that single Scotsman propelling the ball into the net at that particular moment sent 32,000 people into raptures, and another 32,000 into despair. If Hopkin had scored with, say, 15 minutes left and Palace had hung on to win, their fans would still have been incredibly happy, and yes, we'd have been downcast, but there's just something indefinable about getting beaten in the 90th minute.

I can only imagine how the Crystal Palace fans felt that day (although Leicester City supporters would've had a good idea). In two consecutive play-off finals, with promotion to the Premiership and all that it brings as the prize for the victors, Palace followers have experienced the two extremes of the last-minute winner. So at least *they* know how *we* felt. But on second thoughts, perhaps not; after all, their share price didn't drop by 25 pence the next day...

In the aftermath, the common theme is "We must pick ourselves up and start again." But is it that easy? Over 18 months Howard Kendall assembled a squad that, individually at least, looked the equal of anything in this division. His problem was getting those individuals to perform consistently as a team. Not one away win in 1997 tells it all. Kendall will cite injuries, and he is right to do so as he lost Mitch Ward, Dane Whitehouse, Michael Vonk, Chris Short, Doug Hodgson and John Ebbrell for large chunks of the season, as well as countless other players for shorter periods. However, it wasn't so much Kendall's lengthy injury list that drew most attention from Blades fans, but his tactical approach away from home. It seemed obvious to everyone except the boss that telling the team to go out "not to lose" was never going to bring in the points. And not only did we not win away in 1997, we never even took the lead! We only tried to score after the other team went in front.

Whether Kendall changed his tactics because of the injuries I don't know, but earlier in the season, when we had a full squad, United scored four at Stoke and Grimsby and won well at Wolves, Oldham and West Brom. A couple more away wins in the Spring and the play-offs wouldn't even have concerned us.

In the meantime we were winning convincingly at home, if only in terms of the results. Performances in 3-0 wins against Southend, Grimsby and Port Vale left a lot to be desired. Gone was the slick, quick style that had seen us win seven and draw two in the final run-in of the previous season, to be replaced by a hybrid hotch-potch that was neither a long-ball game or a short one. Although Kendall denied that he had changed the way United played, everyone else thought otherwise.

The feeling at the end of the season was that we were lucky to have finished fifth, so I suppose defeat in the play-off final wasn't so bad after all. IF ONLY IT WASN'T IN THE LAST SODDING MINUTE!!

FLY ME TO THE MOON

Middlesbrough

It's June now; outside the sun is blazing and I'm stuck inside staring at an empty computer screen. Dave Jenkins has been on the phone again reminding me that my contribution to *Survival of the Fattest* is now urgently required. Any later and he'll be sending round the bailiffs. But it's not that I'm being lazy; well, no more than usual at any rate. It's just that even now I'm not quite over the trauma that was Middlesbrough's season '96-97. Fantasy and nightmare. Demon rollercoaster that flew off the rails. The very best of times and the very darkest. The season of a thousand 'if only's.

Back in the long, long dog days before chairman Steve Gibson's red revolution, Middlesbrough were the perennial under-achievers of British football. You knew exactly where you stood watching the Boro, from what was so often the terrace of despair, the concrete slopes of the old Holgate End. In over a century of crushed hopes and trampled dreams we had constantly flattered to deceive, only to rise again before another undignified fall. But last season we broke the mould - and how!

It began so well, with the scorching £7 million summer signing of 'The White Feather', Cup Final scorer for Champions League winners Juventus. Amazing! The sheer nerve of it! We had already prised promising Brazilian midfielder Emerson from Porto and were pitching him in alongside Barmby and Juninho, now both firmly settled in for surely a more auspicious second season with us. Suddenly we had high hopes. *Very* high hopes. We had staked everything and we were going for it, big style. And in the end, how desperately close we came.

Look at our achievements: our first major Wembley Cup Final in 121 years, followed by our second and first ever FA Cup Final only a couple of months later. You wait two lifetimes for the bus to paradise and then the things won't stop coming. In between times of course we crashed to our third relegation from the top flight in less than a decade, and what makes it all the more galling is the knowledge that we were banished by a points divide significantly less than the three removed from us by the Premier League for failure to

turn out at that darned Blackburn Rovers game in December. Unbelievable!!
Oh and of course we lost the two cup finals, but I needn't have told you that.
Even in defeat we couldn't accept it in the 'normal' manner. Chelsea's Di
Matteo just had to score the quickest goal in FA Cup Final history against us,
and as for the Coca Cola, well Leicester City were gagging to snatch a last-gasp
victory from us with an equaliser less than three minutes from the end of extra
time. That was how close we came to picking up our first major honour, and
in effect that was how close Middlesbrough came to setting the seal on our
greatest ever season. In the words of my former co-editor Nigel Downing:
"we'd have gotten away with it if it hadn't have been for that Heskey kid."
Absolutely typical! What a season.

OK, but that bare bones outline ignores some unforgettable incidents
and twists of fate. So here goes...

Middlesbrough made a major impact at the season's onset. A 3-3 home
draw with Liverpool featured a brilliant debut hat-trick for 'Super Rav'. In one
unforgettable fortnight in September we hammered four past West Ham and
Coventry, floored high-flying Everton 2-1 at Goodison before destroying lowly
Hereford 7-0 in the Coca Cola. Ravanelli was the Premier's ace marksman and
the fans were swooning in raptures over the immense flair of Juninho and
Emerson. The Riverside was awash with would-be White Feathers, shirts pulled
up over heads, spray-on grey hair and mucho mucho mamma mia's. Game on!

But then just as we were savouring the sweet taste of paradise, that
special Middlesbrough malady struck us back to planet reality. Just as we seemed
to have cracked it, *we* cracked. Our 'Fall in the Fall' began against the powerful
Arse, after which Spurs, Newcastle and Derby all stuck the knife in. And as
ever, the referees played their part. Even Jim Smith reckoned we should have
had at least one of the three clear penalties at the Baseball Ground.

Meanwhile the Boro were shooting themselves in the foot. Both feet
actually. Mr 'Donna Summer' Emerson decided to extend his Brazilian holiday, going AWOL in Rio. "Emo Quits" read the *Sun*, which begged the question, just how did Britain's No.1 tabloid (allegedly) know that Emo Philips had
thrown in the towel? What followed was a shameful episode of will he/won't
he when Middlesbrough became victims of a vicious newspaper circulation
war. A season's jealousies over Teesside's capture of the Latin army now burst
forth in hysterical fashion. The derogatory comparisons between Redcar and
Rio, the Tees and the Copocobana became tiresome, and more than a little
insulting. The *Mirror* capped it all by printing a picture of Emerson's poor little
abode, next day publishing an apology to the gentleman whose sumptuous
suburban villa they'd incorrectly targeted.

In the meantime it seemed like Middlesbrough against the world.

A sound 1-5 thrashing at Liverpool was followed by one of the most
peculiar episodes of a bizarre season. On the Friday before our game with
Blackburn, Middlesbrough sought guidance from the Premier League. Our
squad had been decimated by injury and 'flu. Amazingly no-one seems to
have been in at Premier HQ and the only advice we could get was non-

committal. Middlesbrough decided to take the fateful decision for themselves, according to the FA, "acting in good faith." The consequences
were to be quite appalling.

We weren't feeling too festive over the festive season. Not until the
Boxing day clash with Everton, that is, when everything came together again
as we hammered the toffees 4-2. (I should have known the result in advance -
my brother flew in from Hong Kong to see his usual one game a season, and we
always win 4-2 when the jammy bugger comes to town!)

We followed this up with dire displays at Coventry and Arsenal. One
bright spot at Highbury was Bryan Robson rolling back the years to play a
quite superb final match. How we laughed as Hartson's verbal volley at Robbo
was intercepted by a red card-wielding official. Clearly ginger John wasn't
wishing us a Happy New Year.

So we entered a mad period when we couldn't hit a barn door in the
league, while in the cups we were well nigh unstoppable. We had already
destroyed the auld enemy Newcastle 3-1 in the Coca Cola. Juninho had torn
them apart. Now we added Premier leaders Liverpool to our scalp collection
and saw off Chester City 6-0. We scraped past plucky non-leaguers Hednesford thanks to a saving goal by Jan Fjortoft and then promptly sold him.

In the league we were cast to the bottom of the heap when defeated at
home by basement side Southampton, thanks to a goal from a corner that was
clearly a goal kick. It was to be a terrible week. The Premier panel exacted its
punishment for the Blackburn debacle and docked us three points. The town
was stunned. We were now hopelessly adrift.

Sometimes when you are down a new spirit is forged, and so it was with
us: the whole town of Middlesbrough was galvanised into action. Chairman
Steve Gibson intervened with a major team talk and the fans demonstrated
with postcards and petitions at Lancaster Gate. Middlesbrough were born
again, particularly the foreign legion. For the next couple of months we steam-
rollered our way past much of the opposition. Brave Stockport were beaten
away to set up a Coca Cola Final. We won our first ever FA Cup Quarter Final
at Derby and hammered Leicester, Blackburn, Chelsea and Derby in the league.
Juninho in particular was unstoppable. Even man-markers couldn't tire him
or tie him back.

Although it all went so wrong in April and May, we were still 'privileged' to suffer agony upon agony. Ravanelli's extra time Coca Cola goal at
Wembley was the most incredible moment of my life - I felt as if my body was
going to splinter and fracture into a thousand pieces. A week later, trying to
put Heskey's cruel late strike out of our minds, lightning struck twice. Imagine
the torment of coming back from two down against Chesterfield in your first
ever FA Cup semi, only to have a lead swept away with the last touch of the
game. Nothing ever prepared me for such torture!

How much more of this could we take? Following another all-night
queue we set out to Hillsborough for the Coca Cola replay. The police decided
to divert all 20,000 of us down one single track road. The result was stationary

traffic stretching back beyond Barnsley. The kick-off was put back 15 minutes but thousands of fans still missed the best part of the first half. In extra time of a disappointing game Heskey laid out Boro defender 'uncle' Festa. The Leicester attack exploited the gap for Claridge to convert Walsh's unopposed knock-down and we had lost. Although we swept back to beat Chesterfield, the fates intervened again to disallow the goal of the season by Juninho for the most innocuous of challenges by Beck.

The final four games in nine days saw us bow out of the Premiership. An incredible last seconds penalty against Villa gave us hope. At least half of the crowd had to turn away from Rav's spot-kick; they simply couldn't bear to look. Three-one up away at Old Trafford looked like a lifeline but then Ravanelli hobbled off and out of the season. How we needed his goals.

So, ultimately we failed, but you can't say we didn't try - and try to entertain. The supporters dipped deep into their holiday funds and sang their hearts out. The players went all-out in attack. The media replied with unprecedented levels of flak. At the end I was honoured to be amongst a privileged band of supporters selected as the club's guests for the FA Cup Final. What other club would do that for a humble fanzine editor?

I'm so proud to be a part of my club, Middlesbrough FC, and to have witnessed every twist and turn in this unbelievable season. Whatever happens in our now uncertain future, we will never forget the sight of Juninho in full flight, running at the heart of the defence and taking them apart with consummate ease. Good luck, little fella. It was a dream.

FOLLOW THE YELLOW BRICK ROAD

Mansfield Town

"We've come to spoil your party!" That's what we sang at Wigan's Springfield Park on the last day of the season (and in the pub beforehand, if the truth be told), as Wigan went all-out for victory and the Division Three Championship. And to be totally honest, despite our late surge up the table, the Stags couldn't spoil a trifle by tipping it onto the carpet and dancing on it. But we tried anyway. And did we spoil the party? Did we arse! At the start of the second half, we rolled over and died, were reincarnated and promptly died all over again. Fulham's chairman Jimmy Hill had allegedly promised the Stags a crate of champers if we

THE SMALLEST ISSUE OF
F.T.Y.B.R.
IN THE WORLD.... EVER....

ALL I SAID WAS "NEVER MIND, THERE'S ALWAYS NEXT SEASON!"

This issue belongs to :- ....

ISSUE No. 31½   PRICE : £0.00

pulled off a famous victory, handing them the title. If that bloke from Harrods had took over a few weeks before, we might have gone and done it. The champagne from Harrods is probably better than the cheap stuff that Chinny would have given us!

In the end, 11th place wasn't that bad a finish for the Stags. We didn't get off to one of our greatest ever starts. Three league games in, no goals, no points, out of the Fizzy Pop Cup and then suddenly, no manager. Andy King, once proud hero of Mansfield, was suspended from the ground, only being allowed back in for the chairman to sack him.

With new manager Steve Parkin installed, the Stags turned over high-flying Fulham 2-1 at the Cottage. Was *FTYBR* there to see it? No, we played Watford at footy in the morning and found the comforts of their local pub too great. When we heard the result on the way back up the M1 we were gutted beyond belief. A great day out was then had by all who travelled to Darlington. After much beer and an impromptu game of cricket on the terraces, the Stags went goal crazy and rattled four past the opposition whilst conceding only two.

The away trip to Brighton was one of those really bizarre occasions. The Brighton supporters, who were in dead schtuck at the time, had declared this as the game to stay away from. Blimey, we've had plenty of practice for this, with only 1,600 and 2,200 for the two previous games at Field Mill. Just under 2,000 saw the first half at the Goldstone Ground, but a rush on the gates saw many more for the second half, with a dodgy penalty giving the home side a much-needed point. However, down at their place they said what a great job we did in supporting their cause, but when they came to Field Mill all they did was hurl abuse at us. How two-faced can you get? A cushty draw in the opening round of the FA Cup saw the Stags walk all over non-league Consett. It should really have been more, but four strikes without reply was more than enough.

A decent weekend away in Torquay is all that any true Stags fan could ask for. Ah! The usual itinerary is a Friday night out on the town knocking back the ale, an *FTYBR* victory in the morning and a Stags win in the afternoon. It was all going so well. Beer was drunk and the morning game was won under a heavy blanket of fog. The Stags held Torquay at bay for 37 minutes until the referee decided to abandon the game due to the fact he couldn't see a bloody thing ("So what's new!" I hear you cry). The fog had become a real pea-souper and despite attempts to help play along by using an orange ball (?), he called it off. "We want our money back!" we screamed. And we got it. We were given a voucher which we could either exchange for cash or use to get in when the match was replayed (a Tuesday night and a much needed 2-1 win). Torquay lost money on this day because even those who'd been given complimentary tickets got a voucher and made eight quid on the deal. And so did a couple of photographers! But the ones that I feel sorry for are those who travelled down on the day - five hours on the coach, just about an hour off of it, then five hours back up North.

Despite not being able to rattle the ball into the back of the net too often, the defence stood its ground and slowly the Stags inched up the table, and 'party time' was just around the corner. Unfortunately it wasn't our party. Fulham arrived at Field Mill. One point was all they needed for promotion and one point was all they got. The champagne corks were popping in the visitors' changing room.

Carlisle United and the *Sky* TV cameras arrived at Field Mill. Much waving to the cameras ensued for a brief moment of fame, but to no avail. One point was enough for their champagne corks to start popping as well.

A trip to Swansea saw them take the three points to ensure their play-off place. Well, we think they took the points. The trip to Swansea didn't happen for me and I had to listen to the biased local radio station (motto: If it ain't about Forest we don't give a monkey's). They said we were losing, Ceefax said we were in front. The local radio mob didn't give us the right score until after the final whistle and the result had been on the telly. Then it was Wigan's turn to be done a favour, which takes us full circle to where this review started.

The season could have been a lot better. All we needed was someone to knock the ball into the net. I mean, you're not gonna win much when you're top scorer has a grand total of five goals to his credit, are you?

There were no big money deals coming in to Field Mill this season (a big money deal to Mansfield means a transfer fee of any sort, be it hard cash or the rent of a lawnmower - ours was destroyed in a 'mysterious' fire!). But at the end of the season Manchester City offered a ludicrous fee (which could be up to

£20,000 depending on this and that) for our reserve team 'keeper Nicky Weaver, who'd put in a sterling performance in his last reserve game for us, letting in a respectable nine goals!

Speaking of the reserves, their season was certainly one to forget. After being relegated the previous year, they went all out and finished with a quite outstanding ONE point from 24 games and a good 20 or so points adrift at the foot of the league - Bradford were the only team crap enough not to beat us.

The new season is being looked forward to in anticipation. It is our centenary year. Let's just hope it isn't as bad as at least 96 of the previous ones.

A round-up of this season can't go by without a mention of our scummy rivals' fluke FA Cup run into the semi's. The Anti-Christ himself, John Duncan, said that all the good teams went out early on, so a second round exit to Stockport puts us up there with the best of 'em. I could live with the fact that they beat Forest, but to then go on and reach the semi-final was too much. When the ball found the back of the net to make it 3-3 in the 120th minute at Old Trafford, the swearing in Mansfield and the surrounding area reached an all time high. Still, they got stuffed in the replay, so all was well. Go on, read their review - it'll be FA Cup this and FA Cup that and 'we're better than the Stags'. Just one final word to all those so-called 'Stags' fans who mysteriously turned up on live TV wearing the blue scum shirts - we know who you are!

Epilogue: The Book of the False King

And lo, the King was summoned unto the almighty Stags chairman. And the chairman spake unto the King, "We're at the wrong end of the table. Thou art bloody shite, take thyself out of my sight! And never darken this doorstep again!"

And so the King left and wandered in the football wilderness. The King spake unto himself, "I'll head North, and I'll bloody show 'em!"

After much wandering, the King arrived at Doncaster. A friend named Kerry took the King under his wing, but in a few months all was not well.

And lo, the King was summoned unto the almighty Donny chairman. And the chairman spake unto the King. "We're at the wrong end of the table. Thou art bloody shite, take thyself out of my sight! And never darken this doorstep again!"

And so the King left and wandered in the football wilderness The King spake unto himself again, "I'll head North, and I'll bloody show 'em!"

After much wandering, the King arrived at Grimsby. Another friend took him under his wing, but in another few months all was far from well, and the fishermen were relegated.

And lo, the King was summoned unto the almighty fishy chairman. And the chairman spake unto the King, "We've been relegated. Thou art bloody shite, take thyself out of my sight! And never darken this doorstep again!"

The King once again set out into the wilderness. And he spake unto himself (cos no-one else would listen), "I'll be back! And I'll show the bloody lot of ya! Just you wait! Now, where did I put that application form for the Everton Job?"

FOREST FOREVER

Nottingham Forest

Annus Horribulus...

This, you may remember, is a phrase which was used a few years ago by HM in her Christmas Day speech. She was using it to sum up a turbulent year for the Royal Family. One could be forgiven for thinking that she was actually predicting Nottingham Forest's fortunes in the '96-97 football season!

After all, this was undoubtedly one of the worst seasons in Forest's history. Not only were we (deservedly) relegated from the Premiership, we also got knocked out of the FA Cup by lowly Chesterfield, *and* finished lower than both our local rivals, Derby and Leicester, for the first time in living memory.

Despite all of this, however, the campaign did actually provide one or two memorable moments. So, instead of writing a kick-by-kick account of too many spineless defeats, I have decided to make this review a summary of my top ten memories of Forest's year. Read and enjoy...

1. The opening day...

Picture the scene: it is approximately 4.45 pm on the opening Saturday of the Carling Premiership, and all is well with the world. The August sun is shining, and Forest have just clinched a convincing 3-0 win away to Coventry.

As we leave Highfield Road, the 3,000 travelling supporters sing in unison - "Super super Kev, super super Kev, super super Kev, super Kev Campbell." Now Campbell is hardly the most illustrious striker to have ever appeared in a Forest shirt, but on this occasion he was fully deserving of the prefix 'super'. He had just played the proverbial blinder, putting the ball in the back of the Coventry net no less than three times. But it wasn't just a one man show; the rest of the team were superb as well. Indeed, some of the supporters were so impressed with the display that they started singing "We're gonna win the league." Talk about false dawns!

2. The Mark Crossley sex scandal...

Yes, no misprint here - the *Mark Crossley* sex scandal! Let me explain. On the day of Forest's second game of the season, while browsing through a copy of *The Sun*, I happened to notice a prominent headline which read, 'Forest Goalie Couldn't Keep His Hands Off My Gaynor'. Intrigued, I read on. I quote:

>Soccer Idol Mark Crossley has broken the heart of one of his biggest fans - by scoring with his girlfriend. Sad Simon Miller was ditched by Gaynor Mann after she fell for the £7,000 a week Nottingham Forest goalie on holiday in Crete. Lifelong Forest nut Simon, 21, said last night, "I'm devastated - Crossley's a legend around here, but I feel he's let me down. I feel worse than if he'd let in four for Forest."

OK, the story was just a run-of-the-mill tabloid celebrity sex scandal. However, the funny thing is, Mark Crossley did actually 'let in four for Forest' the very same day the story appeared! Yes, Sunderland duly won 4-1 at the City Ground - and the season went downhill from that point on really...

3. Jason Lee's Shirt...

Once upon a time, *Forest Forever* used to be the official sponsors of Jason Lee's kit. This is the reason why I can confess to the dubious honour of owning a long sleeved Forest shirt with '12' and 'Lee' printed on the back. Anyway, to cut a long story short, on the way home from Forest's Coca Cola Cup tie away to Wycombe, my forfeit for losing at cards was to wear the Jason Lee shirt to Forest's next away game.

So, a couple of weeks later, I found myself sat in the away enclosure at Stamford Bridge wearing said shirt... Suffice to say, with Jason Lee hardly being the greatest of players (to put it politely), I had the piss taken out of me all afternoon by both Forest and Chelsea supporters alike.

However, he who laughs last laughs loudest... With Forest 1-0 down and only a few minutes remaining, Frank Clark brought on Jason Lee as a substitute in a last ditch attempt to get an equaliser. And yes, you guessed it, Forest's No.12 duly turned a 1-0 defeat into a 1-1 draw by scoring an audacious lob with his first touch! Ha!!

4. Student night at Rock City...

For those of you who are not 'in the know', Rock City is a night club/music venue in Nottingham, and every Thursday is student night. Nothing remarkable there. However, Thursday October 3rd 1996 was a student night with a difference. Because on this occasion, Rock City was hosting the debut gig of Merc - a Nottingham indie band, featuring none other than Forest player Paul McGregor on lead vocals.

Thus, myself and several hundred others enjoyed the surreal experience of watching a Forest player performing as part of a band. What's more, in the audience were a number of McGregor's team mates - Kevin Campbell, Chris Allen, Ian Woan, Colin Cooper, Jason Lee, Brian Roy and Mark Crossley! Scott Gemmill, however, was unable to attend, for he was on international duty for Scotland. Shame really, as he had been lined up to do a spot of DJ'ing under the bizarre pseudonym 'Blood Clart Rasta of the Wicked Bitches'. I kid you not...

5. Steve Stone incident number one...

Steve Stone missed most of Forest's season after suffering a serious knee injury. But even so, he still managed to provide more entertainment from off the pitch than many of his team mates on it!

First of all, there was his appearance on *A Question of Sport*. For his first go, Stoney was shown a clip of a goal from Euro '96 and was asked who scored it. "Poborsky," he answered correctly, "although I don't know his first name." "That's correct," said David Coleman, "and for the record, his Christian name is Karel. " "Karel?," the bluff, slaphead Geordie exclaimed in a tone of derision. "That's a *girl's* name. And he's got a girl's haircut as well!"

Quite extraordinary... A priceless moment!

6. Christmas come early...

After the aforementioned victory on the first day of the season, Forest failed to win any of their next 16 Premiership games. Thus, by mid-December, we were anchored to the foot of the Premiership. Frank Clark had clearly lost the plot, and it came as little surprise when he handed in his resignation.

The board quickly persuaded club captain Stuart Pearce to take over as caretaker player/manager. This proved to be a popular choice, but then, 'Psycho' is so popular at the City Ground that most Forest supporters even believe that his shit doesn't stink!

Anyway, Pearce's first game in charge came on December 21st - and it was a baptism of fire if ever there was one. Yes, a home fixture against Arsenal, who at the time were lying second in the Premiership. However, Pearce's inspiration was such that Forest, against the odds, managed to secure all three points. What's more, the winning goal by Alf-Inge Haaland came in the very last minute of the game. T'was sheer bloody nirvana... and I had the hangover the next morning to prove it.

7. Que Sera Sera...

Pearce taking over sparked a brief revival, with Forest winning five of his first seven games in charge. But despite this dramatic improvement in form, nobody seemed to fancy our chances in the next one - a tricky FA Cup fourth round tie away to Newcastle. Oh ye of little faith... as it turned out, two brilliant late goals by Ian Woan saw us come from behind to win 2-1 and claim a place in the last 16.

It was a wonderful afternoon, and with Manchester United, Arsenal and Liverpool also having been knocked out, many supporters began to fancy our chances of going all the way. However, it was not to be. The law of sod ensured that Forest went out to the mighty Chesterfield in the next round...

8. Shit on the Derby...

Now, Derby - or the Sheepshaggers, as they are better known around these parts - have always been our greatest rivals. Forest supporters hate everything about Derby, and the feeling is reciprocated. During this game though, one Forest supporter took this hatred to new lengths. The gentleman in question had somehow managed to smuggle into the ground a paper bag containing a big lump of shit. Yes, REAL shit! And midway through the game, he stood up and hurled it at the Derby supporters sitting directly to the right of the away enclosure! Now I can only assume that those on the receiving end of the flying turd made a complaint, and that the Police subsequently used Close Circuit TV to identify the gentleman who threw it... because about ten minutes later, he was ejected from the ground!

Overall, it was not the most pleasant of incidents. But at least it provided the rest of the Forest supporters in attendance that evening with a legitimate excuse to start singing "Shit on the Derby, shit on the Derby tonight..."

9. Steve Stone incident number two...

Queuing for tickets is usually one of the more tedious aspects of being a supporter. However, there was one occasion last year when this was not the case, thanks to Steve Stone!

On the morning that tickets went on sale for our final game of the season, Stoney pulled up in his car outside the ticket office to park. But instead of applying his footbrake, he accidentally kicked his accelerator and crashed into the City Ground's wrought iron gates! And all in front of a captive audience...

10. Party on down...

Although most of us had given up any hope of survival weeks before, Forest were not officially relegated until Saturday May 3rd 1997. That day, we were playing at home against Wimbledon - and in order to stand any chance of staying up, we needed to win... and also hope that Coventry, Leicester, Sunderland, West Ham, Middlesbrough and Southampton would all lose. Slim chance, eh?

Well, by half time we were a goal behind, and all of the aforementioned teams (apart from Coventry) were winning. So that was it. Barring a miracle, it was all over. However, rather than getting all morbid, the Trend End decided to laugh in the face of adversity. Consequently, during the second half, I found myself partaking in numerous Mexican waves, and joining in with a whole array of ridiculous songs, from "Stockport, on a Friday night" to "We're better than United/We're louder than the Kop/We're bottom of the league/ But we should be at the top." Quite hilarious - although I suppose you had to be there really...

So, that was what I will remember about Forest in '96-97. However - and let me make this clear - the aforementioned ten incidents, as memorable as they were, are no consolation whatsoever for an otherwise forgettable season. Nottingham Forest, please take note of the following: we supporters demand a *hell* of a lot better in '97-98.

GIVE US AN R

Tranmere Rovers

I know that everyone says that watching their own team isn't easy, and watching Rovers definitely isn't. I've got that headache in my eyeballs from shouting to prove it.

You know that Purple Loans TV advert with Martin Clunes' 'voice-over behaving badly': "Name three things that are difficult: quantum physics, brain surgery - and getting a loan..." I don't think so - make that third one watching Tranmere Rovers! Now *that's* difficult. Admittedly, in the last four or five years we've only had one courtship with the world of the relegation trapdoor, when, the season before last, we were close

enough to hear the hinges creak. This has been more than compensated for by the enviable frustration of almost always - *just* - missing out on promotion.

Let me explain what our usual season is like. Do you know that final scene in *Von Ryan's Express*? The one where ol' blue eyes is trying to catch up with the last carriage of the train to escape the clutches of the pursuing SS Infantry? Well, that's our season, that is. The train? That's the Premier League, that is; always just out of reach from us, a 'gravy train' you could call it. Frank Sinatra? That's us, that is. Tranmere Rovers. As most of our team drink more in a season than Franky did in a lifetime it's pretty apt. And what of the Waffen SS trying to ventilate Franky's Air Force leather jacket? That's the referees and linesmen, that is; always trying to shoot us down. And isn't it a coincidence that the SS and referees have the same tailors, specialising in black apparel...

Mind you, Rovers haven't helped themselves. In the last decade we've tried to put together a team crammed with experience, but it ended up as an experiment gone mad, and we acquired a team whose average age was not far off Frank Sinatra's. About a year ago we introduced a number of youth team players to the team to try and bring the average age down to something under 45. I mean, I know some companies are trying to re-employ pensioners, but why do we have to be at the forefront of it?

At the end of the previous season we were saved from relegation by the appointment of John Aldridge as manager: affectionately known by Rovers fans as 'Oldo' due to his advancing years. He quickly got the team playing 'The Liverpool Way' (TLW) using an intricate passing game. We could do hexagons, pentagons, star shapes and parallelograms, then we, erm, gave the ball away. At the beginning of this season when Oldo announced that we would continue to play TLW, I thought he meant we'd have to pop down to the antiques shop and order a trophy cabinet, but Oldo was on a learning curve and the season became more of an exercise in getting things right.

For about seven or eight years Prenton Park had become a fortress. We usually only lost about two or three games a season at home, and they were hard-fought affairs. If you needed one point to go up, away at Prenton Park wasn't the place to be for your last game. We never got promoted though, because our away form was 'lay down and die' stuff. Oldo changed all this. Away from home we became tenacious Tranny and scrapped away for a full 90 minutes, dominating many games even when we lost. But it was as if a giant set of symbolic footy scales had swung the other way and our legendary home form became indifferent, bordering on crap. Our only decent home result of the season was a 4-0 stuffing against the mighty Atletico Charlton, but in previous seasons we'd get half a dozen scorelines like that at home.

A truer measure of our home form was that we beat Shrewsbury 2-0 away in the Pop Cup, but only drew 0-0 for the home leg, and we were lucky to get nil! In the next round Atletico Oldham beat us at home to knock us out. Meanwhile we had some notable away victories in the league at Huddersfield, Ipswich, Manchester City, West Brom and Crystal Palace. The West Brom one was particularly hilarious. Their fans spent the whole morning clearing January snow from the Hawthorns' pitch for the game to go ahead. West Brom scored first with the famous orange ball, but with victory in sight Oldo scored two goals to win the game. One of the Birmingham papers my brother got hold of read 'Baggies sweep up snow, Aldo sweeps up Baggies'. Results like this kept us in or about the play-off group for the first half of the season. After Christmas though we drifted towards mid-table. Copious amounts of alcohol does this to you.

With eight games left though, Oldo pulled off the master stroke of the season (in the First Division at least) and got the elf-like Lee Jones on loan from 'dat Liverpule'. This lad played like he'd eaten the Road Runner: he just couldn't keep still. In his first four games he scored three goals and was in serious danger of getting us into the play-offs. Reality reared its ugly head though with the penultimate game of the season and a 2-0 defeat away to QPR in the smoke. This left us with a final game at home to arch-rivals "Wanky, Wanky, Wanky, Wanky Wanderers" (that's Bolton to you). Now, not a lot of people know this (you can use a Michael Caine voice when you read that bit), but for the last three seasons our final game has been at home to the team already crowned as Champions. Bolton this year, Middlesbrough last (and they then proceeded to smash up all the seats in our recently built Kop), and Sunderland the year before. Bolton needed two goals to reach 100 and three points to reach 100, so at least we had something to play for. We pissed on their party in good style by scoring an equaliser (2-2), denying them their 100 points, with the last kick of the game. It was that lad Lee Jones and he wrote himself into the Tranmere history books. Since the season finished we've signed him permanently, and he now looks likely to fill the famous boots vacated by Oldo.

Incidentally, if you want to make a bet on who'll win the division, the Football League's most sought-after fixture of the season belongs this year to Wolves. On second thoughts, why waste your money?!

Source: *A Load of Bull*

THE GOONER

Arsenal

A fortnight before the '96-97 season started a number of *Gooner* contributors met in a West End pub, as we do every year, to have a chat over a few pints about the forthcoming campaign. There was no doubting the feeling of discontent as we moaned and groaned about the club's inactivity in the summer transfer market, but we were basically there to enjoy ourselves and talk moved on to Bowie's performance at Phoenix and whether Jo Guest is the most gorgeous Arsenal supporter on the planet. However, somehow the popular tabloids, who were well into their 'Arsenal in Crisis' campaigns, got wind of our little get-together

and the meeting was reported the following morning as "a secret gathering of hundreds of season ticket holders to lay down battle plans for a series of high-profile demonstrations after running out of patience with the club's 13-month failure to make a single signing." Isn't it interesting how things can get blown out of all proportion? Whether or not these shenanigans had any bearing on Bruce Rioch's sacking a week later is impossible to ascertain, although there are some fans who liked to claim they played their part by forcing the club to act decisively.

Despite not having a manager, we did manage to boost the squad before the opening game with the signing of two Frenchmen - Patrick Vieira, a £3.5 million capture from AC Milan and Rémi Garde on a free transfer from Strasbourg. However, both players missed the opening month of the season through injury and although we came through this period with two wins, two draws and only one defeat (at Anfield), there was no hint of the thrilling season we were embarking upon.

The turning point was to be the televised match against the early season table-toppers, Sheffield Wednesday. After a month of intense and (for once) accurate speculation, Frenchman Arsčne Wenger was confirmed as the next manager of Arsenal Football Club, although he was unable to take over until the start of October because of commitments to his current side Grampus Eight in Japan. A specially recorded message from him was shown to the

Highbury faithful on the big screens before the game, and it obviously inspired his compatriot Vieira, whose debut was the catalyst which kick-started our season. A goal down when he was brought on as substitute, we romped to an impressive 4-1 victory with Ian Wright notching his 100th league goal for the club en route to a hat-trick.

Even though our league season was now on the right track, Wenger's arrival had not been able to prevent our UEFA Cup campaign being permanently derailed courtesy of Borussia Münchengladbach and a pair of 3-2 defeats - the first leg at home being particularly disappointing for the un-Arsenal-like manner in which we defended.

George Graham returned to Highbury in charge of the opposition for the first time at the end of October, but if he was going to return to haunt us, as many fans feared he would, it would be on another day as we steam-rollered his dreadful Leeds side with two goals in the opening five minutes. The first, by Lee Dixon, was set up by a surging run from 'Paddy' Vieira - the creative talent in midfield we had been waiting for throughout the latter years of George's reign, when all he had managed to provide for us was John Jensen.

Unthinkable as it may have been in August, there were fans beginning to believe we might actually be able to mount a challenge for the Championship, although with November looming and a run of tricky matches against Wimbledon, Manchester United, Tottenham and Newcastle coming up, it seemed sensible to err on the side of caution. One point from the first two games of this run seemed to indicate that the non-believers were probably right, but the visit of Spurs on November 24th provided us with the perfect opportunity to make up lost ground. It had been three years since our last derby day victory and five since they had left Highbury without a point, so we were clearly due a result. When Ian Wright tucked away his 16th goal of the season to move within 19 of the Arsenal scoring record held by Clive Bastin, the feeling around me was that Spurs were there for the taking in a big way - unfortunately we had underestimated just how low the enemy would sink in the hope of getting a result. Vieira had already been booked for having his face slapped by Armstrong, when he was then crunched by a two-footed tackle from the same player in front of the West Stand. No foul was awarded, so the Frenchman lay prostrate on the turf until Lukic was able to throw the ball into touch when it reached his possession. Treatment was provided and the normal practice would have been for a Spurs player to casually throw the ball over the goal-line for an Arsenal goal-kick, but since Campbell and Calderwood were both trotting forward into our penalty area, it was obvious this was not their line of thinking at all. A long throw, a flick on, a Sinton shot which rebounded off the post, against Lukic's head and the cheating bastards had equalised. Three and a half sides of the ground responded with a cacophony of booing. This seemed to urge Arsenal on to a period of renewed pressure, but as the minutes ticked away it seemed Spurs were set to disprove the old adage that cheats never prosper. However, if there is one man in the Arsenal side who would never allow such an injustice, it's Tony Adams, and it was he who scored in the 88th minute with a sweeping left-foot volley to end a move which embodied so much of the new era. It would have been hard to imagine Tony surging forward to join the attack in open play in the closing minutes of a delicately balanced match under the tutorship of George Graham, but Wenger is keen for his players to express themselves more and from the fans' point of view it is a joy to behold. As if that wasn't enough, Bergkamp added an exquisite third to cap what had arguably been his best performance in an Arsenal shirt to date.

There was more controversy the following week when we travelled to Newcastle for a top of the table clash. Lee Dixon had given us an early lead with a header (!), only for Newcastle to equalise when Alan Shearer took advantage of a defensive mistake. When a through ball was played for Shearer two minutes later, the referee and his assistant decided that Asprilla, who was still retreating from the last home attack and about 15 yards further forward than the last defender, was not interfering with play even though the ball bounced between his legs. Adams chased back and had it not been for his enforced detour around the Colombian, would have made a comfortable clearance, but instead he tangled with Shearer (six of one, half a dozen of the other) who gratefully took the opportunity presented to throw himself to the floor and get his England team-mate sent off. Thankfully, we are nothing if not resilient and the ten men fought for every ball throughout the second half, and when a chance did arrive Ian Wright despatched it with aplomb to take us top of the table... Say we are top of the league!

Even the press were hailing us as potential Champions, but unfortunately, once you reach the top there's only one way to go. Suspensions began to arrive thick and fast, primarily due to the expansive collection of yellow cards we had amassed since August, but not helped by a run of five sendings-off in nine games! And if that was misfortune of our own making, then there was little we could do about Frank Clark walking out on Nottingham Forest or Stuart Pearce taking over as caretaker just before our visit to the City Ground. It's strange isn't it how teams in this situation have a habit of winning their next game?

If the league was to be a bridge too far, then the FA Cup was a more realistic proposition. Sunderland were seen off after a replay in round three, thanks mainly to a breath-taking goal from Dennis Bergkamp, which was scandalously left out of BBC's Goal of the Season competition. He executed two perfect 'drag-backs' to make himself the space to steer the ball round a defender, past the outstretched arm of Lionel Perez (fancy having a goalkeeper named Lionel) and into the top right hand corner of the net. Andy Gray was spot-on when he told the commentator on *Sky* to just shut up and watch the replay - words could simply not do it justice.

Ultimately, however, it was to no avail, since Leeds visited Highbury in round four and thanks to a typical George Graham defensive strategy which we knew only too well, went home with a 1-0 win. The victorious manager said afterwards that we had run out of ideas and resorted to hitting long balls - a touch ironic, don't you think?

Wenger had been steadily off-loading dead-wood from the squad for modest fees - Dickov and McGoldrick to Manchester City, Hillier to Portsmouth, Linighan to Palace, Morrow to join up with his chums Stewart Houston and Bruce Rioch at QPR - so although the departure of John Hartson to West Ham boosted the club's bank balance by a reported £5 million, it left the squad dangerously short of experienced cover. Whether or not his absence cost us points during the run-in is debatable, but there is no question that there were matches when his presence would have been an advantage.

Manchester United visited Highbury in mid-February and produced one of their best displays of the season to emerge victorious, although Ian Wright's confrontation with Peter Schmeichel, which had its origins in some alleged racist remarks in the earlier fixture at Old Trafford, dominated the headlines. When Wimbledon inflicted another home defeat four days later, Wenger announced that the title was now out of our reach and although no-one really believed him, it was clear we had suffered a major blow to our hopes.

Three consecutive 2-0 wins, combined with some unexpected results elsewhere and United's fixture backlog (a subject which Wenger and Ferguson were debating publicly in the national press) had forced us back into the reckoning by the time Liverpool came south in mid-March. In a season full of referee's blunders, we were unfortunately the victims of one in this match which was right up there with the best of them. Cheeky scouse striker and scourge of Arsenal, Robbie Fowler, raced on to a through ball into the Arsenal penalty area and dived theatrically over the on-rushing David Seaman. Then, much to the amazement of the watching television audience, he lept to his feet and was clearly seen mouthing "No penalty ref, he never touched me." Referee Gerald Ashby, who insisted on awarding the spot kick, later claimed he hadn't heard Fowler's pleas on Arsenal's behalf which prompted one newspaper to coment that Mr Ashby "must be deaf as well as blind!" When the furore had died down, it seemed that Fowler was keen to see justice done by hitting the penalty straight at Seaman. Typical of our luck, Dave didn't manage to hold it and Jason McAteer, clearly encroaching, reacted first to the rebound to crack the scousers into a 2-0 lead from which we were unable to recover, despite a late Ian Wright goal.

The final nails in our Championship coffin were banged in by Chris Sutton right at the end of our match against Blackburn on April 19th. Manchester United had beaten Liverpool 3-1 in an early kick-off, so victory was imperative and with David Platt's third goal in as many games separating the sides in the 94th minute, it seemed the points were safe. Then Stephen Hughes went down under a heavy challenge from Tim Sherwood and we conceded a throw to allow him to receive treatment. Blackburn, unlike a certain underachieving North London side earlier in the season, followed the correct protocol by returning the ball to Nigel Winterburn, but instead of allowing him to play the ball unchallenged, Sutton decided to close him down and ended up forcing a corner. From the resulting kick, Flitcroft lashed in a spectacular equaliser and the crowd trooped out hardly able to believe that lightning had struck twice in the same place.

To make matters worse, a home defeat to Newcastle on the penultimate Saturday of the season proved crucial in the battle for runners-up spot, which for the first time carried the added bonus of entry to the Champions League preliminary stages. But even though the season may have ended without any silverware, there will be few Arsenal fans who will regard '96-97 as a disappointment. Realistically we are still two or three top class players short of a Championship-winning side ready to mix it with the likes of Juventus, Real Madrid and Borussia Dortmund. So, just like last season, we'll be studying the back pages of the newspapers throughout the summer, eager to catch that first exciting glimpse of an expensive new signing holding an Arsenal scarf aloft, and hopefully there'll be much less moaning and groaning at the *Gooner's* pre-season drink-up than there was last year. The future promises much. Wenger has won the respect of the fans and with a name like Arsčne, he was born for the job, just as Bobby Crapper is sure to be the next manager of Spurs.

GRORTY DICK

West Bromwich Albion

Arrogant, uncaring, out of touch with the public, now, thankfully consigned to the Outer Darkness. But that's enough about the Conservative Party; what about Alan Buckley?

What indeed... When I wrote *apropos* of Mr Buckley in the '95-96 issue of this tome, I made large of our erstwhile leader's shortcomings; the criticism wasn't entirely negative, as I concluded said piece in a self-admitted overabundance of hope plus expectation (twin vices that plague footie followers the world over) that despite The Ayatollah's failings (players' *sobriquet*, not mine), the Baggies would be there or thereabouts come crunch-time in the merry month of May, just like Tony Blair's lot.

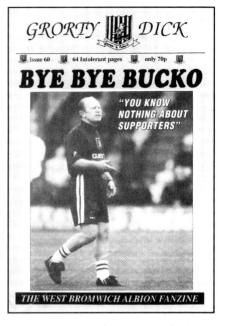

Wrong! In fact, following a brief flirtation with the trap-door, we finished the campaign 16th in the Division One pecking order, minus Buckley and plus Ray Harford. Not quite what we'd expected after the ecstatic highs and depression-inducing lows of last term. The writing was well and truly on the wall from the opener versus '96-97's surprise package, Barnsley, who promptly and embarrassingly turned themselves to a demolition job of which Colonel Tibbetts, the A-Bomb destroyer of Hiroshima, would have been proud. The principal demolition man was one Clint Marcelle, a thorough nuisance whose constant left-wing wave-making pierced our diaphanous defence time and time again. Thanks to a damage-limiting penalty (God must have applied a celestial blindfold to the eyes of the ref), the game ended 1-2. More about the Tykes later.

We suffered an ejector-seat exit from the Coca Cola Cup, despite being one goal in credit after the away leg. As usual, the opposition were lower-league, i.e. Colchester, the home-leg ending 3-1 to the opposition. Was this belated revenge for that dodgy 1968 penalty award to Albion in the dying minutes of our Layer Road third round encounter, thus paving the way for our May appearance at Wembley? As Mulder and Scully would say, "the truth is out there" ...

Time steamrollered on to Christmas, and, just as Barnsley had ruthlessly exposed our general lack of promotion credentials on the opening day, failure when it mattered repeated itself time and time again. On the 'credit' side of the ledger were results at venues such as the Valley, Loftus Road, Selhurst Park and Prenton Park. The debit side consisted wholly (to us) of a monstrous, pusillanimous 2-4 whopping by Wolves, at the Shrine. Tatters please note: Bob Taylor's late 'goal' *was* onside - had the referee not been half-blind as well as half-baked, the last few minutes could have been quite hairy for our chums up the road. However, refereeing cock-ups notwithstanding, we simply weren't performing. Our home form? Abysmal. Reasons? Got a few decades to spare, mate?

Paul Crichton. Oh dear. Signed hurriedly from Grimsby (where else?) by the Bald One, as normal net-keeper Spink had sustained knee damage something awful at QPR. Remember my *critique* of Mr Crichton in SOTF's *passim*? Yep, we signed him, yep, he responded to goalmouth pressure from strikers in similar fashion to an harassed picnicker trying to eject a troublesome swarm of wasps from the vicinity of the spread, with equally unrewarding and painful results. And yes, sensitive soul that he was, he more and more became the unwilling recipient of spectator abuse; football supporters rarely possess degrees in applied psychology, but they do know a "dodgy 'keeper" when they see one. Our 'goals against' total began to rack up like numbers on a pinball machine.

Add to that the unpalatable fact that another ex-Mariner, Paul Groves, was perceived by the Brummie Road as being yet another non-performer, and you've got problems, both on and off the pitch. Our leader's Standard Operational Procedure was to conduct dressing-room post-match inquests in a similar manner to Krakatoa erupting, which when dealing with players already somewhat denuded of confidence, helped not one jot. The consequent negative mood of our finest inevitably spread to our faithful, who rapidly polarised into pro/anti-Buckley factions. The first ugly rumblings of supporter dissent emerged at Roots Hall, Southend. I honestly believe that had Albion not rectified a 1-0 deficit and gone on to win the game 3-2 borne along by a tide of vocal support, then Baggie would have turned on Baggie. I should know - I was seated perilously close to the protagonists.

Christmas. Presents were exchanged, carols were sung, and, despite a temporary surge in our fortunes following favourable results such as a 5-1 home stonking of Norwich plus a somewhat fortuitous yet emphatic victory versus QPR, the nascent year saw Albion firmly rooted at the non-achieving end of the Division One listings. The cup-tie ejector-seat did the biz yet again (at Stamford Bridge this time); consequently, the all-too-rapidly diminishing prospect of promotion via the back door apart, the season had effectively finished for us. And then, hard on the heels of the 3-0 Chelsea surrender came Buckley's nemesis: Molineux.

It's strange how history repeats itself. Two seasons ago, Keith Burkinshaw was ousted from the Hawthorns hot-seat because of a white flag-waving performance from our finest at Molineux. Consequently it surprised regulars not in the slightest to hear chairman Tony Hale imply at a supporters club meeting less than 48 hours following a similar televised 2-0 drubbing that our manager was definitely through the swing-doors of the last-chance saloon. I may add that during this game our tremulous custodian Crichton had given an all-too-passable imitation of a blancmange at setting-point thanks to constant barracking from both away (unfair actually, some of those pass-backs from our defenders!) and *schadenfreude*-intoxicated home supporters (but that's Wulves for you). Having witnessed every step, home and away of the current Albion saga, we estimated a managerial life-expectancy of approximately 28 days for our explosive leader, should adverse results be his lot. Hence my incredulity when my other half screamed over the phone "he's gone, he's gone!!" the Wednesday afternoon following our dismal home 1-1 draw with Second Division-bound Oldham Athletic. My initial reaction of "Thank God he's gone!" softened somewhat. Perhaps our players should examine their own consciences; they were the ones who got Buckley the sack. Obnoxious though he is, it wasn't *all* his fault.

A Hawthorns managerial vacuum now existed. Speculation abounded: who in the football world would have bottle sufficient to grasp the metaphorical stinging-nettle firmly with both hands? Names in the frame included Barry Fry, John Rudge, John Deehan, Chris Waddle, Steve Coppell, Lou Macari, Bruce Rioch, Ian Rush - I leave it to the reader to arrange these in order of ascending improbability. Indeed, one delightful Sunday morn shortly after Mr Buckley's demise, we scanned the *Sunday Mercury* to be informed that Mr Waddle was indeed to be our leader. Delight abounded, only to be dashed in true Albion fashion. The *Mercury* had jumped the gun. Yes, negotiations had taken place, but agreement hadn't. Another false dawn. Next!!

We now skip forward in time to Wednesday February 4th, the venue St. Andrews, the opponents the Bluenoses. Among the thousands who witnessed our last-gasp 3-2 victory (*All together now: Sup-er, SuperBob!...*) was a certain Mr Ray Harford, previous address c/o Ewood Park, Blackburn. Rumours of his presence spread around the away end. Was he to be The Chosen One, The Messiah, or, taking the cynical view so beloved of Albionites, the Next Managerial Muggins? Confirmation of our suspicions came within several days when the man somewhat unfairly dubbed 'Mr Happy' by aggrieved journos was indeed given the job ranked by our supporters, next to the vacancy at Maine Road of course, as the biggest hot potato in the game. While not possessing the coruscating credentials of an Alex Ferguson, or a George Graham, Harford however toted impressive baggage of almost universal respect throughout the game because of his tremendous coaching abilities. We additionally solicited the opinion of Blackburn supporters - and received glowing testimonials by way of return. "He's great with the fans but doesn't like the press!" our 'mole' enthused. "Handled team-talks, coaching, that sort of thing himself: you've got a good 'un." This, to us, was the opinion that counted, confirmation that indeed the board had chosen wisely.

What really clinched it for us was the fact that within a week or so of his arrival, Harford publicly hit the proverbial nail right on the head regarding the strengths and weaknesses of his team and the tactics employed at the time; all matters well-known to concerned supporters since before the start of the season. Trouble was, any rational discussion with the late and definitely unlamented Mr B. was generally abruptly stifled by the latter's charmingly-phrased standard response, i.e. "I pick the team, not you - if you don't like it, Foxtrot Oscar and watch the Wolves..." (much bowdlerised version). Nobody's fool, for certain - big changes were certainly afoot. Ending our totally unrequited annual love affair with the wrong end of the table would do for starters. Appointing former Albion favourites John Trewick and Cyrille Regis as assistant manager and coach respectively assisted hugely in the process of winning hearts and minds.

Amidst all this turmoil, it was business as usual for our faithful. As ever, our away following was magnificent; at venues throughout the length and breadth of the land we saw Baggies at their best in both song and deed. After all the trials and tribulations of recent seasons, Baggies know passion; we've been there, done it, then dutifully queued for the T-shirt from the club shop. And if you've never sat (or, in happier times, stood) with those massed ranks of Albionites lustily singing *The Lord's my Shepherd* - appropriately enough, a hymn celebrating the triumph of faith over adversity - if you've never felt those shivers run up and down your spine, never felt those tearful pangs of emotion, then you're dead from the neck up. We may not have a Premiership side, but we've sure got Premiership supporters. What happened at Portman Road and Oakwell well illustrates my point...

Ipswich. Second half. Four-nil down, no manager, no hope. No singing? Wrong! Just like the previous season's Portman performance, our supporters, relatively quiet beforehand, collectively decided that all those cardboard cut-out 'farmers' sitting mutely in the home end would be galvanised into vocal action, like it or not. There then followed vocal renderings of such 'classics' as "Stand up if you hate Norwich," "We hate Norwich more than you," "You must have come in a tractor" closely followed by those old standbys "You're supposed to be at home!" and "What's it like to make a noise?" And just to remind the world of our leaderless status we were, of course "Nobody's barmy army!" To their eternal credit, the sporting Portmanites not only joined us in a rendering of "Stand up if you hate the Wolves," they actually stood and applauded us at the end of the game.

Thanks to *Sky* TV, our away support at Barnsley became the talk of the nation one Friday night in March. Not because of our singing, although viewers might have noticed unusually loud vocal renderings of "They're going up, they're going up, Barnsley's going up," the enhanced volume being largely due to our lot leading the Barnsley supporters in their pre-promotion fun. It was a heaven-sent opportunity to ridicule nationwide a certain non-automatic promotion achieving, old gold and black-kitted side not a million miles from Wolverhampton! No, the principal *cause célèbre* was that on a night which was gonad-freezingly cold, two or so score of our followers decided to view the proceedings totally topless; not only that, these Black Country exhibitionists then embarked on a conga-dance which threaded its mazy way across, forwards, back, then around the away end. The 'supporting cast' increased the surreality of the situation by their rendition of several somewhat bizarre chants about food; at one point I heard lustily-sung paeans of praise about *cheese and onions* (don't ask). The police were totally mystified by this performance, especially as we were two goals in arrears by this time. The stewards, however, being unused to such eccentricities, totally freaked.

Meanwhile, back at the ranch. Alan Miller. Middlesbrough supporters (welcome back to the *real* world, chaps!) certainly need no introduction to the lad; they sold him to us as a hasty replacement for Mr Crichton, whose confidence, unsurprisingly, was totally shot. Not many league outfits can boast a published author in their ranks. We can; his account of season '95-96 titled (great originality, Al!) *A Miller's Tale* has been on sale for about a year. More importantly, the Brummie Road, on the rebound after Crichton, instantly took to Big Al in a big way - a bonding process which took a quantum leap thanks to a number of spectacular shot-stoppers courtesy of our literary gentleman. He's also something of an astronomical phenomenon in the modern game - a player with more than a smidgen of character, and fully functioning sense of humour glands; his double act with pint-size Paul Peschisolido before a post-season friendly with Walsall had me in stitches - it's not often you see a burly moustachioed six-footer plant a distinctly slobbery wet smacker of a kiss straight on the unsuspecting lips of our diminutive Canadian striker, at the conclusion of a pre-match warm-up consisting of Big Al playing the role of the striker, and 'Pesch' the custodian... Totally loved it; footy takes itself far too seriously these days. More please!

And there you have it. One humble Albion supporter's viewpoint of season '96-97. The verdict? After a shaky start and a change of form master, the class shows promise. A couple of good signings, and - who knows? - our supporters might finally have good reason to hold their heads up high. Albion still have the capacity to surprise. *GD* readers' Player Of The Year was Ian Hamilton, who finally overcame hostility and abuse from supporters by sheer hard work and intelligent, classy midfield play. Our Canadian goal-machine Paul Peschisolido was a worthy runner-up; supporters of other First Division outfits will readily confirm his ability to be a thorough nuisance in the box; a defender's nightmare. One final word: if anyone involved with the club's reading this, can someone please, please, please find Pesch a smaller size playing kit - his present one fits like a Bedouin tent!

GULL'S EYE

Brighton and Hove Albion

At this time last year, I described '95-96 as "an absolute season from Hell." Now I find myself in a hyperbolic straitjacket - so stop me if you think you've heard this one before. Undoubtedly, for ALL Albion supporters, '96-97 was simply the worst season ever. It was Reservoir Dogs - with both ears cut off. The (metaphorical) boardroom robbery had gone wrong and the supporters got the blame. We had, according to them, put our fingers on the self-destruct button and we were the reason the club was on the verge of terminal decline. Only *Meridian* believed their hype, and gave them a televised 'debate' to exploit to the full, during which supporter's arguments were largely ignored or edited out. We got our own back, though. Unable to get *Channel 5* down here (no loss there then) we asked the engineers to de-tune our sets from receiving *Meridian*. And we continued to fight the board by every rule not in the book.

Right at the start of the season things were already bleak, with the motives of the board being questioned by everyone, including the local and national media (*Meridian* no longer count). This was to be our last season at the Goldstone, with the club leaving Sussex for a period in exile at Portsmouth - which was then modified to Gillingham which was then modified to Hove Greyhound Stadium and then Crawley and then Charlton, and finally... Gillingham (again), possibly, probably, perhaps, maybe, definitely, for a short time at least. The planning application for the new stadium in Hove had been rejected by the Borough Council - but the board were adamant that they would press ahead regardless, even if it meant a Public Inquiry. At some stage they might even have got around to buying the land on which the proposed stadium was to be built, as the pigs had been cleared and were now ready for take-off. BUT, and a big but it is too, no-one, not even our crass directors, ever imagined that we would be rooted to the bottom of the Football League for most of the campaign. And I don't mean campaign as a clichéd synonym for season. In the space available I can't do any sort of justice to the efforts of a great number of Albion die-hards, who ran a tireless battle against the way the club was being run (down). Here is just a flavour of said battle, interspersed with the rubbish that the club heaped upon us:

Supporters banned for peaceful and legitimate protests against the board - three supporters threatened with litigation via the club's illiterate solicitors Eversheds - bridge protest signs along the A23 and A27 - a match boycott against Mansfield - a mass walk-out during the Hereford home match to a firework accompaniment - exclusion zones around the directors box - a thousand whistles in the crowd - two points deducted by the FA after a peaceful pitch invasion, followed by a farcical failed appeal by the club months afterwards - posters, pamphlets and car stickers galore - ticket allocation fiascos for the last two home games - a mass visit to chairman Bill Archer's home, just up the road in Mellor, Lancashire - petitions to the FA following a protest march through central London - formation of The Seagulls' Party to ensure David Bellotti, the club's deputy chairman and chief executive lost his East Sussex County Council seat - a supporter imprisoned for eight months for saying to Bellotti what most supporters were thinking - supporters meeting with mediators at the Centre for Dispute Resolution - supporters threatening legal action against the FA for failure to enforce its own rules - fighting fund benefit concerts - red cards - regular demonstrations outside the ground after matches - letters and phone-ins - picketing Focus DIY (one of Bill Archer's 'legitimate' business interests) - establishing contact with other supporters' organisations and fanzines - fly-posting - and the internet...

Computers can preserve your Football League status - shock, horror! Well perhaps not, but they can make a contribution. More specifically the (mis-) information superhighway. A young Plymouth fan by the name of Richard Vaughan suggested, via the guest book of an 'unofficial' Albion site, an event which matured into Fans United - a gathering of supporters from other clubs to rage against the enemy - the corporate machine that has no understanding of football culture, and can, if hungry enough, consume football clubs without even spitting the bones out. This event was nothing short of phenomenal, and was staged to coincide with our home game against Hartlepool. Our attendance doubled as fans from all over the country, Europe and beyond lent us their support for the day. Hove Park, just across the road from the Goldstone, acted as the focus for most of the pre-match activities. An effigy of Bill Archer's head was blown apart by fireworks as we sang and danced, cheered and jeered. In contrast, messages of support were fixed to the railings that bordered the pathways, and as people stopped to read them, the park took on the sombre appearance of a garden of remembrance. A strange day indeed, veiled in a sea fret of dry ice intensity. Needless to say, such an event had the blessing of the target of our protest, as the boost in gate receipts kept the wheels of corporate greed lubricated. And for this one occasion only, so what? On the pitch the Albion took on a look of old and won 5-0. Hartlepool simply went through the motions - the script dictated they could do little more.

How Steve Gritt did not receive the Manager of the Season award is somewhat of a mystery here on the Sussex Coast. When he took over in December, the Albion were 11 points adrift at the bottom of the Football League. Jimmy Case had made an absolute cods of his first managerial post, taking us down after his first season in charge. In his second, he had steered us to the foot of Division Three in time to celebrate Halloween. Trick or treat indeed! We even lost at home to Sudbury Town in the replay of our FA Cup first round tie. It is true that a number of 'experienced' players let him down, badly, but worse still, Jimmy - a folk hero from his playing days at the Albion - let himself down. He should have done the dignified thing and resigned during the close season. Instead, he gave the board the opportunity to claw back an atomic particle of credibility by sacking him - albeit five months late. Gritty arrived to a less than lukewarm reception, with supporters who hold honours degrees in cynicism (most of us by now) thinking he would prove to be nothing more than a puppet of the Bellotti-Archer regime. He was booed as he took his place on the bench for his first game in charge against Hull City on December 14th. We won 3-0. From that day on we were never to lose a game at the Goldstone again. Out of 13, we won 11 and drew two. Coincidentally, David Bellotti never attended one of these games. The CEDR meeting with supporters, combined with 'persuasive' match-day protests, had resulted in his agreement to stay away. Yes it's true - the supporters had effectively banned the chief executive from home games, and he was dumb enough not to realise it. Bill Archer hadn't attended an Albion home game since... who cares? Our directors' box contained more open space than the meat pies at Scunthorpe, and we were oh so grateful. However, the weasel Bellotti, accompanied by his wife, still went to away games where our form continued to be wretched. We won only one game away from home all season. I do not want to take anything away from Steve Gritt's achievement, but I do have this nagging feeling that had Bellotti stayed away all season, we could have gained promotion.

Entering the closing stages of the season, there was a hint of an upturn and the faint whiff of survival - if results elsewhere went our way. Did they heck! We were forever taking two steps forward, immediately followed by one step backwards. The turning point came at Cambridge in April, at our penultimate away game, where we fought out a deserving 1-1 draw. Then, the realisation dawned that fate was, at long last, in our own hands. All we had to do was win our two remaining games.

Regimes come, and regimes go - almost. After many, *many* false dawns, the consortium headed by Dick Knight held a press conference on April 22nd to confirm that although the current owners would retain a 49.5% stake in the club (boo, hiss!), they were gaining a 50.5% controlling interest (cautious hip, hip hooray!). As questions of probing simplicity were lobbed towards the top table by the hacks, Bill Archer came off his line and parried one into his own net by inadvertently referring to the club as Brighton and Hove DIY Limited.

Corporate greed had started to consume itself, and Archer squirmed with embarrassment.

On my way to the last ever match at the Goldstone, I had a religious experience. So *this* is how Jesus felt when he set about the traders who were peddling their wares in the temple, I thought. All manner of opportunist low-life lined the pavements with souvenir this and commemorative that, the worst example being a cardboard cap emblazoned with 'Brighton v Doncaster - I was there' together with the logo of local radio station *Southern FM*. It won the 'kick in the crotch with an-open toed sandal' award hands-down.

Under normal circumstances I wouldn't indulge in boring recollections of individual matches. But sod it, I'm going to this time - after all, it was the last match ever at the Goldstone, and our league survival depended on the outcome. The atmosphere was fraught, and the weather suitably damp and depressing. This was a day of personal last times; the last time I would take my seat in the South Stand (and but for a spanner and a tin of WD40 I would have taken it with me after the game); the last time I would delight in the pre-match cuisine of an E-Coli burger; the last time I would smell the urine that seeped through the brickwork of our 'medieval without the mod cons' lavatories. All this unabated sentimentality was coupled with the fact that by a quarter to five the Albion could be a Vauxhall Conference club, and as a result my medication levels were at Ciba-Geigy wholesale levels. To make emotional instability worse, two Doncaster players paraded a banner before the game reading 'Rovers Players Salute Brighton Fans'. Touches like that are enough to make grown men blubber. I didn't. I just took more medication. The match kicked off after a lone bugler played *The Last Post* to a largely bemused and less than attentive crowd. The game itself was unmitigated torture. Red cards followed fisticuffs between our captain Ian Baird and Doncaster's Darren Moore. All ears strained to hear the half-time scores on our state-of-the-art-wasp-fart PA system. Hereford were also drawing 0-0 against Orient at Brisbane Road - hope was still intact. When in the second half the North Stand struck up with 'One-nil to the Orient', followed soon after by 'Two-nil to the Orient', we knew that even if we lost today, we could still stay up by winning our last game at Hereford. And then, three minutes later, YEEEEEEEAAAAAASSSSSSSSSSSSSS - Stuart 'Adonis' Storer scored. We went ape-shit. The Albion clung desperately to their lead, and at the final whistle there was the inevitable pitch invasion. Emotion and sentimentality took over again for about an hour. I stood in the spot where I'd stood as a kid. *The Carnival Is Over* crackled across the PA. The bloke behind me took his kit off. The West Stand seats were smashed apart. But then the chilling 'back to reality' thoughts returned. In an unbelievably cruel twist of fate, we'd dragged ourselves off the foot of the table for the first time since October and now faced a play-off for relegation against Hereford, the team who'd replaced us there. Pass the pills ...

The stress levels rose with each passing junction of the M4 on the seemingly endless road to Hereford. Do or die. Shit or bust. This was the big one - and if further proof was needed of how big the game was, *Sky* (pause for respectful silence) wanted the game moved to Sunday so it could be broadcast live. Hereford were up for it - we refused. They needed to win; we didn't, and we wanted to hold onto this psychological advantage. Under normal circumstances I wouldn't indulge in boring recollections of individual matches. But double sod it, I'm going to again - after all, our league survival depended on this one. Other than the brief distraction of Hereford parading a real live Bull mascot before the game, it was nothing but tension - tension I have never experienced before, and never wish to experience again. The game was rubbish, park football paraded as Division Three elitism. Hereford stood up to first half nerves better than us and we were fortunate to go into the break only a goal down - and typical to all things Albion, an own goal at that. At half time I sat, head in hands, trying to come to terms with the fact that we were free-falling into non-league football. Gallows humour was no longer funny. Nothing would ever be funny again. The second half showed a degree of improvement on our part. Then came the masterstroke. Robbie Reinelt came on for Paul McDonald in the 55th minute, and eight minutes later Craig Maskell volleyed the ball off the post to Reinelt, who scored the most important goal in the Albion's history. Bedlam, bedlam and more bedlam. The remaining 27 minutes were awful - monumentally awful - with what seemed liked three hours of injury time added. This wasn't football - this was the most vindictive, sadistic and cruel form of torture ever endured by mankind. But then the final whistle, and we were SAFE. Bedlam revisited, bedlam with extra ape-shit topping. We went absolutely fucking mental, and who could blame us? Our uninhibited crowing was tempered, on my part at least, by thoughts for the Hereford supporters. The bottom had fallen out of their world. The sun had set on Sun Valley. At half time I had been 50% of the way there myself. No-one deserved to be on the receiving end of this encounter. Hereford had supported us at Fans United back in February, and the five goals we scored that day had helped to keep us in the league. Had we won that one by scoring only one goal, we would now be in the Vauxhall Conference.

! That was the season that was. To use a feline analogy - of its nine lives, the Albion have now used up eight and a half. None of our experiences during the season were totally unique when taken in isolation; it would be sanctimonious to believe otherwise. What was unique was having it all heaped upon us in the space of ten months. There is one person who is responsible, either directly or indirectly, for the near destruction of the Albion. And he knows it. So, as I crawl up to the bar of the Last Chance Saloon, and order my final measure of the spirit of '96-97 - not on the rocks just yet - one thing remains clear in my inebriated mind before any transformation of the Albion can be complete. The unrelenting message is spelt out by the opening letter of each paragraph above.

GWLADYS SINGS THE BLUES

Everton

When the best win of the season for this Evertonian was red over blue, it serves as an indicator as to how bad things have been at Goodison. That that victory had nothing to do with football - the red being the colour of Labour and the blue being that of the Tories - merely highlights what a dire campaign was waged by the Blues.

Maybe I'm being too harsh. After all, at one point, on the back of a 7-1 win over Southampton, Everton were being tipped as title outsiders. At that time we were fifth in the table, Nick Barmby had just been signed for a record fee and the likes of Tony Grant, Andrei Kanchelskis and Gary Speed were

all showing good form. Yet even though we were playing well, we were still failing to convince, still failing to beat beatable sides and still failing to fulfil the famous 'Nothing but the best is good enough' motto. And it wasn't that we were particularly good; neither were the other sides. That Man Utd should win the title with only 75 points in a season which saw them beaten 5-0 by Newcastle and 6-3 by Southampton proves my point. For a team as utterly mediocre as Liverpool to be their closest rivals for most of the campaign merely underlines it.

However, Everton, despite being part of a weak field, showed their age-old tendency of ending their season shortly after Christmas. Some circumstances were admittedly outside anyone's control: Andy Hinchcliffe, capped in each of Glenn Hoddle's first three internationals and playing the best football of his life, picked up a career-threatening knee ligament injury days before Christmas which kept him out for the rest of the season; Tony Grant, at last showing on a regular basis the skill which earned him the nickname 'Grantona' when captaining the reserves, was also injured around the same time; Andrei Kanchelskis, a veritable steam engine charging up and down the right wing a season earlier was more like a steam roller before he was sold off to Fiorentina for £8 million, the biggest rip-off since, er, we , um, spent £6 million on Nick Barmby. Joe Royle had claimed in one of the understatements of the year that the Russian's poor showing was down to a "Euro '96 hangover." More like a Euro '96 coma, mate.

With these factors already against us, a record-equalling run of six defeats was embarked upon over December and January, which sapped the already depleted and beleaguered squad of any remaining confidence. Attempts by Royle to strengthen the staff met negative responses so often that us Evertonians came to believe that nobody would ever sign for us. Over the early months of 1997 Slaven Bilic, Mark Schwartzer and Tore Andre Flo were added to the pantheon of those nearly bought by Royle in his 28 month reign as boss. In fairness to Joe, he did sign Terry Phelan, who although at first eyed with trepidation proved to be possibly his classiest signing. However, let us not forget that he is also the man who paid money to buy Claus Thomsen. While Bryan Robson was able to bring Ravanelli and Juninho to the living hell that is Middlesbrough, and Ruud Gullit snapped up half of the Italian national team, all that genial big Joe could manage was this poorly co-ordinated pile of pooh. In 20 games, the only two things I can remember about Thomsen were his getting injured when celebrating a goal and his o.g. in the derby.

It was this ineptness in the transfer market which was to lead to Royle's departure on transfer deadline day. During his time as Everton boss he'd managed to elevate cocking up transfers into an art form. There were of course other contributory factors to his downfall: a three week long media ban had forever tainted his perennial cheery red-faced avuncular image; his sides were always lacking in the hallmark Everton flair and adventure; crowd favourites such as Limpar, Samways and Amokachi were axed and then sold, while Royle's own ambitions for the side never really seemed to be on the same level as those of chairman Peter Johnson.

In his place came Dave Watson on a caretaker basis until the board had secured the services of a coach with "European experience." At the time of writing, however, the search goes on, with the one-time targets of Lippi, Van Gaal and Bobby Robson being overlooked in favour of more realistic propositions such as Martin O'Neill, Bryan Robson and, heaven forbid, George Graham. Watson did OK in his seven weeks in charge, steering us from further embarrassments and from relegation and maintaining the proud three year unbeaten derby run while at the same time introducing some highly promising youngsters into the side.

In fact, if one positive thing can be gleaned from this season of discontent then it is the performances towards its tail end of kids like Michaels Ball and Branch, Danny Cadameteri, Richard Dunne and John Hills. Just as Tony Blair, the youngest Prime Minister since Pitt, offers new hope to the people of Britain, these young men give new hope for the supporters of Everton. While the red landslide of May 1st still leaves a tingle of elation, my fingers are now tightly crossed for some wins for the blue of Everton in the forthcoming season. Hopefully, with a new manager, plenty of new players and in a new stadium which has just been promised, I'll be able to toast the good fortunes of the team I love and not just those of the Labour Party.

HANGING ON THE TELEPHONE

Huddersfield Town

Zzzzzzzz!

Sorry about that. I was just basking in the glow of the gloriously entertaining and exciting football that I enjoyed last year when I inexplicably nodded off. Could it be possible that mere reflection upon a season which never really got out of the starting blocks, instilled a sense of complete boredom and went downhill from there could bring on instant slumber? You bet.

Now I'm sure that if you talked to anyone at this club, they'd cite any number of extenuating circumstances for our less-than-average showing, but the fact remains that Huddersfield Town supporters

sensed a general malaise that no amount of double-talk could dispel. As with anything in life, you only get out what you're prepared to put in and Huddersfield Town FC got exactly what they deserved last season: sweet FA.

Back in August though, things couldn't have looked more different. In a bout of transfer market dealing the scale of which was unprecedented in Town's history, the £2.7 million sale of Andy Booth financed the purchases of Marcus Stewart from Bristol Rovers, Andy Morrison from Blackpool and Andy Payton, much to the delight of Barnsley fans everywhere. And that still left over 600 grand in the kitty!

Pre-season hype would have us believe that this was to be a bright new dawn. By September it had started clouding over and before the turn of the year there was a total eclipse that lasted the rest of the season.

It was clear after only a few weeks that all was not well. First of all, Andy Morrison disappeared for the next 40 games with a knee condition (yeah, thanks for mentioning that, Blackpool!). Shortly afterwards, million-pound-man Marcus Stewart joined him with what was initially diagnosed as a bruised shin, revised some weeks later to a hairline fracture and finally identified (in January!) as a bone cyst, which had to be removed by the surgeon's knife. And it wasn't just our two most expensive players who made the trip to the operating table last year; a dozen more followed (a fact totally unconnected with the loss of physio Dave 'Tatey Man' Wilson and his replacement with an ex-military man - I don't think!).

The ever-lengthening injury list meant that manager Brian Haemorrhage had to field an unprecedented 35 players during the season and the starting line-up changed almost as often as the manager's tactics. Now most footballers are not rocket scientists, yet our Brian appeared to have a 'tactics de jour' policy which meant that none of the players seemed to know what they were supposed to be doing from one game to another. Far more depressingly, many didn't appear to care either and all too often we were forced to watch the boys in blue and white apparently going through the motions before skulking off, amply rewarded for the day's ineptitudes, to the town's nightclubs.

Still, we can always rely on Bradford City to provide a counterpoint to the season whatever the circumstances, and this year was no exception. After they'd thrown away a 3-0 lead at the McAlpine in an unparalleled act of generosity, the return at Valley Parade merely highlighted all the recent off-field animosity. With Town scoring after only 56 seconds everyone assumed that Bradford's Gordon Watson was feeling a little frustrated when he purposefully elbowed Paul Reid in the face in an off-the-ball incident, which the referee missed. A minute or so later he suffered the misfortune of a broken leg in a challenge for the ball with Kevin Gray. The dignified and controlled actions of the much-liked (!) Bradford manager Chris Kamara, who did a wild Basil Fawlty impression in the centre circle in an (unsuccessful) attempt to get Gray sent off, only served to confirm most Town fans' opinions of him. Our feelings were reinforced 48 hours later when Bradford announced that not only were they suing the player and the club for compensation in a civil action, but also that Gordon Watson (against PFA advice) would be pursuing a criminal action against Gray ("cos he meant to do it" screamed hysterical City fans, baying for Huddersfield blood).

The whole sorry affair might have dominated the local headlines had it not been for the ever-degenerating fortunes of the club as a whole and midfielder Darren Bullock in particular. Psycho, as he was affectionately known, was proving to be as aggressive and uncontrolled off the pitch as he was on it. His appearance in court for assaulting a police officer came hot on the heels of unsubstantiated stories of training pitch brawls, attempts to strangle the manager in the dressing room, infidelities in any number of town centre nightclubs and it came just before a further arrest on yet another assault charge. Unsurprisingly his form (and with it that of the entire side) suffered, and he was packed off to Swindon with unseemly haste at the end of February.

By the time the final game of the season came around we had watched too many inept performances from half-interested players, witnessed indiscipline on an unparalleled scale resulting in four sendings off in the space of five games, seen open dissent for the manager from substitutes warming up on the sidelines and had looked on as a seemingly never-ending tide of half-fit players limped from the field of play, forcing an increasingly exasperated manager into ever more bewildering team selections.

As the final game unravelled in familiar fashion, I dozed between torrential downpours and tried to amuse myself by thinking of a more appropriate tune for the side to run out to instead of the dreadful dirge of Smile *A'While* which is what we have at the moment. At the final whistle the players trudged off to lukewarm applause whilst Swindon midfielder Darren Bullock, resplendent in a blue and white shirt and scarf thrown from the crowd, did a personal lap of honour that brought the house down. Despondently, I racked my brains for a song to sum it all up.

Sadly, the best I could come up with was The Stranglers' No More Heroes.

THE HANGING SHEEP

Leeds United

After a summer of discontent in the ranks, Elland road was host to a scene reminiscent of the plains of the Serengeti. Outgoing chairman Leslie Silver (the lion in all of this) eventually decided he'd had enough of standing over the carcass that is Leeds United and wandered off to pastures new. What he left was a squabbling pack of hungry hyenas (the directors) ready to battle for what flesh remained. Their infighting in the High Court made the club a laughing stock as Gilman, Fotherby, Silver and rival Conrad and Caspian groups fought over the bones of this beleaguered club of ours.

All this left the position of Howard Wilkinson (let's call him the leopard) in severe doubt. He was left to sit up in his tree and watch the proceedings unfold in front of him, never quite sure when the next scrap, in the form of badly needed financial sustenance for team building, would be thrown his way. His end would surely be near...

The lack of cash since the Championship of 1992 meant that only the odd signing was sanctioned by a boardroom preoccupied with maximising the value of their own shareholding prior to the club being sold. Why bother to spend more of your own money when all you're looking to do is cash in? Never mind the fact that the team and fans were floundering in a sea of mediocrity week after week, this is the real world chaps, so let's not get too involved with it, eh?

Fotherby was now chairman and his appointment was greeted with a plethora of spray-painted slogans across the fine city of Leeds - from billboards to bridges these messages proclaimed him to be a crook, liar or thief, and invariably all three! How this man could ever attain such high office at our club I am at a loss to explain. Unpopular is the most charitable description proffered by most Leeds United fans regarding this man. Alex Ferguson would stand more chance of getting a pint bought for him in Spencers on matchday.

Wilkinson had been allowed to spend a combined total of some £9 million on Bowyer (don't mention Big Macs), Nigel Martyn and a certain Lee

Sharpe. That outlay was offset by (thankfully) getting rid of Speed for £3.5m and Gary McAllister for £3m. The latter found Coventry's offer of a reported £20,000 a week just too much to resist.

Funnily enough, the season started brightly (weather-wise that is) as we romped to a 2-0 lead at Derby. Later, when we were 3-1 up, the first of many re-hashes of Three Lions was being delivered from the Leeds end. A minute later and it was 3-3... Two wins and a display of synchronised swimming at home to Sheff Weds in a downpour of monsoon proportions later, it was the scum at home...

It was a very sad day all round for the Whites. On the pitch we were pissed on 4-0, and off it there was violence throughout the day, with those fans less able to control themselves doing just that; shops, bars and Wilkinson's career were all wrecked during one September day. Less than 24 hours later Howard was history. For the Caspian boys the drubbing was perfectly timed because they could wheel Fotherby out to read their prepared statement about how much Howard had done for us (true) and that he wasn't getting things right (true) and had to go (true).

The rumour mill immediately started grinding away. Smiling Kenny D's mug was in the frame for a while as was the 'resting' George Graham. Mind you, given that George had consistently turned down a string of top jobs (and the one at Man City) and that he was buddies with the Caspian chairman, his appointment wasn't exactly a secret around these parts. The fact that he was warming his backside in Wilko's chair less than 24 hours later smelt somewhat, but that's the way of big business I suppose - line the new guy up before handing the old one the revolver.

He of the large back pockets and brown envelopes fame (I don't even have to add 'allegedly' 'cos he got caught) breezed into Elland Road following his twelve month exile proclaiming that he was glad to be back. Hardly surprising really considering his reported salary... making up for lost time perhaps? Graham's reputation at Arsenal had been built on solid defensive qualities, which was exactly what we needed given our back four's continued attempts to give the ever-excellent Nigel Martyn heart failure. In short we were leaking goals quicker than the Titanic's engine room. To cap it all, free signing Ian Rush had failed to find the net by the end of November.

I should have predicted as much when I picked up the News of the World last summer and read that new signing Rush "liked to score regularly" with some Welsh waitress in a broom cupboard or restaurant, I'm not sure of the exact location. Much like our Welsh wizard actually. If there was an ounce of truth in the tale, why the fuck didn't Leeds contract the girl to pose in the back of the bloody net every week. That way at least Rushie would have had some idea where he should've been heading. Instead, I watched as the former goal-grabber-supreme struggled forlornly to achieve any success in the now ultra-defensive Leeds set-up. For the record he finished with a paltry three goals (or joint fourth if you mockingly prefer). With that scoring prowess it's doubtful whether the aforementioned waitress would have had her underwear ruffled, let alone been given a good seeing to.

Comparisons between the old and negative but super Leeds team of yesteryear, the slightly more modern and negative Arsenal team, and the all new and very negative Leeds team abounded in the press week after week. Yes, at times it was dire, very dire, and yes the bloody hyphen in 0-0 was about as exciting as it got in a lot of the matches. But at the end of the day Premiership survival was achieved through those tactics (and Martin's total of 20 clean sheets), something which would have been beyond Leeds had Wilkinson still been in charge. Just how much more the fans can take I'm not sure, but we'll be looking for the entertainment value to rise in a similar fashion to the season ticket prices.

By the way, are we the only set of fans (Newcastle excepted) who are pissing ourselves over near-neighbours Sunderland and Boro being relegated? 'Oh, isn't it a shame' proclaimed the tabloids. Bollocks! I nearly wet myself along with the other 35,000 Leeds fans present at the final home game against Boro; it's just a pity they couldn't drag Coventry (McAllister and all) down with them. By the way Mackems, you can now chant 'Wembley '73' in the Nationwide, in your nice new £ full stadium...

So what of the future? We've still to sort out the Brolin saga and Yeboah might be staying, or then again he might not. Deane and Dorigo are stalling on new contracts as I write, and Carlton Palmer could be on his way too, along with a string of other players. Major surgery is needed both on and off the pitch, and George has already started by bringing in Halle, Molenaar, Lilley, Laurent and Robertson. Just where his spending spree will take him next I'm not sure, but the supposed Caspian millions don't look to be as readily available as we first thought, especially as their shares are up and down like a whore's knickers at the moment. On the slightly brighter side, the youth team completed a league and cup double, only for manager Paul Hart to leave and take a side swipe at Graham's apparent disinterest in our up and coming youngsters. Quite frankly, while understanding Hart's frustrations, George has got to concentrate on sorting out the first team right now.

Off the pitch there were a number of unreported incidents involving our travelling support, much to the club's dismay. The much-maligned membership scheme has been reintroduced to try and put a halt to the problem.

Caspian have been given planning permission for a 15,000 capacity ice hockey arena and conference and leisure centre next to Elland Road to further galvanise their investment. In an effort to compete with the top clubs they've also started the process of enlarging the stadium; 5,000 seats will soon be available to be filled by cute Yorkshire posteriors. But the alienation of many fans over the last three to four years means that the team must be worthy enough to persuade them to part with their pennies. Oh, and we ballsed-up in the FA Cup - as usual...

THE HATCHET

Bury

Bury are up (but don't tell anyone...)

The story of '96-97 for Bury is one of quite breath-taking achievement (now there's a sentence we don't hear very often!). Manager Stan Ternent and his previously somewhat maligned assistant Sam Ellis led the Shakers to promotion yet again, confounding critics, prophets of doom and bookmakers alike by clinching the Championship with a team assembled on the proverbial shoestring budget. Just in case, however, you somehow managed to miss the barrage of publicity and praise lavished upon us by the nation's sports media, the Hatchet

has pleasure in providing the following fascinating facts about Bury's season:

WE HAVE JUST BEEN PROMOTED FOR THE SECOND SUCCESSIVE SEASON!

This is an achievement unparalleled in the 103 year Football League history of the club. Of course, it has been suggested that it bears some similarity to another storming season just a few years ago - in 1895 we were promoted to the top flight at the end of our first ever season in the league - and Granada TV never mentioned us then either...

WE HAVE JUST WON OUR FIRST CHAMPIONSHIP IN 36 YEARS!

The last time we lifted any serious silverware was the old Division Three Championship in 1961. Last season's trophy is only the third in our entire history. Not counting the Midland Senior League of course...

WE WERE UNBEATEN AT HOME IN THE LEAGUE ALL SEASON!

Bet you never knew that, did you?

WE'RE OUT OF THE BOTTOM TWO DIVISIONS FOR THE FIRST TIME IN 29 YEARS!

As well known Shakers fanatic Gary Glitter once said "Hello, hello, Bury are back!" We've returned to the land of the living for the first time since 1968. The most important aspect of this for most Bury fans is that it means we're still within hailing distance of our old pals Horwich Wanderers - which is more than can be said for their new ground of course.

OUR LAST MATCH OF THE SEASON WAS THE FIRST LOCK-OUT AT GIGG LANE IN LIVING MEMORY!

A staggering 10,000 fans (or should that be 10,000 staggering fans?) turned up on May 3rd to witness the Shaker's metamorphosis from lower division tiddlers to Premiership pretenders. How fitting that our victims that day were Millwall, beloved of Danny Baker who once alleged on Radio 5 Live that Bury didn't actually exist. Was 2-0 real enough for you, Dan?

Success on the football field has given the whole town a lift of course. The last 30 years has been a story of decline, common to most of us in post-industrial Britain: loss of traditional industries, gradual erosion of regional identity, even the spectre of pub closures. But now that Bury FC have been promoted, things are looking up. Can it be purely coincidental that by the start of the new season we could have no less than four new bars in the town centre? The local economy was also given a massive boost during May, when one supermarket announced a 600% increase in the sale of face paints (yes, nearly a dozen boxes this time). All we need now is a government subsidy to re-open the old black pudding foundry and Bury will be truly back on the map.

But I digress. Many of us die-hards have of course been in much bigger crowds than 10,000 at Gigg in the past. Twenty-thousand plus against Forest and Burnley in the '80's, 16,000 against City and Leeds the decade before. Nevertheless, in anticipation of big crowds next season, Bury's season ticket holders now have the novel experience of having to reserve a seat - a totally alien concept to the most of us who grew up with Gigg Lane as the quintessential open-plan stadium (sorry, ground). Not only could you move around at will, but we even used to swap ends at half-time! Progress always comes at a price...

The only down-side to our remarkable season was the coverage - or rather lack of it - we received in the media. Apart form local outfits like the Bury Times and GMR Radio in Manchester, we were treated to the kind of apathy that would have reduced any committed fan - or even any fair-minded neutral - to throwing bricks at the screen.

The national press virtually ignored us... "So what?" you might say. Thing is, do you think it would have been the same story if Watford, Brentford or even (God help us) some 'Sleeping Giant' like Preston or Burnley had taken the title? The PFA awards night towards the end of the season summed it all up - not a single member of the side that won the Championship made it into the select X1 for Division Two. David Jones of Stockport got Divisional Manager of the Year (and Stocky finished second).

Worst of all, though, was Granada's Elton Welsby's performance on the day we secured promotion: it was illuminating. "And Bury are up" he flatly announced, doing his best impersonation of a sick parrot. Then again, maybe we cynics have got Elton and his chums all wrong... maybe they really love Bury, and they're deliberately trying to keep quiet about us, because they know that - like Monty Python's Spanish Inquisition - the Shaker's most lethal weapon has always been SURPRISE...

Bury's promotion last season signalled a change of seismic proportions for the club. But it must surely have sent a few small after-shocks reverberating around the entire league as well. We have provided hope to all the so-called small clubs that success could be just around the corner. The message to all of you is clear: Don't give up - next season it really could be YOU! Then again, I've just seen the European Cup Final on telly, and heard Brian Moore describe Borussia Dortmund as "Unfashionable." If that's what he thinks of the European Champions, then Bury clearly have a little way to go just yet...

ELTON WELSBY PRESENTS

GOALS EXTRA 1996/97

GRANADA'S STORY OF THE SEASON ON VIDEO

SPECIAL EDITION for BURY FANS!

Yes, all you Shakers, this high-quality video contains all the highlights of Nationwide League football in the North West, as shown on Granada during the season - *and the great news is that we've cut out all the bits featuring Bolton!*

Just sent £12.99 to the usual Granada address and we'll send you one by return.

WARNING: THIS VIDEO *MAY* LAST IN EXCESS OF FIVE MINUTES (BUT WE SERIOUSLY DOUBT IT).

HEAVEN 11

Reading

Reading between the lines

No-one really wants to read a review of a fellow team's season, unless you know your team stuffed them, knocked them out the cup or in Brighton's case jettisoned the opposition into the abyss. Hereford... bless 'em... nose-diving into the far and beyond (green parkas 'n' all).

So without going into a match-by-match account of the whole campaign, it will make better reading (or is that Reading better?) if the season was dismissed as a total non-starter from the time we acquired the services of Paul Bodin, to the moment when chairman JM announced Jimmy Quinn and Mick Gooding could no longer be holders of a joint account.

Reading's resident Aussie Andy Bernal, really knew how to take a leading role Home & Away. He got sent off in game no.1, went in goal for no.2, and returned for the early bath in game no.3 - he definitely has a liking for Soaps! Poor bloke even got red-carded later versus West Brom, when Paul Peschisolido decided that diving in the away area was a lot more fruitful than going down whilst at home (phnaar). Andy was sent down the tunnel to run the taps again, but some days later a spotlessly clean Bernal was given a reprieve by a referee who realised the little Canadian's sudden fall had been caused by progressive jet lag.

So what else happened which was of any interest? Well, we got beaten at Wycombe in the cup in an evening fixture containing a catalogue of errors on and off the pitch. The biggest blooper concerned the Adams Park ticket office, who'd sold us more tickets than there were seats. So what was supposed to be the historic opening of a huge stand full of the Wycombe faithful ended up with all us lot in it.

Next on the agenda was a 6-1 defeat on our own patch by Crystal Palace (our worst home defeat for 50 years). The fans invaded the pitch after the game demanding the heads of Quinn and Gooding. This incensed the Irishman who couldn't understand the mentality of home supporters cheering Palace's fifth and sixth strikes. The chairman re-assured the duo that he had every faith in them and allowed them to purchase another 'keeper on loan. Well, he had to really, Bobby Mihaylov didn't want to know. In a nutshell, the bloke was bollocks and only put in a performance worthy of his talent when the Bulgarian coach was announcing his international squads. Tommy Wright (Forest and Northern Ireland) then arrived on the scene, and with the help of James Lambert (ex-Blackburn and Monaco training sessions), won us three points up at McGhee's cosy nest. This tied them over till the next bad run, then just as it seemed the writing was on the wall, Lambert would be brought in from the cold, save their bacon, then get shelved until it was time to be their saviour again. This became a regular feature, and Lambert was eventually given a new contract after he'd destroyed Southampton. However, there was unrest in the camp; the players just didn't want to play for the bosses, which was plain to see to the paying fans.

Billy Bonds then took the bull by the horns, and all of a sudden it was a case of 'Quinn and Gooding taking a back seat' as the former Hammer's influence spread. We even managed to beat Bolton 3-2 (with Jimmy Quinn in goal), then to top it all we completed a rare double by beating Wolves 2-1, having been one down when the 90 minutes were up! This game gave the club record gate and catering receipts. Could this have had anything to do with the visitors bench and their consumption of pies? Oh yes, he ate 'em all.

The season then ground to a halt. We'd earned the right for another year in this division, and at the end of a topsy-turvy campaign, not a lot more could really have been expected. So in a not too memorable season on the pitch, statistics nevertheless show our best home record ever in Division 1 (and old Div 2), 23 goals by a striker with a metal plate in his head, seven sent off, and Nestlé bringing out a mint-flavoured KitKat The managers thought they'd done enough to earn a new contract and paper talk led us to believe likewise. However, following the decision for Bonzo to take centre stage at the New Den, his departure was soon followed by that of Quinn's and Gooding's, but to where no-one yet knows.

Of more importance, the club's final ever season at Elm Park is upon us. Come '98-99 we're off down the road to a 25,000 capacity stadium. Gone will be our infamous bogs, historic terraces, inaudible tannoy system and wonderful parking facilities. The new ground will be named after our chairman John Madejski, basically 'cos he's ploughed an absolutely huge wedge into it; can't really argue with that I suppose. The Madejski Stadium will hopefully provide the people of Reading with a ground to be proud of, although success on the field will obviously be the telling factor when it comes to filling the joint. Or as a fan pointed out, we might need to change its name by deedpole to the Madejski Tribute Stadium - MT for short (geddit?)!

So as it stands at the moment, it's a few weeks from pre-season training and we haven't got a manager or coach. Everyone has been linked with the post but it's the local evening paper The Post which seems to be playing all the right cards. They have well documented the fact that Colin Lee (our ex and McGhee's current No.2) is a leading candidate for the job; however, there are a few stumbling blocks. The Wolves chairman won't allow Lee to talk to our chairman and Lee himself will not walk out on his club (practice makes perfect, mind you!), so it's a basic stalemate scenario. However, the newspaper has launched a campaign-petition-like-thing with the aim of getting enough signatures to sway the Wolves board into at least allowing Lee the opportunity to talk to Mr Madejski.

The outcome of this rather unusual approach work is a long way from reaching a final conclusion. Ever since McGhee, Lee, Hickman, Osborn, Williams, Gilkes (and whoever else might have been recruited while I've been putting this piece together) joined the Wolves, they have never been allowed to forget it; suffering verbal abuse to the extreme whenever setting foot in Elm Park. During this season Lenny Henry made a visit to Elm Park to do some filming. He asked the Reading fans to get their vocal chords in tune and to chant their most passionate song. If I said 'Mark' and 'McGhee' were the third and fourth words, you can understand why this documentary remains unbroadcast. At least I presume it was for a documentary, it most definitely wouldn't have been for the Chef series; our menu starts with rubber burgers and ends up with a considerably more fluid version hours later!

It therefore seems really astonishing that Colin Lee could be returning as manager, but I for one wouldn't mind. The bloke's got a decent footballing brain, he just lacks a certain amount of allegiance. Without being biased, it should be a pretty attractive job for the right person 'cos there are definitely exciting times ahead for Reading Football Club (they'll even be luxury quilted soft blue and white bog paper to replace the traditionalists' favourite: Izal Medicated). But who fills the vacancy is very undecided at the moment. Next season could and should be the most important in the club's history. Come next May we might even be on our way to the Premiership. However, my money's on the launch of a mint-flavoured Crunchie bar!

HEROES AND VILLAINS

Aston Villa

Fans of Nottingham Forest, Oldham, Grimsby and especially Hereford will find these next few sentences a bit hard to understand. After all, qualifying for Europe and getting your best crowds for 20 years is, to the untrained eye, hardly the sign of failure. So why was it that Villa supporters regularly filled the local newspaper letters pages and radio phone-ins with criticism of team and manager, whilst the final whistle of the '96-97 season was greeted with relief that the whole thing was over? Maybe it was because we expected to do badly. Or because our fans have witnessed the occasional triumph followed by years of failure for so long that we

STAUNTON IN VAIN ATTEMPT TO DISPEL "ONE-FOOTED" MYTH

No. 47   December 1996   £1.00

decided in advance that the season would be one to forget. Or possibly it was because the football was for the most part uninspired and the team capable of so much better.

We started disappointingly with defeat at Sheffield Wednesday, but three consecutive wins and the impressive introductions of new signings Sasa Curcic and Fernando Nelson gave cause for optimism. Two up against Arsenal wasn't a bad position with 20 minutes to go, but poor finishing, panicky defending and a referee's eccentric time-keeping set the standards for the rest of the season.

The UEFA Cup came and went as a few seconds of unprofessionalism let Swedish side Helsingborg leave Villa Park with a 1-1 draw, and they belied their supposed part-time status with 90 minutes of defensive efficiency in the return leg to leave the Villa with an embarrassing exit from a competition which we've never exactly shone in. Newcastle beat us 4-3 in a classic with Dwight Yorke scoring a hat-trick, and suddenly things weren't looking too clever.

It was at this point that events started to take a turn for the worse off the field, when Paul McGrath fell out with the management over not getting a regular place and eventually left for Derby. End of an era? We'll never see his like again! All the old clichés were trotted out, and if anything they were understated. If I ever see a better footballer than McGrath playing for the Villa again, then both me and the club will be very lucky.

The next little drama saw Mark Bosnich upsetting a few Spurs supporters with a Hitler impersonation at White Hart Lane. A few years ago it would have been laughed off, but in the newly sanitised world of football there's always somebody looking to be offended, and Bosnich stepped unwittingly into the moral low ground.

The season blundered along on its way. Savo was off to Italy, then he wasn't. We won, drew and lost regularly to maintain a top six position without looking particularly convincing. We were buying Stan Collymore, then we weren't. A League Cup defeat at Wimbledon meant that we'd gone out of two cups to teams who'd had two attacks between them in three games. Then five league wins in a row, culminating in a 5-0 thrashing of a Wimbledon side who hadn't lost for about 20 matches. But just when it looked like things were going right they went into decline: home defeat to Chelsea on Boxing Day, three draws in a row, a defeat at Anfield and out of the FA Cup courtesy of Derby County. The Rams' new defender had a magnificent game. Not that he had much to do, his most difficult job being to acknowledge the ovation he received at the start of the match.

By now Mark Bosnich had used up most of his post-White Hart Lane sympathy thanks to a series of poor performances, and seemed to be getting the blame for every goal the team conceded. Mind, most of them were his fault. Sasa Curcic wasn't Mr Popularity either. A promising start was followed by a string of lacklustre performances, an extended run on the bench and consequently a promptly tabled transfer request.

There were a few more inconsistent performances, the highlight of which was a 1-0 victory over Liverpool, and by the time March came round we were looking at things with more optimism. The injury crisis had cleared up and the Villa were faced with an easy run-in. The title was out of our reach, but with every other team doing themselves no favours, the possibility was still there of a runners-up spot and a place in the seriously devalued Champions League.

'Twasn't to be, though. That old devil called inconsistency, coupled with some very dodgy refereeing, meant that we went into the last game of the season needing a point to qualify for the UEFA Cup. We got a 1-0 win over a Southampton side who were almost certain to stay up regardless of the score, but it was a hollow celebration. We knew the team could have done better; so did they.

Attendances were ridiculously high - more capacity crowds than any other season in the club's history. We even sold out against Leeds and Everton. There was a successful flotation on the Stock Exchange - successful that is if you sold your shares before the price began to slide when the money men started to realise that football is a bubble waiting to burst. Yes we did qualify for the UEFA Cup (the first time the Villa have ever finished high enough in the league two years in a row), and 87 clubs would have swapped places with us. We were no worse off than Liverpool and Arsenal for all the millions they spent.

So again, why the disappointment? There were a few reasons. The football was quite often unexciting. Villa had a team who on their day were good enough to beat anybody, but lacked the strength in depth to cope with a series of injuries or to change the pattern of the team's play. Put simply, there was no plan B.

The style of play, which had often come as a surprise to the opposition in the previous season, had been worked out. And with such a small squad there just weren't the replacements available for players who were out of form or just happy to put in substandard performances knowing their place was still secure. For sure (as our illustrious manager would say) we had some bad luck. In fact, I simply wouldn't believe that any club has ever been victim of so many diabolical refereeing decisions over the course of the season. But if only we'd had a regular partner for Dwight Yorke, or even a goalscoring midfielder; we might not have won the Premiership, but looking at the way results went, we'd have certainly been in with a shout. And to compound the agony, what happens less than 24 hours after the season ends? We sign Stan Collymore for £7m. I defy you to find anybody who believes that this particular deal wasn't agreed months previously.

And that's the bottom line. The nagging suspicion that when it comes to the big prize, we'll never have a better chance.

Big Ron left Highfield Road with not quite the trophies he had hoped for

Source: In Dublin's Fair City

HEY BIG SPENDER

Derby County

Despite the fact that we only won two away matches all season; despite the fact that we were entertaining the prospect of joining F****t in the relegation dog-fight since before Christmas; despite the fact that we were knocked for six by the useless Middlesbrough at the Riverside Stadium and denied an all-Derbyshire FA Cup semi final spot three days later by the same motley crew AND despite the fact that this was the last ever season at our historic and famously atmospheric little Baseball Ground, '96-97 has been a good year for the particular species that is the Derby County fan (Sheeperus Shagursaurus to use the correct terminology).

So, why has it been so good, you may ask. Well, because it's been pretty much an uneventful season. Since I started supporting the Rams at the beginning of the seventies, there has always been something or other cracking off at DCFC. Such as (take a deep breath): two League Championships within three years under different managers; a European Cup semi final (and there should have been a final against Ajax - Juventus had to resort to bribing officials to knock us out!); famous victories in Europe over Velez Mostar, Benfica, Real Madrid and Athletic Madrid; Clough and Taylor totally turning around the fortunes of the club, and their subsequent resignation; an FA Charity Shield win; relegation, after years of trying for it; Tommy Docherty's ten minutes in charge, during which he sold an entire international squad and replaced them with a bunch of nobodies from Eire; a winding up petition or two, and losing an FA Cup quarter final at home to bloody Plymouth (on the same day); another relegation and two years in Division 3 (old money); Arthur Cox, Robert Maxwell and two subsequent promotions; finishing fifth in the old Division 1 with Deano Saunders and Ooh-Mark Wright; Robert Maxwell, Arthur Cox and relegation; Roy McFarland and a failed play-off final against hated local rivals; Jim Smith, the Croatians and promotion; not to mention Texaco and Watney Cup wins and an Anglo Italian Cup Final appearance. Being a Derby County fan, yer see, is either very exciting or very worrying and often both at the same time. This season should have been no different - we were one of the favourites to 'do a Bolton' and the Bald Eagle was the bookies' favourite to be first boss for the chop. So what went right?

We got off to a good start, against all the odds, with a thrilling 3-3 draw at home to Leeds. A few days later at White Hart Lane our defence held out, except for a pointlessly re-taken Teddy Sheringham free kick, and a second point was gratefully bagged when Christian Dailly (we've not thought of a song for him yet) grabbed a late equaliser. We were defeated at Villa, but only after half of our defence (i.e. Gary Rowett) was carried off injured in the first ten minutes. Things were still looking promising when we went ahead against Manchester United at the Baseball Ground the following Wednesday, Denmark's No.2 teaching Denmark's No.1 a thing or two about covering your near post from 40 yard free-kicks - funnily enough the BBC didn't show that amazing goal in their end of season Premiership round-up, preferring instead Beckham's toe-poked equaliser. Then again, the BBC never bother screening anything to do with Derby - apparently, navigating your way to the East Midlands is a difficult task made doubly tricky when you've got your tongue simultaneously stuck neatly up the arses of Liverpool, Arsenal, Newcastle United and Manchester United FCs. Ahem!

Then I went on holiday for a week and we won at Blackburn - our first ever Premiership win and I listened to it on a car radio in the pitch black on a Dorset camp site - what memories! It was obviously going to be a good year. With all the worries of a desperate promotion battle cast aside (that's all we've done for the previous five seasons), it was just a case of keeping it tight at home whilst picking up the points on our travels from the weaker Premiership teams, such as, er, Arsenal and Manchester United. Both were respectively top of the table when we visited them. At Highbury the Gunners grabbed a late equaliser after Dean Sturridge had totally outshone his all-time hero Ian Wright, and at Old Trafford... well, if you haven't seen teenage Costa Rican sensation Paulo Cesar Wanchope Watson's goal, where have you been? If you get the chance to watch it again on TV, don't follow Paulo's goal celebrations, but instead look at the horror on the faces of the United fans in the crowd behind him; there's a young girl who turns to her mother bearing an expression that says, "look what that horrible big man's done to our lovely football team, mummy!" Priceless! Oh, and guess what? It didn't even win Goal of the Month. What a bloody surprise!

While all this was going on, just 14 miles down the road at the City Ground, Nottingham F****t were digging themselves deeper into the relegation mire, sacking managers and struggling off the field with boardroom takeovers and the likes. Of course, they were first to fall. It was just a pity that it wasn't made mathematically definite when they visited our ground for the last time in April, but it didn't stop the Popside making one last effort to humiliate the away following at a floodlit match; highlights in the Lennon and McCartney category were "Going down at the Baseball Ground," "Again, you'll never play us again, you'll never play us again!" and the subtle "Que sera, sera, whatever will be will be, you're going to Grimsby, que sera sera!" (Grimsby was later changed to Bury, when we realised the Mariners were as good as relegated themselves). We thought it was funny anyway.

The biggest event of our season was of course the construction of the new ground a mile to the north of the old one. Built by Taylor Woodrow on some waste ground by the river, the new stadium will hold around 30,000, and was designed as a free-standing two-tier main stand opposite a horseshoe-shaped North, West and East stands. We've heard rumours that Cellnet could be the stadium sponsors. Anything sound familiar about this project? Yep, it's the Holiday Inn of football grounds; every town's destined to get one, and they're all built the same. Ours is virtually identical to Boro's Riverside home, to such an extent that the club went out of its way to list the differences in a recent ground update publication. They could only come up with a list of 30 items and I thought they were trying a bit too hard when I noticed 'No.26: Voltage of street light bulbs in adjacent side street 10v less than those at Middlesbrough'. (Made that bit up actually, but that's how feeble the arguments were). Of course there is a downside to moving to a brand spanking new state-of-the-art stadium, with (hopefully) a club shop and ticket office slightly larger than the cornflakes box replicas we've had up until now. This is that you have to leave your familiar seat in the old, compact, intimidating little Victorian relic you're used to and which holds so many memories. The move was long overdue in reality; there was nothing to stop a Bradford-type disaster happening in any one of the three wooden stands along Shaftsbury Crescent, and the surrounding industry, housing and roads (or 'infrastructure' as they're referred to these days) dictated that the old Baseball Ground really wasn't the ideal site for top-class football. Virtually the only aspect of the new ground that has received little local publicity is what it will eventually be called. The 'Racal Vodaphone Riverside' has been suggested to put us in direct competition with Boro; 'Pride Park' is the name of the rejuvenated business park upon which the ground has been built, and that's a likely contender, but with QE2 coming to officially open the place over the summer a royal title is not yet out of the running. I believe that if we must have a sponsor in the name then it should stay local. It would also be a nice thought to follow the tradition at Derby of playing at a ground named after a totally different sport (the Racecourse/County Cricket Ground was our home before the Baseball Ground). Bearing these two points in mind, my suggestion in the official club poll was something along the lines of 'The Birds The Confectioners Royal World Superbike Championship Mega Dome'. Catchy, don't you think?

So what will next year bring? Probably the departures of Paul Simpson and Marco Gabbiadini, together with Martin Taylor and other long-time servants of the club, all of whom played a big part in getting us to the promised land. One man whose presence, flair, skill and experience as well as good humour on the park will also be sorely missed is Paul McGrath. He was a revelation and a pleasure to watch; his signing was a stroke of genius and a Godsend. Good luck, wherever you might be, Macca.

On the positive side we'll expect more genius from Jim Smith and Steve McClaren and no doubt we'll get it too. Hopefully next season will see a few more influential appearances from Igor Stimac, whose '96-97 was ruined by various injuries, and more of the same from Dean Sturridge, a subject of several multi-million pound bids from the 'bigger' Premiership clubs. Not bad for a bloke in only his second full season who we couldn't offload to Torquay a few years back for £100,000! While the defence looks pretty secure (tip of the summer - our Player of the Year Chris Powell will be the regular England No.3 within a year), and the midfield's taking shape nicely, only the forward line needs a little work. Ashley Ward and Ron Willems have scored their fair share of goals without ever really looking the part and when Studger's been out (usually suspended due to his big gob) his absence has been felt the most. Ravanelli should do. Is a European place beckoning at the end of '97-98? Aye, I'd say so. Up the Rams!

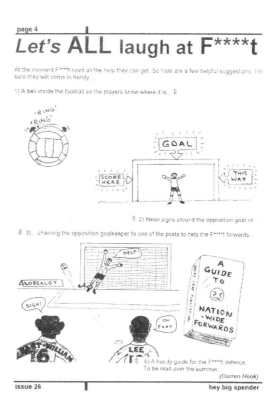

HIGHBURY HIGH

Arsenal

Allez les rouges!

It was the Monday before the start of the league season and like every Arsenal fan alive I was despondent, disillusioned and not to say downright brassed off.

Shearer had gone to Newcastle, Ravanelli to Middlesbrough and Vialli to Chelsea; at Highbury we'd acquired the services of John Lukic on a free transfer. Something was strangely amiss. Rioch was producing a 'players wanted' list which read like a 12 year old fantasy football team and we were getting nothing and nowhere fast.

Steve Ashford of the Goon-

Arsene lays out his plans...

Leezen very carefully I shall say theez only once

HIGHBURY HIGH

UEFA Cup Preview
Rioch – Wonder Year or Blunder Year?
The French Connection
Shareholders Meeting

Issue 11 £1.50
September 1996

er went to the press to talk of revolution amongst the fans. "We are not happy, we will mount a demonstration at our pre-season friendly at Birmingham City" he exclusively told the *Daily Mirror*. Steve was so militant and incensed he stayed at home, favouring an excursion to B&Q. Some revolution... or so I thought!

At just after 4pm on Monday August 12th the local radio station flipped over to a 'sensation at Highbury' report. Now what, another signing? Had we re-captured Perry Groves for £1.50 plus bonus for number of haircuts received? Nope, Rioch had been sacked! I was shocked but delighted; the jury had been out for some time on Rioch; some felt he was Highbury material, others, myself included, felt he was not high profile enough to manage a club as big as Arsenal.

Speculation was rife around the office about possible successors. From my window I saw a mate of mine walking down Roseberry Avenue; Mike looked like he'd lost a pound and found a tenner. He'd also heard the news, and like me was no Rioch fan. Outside we pondered; who would it be? Would 'kin George return? Bobby Robson perhaps? No, this was all folly, there was only one man big enough for the job and his name was Johan Cruyff. He was high profile enough for anyone and he was also my boyhood hero. It was sublime; that night I went to sleep like a child excited about his birthday.

Every paper the following morning agreed: Cruyff was coming to Highbury. Alarmingly the small print kept mentioning somebody who had a name that sounded a bit like Arsenal. Something was beginning to nag - why wasn't the Dutch one here already signing forms and holding up scarves and shirts for the usual rabble of photographers? By lunchtime the *London Evening Standard*, not known for sports sensationalism, was confidently stating the new boss was to be Arsčne Wenger. Who the hell was he?

Cruyff officially put himself out of the running and the Arsenal board began to stumble over the worst kept secret in the club's history. Wenger was of course coming to Highbury, but because of his contractual complexities in Japan the club could not announce his arrival officially. The Arsenal board took a hammering from fans not too enamoured at the way in which Rioch had been dispatched, with no official replacement installed. Dein and Hill-Wood were not flavour of the month.

So why had Rioch been so unceremoniously sacked? It's alleged that Mr Dein had very quickly recognised his mistake in appointing Rioch; he didn't rate him and the grapevine tells that Rioch had a mutual level of admiration for Dein. Something had to give and it was never going to be the vice-chairman. Some of the other Arsenal fanzines predictably began their usual campaign of indignation, but at Highbury High we were more optimistic. There was no reason to criticise the change in personnel.

Rioch wasn't good enough, the club wanted to replace him and they approached Wenger. If they'd sacked Rioch in May they would have spent a managerless summer never off the back page of the tabloids, and would still not have been able to announce a successor until September. It didn't, and still doesn't, paint the club in a good light, but the board were clearly not letting Rioch spend money and reasoned it would have been even worse to let him start the campaign and then sack him. It may have looked nasty, and it was, but the long-term strategy was the important thing and the board were getting that right.

The first game brought West Ham to Highbury. The papers were full of stories of riot and revolt amongst the fans, but the truth was that in shirt sleeve weather we walked all over West Ham and most of us went home joking that we were better without a manager. Stewart Houston took over the caretaker role but whispers were that he wasn't impressed at the treatment of Rioch. The rumours were true and before you could say 'Spurs are crap' Houston was off to QPR to ultimately swap roles with Bruce Rioch... Enter manager number three Pat Rice, and a quick climb up the league table. For a crisis club we weren't doing too bad at all. Perhaps this changing managers every few weeks was the revolutionary new strategy?

Wenger finally got here from Japan in October with Frank Skinner observing that "Prisoners got out of Tenko quicker than Wenger got to Highbury." Unfortunately he was too late to stop us going out of Europe at the first hurdle; we scored four but let in six against Borrussia Münchengladbach. Still, we weren't the only English side undone by Germans in Europe so at least there was something to feel good about!

Two weeks into his Highbury tenure Arsène Wenger was pitched against the newly-appointed Leeds boss, a certain Mr George Graham. The press loved trying to crank this one up but were disappointed to see George cheered home like the hero he still is at Highbury. Arsenal steam-rollered Leeds with an ease that was soon to disappear, and George came back in February to gain his revenge with a 1-0 defeat in the FA Cup. Everyone left Highbury stoney-faced, asking "did we really look as boring as that for all those years?"

November would be a big test for the new boss with a daunting away schedule facing Newcastle, Wimbledon, Manchester United and a home game against Tottenham. But Wenger was beginning to win everyone over at Highbury; his acquisition of Patrick Vieira was inspired and the whole team was playing with a new zest. We drew at Wimbledon 2-2 and then travelled to Old Trafford to take on everyone's favourite 'rent-a-fan' club. That much-loved cheating red-nosed illegitimate Schmeichel endeared himself to us yet again by getting Wright booked for daring to go for the ball. There televised set-to also stoked the on-going 'racism in football' debate. We played well, competed for everything and saw Vieira display just how good he is. But we still got tanked courtesy of an own-goal by Christie Brown, otherwise known as *My Left Foot* star Nigel Winterburn.

Still in third place and not at all downhearted, we eagerly awaited the arrival of the sadmen from up the Seven Sisters Road. It poured with rain all afternoon but who cared? Wrighty dispatched goal number one from the spot and all looked well until Sinton bounced one in off the back of Lukic's shoulder. This after Spurs had shown what cheating lowlifes they are by refusing to return the ball to us after it had been kicked out to allow treatment to Vieira. With only a few minutes to go Wenger gambled on throwing in Hartson (no George caution there then) and was rewarded when Adams then Bergkamp scored sensational goals in the last three minutes to send the red sides of the stadium into ecstasy. The Spurs contingent scurried away into the rain-swept November evening, preferring not to stay and enjoy the after-match celebrations. Sky awarded Tony Adams the Man of the Match award and sensitively gave him a bottle of champagne...

A week later and we were at St. James' Park enjoying the serenading of supporters whose ability to whinge can only be bettered by the rantings of Moan Utd players. I hope those two never get together! Adams was sent off for a Shearer dive as the referee gave a whole new interpretation to the professional foul. But we were not to be denied, even down to ten men and with only three players not in the ref's book, we were magnificent. The 2-1 victory was probably one of our finest moments of the season, and it put us top of the league.

From here on in we flirted with the Championship and never dropped lower than fourth, and for a club who'd started the season in crisis we were extremely happy. Up the road at Tottering there were so many injury excuses we were half expecting to hear that Darren 'Sicknote' Anderton had been forced to retire from the game with a broken eyelash.

The feud between Schmeichel and Wright boiled over again following an undoubted accidental two-footed GBH tackle on red nose's left leg. The referee and his assistant somehow contrived to miss the incident, but even they couldn't miss the hoo-hah at the end: Wrighty being restrained by team mates, the physio, the army and half of the Metropolitan Police was a bit of a tell-tale sign that all was not well between he and the nasally over-endowed one. To say that bad blood exists between Arsenal and United would be the under-statement of the century, but you know what, we wouldn't have it any other way!

As if that wasn't enough, Liverpool's visit to Highbury brought more controversy. 'Honest' Robbie Fowler dived over David Seaman and immediately jumped up to acknowledge it. Seaman and thirty-odd thousand voices made it plain that this shouldn't be a penalty. The referee - the arrogant, incompetent, degenerate - decided he knew best, over-rode popular opinion and pointed at the spot. Fowler did the gentlemanly thing and missed, only to see his 'Mickey Mouser' team mate bang in the rebound. Championship over!

This was the season of the yo-yo; we were in and out of the Championship so many times it defied belief, but at least it made it interesting to the last. The last came at Derby where 20,000 football fans danced around to the Spice Girls in a party celebration for the passing of the Baseball Ground. It is a sight that will live with me forever. We finished third and qualified for the UEFA Cup, which, given our ridiculous managerial beginnings, wasn't bad at all. If that cheating heathen Chris Sutton hadn't robbed us of two points at Highbury we might even have made it to the Champions League.

Still, as we say at Highbury, *C'est La Vie!*

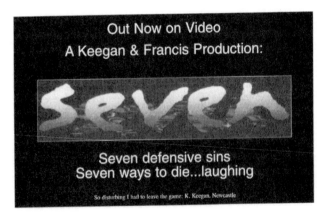

THE HOLY TRINITY

Aston Villa

To be truthful, '96-97 was hardly a vintage year for the Clarets. Finishing in fifth position and qualifying for Europe covered up far too many poor performances and a complete failure in the three knockout competitions that we entered.

In my opinion, our high finish was largely due to the inferior standard of the Premiership. It was a season when Manchester United won the title without breaking sweat. Leicester City - who only escaped relegation on the penultimate weekend - finished ninth, only one place behind a Wimbledon side highly-praised for their success. Further evidence, if

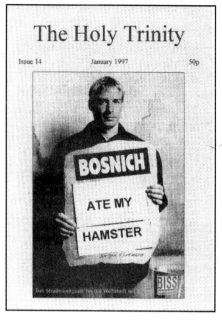

any was needed, was the progress of lower league clubs in both domestic cup competitions.

After the triumphs of the previous season (fourth in the Premiership, Coca Cola Cup winners, FA Cup semi-finalists), Brian Little had set himself a hard act to follow. Just to make things interesting, he also had to deal with a few players who did more talking on the back pages than they did on the pitch. Add to that the odd questionable decision by the man in a severe need of a bottle of 'Just for Men' and you had a recipe for a very frustrating season indeed for Villa supporters.

The first disappointment was our ignominious first round UEFA Cup exit (shown live on BBC) to Swedish side Helsingborgs. Fellow work-mates and so-called friends who supported one of the other (far inferior) Midlands sides took great delight in our defeat by an assortment of social workers, bank clerks and the obligatory postman. The truth is though, that Helsingborgs finished second in their domestic league behind Gothenburg, consisted mainly of a full-time squad (a few of whom had been targeted by Benfica), and went on to beat Swiss side Neuchatal Xamax in the next round before losing narrowly to Anderlecht. But this still doesn't excuse our two performances against them which stunk of complacency.

The return game in Helsingborgs marked the end of an era, being Paul McGrath's last appearance in a Villa shirt. Little had left him out of the starting line-up at the beginning of the season in favour of Steve Staunton. Frustrated by his lack of opportunity at Villa, McGrath moved to Derby where, once again, he was allowed to display his pure genius. Injuries soon followed to both Southgate and Staunton, so instead of watching the genial Irishman we got... Carl Tiler. There simply is no comparison. In fact, unsurprisingly, after only five starts, Tiler was demoted once again to the substitutes bench and he soon went crying to the media uttering the words 'transfer' and 'request'. Some gratitude after Villa had nursed and paid for his return from injury during the previous twelve months.

Tiler was dropped after a 1-3 home defeat to Leicester City. It was only November, yet this was already Villa's fifth league reverse of the season and we were occupying a disappointingly low ninth position. Further teeth-gnashing was to follow only ten days later as our hold on the League Cup was ended at Wimbledon, despite having most of the play.

The Wimbledon game was also significant in that it began a run of games in which Sasa Curcic did not figure in the starting line up. Curcic was our record summer signing at £4 million - apparently Little had been tracking him for months. But after a superb debut, when he received a standing ovation as he left the pitch, it all fizzled out into a bit of an anti-climax. His form had been disappointing and many observed that he was too similar a player to Mark Draper. It wasn't long before Sasa got fed up with splinters in the bum and went running to the press saying that he had made the wrong decision, that he was very unhappy at Villa Park, that he wanted to return to the North West and that this was the biggest mistake that he had ever made. This little outburst hardly made him flavour of the month with Villa fans, and when he did return to the first eleven against Liverpool in mid-January, he became the first Villa player that I've heard jeered for a long time.

Looking on the bright side for once, between the Wimbledon and Liverpool games we had embarked on a bit or a run. First of all we collected four wins on the trot - all with clean sheets to boot - then drew three and lost only one of the next four. The second set of statistics may not seem that impressive until you realise that the opposition were Chelsea and Newcastle at Villa Park along with Arsenal and Manchester United on their own patches, so we could still feel satisfied by the results and the performances. The draw at Old Trafford also meant that the 'mighty' United had now failed to beat us for the second season in succession.

These eight games marked a return to the side, and to form, of Savo Milosevic who scored four goals in this spell. At the start of the season Savo had once again struggled and was constantly being made the scapegoat in the media, being blamed for anything from our latest defeat to the recession. Understandably he was very unhappy and asked his agent to set up a long-yearned for move to Italy. Perugia showed an interest - then they didn't - then they did - then they didn't (this went on for several weeks). Eventually Savo decided to pull the plug and stay at Villa Park, but had he gone to Italy his replacement would have definitely been a certain Mr Collymore! When Savo stayed put, so did Stan. This angered many Villa fans; why should a club of our status have to sell before we can buy?

Although Savo had his temper tantrums and his mood swings, he never said a word against the club, management or fans, so most supporters were always on his side. Unfortunately, the same cannot be said of Mark Bosnich. He returned to the side during the aforementioned eight game spell after understudy Michael Oakes had kept three clean sheets on the bounce! In fact Oakes had played consistently well for the first team and conceded only 15 goals in his 17 starts, and it came as a shock to many to see the eccentric Bosnich put straight back in the side.

In an FA Cup replay against lowly Notts County, Bosnich kicked a ball straight down the pitch to another Villa player (believe me, this is a rare occurrence) and the Holte End struck up a very loud and prolonged sarcastic cheer in recognition of the feat... our Antipodean was not amused and went on the attack. In the national press he said that we needed to be more like Manchester United supporters (!) because true Championship fans always got behind their team and were never critical. His outburst was condemned by Brian Little, and really angered us. Needless to say the special rapport which should exist between 'keeper and the faithful behind the posts has all but disappeared in our case. Bosnich now pays far more attention to the opposition fans, laughing along and applauding them when they give him stick about his 'oh so funny' Nazi-style salute at Tottenham; on the last day of the season he even threw his shirt to the travelling Southampton contingent.

Our run-in was unspectacular in the extreme. The last few months were spent hanging on to European qualification and waiting for the summer when signing new players would be a lot easier. Of the last 15 games, we won seven, drew four and lost four, but the measly 16 goals scored in that period showed where our weaknesses lay. Although you can't blame the front two of Savo and Yorke, who hit 30 goals between them, the real problem was the lack of support from midfield. The usual line-up of Ian Taylor, Andy Townsend and Mark Draper only managed to muster five goals between them in over a 100 combined starts.

In recent years Villa have always seemed to have one excellent season followed by one bad. The trend continued this year, but instead of finishing 17th and just avoiding relegation, we finished fifth and we're off to Europe again. This shows just how much progress we are making under Brian Little who is undoubtedly one of the best managers around. With Stan the Man on board (at last) and fortune pointing towards a good season, just watch us go in '97-98.

IN DUBLIN'S FAIR CITY

Coventry City

"The finest plans have always been spoilt by the littleness of those that should carry them out. Even emperors can't do it all by themselves" Bertolt Brecht - 'Mother Courage'

Although these were not Big Ron's parting words on his dismissal from Coventry City (sorry - promotion upstairs), they easily could have been. When this larger than life character swanned into Highfield Road he immediately put a couple of thousand on the attendance of each home game. That perennial strugglers like the Sky Blues could even attract such a big name was heralded as a triumph for chairman Bryan Richardson.

In **DUBLIN'S** *FAIR* **CITY.**

THE UNOFFICIAL FANZINE OF COVENTRY CITY F.C.

Claridge celebrates his winning goal

Hello Boys

ISSUE **10** End of season 1996/7 **£1**

Few fans cared that he was a reject from our fiercest rivals, Aston Villa. Fewer still voiced disapproval of a self-proclaimed boyhood Villa fan taking controls of the Sky Blues. Instead the buzz was that Big Ron always won things. More specifically he won cups, which is all any realistic Coventry fan dare aspire to. So we turned up and waited for the inevitable triumph, secretly hoping that it would be a second victorious campaign in the FA Cup rather than a first success in that lesser competition, the one with the fizzy drink title.

Now the orange tan of the once great man has faded. To spend £16 million on a squad that only managed to avoid relegation on the final day of the season (and only then on goal difference) seems faintly scandalous. When this season kicked off Big Ron had a new parade of glittering stars from exotic climes to dazzle us. On the Saturday before the kick-off proper, the latest signing Regis Genaux was introduced to the fans before a friendly against Benfica. Surely this was just a taste of the great European adventures we would soon to be embarking upon. That sunny afternoon the reality of our true situation was brought home as Benfica destroyed the Sky Blues 7-2 without really trying; even bringing on nine substitutes in the second half to emphasise the difference between their weakest players and our strongest. Needless to say, Regis didn't stay long.

The problem in City's defence and lack of bite up front were re-emphasised the following Saturday when a very poor Forest side beat the Sky Blues with a Kevin Campbell hat-trick. They could've scored another six. Still Big Ron failed to face the truth and argued that success was just around the corner. The fans, however, had learnt that just like in the Hans Christian Anderson fairy tale, this emperor's gowns had no fabric to them.

Our season's condition deteriorated as weakness turned to utter feebleness. The only real passion came from the management team as they fumed about referees' inadequacies without quite noticing the irony of their comments. The best of these displays of playground sulking came from wee Strachan who refused to leave the pitch for 15 minutes after being dismissed in a crucial reserve game against West Brom. If only such fire and commitment could have been exhibited by the team we might not have had to rely on others losing their final game to guarantee our Premiership salvation. Finally the 'Big Man' had to go. A Cup exit at home to Gillingham and a draw with mighty Woking signalled the transfer of leadership from Big Ron to Little Gordon.

In the end, Ron, that great media manipulator, wasn't even able to stage-manage his own departure. News was leaked, possibly through a director, to the Mirror newspaper. Big Ron was not happy. In a display of purposeful aggression that has been sadly lacking from his team, he pointed the finger at Geoffrey Robinson, the Labour MP whose funds helped buy club captain Gary McAllister. "It was leaked by a member of the board," he fumed, "I shan't name the person, but put it this way, I shall be voting Tory at the next election." And there we were assuming he was a member of the Socialist Workers Party...

As for Big Ron's history at Coventry; he presided over 14 wins in 68 league games and early cup exits in all attempts. On passing over the mantle to his assistant he left the club firmly embedded in our second home - the relegation zone. For all Coventry's three decades in the elite of English football we have had to struggle on minimal resources and players nobody else wanted. Our one moment of triumph, the FA Cup win of 1987, was achieved with players other clubs had either rejected or overlooked. Our only other successes have been the perennial last minute escapes from relegation.

It wasn't really the sort of history that had room for a character with the moniker 'Big'. The only big thing in our history is Jimmy Hill's chin and even that left us for the glamour and bright lights of Fulham.

On Atkinson's departure Gordon Strachan said "Ron has been a one-off, the last of the great character managers who can run a club on their personality and knowledge. His like will not be seen again."

Phew... Let's hope not - in Coventry at least.

On the night of his departure Ron hosted a party for his players (many supporters held similar celebrations of their own). Even Ron's parties, however, are not without problems and sure enough the players showed the same lack of judgement, team spirit and responsibility off the pitch as they had on it. Allegedly, Dion Dublin and Noel Whelan had a fight after a 'love-bite' prank by the latter, while Noel added to his problems by driving home under the influence of alcohol. His resultant court appearance showed he'd had as much success shaking off the police as he'd had losing opposition defenders during the season.

After a few teething troubles Gordon's new, more puritanical regime seemed to be working. His purchase of Darren Huckerby was inspirational. The year ended with four wins in a row (our best run for ten years) and a Manager of the Month award for the little Scot. Had we finally turned the corner? Had we heck! Our best chance of a return to Wembley was thwarted on the mud at Derby. In the league our new captain McAllister played with himself while our new international defenders Breen and Evtushok threw games away, and only the return of Gordon onto the pitch at 40 years of age brought any glimmer of hope for our Premiership survival. Evtushok even suffered the indignity of a first half substitution at Old Trafford after our expensive new back four - no, back three, no sorry, back five - scored two cracking own goals in the first five minutes to ensure the Champions weren't put under any stress. Unexpected wins away at Liverpool and at home to Chelsea threw us a lifeline, but the players' attempts to grab it failed miserably and we lost our last home game to Derby. As a result Coventry City indulged in their perennial last day 'must win our own game and others must lose theirs' struggle. Incredibly, for the tenth time in our 30 years at the bottom of the top, the Sky Blues shone through at the final hurdle. While Middlesbrough and Sunderland floundered we managed an incredibly tense win at Tottenham to ensure another season at the trough of TV gold.

Ten years ago Coventry City won the FA Cup and looked to a brighter future, hinting at European adventures and fighting off a predatory approach for Cyrille Regis from Ajax manager Cruyff. So it is a bit of a shame that the name still most associated with the Sky Blues is not a footballer at all, but that of Harry Houdini. At the beginning of the season Total Sport magazine asked for my ambitions for the forthcoming campaign. I replied that I merely hoped for survival on goal difference, and at the final reckoning the Sky Blues went one better than that. As a result, Coventry will not be playing first division football next year, even though most of the squad were playing first division football this year - and there lay the cause of our problems.

INTO THE O'S ZONE

Leyton Orient

In this very book last year, I was full of optimism. The O's had just beaten Wales 2-1 and we had signed quality players in Alvin Martin and Les Sealey. What a prat! (Me, that is!) Nothing had really changed.

Les Sealey played just 12 league games and returned to West Ham, whilst Alvin Martin managed a massive 16 league appearances before he quit the game! Other new signings included Martin Ling (a quality player, or so we thought), Justin Channing and Dominic Naylor. There was also Dave Martin, who'd apparently won promotion with nearly every club he'd ever played for. His Orient

Into The O's Zone

THE FANZINE FORMERLY KNOWN AS FRANKLY SPEAKING

Issue Number 40   Month: September/October 1996

Just 60p

THE ORIENT FANZINE

Les: Alvin, Why Are We Joining A Club Like Leyton Orient??

Alvin: Don't worry, Les. By Christmas, I'll be Manager and you'll be my Assistant!!

career was, er, brief, when the club discovered that Dave was a bit of a thug. Two of the best rumours surrounding his sacking involved a fight with Alvin Martin and the scrawling of graffiti on the bog walls and in the dressing room.

And who'd given us all these luminaries of the modern game? None other than our manager Pat Holland. He'd stated on a number of occasions his ambition to take us out of the Third Division, and *ITOZ* reckoned that with the squad he was assembling he'd probably do it... Now where do Rushden and Diamonds play?

The season began with a 0-1 home defeat by Scunthorpe, and it sort of set the tone for the season. We dominated and had loads of clear chances, but there was no-one capable of putting the ball in the net. For ages, it looked as if our top scorer was going to be Colin West with a massive three goals; and he'd been injured from January onwards!

The Coca Cola cup came and went (it never seems fair that a club with our away record has to play a home *and* away leg). At our second league match we witnessed the sight of Lincoln manager John Beck being arrested (honest!) just before the kick off at Sincil Bank. Deep into injury time, Lincoln were holding onto to a 1-0 lead and their 'keeper was penalised for time-wasting. Ian Hendon stepped up to take the free kick and wallop! The ball flew into the net for a late, *late* equaliser. At the final whistle their 'keeper went mental, and I'm not sure which bit of the ref he wanted to shake.

I've already touched on our away record, but for those of you unacquainted with the O's on their travels you might like to know that since 1993 we've won just once: Northampton away (with a last minute winner) in September 1995. This season the kind fixture computer had given us a September away fixture on exactly the same day. Surely we couldn't win again, could we? At 0-0 in injury time it looked highly unlikely, but then Danny Chapman fired in a shot from the edge of the area, the 'keeper was beaten all ends up, and the ball struck the inside of the post before nestling in the empty net. Unbelievable! The away end erupted and the O's had recorded their second away win in just under three years. And if you hadn't already guessed, our opponents that night were none other than Northampton. *Double* unbelievable!

We followed this up with a 2-0 win at Mansfield, but we weren't fooled; we were a crap side going nowhere, and changes were needed. After Mansfield, a run of one win in eight saw Pat Holland sacked and replaced, temporarily at least, by his assistant Tommy Cunningham. Tommy's first game in charge resulted in a 0-1 home defeat by Scarborough and all sorts of stories about how Barry Hearn had announced that he'd picked the team only to deny it once we had lost! Whoever *had* picked the team, they'd given a debut to Luke Weaver, our England Under-19 goalkeeper. This kid is one of the O's best ever prospects and by the season's end he'd trained with Manchester United and West Ham. We all realise that it's not a case of 'if' but 'when' he goes, and how much we get.

Then it was all change at the top, as ex-O's player Tommy Taylor bid farewell to Cambridge United and took up the reigns. One of his first actions was to raid his old club and bring back Scott McGleish, who'd been banging in the goals for Cambridge. After just three games in charge Taylor took his new team back to the Abbey Stadium, and in a hostile atmosphere, McGleish missed a sitter as we lost 2-0.

Taylor's next signing has to go down as one of Barry Hearn's most successful publicity stunts, when Peter Shilton joined us tantalisingly close to the magic figure of 1,000 league appearances. *Sky* got very excited about the prospect of witnessing such a milestone and televised our last home game before Christmas against Brighton. Whatever you think about Shilton as a man, it was a truly remarkable footballing achievement and 9,000 people turned up to pay their tributes. Whatever you think about Barry Hearn, there was no denying that it was a brilliant publicity coup.

Despite the signing of Shilton and other old pros such as Chris Whyte, Roger Joseph and Ray Wilkins, the O's continued to be crap; three wins in four games over Christmas was followed by a run of one win in ten games... then came Brighton away.

The game was a thriller. The scoring went Brighton 2-0, then the O's led 3-2 and 4-3 before Brighton grabbed a late equaliser. The afternoon, though, will be remembered for all the wrong reasons. When we scored our fourth, Scott McGleish celebrated with his customary somersault. Inciting the crowd? Hardly; he celebrates *every* goal this way. On came three Brighton idiots; their targets were McGleish and the ref. Ray Wilkins put in his best tackle in an O's shirt to stop one bloke reaching the ref, but these were disgraceful scenes. Celebrating goals is all part of the game; Peter Beagrie and Asprilla love a somersault, Fowler, Wright, Klinsmann and Ravanelli are not averse to a bit of theatricals, but none of them have ever been attacked for doing it. Yet all we heard was "Orient players incited the crowd."

The FA launched an enquiry into the pitch invasion and charges of crowd incitement against the O's players. There are a couple of major problems with the case against the O's: (a) Why was the ref attacked? And (b) Why did the ref praise the Orient players for their actions? If you ever get the chance, check out the TV coverage of this incident. A packed stand of Brighton supporters shows nothing but horror as the events unravelled before their eyes. Surely, if the O's players had been inciting the crowd, the Brighton fans' reaction would have been different. Anyway, enough's enough and let's hope our games with Brighton this year still attract close on 20,000 people, but without any problems at all.

Our season drifted on after this. Surprising wins over the Easter weekend away at Scunthorpe and at home to Carlisle secured our place in the Football League, and under Tommy Taylor things seem to be falling into place. So on the playing side at least we can feel a little more optimistic.

Off the field, things aren't looking so good. Our ground redevelopment plans were based on funding from the National Lottery, but this has been turned down. Still, we do have Leyton's most expensive car park in its place. And while you need fans behind the goals to really liven things up at the ground, no-one among the 3 to 4,000 O's die-hards can ever say that life is ever dull with Barry around!

IRON FILINGS

Scunthorpe United

A review can be a little repetitive when your subject is a team that has won nothing for nearly 40 years, been stuck in the same division for the last 13 and whose only claim to national fame in the last twelve months was as the subject of an embarrassing TV commercial by the Royal Mail.

So, leaving the usual tale of woe about yet another boring, mid-table season until a little later, let's get the few vaguely interesting bits out of the way first for the 'stattos' amongst you:

1. We won the Lincolnshire Cup for the first time since 1977.
2. We won at Exeter for the first time in 18 visits since 1965.
3. When our youth coach Paul Wilson was pressed into action as a substitute at Cardiff at the age of 36, he became the oldest player to make his Football League debut since 1929.

And that was about it really. Nothing much else out of the ordinary happened. Oh, we did sack the manager but that's now an annual event, of course. And Samways did make that monumental goalkeeping error against Wrexham to get us knocked out of the FA Cup with West Ham waiting in the next round - but I'm sure it's in the competition rules that Scunthorpe aren't allowed to reach the third round anyway.

And so, back to the boring bit and the team's fortunes in the league. 'Water' and 'treading' were the two words that sprang to mind as yet another Iron season ground to a mid-table conclusion. In the aforementioned 13 seasons it's now five years since we even came within touching distance of the promised land of Division Two. And this campaign pretty much followed the pattern of the previous four - high hopes to begin with, largely uninspiring throughout and ending in the usual undignified and unsuccessful scramble for the last play-off spot.

For those unfamiliar with a typical Scunthorpe season, I can offer a brief résumé:

August: Almost always yields an away win on the first Saturday, a good home win in the Coca Cola against higher grade opposition but then a swift exit after a defeat in the return. League forms tails away towards the end of the month.

September/October: Normally indifferent as we settle into our customary mid-table position. Money often squandered on an ageing lower division journeyman unwanted by any other club, as manager realises team isn't up to it.

Pre-Christmas: Several games without a win, followed by several games unbeaten. Still mid-table. Exit FA Cup in round two after a replay having landed a 'biggie' in round three.

Post-Christmas: Several games without a win, followed by several games unbeaten. Mid-table, but manager making "don't panic, we can still reach the play-offs" noises.

February/March: Sack manager (not unheard of to dish out the P45 only a fortnight after he's received the Manager of the Month award).

April/May: New manager inspires a lengthy unbeaten run to falsely raise those play-off hopes. Fall short by a considerable margin and finish in mid-table with everyone thinking "it's looking good for next year."

In a nutshell, that was the story of Scunthorpe's '96-97 campaign - and one or two others before it, come to that. We are now in exactly the same position as we were twelve months ago, with a new manager preparing to start his first full season at the helm in charge of a mid-table team. Perhaps things will get better. But we thought that this time last year, too.

To be fair, there did seem some cause for optimism. Mick Buxton wasn't everyone's cup of tea but having succeeded Dave Moore as manager he'd steadied a sinking ship at the tail end of the previous season, and looked to have strengthened the side with a couple of decent acquisitions. In came Mark Sertori from Bury, reputedly a reasonable lower division centre-half, and part-timer Dave Moss from Chesterfield, who was expected to boost the midfield (he lasted little more than a month after moving to Scotland to work and signing for Partick Thistle!).

Initially, things did look promising as we opened with our now customary away win on the first Saturday, Phil Clarkson scoring in a 1-0 victory at Leyton Orient. Clarkson, in fact, was to score in each of the first three games as we followed the Orient success with a 2-1 home win over Blackpool in the Coca Cola Cup and, incredibly, a 1-0 triumph over Torquay in the Glanford Park league-opener. I say incredible because it was the first time Scunthorpe United had ever won both of their first two league matches since becoming a Football League club in 1950!

At this point, the Third Division table provided the rather unnerving sight of Hartlepool and Scunthorpe setting the pace as the only two sides with maximum points. 'Pool were top by virtue of having scored more goals, thus depriving us of appearing at the head of any league table since November 1982. Alright, so it was only after two games but these things matter! When they failed to win their third outing, we could have gone top by beating Scarborough at Glanford Park. For the first 15 minutes, United played like men possessed, pinning the visitors back into their own penalty area with some tremendous football. But games, of course, last considerably longer than a quarter of an hour, and we went on to lose 2-0. We would never reach the giddy heights of second again.

The Scarborough defeat burst the bubble of early season optimism and a run of only one win in eight league games suggested all was not right. The team was struggling to score goals, with the recognised strike force of Andy McFarlane and John Eyre failing to come up with the goods, and looked vulnerable at the back, conceding two goals virtually every game. For the second season running, a low point was reached at Hereford's Edgar Street. Last season we'd been gubbed 3-0 on a wet and thoroughly miserable Tuesday night in December; less than a year later, we again faced the long trip to cider country in midweek, and slumped to 19th after going down 3-2.

It was obvious that something had to be done as this was getting serious. No-one dared mention the prospect of relegation. To their credit, Buxton and the board actually did come up with a signing. Much-travelled striker Paul Baker wanted a move from Torquay to be nearer to his roots in the North East and wound up at Glanford Park, scoring on his debut in a memorable Humberside derby win at Hull. He went on to solve the goal-scoring crisis for a while (finding the net 14 times before moving on again in March to rejoin his old club Hartlepool) and helped inspire a run of five games unbeaten in October.

This was only following our typical pattern, however. After a blip of three defeats in a row at the end of October and beginning of November, we then won four on the trot to climb as high as fifth by mid-December. Cue the inevitable slump (only one win in 11 league and cup games) and Buxton - the right man for the job less than a year earlier, according to the board - was out of that job by mid-February, sacked by Scunthorpe for the second time in six years. His last game in charge was a 2-0 home defeat by Chester in front of the lowest ever crowd for a league game at Glanford Park. Things could only get better, and they did - immediately.

The new 'right man for the job' was already on the playing staff as the board turned to Brian Laws, formerly the boss of our much-loved (not) local rivals Grimsby and signed by Buxton as a player little more than a month earlier. Five wins in six games, four of them away, promptly revived the season, so much so that going into the Easter programme we were only four points off the play-offs with a game in hand.

"Would this finally be our year?" wondered the few remaining optimists amongst the Iron faithful. "Unlikely," thought the realists, who were quickly proved right when the team's old inadequacies resurfaced in a disastrous 2-1 home defeat by Leyton Orient. A 3-2 defeat at Scarborough on Easter Monday effectively ended the season, and with defeat at Lincoln even the 'mathematical chance' had passed.

So, what is to be made of yet another ordinary season?

Finishing 13th could certainly be described as disappointing but was no more than we deserved. Nine home defeats was only one short of the club record and no team can possibly expect to win promotion when losing so many on their own pitch. The away record stood comparison with most in the Third Division, though four of our seven wins on the road came in successive games straight after Laws' appointment. Has any other manager ever won his first four away games, I wonder?

It was soon clear from an early stage that the ageing defence pieced together by Mick Buxton was not up to the task and some were discarded well before the end of the term. One club record that was smashed during the season was for the most number of league games without keeping a clean sheet - which just about sums up the inefficiencies at the back. Up front, McFarlane was off-loaded to Torquay in January after scoring just three times; Eyre, not exactly a recognised scorer anyway, mustered only eight, which left two players who didn't even finish the season in Scunthorpe colours as the leading scorers - Clarkson, sold to Blackpool in February, with 13 and Baker with 14.

Laws has clearly recognised the need for a major revamp, releasing eight players and introducing a number of new, younger faces such as defender Sean McAuley from Hartlepool, midfielder Justin Walker from Notts Forest and striker Jamie Forrester from Grimsby.

Yet again, we will go into a new season hoping 'the right man for the job' will actually get it right for once.

This Valentine's Day why not treat your loved one to a box of Scunthorpe United Chocolates...

Available from
Son of a Referee Products Ltd

JAN 3RD 1988

Portsmouth

What do you do when you've just escaped relegation by the skin of your teeth, failed to significantly strengthen the team or improve the ground and some of your fans have forced the abandonment of a pre-season friendly in France with an on-pitch protest against the chairman and the state he's got the club into? Easy. You merely recruit a man who has just become a national hero by leading England to the semi-finals of a major tournament. An unlikely scenario, admittedly, but it's what Pompey managed last August. And one year on, we have to say that it worked.

Terry Venables arrived at

January 3, '88 says: "Oh Stockport we love you..."

VENABLES PICKS UP ANOTHER BARGAIN

Inside: FC Martigues: Special Report, My Hero, Souness Tory Poster Rip-Off, Dodgy Haircuts (No, not the editor's!), De Sisto plus all your old favourites and much, much more!

Fratton Park only days before the new campaign got under way in a blaze of publicity. Even after his high profile introduction (at home to Bristol City, I'm afraid) many believed his stay would be as short as the odds on the Scummers struggling in the Premiership.

But the doubters have been proved wrong. During the season he took up the option of buying majority control for £1, not such a bargain when you realised how much debt the club was in, and became chairman. How long he'll be around for remains anyone's guess, but the fact he's stayed this long has already surprised many. And few would disagree that El Tel's involvement was one of the major factors why a bottom four finish in '96 was replaced by a top seven finish last May.

There were times early in the season when his arrival appeared to be making little difference. True, we played some pretty football, but while that was good enough to see off Leyton Orient in the Coca Cola Cup it wasn't going to stop us leaking too many goals and hitting an alarming slump in results away from home. But things began to turn around when, for once, early season transfer activity saw decent players arriving rather than leaving. David Hillier joined from Arsenal and Mathias Svensson came from, er, Sweden to become an instant cult hero. Shock horror, the squad was getting an unusually solid look about it.

Watching Pompey at Fratton also gave a new perspective because we all had to sit down. For ages the atmosphere was dreadful as only half the former terracing was covered by seating, but gradually enough loose change was unearthed from beneath the sofas in the Patrons' Lounge to pay the workmen to install some more. By the time Manchester City were beaten by one of the goals of the season from Fitzroy Simpson, the new-look and near-full Fratton was looking and sounding much better.

It was around this time that the presence in the team of rookie goalkeeper Aaron Flahavan began to cause more than a murmur of protest. He had been preferred to legendary crowd favourite Alan Knight from day one, but had begun to drop clangers (not to mention shots and crosses) too often. When his worst mistake of the lot cost us a home defeat by Swindon on Boxing Day, even Terry Fenwick had to admit it was time for the regal one's return. Two days later at Port Vale and a rousing *Three Lions* chorus of "He's back in goal, he's back in goal, he's back in, Knightsie's back in goal" welcomed back our favoured custodian and with him a dramatic improvement in our fortunes.

For two months we found ourselves watching a Rolls Royce of a team; January saw us claim a cup victory at Wolves and three points at Palace - a particularly satisfying experience made even more enjoyable by the inept finishing of Scummer Neil Shipperley - plus wins against a handful of mediocre teams at home. We were now in the fifth round of the FA Cup and getting dangerously close to the nosebleed territory of the playoff zone. What a contrast then to our usually dependable but prone to breaking down C-reg Escort squad.

Could it continue? Well, despite the cup draw sending us to Leeds, yes. We were on a roll and tight Premiership defences weren't going to stop us. Even George's miserly Leeds couldn't stop us scoring three times on a glorious afternoon that was as good as any of our big occasions of recent years. When a week later we cruised to another away league win at West Brom, people were being excused for getting carried away. "The best team we've had in years." "Automatic promotion could still be on." Such words didn't appear an exaggeration. Boss Fenwick, never the most popular figure among Pompey's fans, even got to hear his name sung instead of used in the same sentence as a stream of expletives. Progress indeed.

We were riding the crest of the wave but we almost expected to fall at some time. Sheffield United and Manchester City gave us a gentle nudge by drawing successive games, then Chelsea came along and ducked us under the surface for a full 90 minutes... annihilation in the cup quarter-final was numbing and humiliating. And it was a moot point afterwards whether we ever really fully recovered from the beating.

In our hearts we probably knew we wouldn't finish in the top six; Pompey aren't the sort of team to put a stunning run together and then keep up the momentum. We like pressure and produce some of our best displays when the heat's on, but when it's off then we're all to ready to ease down a gear; witness a run-in that regularly featured a sequence of WLWL. So when we beat Barnsley in one of the most exhilarating matches Fratton Park had seen for years, it was too little too late - not that we admitted as much during our post-match euphoria. Our final home game against Ipswich three days later couldn't have been more different. Three things always happen at home to Ipswich: it always rains; they always nick a goal; we never equalise. Guess what the final score was? And yes, it rained.

The only way we could win promotion now was simple: Palace couldn't pick up more than a point from their last two games, Port Vale had to do the same and we had to score 18 goals at Wolves. See, simple! I even contemplated the impossible in my darker moments of desperation... and now it's off to the videprinter - Wolves 17 (seventeen) Portsmouth 18 (eighteen), extraordinary. Our plans to play eleven up front were just taking shape when Palace went and beat Swindon - why are they always involved in our failures? - to make promotion mathematically impossible.

While Pompey fans could've been excused for slitting their wrists on a sharp piece of North terrace plastic seating or throwing themselves off the South's TV gantry, we actually took this narrow miss quite well. No doubt something to do with the fact that we were clearly much better off than we had been twelve months earlier.

So although it started out a bit flat at Molineux, we soon realised that Wolves were poor enough to allow us to enjoy ourselves and let our hosts know in no uncertain terms that while we weren't going anywhere, neither were they. "Down with the Pompey, you're staying sown with the Pompey," we sang as we eased to a 1-0 win. "We'll be back again next year," we told them, and of course we were right.

So off we went for our summer break with Barnsley's unlikely, and surely for one year only, elevation making us the division's longest-serving members. And yet the prospect of Prenton Park, the County Ground, Bramall Lane and Carrow Road doesn't seem quite as depressing as usual. Maybe that's because we have quite a handful of new grounds to visit - thanks to relocations as much as an unfashionable-looking Second Division promotion frame - or perhaps it's because our hearts are telling us that if a summer without hope can turn into a near miss, then a summer *with* hope might just result in glory.

With a chairman and manager taking the club in the right direction, Pompey fans for once can look forward with justified optimism. No more demos and a bit of stability (shit, what are we going to put in the fanzine next year?) has some of us thinking that the future's so bright we gotta wear shades (who *did* sing that?). So if you're down the bookies this summer put a few quid on a Pompey promotion. But you might also want to have a side bet on us still being in Division One come August 1998 with an opening fixture against, er, Wolves.

KEEGAN WAS CRAP REALLY

Doncaster Rovers

The Only Way is Down

The '96-97 season started with a bang for the Belle Vue boys. After Graham Jones was sold in a much publicised move to Wigan, Sammy Chung and assistant George Foster were sacked upon turning up for the first game of the season. Veteran striker Kerry Dixon was put 'in charge', and the season got off to an uneasy start. This was illustrated by the disastrous defeat at bottom of the table Rochdale, who despite having two men sent off came back from behind to win 2-1.

The season was also hard on the supporters. Prices remained at a division high of £8 to stand and a tenner to sit in what is arguably (not!) the worst ground in the league. We also had to contend with Tuesday and Friday night trips to Exeter, Torquay, Cambridge, Swansea and Cardiff. Who programs the bloody fixture computer? Couldn't they supply them with a copy of *Autoroute*? Six hundred plus miles on a Tuesday night? Do me a favour!

Another season with 40 plus players didn't provide much stability. Some of the good 'uns included Darren Moore, Colin Cramb, Paul Birch, Dean Williams and Ian Gore. Some of the bad 'uns were Simon Black, Alan Fahy, Darren Esdaille (this man is just so poor it's unbelievable; ask anyone who witnessed him at Brighton), Lee Warren, David Larmour and Steve Walker. Unfortunately some of them never even played for the first team and just took money every week for nothing. We've also been to see those nice men at FA HQ over alleged illegal approaches to players by Droylsedon and Hyde. I wish I could say that it was worth it but the players that we got were no better than the ones we already had (and in some cases far worse).

Games that stand out in the memory include, much to our surprise, a few wins. A 2-1 over Scunthorpe, while not a shock was still a pleasant experience, as were our away wins at Cardiff (Utley from the *half way line!*), Cambridge (how did they get to third?), Darlo and Hartlepool, not to mention a brilliant home win against Wigan (suck on that Jonesy!). The defeats that stand out include (spoilt for choice really) Rochdale away, Chester away (0-6),

Torquay away (my personal favourite, non-stop party) and Leyton Orient for the demonstrations.

The main breaking point came in February at a supporters' meeting. Kerry Dixon and general manager Mark Weaver admitted that Kerry was "not in charge of team affairs." Later they claimed they'd been misquoted by the press, but those present knew the truth. The team was instead being picked by the interesting character know as Ken Richardson, who likes to be called the club's 'benefactor'. He is in fact a major shareholder and adviser to the majority shareholder Dinard (who incidentally no longer support the Rovers financially). It was also revealed that popular midfielder Paul Birch was not being allowed to play because of an alleged argument with Mr Richardson.

The season finished on a high and then came down with a thump. The game at Brighton, where we thought violence would never be far away, was great to see, especially when at the end the fans joined together singing and digging up lumps of turf. But the last day of the season was the main one for us. In the programme Mark Weaver claimed that Dixon's first year in management was "A Disaster" and it was only Ken Richardson's involvement that saved us. Funny then how the fans gave Dixon their full backing while calling for the removal of Richardson and Weaver, a saga which looks set to continue next season.

As the season finished it became more and more clear that our star players (yes we did have some!) were out of contract and reluctant to sign new ones. At the time of writing, Darren Moore has signed for Bradford and Colin Cramb and Dean Williams are almost certain to leave. Moore's departure is a mixed blessing. Although it has probably damaged our chances of staying in the league (yes, we are that optimistic) it should pay for the £100,000 safety work needed for the San Siro of Yorkshire. To anyone visiting our fine home next year, do not expect any improvements (especially you, Scarborough). Belle Vue is without doubt the worst ground in the Football League (we won something at last), but we love it and it's our home. At least it's not the Lego sets of Scunthorpe and Chester. It also has a nature garden that masquerades as the Town End Terrace which has been closed for over two years. We're expecting Swampy to come round when we eventually get round to clearing it up.

And for those of you that don't think that Rovers are a fashionable club, we can jump on the bandwagon with the best of 'em. Like so many other small clubs, we too have acquired the ultimate street-cred accessory - an administrator - after the Inland Revenue took us to court over £250,000.

KICKER CONSPIRACY

Burnley

At the source of the fountain of all football, all we got was another season in Division 2

Following England's success in Euro '96 we were on a high. Moves were afoot to sign an unlikely-sounding Portuguese player named Bambo, season ticket sales were up and the air was thick with optimism. There was talk of changing our traditional strip for one designed by Adidas featuring Claret and Blue quarters, and the CISA (Clarets Independent Supporters Association) was formed to promote dialogue between the club and the fans (thanks go to PNEISA for their guidance). The

Kicker Conspiracy

I bet you hate us now Stockport!

BARNES' FIFTH SYMPHONY PERFECT TIMING !

The BURNLEY fanzine produced by the HUDDERSFIELD CLARETS

Issue No 2 : October 1996

Fans !
Remember !!
Still only £1

two new double-decker stands that took the place of The Longside and The Beehole added a new dimension to the home of football, and despite the club insisting that they be called the North and East stands, they retained their traditional names to the fans.

By October, things on the pitch were going reasonably well, but the team was a bit inconsistent and it was obvious that more new faces were needed to maintain a serious promotion challenge. The Barnes and Nogan partnership was showing signs of working well, and Barnes scored five goals against that sorry bunch whose fans think we're some sort of rivals. Look Stockport, we don't care about you! Rivalry is about tradition not jealousy, and we still only hate Bastard Rovers.

Despite our smart new stands there were still some constant annoyances at home games including crap stewards (if you pay peanuts you get monkeys), expensive food and drink and, apart from Preston, a general measly away following at Turf Moor which did nothing for the atmosphere. But it was good to hear *Tom Hawk* by the Piranhas being played when the team came out.

By Christmas we were looking good at home, but the away form was again letting us down. Yet the team couldn't complain about the backing they received on the rare occasions they actually attacked the home defences. Never more so than when we went to Anfield in the third round of the FA Cup and only lost to a solitary Stan Collymore goal. The short-sighted press may have criticised Adrian Heath's tactics for being too defensive, but what we were supposed to do, throw caution to the wind, get murdered, and in the process lose all dignity and self respect? I think not.

The media exposure continued with our televised *Sky* game against Bury. We turned on a treat for the cameras and stuffed the eventual Champions 3-1 in front of a big crowd.

Meanwhile Kurt Nogan, whose alleged drinking habits became legion in his short stay, got all primadonna-ish and threatened to leave in the summer under the Bosman ruling if the club didn't cough up some extra dosh. Thankfully the club reacted dead right to Kurt's tantrums by putting him on the list and allowing him to sod off to Preston for whatever they could get. No player is bigger than the club, especially not a big-headed one. With Nogan gone, the door opened for a rising young star Andy Cooke, and he did a fine job strutting his stuff.

Anyway, it was a pretty ordinary season for the Clarets mainly due to the fact that most of the bottom clubs took points off us (York gleaned six!) though the side is beginning to look stronger and younger, and is trying to play attractive football.

Which brings us onto an event that was anything but ordinary. In February Brighton and Hove Albion supporters hosted their 'Fans United' day and gave supporters from all over Britain (and Europe) the chance to show their solidarity and commitment to football in one voice, in all colours. For us it was a 500 mile round trip to see a woeful team at the bottom of the Third Division. Of course, as Burnley fans, we felt some affinity with followers of a club faced with the prospect of extinction because it almost happened to us ten years ago.

It was a truly fantastic day. People were jumping out of cars to take photos of each other as fans of all ages, from all manner of different clubs walked down the street arm in arm (we had a massive Burnley FC Union Jack). I've never experienced anything like it before at a match, and I doubt I ever will again... it was genuinely moving.

Of course there was a serious message amidst all the camaraderie. The 'greed is good' mentality pervading the modern game and perpetuated by the Premier League needs to be curtailed in some way. If not, you can be sure that there will be more cases of absentee landlords trying to run clubs like Brighton into the ground in the hope of making a fast buck. At the end Brighton supporters came up to us, shook us by the hand and thanked us for coming. Well, thank you for the memory Brighton, and good luck!

As far as the forthcoming season is concerned we're going to be really bold and confidently predict that we will be promoted as Champions with Fulham trailing us home as runners up. We'll then take up our rightful place in Division 1, and with a bit of luck Blackburn will have been relegated and we will once again be able to play our much-loved derby games. THE CLARETS ARE GOING UP!

KING OF THE KIPPAX

Manchester City

Last year Alan Ball enhanced his reputation as a relegation specialist by taking Manchester City into the real Second Division. The fans had stood by the club in their hour of need, but they'd failed to deliver. No surprises there then.

A few weeks later the bookmakers forgot how hapless we were and installed City as favourites for promotion. On the surface they had good reason. We had potentially the biggest crowds in the best ground, and our overall record for winning major trophies was better than any other Nationwide League team. Don't laugh at the last statistic; it may be hard to believe but it's true.

Unfortunately grounds, crowds and trophies won over 20 years ago don't guarantee points, so what else did we have going for us? Well, there was Niall Quinn, good in the air and underrated on the ground, who would be a handful for defenders and Keith Curle, whose pace would snuff out the opponents attacks. And of course there was Kinkladze, the most gifted player in the division, who would do whatever he wanted in midfield. Chairman Lee and manager Ball told us that the squad were good enough to bounce straight back, and that team strengthening wasn't needed. All this made more sense.

So what went wrong, you may ask. Basically, Quinn and Curle went before the kick-off and we set about trying to gain promotion without a hint of pace anywhere in the team. More to the point, we retained the services of Alan Ball. Only two people rated his ability as manager: Franny Lee and Ball himself.

Friday August 16th. A chance to try out my seat in the new Kippax Stand as City and Ipswich convinced the nation that *Sky*'s Friday night *Nationwide League Football* is a great cure for insomnia. Despite the best efforts of our defence, a bit of magic from Gio and the head of Steve Lomas gave us a 1-0 win.

But Bolton immediately put paid to our 100% record and by the end of our third game, with City 2-0 down at the Victoria Ground and with both sets of fans suggesting that the squeaky loser should seek alternative employment, Ball was gone: sacked or resigned depending on who you believed. Asa Hartford reluctantly took control (he'd stated he didn't want the job full-time even though Lee's programme notes said he did!) and for six weeks speculation was rife about who might take charge. All the usual names were mentioned: George Graham, Dalglish and Big Fat Ron but in truth very few fancied working with our ex-England International chairman.

Just when we thought it couldn't get any worse, along came Lincoln City in the Coca Cola and Dave Bassett. Still managerless, but with strong rumours of Bassett's imminent arrival, we arrived at Sincil Bank and were 1-0 up within 60 seconds. Eighty nine and a bit minutes later we were 4-1 down, and the following morning Bassett decided to stay at Palace. In the return Lincoln won 1-0 at Maine Road and 5-1 on aggregate, which gave us our heaviest two-leg defeat in nearly 20 years.

If Franny was desperate before, he was apoplectic after Coppell came, saw, panicked and ran away after less than five weeks, leaving Phil Neal to pick up the reins till Christmas. Coppell's departure is still a mystery. He simply claimed he was not the man for the job, but we suspected something else was getting to him. Rumours spread about his sex life, gay friends and rent boys. It may have been nonsense but it was marginally more palatable than accepting that we were broke and Coppell had left because money promised for team strengthening had not been forthcoming. The fans who had stood by Franny and Ball were getting more than a little upset. Home defeats by Oxford and Tranmere were followed by after-match protests, and it was only the sudden appearance of a £10m share issue which enabled Lee to survive the AGM.

On the pitch things continued to slide. We didn't even have an unbeaten run to speak of as every win or draw was followed by a defeat. We had expected this to be a tough division; we had expected to be kicked out of a few games, but we never expected to be beaten fairly and squarely by Barnsley and Reading. The final straw came during the so-called festive season with losses against Oldham, Port Vale and Barnsley. Earlier in the month Phil Neal had issued a "Back me or sack me" statement. Oops, timing is everything Phil. And so it came to pass that as 1996 became 1997, Frank Clark was appointed as the latest incumbent of the Maine Road hot-seat.

The first two games of the year were postponed (although we did win a cup tie at Brentford according to the Pools panel), and Frank eventually opened his account with a draw against Palace. Time for a cup run, we thought, but Brentford had similar ideas and were kind enough to have their pitch declared unfit only 90 minutes before kick-off, ensuring that a couple of thousand City fans would endure the misery of the M6, M1 (or M40), M25 and M4 for nothing. Our first trip to the McAlpine Stadium saw another 1-1 draw and the start of our first unbeaten run. Brentford finally staged the FA Cup tie at the third attempt and Nicky Summerbee put us into round four.

A dour and disciplined draw took our unbeaten league run to three games, but the match against Sheffield United will be remembered for the pathetic comments made by Alan Ball on *Granada Soccer Night*. Our performance may have been uninspiring, but the players Ball criticised were either bought or regularly picked by him. Elton Welsby, the GSN presenter, has no time for City and was quite happy to encourage Ball. All this was too much for Frank. The gloves were off.

Four days later we went to the Manor Ground for a live Sunday game. The Granada TV region were about to get a shock. So were Oxford United. Come to think of it, so were the City fans. An own goal gave us the lead before two classics from Kinkladze made it 3-0. The travelling fans alternated between "What the F**k is going on?," the club anthem over the past decade and "3-0, it's just like watching Brazil," etc. Silly defending made it 3-1 but Uwe poked home a fourth for us just before the end. We also hit the woodwork twice and had a clear penalty turned down. Are you watching Alan Ball?

Watford were removed from the FA Cup without too much bother and Southend went home with a 3-0 defeat as our unbeaten league run reached five games. Finally our fears were realised, when we were kicked, punched and cheated out of a match. Ravanelli kicked Brightwell, Festa punched Lomas, Brightwell had a goal disallowed for offside and a foul on Dickov in the area was ignored. If you want to know what tips Robson picked up from Ferguson, ask any City or Chesterfield fan, or maybe a referee's bank manager (allegedly).

The Boro game also reminded us of the turmoil that can be created by our ticket office. Twelve windows but never all open, a dial-a-seat service which is permanently engaged and a fax-a-seat service which forgets to take the faxes to the ticket office. Some companies use technology to improve services. At Maine Road we use it to spread chaos.

Away from the general administrative mess the team whacked in six goals and secured six points from our next two games. That's the problem with being a City fan, there's rarely any middle ground. When they are bad they are unbelievably awful, but when they are good they are brilliant. Mediocrity is a word seldom used at Maine Road, so panicking about relegation or dreaming about the play-offs was always going to be the order of the day. After a hiccup against Pompey we beat Oldham and that meant nine games undefeated. Now for those play-offs!

Alas it was not to be. A mixture of good, bad and generally indifferent displays saw us fade at towards the end, and we finished in 14th place, our lowest ever league placing. Nevertheless, the top 12 (and highest average) Nationwide League attendances were at Maine Road; not bad considering we were in the bottom half of the table for most of the season.

As well as having tremendous home support, our travelling fans also made a lot of noise and money for the clubs good enough to give us a decent allocation of tickets. However, some just took the piss. OK, Bolton and Oxford do possess ramshackle grounds, but at least they're building new premises, so the F**k Off and Die award for '96-97 goes to Swindon Town for their ridiculous policy of herding visiting fans into uncovered seats but not allowing them to carry umbrellas when it's pissing down on them. Didn't a House of Commons Committee say something about the rights of visiting fans?

So what of the future? We are keeping Kinkladze, and if we can strengthen the team in the right areas to complement his skills, then we can challenge for promotion. Anything less just doesn't bear thinking about

LATIC FANATIC

Wigan Athletic

To coin a well-known phrase used by Del Boy in *Only Fools & Horses*: "We've done it, we've only gone and bloody well done it!" Yes, the Latics have become Champions of the Third Division for the first time in our history. We've had red letter days before - good cup runs, inaugural winners of the Freight Rover Trophy, promotion under Larry Lloyd - but never before could we say we were Champions, and what a great feeling it is!

Yet at Christmas, with Fulham holding a 15 point lead, most Latics supporters weren't talking about the Championship and would've gladly settled for automatic promotion.

And who could blame them, having been through thick and ever-thinning times during recent years? But for the players and management that wasn't good enough and the message from the dressing room was always very upbeat; "the title's there for the taking" they thundered, and when Fulham and Carlisle developed the sort of hiccups normally associated with Paul Merson on a piss-up, Latics seized their chance and grabbed the silverware. Yessss!!

However, the run-in gave us one or two heart-stopping moments to say the least. We had the usual bout of injuries, players' nerves started to jangle, but while nowhere near our best we still managed to grind out the results. Credit has to go to John Deehan for forming a strong squad of quality players, including the country's leading scorer in 33-goal Graeme Jones, but all the players came good as well and proved the bookies, who made us 6/1 favourites at the kick-off, right.

Although our away form was by no means brilliant, Deehan had at least recognised that we had to be more attack-minded if we were to avoid the instantly forgettable away trips of last season (which had cost us a play-off place). Our finest result came in a 3-0 victory at Carlisle, while the most bizarre was a 1-1 draw at Hartlepool in which we scored in the last minute and they equalised in injury time.

Promotion was gained with a tense 1-0 win over Colchester, but the title was only secured on the last day. As long as we beat Mansfield, it didn't matter what Fulham had done, but the biggest question regarding this match was whether the fanzine should go on sale beforehand. Out of 15 editions of *TLF* the embarrassing record reads: 13 matches lost, 1 won, 1 drawn. Some spectacular results attributed to the jinx include a 6-2 home defeat against Mansfield two years ago that led to the sacking of Graham Barrow, and a 2-1 home defeat against Northampton on the corresponding day of the previous season which meant we missed out on the play-offs. But this time we found ourselves in a Catch-22 situation: there were no other matches left at which to sell 'em! So, despite numerous threats and with churches throughout the district holding special prayers for our personal safety, we went ahead, and had sold out 40 minutes before the kick-off. At half-time we were still being held to a 0-0 draw and Fulham were leading 1-0 at Cambridge. Fortunately, thoughts that the jinx had struck yet again were wiped out in the second half when Graham Lancashire scored straight from the kick-off and David Lowe added a second just before the end. We'd won the Championship and the voodoo had at last been beaten.

Awards for the season are as follows:

Best performance: This would have to be the record 7-1 victory over Scarborough. Remarkably Graeme Jones didn't get on the scoresheet.

Best visiting teams: Brighton, who played good attractive football but didn't have a Graeme Jones up front to finish it off, and Swansea, who seemed to rely on Jan Molby a bit too much, and lost their way once he'd gone off at half-time.

Worst visiting team: Lincoln, who resembled a school team playing caveman football in a playground. They came to Springfield Park intent on kicking the opposition more than the ball.

Best goals: The brace by Issy Diaz in the 3-0 win at Carlisle were the most memorable. Sadly it looks as though the Spaniard will be returning home as the club seems a wee bit indifferent about keeping him, although they do seem determined to hold on to Martinez.

Player of the Season: No surprise here: Graeme Jones, simply by the number of goals he scored. Also worthy of mention are captain Colin Greenall, Bob Martinez and Graham Lancashire who made a fantastic start before getting injured, but battled his way back from the treatment table to end the campaign in the same manner in which he'd begun.

Best opposition player: Wiganer and former Latics star Warren Aspinall, currently plying his trade at Carlisle. He may have lost most of his pace (and his hair come to think of it) since he last stepped foot on Springfield Park, but the quality of his passing and ability to read the game make him an easy winner.

The other big talking point at Springfield Park during the season was the ground move pantomime, which at one point reached farcical levels. We started the season expecting to eventually be ground-sharing with Wigan RL at a 30,000 all-seater Robin Park stadium. Then our chairman Dave Whelan fell out with the council and decided to take us ground-sharing at a 25,000 all-seated Central Park with Wigan RL. They in turn fell out with Whelan over the proposed deal, and decided to flog Central Park to Tesco's and take themselves off to Horwich to share at Bolton Wanderers' new ground (and good riddance too). Whelan then went back on his word to develop Springfield Park if the Central Park deal fell through (obviously expecting it not to), and we're currently back on track to finish up at Robin Park, this time sharing with Orrell RUFC. Sounds confusing? This whole fiasco has been to sport what spaghetti junction is to motorways and we've had more artists impressions than the Tate Gallery.

Don't be surprised if Wigan RL also finish up at the new Robin Park ground as well, provided that the current vendetta between our chairman and Jack Robinson (Wigan RL Chairman, or O.J. Robinson, as he's better known in these parts) can be resolved.

Latics' success is no doubt due to Dave Whelan's cheque-book (he's worth about £180 million) and John Deehan's eye for a good player. Time and time again the club's transfer record has been smashed; at the time of writing we've paid Hull City £360,000 for highly rated goalkeeper Roy Carroll, Jones cost (a bargain) £150,000, Andy Saville (not so much of a bargain) £125,000, David Lowe £125,000, Kevin Sharp £100,000 and Whelan has already promised a further £3 million spending spree for the assault on Division Two.

Whelan seems hell-bent on getting Latics into the First Division and from there into the Premier League, and he is a man who normally gets what he wants. His football knowledge is considerable, having been a top professional and an FA Cup finalist with Blackburn (they only lost after he'd been stretchered off). He certainly has the money (he owns half of Wigan) and the business acumen that has made him such a success. He's also a very ruthless man who cannot stand failure, so it's good to know that Latics' financial future is secure, but of course like everything else, at what price? Whelan has the power and wealth to do whatever he wants with Wigan Athletic so we cannot be complacent. When he came up with the ill-fated ground-share plan for Central Park, fans were never consulted about the move, which most of us viewed as sacrilege considering the amount of rivalry that exists between the rugby and football clubs. We were basically left to like it or lump it. At the end of the day we just hope that there is conviction in his statements about having "the best interests of Wigan Athletic at heart." He said he would get us out of Division 3 and it took him 18 months, and still maintains that we have seen nothing yet, so on that promise you have to believe him.

It's taken us 19 years to win the Championship, and the recent past for the Latics faithful has not been a happy one, but the memories of last season and particularly the final day will remain with every Latics fan for the rest of their lives. Whatever we do or wherever our future lies, the song remains the same: "Things can only get better..."

LEYTON ORIENTEAR

Leyton Orient

A glance at the final Division 3 League table for the '96-97 season gives the impression that Orient's followers suffered a pretty uneventful nine months. In fact, nothing could have been further from the truth.

On the whole, the standard of football that was put before the discerning Leyton public was at best laboured and at worst an insult to the intelligence. However, the real entertainment came from the off-field shenanigans in which the club's personnel found themselves embroiled. From the very first day of the campaign up until the back end of May, life at Brisbane Road had all the twists and turns of a John Grisham novel.

The start of the season highlighted the team's lack of punch up-front. With Portsmouth ending our Coca Cola interest in round one, the last thing we needed was to occupy the bottom spot 'early doors', but after three games that was the case. Although the club had splashed out on a number of experienced campaigners during the summer (including ex-Hammers Alvin Martin and Les Sealey), it seemed that manager Pat Holland was having difficulty in getting the best from his new faces. Rumours began to circulate that Alvin Martin would be in charge by Christmas, although these subsided when the O's put together a good run during September that included two away wins in a row (Northampton - we love you!). The club celebrated by knocking down the away end without having the cash to build a replacement, leaving us with the most expensive car park in the league. Let's hear it for Britain's first drive-in football stand!

By October things began to go seriously pear-shaped. The unpopular but effective midfielder Dave Martin was fired in mysterious circumstances, and with injuries to namesake Alvin and crazy Les, the team was sinking to new depths of ineptitude. An horrific performance and subsequent defeat at Cardiff spelt the end for Pat Holland. The trip to Wales almost spelt the end for some of the *Orientear* crew too, when a few of the home team's more neanderthal support came looking for a bit of action in the pub we were visiting before the match. Mercifully they didn't think we were worth the trouble of getting their boots bloody.

As soon as the poisoned chalice (i.e. the manager's job) became available, a whole host of names - mostly ex-Hammers - cropped up. One of the most ridiculous candidates was sad old man Alan Hudson, whose appearance on L!ve TV almost rivalled George Best's on Wogan in his attempt to bullshit his way into the job. Eventually Tommy Taylor took charge after an acrimonious departure from his former club, Cambridge United. Indeed there hasn't been such a sense of outrage since Val Doonican found out what his initials really stood for. Just to rub salt into our neighbours from up the M11's wounds, Tom took top scorer Scott McGleish with him, although the U's had the last laugh as they recorded a 2-0 win over us a fortnight later.

Things got a lot worse when Stevenage Borough dumped us out of the FA Cup, despite former England goalkeeper and failed professional gambler Peter Shilton's presence. Meanwhile chairman Barry Hearn was spending some quality time on holiday in the Indian Ocean, contemplating those mugs who'd bought near-worthless stock in the Autumn share issue.

In the words of the song; things could only get better, and an unbeaten run throughout December and most of January (including Shilts' 1000th game against a truly awful Brighton side) saw Orient climb to the fringes of the race for the play-offs. Three defeats on the trot killed the dream in its tracks and also saw the club's leading marksman of the previous three seasons, Colin West, pick up a serious leg injury which put him out for the rest of the campaign. Westie may not be Mr Popular at Brisbane Road but at least he knew where the goal was. Taylor made a big mistake in not finding a replacement until early March, by which time a dreadful slump in form had seen the club drop into a bottom six position.

The game at Brighton on March 8th took on real significance as a defeat for Leyton's finest would mean the Seagulls would only be two points adrift, leaving *us* staring at the Conference. Luckily, Carl Griffiths had been signed after a successful loan spell, and his two goals in the opening minutes of the second half brought us level. The atmosphere began to really hot up when after we took a 4-3 lead, some of the disgruntled locals mounted an assault on our players as they made their way back to the half-way line. Another ex-England international, Ray Wilkins, found himself on the wrong end of a kicking as kung-fu became the order of the day. Whoever was to blame, the atmosphere was now white hot, and a penalty in the 85th minute gave Brighton a lifeline which they accepted with relish. When the final whistle came, we were white and emotionally drained, looking like Barbara Cartland on smack. Nevertheless, it was a hell of a game.

Come April, Orient were still in relegation trouble despite a battling performance against promotion-chasing Carlisle that gave us a 2-1 win. We lost at Ape City, sorry, Hartlepool, but three wins out of the last four assured my beloved O's of league football for next season. But make no mistake, it really was touch and go. By the time May had arrived all the big signings made by Holland (and Hearn?) had either departed or had been dropped by Taylor. A major feature of yet another season of shame was that too many of the new players thought they'd get an easy ride on the back of Leyton Orient. Luckily they were found out, but how long must we continue to be an easy touch? At least Taylor has the right idea and is building a young and hungry side. Pity about the hoof-ball tactics, though. Hopefully the club's long-suffering support will get some real value for money next season.

So what now? It seems that uncertain times are ahead for Orient and their like. The spectre of nursery clubs and part-time soccer is never far away, and seeing that Spurs have signed a three year deal to play their reserve fixtures at Brisbane Road I can't help feeling a little uneasy as to where all this is leading. As for the ground developments, the national lottery's decision not to push any cash Barry's way means that our state-of-the-art car park will be around for a good while yet. And the less said about the new lease the club has been on the verge of signing the better, although the longer it remains unsigned, the more people will doubt Hearn's commitment to the Orient cause.

So it's all aboard the rollercoaster for next season's thrills and spills at Barry's East End paradise. Let's hope I don't throw up!

THE LION ROARS

Millwall

The '96-97 season proved to be a traumatic time for all concerned with Millwall Football Club.

As well as failing miserably on the pitch, off the pitch matters were even worse. The very existence of our club was even threatened, as we hurtled head-first towards receivership. Whilst the nation sympathised with the struggles at Bournemouth and Brighton, few would have shed a tear if Millwall had disappeared from the Football League. However, the very fact that a club like Millwall could have gone to the wall provides many lessons for the rest.

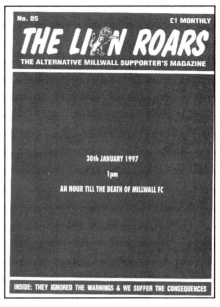

No. 85   £1 MONTHLY

THE LI🦁N ROARS

THE ALTERNATIVE MILLWALL SUPPORTER'S MAGAZINE

30th JANUARY 1997

1pm

AN HOUR TILL THE DEATH OF MILLWALL FC

INSIDE: THEY IGNORED THE WARNINGS & WE SUFFER THE CONSEQUENCES

Yet it could have been so different. Despite having been relegated on the very last day of the previous season, which led inevitably to the departures of Rae, Keller and Thatcher to Premiership pastures new, hopes were still high. With the majority of a team which had previously looked so much like Premiership candidates intact, plus a few of Jimmy Nicholl's Scottish Cup-winning favourites, surely the Lions would bounce straight back up. Or so we thought, as did the bookies, the pundits, etc., etc...

Little did we know it at the time, but one of Nicholl's acquisitions, Dave Sinclair ('Sinky' to his drinking partners), would sum up Millwall FC under the Scot's management. Nicholl's description of him as being so hard he had "tattoos on his teeth" was an attempt to endear him to The Den faithful, in spite of his obvious lack of talent. Having researched into Millwall's history and seen that players like Hurlock and Cripps were immensely popular in South East London, he had failed to observe that they could play a bit too. Aah, poor old Sinky. He was indeed a character, but it didn't take long for us to see he was simply out of his depth. The manager had made the grave if unintentional mistake of failing to understand what we expect from our players. He reasoned that if it was good enough for Raith, it was good enough for Millwall. He couldn't have been more wrong, and by this error of judgement Nicholl had sown the seeds of his eventual departure.

If Sinclair was a red herring, another of the Raith old-boys Steve Crawford scored on his debut on the opening day of the season in a 1-1 home draw with Wrexham. The crowd of 9,371 was the highest in the division, which showed the supporters' faith in Nicholl, who was not (yet) being held responsible for our relegation. Crawford immediately forged a solid striking partnership with Chris Malkin and after a few games, despite a blip at York, Millwall were neatly tucked in behind early pace-setters Brentford.

Then the first disaster struck: inspirational captain Keith Stevens was put out for the rest of the season by an injury resulting from a misplaced pass against eternal jinxes Bristol Rovers. With Sinclair already crying off injured it left a gaping hole in the Lions' defence; one they would not be able to fill. The same game saw the debut of Darren Huckerby, who'd arrived on loan from Newcastle. Huckerby became the second Millwall forward to score on his debut in a couple of weeks, and looked a class above anyone else on the pitch. Even with a hole in our defence, it didn't matter, Huckerby was the man who would have taken us up, without a doubt. The fans knew it, Nicholl knew it, the board knew it. Kevin Keegan had dispensed with Newcastle's reserve side, so Huckerby was just kicking his heels on Tyneside, and openly declared in a *TLR* interview that he would love to come to The Den if Millwall could stump up the money.

Chairman Peter Mead made the right noises, and said he was doing everything he could by Huckerby, but he knew the writing was on the wall. Not only could we not afford one of the brightest prospects in the league, but creditors were growing impatient. It's one thing promising promotion in August, but unless you're 30 points clear by Christmas people are going to get a bit tired of waiting for their money. One of these creditors even forced the sale of Chris Malkin. Despite rumours that Malkin wanted to return North, the truth was that Millwall didn't have a pot to piss in, and owed everyone and his dog a fortune. It was this fact that began our on-pitch demise.

To add to Nicholl's injury-depleted defence, he had now lost two key attackers at the same time. Realising that financial constraints would clearly restrict his plans to improve the side, he was forced to use the loan system again. Wimbledon's Scott Fitzgerald arrived and was an instant success. Having now used several thousand players, Nicholl's Millwall side went into November in top position, albeit unconvincingly, but there didn't seem a better team in a very mediocre division.

At around this time, *TLR* began calling home games 'Groundhog Day Games'. Every match was the same: the opponents would take an early lead, Millwall would then play well for 20 minutes, full-back Anton Rogan would score his customary goal (his performances earning him a deserved recall to the Northern Ireland squad) and Millwall would win 2-1. This continued until we drew Woking in the FA Cup. An exciting 2-2 draw, including two of the best televised goals of the season from Savage and Crawford in front of the *Sky* cameras at Kingfield, led to another televised bite of the cherry for Woking. Viewers around the country saw former Chelsea hero Clive Walker waltz round the Lions' static defence to score the only goal of the game after nine minutes, thus sending the minnows into round four. Jimmy Nicholl was blamed; the players were blamed; the board was blamed. Supporters were angry, and justifiably so.

Another *Sky* game immediately followed. Leaders Brentford arrived at The Den and somehow escaped with a lucky 0-0 draw, as we gave our best performance of the season. Apart from the rare excitement, this match was notable for the *Sky* graphics displaying a 94% to 6% ratio in favour of Millwall's penalty area possession in the second half. The unreality of the performance was proven in the following game. A freezing cold night at Adams Park, home of Wycombe Wanderers, saw the Lions' worst performance of the season. Our TV show-ponies were simply not interested. To add to the problems, Scott Fitzgerald had been injured a couple of weeks earlier at Bristol City and would miss the rest of the season.

Jimmy was doing his best, but with a team low on confidence and the club's financial plight, it was an uphill task; one which was beginning to prove more impossible each day. Further loan signings arrived, Mark Bright and Ray Wilkins by now doing the rounds of beleaguered clubs for about four grand a week each. Bright scored on his debut at Bournemouth but did little else, and Wilkins was a very good corner taker, and that's about all.

Defeat just after Christmas in the AutoWindscreens at home to Colchester (2-1 up with two minutes to go, then 2-2, then 2-3 in the very first minute of sudden death) led to a heated demo against Nicholl and the board outside the main stand. A larger protest followed after defeat against Bristol City, and Nicholl was now running out of time. But all this had been overshadowed a few weeks before by news that the club's bankers had advised Mead to withdraw Millwall Plc from the stock market. Oh yes, things were very grim indeed. Quite simply, we'd paid the penalty for being over-ambitious. In building a Premiership stadium, its then chairman Reg Burr gave the club a Premiership structure, and with Millwall relegated to the League's Third Division and no more million-pound players left to sell, something had to give. It did. Millwall's financial crash was a disaster just waiting to happen.

Events on the pitch were now of little importance, and far from talking about promotion, people were relieved to have avoided relegation. Administrators Buchler Phillips were brought in to try to maintain Millwall's Football League status, and to find a way to meet the demands of the club's numerous creditors. Guarantees were given that we would be able to fulfil our remaining fixtures, and they prepared plans for a Rights Issue, which it was hoped would solve Millwall's precarious financial position. There were of course job losses (aren't there always?), which included Nicholl and his assistant Martin Harvey.

In such a dramatic season, there was still time for a further twist. To fill the managerial void, John Docherty, the club's most successful manager ever, was coaxed out of his potting shed. Was there yet something left?

Performances by now were consistently poor, but Docherty's arrival coincided with a run of easy fixtures, and after an amazingly fortunate 2-0 win at Luton, who were seemingly on course for the title, Millwall suddenly found themselves third in what was proving to be a tremendous ruck at the top of the table. However, any lingering promotion hopes disappeared, as Bournemouth, by now in bigger financial shit than we were, arrived at The Den in what could have been their last ever league game. The Cherries beat the Lions 1-0 in a much easier fashion than the scoreline suggests.

Docherty's long-ball tactics quickly failed and the slide down the league was rapid. During the last 11 games, not one win was registered. By the end of the season fans had lost interest and our former hero's bubble had well and truly burst. Prior to the final game he handed in his resignation to the new board.

At the time of writing under the leadership of the new chairman, Theo Phaphitis (who made his fortune by turning around financially stricken businesses), Millwall have provided the stock market with underwritten plans to pay off their creditors. Theo's even managed to get *L!ve TV* to sponsor the shirts and Fosters to sponsor a stand, already a vast improvement on the previous regime's business achievements. It's even rumoured that Brighton will be paying us rent for a couple of years!

It's a new dawn (as they say) and Billy Bonds is the new manager, which may or may not be a good thing. It's whether or not the fans care that matters now.

LIVERPOOL ARE ON THE TELE AGAIN!

Norwich City

Walker is back!

The summer of '96 was a period of pure fantasy for every Norwich supporter. The corrupt administration of Robert Chase was now a distant (bad) memory and the return of Mike Walker was like a breath of fresh air. We may have been £5m in debt (thanks to Chase) but it didn't matter, there was hope. 'The Saint' turned Norwich City into one of the most entertaining and respected teams in England and Europe during his first spell in charge. But the circumstances were a bit different this time and we were under no illusions. Walker had a very difficult job ahead of him.

However, the season initially went beyond all our expectations; we even led the table on a couple of occasions. Unfortunately a succession of injuries, a poor disciplinary record, a leaky defence (a problem Walker has never put right, which is curious considering he used to be a goalkeeper) and the lack of a prolific centre-forward were the main factors in City's eventual slump down to 13th place.

In February two players were arrested after an 'incident' with a taxi driver, who accused Andy Johnson and Carl Bradshaw of damaging one of his doors and injuring his little finger. 'Johno', allegedly a bit of a womaniser and piss-head off the field and crowd favourite and highly gifted player on it (when he's fit), and 'Butch' (nicknamed after the thicko in TV's *Emmerdale* and more injury-prone than Johno, if that's possible), had been out celebrating a 3-2 victory at Sheffield United. They got into a cab in the city centre and asked to be driven to the club's training ground at Colney on the outskirts of Norwich. Why the bloody hell did they want to go to there at one o'clock in the morning, you may ask? Not for some extra training surely? Well, yes, in the car park actually! Apparently, the cabbie went in goal, and he deflected one of Johno's shots onto the door of his hackney carriage, denting it in the process and injuring his little finger too. A friendly little kick-about just got out of hand, that's all.

Another player likely to be leaving Carrow Road during the summer is Bryan Gunn. Gunny will be remembered as one of the Canaries' all time greats, no question. But he is now a shadow his magnificent former self and has been making too many mistakes. Sadly the finger has got to be partly pointed at the gaffer because he kept selecting Gunn, even though it was plain to see that the Scotsman's alertness was bordering on the non-existent and his confidence was declining match by match. Quite frankly he was becoming a bit of a joke amongst the Norwich faithful. This fact was made evident during a special screening of the Canaries' dismal 2-0 defeat at Ipswich (for supporters fortunate enough not to get a ticket for Portman Road) at the International Carvery at Carrow Road. Gunn's appearance (on screen) just prior to the game was greeted with a crescendo of boos that was almost deafening. What a way to end a testimonial season!

The appalling form of Bryan Gunn may well have been a hindrance to the Canaries' quest for Premiership football, but the disgraceful standard of refereeing in the Nationwide League didn't help either. One of the bastards in black, Terry Lunt (shouldn't that be a 'c'?), disallowed a Robert Fleck goal against Barnsley after Darren Eadie had shaken off an innocuous challenge. A TV replay confirmed later that the Barnsley player's boot barely touched Eadie's leg. Lunt the c**t made Norwich drag the ball all the way back for a free-kick which as you would expect came to nothing (hugely frustrating). Then to add insult to injury, Lunt sent off Fleck for his second bookable offence. No-one knew what the first one was for.

Although winger-come-striker Darren Eadie finished top scorer for City with 17 league goals, the best that the rest of our so called 'strikers' could manage was a paltry nine between them (13, if you include Keith O'Neill who's more recognised as a winger.) Robert Fleck was the top scoring 'proper' striker with just FOUR! Flecky was a class player in his heyday (six or seven years ago) and he's still half-decent now. A superb team player who lays on opportunities for others, he's never been a prolific goalscorer and to get out of this hell-hole called the Nationwide League, you're gonna need someone like John McGinlay, Nathan Blake or both. Hopefully Delia will give some of her £17m fortune to Walker during the summer to buy a goalscorer!

During the campaign Walker sold two strikers, Jamie Cureton and Ade Akinbiyi, and loaned Keith Scott back to his old club Wycombe. Cureton has got talent but he was too much of a jack the lad for Walker's liking. It's rumoured that he'd turned up for pre-season training a stone overweight and stinking of beer. Walker ran out of patience and sold him to Bristol Rovers. Few Canary followers would have been sad to see Akinbiyi leave. He was hopeless and is now a certainty for any fan's all-time worst X1. Quite how Mike Walker managed to sponge a quarter of a million out of Gillingham I'll never know. It was daylight robbery and a brilliant piece of business by the silver-haired one!

Rob Newman had a particularly good season (by his standards) at the heart of the Norwich defence. Newman, nicknamed 'The Charmer' by his team-mates (because he's got a gigantic manhood - allegedly), is a big favourite of Walker's who told *LAOTTA*! readers last August, "If Rob had more pace, he probably wouldn't be playing for us, he'd be playing for Manchester United or someone." Newman is a character and a top bloke. He met his wife at Pontins in Weston-super-Mare during a netball weekend and told her he was a plumber! Big Rob received some shocking treatment from some sections of the Carrow Road faithful towards the end of '95-96 but showed great character to be one of the club's most consistent performers during Walker's first season back. (A Weight Watchers diet was surely a significant reason for Newman's improved form.)

The highlight of the season for me besides the 3-1 home win against Ipswich was the scum's elimination from the play-offs by Sheffield United. I wish I could have seen the look on Alan Brazil's face at the final whistle. 'Fathead' was co-commentator for *Sky* during the Ipswich v Norwich clash which ended the Canaries' own play-off hopes. "I'm not biased," he said. However this statement seemed somewhat dubious after comments like, "Oh, that's a marvellous goal by Taricco! What a terrific move!" and "That was clearly a shove by Eadie!" Both total exaggerations. In fact, the only true thing Brazil said all evening was that "Ipswich fans hate Norwich fans and vica versa." He declined to mention the over-zealous refereeing of Uriah Rennie of Sheffield who booked seven Norwich players. I bet he wouldn't have liked it if it was the other way round.

I had the misfortune to meet Brazil at a supporters' club meeting last year. He had me fooled for a minute; I thought he was a decent bloke. He slagged off Robert Chase and even bought me and my mate a pint. However Brazil had brought a so-called 'comedian' with him who began to 'entertain' the audience with sexist and racist jokes. The racism got worse and at one stage he stood on his chair to see if any black people were present. Brazil was practically falling off his chair. Some of the audience (which included families) left the room in disgust. Apparently Brazil and his malodorous mate were hoping to tour the country with their 'act', but not surprisingly it didn't materialise.

Mega-bucks TV cook Delia Smith came onto the board on November 28th and her arrival initially seemed a bad omen as the Canaries went six games without a win. The sequence included shocking 5-1 and 6-1 thrashings at West Brom and Port Vale respectively.

Delia was to cause a bit of a stir at the end of the season when she was one of the main influences behind a new Norwich kit designed by Bruce Oldfield (no relation to Mike but allegedly a highly respected name on the catwalk), and a shirt sponsorship deal with the local Colman's mustard company. Delectable Delia even modelled the new strip at a press conference launch in London. (Luckily she didn't 'get her kit off'!) The club has ditched its traditional green shorts for vomit yellow, which will upset a lot of people.

But who cares, as long as we're winning?

LOADSAMONEY

Blackburn Rovers

Well, it's that time of the year again, and it's been a long hard season for most Rovers supporters.

In a nutshell, most of the goings on around Ewood have concerned the manager's job. Ray Harford resigned in October and Tony Parkes took over for a third time in the capacity of caretaker manager, while the board searched Europe for a replacement. On December 16th Rovers announced that Sven Goran Eriksson would be coming to Ewood at the end of his contract with Sampdoria. Serie A suddenly became a talking point with Rovers fans, mainly because there was bugger all to talk about in the Premiership! Could

Sampdoria catch Juventus, and if so would he still turn up?

As time passed rumours grew that Eriksson was going to renege on his promise. Robert Coar denied it, but with his track record on Shearer and Dalglish, things looked bleak. February 21st, and the rumours were confirmed. Eriksson was staying in Italy, but moving to Lazio. The search was on again... Once more Rovers went to Italy, this time to Inter Milan and it was Roy Hodgson who was getting the job. The announcement was made on the day of our AGM in the hope that this would keep the punters happy. Hmm...

But back to the football. Before the season started I was enthusiastic about what the coming campaign had in store for us, predicting a top three spot and possibly even a cup final. All this went out the window when Shearer pissed off to Newcastle and Graham Fenton took his place! There was nothing to cheer about in the pre-season friendlies either, as we struggled against Colchester, Seville, Vitesse Arnhem and the mighty Preston North End. We did beat Cambridge and Volendam, though. Huh! Who needs Alan Shearer?

When it kicked off for real, defeats against Spurs and Villa started the alarm bells ringing. 'Club In Crisis' was a common headline in the sports pages, and I couldn't really disagree. It wasn't the losing that bothered me, but the manner in which we did it; creating nothing, with no goals and not even any shots on target. And then there was more disappointment on the way back from Villa, when we found out that the board had told King Kenny that his services were no longer required. It seemed that they had informed Dalglish of their decision by recorded delivery letter, and since the King was on holiday, his son had signed for it, and Kenny only discovered that he was surplus to requirements by reading about it in the morning papers.

Next up, a trip to Old Trafford, the 'Theatre of Dreams' and a 2-2 draw. Bohinen scored the goal of the season while Pallister played hand ball in his own penalty area (something the referee chose to ignore). What a display! Finally, something positive! However my lasting memory of this match was not the football, which was excellent, but something that happened on the way. About one mile from OT, with our coach stuck in traffic, a car pulled up alongside sporting the usual MUFC regalia: loads of stickers, 27 mini kits (at the time of writing) and the requisite red and white scarf. Nothing unusual about that, until you realised that we were within spitting distance of OT and the two passengers were busy studying an A to Z of Manchester. Seeing was believing!

Something else that took some believing was the lame excuse offered by our players following a couple of limp displays. They put it down to the music which was played to welcome the teams onto the pitch! They reckoned that the previous season's *We are the Champions* was more inspiring to the visitors than to the Rovers players. Alex Ferguson eat your heart out! Current choice, Van Halen's *Jump*, apparently "didn't have the same feel," so Europe's *The Final Countdown* got the vote, one caller claiming on Radio Rovers, "We always seem to win when the players walk out to Final Countdown." I hope he's reading this!

An away game at Newcastle, and again Rovers raised their game. One-nil up after a disputed (Shearer) penalty, the Geordies finally woke-up, chanting "Shearer, Shearer." We responded with "Judas, Judas," "There's only one greedy bastard" and "Did you cry when Fenton scored?," referring to last season's goals against Newcastle. Ferdinand made it 2-0, and although Sutton pulled a goal back the equaliser wouldn't come. Coventry won at home and we were bottom of the Carling Premiership after six games, with just one point. Another dismal display against Arsenal and three other draws brought our points total to four! A few days later and we were out of the fizzy drinks cup with a 1-0 home defeat to Stockport. Believe me, the scoreline flattered us!

By now, some supporters were calling for Harford's head, and the Friday after the Coke Cup defeat they got what they wanted when he resigned. But why was Harford left to shoulder the blame alone, when there were others who surely should have stood up and faced the music too? I mean, how much money had been available for him to spend? Had he been stopped from signing players by the board? Why was Shearer allowed to leave? These and other questions demanded an answer.

Tony Parkes was given the job of caretaker manager, and for the game at West Ham he brought back Le Saux, Marker, Fenton and McKinlay. Out injured were Hendry, Gallacher and Sutton, leaving the manager with a 4-5-1 formation. New boss, but the same old luck: 1-1 with five minutes to go and Henning Berg put the ball through his own goal.

November saw a definite up-turn, beginning with a 3-0 win over top-of-the-League Liverpool. Two draws (including away points unluckily lost when Forest equalised with the last kick of the game in injury time) were followed by another win, this time against Southampton. Oh, why couldn't all months have been like November?

The season of goodwill to all men was anything but, especially in Bryan Robson's case. On the back of our comparatively good run the club were looking forward to a bumper crowd with the visit of Boro's foreign legion, and the chance to put one over fellow strugglers. However as we all know, Robbo, Steve Gibson and the rest of the Riverside congregation decided that they didn't have enough fit players to put out a side, unilaterally called the game off, and were then gutted when the FA actually took three points off them rather than fine them the equivalent of a Ravenelli pay packet. What idiots. Even a pub team wouldn't have acted in that way. Of course they continue to protest their innocence and have engaged the finest legal minds to defend them. As it happens they would have been better advised to have paid George Carmen QC to pull on some boots and actually play the game before Christmas.

Boxing Day saw the media circus in full swing as various hacks speculated about the hostile reception Shearer would receive on his return. In fact it wasn't that bad, especially as Berg denied him a single kick all afternoon. However, he still had the temerity to question *our* loyalty on *Radio Lancashire*; this after Rovers had voluntarily rested him at the end of last season so he'd be fresh for Euro '96. And of course he repaid our loyalty by buggering off in the direction of John Hall's millions. Bastard.

On New Year's day we recorded our only away win of the season, 2-0 at Everton. We were so good that day that many of us were left scratching our heads and asking why were we in such a shitty situation. Needless to say, if you ask a question you usually get an answer, and the utter crap we served up at Tottenham in losing 2-1 to a depleted (take note Robson) Spurs hammered home what our problem was - inconsistency.

Given the up and down nature of our league progress, there was at least the hope that we could do something in the cup after pulling Cov out of the velvet bag. Big Fat, Big Spending Ron had been steadily steering them to Nationwide oblivion and surely they'd be ripe for the taking at Ewood... Oh, bollocks.

Still, after a demoralising defeat what better place to lick your wounds than Anfield. It was on the eve of the Liverpool game that Eriksson had confirmed that for some reason he preferred Signori and Lazio to Fenton and Blackburn, but at least another Scandinavian did pitch up in the form of the £2.5m Per Pedersen from Odense. The game at Anfield was unbelievable as the Collywobbles hit the koppites and with over 20 Fowlups in front of goal we grabbed our point and ran for the hills.

The competition at the foot of the Premiership was intense and given our inconsistency we never felt really confident about the eventual outcome to the season. Highlights such as Billy McKinlay completing a game without getting booked (even outshining Kevin Gallacher's hat-trick against the Dons in the same game) were offset by niggling defeats just as we looked like finally escaping. And it certainly didn't help when after making the effort to travel to Middlesbrough (don't scoff, it was touch and go at one point; we'd had at least two players sneeze and one report a nasty tummy ache), so-called Boro supporters bricked the Rovers team bus after the game. What would have happened if we'd won?

We were also involved in probably the worst *Sky* game ever broadcast. Why they chose to cover our game at Elland Road no-one knows. Leeds hadn't scored for about two years and we arrived sporting a 1-9-1 formation. If I'd been calling the shots at *Sky* that evening, I'd have pulled the plug and shown Detective in a Wheelbarrow ("this time it's personal") instead. Even Andy Gray struggled to say anything positive about the game.

The final game in April was a real carnival affair. Mind you when the Sheff Weds band met the Ewood band there was always going to be a party. The atmosphere was brilliant and even the Jack Walker Stand joined in; there's more life in Pleasington Cemetery than in that part of the ground. The kill-joys at clubs who ban these guys need their heads tested. There was an equally manic atmosphere when, ironically, the invalids of Teeside turned up for a rematch which saw us needing a solitary point to ensure our survival. Thankfully for us, with Beck's goalscoring prowess (!) up-front, Robson's unwillingness to go for broke on the night and Tim Flowers' brilliant save from Juninho we got the required point.

Say your farewells to the San Siro, Roy. It's time to go to work.

THE MIGHTY SHREW

Shrewsbury Town

Two members of the foreign legion were brought in for the '96-97 season: Danish pair Thomas Nielsen and goalkeeper Benny Gall. It was Gall who made the bigger impact by punching team-mate Dean Spink after a defensive mix-up. The big Dane later apologised and gave his reason for the sudden outburst: "He put two fingers up at me" was the explanation. The rumour that Prince Naseem was next in line never materialised!

Apart from possible world title fights, this was a season of bad results, bad tactics and eventual relegation. Mind you, after three games, promotion and the First Division looked a lot more likely.

Town had earned a 3-1 away victory over Burnley, a team they later did the double over, with key players missing through injury and with striker Steve Anthrobus playing in defence. This was just too easy! We'd reached the dizzy heights of third place, and although early doors, there was no stopping delirious fans: "We hate Burnley..." could be heard long after the final whistle. After a Brentford give-away, Shrewsbury went on an unbeaten run of six games, the best of the season, and by the end of September were handily placed fifth.

However, fans' huge smiles were just as quickly wiped off their faces by a run of unbelievably bad results. Although 'goal-machine' Ian Stevens was regularly hitting the onion bag and Paul Evans scored some truly memorable goals, most from 20 yards plus, Town slipped down the table via six straight defeats. This slide signalled the arrival of two loan players: Junior Bent from Bristol City and Frankie Bennett from Southampton. Bennett, coming on from the subs bench, scored twice at Peterborough to give us our first point out of a possible 21. He then went on to score the winner at Notts County on November 2nd, which unbeknown to the travelling faithful was the last away victory they would celebrate all season! During his time at the Meadow, Bent won a place in the fans' hearts and will always be welcomed back. The respect they have for him was shown later in the season at Ashton Gate, when he received a standing ovation from the travelling Shrews - and all he did was warm up! Bennett on the other hand signed for Bristol Rovers instead of Town and is sure to receive a hostile reception when our paths next cross.

Shrewsbury, following a home victory over Bristol Rovers, then went on another no-win marathon. A run of nine games without a victory, which included a first round FA Cup defeat to lowly Scarborough and a humiliating 5-1 defeat to Crewe, was ended with a 2-0 Gay Meadow victory over Tim Clarke's York City. The ex-Town goalkeeper was only too happy to help out his old team-mates by gifting them two goals. But ironically the biggest cheer of the afternoon was not for his endless flapping at crosses, but for goal kick after goal kick that Clarke hoofed out of play!

The new year saw the rarity of an orange ball used on the snow-covered Gay Meadow, and despite Town's appalling league form, we had progressed to the area semi-finals of the AWS Shield. An immediate return to Wembley was certainly on the cards. Wigan Athletic in round two and Scunthorpe United in round three were both disposed of by Paul Evans' golden goal extra-time penalties, but the second trip to Wembley was sadly not to be. Carlisle United, aided by a very dubious penalty (he never touched him ref!), won through to the next round via a 2-1 victory. By this time we were 16th in the league, slipping fast, and all we had to play for was Division 2 survival.

We thought that we'd stopped the rot with a 2-1 victory over Millwall, but Darren Currie's winner was ruled out by referee Brian Coddington who blew the final whistle just as the ball crossed the line. What a prat! Surely common sense should've told him to wait for Shrewsbury to win before blowing the final whistle... Mr C. needed an escort off the pitch, but even this did not stop one 'fan' who raced across the turf to tell the referee exactly what he (and everybody else) thought of him.

By the time we had lost to three of the four teams below us (Plymouth, Rotherham and Wycombe), we were 20th in the league and the fans were not happy. After crowd favourite Steve 'Throb' Anthrobus had been sold to Crewe for £75,000, terrace unrest grew further and calls for the manager's head were heard after games. But that's not to say that the fans were not behind the team. We were 110% behind the players and cheered every one of them. (Fred Davies: We never booed Shaun Wray...) After a ten man defeat to border rivals Rectum, sorry Wrexham, due to a red card for captain Dean Spink, Town finally succumbed to their fate and were relegated following a 1-0 home defeat to Preston.

The season finished and wholesale sackings followed. Manager Fred Davies and coaches Richard Pratley and Kevin 'pointer' Summerfield were all shown the door, which at least points to a brighter future for the club. With ex-captain Jake King now at the helm, the word from Gay Meadow is: Division 3 watch out, you have been warned!

MISSION IMPOSSIBLE

Darlington

Over a season there are always amazing peaks and troughs to consider. In September, sitting in Leeds United's plush Elland Road Stadium, thoughts of relegation from the Football League for a second and probably more permanent excursion were a long way from supporters' thoughts. Little did we know that the splendid 2-2 draw against George Graham's Leeds side would be the pinnacle of a season that promised so much, but once again in the turbulent history of one of the most unstable professional football clubs, failed to deliver.

The opening matches produced a mixed bag: excellent home

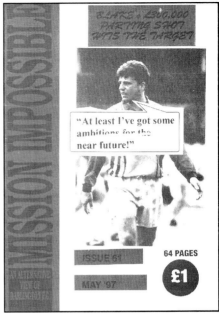

"At least I've got some ambitions for the near future!"

ISSUE 61   MAY '97   64 PAGES   £1

victories recorded against promotion favourites Swansea and Wigan were negated by two infuriating defeats at Hull and Doncaster, doubling last seasons's number of away failures - and this was only August! The away form was to be the Quakers' achilles' heel all season long, but then players sold for a vast profit and replaced by free transfer signings earning £150 a week was never going to be a recipe for success at an ambitious football club.

The first casualty off the pitch was former Middlesbrough and Hull City player Billy Askew who was unceremoniously sacked as youth team coach so that one of Reg Brealey's boys, Tony Kenworthy, could resume his duties at Feethams. Also along for the rollercoaster ride was former Sheffield United and Stockport manager Danny Bergara. In effect Bergara lasted less than two months when it was revealed that he had not been director of coaching Jim Platt's choice but rather that of 'the majority shareholder' Brealey. The departure of Bergara saw the club issue a bizarre press release in which general manager Steve Morgon appeared to be more supportive of Bergara than Platt! Anyone familiar with goings on at Darlington will know of our dislike for Morgon, and the feeling's probably mutual seeing as he tried to put MI out of business this year. Until his hasty departure the fanzine's sale was banned at the ground and that was why away supporters couldn't buy a copy.

Despite all this, Darlington supporters had good reason to be optimistic for the '96-97 season. Granted, we'd sold defensive lynchpin Matty Appleby to

Barnsley for £180,000 (plus £50,000 if the Tykes got promoted to the Premier League - how we all laughed at that one!) and influential player/coach Gary Bannister had retired and then announced his intention to leave the club. But these two departures didn't unduly worry Jim Platt who had been told by Morgon that he could have a bigger squad of players on one proviso: they had to be freebies!

Off the pitch the club's much publicised East Stand redevelopment to seat 4,100 never got beyond the 'things will be ready in a couple of weeks time' stage and Soccerdome; the shirt sponsors for the season, who according to Morgon had put £50,000 worth of investment into Darlington FC, were no further forward with their plans for a leisure complex on the outskirts of town. Interestingly, Soccerdome are set up as a limited company but aren't listed in the phone book and appear to have no premises.

The departure of Steve Gaughan to Chesterfield for £30,000 had been predicted as far back as the previous January so nobody was surprised when it happened, but fans' favourite Robbie Painter had refused to sign a new deal and was often only given the last ten minutes as sub. The first (last?) big event of the season was our David v Goliath cup-tie with Leeds at Elland Road. United were low on confidence and our lads were really up for it as we clinched a 2-2 draw (could've won with a bit more luck). It certainly shook the foundations of the *Yorkshire Post* who tucked the report onto the inside back pages. Chairman Bernard Lowery was excited enough to utter the immortal words that Jim Platt "could have a job for life at Feethams." In the return, Leeds secured a two goal victory, but our cause wasn't helped by having three key players injured in 15 minutes at home against an over-physical Fulham side.

Bereft of experienced players, Platt was forced to turn to youth and the reserves, but the results didn't come. The team started to plummet on the back of a spell of one victory (at arch-rivals Hartlepool) in 11 matches. Robbie Painter had gone on loan to Rochdale and John McClelland, brought in by Platt to coach the team, was forced to make his one and only appearance at Hartlepool and broke his leg in the process. Now the boardroom reverberated to a different tune and Platt was asked to resign three times just weeks after Bernard Lowery had, erm, offered him a job for life. What a shocking way to treat a bloke who only six months previously had taken the club to Wembley.

The blame for all this was laid squarely at the feet of GM Steve Morgon who was refusing Jim access to the players he wanted, while denying any interference. Following a third home defeat in four matches against Barnet, around 300 supporters gathered in and around the East Stand to voice our disapproval. For half an hour we sang and demanded the heads of both Morgon and majority shareholder Brealey. Guess who got the blame for the demo?!

As a result of this hostile direct action, Morgon flew to Gibraltar (Darlington's majority shareholder St. Philip's Ltd being based offshore) and announced that he would be leaving the club at the end of the year. What he didn't tell anyone was that he had transferred the shareholding from St. Philip's to Soccerdome, the club's so-called shirt sponsors. This 'little' point was only revealed when the *Northern Echo*'s Chris Lloyd put together an article on the club's ownership. Morgon didn't divulge this information to anyone but when questioned at the club's AGM said that shares could be transferred by the owners to wherever they wanted. It later transpired that Soccerdome's investment in Darlington FC was zilch, with Morgon only admitting this at a shareholders' meeting FOUR weeks after he had left the club!

This all pointed to the fact that Morgon's role at Feethams was purely to make money for the benefit of the 'majority shareholder' by maintaining strict financial controls. Money generated from the playing side (transfers, Wembley, Leeds) would not be used to buy the club out of trouble however far we dropped. More than anything it was his arrogant, pompous and contradictory nature that upset people. He claimed the club was "open and friendly" but at the same time issued all manner of threats and solicitor's letters to *MI* editorial staff. The club had generated an estimated £400,000 in the six months yet not one penny had been re-invested. But when we shouted and screamed about it, all he could do was try to intimidate us.

After the demo Platt lasted two weeks. Bernard 'Job for life' and 'If Jim goes I go' Lowery did the dirty deed in a somewhat cowardly fashion over the telephone following a 2-0 defeat at Lincoln. Platt was told never to darken Feethams corridors again, yet ironically the supporter's club had organised an evening to commemorate the players' achievements on reaching Wembley last season just 36 hours later. It was an emotional night and 300 supporters gave Jim a standing ovation. The outcry in the local media was unprecedented; never in all my 21 years of watching football have I seen such condemnation for the way in which Jim was dismissed.

To replace him, the club offered former coach David Hodgson and his assistant Gary Bannister their jobs back. Unhappily it was mooted that they'd been approached four weeks before Platt's sacking, so many supporters quite rightly questioned Hodgson's motives and distrust was prevalent. Early results under the new pair were sketchy, but at least Brighton were accounted for at the Goldstone Ground: an important victory as Darlo had slumped to second bottom and it gave us some welcome breathing space. Carlisle did for us in the FA Cup, and Second Division Champions Bury put paid to our chances of a Wembley appearance in the AutoWindscreens. Christmas didn't bring much cheer but at least the introduction of Teuvo Moilanen and defender Richard Hope produced a remarkable turn around, particularly when two late goals killed off promotion-chasing Cambridge, which lifted everyone's spirits.

February, and Darlo were at it again as two excellent victories over Lincoln and Scunthorpe were nullified by defeats at Scarborough, Exeter and Wigan and a point at Hereford. The Scarborough match showed the black art of refereeing at its best. Three Darlo players were dispatched for the early bath while the Seadogs' players, equally willing to commit similar offences, received only the yellows. Eddie Wolstenholme caused a near riot that particular day and certainly robbed us all of watching a competitive game of football.

March saw David Hodgson pick up the Manager of the Month award for an unbeaten spell of six matches, culminating in three victories over Brighton, Hull and away at Colchester. Robbie Blake filled the Feethams' coffers by a further £300,000 as he departed for Bradford, but no sooner had March disappeared and it was back to normal with a handful of dreadful performances. However, there was real pleasure at the bitter end when a 2-1 victory over play-off contenders Cardiff City saw us leapfrog arch-rivals Hartlepool and continue our impressive record of finishing above them in the league. What a great way to finish a season of epic contrasts: scored 64 goals but leaked 77; a 2-2 at Leeds, a 2-1 victory at the Chimp Stranglers and a leading goalscorer in Darren Roberts in the top ten. It was also the first since we started that MI never sponsored any aspect of Darlington FC. Little surprise really when the season opened with us being threatened with arrest for breach of the peace on two occasions; dangerous hobby, selling subversive literature to fellow football fans... The hated Morgon departed Feethams, although he remains involved behind the scenes as a paid employee of Reg Brealy.

One of the more positive aspects of this season was the introduction of yet another Darlo fanzine entitled 'Darlo, It's Just Like Watching Brazil' which takes the total to four if you include the club's own production. Attendances averaged around the 2,750 mark, not bad after such a calamitous campaign, but by far the club's biggest asset is its ever-increasing fan base thanks to the work of the Darlington Away Far Travelling Supporters (DAFTS) who sponsored matches, the player's kit and tried to ensure that there were at least 300 fans at each away game. If only the club hierarchy could match such impressive figures.

Source: Monkey Business

MONKEY BUSINESS

Hartlepool United

We only used two managers this season. That's a mark of qualified success for us!

This rest of '96-97 just proved the old adage that what goes up must come down. Peaks and troughs came thick and fast, with the emphasis mainly on the troughs. If Harold Hornsey wants to redesign the club badge (please God!) and is looking for a club motto, I think he'd do a lot worse than 'For every silver lining, there's usually a cloud hanging around somewhere'. Either that or 'Just when you think you can see light at the end of the tunnel, you realise it's a train coming the opposite way!'

Just prior to the start of the

No 38   Feb 97   Only **£1**

First issue of the Tait era (Part 2!)

SUPPORT THE POOL

Bring a friend - or even bring someone you don't like!

Season Ticket holders pay on the day
(you've already got several 'free' games as part of your ticket)

Support Brighton fans' campaign to get rid of their Board -
BOYCOTT FOCUS DIY
After all, Pools have already done more to help save Brighton than any other
club in the Division - we've given them six points !!!

season Peter Reid had stolen our leading youth player Paul Conlon on a technicality. He then proceeded to 'sign' Steven 'Buddy' Halliday who was delighted at the prospect of joining his home town club and possibly playing in the Premiership. The clubs failed to agree on a fee: Blunderland offered £50,000; we wanted ten times that. The tribunal valued him at £375,000, and Reid, showing his true colours, backed out of the deal and sent home the disillusioned Halliday.

An opening day victory at Colchester seemed to augur well and by August 24th, after two league games, Pools were top of the league for the first time in their history. Ever! It lasted until the Tuesday home game against Mansfield, but by the following Saturday at Orient, the ever-pragmatic Pools fans were singing "We're not top, we don't care, we'll be back in forty years." They just about summed up the season.

In the first few months, Keith Houchen led the team on a sometimes bewildering series of formations and tactics which seemed to confuse both players and fans alike. He told the press that he believed in tailoring each game's formation and tactics to suit the opposition. Sadly, most of the playing staff couldn't cope with understanding *one* of his formations, let alone a different one for every game. But we played 'good football', with a relentless passing game that often petered out because we had no-one able to make the incisive pass or a forward with enough confidence to finish.

Manic refereeing decisions didn't help Houchen's cause either. At Cambridge we were denied two blatant penalties for no apparent reason, and at home to Dar-low, refereeing of the highest incompetence led to two points being stolen from us. Scarborough's Bill Burns blew his whistle after a Dar-low player threw the ball in from the wrong place, but then changed his mind and waved play on. For once in their lives, Pools' players played to the whistle, stopped, and looked on in amazement as a Dar-low player swept the ball home past a static 'keeper. Little did we know at the time how significant those points might be.

Houchen, for one, certainly let referee Burns know what he thought about that particular decision, and got red carded from the touchline as a result. He later escaped punishment for this offence, as he was no longer employed in football. Near the end of his tenure Houchen gave trials to two French First Division players on the advice of an agent. Club commercial executive (and part-time comedian) Frankie Baggs was sent to Newcastle Airport to meet two six-foot-six strikers who were fluent in English. Baggs, who struggled with his native tongue, was somewhat nonplussed to find two five-foot-six midfield players who didn't speak a word of English! In better circumstances, two eminently talented midfield players may have been welcome, but unfortunately they weren't going to dig Houchen out of the hole he was rapidly excavating.

Injury prematurely ended his playing career, and his managerial career went downhill soon after, culminating in the home debacle against Brighton. Houchen and Tait should be summoned to Brighton, or Hove actually, to receive the freedom of the town. After all, no other club did more to help keep Brighton in the league - we gave them 6 points... on a plate! The writing on the wall was written large and clear for Houch, and he effectively resigned by leaving the bench and walking away before the game finished - the first time in my long football watching career that I'd ever seen this happen.

Tait was given ten games to prove himself. Ably assisted by all-time-hero Brian Honour, he put together a great string of results starting with a cracking 4-2 away win at Scarborough the following week, having given them a two goal start! The following week we played our most convincing and composed 90 minutes of football all season at home to York in the Cup. However, and rather tellingly, we failed to score, and a much relieved York escaped with a draw only to beat us comfortably 3-0 in the replay.

The better league results continued, and during the Christmas holidays Tait was duly appointed manager till the end of the season. Shortly afterwards we had the rather bewildering spectacle of Tait resigning on a point of principle (the proposed elimination of the club's youth policy and reserve teams to save money). The chairman denied any knowledge of the resignation even though 99% of the fans knew about it. The dust soon settled and Tait was back in place by the Monday lunch-time. Small earthquake in Hartlepool - not many injured.

As suddenly as Tait had improved the performances and results, they started to decline, and rapidly went into a free-fall descent into the danger area. This combined with Brighton's media-hyped recovery started alarm bells ringing at the Vic. No matter how badly we played, we'd all convinced ourselves that Brighton could never bridge the gap between themselves and the rest of the division; so why worry? As the weeks rolled by and the incompetence and ineptitude on the pitch was matched only by the increasing depression off it, the South-coasters started to intimidate the bottom half of the table with a string of home wins.

Brighton supporters arranged a 'Fans United' day at The Goldstone, theoretically to show that all fans were united against what their board had done to them. To the increasingly paranoid Hartlepool faithful, it seemed like 91 clubs united against us! The day itself was a fantastic confirmation of the fact that 99% of all football fans love the game itself as much as their own team. It would have been an ideal opportunity for our players to go out, play good football and make a lasting impression on that multi-club, multi-national gathering, most of whom were seeing Pools for the first (and probably last) time.

We bottled it. We lost 5-0 and were lucky to get nil! Yet again we seemed to be on the receiving end of a somewhat eccentric refereeing decision, when Chris Beech was sent off for fouling a Brighton player. The fact that said player proceeded to grip Beech around the throat and bounce his head off the pitch several times seemed to escape the attention of the official, or was it referee's discretion (i.e. don't for Christ sakes give decisions against Brighton in case the fans invade the pitch again). Come to think of it they did exactly that against Orient a few weeks later when the O's had the temerity to score against them. Once again Fat Man Kelly invoked special rules stating that "it was not in the best interests of football to punish Brighton." Let's see what happens to a club who tries that as a defence next season!!

Heads dropped and even players who could've previously have been relied on to give 100% seemed to lose direction, and more critically, commitment. Senior pros who should've been seen at the front leading by example, were soon going absent without leave. Joint leading goalscorers Mark Cooper and Joe Allon (not two of the highest paid players at the club) were dropped for disciplinary reasons. Cooper who'd been instrumental in all of the good things in the first part of the season took little part in the remainder, and Allon, a goalscoring hero who could do no wrong in his first spell with the club, had a rocky time in his second. We weren't exactly inundated with offers when both were subsequently transfer-listed, even on deadline day. Managing prima-donnas is an essential management skill, even at Hartlepool, and the last two seasons have shown that we haven't quite cracked it yet at the Vic.

A spate of deadline day signings added much-needed backbone and commitment to a side which now bore no resemblance to that which had reached the heady heights in August. Probably the most significant signing was that of local boy Michael Brown on loan from Manchester City. He arrived after the club received encouragement from fans: Brown's father is steward at the Supporter's Club and had indicated that Michael would be delighted to play for Pools. This surely had to be one of the strangest backgrounds to a transfer deal since the days when we signed a player for £10 and a box of kippers in the 1920's!

The atmosphere at the first game with the new blood was electric, and we ground out a 1-0 win over Colchester in seemingly cup-tie conditions. Well, at least the reaction to the win made it feel as though we'd won a cup, and a further home win against Orient meant that at least we were keeping pace with Brighton. But a home reverse against Cambridge - surely the most composed and skilful team we had seen at the Vic all season - meant further jitters.

Then came what is even in normal circumstances the highlight of many fans' season: the away trip to Dar-low. Intense local pride is usually all that's at stake on these occasions, but this time it was still possible that either club could end up in the Conference, and having been there before Darlington were not relishing the prospect again. In a tight match with few chances, Michael Brown gave us a dream start with a stunning free kick in the seventh minute. But when Dar-low equalised, it was just a case of hanging on grimly for a point. As we entered injury time we were all trying to work out what the result would mean when Joe (Phoenix from the Ashes) Allon, a recent arrival from the subs bench, did the business from a prone position. Wild celebrations, combined with hastily revised mental arithmetic, followed from somewhat stunned fans.

The other results clarified the league table and we simply needed to beat Barnet in our penultimate league game. Barnet were comfortably in mid-table, with apparently nothing to play for. For 25 minutes they showed some real interest, but eventually cracked and we ran out 4-0 winners. Safe!

The unthinkable drop into the Conference came too close for comfort this year. Survival, whilst most welcome, should not be seen as success. We've got to learn the lessons of this, and the previous five seasons or will find ourselves in the midst of another grim and draining relegation struggle next time around.

Is that light I see at the end of the tunnel?

MOULIN ROUGE

Rotherham United

Reading through last year's review I can't believe how happy I was. We'd won at Wembley on arguably our greatest day and we were looking forward to a successful league season. Looking back, things began to go wrong shortly after sending in my article for SOTF2!

Basically, our quality players started leaving for ridiculously low prices and were replaced by freebie no-hopers. The big departures involved Matt Clarke who was stolen by Washday for £300,000 and Shaun Goater who joined Bristol City for a ludicrous £175,000. In came fat-boy Steve Cherry, old-boy Jim Dobbin and the player Brighton were most pleased to offload, Junior McDougald. Several other nobodies were taken on and the only player of any 'pedigree' to arrive was Lee Glover, but he was to prove our worst ever signing at a reported record fee of £150,000. By far our biggest mistake was the failure to land Nigel Jemson for a knock down asking price of £60,000.

So as far as we were concerned the writing was very definitely on the wall, even though the club attempted to hype our prospects with predictions of a rosy future. At the Coca Cola first round tie at Darlington, Russ of the Muns, a Miller of many years, staged a one man sit-in on the terrace and refused to move despite the best efforts of police and stewards. Being a stout fella he took some shifting and was eventually arrested for speaking his mind. He got a refund on his season ticket the next day and hardly went to a match all year. If you needed a prime example of what chairman Booth and his board were doing to genuine, die-hard fans, this was it. Needless to say, Russ was not alone in his thoughts.

Darlo had no problems disposing of us over two legs and we were soon experiencing our worst ever start to a league campaign. Something had to give, and it did when Archie Gemmill and John McGovern were sacked after a draw with Bristol City. Ironically it could have been Joe Jordan getting the boot if we'd held our two goal lead. What we needed was someone who could scrap for results. What we got was Danny Bergara who could scrap with chair-

---

MOULIN ROUGE

THE ROTHERHAM UNITED FANZINE
Sponsors of Mark Druce's football kit... or whoever's still here!

Phil Henson gives it to us straight!!

Well... err... as I am led to believe... err... it would seem, as I understand it... err... that ... err, err... well.......... that we have no idea!!

ISSUE 17   SUMMER '97   £1

men. And while he wouldn't have been our choice, he had launched Stocky on their journey to the upper reaches of the Nationwide so we had to give him a chance.

At first our new boss made an impression; mainly because his tactics and programme notes were impossible to fathom. Given what was happening on the pitch it was reasonable to suggest that the players were having an equally difficulty time understanding him. The FA Cup was a temporary distraction; we crashed out at Scunny despite a large Millers following, and our brush with the AutoWindscreens was similarly brief.

And to cut a long story short things didn't get any better. We were in a relegation fight from first to last and never looked like pulling away. Yes, there were some notable victories, particularly a win at Bristol City that finally finished Jordan off, and another at Shrewsbury, but it was too little too late and we returned to the basement division for the third time in ten years. What's worrying though is that the previous two times we've been able to bounce straight back because we had some quality in the side together with promising youngsters. Now the kids get sold for little or no money and the quality players want out immediately. This time the vultures will no doubt be circling for a couple of boys with big potential. 'Keeper Phil Barnes and Irish youth player Paul Dillon have both made a big impression and look set to hold down a permanent first team place next year - if we can keep hold of them!

One thing's for sure, someone else will be picking the team now that Danny Bergara has been given his marching orders. The question was who would replace him? The overwhelming fans' choice was Ronnie Moore, our charismatic goalscoring centre forward of the early eighties. A recent newspaper poll revealed that 77% wanted him as boss but that we were unwilling to meet the Southport chairman's compensation claim. For a few weeks it looked like we might end up with yet another Washday connection as Steve Nicol, Chris Waddle and Nigels Pearson and Worthington were touted about. (I've got a feeling the Fowls actually own RUFC and call the shots but what do I know?) Then just when we had all but given up hope, the club did a U-turn and negotiated a settlement with Southport... Ronnie's coming home, he's coming, Ronnie's...

Now that we've got our man, I just hope and pray that the board give him the financial backing required to get us back up.

So that was our season. But there were a few other non-Rotherham footballing incidents to report that I'd like to tell you about.

One of the great things about putting a fanzine together is that you meet some brilliant people. For instance I finished the English season at Wigan and Oldham with my old Norwich supporting mate David Thornhill who came to Wembley with us last year. We'd met up again at Huddersfield in December and made a plan to go and see the Canaries playing on the last Sunday. He pitched up with SEVEN mates, and tents were needed in the back garden to house them all. I decided to cancel a boozy trip to Bristol Rovers to accompany them to Wigan for the Championship party (John Deehan and John Benson being the reason for the journey). They loved the ground (shit heap!) and standing on the terrace again. After a drunken night in Skipton, we sauntered off to Oldham for a miserable 3-0 defeat that didn't mean a thing. We've pencilled in a few more trips next year and I'm hopeful of meeting a few other fanzine people again, like Jackie Mooney of the *Seaside Saga* in Brighton. Mind you, that could be difficult because they don't have a clue where they'll be playing.

My season didn't quite end there because Kilmarnock had made it to the Scottish Cup Final, and with their manager Bobby Williamson being another ex-Rotherham goalscoring hero I had to get up there to support them. It was billed as the 'family final' in the absence of the old firm, so I took my wife Lorraine and our nine year old son Jonathan for the weekend. It had been 23 years since I'd last been to Ibrox (stairway 13 was still intact) and it scared the shit out of me, but now it was almost completely rebuilt, with superb views and a terrific atmosphere guaranteed by 49,000 fans.

Decked out in our Rotherham shirts we got a few weird looks, but once the Killie fans understood the Bobby Williamson connection they welcomed us with open arms. They thought it was great that we'd made such an effort to go up and support them and there's now an unofficial Rotherham supporters club in Kilmarnock. A 1-0 scoreline in Killie's favour meant the party began with a 25,000 strong lump-in-the-throat rendition of Paper Roses, the Lillie anthem. The Falkirk fans deserve a mention as well because they were brilliant in defeat; applauding the presentation of the cup and shaking hands outside the stadium. They were right, it really was the family final.

I had asked Richard Cairns of the *Killie Ken* fanzine what was planned if we won. He explained that there would be an open top bus tour win or lose, so we drove down and joined about 35,000 on the streets of Kilmarnock for a big old knees-up. We were even smuggled into the 'members only' Killie Club after being described as 'family who had travelled up specially from England.' It was a fantastic private piss-up during which it was revealed that Richard's dad was in fact born on Scottish Cup Final day in 1929, the last time Kilmarnock won the cup; couldn't lose, could they?

As I drove back home (with a permanent smile on my face) I reckoned that two end-of-season experiences away from my own supporters had in fact made up for a lot of the heartache of my own team's failings. It really is amazing the spirit that can be engendered by genuine football people who just want to have a laugh with other supporters.

Oh, one last thing. You may think that we had no interest in the play-offs but you'd be wrong. If Sheffield United had gone back to the lager league it would have meant heaps more Yorkshire derbies (Washday, Leeds and Barnsley is quite enough thank you). Our matches with Donny Rovers will take on more importance in South Yorkshire now!!

MOVING SWIFTLY ON...

Walsall

For a season that promised so little back in August, '96-97 turned out to be a surprisingly decent campaign for Walsall FC.

Especially when compared to Peterborough, who 'stole' our two star men, Martin O'Connor and Scotty Houghton, spent a fortune on other players, and still got relegated. The Saddlers in contrast threatened to make the play-offs all the way up until the final week of the season, with a modestly sized squad and only £60,000 spent in total, and even that was all blown on just one decidedly average player! Sadly, the dream died a very painful death following two desperately disappointing performances at Gillingham and Preston; all the good work that was done in the run-in to the 'big finish' was ruined by 180 minutes of seemingly 'couldn't care less' football.

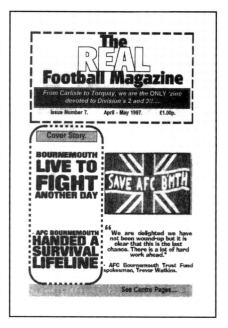

As we trudged away from Deepdale on the last day the mood was that of sheer gloom. The hard facts showed that Walsall FC had ended the season in 12th place, which in the cold light of day meant mid-table mediocrity and a step backwards from the previous campaign's 11th place berth. What it didn't show was that just five days before the season's climax, a top six finish was well within our grasp and many believed that we were more than capable of achieving it; something which couldn't have been said at the same stage last year.

I have to admit that I was among those who doubted that we'd be involved in the end of season lottery that is the play-offs. In fact, looking back I doubted the team's ability at regular intervals from day one, so I must take my hat off to the players and management for keeping the interest very much alive, right up until almost the bitter end. It really was no mean feat that our selection of free transfer captures and up-and-coming youngsters could compete so well in the division, especially when all around us clubs with greater resources were spluttering.

What made our rise into the dizzy heights all the more commendable was that it was born out of the stickiest of starts, which saw us hit rock-bottom after the first four games. A scrappy point from an opening day home draw with the pre-season favourites (for relegation) Rotherham set the tone for the first couple of months, as the club loitered with intent around the relegation zone. Chris Nicholl's summer of indecision (he couldn't decide between the club and the tennis court) cost us dear as we were left in limbo for much of the pre-season, and it showed when the real action got underway.

A host of trialists came and then disappeared off the face of the earth, and we were left with virtually the same group of players who weren't good enough to mount a serious escape bid out of the division last time round. Once again we were left frustrated by the club's reluctance to loosen the purse strings. As a result of this, we missed out on signing a tremendously talented player by the name of Fabio Nigro who looked a couple of classes above anything else that we'd seen during the pre-season games. Coupled with a rather predictably slow start, tensions were running high during our 4-1 defeat at Bristol City in mid-September, and things came to a head when the "Nicholl Out" chants made their debut. The large amount of time it took to persuade him that Walsall was the place to be for another year had not endeared him to the fans and the word from the terrace was that Nicholl wasn't 100% committed to the job. At this point we felt we were being led down the road to nowhere, or in the worst case scenario, the road back to Division Three.

The club complained about the lack of numbers coming through the Bescot turnstiles and cited this as the reason why no money had been spent on new blood. But this argument was a two-way street and when the club went on record as saying that all money generated from the sale of O'Connor and Houghton would be used on team strengthening, only to keep the cash tightly under lock and key, you could understand why some disillusioned fans lost interest and stormed off into the woods. And there's always the danger when you're in the wilderness of being gobbled up by the wolves... or Albion... or Villa... or the Blues!

Meanwhile back on the field, October brought about a slight improvement but little progress up the table, and as such the stay-away fans continued to erm... stay away! One of the few new men in the side, Mark Blake, was failing to live up to the high standards set by O'Connor, and the midfield as a whole looked like a very inexperienced and weak unit. At least we'd now found a more than adequate replacement for Scott Houghton in the form of John Hodge who flew in from Swansea. He was joined for a handful of games by Louie Donowa on the other wing, and despite both players being your typical wingers - when they were good they were very, very good, and when they were bad they were horrid - they at least gave us hope that the management had recognised, and were trying to rectify, our weaknesses. Sadly, after helping to destroy Peterborough in a very sweet 4-0 victory - following which Barry Fry put his entire squad up for sale - Donowa literally disappeared and no-one could find him until he turned up on loan at... wait for it, Peterborough of all places! Suggestions that Barry Fry kidnapped him and forced him to play for his struggling side are still to be confirmed, although I wouldn't put it past the cheating fat bastard!

There was a good degree of festive cheer as December marked the beginning of an impressive rise up the table. Yet, as usual, it was tinged with disappointment and bitterness, but this time it had nothing to do with our players or management. With a mouth-watering tie at Liverpool awaiting us in the next round of the FA Cup, we went into our second round replay at Burnley full of confidence that we could remove them from the competition for the second successive season. Sure enough, after totally outplaying them in the first half, we deservedly took a one goal lead into the interval when, lo and behold, the floodlights went out and we were plunged into darkness! A dodgy tannoy meant we were then left for an hour without having a clue what was going on, until news filtered through that the game was being abandoned. Well, the huge cheer from the Burnley faithful kind of gave it away! If this wasn't bad enough we were then victimised from three different sides when *we'd* done absolutely nothing wrong. First, despite informing us on the night that we would be able to gain free entry into the rearranged game, Burnley proceeded to charge us again (albeit half price, but that was no consolation, believe me). Liverpool then stuck their oar in and insisted that the game was played before Christmas to ease their precious fixture congestion. Cheers, you bunch of overpaid, posing prats - what about *our* five scheduled games in just 12 days!

Finally the FA, in their infinite wisdom, decided that the original 45 minutes never actually took place, so therefore the goal was wiped from the records, yet rather interestingly we'd still had to pay to watch this non-event. On top of that Burnley were cleared of any blame, and so we weren't even in line for any compensation. In effect this decision gives clubs the licence to simply flick off the lights when things aren't going their way. If it wasn't Burnley's fault then who the hell was responsible? If they can afford to build two impressive new stands and splash out large amounts on new players, then surely they could've ensured that there was some kind of back-up system in place to cope with this kind of situation; a decent tannoy system wouldn't go amiss either. Oh, and to top the whole thing off we bloody ended up losing the tie on penalties - of course. Football can be a cruel game!

One good thing to come out of the FA Cup debacle was that it spurred us on to win the next six league games, with Adi Viveash emerging as a prolific goalscoring centre-back. In fact, the Burnley story was quite typical of how the season went for your average regular Walsall traveller like myself. I've never known a season which brought so many disappointments on our travels, and I am not necessarily just talking about matters on the pitch. First of all we battled through the elements and some unforgiving tea-time traffic to finally reach Bootham Crescent, home of York City, only to find the ground bathed in darkness and the match off. Then two separate journeys to Peterborough for an AWS tie brought no joy, and finally we struggled through thick fog to arrive at Gillingham for another night game, only to be greeted by a large group of giggling school kids who took great pleasure in informing us that the match wasn't going ahead. It is hard to find the words to adequately explain how you actually feel at moments like these. I suppose that 'empty, tinged with a bit of foolishness' would sum it up.

At least things were starting to come together on the field and we were at last being given something positive to shout about as the home straight saw us emerge as serious play-off contenders. Having said that, we only crept into the play-off zone once over the course of the season, and the rest of the time we were content to lurk just on the edge. Unfortunately our planned late move never came, and instead we plummeted to finish 12th - our lowest placing since early February.

With the majority of the squad having been together for several years - a rare thing in today's harsh football world - it is hoped that with Chris Nicholl's departure we can bring a bit of zip back to the club. Fresh ideas, fresh faces and fresh impetus is what's required, but implementing change can take time, so whether we can mount a promotion challenge this season remains to be seen. Still, things could be worse... I could be a Shrewsbury or Peterborough fan. Commiserations lads, but we'll meet again, don't know where, don't know when...

"Can I get my money back, if I'm not satisfied?"

Source: Zulu

NO MORE PIE IN THE SKY

Notts County

THE BITTEREST PILL (we've ever had to swallow) [Mass Appeal Mix]
-: The Sound Track To The Season :-
Prologue: The club was packed, bouncing like fuck to the hard-edged dirty rampant sound from the fusion of Old Skool break-beats, Rap and R'n'B that were mashed together with the sonic at-tack from the underground trip-hop tunes that 'Fatboy Slim' pulled with precise skill from his flight-box be-hind him. Heather loved it. She knew her Rap and appreciated the knowledge of the man on the Wheelz-Of-Steel. The packed are-na reminded her of the vibe on the

NO MORE PIE IN THE SKY

Presents

ISSUE NO.20 (OR WAITER, THERE'S SOME SOUP IN MY FLIES.)

(Oct. - Dec. 1996)

A NOTTS COUNTY FANZINE...   Still only 50p

NOT EVERYTHING IN BLACK AND WHITE MAKES SENSE.

Is it the GUINNESS or The MURPHY's Speaking ?

ALSO INSIDE : Noel Gallagher down the Lane, The Statto Zone, Match Reports, Why we keep losing, Join the F.S.A., Your views and loads of other rubbish to fill up the space....

terraces, of her other love - the beautiful game. She could hold her own in a so-called man's world. Home and away, week-in, week-out, her religion: follow-ing her boys. Added to this was her uncompromised hatred of F***st. No reason, no logic, just an E-motion of unremitting hate. She had a dream, a wish, a hope... that the 'The Children Of The Devil' from 'The Temple Of Sin' would be relegated.

The pill was kicking-in and as her mind drifted away from reality, she slowly became aware of an unrecognisable presence. She felt a shiver down her spine, then an almighty scream rang inside her mind. And as her eyes slowly opened, the dark pools of her pupils began to focus on the enticing figure. Lucifer himself stood before her in a dark red glow that engulfed all. Her wish would be granted, he said, but there would be *A Cost Of Loving*. Everything has *A Price To Pay*... Her mind then sped off on another tangent as the beat changed once again, the DJ taking the rhydum to yet another dimension.

Side A: The First Half

Track 1: Headstart For Happiness - The Style Council

A pre-season, again unbeaten, included trophy success over F***st in the County Cup and a useful win over Palace that gave genuine optimistic hopes for a successful sojourn. The campaign kicked-off with a 2-1 victory over newcomers Preston, but August concluded without a second win. An analysis of 'Wembley Blues' from manager Colin Murphy was dispatched to quell any disquiet among early doubters in the ranks.

Track 2: The Man Who Sold The World (Unplugged Version) - Nirvana

September's story was to be one that would be a yard-stick for the saga ahead. Out of the 'Eat Football, Sleep Football Cup' to Bury (fuckin' *Bury* for God's sake) with a performance that was as effective as Olderan vs The Death Star. The long trip south to Home Park saw the spineless match-day officials totally bottle it as they ruled out Robbo's cheeky 'Gary Crosby goal-scoring tactic' on Bruce '£10 and it's sorted' Grobelaar. Initially the goal had stood until the home side and fans' protests changed their minds. Notts then began their first of many journeys into the Late Goal Zone (LGZ) as both Watford and Millwall returned south three points the better with late strikes. We did win away at Bournemouth but we always win there; it's not hard is it? Even for Notts!

Track 3: The Third Decade, Our Move - DJ Shadow

An onerous October saw more misery as the Gills and The Adams Family clinched 1-0 wins. The "Murphy Out" chant was released and began its rise up the Meadow Lane hit parade. Available in limited 7," CD digi-pack and 12" (Chemical Brothers remix) formats in late September, it gained a full prime-time spot in the defeat away at Adams Park, although a 3-1 win away at Posh (another happy hunting ground for the Pies) gave Murphy some respite. This was to be only a hiccup though, as the chant entered the Top 40 after yet another 1-0 reverse, this time away at Burnley. "Murphy Out" was picking up pace, gaining support all the time. The pluggers reckoned Top 20 beckoned with a crushing 4-0 annihilation at Ashton Gate. If the Robins had any compassion they would have declared at half-time. If that seemed bad then the end of the month wrote October's obituary; the final sacrifice of the Stone Roses as Mani joined the Premiership Primals. Was there to be a *Resurrection*?

Track 4: Exodus (Movement Of Jah People) - Bob Marley

November's fireworks began with a rare home win, but as the bonfires burnt down normality resumed against The Shrews (beaten with the now obligatory late goal -Bennett, 88th). The debacle at Luton (*A Town Called Malice*) gained media attention as the band of anti-Murphy protesters gathered force; the team was in disarray and even the fans began to split into For and Against factions. A non-league encounter in the FA Cup could have seen the final nail in madman Murphy's coffin, but he escaped his fate with a 2-0 win. But we knew that we couldn't lose sight of the real incubus. Murphy was treading water now, but the ship was in danger of sinking with the crew thirsting for mutiny.

Track 5: Bye Bye Badman - The Stone Roses

December doom began with Brentford shooting another cannonball into the bow as County joined the relegation battle royal. Two cup victories (wow!) and UFO sightings at Scarborough (even bigger wow!) detracted from the real deal. And as Christmas drew near "Murphy Out" entered the Top 10 with its sights firmly set on a festive no.1. December 20th provided the season's nadir: a 3-0 trouncing at Gresty Road with a performance devoid of skill, fight, honour, passion - you name it, all had gone AWOL. The chant (now in remixed form as "All we want for Christmas is Murphy Out Murphy Out") hit the top spot. Santa arrived early for the long-suffering supporters when Derek Pavis, himself under immense pressure, had no option but to release Murphy n' Thompson from their multi-album deal. There was time for a compilation though: *Colin Murphy, The Worst Manager in Britain - EVER!* had tracks dedicated to his total lack of knowledge, compassion, his eccentricities and the scars left on us that will take years to heal. Thank Marley that these artistes are no longer signed to County...

— **End of Side One** —

Side B: The Second Half

Track 6: New Religion - Duran Duran

Still full of turkey and Christmas pud, we set off for Vicarage Road with our hopes now in the hands of three wise men; Tony Agana, Gary Strodder and Mark Smith were now calling the tune. A 0-0 saw the Magpies full of fire and steel, and hopes of a New Year renaissance were in the air. Then on to the Racecourse Ground for undoubtedly the game of the season and a stomping 3-3 draw. The Magpies continued to flourish under their new-found confidence and pulled off a 0-0 against the mighty Villa in the third round of the FA Cup, and if truth be known should have won. Two days later Pavis and his puppets unveiled the latest member of the Notts management circus when Sam Allardyce, formerly at Blackpool, was chosen to lead the fight-back out of the inherited mire.

Track 7: Black Steel In The Hour Of Chaos - Public Enemy

High-flying Luton glided into the Meadow. At 1-0 up you'd have been hard-pressed to say that it wasn't County who occupied the higher perch. But then Sam played it again, or to be precise, made one of his wholly uninspired substitutions and gave Luton the impetus to draw level within seconds. Then with the fat lady drawing breath it was time to enter the LGZ. *Bye, bye baby...* Not even the loan deal to bring back former striker 'big' Dave Regis could save us from beginning an embarrassingly shite run of defeats.

Track 8: That Joke Isn't Funny Any More - The Smiths

The March parade began with two points thrown overboard against Brentford, and with survival time running out we were in dire need of help. The infamous Rodger Stanislaus failed to come down to the Lane and floated off to Peterborough; instead Devon 'Bruno' White returned in a final quest for the great escape. But re-entry into the LGZ against Crewe, Rotherham and Stockport left us in need of miracles. Another 1-0 defeat by Bury (yet again) saw us into club record-breaking territory as 18 games without a win soon became 19, then 20... Would we ever win again?

Track 9: Beat Surrender - The Jam

April began in bizarre fashion. A win! But it was too little too late, and a home defeat by Wycombe finally closed the book on life in Division 2. All that was left to do now was to turn our gaze to the shambles over the Trent and hope that F***st's equally pathetic attempts to escape the clutches of the Nationwide would fail. What a nightmare that we had to look to them to put the smiles back on our sad faces.

Track 10: Play That beat Mr DJ (The Payoff Mix) - MC Globe and DJ Whiz Kid - (remix by Double D and Stienski)

F***st had lay in the Premiership doldrums for most of the season and a 0-0 draw with the sheep had left the trees all but felled. Now Wimbledon, those masters of the upset, visited the shitty ground ready to administer the fatal blow. They didn't shirk from their responsibility and cleared the deadwood from the top flight.

Bonus Track: WFL (Think About The Future) Perfecto 12" Mix - Happy Mondays

The scars are deep, confidence blunted and the future uncertain. Managing director Geoff Davey has called for everyone to pull together, and while this is an ideal we can share, we still believe that someone has to view the whole picture. *No More Pie In The Sky* is not the voice of a generation or any of those cute clichés; we are part of a generation, part of a growing mood and most of the future. But when the squares upstairs keep complaining about the noise grooving off my portable then what do they expect me to do, other than crank up the volume, shut out their dreary grumblings and get out onto the floor!

Epilogue: Heather walked into the open, the bright light of the new day lit up the world again. The vibe had changed though; *If You Wanna Be My Lover* could be faintly heard from a Car Stereo. She saw the headlines in a Sunday paper: 'F***ST SLUMP', and realised that her wish had been granted. But there had been a price: the debacle at the Lane - the music of Oasis, Weller and Stone Roses replaced by the satanic verses of the Spice Girls. The '96-97 season had been one to forget. As she walked back through the deserted streets of Nottingham, thoughts of the future milled around inside her mind; would she make the same deal or was it time to forget the rest and concentrate on her true love? There is hope though; 1997 brings new material from The Chemical Brothers, Prodigy, Oasis, Weller, The Seahorses, Depeche Mode, Wu-Tang, Primal Scream, Charlatans and Bentley Rhythm Ace – so perhaps the future does look bright...

- End of Side B -

NO-ONE LIKES US

Millwall

The real horror story

Never mind Boro and Brighton whinging about their problems; for this third issue of Survival of the Fattest, it's your old pals from Sarf London who've been through real hell. The first *SOTF* told of beating The Arse, Chelsea and Forest in cups, and league disappointments, while the next told the story of our trip from top of the table to relegation. This time it's mid-table obscurity, cup disasters and losing two managers on the way. And to top it all (and make us feel like topping ourselves) the club nearly went bust.

Jimmy Nicholl faffed about at the end of '95-96 and when rele-

THE ALTERNATIVE **MILLWALL** MAGAZINE £1

ISSUE 51

MANNING MEETS THE FANS
◆
A SUPPORTERS CLUB - WHO NEEDS THEM?
◆
THE LIONESSES - SORTS WITH ATTITUDE
◆
NICHOLL OUT - DOC IN
◆
CARTER JOKES OUT - HORNE JOKES IN

STILL LIFE IN THE LIONS?

gation finally became a reality, most of the Millwall faithful felt that the blame for it lay with ex-boss Mick McCarthy. The balance of opinion later shifted, however. Jim sold the agile Kasey Keller and our most exciting midfielder Alex Rae. In came the Raith trio of Stevie Crawford, newly-capped and scoring on his national debut, Dave (Sinky) Sinclair, infamous defensive hard man, and Jason Dair, gifted nephew of Slim Jim Baxter. They were accompanied by tricky Jocko winger Paul (JR) Hartley.

Our curtain-raiser with Liverpool had been agreed as part of our fee for Mark Kennedy, and we held our own against the Anfield giants. We'd been caned by Ayr United on a pre-season tour, but as every fan does, we chose to believe we were as good as Liverpool rather than on a par with Stanraer.

From the start our league form was patchy; we were top of the table and then down again, while the cups were disastrous. Peterborough (later relegated, and bollocks to you, Barry Fry) dumped us out of the League Cup. And in the FA Cup first leg at Woking, we were cruising to victory but let the non-leaguers force a replay. In the return we capitulated in shameful fashion. The most damning aspect of the whole evening was Jimmy's pessimism on *Sky* before the game; his inability to motivate our lads was obvious to all, and soon after we went out of the AWS to a golden goal by Colchester.

Millwall's greatest asset is the fans - OK, they can get carried away, notably the so-called supporters who attend two games in a season, intent on trouble. So when Jimmy started slagging us off he'd committed the cardinal sin. We demanded his immediate departure - we were here before he came and we'd be here long after he'd gone. His bunch of gutless wonders were a disgrace to our name and we'd had enough. Butch Wilkins and Mark Bright came, and - thank God - left.

Of the signings, Sinclair proved to be a bloated, clumsy twat, and Jason Dair was described by *Time Out*'s sports writer as the worst professional he'd ever seen. Crawford scored a few but spent a lot of time posing about; only JR Hartley looked up for it. But the biggest blow was our failure to sign Darren Huckerby, who we'd all instantly spotted as an outstanding talent in his all too brief loan spell. And of course he did become a star... at Coventry. Perhaps that was the turning point of our season.

In the shit - it's official

The club then made an announcement. Not the widely expected statement thanking Jimmy for all his hard work but politely telling him to fuck off, but about massive and grave debts, which had to be met. The administrators arrived and the board surrendered control rapidly, completely and utterly. We knew things were bad, but it was still a shock - how had it come to this?

A new and under-utilised stadium was probably the main cause. At first we'd complained about their proposals to host 40 non-footballing events a season, fearing that our beautiful game would become a side-show (the lack of Millwall signs and the name New London Stadium did nothing to ease our misgivings). Our American promoters promised visits by the giants of rock, *mate*, and demanded the installation of state-of-the-art pizza ovens. Well, the grand total of events in three years was one boxing match (a free copy if you can say who was in it), which lost £˜ million.

The naïvety of our board was appalling. We were trying to deal with people who were far more clued up than our incompetent and divided amateurs. Our car park saw a Speakers' Corner style set-to between our current chairman and his predecessor - unfortunately it didn't come to blows (we'd probably have lost money on it anyway).

Previous purse-tightening had already seen the departure of clerks and receptionists, but this was the big one: the chief executive, a detested character, was dismissed. But unfortunately we lost some good Millwall people too. Tragically, we couldn't unload the lazy, spineless overpaid bastards who had the cheek to place their unworthy bodies in our shirts. Contracts had to be 'honoured' and the players refused to take a cut in wages to aid our survival. Understandable maybe, but they were leeches compared with the more laudable Bournemouth squad.

Off the pitch it was all change. Jimmy Nicholl was dismissed at last. John Docherty, who had once taken us up to the top division, returned, while our ever-loyal hero Keith (Rhino) Stevens stepped up to management. Doc produced an unbeaten run which only ended because he didn't have enough (some would say any) decent players. (I am sure that every fan has seen the farcical situation of a centre back being played as a centre forward.)

For me, the final straw came at our last home game. The humiliation dished out by Gillingham was too much; I could take no more pain and left at half time. Docherty had also had enough; when it was suggested that we sell our only star Lucas Neill to Glasgow Rangers, try as they might to dissuade him, and they even succeeded for a short time, John eventually threw in the towel.

The new chairman is Theo Paphitis, who made money out of turning around the Ryman group. Apparently he is more willing to listen to good advice and run a sound set-up. Perhaps it'll be better having a real businessman in charge rather than the amateur types who got us in the shit in the first place.

The final shock for the Millwall faithful was the announcement that our new manager was Hamster legend Billy Bonds, who also brought in Pat Holland. They have an awful lot to prove, and success will depend on whether they can produce a quality and committed team on very little money. A clearout has begun but some parasites are still on juicy contracts, so it could be two or three years before we are a competitive outfit. Still, if Bonzo acts with a common sense sadly lacking in his predecessors then at least he can count on our magnificent support.

NOT THE 8502

AFC Bournemouth

An unforgettable season... and then there was some footy!

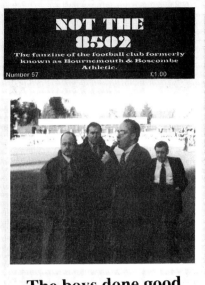

Money problems have blighted lower league clubs for many years and when the Premier League was formed there was genuine concern that the gulf between the elite and the rest would widen, perhaps even forcing some clubs out of business. This state of affairs can be jointly attributed to the spiralling wages at all levels, the concentration of sponsorship and TV money at the top of the game, and most worrying of all, the Bosman ruling which has opened the floodgates allowing cheap foreign imports to be favoured over the purchase of talent from the Second and Third Divisions.

I think most readers would agree with that sentiment, but it still comes as a shock when the reality of financial ruin visits your club. And this season, the reaper came knocking at the door of mine. The dark clouds had been growing around Dean Court for years. When we tried to compete with the bigger clubs in our three year spell in the old Second Division, the seeds of ruin were sown when relegation meant less income through the turnstiles and a squad full of mediocre players on long contracts and large wages. The club limped on, getting further into debt as a succession of 'White Knight' chairmen came full of promises and left fulfilling none of them.

Things were spinning out of control. The last chairman was Ken Gardiner, a man who was both passionate about AFC Bournemouth and who loved being in control. In November 1996 he went on holiday to Kenya and on his return resigned from his post due to alleged 'ill health'. At the same time, the majority shareholder and former chairman Norman Hayward sent in his men to investigate the club and the alarm bells were deafening. However their mutual dislike for each other made establishing the truth very difficult.

The local paper was full of doom and gloom with regular headlines proclaiming 'IS THIS THE END OF THE CHERRIES?' Most Bournemouth fans had heard it all before and although there was concern, the feeling was that it would all be alright and the cracks would once again be papered over.

But on Friday January 4th reality struck as the receivers were called in. They made it clear that the following day's match at Bristol City would very likely be the last in the history of the club. The players would not be paid and weren't obliged to play if they didn't want to. Many people didn't attend the game; either they couldn't face up to the facts or they knew it would be too upsetting. The ones who did were walking around in a daze before the game, asking "Is this it? Is this the end?" There was a huge feeling of togetherness which lifted everybody during the game, especially as Bournemouth pulled off an unlikely win. But then afterwards...

It's very hard to describe. We'd just won away from home, yet the feelings were of complete deflation and utter despair as we thought we'd just witnessed our club's last ever game. No more Saturdays at football, no more travelling miles with little hope of a win, the end of something that is a huge, important part of your life. The following day I received a phone call to go to a meeting at the ground. Supporters gathered and the Trust Fund was formed. We had to get enough money together to buy time so that the next game could be played. This event was to escalate into an unforgettable time for the town. On the Tuesday a public meeting was planned to tell people what was going to happen. The venue held over 1,800. The thought crossed our minds that it was too big.

AFC Bournemouth and passion are not usually associated with each other. Knowing this worried me, but turning up at the Winter Gardens 45 minutes before the meeting started I realised that Bournemouth people *can* be as passionate as anyone. All you could hear on that crisp February night was the sound of Bournemouth fans singing. I've got good eyesight but I certainly couldn't see the end of the queue. Every seat was full, the aisles were packed and a PA system was put up outside for the hundreds who couldn't get in. Mel Machin shed a tear on stage, and he wasn't alone - there was hardly a dry eye in the house. This wasn't about eleven men v eleven men. This was about the heart and spirit of a town. This was about a community coming together to try to preserve something that meant so much to so many. An incredible £30,000 was put into buckets that night. The League took notice and allowed us to play against Blackpool the following Saturday. Thousands turned up. Even though many of the crowd were there to show their allegiance and would probably only return for the visit of a Premiership side or if success came to the club, it at least showed our potential.

The game was a disappointing 0-0 draw, but that didn't matter. The sight of season ticket holders paying to get in summed up the feelings. And although attendances continued to be around 1,500 above the previous average, we needed more, and three nil-nils in a row didn't inspire the less committed to attend. Behind the scenes, the Trust Fund announced that instead of just tiding things over until a benefactor came along, they wanted to turn AFC Bournemouth into a Community Club. It was a brave move and one that would be very difficult to pull off. Local firms were asked to buy in by contributing a minimum of £10,000. The main stipulation to avoid all the past mistakes was that no one person or company could have a 51% controlling interest.

We even witnessed the impossible during this time. Southampton came to Dean Court for a fund-raising friendly, *free of charge*. Nearly 9,000 turned up and Bournemouth fans actually applauded their much-loathed rivals.

The season came to the end with winding up orders being put back time and time again. Local firms agreed a Creditors' Voluntary Agreement and many lost thousands, but this was the vital step. The League agreed the deal on June 18th, and for all of us in so-called sleepy Bournemouth, Teletext reporting that our first game of the season would be at Northampton meant that the dream had been kept alive: the supporters had taken over the club.

And here's the stark truth: AFC Bournemouth would have ceased to exist had we, the fans, not put our hands in our pockets, not walked mile upon mile on sponsored walks, not seen local rock bands perform for nothing, not had children sending in their pocket money and fund-raising at virtually every school, not had unemployed people donating their giros even though this meant they couldn't afford to go to the games. There are many stories of people's dedication to the club and all had one goal: keeping the dream alive.

We are victims in AFC Bournemouth of the Premiership marketing campaign that targets children to wear licensed products. Our situation will never be repeated at Manchester United, Spurs, Arsenal, Liverpool, etc. but we have proved that if you really support a club, it can be the most rewarding thing in the world. I know we're not world-beaters and probably never will be, but it is our club now and no-one can deny that fact. Could a supporter of a big club say that?

Oh yes, on the pitch! It was a comfortable season which could have been better if we hadn't lost our first six home games. We gained some superb wins on the road at Millwall, Watford, Stockport and Bristol City and also had a brilliant defensive record. It didn't matter what happened on the pitch, though, not even if we'd been relegated. What matters is that we still have a football club to support. *Our* club.

THE NUMBER 9 ·

Newcastle United

After the depression of last season was finally erased by sinking countless crates of Newcastle Brown Ale during the pre-season, Geordies up and down the country anticipated that piece of silverware we so desperately craved. The arrival of the prodigal son Alan Shearer was greeted with the same euphoric enthusiasm that was bestowed upon a certain Kevin in 1982. But £15 million! I ask you...

Having been lambasted by pundits up and down the country for naïve tactics and poor defending, many anticipated a defensive signing. It didn't arrive, and with that, many declared that the chances of silverware for the Toon Army

Thank You - Good luck -

THE ALL NEW NUMBER NINE ISSUE 27 JANUARY 1997
INSIDE THIS ISSUE
AUF WIEDERSEN KEV PART 2
DEREK WRIGHT INTERVIEW
DALGLISH   ONLY
MORE CHANCES TO WIN MORE VIDEOS!!

NOW 4 EXTRA PAGES   **99p**

were now slim. Opening the season at Wembley in the prestigious curtain-raiser that is the Charity Shield, we were thumped 4-0 by Champions Manchester Utd. We enjoyed the day, though, and once again Newcastle Brown Ale proved to be our saviour.

The opening games of the season, and things seemed to be getting worse. Defeats at Everton and at home to early leaders Sheffield Wednesday had Alan Hansen, Trevor Brooking and Jimmy Hill slavering at the jowls to criticise Keegan's team. "The bubble's burst," they whined. "Puir defending" cried Alan. Bollocks! The visit of Manchester United in October left them all speechless. The previous season had seen us dominate the game against the Manc scum, only to lose 1-0, a result which for me turned our title ambition and dreams into a nightmare. The 5-0, yes *five-nil* thumping of Cantona & Co was truly the best game I have ever experienced as a Newcastle follower, although the win over Brighton in our promotion season ranks alongside it (for the record: '83-84, a 3-1 win with goals from dream team Beardsley, Waddle and Keegan). Our European adventure again threw up some fascinating games: Metz, Ferencvaros and Monaco, the latter finally getting the better of us, due mainly to injuries to Shearer and Ferdinand.

The bombshell of Keegan's departure from the club he loves so much still angers me, and I, like many other Toon fans don't like talking about it too much. He made his choice; he awoke the sleeping giant that was Newcastle

United for the second time, and he should be given the highest honour the City of Newcastle can bestow upon him. Good luck Kevin, we still love ya!

King Kenny took over the reins at the turn of the year and with Dalglish's record as a player and manager he was the only man with a suitable CV. Although not as emotional as Keegan, Dalglish made it clear that he would not put up with prima-donnas... and Ginola found himself on the bench. The run-in saw Liverpool, Arsenal and ourselves challenging for second spot and a place in the prestigious Champions League alongside the Champions-elect Manchester 'bloody' United. With Arsenal and Liverpool having an inferior goal difference Newcastle earned the coveted second place with a 5-0 thrashing of relegated Nottingham Forest.

How times change, and how ironic that twelve months earlier we had been devastated at finishing second. This year St James Park had its own party for finishing in runners-up spot. So, overall a successful season, especially after Kevin's resignation, and I think you all know now it is only a matter of time before Newcastle United win something! Please!!

THE OATCAKE

Stoke City

The '96-97 season should have been memorable for Stoke City supporters, not just because of our unexpected feat of reaching the play-offs the previous year, but more importantly for the fact that it was to be our last ever at the Victoria Ground.

Supporters of any club, be they in the Premiership or the Conference, will tell you that their ground is special, but for the Stoke supporters the Victoria Ground was more than that. It wasn't just where we watched our team play, it embodied everything that is Stoke City; although a run-down relic and a shadow of its former self, the ground represented treasured memories and was still precious to those who loved it so dearly.

THE OATCAKE

STOKE'S SAS
Who dares wins!

80p Wednesday 15th May 1996
Play Off Semi Final 2nd Leg v. Leicester City 142

We all hoped that the club could build on the progress on the previous year and give 'The Vic' the kind of send-off it so richly deserved. Those of us with more furtive imaginations foresaw full houses every week and a final triumphant farewell as the team celebrated their promotion to the Premiership on the last day of the season. The more realistic amongst us predicted another hard slog, and as usual it was they who were proved to be right.

For a very short while it did seem that the dream was on, though. We lay to rest a ten-year jinx against Oldham by winning there on the opening day of the season, and then inflicted on Manchester City the defeat which saw Alan Ball shown the exit at Maine Road. You have to be a supporter of a club that Bally has managed to fully understand why this should be such a joy for us. The squeaky-voiced one took us to the lowest league position in our history, and this was our long-awaited retribution.

After the fourth game we were top of the table, but that really was about as good as it got for the Potters. Successive three-goal defeats within the space of four days at Barnsley and Birmingham put a spoke in our wheels and gave a more realistic complexion to our better-than-expected start to the campaign.

The defeat at Barnsley not only showed that the Tykes were a far better side, it also saw injuries to two key Stoke players, striker Simon Sturridge and stalwart defender Ian Cranson, which put an end to both of their seasons. The loss of these two showed once again just how wafer-thin our squad was, and for the next 40 games we were papering over the cracks in the team.

Unusually, the club did actually take steps to rectify our shortage of numbers, by signing Irishmen Gerry McMahon and Graham Kavanagh from Spurs and Middlesbrough respectively. Unfortunately, neither player really did themselves justice over the course of the season, and their addition to the first team squad did little to cover the woeful shortage of numbers in the defence and forward line.

Except for the odd hiccup here and there we were pretty invincible at home, at least as far as results went. Sadly, even in victory we rarely looked convincing and that lack of killer form manifested itself in truly dreadful fashion away from the Victoria Ground. Following on from that well deserved-opening day victory at Boundary Park, we recorded just two more away victories all season - at West Brom (we always win there though, so it hardly counts!) and at Charlton. As a pointer to just how bad our away form was, Mike Sheron's two strikes at Charlton on January 18th turned out to be the last goals scored by a Stoke player in an away game for the rest of the season!!

Other horrors on our travels included a 1-0 defeat at Swindon (despite playing against ten men for over 60 minutes and with a final shot-count of 26-4 in our favour!) and a two-goal defeat at Manchester City (where we set a new standard for crapness). However, those nightmares were eclipsed by another two-goal loss at Carrow Road, where we went into the game seeking to end a sequence of games that had seen us concede early goals. We held out for... wait for it... TEN seconds. And we kicked off!

Those of us who follow Stoke to every away game began contemplating the wisdom of blind loyalty in the face of such a miserable return. In fact it wasn't until the last game at Sheffield United that we finally had something to cheer about - we give our sincere thanks to the large-breasted young lady who enlightened the evening by streaking topless across the pitch. The way some Stokies were gawping and salivating you'd think that they'd never seen a naked woman before... but that's enough about me and my mates!

For a while it seemed that our home form might compensate and keep us in the play-off hunt, but that hope went up in smoke with successive home defeats to Bolton and Norwich. The match against champions-elect Bolton removed any illusions we were harbouring about promotion. They had Nathan Blake sent off in less than half an hour but still completely dominated the match and should have finished with a more convincing victory than 2-1. Defeat by a similar score to Norwich a week later may not seem too bad, but bear in mind that it came at a 'crisis' time for them, as they'd conceded 14 goals in their previous three away games, including 5-1 and 6-1 defeats at West Brom and Port Fail!

With our play-off prospects disappearing over the horizon, the combination of poor results, poor form, poor league position and unacceptable quality of football led to the previously unthinkable - supporters began to question

Lou Macari's position as manager. For those who don't know Stoke City too well, Lou Macari is/was revered by Stoke fans for the work he did in saving the club in the wake of Alan Ball's disastrous spell in charge. There has never been a shortage of people queuing up to take a swipe at Lou, but at Stoke we would have none of it. The fans loved him and he could do no wrong. There have always been critics of his style of management and the football he likes his teams to play, but what did those people know? Lou has a proven style that works, and he can boast a record of never having managed a team that finished lower than halfway in a league table!

However last season's failings illustrated that Lou was not the pragmatist we had previously believed him to be, but was instead totally dogmatic in his belief on how football should be played. Having signed four players from Premiership clubs, Lou still sent the team out to play in its customary fashion, despite the fact that everybody could see that it wasn't working. Lou's answer to repeatedly poor performances and the unavoidable fact that other teams were playing much better was to insist that we had to work harder and run around the pitch at 100mph! The question was soon asked as to why we should be signing players from the Premiership and then asking them to play Third Division football!?

The consensus of opinion among Stoke supporters (and if rumour be believed, the board too) was that Lou had lost the plot and had taken the club as far as he was likely to. Despite this, it still came as an incredible shock when on the eve of last ever Potteries derby at the Victoria Ground, Lou announced that he was stepping down. He cited his main reason as the ongoing court case with Glasgow Celtic and Fergus McCann, which had already seen him spending a lot of time in Edinburgh and which would occupy even more of his time in the future. Fair enough - maybe - but many fans believe that Lou sensed the wind of change at the Victoria Ground and jumped before he was pushed.

Whatever the case, it meant that our preparations for the home match against hated Burslem neighbours 'the Fail', our penultimate fixture at the Victoria Ground, were less than ideal. And it was to be the most important derby game for years, as they were - incredibly - in the running for the play-offs. They only needed to extend their four year unbeaten run against us by one more match to give themselves a really good chance of having a shot at the Premiership.

The very thought of the Fail making it into the elite of English football (for what would be the first time in their history) off the back of a win against us was too gruesome to contemplate. We prayed that the players would be able to rally themselves to give us something to smile about. And they did. The final score was 2-0 to Stoke, and it should have been more. Our local rivals showed themselves to be 'Fail by name, Fail by nature' as they choked and blew their chance of the Premiership. This of course meant that we could leave the Victoria Ground with a smile on our faces.

The stage was finally set for the last competitive match ever at The Vic. The first league game to be played there had been against West Brom on September 4th 1888. By an incredible quirk of fate the Football League's computer had determined that the last team to provide opposition would once again be the Baggies; this as good as guaranteed a good send-off for the old place. It is now nearly nine years and 17 games since West Brom last beat Stoke City, and though some of us worried that the run might end at the most inopportune time, we needn't have. Goals from McMahon and Kavanagh led us to a comfortable 2-1 victory, though the record books will show that the last goal scored at the ground was by West Brom's Andy Hunt, courtesy of a late penalty.

When Stoke had first voiced plans to move to a new stadium it all seemed so far away and you never really thought that the last day against West Brom would ever come. Come it did though, and there were some very mixed emotions on the day. The excitement at the prospect of a move to a new home was tempered by the loss of the only place any of us has known as home. The Vic was the only football ground to be used constantly since the formation of league football in 1888 and it held the record for being the longest occupied league ground in Great Britain (and therefore the world!?), with Stoke having been there for 119 years. With its passing, Stoke lost a home, and English football also waved a final goodbye to a piece of history.

For sure, '96-97 was a strange season. None of us had really expected that the team would be battling for automatic promotion, but a shot at the play-offs had been almost taken for granted. A failure to achieve that had taken away from what was supposed to have been a very special season. There are however, silver linings to most dark clouds. Our side is a very young one and with a few additional new faces, it has the potential to give a much, much better account of itself. Hopefully, our fourth contribution to Survival of the Fattest will tell of a glorious first season at the Britannia Stadium. Knowing Stoke though, I won't be holding my breath...

ON THE TERRACES

West Ham United

Following the tremendous conclusion to the previous season (when West Ham finished tenth, ahead of the likes of Blackburn, Leeds and Chelsea), hopes and expectations for the new campaign had never been higher. "Forget about any fears of relegation, it's European qualification we're aiming at, be it via one of the cup competitions or the UEFA Cup from a top eight Premier League spot" was how *On the Terraces* saw it. But how were we to know that Harry Redknapp had made some serious errors of judgement over several of his new (and not so new) former Eastern bloc squad members?

Florin Raduciou joined us for the not inconsiderable sum of £2.3m and was introduced to the media amid a great fanfare of publicity. Pace up front had been as lacking as silverware in the Hammers' trophy cabinet, and here, so we reckoned, was just the man to supply it. Paulo Futre, whose mercurial talents once earned him the accolade of 'the next Maradonna', was signed on a free but with wages of a £1m a year (*that* helped to raise the club's profile). Completing the set were Mark Bowen, Richard Hall and Steve Jones who returned from Bournemouth.

An all too familiar catalogue of pre-season injuries decimated Redknapp's options for the opening match at Arsenal. Raduciou was the victim of a disgusting elbow in the face on his debut at Torquay (an incident that I feel had a lot to do with his eventual quick return to Espanol), Richard Hall broke a bone in his foot on his debut at Carshalton (echoes of the ill-fated Simon Webster three years before) and centre-backs Slaven Bilic and Marc Rieper were still not fully fit after their European Championship exertions.

It took just 90 minutes for the optimism to ebb away. While John Hartson (more of him later) grabbed Arsenal's first, it was clear that while the defence looked pretty robust, scoring was still going to be a big problem. There were intermittent flashes of brilliance from Futre, but his knee clearly wasn't going to hold up to the rigours of a jam-packed English fixture list.

Then the rumours started. By all accounts Bilic doubted the club's potential or Redknapp's managerial ability and wanted away, while Redknapp himself was having equally serious doubts about Raduciou. In Bilic's case, word was leaked to some covetous clubs that he had a clause in his contract allowing him to talk to anyone offering more than £2.5m. So to dissuade him from talking, West Ham doubled his wage! Of course, we knew nothing of these clauses and a lot of anger was vented over what was felt to be a betrayal by Bilic. As far as I'm concerned he'd shown his true colours and I wrote as much in *OTT* saying that I'd streak around Upton Park if he saw out his contract. So when he did finally leave for Goodison, the pain of losing a top class defender at least meant that the Upton Park faithful were spared the sight of me stark bollock naked!

Things bumbled on in a low-key fashion. Goals were thin on the ground, yet Redknapp was increasingly reluctant to play Florin Raduciou, happy instead to stick with the free-scoring (!) Iain Dowie up front. Our frustration simmered as the recalled Raduciou helped us to a stirring 2-2 draw at home to Manchester United and was then instrumental in the defeat of Sunderland. Meanwhile Dowie helped Stockport knock us out of the Coca Cola Cup. Boiling point was reached when the board's refusal to accept Michael Tabor's offer to pump over £20m into the club coffers was followed by Wrexham bundling us out of the FA Cup. Some found it all too much and invaded the pitch to make their point to chairman Terence Brown. Redknapp also seemed to have had enough by offering his resignation. Tabor, a friend of Redknapp, had his bid and offer of exploratory talks rejected out of hand. This only inflamed supporter emotions and the demonstration after the Arsenal game went on for hours (the local police got plenty of overtime that day).

However, as details emerged about Tabor's 'kind offer', especially the key one that the £20 mill was in fact a loan, his name disappeared as quickly as it had arisen. Why then hadn't the board screamed blue murder about this? They are so out of touch!

Mind you, even they finally realised that Nationwide football was guaranteed unless we signed a couple of strikers. But where would the cash come from? Personally, I think that they raided the ground development kitty, although it was said that a new share issue had realised £5m. Wherever it came from it undoubtedly saved Harry's neck and temporarily alleviated the pressure on the board, as John Hartson and Paul Kitson arrived.

The media, unsurprisingly, were more interested in the details of their respective contracts than their undoubted potential. And they really do have what it takes to be as good as any striking duo in our history. Hartson is a powerhouse in the air and holds the ball up brilliantly, while Kitson is quick, makes intelligent runs off the ball and opens up spaces for others to exploit.

Perhaps the only other positive thing to happen on the pitch was the emergence of 19 year old Rio Ferdinand, a player of frightening potential. A quality centre-back, he is equally comfortable in midfield or up-front, and certainly has a bit of the Beckenbauer about him. Let's hope that Rio goes on to be as successful for England as the German was for his country in the 60's and 70's. And this isn't just your usual over-excited fan talking; both Alex Ferguson and Arsene Wenger have had bids of £5m rejected. Rio recently signed a five year deal and has pledged himself to West Ham for the foreseeable future, but we should make the most of his career in claret and blue, because soon enough it'll be the likes of Juventus and Barcelona who'll be offering the £15m that one top football pundit reckons Ferdinand will be worth by the millennium.

This was my tenth season editing *OTT* and my 13th as a Chicken Run regular, and I have the distinct feeling that as far as both are concerned, it may well have been the last. I've become increasingly disillusioned with the Premier League, and feel somewhat like a football relic from a bygone age (editing a fanzine called *On The Terraces* in this all-seater era can't help). No longer do I get the same pleasure or enjoyment from the game I've been hooked on since Bobby Moore held aloft the Jules Rimet trophy in 1966. Even sadder is the fact that I really don't feel much pain at the prospect of letting it go. The Premiership is *all* about money, profits, players who get paid astronomical sums and fail to deliver and sodding about with kick-off times and dates to suit television - it has bugger-all to do with the people on the terraces.

I will always be a West Ham fan, but my support might not be of a financial nature for too much longer, and believe me, I know I'm not alone in feeling that way...

The Bish Bosh School of Soccer Skills

A banana shot

Source: *Over Land And Sea*

ONE MORE POINT

Crystal Palace

The rollercoaster keeps on rolling!

For the second year on the trot, the final outcome of Palace's season was unknown going into the final minute of the entire football season. Three hundred and sixty four days previously we had lost to Leicester with two seconds to go; this time the opposition was Sheffield United, a team who'd beaten us 3-0 just six weeks earlier. If the last 30 years have been a rollercoaster for Palace, our path to Wembley this year was The Big One.

Following our desperately near miss at reaching the top flight in 1996, this season began with several new signings, and just one major departure. 'Keeper Nigel Martyn had been loyal through previous disappointments in the '90's, and left for Leeds with our blessings. Unlike Armstrong, Thomas and Shaw, his move was vindicated as he regained his England place at the end of the season.

The campaign started slowly with just one win from the first six games, despite the fact that our football was nearly as sexy as our smart new Adidas home shirt. A surge in form coincided with the widespread rumours that the extremely popular manager Dave Bassett was being lined up to take over surprise strugglers Man City. Ironically, we played City at this point and wiped the floor with them, although their fans appeared to have the last laugh with their chants of "we're getting Bassett." However despite fevered press speculation, Harry thankfully came to his senses.

It got even better over the next week as Palace notched up a 6-1 win at Reading, followed by a midweek 4-0 thrashing of Bury to complete a 7-1 aggregate victory (all the more remarkable when you consider they would eventually win their division), which in turn was followed by *another* 6-1 win over Southend. It was a truly great time to be a Palace fan, unless you were my mate Andy who'd had a tenner on us to win 6-0 at 100/1. With eight minutes to go he was on for a grand, when up popped Palace reject Paul Williams with a 'consolation'. Not to Andy it wasn't!

Having started the season wondering where the goals would come from, the answer was - everywhere! Palace were not only the top scorers, but in each of those three big wins, no single player scored more than once. What was funny was that another friend of mine managed to coincide her two week holiday with our greatest scoring run in nearly 40 years! Unlucky, Keeley!

October saw Palace slow down a little, with the woodwork denying them all three points at Pompey and sloppy refereeing doing likewise at Barnsley. Our unbeaten run had reached a seven year record of 13 games when Swindon visited Selhurst. Despite taking the lead we were kicked around the park in a very ugly game and eventually lost 2-1. It emphasised that no matter how skilful and pretty our play was, we didn't have any cloggers to combat such opposition. The following game saw us get thrashed at Ipswich in the Coca Cola Cup and suddenly the hue of the season had changed. Bassett moved quickly and bought Southampton's Neil Shipperley for just over a million. It did the trick as we won the next four matches, a handy goals for and against ratio of 13:1, Shipperley bagging three goals and setting up others.

November 16th saw first-placed host second as we visited Bolton. In the first 30 minutes we got ripped to shreds and they went 2-0 up. Somehow we held on, despite not being able to string more than two passes together. Just before half time, a 20 pass move ended with Hoppo slamming in a 25 yarder to give us hope of a comeback. Two minutes later and our terrace was going mental as Freedman raced through on his own to level the scores. There was minimal danger in the second half and walking back to Bolton station I couldn't help thinking that Palace's escape was even better than my effort of getting out of The Den unscathed when we beat Millwall 4-1 back in March!

But any thoughts of our invincibility were quashed as we embarked on a miserable run of just one win in 11 games, the first of which was at home to Wolves, which proved to be a watershed. England U21 'keeper Chris Day had been given the seemingly impossible task of replacing Nigel. Yet only the harshest of judges would have said that he was failing to fill the great man's gloves; indeed, we had the division's best defensive record. However, the Wolves game saw us 2-0 down within 15 minutes and Day, along with the hapless Leif Anderson, our cult (more cynical fans would suggest there should be a 'n' in there somewhere!) figure from Norway, was largely responsible for both goals. We fought back to 2-2 only for old boy Geoff Thomas, returning from long term injury, to pop up and score their winner.

The following week saw us blow another lead and lose at poxy Grimsby. All the more galling when thanks to BR I'd had to get up at 5.00am and then missed our goal by a matter of 20 seconds. When we got back to London, despite having been drinking for 15 hours we decided to go clubbing in Camden. My only memory of that night was trying to convince some bird that my trip to Grimsby and back was not, as she thought, "a sad way to spend Saturday." However, I had to agree with her when she asked why my mate Jay had come with me when he's a Spurs fan. I still haven't worked that one out myself!

This shabby run during winter was only brightened up by a (lucky) win against the eternal idiots from The Valley. They thought they were so funny with their 'hilarious' "Claridge in the last minute" chant but Clownton were laughing on the other side of their faces when Shipperley squirmed a very late shot over the line.

However, that solitary win did little to cover up the fact that Bassett was facing his first test since arriving at Palace. Chris Day's confidence having been dented in the Wolves game was now shot to bits. Postponements at the turn of the year led to frustration as people questioned the viability of ground-sharing with Wimbledon given the state of the pitch. Leeds knocked us out of the cup, thanks in no small part to our Nige who came back to haunt us with a last minute penalty save to force a replay, which we lost.

February marked a change in our fortunes, as Carlo Nash, another of our summer goalkeeping signings, came in for Chris Day. A fine show from Nash and a great goal from Hoppo saw us win 1-0 at QPR followed by two more wins, the latter being a superb 3-0 thrashing of those w*****s at Molineux. Despite all the business with Cantona and Man Utd and our traditional rivalries with Brighton and Millwall, there's no team I hate more than Wolves. There was some serious partying that night!

The most remarkable event in Palace's season came at the end of February when Dave Bassett resigned and joined Forest. I heard the news just before I left my house to join the studio audience for *Carlton's* footie chat show *Do I Not Like That*, on which Harry was due to guest. I didn't actually bear any grudges against him; he'd moved on to further his career and had left Palace in a better position than when he took over. But I was apparently in the minority, most others labelling him 'Judas', and I ended up in a bit of a row with other Palace fans during the ad breaks. As the weeks went by even fewer agreed with my viewpoint, and Forest's eventual relegation was greeted with a lot of cheers in Croydon.

Steve Coppell was immediately appointed caretaker manager, although not before coach Ray Lewington, widely accepted as the architect of our passing game, had been offered the job. However, Coppell represented stability and most fans were content with the appointment. His first game in charge saw us win 4-1 at Oxford on our way to collecting ten points from the new regime's first five games. However, a diabolical run at the beginning of April, culminating with a 3-0 defeat at Sheffield, led to discontent and even a few calls of "Coppell Out." Oh, ye of little faith!

We'd slipped right out of the play-off bracket at this point but another good run coupled with Wolves winning a televised game at Port Vale 2-1 (the only time you'll ever see me cheering them on!) secured our place in the 'end of season lottery' (Cliché Vol. 24 No.13) with a week to go.

Ironically, it was Wolves who were to be our play-off opponents. With two minutes to go we were 1-0 up, then super-sub Dougie volleyed home a superb goal. Two-nil up, we were nearly at Wembley and I was almost crying with joy! One minute later and the away end erupted as Wolves carved a goal out of nothing. Two-one and all to play for at Molineux. Bollocks! Just as we were thinking a draw up there would be OK, Dougie popped up again to make it 3-1. Selhurst went ballistic! Wolves fans did their best to mess up the day, kicking it off on Whitehorse Lane, but we got through unscathed and set our minds to the return.

Molineux provided the most intense night of my Palace-supporting life. Despite my hate for them I have to concede that they create an awesome atmosphere. When they went 1-0 up after half an hour I was nearly physically sick with worry. On 66 minutes, Player of the Season and top scorer Hoppo (aka God, the greatest human being on the planet, etc.) won the ball and raced through the middle before powering it home to virtually assure us of a Wembley visit. The away end went crazy. Wolves pulled one back near the end thanks to diabolical refereeing and despite an exceptional amount of injury time, we held on.

And so to Wembley. From the moment I woke up everything seemed to go to plan - the weather was superb, the drink at Palace's now traditional pre-Wembley party at Victoria was flowing and unlike last season, I was convinced we would do it this year. Upon arriving at the ground, it was immediately evident the atmosphere in the Palace end was a lot better than that for the Leicester game.

The first half offered little for the neutral although it was fair to say Palace shaded it. At half time I was introduced to an American guy over here on holiday who'd been on his way to Wembley to take a photo of the stadium, unaware there was a match taking place! He was persuaded to come to the game and had managed to get a ticket outside. I spent the second half chatting to him and it turned out he had never been to a 'soccer' game in his life.

With ten minutes to go, we seemed to step up the pace and in turn the Palace fans collectively raised the volume. It just got louder and louder. STEVIE COPPELL'S RED AND BLUE ARMY. "I can feel a goal!" I said to my American friend. STEVIE COPPELL'S RED AND BLUE ARMY. "How d'ya mean?" he asked. STEVIE COPPELL'S RED AND BLUE ARMY. "Just make sure your camcorder's on," I replied. STEVIE COPPELL'S RED AND BLUE ARMY. Never in the past 12 years has this chant been sung so loud. Then it happened. Hoppo picked up the ball on the edge of the area and realising there were only seconds to go, shot for goal. The result was one of the most brilliant curling shots of all time. IT'S IN! WE'RE UP! The place went barmy. My overriding memory will always be of the American guy desperately trying to keep his balance whilst filming the mayhem.

The party went on well into the night, as did the debate as to who was going to be the first to have Hoppo's children (and that was just the blokes!). As I staggered home and into my bed I made sure the last thing I did was place my copy of the early edition of *The Sun* in such a way that the first thing I'd see when I awoke was Hoppo with the play-off trophy high above his head.

Now what was it that bird said about football fans being sad?

ONE-NIL DOWN, TWO-ONE UP

Arsenal

One-Nil Down, Two-One Up is renowned for its hard-hitting and profound analysis of the truth. Sometimes we are too near the knuckle for the club's comfort, sometimes too brilliant for our readers' intellects to grasp - a bit like Richard Keys summing up a Coventry vs Blackburn match.

Although this piece is supposed to be a general review of Arsenal's '96-97 campaign I see no reason to compromise our reputation here. Those readers, therefore, unfamiliar with the main strands of western philosophy and culture of the last 200 years will be better off turning the page to *One Team in Bristol's* essay on City's current predicament.

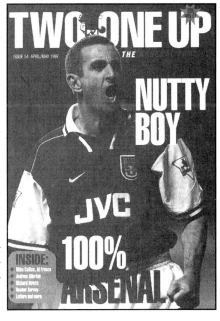

Here goes then, and please think hard about each of the following propositions:

1. Bruce Rioch and Stewart 'Coneman' Houston are a proper pair of twats.
2. Dennis Bergkamp is a rather good footballer and we're jolly glad he's on our side.
3. Ian Wright sometimes lets his temper get the better of him. Indeed, some psychologists have diagnosed 'Ian Wright Temper Syndrome' in our best-ever (almost) striker. He also doesn't like Peter Schmeichel much.
4. Nigel Winterburn is an android assembled by advanced beings in a far distant galaxy, but his creators forgot to include the power of speech, or a right foot.
5. Arsene Wenger is a tall thin Frenchman with spectacles.

To take the last statement first, it is obvious that Arsene Wenger is a tall thin Frenchman with glasses as even a cursory glance at his pre-match speeches on Highbury's magnificent Jumbotrons (bloody great tellys, for the uninitiated) will confirm. "Ah waz az seek az un oiseau zat can speak after ze Weembledon beat uz," is a typical statement, which, roughly translated, means "The Dons did a proper job on us, Barry." There is no argument about his tallness, thinness and Frenchness, then. He's also a very clever man who makes the average English gaffer look like the thickest plank in the timber yard. This geezer quotes Flaubert in the team talks, which may explain why the Merse looks so baffled lately - "So, oo'z this Bovary bird again, Bouldy?"

Now we come to the mystery that is Nigel Winterburn. Our Nige has been a fixture in the side since Noah chucked away the scuba gear and was this year rewarded with an end-of-term testimonial against Glasgow Rangers, a fixture that ended 3-3 and boasted a rather sad Scottish streaker - no wonder they're so coy about what's under their kilts!

Although Nigel played as well as ever this season, it's noticeable that age is catching up with him (rather like the mascots in the pre-match kick-abouts), and whereas the other lads take slugs of Lucozade whenever they get the chance, our No.3 has a cup of steaming Complan brought on by a very pleasant nurse from the Happy Autumn Lodge where he currently resides. Still, he did well enough overall to earn another year's contract from Wenger and was no doubt grateful for this token of confidence. Unfortunately, as mentioned above, Nigel has not uttered a word in public since he joined the club many years ago, so I cannot record his feelings on this happy occasion.

Ian Wright had another productive season, both for the club and the London cabbies who took him to Lancaster Gate on the many occasions when the senior common room summoned him to their study. In October, for example, he called the ex-Spurs boss David Pleat a "pervert," for what reasons we can only guess at. Although he later said that his comment had been "a joke," many Highbury regulars were so upset by the incident that they tore up their season tickets and made a pilgrimage to Lourdes. Despite appearances, we have close ties with our pals up at the Lane and anything that alludes to their total uselessness doesn't go down too well.

Wrighty also made a big impact in February - on Peter Schmeichel's knee. In chasing a 0/100 (in PS's favour) ball, Ian accidentally jumped on the Dane's patella and then squared up to him in the tunnel. To add fuel to the flames, he accused the Man Utd mutant of being a "racist," which Schmeichel clearly is not. A hysterical whinging blonde prat, yes; a racist, never.

Just to show everyone that he hadn't lost the knack of upsetting most of the people most of the time, he then got collared in May for making obscene gestures to the Coventry crowd. However, as this is a common pastime for most of us, and recommended by many doctors, the FA let him off the hook.

In between these amazing feats, he notched 23 league goals and closed in on Cliff Bastin's all-time scoring record for the club. Many junior Gooners will talk in learned tones about this, even though Bastin existed in Jurassic times and might well be exhibited as a fossil in the Natural History Museum as far as they're concerned. Surprisingly, Wrighty also found time to play like a turnip in a lot of matches and many a fan's patience wore thin with our mercurial No.8. But, let's give credit where it's due - he's been the most exciting player seen at Highbury in generations, and who hasn't occasionally dreamed of clumping Schmeichel? I bet Gary Pallister has! Overall, our disciplinary record was rotten and this will have to be improved next time. Still, at least

John Hartson is now biting ankles for West Ham, so there's a few less red cards to worry about.

As for Dennis Bergkamp - what can one say? As Dutch as Wenger is French, Dennis has won a special place in Highbury's collective heart and his command of spoken English is far superior to Winterburn's. Two moments of Dennis magic stand out from the season and deserve further analysis.

The first came on a rain-swept Sunday in November. We were beating Tottenham 2-1 at the time and I was commiserating with the MENSA branch of the Spurs Supporters' Club (he's not a bad bloke, considering) when Wrighty pulled off some fine trickery on the right and sent in a long high ball to the far post. Dennis watched it come over to him, dummied the nearest defender and smashed it into the far corner of the net. Cue ecstasy in the North Bank, the East and West stands and the Arsenal section of the Clock End. Cue damp and dismal dejection amongst our visitors, many of whom were due back in their rubber bedrooms within the hour. Dennis celebrated his achievement like a real man.

The other glorious moment came a few months later at Sunderland in an FA Cup replay. Dennis got the ball in or around the area and faced a wall of Wearside defenders. With a little feint here, a jink there and an audacious drag-back, he then chipped the goalkeeper with the most exquisitely controlled shot you'll ever see. George Best is the only British player who might have tried it and gotten away with it. The Dutchman made it look as simple as peeling an orange, however, and it was a highly significant goal as it cleared the way to being beaten by George Graham's Leeds in the next round. Such is life.

On to our pre- and early-season managers. Now, I'll bet any one of you that the other Arsenal contributors to this marvellous book begin their articles with a po-faced analysis of our 'crisis' at the start of the season, the procession of managers that filed through the Marble Halls and the low expectations of the fans in those far-off days. But why bother, boys? Rioch was a disaster from start to finish, and Stewart 'Coneman' Houston (so called because of his, er, responsibilities at the training ground) a hopeless pretender well out of his depth at the top level. Pat Rice proved an able caretaker when Coneman bade his polyurethane pals farewell to guide QPR to mediocrity (and we didn't miss him one bit). Arsenal went through a bad patch, for sure, but then Spurs do as well from time to time, although it's usually called 'the season' in their case.

No, all that's sorted. Wenger has started the French Revolution at Highbury and all the rest is bunk. Witness the improvement in journeymen like Parlour, Keown and Bould, the rejuvenation of Merson and Dixon, and the introduction of the phenomenal Patrick Vieira to the team. Pat won this fanzine's prestigious Player of the Season award (a weekend for three at the Dunstable Holiday Inn) and he can only get better. He tackles like Norman Hunter, passes like Hoddle in his prime and swipes in the odd belter, such as the equaliser against Derby County at Highbury. Steve Hughes looks like one for the future as well.

Unfortunately, there is one outstanding hangover from the season before last still troubling the red and white hordes, and this is called David Platt. It's bloody bad luck when you lose players of the calibre of Dave Seaman and Tony Adams to injury and suspension for long periods, but we really wouldn't mind all that much if Platty dematerialised in the Tardis with Doctor Who for the rest of recorded time. His four goals in 27 appearances tell of his real worth to the team and there was talk of a move to Blackburn towards the end of the season. Many Gooners relate how they have never seen such a bad passer, although during the Liverpool match he actually managed a perfect through-ball - to Stan Collymore! David, go away. To Antarctica preferably.

Anyway, we finished third, better than many of the pessimists expected. We went out of all the cups early but Wenger showed enough savvy to suggest that things could get much better next year. In football, it's both what you do and the way that you do it that count and the Frenchman definitely has it in him to take Arsenal to the title. And, of course, Wrighty could break the record, if only for carpetings by the bods at the FA.

It all begins afresh each August. Well, it keeps me young anyway.

It's nice that we can share everything............ like relegation!

Surce: One team in Bristol

ONE TEAM IN BRISTOL

Bristol City

Bristol City Football Club's centenary season will be remembered for all the wrong reasons. On the pitch the side narrowly missed out on promotion to Division One when losing to Brentford both home and away in the play-off semi-final. Off it, the club received national coverage of the wrong kind when the home televised derby game with Rovers was marred by crowd trouble.

Now of course tensions are always running high on derby day, and nerves were getting frayed as ten man City hung on to their one goal lead as the game entered injury time. Suddenly, Jamie Cureton broke down the left for Rovers and

The fanzine for the only permanent team in Bristol

ONE TEAM IN BRISTOL

It's ok, we've got enough points in hand for a good punch up!

still only

41

Tino Interview
Kuhlie
The Seventies
Hooligans Named

£1

32 points from the play offs!

Tino Interview

GWR Compt

crossed for the unmarked Peter Beadle to stab home the equaliser with City claiming in vain for off-side. The goal understandably sparked joyous scenes amongst Rovers small contingent of travelling fans while their counterparts in the other three sides of the ground held their heads in despair. But then a handful of Rovers fans took their celebrations too far and decided to invade the pitch to congratulate the delirious Rovers players. Regrettably, this prompted a copycat response from around 300 or so City fans situated in the neighbouring Dolman Stand.

The fact that most of the invaders ran onto the playing area covering their heads with baseball caps and scarves made it clear that the trouble had been premeditated. Thankfully, the stewards did a sterling job in managing to keep the majority of the hooligans away from the Rovers supporters before any serious fighting had taken place. Then, following the final whistle, a second smaller pitch invasion occurred forced the visitors to bolt for the dressing rooms with a great deal more haste than they'd anticipated, leaving one tardy Rover to later publicly state how he "feared for his life."

Yet again a moronic minority had dragged the good name of our club through the mud.

It was nearly all too much for pop star, turned chairman, Scott Davidson who promptly announced that he felt like "slamming the door and walking away." He vowed to get tough with the offenders and 44 City 'fans' have since been handed life bans from Ashton Gate and made a brief appearance in Bristol Crown Court.

Apart from the derby bother we also had another change of manager when the fearless Joe 'Jaws' Jordan was replaced by John 'Media Man' Ward. In recent years not many City bosses have lasted longer than a couple of seasons and Joe Jordan paid the price for a dismal Easter which saw defeats at promotion rivals Watford and Walsall and an embarrassing home surrender to Division Three-bound Rotherham.

The new manager did nothing to hide his murky past as an ex-Rovers boss, but he surprisingly won 50 per cent of the vote in a local newspaper poll which clearly demonstrated he was the fans' choice. Mind you, more than a few of the Ashton faithful were worried by Ward's friendship with ex-England coach 'Turnip' Taylor. In an exclusive interview with *One Team In Bristol* just after his appointment, Ward put everyone's mind at rest when asked to explain his football theory; he said: "I'm a very keen counter of shots and crosses because whatever you say about systems, I know if you can get a higher number of crosses in, you will get a high number of shots in with a good chance of scoring goals. You put crosses in a penalty area and it turns defenders around; They're at a disadvantage because they're facing their own goal; You're at an advantage because your facing the way you want to go." Bill Shankly always said football was a simple game.

Rumours had abounded all season that Joe Jordan was living on borrowed time, having been appointed by a previous board. He was almost chopped in late October when defeat at bottom placed Rotherham was unthinkable. At one stage City trailed 0-2 but two late goals from the skipper Gary Owers earned a precious point and temporarily saved big Joe's neck. The ex-Scotland International could be a little too direct for some players and it could be said that he spent the majority of the season successfully alienating himself from his first team squad. For instance, goalkeeper Keith Welch, defender Mark Shail and forward David Seal had all been told they had played their last game for the club.

This type of approach was never going to square with the new board who wanted a media-friendly manager to help sell the club to the community. While public relations was never one of Jordan's strong points, there was no denying that he was a man of considerable presence and hard through and through. By all accounts dressing room banter was toned down or halted whenever the manager neared, but the majority of players and fans held him in great esteem.

On the other hand 'Media Man's' style of management was very much laid back and the players visibly relaxed after his appointment. This helped them to embark on a five-match winning run which catapulted the club into the play-offs when all hope seemed lost following Jordan's departure.

Brentford did not read the script though and the busy Bees bustling stung (ooh) the Robins in the first leg. The division's long-time leaders deservedly returned to the capital with a 2-1 lead thanks to goals from midfielder Paul

Smith and the ever-dangerous Robert Taylor. However City came back strongly at Griffin Park and took an early second half lead through our marauding full back Darren Barnard. Brentford's recent home form had not been impressive and the Robins looked all set to force extra-time, but tragically, a long punt forward rebounded off the shoulder of the unlucky Shaun Taylor, leaving that man Taylor to drill home the killing equaliser.

'Media Man's' response was to make a dramatic last-throw-of-the-dice substitution. He took off the substitute centre-half Louis Carey as City were defending a throw in deep in their own territory. Even worse, the player that Carey was supposed to be marking, Marcus Bent, then proceeded to run into the open space he'd vacated and calmly slotted the winner passed a bemused Keith Welch. Wardy threw for double-six and got three! The game was up and shortly afterwards the referee blew the whistle on City's season leaving a dejected team to trudge off the field and us shattered.

Now, the early pre-season activity points to a much-revamped City side taking to the field for the start of the '97-98 campaign. Australian ace Paul Agostino has already left the club for pastures new, opting to join German side 1860 Munich under Bosman rules, star defender Darren Barnard, captain Gary Owers and Welsh International defender Rob Edwards are also all out of contract and have rejected the club's initial terms. Old timers Paul Allen and Martin Kuhl have also been shown the door as new manager Ward aims to give youth a try next season. It's not all doom and gloom though, especially as master marksman Kevin Nugent wants to re-sign, thus ensuring that Second Division defences will again be on red alert again next season!

THE ONION BAG

Chester City

The season before last, Chester seemed to be cruising to the play-offs, if not promotion, until a disastrous New Year run saw them plummet down the table like a sperm whale thrown from a Jumbo jet. In '96-97 Blues fans were treated to what constituted a virtual mirror image performance. With the side seemingly destined for mid-table mediocrity, watching 'the lads' was proving about as enjoyable as listening to the Brazilian national anthem played backwards. However, a dramatic up-turn in form towards the latter stages of the campaign, which was as entertaining as it was unexpected, launched Kevin Ratcliffe's men into an historic first ever play-off berth. More of that later though.

The Onion Bag

The quite bizarre Chester City fanzine *Issue 21 September 1996*

Funny? We've not seen much of the Wrexham boys lately.

Eighty Pence

Mad Cow Disease Spreads to Sheep

Inside This Action Packed Issue:
Doodled goals, "They've Scored Against the Wrexham", boring match reports about games you'd long forgotten about, Julian Alsford showing us around his newly fitted Elizabethan rosewood kitchen, the long range Cyrille Regis forecast plus loads of other articles which will be hopelessly out of date when this bloody thing gets printed.

Back to August and as usual the close season brought little activity in the way of squad changes. There was some panic when long-established goalie Billy Stewart buggered off to Southport leaving us in the lurch - Ronnie Sinclair (destined to win Player of the Year) arrived from Stoke to fix that - but that was about it really, although we'd also better mention the additional signing of failed Everton apprentice Mattie Woods for fear of upsetting his family.

So after a series of low-key friendlies, Chester began the season in their customary inauspicious manner. First there was defeat at a baking hot Goldstone Ground (City couldn't even blame predicted crowd trouble for this one - the only pitch invasion being a streaker who was completely ignored by police and stewards until he tried to pose for photos with the match officials and mascots) and then three days later, as well as a mere 353 miles up the road, the groundwork for a first round Coca Cola Cup exit at Brunton Park was put in with a 1-0 loss to Carlisle. With the difference in class between the two sides so self-evident that even the most optimistic Blues fan would have felt instantly obliged to water down their ambitions for the weeks that lay ahead. Thereafter Chester played in fits and starts. There were a few highs (wins over Swansea 2-0, Lincoln 4-1 and Northampton 2-1) and a few lows (defeats to Wigan 4-2 and 3-1 at home to Hereford) but sandwiched in-between was some real dross.

Fans' frustration focused on City's gifted but seemingly lazy midfield trio of Neil Fisher, Nick Richardson and Chris Priest. The latter could possibly blame a foot injury for his lethargy (incurred, rather bizarrely, by treading on broken glass while wearing flip-flops after the game at Brighton) but what of the other two? Fisher, deluded fool that he is, played with the arrogance of a man expecting to be summoned to the Premier League at any moment, while poor Richardson spent his time chasing shadows. Mind you, he didn't deserve the cheers which greeted him being stretchered off at Hartlepool after one solitary tackle terminated his season, leaving him with concussion, ruptured knee ligaments and a sprained ankle to boot.

Up front things were hardly better (the lads managed a cracking nine goalless draws in all) despite plenty of huff and puff from Andy Milner and Stuart Rimmer. To rectify this, October marked the arrival of Ian Helliwell on loan from Burnley. Now Ian for all we know may have been a real good bloke - you know, the kind of guy who would save baby hedgehogs from the middle of the road or wipe the wet bits off the toilet seat before his wife used it - but in footballing terms, he turned out to be a useless, lanky, streak of piss. Oh how we didn't laugh!

Although we didn't realise it at the time, the season's salvation came with a rare home defeat during the visit of Cardiff in November. Making their debuts that day were Rod McDonald (his chief claim to fame was once being sent off for crossing himself in front of Rangers fans after scoring for Partick) and, far more significantly, Shaun Reid. Shaun was soon to transform the centre of the park into scenes akin to the climax of *Platoon*. His combative performances, allied with an almost maniacal enthusiasm for celebrating goals, made him an instant hero with the fans. With a playing style identical to that of his more illustrious sibling, Sunderland boss Peter, we reckoned the brothers used to spend their youth honing the art of tackling by sliding into stampeding rhinos at Knowsley Safari Park.

Suddenly the team had spirit. Excellent displays against Fulham and a fine win at Barnet (a beauty from Rod to thank there) gave everyone renewed optimism. Until that is we ran up against Middlesbrough in the FA Cup. Although the 6-0 scoreline was hugely flattering to the Teesiders, confidence was knocked, quite literally, for six and Chester slumped horribly through January reaching a nadir with a 5-1 twatting at Northampton. A further loss at Hull in February prompted the most vociferous cries of "Ratcliffe Out" so far, but the side responded by embarking on a glorious 12 match unbeaten run. Doncaster were thrashed 6-0 (Milner grabbing four), there were assured wins at Mansfield and Scunthorpe, while Cambridge, Carlisle and Fulham were all given a real run for their money.

Much of the credit went to the almost demonic Reid, but other star performers were also starting to emerge from the shadows. Ugly duckling centre-half 'Eric' Alsford (well, you can't call him Julian can you) had matured into a cracking player, as had full backs Ross Davidson and Iain Jenkins. Jenks went on to gain an unexpected Northern Ireland cap in April (unexpected because it was Bryan Hamilton and not Iain who found out his great, great grandmother on the distaff side hailed from the province). Also wowing the crowds was Sam Aiston who was on loan from Sunderland. His gangly somewhat ungainly run, littered with dropped shoulders and nonchalant step-overs, were reminiscant of a young Chris Waddle - just a shame we couldn't afford him permanently.

By April this dramatic change of fortune had seen City surge into the top seven, climaxed with an almost magical 5-1 victory at Exeter where that dream spot in the play-offs was clinched. Trailing at half-time the boys went nap in an orgasmically enjoyable second period, with every goal being celebrated in almost apoplectic style by Blues fans undeterred by standing on open terraces in torrential rain. Sadly the play-offs were to prove a massive disappointment. There was no sweet taste of victory - more the flavour of rancid Caerphilly cheese - after the 3-0 aggregate defeat by Swansea.

What really disappointed was not so much the third successive failure to make it to Wembley when only 90 minutes away, nor the thoroughly inept performance at the Vetchfield, nor Chris Priest for being an absolute dickhead for getting sent off so early. What really rankled was that the whole novelty value of participating in the play-offs were lost in a fear factor of being pummelled by the many bruisers that constituted a significant part of the 2,000 Swansea support at the first leg. Fights in town, pitch invasions, mounted police charging around the car park, gangs wielding sticks urging you to have a go! Dear, oh, dear - it was like being back in the bad ol' 70's and early-80's again. For big games you always expect a few wankers but not to this extent.

Ah well. Never mind, eh. So what are our hopes for the new season? Seeing as the likelihood of Chester gaining promotion, as well as winning all the major competitions (knocking Wrexham out in the semi's of course), is only marginally more probable than Zoë Wannamaker winning the next Miss World competition, we'll settle for having another shot at the play-offs. However, with speculation that some of the better players are set to leave the Deva Stadium for pastures new (and with *Onion Bag* funds insufficient to subsidise an audacious club bid for Ronaldo), maybe we're being too ambitious. Hereford, after all, made the play-offs the year before us and look where they are now. Poor sods.

OVER LAND AND SEA

West Ham United

Last season, I wrote in this very book: "I can honestly say that for the coming season there is a real feeling of optimism around the place, and if we don't make Europe we'll feel that we have failed." But, with the strange pessimistic foresight that only a real West Ham fan can have, I cautiously added: "but every Hammer will also tell you in the same breath - we also wouldn't be surprised if we went down." How close that came to the truth is uncanny.

All in all, season '96-97 was much the same as any other I can remember at Upton Park. The fans were all bubbling with excitement right the way through to... the first

full-time whistle of the season, when we'd lost at Arsenal. The key difference though, was the pre-season hype. People were genuinely tipping us to be the surprise package of the season. And, rather foolishly, knowing our own history, the majority of us took the bait - hook, line and sinker.

We were going into the season with probably the most exciting line-up in the last two decades: World Cup stars Florin Raducioiu of Romania and the Portuguese wizard Paolo Futre had joined, along with the other young Portugeezer Hugo Porfirio and the already-signed Ilie Dumitrescu. We added the strength of England centre-half Richard Hall to an already impressive defence that included Dane Marc Rieper and Croatian Slaven Bilic, and brought in Wales skipper Mark Bowen to join Julian Dicks in defence. And with the rest of the squad being more than useful - especially with the emergence of a couple of the previous season's youth side - we really did look capable of challenging for honours. Yeah!

So where did it all go wrong? Why were West Ham fighting relegation for most of the season? Basically, there is no straight answer. But everyone has their own opinion as to why it was such a nightmare. Some blamed Redknapp; some blamed the players; some blamed the board of directors. But the truth, probably, is somewhere in there amongst all three.

Football is certainly a strange game. A tenth place finish the season before last had people talking in the following terms about Harry Redknapp:

he was the right man to lead us to greater things; he was a tactical genius and someone who could spot a player from miles away. But last season, according to some, he was the worst manager in the club's history, he was as naive tactically as they came, and he couldn't spot a player to save his life. The guy couldn't win!

But if he deserved support for most things, at other times his actions were unforgivable. One thing that really sticks in the throat was the way he treated Florin Raducioiu. To this day Redknapp defends himself, and always will, when it comes to the Romanian. But the truth remains that Raducioiu was never given a fair chance at Upton Park and he was handled quite appallingly. His three goals in a West Ham shirt will always be remembered by Hammers fans, who remain convinced that had he been in the side more often, his record would have been far more impressive.

A prime example of Redknapp's strange and unmistakable dislike for him came after Raducioiu had scored an absolute blinder of a goal against Sunderland. On the halfway line he'd allowed the ball to go over his and his marker's head, before turning the player and racing away a full 40 yards before slotting the ball past the 'keeper. A magnificent goal. Redknapp's verdict? He was petrified of being kicked by the defender and only scored because he was running away. Ridiculous or what!

If this was some sort of vendetta, it carried on until Raducioiu finally quit and headed back to Espanyol. As a parting shot he opened his heart to the *Sun*'s Ben Bacon, saying how he thought that Redknapp was the worst manager in the league. Redknapp retaliated in the same paper by saying that the Romanian had failed to turn up for the team coach for a midweek cup game at Stockport, and had instead been shopping in London store Harvey Nicholls with his family! Of course Raducioiu denied this, and the whole sorry saga carried on in the tabloid for a good few days. *Sun* man Bacon also took his share of the blame for stirring up the furore and Redknapp banned him from the club's training ground.

Meanwhile the magnificent Paolo Futre decided to call it a day when his dodgy knee failed to heal as hoped, Richard Hall, injured pre-season, hadn't seen the light of day and Ilie Dumitrescu looked so poor when he did play that he was soon jettisoned to that footballing hotbed (not) Mexico! Mark Bowen also moved on, going to Japan, but the clearout wasn't finished: Tony Cottee, who wasn't having the best of seasons anyway, was allowed to head for Malaysia and in so doing left the club without a recognised goalscorer. Apart, that is, from Iain Dowie, who *is* instantly recognisable, but not for being a goal-grabber: no goals in twelve... *months*!

By now we desperately needed some fresh blood up front, our Premiership existence depended on it, but as usual the club were pleading poverty and no money was forthcoming. Then, as if by magic, a man stepped from the crowd and offered to become the club's saviour. Mr Michael Tabor, ex-East London bookmaker and breeder and trainer of successful race horses, announced that he was quite happy to *give* West Ham a cash injection of something approaching 30 million pounds.

The West Ham United's board of directors response couldn't have been cooler; they stated that (a) they had no intention of talking to Tabor, (b) were not remotely interested in his offer, and worst of all (c) they wouldn't let on why. We couldn't believe it. That was all we needed to hear! It was time to take the matter into our own hands. I personally decided that we had to make a real stand. We had to declare war on the club. As fans, we had to make ourselves heard.

A few years ago, we'd successfully taken the club on over their wicked bond scheme. We won the battle hands-down and I felt sure we could do the same again. However, this time, we needed to get it over with quickly, because Michael Tabor had put a deadline on his offer and was more than willing to walk away.

So *OLAS* set about re-enacting one of our previous demonstrations and decided to 'Red Card' the board. First things first: get the story into the papers, across the airwaves and onto the TV screens: *maximum* publicity. Then set about the task of having 25,000 red cards printed with one simple message on the front: **It's Good To Talk**. The message was plain; if the board were not prepared to talk to Tabor, then they should tell us why. That was it; that's all I wanted. The protest wasn't about sacking the board or the manager, it was just born out of sheer frustration at the lack of communication.

The big demo was organised for the night of January 29th: Arsenal at home. The fans were generally wound-up; there'd been a small demo after being beaten by Wrexham in the FA Cup the previous match. Needless to say the media had started saying that things were out already of hand and to expect something akin to the start of another world war. Nah! We had it well under control. Then at six o'clock that evening in a radio interview, managing director Peter Storrie opened his mouth on the subject for the very first time, and took the sting out of the evening with superb timing. He announced that the deal wasn't all it looked, and in fact the 30 million pound 'gift' to the club had conditions attached. The investor wanted to buy a third of the club for eight million pounds, and lend the club the rest at an interest rate worse than the bank's!

So why the hell didn't they tell us that in the first place? Anyway, the evening still went ahead with the red cards, and we stayed behind for an hour after the match to have our say once again.

So whose was the victory? Storrie would claim that club came out on top after his eve-of-demo speech defused the protests, but we'd counter with the fact that without our protests he'd have never opened up about the whole affair in the first place (1-1 after 90 mins). And, more importantly, a few days after the big demo, West Ham went out and bought Paul Kitson from Newcastle and John Hartson from Arsenal for around seven million pounds. Would they have done that had we not kicked up? I don't think so! (we win by the golden goal).

All told, it was a horrible season for West Ham, and I couldn't wait for it to end. All the poor performances, going out of both cups to Second Division opposition, and scrapping away until the last week of the season to avoid the drop was something I really didn't expect or enjoy. Another downer was the departure to Everton of Slaven Bilic: a great player, world-class in fact, but a footballing mercenary of the highest order. I'm not alone in feeling betrayed by him, and the welcome he'll get upon his return will not, I would think, be too friendly.

But to be fair, there were one or two real plus points. Paolo Future's one magical performance against Southampton will live long in the Hammers fans collective memory, and the magic of Paul Kitson is another. There were one or two, including me, who didn't fancy Kitson much, but he looked brilliant from the time he joined us. And he, perhaps more than anyone else, is the reason we are still in the Premier League this season. Rio Ferdinand is another who made a name for himself last term. The 18 year old will certainly gain an England first team cap during the next twelve months and will thoroughly deserve it.

Can West Ham do anything different for the coming season? That's anyone's guess, it could go either way. However I can give you a 100% sure-fire prediction: when the curtain comes down next May, West Ham will not have their hands on the Premiership trophy...

"Harry's press conferences are getting much shorter lately.!"

THE PETERBOROUGH EFFECT

Peterborough United

The strange hypnotic world of Barry Fry

THE **PETERBOROUGH**
EFFECT
ISSUE: 52   PRICE: £1

ERE MAVIS WHEN'S BARRY GONNA DROP DONOWA AND BODLEY AND GIVE US A GAME?

The *TPE* editorial team received the news of Barry Fry's arrival at the mighty Posh whilst quaffing a few pints of the Czech Republic's finest produce in a Prague bar during the summer break.

Plastered all over the *International Guardian*, the reaction to his take-over as the league's first owner/manager was, to say the least, mixed. Wasn't he the man who had taken every club he'd managed to promotion? Wasn't he the man who had the knack for buying cheap and selling for massive profit? Wasn't he the man who signed three or four dozen players a season regardless of their ability or the club's means?

Most of these assertions were true, but more importantly, insignificant little Posh were splashed all over the national and regional press, TV and radio. You name it, Baz was there.

"I'll head this club out of the Second Division," he proclaimed. "The fans will see plenty of goals now I'm in charge," he enthused. He was not wrong on either prediction: we got relegated, were one of the higher goalscorers in the division and conceded more than any other team in the league. Heady stuff. Everybody has an opinion on Baz. Love him or hate him; few ignore him. Numerous mates from Bury and Southend fanzines told us how some fans still adored him, whereas others wished him dead. No "no comment" when your club is run by Big Fat Baz, then.

The start of his reign was unreal; sales of season tickets and merchandise rocketed, clubs were robbed blind in the transfer market (ask any Walsall fan about O'Connor and Houghton), ridiculous sums of cash were changing hands for players (by our standards) and bus-loads of new recruits were arriving by the day, most of whom were ex-associates of BFB such as Willis, Payne and Bodley (Southend), O'Connor and Houghton (Walsall), Boothroyd (Mansfield), Rowe (Chelsea), Donowa, Otto, Griemink and Edwards (Brum). The list, if not endless, was bloody long all the same.

The season started on a long hot day in August with a 1-0 defeat at Bristol Rovers and was followed by a first leg deficit at Millwall in the Coca Cola Cup. But our spirits were not dampened by these minor hiccups as an unbeaten run of six games saw Posh safely into Coca Cola second round action with Southampton and comfortably placed in the table. The Saints duly dispensed with us, but in the league Wycombe were dumped 6-3 at home and Preston 4-3 away to leave Posh eyeing a play-off position with three home games coming up.

You don't really need me to tell the next bit, do you? 1-3, 1-2, 0-1 against Notts, Bury and Brentford respectively. Don't you just hate football? This mini sequence turned into a run of 11 games without a win, whilst off the pitch Baz announced he didn't really own the club and that the inherited debt of £600k was actually £3 million! I suppose it's an easy mistake to make, isn't it?

The natives were definitely restless; O'Connor went to Birmingham for £750,000 (or a bloody site less according to Brum fans) but an FA Cup replay against Cheltenham got Posh back to winning ways. This was followed by the second six-goal haul of the season against a truly awful Rotherham (who had beaten us earlier in the season incidentally). This proved light relief for the fans as it was the second time that local VW dealers Cooks had to stump up a brand new Golf as part of a 'score six and win' promotion. It must have seemed like a sure thing when the idea was hatched, since apart from mauling Aldershot 7-1 in the early eighties we'd never looked like getting half a dozen in over 15 years! By the end of the season Cooks had handed over three sets of keys! So if Baz gets the sack, I know of one marketing vacancy in a local car dealership...

Eleven games without a win became one defeat in 13, most of the victories unfortunately came in cup competitions, as Posh entered the new year hovering precariously above the relegation places. Four straight defeats in February meant we were in the dreaded drop-zone and despite other clubs trying manfully to perform more pitifully than us, we easily managed to be more shite than the rest. All this despite a take-over by local entrepreneur and all-round good egg, Peter Boizot, who made his pile from Pizzas - each to his own I guess - bailing out the club and installing Phil 'yes boss' Neal as Baz's No.2.

More players arrived: DeSouza (Wycombe), Ramage (Watford) and Ashley Neal (yes, son of Phil), but even stranger, clubs were queuing up to pay stupid money for untried or incapable players - McKeever and Billington, aged 17 and 18 respectively and virtually untried, went for £500k each to Sheffield Weds with another £500k each in appearance clauses, etc. Ebdon went to Chesterfield, Charlery to Stockport and Griffiths to Orient, all for £100k each. Bloody cash was being thrown at us from all angles. Little of it was re-invested in the team however and although the season mathematically finished on our last game at home to Luton, we were down long before, blowing a series of matches against fellow strugglers that could have saved us.

The final match was away at Brentford and we indulged in that peculiar English habit: hundreds of Posh fans descended on Brentford to get well and truly shredded and sing their hearts out for the lads. All the old faves were rendered: "He's fat, he's round, he's f**king took us down, Barry Fry" and "Holland's, Holland's number nine" to our No.1, the Bart man; you know the sort of stuff. Brentford fans were just amused and baffled; they'd been there, they knew the feeling. Oh yes, of course, we won. Adam Drury, another starlet from our most productive youth set-up ever, scored the goal, and youngest ever Football League debutante, 15-year-old winger Matthew Etherington, starred. It was that sort of day, really.

In fact, it was that sort of season. Record season tickets sales, record transfers, record number of players, two six-goal hauls for, a few five-goal hammerings against, a dismal AutoWindscreens area final defeat after a 2-0 first leg lead, a rained-off game in August, a couple of new owners, increased attendances and ultimately relegation.

Adrian at Blues fanzine *The Heathen* and Mike at *Roots Hall Roar* had both warned: "You'll love him or you'll hate him but you're lucky 'cos life will never be dull with him around." Too right. Funny thing is, even after relegation *TPE* still loves him to death, although the feeling isn't shared by all Posh fans. We haven't had so much fun in years! For one you're never short of articles or front covers, and for another it's great reading teletext and seeing we've bid £1m for some Premiership player who isn't even going to bother to find out where Peterborough is, never mind join us. Who cares? It's been one of the most interesting seasons in a long time and personally I adored it, we've got nine internationals in the youth team to flog to muppets like Sheffield Wednesday and there's bloody thousands of useless journeymen that Baz can buy to replace them.

Don't forget it all starts again in August and it'll be the best party in the league. Be there if you can, but if you can't, don't worry. I'm sure the media will capture every moment for your delectation. Up the Posh!

THE PIE

Notts County

Even the scoreboard's crap!

When the letter dropped on the mat about a book called 'Survival of the Fattest 3', I thought they were writing a book about my old man, although I wasn't sure who the other two fat guys were. Well anyway it turns out that they wanted him to write for a book which apparently is something to do with football. I don't know why they asked him then; he isn't interested in football at all, that's why he's a Notts County supporter he reckons.

It's all because he is co-editor of this flan-zine thing called *The Pie*, which for a long time I thought was about food, since eating is his second hobby after drinking real ale. I thought it was odd though as he is hopeless at cooking; thinks it's women's work, which is tough titties in our house as I reckon it's a man's job. Perhaps explains why he's always in the pub...

Turns out that *The Pie* is about Notts County, which figures as he's been moaning about them for the past 40 years. It's about time others had to hear the crap I have to pretend to listen to when he comes home from the match. He writes under a pseudonym, Electric Steve he calls himself - you wouldn't catch me using a stupid name like that! He reckons he has heard Notts fans referring to him as a bit of a cult. The poor old sod's hearing's going as well!

This fatman book thing wanted him to write a review of last season, but he says he's too depressed and can't bear to do it. Hungover more like. They got relegated you know, to the Fourth Division as he still calls it. They finished bottom of their league and he blames a bloke called Murphy, but more about him later.

The old man's always been a miserable whinging git but last season made him worse than ever. He went to Wembley for the play-off finals last May and that is where the rot set in. In the past he has set off full of enthusiasm, with scarves trailing from the windows and a black and white wheelbarrow strapped to the roof. The wheelbarrow song is the Notts anthem. It goes

ONE POUND   No. 47
February 1997

The Original Notts County Fanzine

SACKING ROCKS NOTTS DRESSING ROOM

"Okay, who had 23rd December in the sweepstake?"

"I had a wheelbarrow the wheel fell off, I had a wheelbarrow the wheel fell off. (*Chorus*) I had a wheelbarrow the wheel fell off, I had a wheelbarrow the wheel fell off. (*2nd verse*) I had a wheelbarrow the wheel fell off, I had a wheelbarrow the wheel fell off." *Etc., repeat ad nauseum.* Boring eh? Just like my old man!

Well last year he was real miserable when he set off for Wembley - no scarves, no wheelbarrow, nothing. Reckoned they hadn't got a chance. He was right; came back sober, moaning about the car-parking and never discussed it again. He figured the team was poor and that Notts were in for a bad season, and was casting all sorts of nasturtiums about the manager Colin Murphy, who I gathered wasn't his favourite person.

When the season kicked off, he started moaning even more, going on about selling good players and buying crap ones. The Notts fans started a 'Murphy Out' campaign in October and Steve got to wailing more and more about "lack of entertainment," and "useless strikers." I asked him why he didn't just stop going to the games. He didn't reply, but looked at me with contempt and didn't speak to me again for a month - I must try that one again!

The only time he laughed all season was when he was talking about the electronic scoreboard down at Meadow Lane. Apparently it tells you the names of the teams, the score and how many minutes have gone. Only this one has a mind of its own. Not only does it give the wrong score and the wrong time, it sometimes flashes back to games two months ago so even the teams are wrong. "Only entertainment all season" the old fart barked.

Meanwhile this 'Murphy Out' campaign really heated up as the team's league position worsened. The chairman said he wouldn't bow to the supporters' protests and some fans believed the demonstrations were making the team play with even less confidence, further adding to their plight. My dearly beloved actually stopped moaning and went into mourning (down the boozer of course).

But he actually cheered up at Christmas, which being a miserable sod he normally hates. Reckoned the chairman had given him a cracking prezzie by sacking Colin Murphy two days before - December 23rd to be precise. I remember it well because the generous old git bought me a barrel of real ale to celebrate. I don't actually drink beer you understand, but it's the thought that counts he says. According to a mate of his, who knows a man who knows the chap who cleans the toilets down the ground, the players ran a sweepstake on the date their manager would get the sack, so that's bound to be untrue then.

Trouble is his world didn't get any better, it got worse. Some players took over as manager for a few weeks and then they appointed this bloke with an unspellable name who he calls Big Sam, comes from Bolton I think. Results on the pitch got worse and Steve got to ripping the sports pages out of the Sunday papers and burning them the minute they dropped through the door.

His solitary bright moment was one day when he said they had signed Big Devon back. I asked him what good a fast bowler would do them and he stopped talking to me again - I wish I could think of more things to say like that. Turns out it was this bloke called Devon White who Steve used to say was "shit hot" when he played for them last time. Funny thing is, he hasn't mentioned him since.

Well, the season finally ended - thank God. This bloke Big Sam only won about two games out of twenty-odd in charge and now Steve's moaning about him as well. Never satisfied, some blokes!

So there you have it. I now have a suicidal husband who keeps talking about going down to the Conference, wherever that is; must be near the pub as he goes there often enough, and he refuses to talk about football. He is still producing this flanzine thing though. "I thought you'd given up on football?" I asked him, "so why are you still writing that thing?" "It's about Notts County," he replied, "what's it got to do with football?"

So, sorry, he's too depressed and can't write your fatman thing for you. *Electric Sue.*

Source: *Spitting Feathers*

PIE MUNCHER

Preston North End

This time last year, and for this very book, I was fortunate enough to have the enviable task of providing 2,000 words on a Preston North End team that had carried off the Third Division Championship and built a spangly new 8,000 seater stand: all in the space of a few months. The '96-97 season was considerably less productive, but as the near 10,000 Deepdale regulars will testify, it was far from dull. Well, most of the time anyway.

After the euphoria of promotion, much of the pre-season talk centered around words like 'momentum', 'potential' and 'if'. By far the biggest 'if' concerned our man-

ager Gary Peters, because most of us felt that if the squad were strengthened then we might be in with a shout, come May. The manager probably knew as well as we did that the team needed freshening up in key areas, especially when five of the first eleven were the wrong side of 30 before a ball was kicked - not a good omen. And strengthen he did, although it wasn't the upheaval we expected. Andy Fensome (the fans' choice right-back) was drafted in along with Blackburn's teenage 'keeper Michael Holt who replaced the departing John Vaughan.

With some trepidation we travelled in our thousands to Notts County for the curtain-raiser and lost. While it wasn't the start we wanted, the outcome didn't seem so bad at the time and in hindsight was nowhere near as bad as the fate awaiting our opponents; those three points were to hoist County to their highest league placing of the season. Still, the first three months were fairly drab apart from our deserved 1-1 draw with Tottenham at Deepdale. It was a great result achieved with a squad ravaged by injuries to a far greater extent than was Spurs', although you'd never have known it from the column inches their casualty list generated. We had to wait until the last Saturday of November for our first away victory. Arriving at Adams Park we'd only taken a single point from a possible 27, but Wycombe were in kamikaze mood that afternoon and decided that they'd rather take us on with eight men. As the red cards flew we grabbed the points. Lovely!

However, there was no disguising the fact that the house needed shoring up so in came Bobby Mimms, defenders Michael Jackson and Sean Gregan, midfielders Mark Rankine and Lee Ashcroft, and strikers David Reeves and Kurt Nogan. The combined transfer fees of over £1 million were offset in part by the sale of Andy Saville, Allan Smart, Mickey Brown and Gary Bennett for £375,000. To be fair, the signings were, in the main, superb. All acquitted themselves well and fitted into our style of play, with the possible exception of Nogan and Rankine: Nogan arrived too late to make any sort of worthwhile contribution whilst Rankine was so ineffective that he was put on the list as soon as the season's last ball was kicked.

Gregan in particular had a phenomenal impact. His debut coincided with the televised rout over neighbours Blackpool, and the success of his conversion to a midfielder in February led to a £600,000 'double your money' bid from Brian Little at Aston Villa. Needless to say it was rejected.

As the rebuilding continued our home performances improved, even if we remained abysmal on our travels. A win at rock-bottom and sinking fast Rotherham was nothing to get particularly excited about, and the 2-1 victory at Burnley was as surprising as it was spectacular: we walloped them and should have scored more. No, what was most pleasing was getting the three points from our final away game at Shrewsbury, where a bit of tactical experimentation and a solid professional performance saw us usher the Shrews off to Division 3 with a 2-0 defeat. We didn't really get any satisfaction from sending them down, but it was good to hear Peters claiming that we were going to try some new tactics that we could apply for next season. These tactics involved soaking up 45 minutes of pressure then throwing on another striker in the second half to have a real go at 'em. The win was complemented by Gregan's 30-yard screamer (goal of the season) and the manager's pre-match foray into the away terrace to apologise personally for our travel sickness.

The team's transformation over the course of the season is best illustrated in two ways. Firstly, only four members of the side that faced Notts County in the opening match of the season figured in the final game against Walsall. Second and more impressive was the fact that in our opening 12 matches we took under a third of the available points (relegation form for sure) but in our final 12 games we secured nearly two-thirds of the points on offer, good enough to have put us on a par with Champions Bury if we'd kept going at that rate throughout the campaign.

Amidst all this end of season optimism, our reserve side, including all the thirtysomethings we abused at Meadow Lane on the opening day, pipped Aston Villa to the Pontins League Division One title in front of gates as high as 3,000. However, Peters clearly learned his lesson in the summer transfer stakes and many of the stalwarts of the reserve side won't be around to play in the Pontins Premiership next year. The Manchester United defender Colin Murdock, who had been so impressive as a trialist for our second team, joined us for £100,000 within a week of the season's end. Furthermore, Peters has promised the arrival of the 'three other missing pieces of his jigsaw' sooner rather than later. That and the start of building work on the 6,000 seater to replace our crumbling Kop, means we'll go into next season fired with fresh optimism. Much more than last year anyway! No doubt we'll continue to be a handful for anyone on our own ground so away form is the key; just a few victories on opposition soil would hoist North End into the promotion frame. Let's face it, if a team assembled for a comparatively huge £1.5m can't challenge for honours then perhaps the manager will get a 'free' at the end of next season!

RAGE ON

Oxford United

On the pitch

Right. On the pitch. "On the pitch, on the pitch, on the pitch." Or not. 'Cos you'd get ejected from the ground and have your season ticket cut up into a hundred tiny pieces - but at least you wouldn't have to endure the pain of watching your team slowly destroyed by a member of the board of directors.

An Independent Voice of Oxford United Supporters

RAGING BULL

Issue 45
May
1997

£1

soon to be known as RAGE ON

**So farewell to the Manor...
...until next season**

Nothing new there then, I hear you say. Well the twist is that at Oxford United Football Club the Conan who is sucking the confidence out of the squad is the director of football, Denis Smith. The coach. The manager. You know, the one who is supposed to be inspirational in his buying, selling and team selection. Hmmm... Not our Den. He would never reach second interview for playground monitor, let alone master tactician. Let's take a lickle looksee at what Mr Smith Out has achieved over the '96-97 season:

Buying: Well he bought Brian Wilsterman, some Dutch guy playing in the nether regions of the Belgian League. He was thrown into the team in the now famous 6-3-1 formation at home to Palace. Fortunately I was out of the country for this debacle. Poor old Bri looked well out of it, apparently.

His loan signings consisted of a certain fat, lazy Marco (get off the parko) Gabbiadonkey. Five grand a week we paid that waste of breath to do nothing for a month. He's not just pants, he's the whole underwear section of the M&S menswear department. And Chris Whyte, too. Though he actually was OK, filling the gaping hole we've got in the centre of our defence. He did so well that his contract has not been extended. Still, he'll go into OUFC history as the oldest player (so far!) to have pulled on a U's shirt.

Selling: David Rush went to York. Shame, I liked the way he ran. A bit like a Prodigy dancer, bless him. And that other chap, can't quite remember his name. You know the one; the best English central defender around at the moment. His skill, vision, control, strength, aerial power, coolness and passing make him an obvious first choice for the national squad. Come on godbotherer Glenn. Sort it out.

So we sold Matt Elliot for a song. More like a joke. A joke with all the humour taken out. OK, Matt is no spring chicken and he had to be sold to pay the contractors of the new stadium. But half price, with so sell-on clause, and no bonus for number of appearances or internationals. That's not astute management. More like a stoat - and the weasly Smith has got himself a new three year contract. Hur-bleedin'-rah.

Team selection: In the London Road stand we have a theory that the first player to turn up in the dressing room gets automatically picked, which would explain why no-one has ever seen Martin Gray arrive at the ground on match days. He must treat every game like the January sales - at least that's the only way I can see him getting a first team place.

Most of the team do pick themselves in as much as they are obvious choices. The problems started when Den Boy decided to leave his best player Joey Beauchamp on the bench. Even when he did play Joey he seemed to discourage anyone from passing to him, maybe to justify his non-selection for the majority of the season! And Martin Aldridge not even getting in the squad after scoring a hat-trick two games earlier against Sheffield United... And Bobby Ford on the wing instead of central midfield... Ludicrous! The three games when Joey was on the right wing from the start and Bobstar was in the middle, we won. Seems obvious to me.

And his negative away tactics were unforgivable.

SMITH OUT NOW! COME ON YOU YELLOWS.

Behind the scenes.

Off the pitch Oxford United have either misled supporters completely or (as has more recently been the case) said as little as possible. The arrival of Robin Herd as chairman in 1995 was widely welcomed as a positive move; a life-long Oxford supporter, he was eminently affable and willing to plough his money into the club. Shortly after this, former fanzine editor Ian Davies was appointed as general manager, and after years of appalling administration, United appeared to be getting its act together behind the scenes.

How naïve we were. The club were ten months late in submitting their accounts for the '94-95 season, and subsequently incurred a fine through Companies House. When the records finally appeared they revealed an operating loss of £1.75 million, a figure acknowledged even by Robin Herd as disastrous.

Then there has been the issue of our new stadium at Minchery Farm, on the south-eastern fringe of the city, which should have been ready in time for the coming season. Unfortunately inept financial planning has put paid to any thoughts of a move for the time being. The seeds of doubt were first cast during the summer of 1996. Although construction was due to commence on May 4th (the day we won promotion back to Division 1), nothing happened until August. Due to this delay, management reported that we would start the '97-98 season in a three-sided stadium, with a fourth being added soon after. This would bring the total capacity up to an all-seated 15,000. They also assured supporters that the finance (£15 million according to most reports) had been taken care of. Sponsors supposedly existed, although the club were at pains not to name names.

When construction finally started the progress was encouraging. Nothing to get too excited about, but the ground started to take shape; pictures of girders appeared in the programme, then more girders, then some concrete, and supporters were led to believe everything was going to plan. However when Taylor Woodrow asked for the first instalment of £5 million the club couldn't produce the beans, claiming a cashflow shortage due to the constructor's premature progress. Not surprisingly, workers were gradually taken off the site until construction ground to a halt.

The aforementioned sale of Matt Elliott to Leicester City for £1.6 million (a fraction of his true value) almost certainly resulted in a payment of around £1 million to Taylor Woodrow, although with so little information emanating from the Manor, we can only guess. As things stand the as-yet unnamed stadium remains a forlorn unoccupied building site.

A glimmer of hope came towards the end of the season when it was announced that Benetton chairman Flavio Briatore was ready to buy a major stake. Apparently this deal could also lead to an alliance with Juventus, allowing an exchange of players. More importantly it would generate the finance necessary to complete the new arena. Since this statement, though, little has been said on the matter apart from "Negotiations are continuing," their typically ambiguous response to any questions, and although an open meeting was scheduled towards the end of the season this was cancelled at the eleventh hour.

So while Bolton, Derby, Stoke and Sunderland gear themselves up for their gleaming new stadia, Oxford United once again find themselves back at The Manor, with its capacity of under 10,000 and an away end widely regarded at the worst in league football. In the meantime we can only hope for a move either around Christmas 1997 (as the club would have us believe) or maybe in time for the '98-99 season.

Good things come to those who wait, apparently, but don't expect us to hold our breath.

RANDY ROBIN

Swindon Town

When in a few years time, some poor misinformed young media graduate-cum-wannabe British film producer decides to emulate those great soccer cinematic works *Fever Pitch*, *Escape to Victory* and *When Saturday Comes* (?), takes his national lottery grant and sets about making 'Steve McMahon - The Swindon Years', how will '96-97 fit into the narrative?

It didn't have the controversy, despair or shattered dreams of '94-95, when Steve took the Swindon reins. Getting himself sent off in his first match, leading us first to a League Cup semi-final and subsequently to relegation to the Second Division, (under) selling our most talented player on the way. Neither did it recapture the glory of '95-96 when Swindon waltzed their way to the Second Division Championship, sweeping away all in their path, with the unfortunate exception of hated local rivals Oxford United.

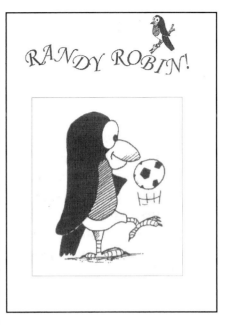

Despite this, '96-97 still had a bit of excitement. Not the kind you get in an all-action blockbuster, more your romantic comedy sort of excitement. In October, we beat Oxford at home for the first time in donkeys' years, to restore a little local pride. The victory was particularly sweet as playing for Oxford that day was a certain Mr Joseph Beauchamp. To say Joey is hated by Swindon fans is like saying that Jimmy Hill is slightly irritating. If on May 1st Joey Beauchamp had stood for MP against Adolf Hitler in Swindon then there is no doubt of the result. The plucky little fella from Austria would have won it by a landslide.

There were other highlights: the 6-0 stuffing of Huddersfield at the County Ground (possibly the most surprising result of our season) gave supporters false hope that this could be another successful league campaign. The trip to Man Utd in the Hokey Cokey Cup was our reward for a second round victory over QPR. Even though Swindon lost at Old Trafford against a Red Devils team nowhere near full strength, it was a game that will live long in the memory. After Karel Poborsky (surely one of the ugliest players ever to grace the English game) had put United ahead in the front half, we thought we were in for a whitewash, but then Peter Thorne headed home the equaliser in front of 8,000 overjoyed travelling fans. Despite Paul Scholes' late winner, not even Meg Ryan could portray the ecstatic feeling of Swindon fans after Thorne scored.

And that was as good as it got. Midfielder-cum-left back-cum-centre back-cum-most complete young player Swindon have had for years, Kevin Horlock, was sold to Manchester City for a paltry £1.6 million. In his place Macca signed Huddersfield hard-man Darren Bullock. Replacing Horlock with Bullock is like axing Claudia Scheiffer from a modelling job and replacing her with Jo Brand. We were given some idea of just what sort of player we were getting when it was revealed that Darren would only be able to sign for us if he didn't receive a custodial sentence for an alleged assault. As if this wasn't enough to endear him to the Swindon fans, Darren then committed a PR own-goal on his return to Huddersfield on the last day of the season. Cheered on by the home fans, Darren removed his Swindon shirt upon the final whistle and whilst seemingly stamping on it, put on a Huddersfield shirt handed to him by a member of the crowd.

The sale of the inspirational Horlock and the off-loading of Swindon legend Shaun Taylor to Bristol City was a combined blow from which we never quite recovered. Oxford regained their local supremacy by beating us 2-0 at the Manor ground. Forget Meg Ryan, Swindon's performance was so passionless that day that an Ozzie soap actress could do it justice. The FA Cup brought another glamour tie, this time away at Everton. Any hopes of a giant-killing though vanished after 52 second when Ian Culverhouse was given his marching orders for hand-ball. Andrei Kanchelskis scored from the resulting penalty, and the final score of 3-0 flattered us.

As for the league, a finish of 19th disappointed most Swindon fans, even those who had spent the season constantly reminding anyone who would listen that "consolidation was the name of the game." Nevertheless, hopes for next season are high. McMahon has promised to refund the price rise in season tickets if Town fail to reach the play-offs, proving that despite popular belief, jeering your team and shrieking "what a waste of money!" as they slip to yet another defeat in a meaningless end of season game *does* have its benefits.

Many Swindon fans believe that '97-98 is do or die time for Macca. Anything lower than sixth place will hit the Swindon board in the only place it hurts, their pockets. That Steve McMahon film could have a rather abrupt ending.

RED ALL OVER THE LAND

Liverpool

Strange Love

Ever had a woman who's led you up the garden path, promised you everything you ever wanted, but when the time came you got nothing except a broken heart? That's probably the only way I can sum up Liverpool during the '96-97 season; they promised everything, gave nothing and left us in tears and with a dull ache in the chest. If a woman does this to you, you learn your lesson, but if it's your football team you go back for more... and more.

Liverpool were a team that were at odds with themselves. Even the pre-season tour went a bit wrong. It started with a half-baked four team tourney involving Borussia Münchengladbach, Porto and our 'lovely' neighbours from over the park. Stuffed by Porto and playing out a goalless draw with Everton, for some daft reason a lot of us travelled up to Liverpool to watch this uninspiring crap (we didn't even put out a full-strength side) and paid a few quid for the 'honour'. But you do throw your money about when you're in love, don't you?! It was then over to Ireland and a meet with 'Belfast Jimmy' to watch our beloveds play against Linfield. It ended 2-2, and we were lucky. Rumours were floating in the breeze about discontentment in the camp. The manager was even reported to have copped one which left him nursing a black eye. Idle gossip? Maybe... We then ventured south to Dundalk, which at least proved worthwhile, if not for the football then for the night out at the 'Wee House', despite the hangover that followed.

When the season proper kicked off at the Cellnet, some people were ecstatic with our point from a 3-3 draw. "But Boro will be challenging for the title," they said apologetically. "Bullshit," we replied, having been down this particular garden path more than once. The Reds had flattered to deceive, something which was to become a pattern for the following months.

The manager even joined in the teasing game. He signed Patrik Berger from German Champions Dortmund for about £3m and then left him on the subs bench (which Berger would become accustomed to, much to the disgust of the Anfield faithful). We eventually found out what Patrik was like when he

Fergie Celebrates Ten Years at The Theatre with Turkish Delight!

RED
ALL
OVER
THE
LAND

THAT'S ODD IT'S MY ANNIVERSARY AND EVERYONE IS HAPPY!

UNITED CLUBCALL 0898 . 5·0 . 6·3 . 1·0 . 2·1

A LIVERPOOL FANZINE, ISSUE 11, NOVEMBER 1996 £1.00

burst onto the scene in devastating style as a second half sub at Leicester. Two goals in a 3-0 win - wow, we had a star! It got better: at home v Chelsea, the Berger-King got two more in a 5-1 rout, and we then beat West Ham at Upton Park. We were on a promise; drunk and in love, and our beloved team were about to deliver.

No! It was just another tease. We lost to Manchester United, drew with Everton (who were absolute shite) and drew with Wimbledon... at *home*. How could someone we cherished so much do this to us? We got told that we were expecting too much, that we were impatient; yes, I've heard that from a woman as well. Duly chastised, we went to Tottenham on a Monday night, and did them 2-0. The affair was back on... Stupid! Stupid! Sheffield Wednesday came and turned us over at Anfield, and once again we were left high and dry. You know the feeling? You hang around waiting in the rain for your loved one and she stands you up. Everyone's looking at you; they know, they're all whispering; you're being taken for a ride, but they're not going to be the one to tell you. You just think that it will be different next time.

And for us that 'next time' came over Christmas. Now to let someone down at Christmas is unforgivable... usually. Leicester - 1-1. Despite this we went to Southampton on a Sunday in the middle of the holiday period. It was bloody cold, blood freezing in fact, but when you're smitten you do daft things. We won 1-0. Lucky? Yes! But somehow we were five points clear. In the world of the strange love for our football team we accepted this on face value; maybe this time they were really going to take us all the way... the ultimate climax!

New Year's Day at the building site that is Stamford Bridge saw us lose 1-0. But hey, we could kiss and make up in time for the Coca Cola quarter final against Boro; let's face it we'd beaten them 5-1 a few weeks ago. Frustratingly, a collective headache saw our team show no interest in our desires and overtures, and we went out 2-1: we were worse than bloody awful. Just when we were starting to think "sod this - we'll find someone else," they whacked Villa 3-0! The boss was forced to make changes and he brought in a young kid called Jamie Carragher; he had a blinder, was easily man of the match: scored, got booked and bounced Andy Townsend all around Anfield. Passion indeed!

A week later we were back at the building site and were leading 2-0 against the Dutchman's team of mercenaries, and looked something special. This was going to be it, at last. But no, we were pushed away and blown-out as the Blues returned (they rammed in four in 15 minutes). Now the whole world was laughing. But love is deaf (or is that blind?) and we couldn't hear their chuckles. But it did beg the question, "why did we do this?" There was no answer. So we asked ourselves "why keep bothering, it takes two to tango, and this lot just aint dancing." By the way, Jamie Carragher had vanished into thin air.

Tension and torment personified was the result of a passionate midweek date with an old flame. King Kenny returned with his new partner, Newcastle United, but we destroyed them both. At three up we were taking the piss... but out of who? The Geordies gave us the answer as they rolled in three themselves without even trying. David James gave it all away, well nearly, until last-minute Robbie nipped in to give us the points. Does real love do this to you? I doubt it.

The height of our frustrations came on Grand National weekend, but it had nothing to do with the race. Manchester United lost 3-2 at home against Derby. We were elated and serenaded our lads with songs of love and praise, confident in the knowledge that we only had to beat Coventry at home to claim that coveted top spot. "That lot've hardly won away all season," we crowed. Oh, David! Jamesy dropped a few bollocks again and it was goodbye my love.

Our relationship, almost at breaking point, was to be tested further. We fell against Everton when we needed to win; the manager deeming that the last ten minutes should be played without a goalscorer on the pitch, and then just a few days later Manchester United rode into town, beat up the Sheriff and took the girl. All that was left to fight for now was second spot and the consolation of a place in the (not so) Champions League.

The rest is history. Like somebody said, "Liverpool finished fourth in a two horse race and the winner wasn't even trying." It was the same in the European Cup Winners Cup. Our hopes were high, but in the world's most romantic city our hopes came tumbling down. Beautiful Paris, what a heart-breaker...

It's difficult now to even laugh at Everton's problems. Look at their year: another season without any sign of success (other than just avoiding the drop - again!), loads of money spent on players that were shite before they joined the blue-noses and got even worse after they'd arrived, and they went on to achieve absolutely nothing. It shows your standing in world football when you have to call Paul Rideout back from a spell in China to help in the fight against relegation!

You know, there used to be a time when it was them and us contesting the Championship or the cups. If they beat us they celebrated, and likewise when we beat them. If we got a draw at Goodison (aka 'the Pit') then we were quite happy, it was a good point, and their lot would go home a bit disappointed. How things have changed! If we draw with them now, we're pissed off, even at the Pit. This season saw a remarkable event, when their fans spent most of the derby singing songs of praise... for Man United! Yet a couple of weeks previously they'd been screeching abuse at the very same team they were now fawning over! Sad or what, these modern day Evertonians? With us devoted Reds we finished fourth, reached a European semi, qualified for the UEFA Cup and we're still not that pleased about life. They on the other hand, just managed to stay up, played shite for most of the time, sacked (by mutual consent) yet another manager, another 'hero', and they went on to the streets for a celebration that would've put a king's coronation to shame, just for getting a point against us at home! On the last night of the season they were even out on the town getting high on yet another defeat and singing the praises of the 'drunken one'. But like I said, who gives a toss about a meaningless football club like Everton?!

Yes, who cares about them; we've got our own problems with our own team. God, we're devoted to them, but shit, they abuse our love. In '96-97 they led us up the garden path so many times we got to know the flowers personally. Basically, they faked it more times than an unfaithful partner last season. The daft thing is, we went through the same level of deceit in '95-96, and it wasn't much better in '94-95! But will that stop us going back for more next year? Isn't love strange...

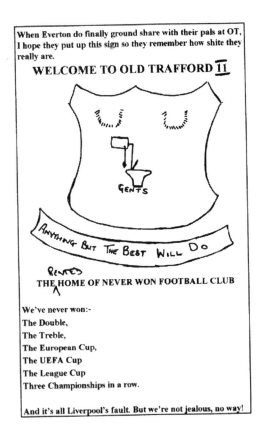

RED CARD

Chelsea

In many peoples' eyes Chelsea were a club who promised much and delivered little. Even Chelsea supporters had to admit that Arsenal fans taunting us with chants of "No silverware, no silverware..." did have a point.

But all that was to change - and how!

The new season began even before the old one had finished. Chelsea's last game at home to Blackburn was the day that we said goodbye to Glenn Hoddle, who had accepted the England job. Chelsea fans told Bates just what he could do with George Graham, chanting Ruud Gullit's name for half an hour

RED CARD No. 80
The Chelsea Fanzine 80p

Matthew Harding's Blue & White Army

Matthew Harding's Blue & White Army

INSIDE: Sherlock Holmes and the Mysterious Disappearance of the Portsmouth Tickets; Strike it Rich, Top Middle or Bottom; One Man Went to Moan; Letters and loads more!!

THE COOL AIR COMPANY Keeps London cool

before the game, throughout the match and for half an hour afterwards. And so it was decided: Ruud was the man.

Few seemed to make anything of it, but Ruud was the Premiership's first black manager. He set about changing the side with an influx of major European stars. The timing of the arrivals seems unimportant now, it all happened so fast. I think the first was Vialli, captain of European Cup-winning Juventus, who joined on a free under the Bosman ruling. Considering he would earn a million pounds a season for three years, he was hardly 'free', but was still cheaper than the players who commanded a fee, such as £4.7m Roberto Di Metteo and £2.5m Frank LeBouef. Both players were foreign to me (excuse the pun). I've about as much interest in watching European club games as I have in films with subtitles, but the tidal wave of players now appearing in the Premiership means that someone must be watching them. And we were right to trust Ruud's judgement because all of our signings have been of exceptional quality.

So whilst Ruud was becoming the star of the BBC's Euro '96 coverage with his comments like "I want to see England win," " I want some sexy football" and being graceful in defeat after we demolished Holland, I was quickly scanning the Euro '96 magazines in case Chelsea signed anymore players from abroad. We did, but not until November.

The pre-season friendlies had been all hype with Vialli appearing on the pitch at various sold-out games although fully dressed and apparently injured.

However when the opposition was Notts Forest rather than Kingstonian or Exeter, he made a miraculous recovery, coming on as sub to help us win the Umbro cup (whatever that is).

Chelsea kicked off a day late at Southampton, courtesy of *Sky*, and then we found out just what our new players could do. Vialli was like a dog who had slipped his lead. He chased everything, tumbled spectacularly every time he was tackled and spat a lot, but what he didn't do was score. Did we care? No, of course not! Chelsea had a new hero; everyone loved him and his shirts were outselling Gullit's six to one. At home for the next two games we won without conceding a goal and sat proudly second in the table. But joint second after beating Coventry was almost irrelevant as Vialli scored his first Chelsea goal and Stamford Bridge went berserk.

Our first real test was at Arsenal and we tore them apart, going two up inside half an hour, but then conceded a goal just before half time and Arsenal's come-back was complete with two more in the second half. Dennis Wise gave Chelsea the last laugh with a last-second equaliser.

In September, our No.1 'keeper Dmitri Kharine injured his knee and would miss the rest of the season. Two weeks later we were thrashed by Liverpool 5-1 and were embarrassed by Blackpool 3-1 at home in the League Cup (only going through by virtue of our 4-1 first leg win). In the next round we were drawn away to Bolton, who were in superb form and well clear at the top of the First Division. The Hughes/Vialli partnership wasn't exactly prolific either, having scored just six goals in 12 games. Chelsea lost 1-2, but this turned out to be incidental.

As we travelled back South we were unaware of the tragic news we would wake up to. Matthew Harding, our vice chairman and owner of Stamford Bridge, had been killed in a helicopter crash shortly after taking off on his way home from the match. Chelsea fans were stunned. Matthew was adored by everyone, and despite a boardroom bust-up with Bates he looked set to become chairman and lead Chelsea back to the top. His boyhood support of the club had grown into an obsession and he had used his wealth to buy Stamford Bridge as well as funding the building of the North Stand and providing money for transfers. Four days after his death Chelsea played Tottenham. Everyone respected the minute's silence - and I mean *everyone*; not a single sound was heard as grown men sobbed in silence, paying their respects to Chelsea's greatest ever supporter.

We beat Spurs 3-1 in a game described by Gerry Francis as one they couldn't win, and although Spurs looked to be trying it did appear as though they gave the game to the memory of Matthew.

Beating Man United at Old Trafford was a bit of a fillip, and in November Gullit went spending again, buying Gianfranco Zola for almost £5m. This time I had heard of him, but for the wrong reasons. He was the player who missed a penalty for Italy against Germany in Euro '96.

If Zola's debut at Blackburn was quiet then his home debut against Newcastle was spectacular. He was everywhere and became an instant hit with

the fans. Zola's curling free kick looked to have crowned a stunning performance until Vialli claimed the goal, saying that he'd got a touch. And by then
Vialli needed all the goals he could get as his place was under threat from the
burgeoning Hughes/Zola partnership. He was going to get used to being the
team super-sub.

It was the new year, the FA Cup and Baddiel versus Skinner. The press
covered the story of the flatmates' Chelsea/West Brom rivalry, but much more
was made of players and supporters saying "We will win the cup for Matthew."
Even if this type of coverage apparently irritated Ken Bates, there was little he
could do about it, and he had even less chance of stopping us singing "Matthew
Harding's blue and white army" throughout the game. A comfortable 3-0
victory left Frank Skinner plotting domestic revenge and Chelsea fans looking
forward to Liverpool coming to the Bridge in the fourth round. But at 0-2
down at half time, the dream looked over. Liverpool hadn't lost after being 2-
0 up at half time for 33 years, and some Chelsea fans were so upset they'd
actually gone home. They missed the Chelsea comeback of all time as the
inspired Mark Hughes, risked for the second half by Ruud, became the focal
point of a second half blitz that saw Vialli (two), Zola and Hughesy himself
score the goals that left the Liverpool players arguing and in total disarray, and
Chelsea players and fans celebrating long into the night.

League games became almost secondary as the cup run gained momentum, and whilst a European place was Gullit's priority, Chelsea fans only wanted to get there one way: via Wembley.

Changes were needed in defence after Michael Duberry's achilles ruptured (ooh, nasty) as he ran round a frozen training pitch, and Ruud also
decided to give Frode Grodas (hardly from Hammersmith with a name like
that) an extended run in goal that coincided with Zola's debut at Blackburn.
Unfortunately, the sight of Grodas conceding goals from 30 yards didn't help
his cause and Kevin Hitchcock returned to share the duties just before the
Liverpool game.

But Chelsea had strength in depth and at Leicester in the fifth round we
cruised to a 2-0 lead, only this time it was Leicester's turn for a come-back, and
after drawing level they nearly snatched the game with a free kick that went
everywhere but in the net. The replay was famous for *that* last minute penalty,
and while Leicester were furious, at least justice was seen to be done after they
went on to Wembley to win the League Cup.

In the quarter-finals Chelsea became the cup favourites, despite the draw
at Terry Venables' Portsmouth being seen as a possible upset. But the fans
were never anything less than cast iron certain that this was finally going to be
our year, and as the mist came in from the sea, Portsmouth were summarily
dismissed 4-1.

Before the semi-final with Wimbledon, Chelsea won two and lost four
league games but only slipped one place. So with Europe still a possibility from
two routes we went to Highbury for the High Noon shoot-out. And shoot-out

it was, with three fabulous goals, two from Hughes and one from Zola, letting everyone know just how serious Chelsea were about winning the cup.

The last lingering doubts concerning Chelsea's determination to grab the trophy for the first time since 1970 were dispelled just 43 seconds into the final when Roberto's spectacular effort ripped the heart out of an already relegated and broken-spirited Middlesbrough team. Chances were few and far between for most of the game, and as the minutes ticked towards a Chelsea victory, Eddie Newton made certain, bundling the ball over the line after Hughes and Zola had combined yet again to make certain of Chelsea's first major trophy for 26 years.

And as we reflect on a memorable season with the prospect of more success to come, no-one can say that we haven't waited long enough. There has been great progress both on and off the field: a new stadium nearing completion, Gullit's ability to buy quality foreigners who have all been successful (even Vialli - it's just that he can't play with Hughes, but that's not his fault), the FA Cup in the trophy room and another campaign in Europe looming. And none of it would have been possible without the contribution of one man. Hope you're still watching, Matty.

Source: Chelsea Independent

ROOTS HALL ROAR

Southend United

I knew we were doomed from the moment we set foot inside Roots Hall to see the Blues take on Spurs in a pre-season friendly in August. My brother was a few steps ahead of me and emitted a noise I had not heard since the days when we used to dive behind the sofa whenever the *Doctor Who* theme music came on. "Just look at this kit!," he groaned. Sure enough it was hideous; our traditional blue shirts had been soiled with a bright yellow splash of vomit and the white band that separated the shirts from the shorts looked like the players needed to turn them down at the waist for them to fit properly. The *Roar* immediately labelled it a

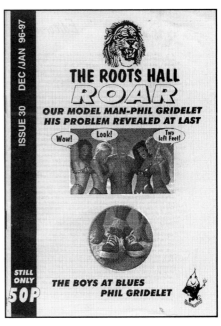

relegation kit. Only the heroics of our custodian Simon Royce had kept us in Division One the previous season, and the fact that we were again going into the new campaign without a decent strikeforce, plus *that* strip, made us certs for the drop.

The first issue of *RHR* the season was full of dire warnings of troublesome times ahead. The Tranmere game had just kicked off and I was hurriedly packing away my wares when a Roots Hall roar went up heralding our (and indeed the entire league's) first goal of the season, courtesy of the bustling Andy Rammell. Were we to withdraw all our unsold copies? Were we going to be pilloried for our unjustified messages of doom and gloom? Not at all. Tranmere equalised and looked more than comfortable in earning a 1-1 draw. Then third Division Fulham dumped us out of the Coca Cola Cup and newly promoted Oxford humiliated us 5-0 at the Manor Ground. That game was significant because it roused our traditionally apathetic supporters into something approaching outright revolt. Ronnie Whelan's honeymoon period appeared well and truly over as stories began to surface of him and his players propping up numerous bars in south-east Essex, many of them laughing and joking after galling defeats, some getting involved in scraps, while others were seen being carried into taxis. The alienation process between the 'mercenaries' and local townsfolk had begun.

We appeared to turn the corner in September when the Blues unbeliev-ably hammered Champions-elect Bolton Wanderers 5-2. It was one of those games where everything we tried came off. Typically it was the only home game I missed. I followed the match on the World Service while taking refuge from a typhoon in not-so-sunny Spain. I'm sure the big fella upstairs targets Southend fans, even on holiday, knowing how much we enjoy suffering. But normal service was resumed when Palace thrashed us 6-1 at Selhurst, one Blues fan near us being accused of child cruelty as he led his disconsolate son out long before the end.

There then followed what we thought was a barren period. Little did we know that four mind-numbingly boring 0-0's and a couple of home victories were to constitute our best sequence. It was obvious that chairman Vic Jobson was not prepared to sign the goalscorer that we craved, or a decent midfielder to relieve the pressure on our overworked skipper Mike Marsh, and we were soon back in our familiar habitat of the bottom three.

It was now clutching at straws time, never more so than when a superb chip by John Hendrie during our 3-0 drubbing at Oakwell was described by our dug-out and by woefully out of touch local hack Howard Southwood as a "fluke." "Played quite well for 15 minutes" was the report after our 4-0 shafting at Loftus Road just before Christmas. Get real - relegation was already staring us in the face but nobody with any influence wanted to admit to it, let alone do anything about it.

As ever though, there was always the prospect of the FA Cup to divert us from the stresses of our league predicament. Leicester City away didn't exactly have us salivating. Nevertheless just under a thousand of us made the midweek trek through icy fog and with little expectancy; you could say we were performing some sort of morose duty. Our pessimism was well founded as we lost 2-0 and gave Kasey Keller the sort of evening where he could quite easily have leaned on his post and read a good book. Another cup exit and another blank scoresheet. Our last FA Cup goal was scored when the Berlin Wall stood and Ginger Spice was still a virgin (yes it's been that long).

Back to the league and the day that summed up the 'professionalism' within our camp. I refer to yet another dour 0-0 draw at home to Ipswich Town on February 1st. A minute after the restart people started nudging each other as fingers were pointed at the pitch in counting-like gestures. Murmurs soon turned into probably the biggest noise heard all season at Roots Hall when it became obvious that only nine Southend players were on the green stuff. Er! Moments later Andy Rammell and Phil Gridelet came 'sprinting' out of the tunnel. Apparently Rammell had lost one of his contact lenses while Gridelet, whose superstition forbade him to cross the touchline before the rest of his team-mates, insisted on waiting for him!

While we're naming names, let's dwell a minute on Phil Gridelet. Now Phil fancies himself (full stop) as a part-time model and was once described as one of the top 50 most eligible bachelors in Britain. Personally I'd have pre-ferred him to have been labelled one of the 50 most competent midfielders in

Britain. Yet, there ain't much chance of that especially when his strike rate is around a goal a season and he generally prances around dressage-style playing piggy-in-the-middle. His continual inclusion, plus the fact that no disciplinary action was taken over the Rammell no-show episode, speaks volumes about the not-so-tight ship Whelan was steering towards the rocks.

Jobson began dropping hints to the local press that performances on the pitch or the standard of coaching were not up to standard. Rumours that either Whelan or his sidekick Theo Foley - Mr Blarney himself - were facing the chop. Vic did not have to wait long for his opportunity to pounce, thanks to an incident at Maine Road during a 3-0 Kinkladze-inspired hammering. Kinky definitely thumped Gridelet round the back of the head (the nearest Philip had got to him all afternoon) but despite our howls of protest no action was taken against the little Georgian. Whelan and Foley went ballistic, so much so that both were ordered from the dug-out. Whelan was duly suspended by the club, only to be re-instated a week later, while Foley was dismissed. The official line was that he was the senior man and should have exerted more control over his fledgling manager. Their scapegoat had been found.

Despite completing our only double of the season against Stoke (boy, they must have been miffed), a run of four games without a win now had only the die-hards predicting survival. It was imperative that we took all three points against Oxford towards the end of March. Unbelievably we led 2-0 with only ten minutes remaining when referee, Mr S.G. Bennett condemned us to the drop. There was a melée in the goalmouth, for which our promising young black defender Leo Roget was heading having just been booked. The man who actually initiated the dust-up was our gangly *white* Dutchman Jeroen Boere, yet to everyone's amazement, the Oxford players included, Bennett sent Roget off. Oxford grabbed two late goals to earn a draw, with an incensed Whelan demanding to know how the hell the official could confuse two men of different race. Forget that - how could he confuse a talented player with one devoid of any?

The transfer deadline came and went, and while our relegation rivals desperately splashed out, our club (bless 'em) managed to keep the coffers tightly under lock and key. Our Scottish centre-half Mark McNally was sold to Stoke though, and vice-chairman John Adams thought it somewhat amusing that Lou Macari immediately dragged him in for extra training upon his arrival. I failed to see the funny side.

On the subject of suspect fitness, the biggest scandal centred around the talented, yet rotund Paul Byrne. An Eire international who we signed from Celtic has previously been able to skin defenders for fun. This term however he has been out injured a lot and appeared to be suffering from a Gazza-type refuelling problem. So bad was Byrne's case that we were pressing for the season to be moved to the summer months so that he could benefit from solar power. I couldn't help but chuckle when one wag behind me shouted out "get your chins up Byrne!" The club in their infinite wisdom decided to write to

him warning that he had to pull his socks up (but not his shorts you understand), or else!

Our inevitable relegation was confirmed after our penultimate game
of the season at home to Huddersfield. I sat behind for quite a while
afterwards. Even though I'd known we were doomed back in August I was
still downcast. All the hard work in getting us to Division 1 for the first
time in our history had been wasted and what really hurt was that not
even at the death did the majority of the players appear to care. I've seen
us relegated a few times before, but this season was one of the worst in
living memory. We scored a paltry ten goals on our travels, we even applied blanket defence at home for God's sake, and when *Sky* screened Division One's highlights the only Southend action featured one of our players pushing a Wolves opponent into the perimeter fence.

At least Vic has already acted by sacking 27 members of the staff (including his brother) and has warned that several players will follow. Personally, I would have thought that he could have dispensed with the services of the
board (there for nodding purposes only) or given up the generous consultancy
fee he allows himself on top of his salary if he was so desperate to slash costs.
The realisation that *Sky*'s money will dry up and crowds will decrease even
further has forced him to act, yet during the season he didn't appear to give a
flying fig. Whelan meanwhile, for the passion he installed into his troops and
for his tactical genius, has been retained.

Only this morning, before the goalposts had been taken down at Roots
Hall, a letter arrived from Vic thanking me for my support and asking me to
renew my season ticket next year. I will, begrudgingly, but I fear many other
sheep will resist the temptation. Many of our fans are already predicting a
rapid slide to the Conference. What about me? Well, it's obvious, we'll enjoy
a season of consolidation in Division 2 (the lack of goals preventing us from
securing a top ten spot) only for us to qualify for the play-offs the following
season - the year they'll stage them at Twickenham while Wembley is being re-
vamped... now that would be typical Southend.

RUB OF THE GREENS

Plymouth Argyle

Pilgrims' Progress?

After the horrors of the basement division, most Argyle fans were looking forward to '96-97 with something akin to relief.

However, the more seasoned of us viewed the lack of transfer activity with mounting apprehension, as we were painfully aware of the limitations of the squad. Some late strengthening did take place as Tony James joined from Hereford and, most amazingly, the circus really came to town when Bruce Grobelaar joined the week before the action proper started.

The promotion wagon was obviously still rolling because we

RUB of the GREENS
The original Plymouth Argyle fanzine
No. 36 March 1997

50p

IS THERE ANYBODY OUT THERE?

Inside: Harley Lawer is an Alien
Peter Bloom Speaks
OPINIONhated - Kevin Keegan

RotG36

avoided defeat in the league during August. We won on the opening day for the first time in ages, drew an amazing game 4-4 at Wrexham (despite leading 4-1 with 20 minutes to go!) and the whole nation (or that part who bothers to watch the Nationwide League on *Sky*) saw us gain revenge over Preston.

However, we soon found our true role as we provided Stockport County with their first win of the season, and the springboard for their success. Due to a row between Neil Warnock and chairman Dan McCauley over hotel accommodation, the players had driven to the game in true Sunday League style, and proceeded to play in a similar fashion. Of course the real losers were the poor fans who'd travelled great distances to, in effect, see us defeated before we'd even kicked off...

A home defeat by Bristol Rovers in our first 'local' derby, followed by a comprehensive hammering at Gresty Road, saw us tumbling towards the floor more quickly than Baby Spice when she dived off her platforms. But we steadied the ship somewhat in October with two home draws and a first victory in eight attempts by stealing the points from the Bescot Stadium. This result so enraged the Walsall support that they held a demonstration whilst we supped an after-match pint in the social club. Very pleasant!

A jet-lagged Carlo Corazzin (we've got a few internationals) wandered aimlessly around Bournemouth's Dean Court as normal service was resumed with a 1-0 reverse, and Argyle then endured the journey from hell to get to

Turf Moor and lose yet again. And this was after the team had actually stayed at a half-way house in the Midlands. At one point we were ready, boots in hand, to take the fight to Burnley, but the team finally arrived with barely half an hour to spare.

Still, with a 2-0 victory over Gillingham, we entered November in slightly better heart and then saw probably the best league game at Home Park, as we twice came from behind and threw away a lead in a 3-3 draw with Luton. After notching up five goals in two games, having taken the previous nine to get that many, we hoped the scoring drought was over.

Oh dear, it was just a shower, as were we in a diabolical performance at Wycombe. The team played with as much fight as an English Rugby League team when meeting its Australian counterpart. It was around this time that the thought of another relegation dogfight started rearing its ugly head in the minds of the Argyle faithful.

Perhaps the FA Cup was what we needed to get our season going? It certainly looked like it after we avenged last season's four-goal hammering at Craven Cottage in beating the Division 3 hot-shots Fulham. Let's go on from here, we thought. Oh bugger! Three days later Chesterfield nabbed another three points and Neil Warnock left the ground with 20 minutes to go. This provoked another war of words between the manager and chairman, and it was plain for everyone to see that their relationship was getting rockier by the day.

The acrimony between the two men seemed to boil over again at the televised FA Cup game at neighbours Exeter. The pre-match jousting saw chairman Dan contradict anything Warnock had said and then claimed that there was no problem! This was even better than the game, which we won with something to spare to end any thoughts they might've had of a magical cup run at the other St. James' Park.

Around this time I was also disturbed about the number of times that Ronnie Maugé's recent contretemps with the Boys in Blue received a mention. I'm sure that if we'd been a 'bigger' club, it would hardly have rated a mention. (Paranoid, me?)

As Christmas approached we had a 'short' trip to that jewel in South Yorkshire's crown, Rotherham. We quickly snatched a two goal lead and spent the remainder of the game grimly hanging on, despite some antics from our favourite clown between the posts. But the joy from that welcome victory disappeared with the turkey on Boxing Day, as Brentford took advantage of some dubious refereeing and some even more dubious defending to dish out a stuffing (!) that left us dreading the new year.

The weather then saved us for a bit (some of us who travelled to Notts County diverted to Coventry and witnessed some real football skills as the hosts entertained Middlesbrough) but wasn't able to help us, despite the best efforts of our manager, when we returned to cup action against Peterborough. Neil Warnock psyched us out of a result by complaining about the state of the pitch and Mr Fry took full advantage. The gap between the boss and the chairman grew ever wider, and there were the first signs of a rift between the Warnock and the bulk of the support.

In fact it would only be a few more games before McCauley and Warnock finally decided to stand face to face and settle their differences manno to manno. Actually they did nothing of the sort, because after another poor draw, this time against Wycombe, McCauley called up Warnock on his mobile and gave him the bullet. The manner of his sacking provoked a big outcry in these parts.

The local press, most of whom had had their run-ins with McCauley, rubbed their hands with glee and ran campaigns calling for the reinstatement of Warnock. To be honest this only strengthened Dan's resolve to hang onto his control. His refusal to talk to anyone interested in taking over, especially if they even mentioned the Heaynes family (his most vociferous opponents), became the stuff of legends.

So, it wasn't really the best time to visit an in-form side like Luton, but, in best third round tradition, even if it was the league (stay with me), the rule book was thrown out of the window, and a fighting performance earned a 2-2 draw. The best part of the day was the constant chants of "Neil Warnock's Green and White Army" and "We want Dan out!"

After a victory against eventual Champions Bury, we travelled to Saltergate to witness the sort of action that *Sky* make you pay extra for on a Saturday night. There was already some needle to the proceedings after Ronnie Maugé had been sent off for a wild lunge in the first half. At 2-1 up we were threatening to put a nice big dent in Chesterfield's promotion aspirations, when a 20 player melée erupted after Bruce was flattened in an aerial challenge. It was Naseem and Tyson rolled into one, but probably with more punches! Just to show he wasn't totally biased towards the home side, and to maintain a pleasing symmetry, the ref showed the red to both number sixes and number eights. While it was really exciting to watch, it is the sort of thing that's best kept in the ring, and we were also worried about the possibility of a points penalty. Fortunately, the FA dithered until long after the season had finished, and the eventual fine will only hinder any transfer activity.

Amidst all this pugilistic fervour and managerial upheaval, our main striker Michael Evans must have been doing something right, because Graeme Souness decided to lighten the Dell bank account by 600 grand to get our man on board. Despite being injured earlier in the season, Evans still finished our top scorer with nearly double the strikes of his nearest rival. What did that say about the rest of the team?

For a while things looked really grim for Argyle, but vital wins over relegation-haunted Rotherham and Shrewsbury eased the fears. Brucie gained more notoriety at Gay Meadow by refusing to take a goal kick until a racist Argyle fan had been arrested. Despite my criticisms of him as a 'keeper, I heartily applauded his actions in this particular case, although I was disappointed that some of the offender's colleagues took exception to our article on this incident in the next issue of *ROTG*.

The rest of the season seemed to fizzle out into boring draws. We made certain of our continued Division 2 status with a victory over Walsall, proceeded to lose heavily at Ashton Gate (not a good thing for those of us trapped in Bristol by work), and closed the whole thing off with a tame home draw against Bournemouth: the return of the "Dan Out" chants were not unexpected.

Analysis of the season? In a nutshell we failed to score in eighteen games and drew ten games 0-0. Our main priority for next year then has to be a striker (or two) who knows that the round leather object is supposed to go in-between the white sticky-netty things. We could also do with an experienced midfielder to spray some decent passes around and we could also do with saying goodbye to Bruce and getting a really decent 'keeper (oh please!).

Same old Argyle - NEW DANGER

THE SEADOG BITES BACK

Scarborough

When the season ends in a seven the omens are invariably good for Boro. In 1977 we had our last winning trip to Wembley and in 1987 our elevation from non-league football to the professional ranks was completed. So would lady luck smile on us as we prepared for our tenth season in the football league? We were about to find out.

The summer break saw the Bulgarian Euro '96 squad staying at (and whinging about) their Scarborough base. But this wasn't the big talking point in the town; oh no, we were more interested in who was going to replace Mitch Cook in the manager's well-worn office. Actually the whole process was a bit of a

lark: first choice Gordon Cowans pulled out to continue playing, John Ward pulled out because of family matters and David Hodgson pulled out because he allegedly wanted to bring in Gary Bannister from Lincoln City as his assistant but chairman John Russell said "No way." At one point it looked like every unemployed manager in the country would turn us down!

Eventually, former Carlisle boss Mick Wadsworth decided to leave his deputy's post at Carrow Road and take on the mountainous task of lifting Boro's fortunes. The moustachioed former England coach was positive right from the start, particularly when steamrollering over a club official who'd refused him permission to buy a flip-chart to demonstrate tactics. His powers of persuasion were also equally well used in some hectic transfer market activity throughout the season. Familiar faces such as Jason Rocket, Andy Ritchie and Ian Ironside were joined by some classy cast-offs picked up for nowt. Gareth Williams and Gary Bennett were probably the most effective on the pitch, while young Scottish striker Jamie Mitchell gained the reputation for being the teen girl idol. Ian Thompstone from Rochdale also deserved a mention for being, er, big and useless. Bennett was christened 'The Black Prince' by Wadsworth, because of his colour and his ability to rule the midfield with an air of regal authority!

Pre-season was magnificent. Man City, complete with Kinkladze, Rosler etc., and Leeds were both held to draws. Others were put to the sword and only two local derby cup defeats by Dork City dampened the mood. Then it was time for Wadsworth and his assistant, ex-boss Ray McHale, to lead the Boro team, suitably attired in their new-look Le Coq Sportif strip, into battle against Cardiff City. Ninety minutes later the optimism had taken a Klinsmann dive as a 0-0 was ground out. Never mind, the first round of the Better-Than-Pepsi Cup offered up some encouragement as we travelled the 40-odd miles down the road to Hull City. The half-injured, half-brain dead striker Tony Daws scored his one and only goal for the club and Andy Ritchie added another as we drew 2-2.

The trips to Exeter and Scunthorpe were notable for a couple of reasons: first, sub Ben Worrall's 86th minute headed equaliser was quite a feat for a player little more than 3ft tall! Then Ritchie continued his Graeme Jones (or should that be Alan Shearer?)-like goalscoring exploits at Scunthorpe, as we won 2-0. Not everyone was happy at Scunny because Ritchie's goal, coming as it did just before half time, meant that the 30 or so Boro fans queuing at the refreshment kiosk missed it! More upset than anyone was fan Phil Clarkson who had also missed Andy's pre-season away goal at Dork for similar reasons.

September rolled along steadily without incident. Not! First we dumped Hull City out of the League Cup 5-4 on aggregate with Gareth Williams scoring a fabulous over-head goal in the 3-2 win at the McStad (ultimately rated second in the goal of the season honours). Our reward was a tie with the eventual winners Leicester City, and although we lost 4-1 on aggregate, aided and abetted by the diving Emille Hesky, we did give them a fright at Filbert Street. In the League we hovered around 12th place on the back of some up and down form. We lost at Brighton, beat Donny and pulled off a dramatic last minute draw at Carlisle; a strike which made me pee myself. Thankfully I was in the toilet at the time and missed it. The goal that is, not the trough. You know what I mean!

After a 2-1 defeat at Cambridge United, Wadsworth moved to stiffen things up at the back. John Kay from Sunderland and a tongue-twisting midfielder called Michael McElhatton from Bournemouth were introduced. The match against Wigan proved to be one of the best of the season. Kay set up Ritchie for his sixth goal of the season after just 90 seconds. Ritchie added another and Bennett also notched one as we trounced the eventual Champions 3-1.

The early season also heralded the introduction of a couple of off-field 'improvements' as the club unveiled its own range of soft drinks and a mascot. The drinks, Ritchie Cola, Rockett Fuel and Ironside Brew, were a big hit, despite tasting like cow dung and being flatter than an anorexic's stomach! 'Gulliver' our new seagull mascot, or to be precise a YTS player dressed up in a stupid costume, also proved a huge favourite with the home support. However, the Scunthorpe fans, on a day trip to the coast in March, took umbrage to Gulliver's threatening tail waving. Four arrests were made as the Scunny crew attempted to invade the pitch and slaughter our bird!

There was then an about-turn in our fortunes. Barnet away on a Tuesday night isn't the fixture most Northern fans would look forward too, but our 3-1 win set us off on a run that almost matched the club record of ten unbeaten. Trust Hartlepool, of all teams, to piss on our bonfire. They thrashed us 4-2 at the McStad and even Andy Ritchie's last ever home goal couldn't save us. To coin a phrase from Ugly Bloke Steve Vermont of TFI Friday fame; "We tried, but we failed." Our next League victory would not arrive until Boxing Day.

The FA Cup provided only brief respite: Shrewsbury were accounted for in the first round before eventual semi-finalists Chesterfield ended our interest. We also lost out in the AutoWindscreens Shield at home to Notts County. So now, to use a gaffer's favourite cliché, we could concentrate on the league!

During this time the player merry-go-round continued. Tony Daws, an injured and crap striker who no one liked, left. With him went Jon Sunderland who'd signed last season and couldn't make it in our first team, but then went to Hartlepool and scored on his debut! In David Coleman's words, 'remarkable!' Arrivals included 'keepers Teuvo Moilanen (a tall Finnish lad from Preston who couldn't catch) and John Burridge (a small and clinically insane man from every club in Britain). Striker Steve Brodie (freed from Sunderland) knocked in a few goals to become a crowd favourite and Colin Sutherland (a very hard Scottish defender who cost £20,000 from Clydebank) made his mark, especially in referee's note books and on the town's nightclub bouncers. Col's Saturday night exploits haven't been publicised because we couldn't handle more than two scandals in a season. The cow dung drinks and riot-inciting Seagull were quite enough, thanks!

As the New Year got into its stride so did Boro with two wins and a draw. But then another new face, loanee David Currie, did something that had only been done twice before. No, he didn't start a World War but he did score a league hat-trick, the first Boro player to do so since Darren Foreman rattled in a triple against Dork City four years previously. Three class goals they were as well as we trounced the eight man Quakers 4-1 for our biggest win of the season.

Soon after, Boro said goodbye to Andy Ritchie as he returned to the Latics and good riddance to Ian Thompstone. Mick Wadsworth then had to avert a goalkeeping crisis by turning to the reserve team and giving Kevin Martin his chance. He didn't waste it and was to make two further appearances before the season's end. Luckily for him they weren't against Fulham and Wigan.

First of all we travelled to promotion certainties Fulham on March 8th, and lost 4-0. The worst result of the season? Oh no. Three days later we travelled to Wigan Athletic determined to get the Fulham game out of our system. Ahem. Wigan shagged us 7-1! But the night wasn't a total loss; Jason Rockett scored his fifth goal of the season, and... err, well, that was it really. The worst result in the club's league history took us back down to ninth place with a very inferior 'goals against' column. Eleven goals in two matches may be a statistician's dream, but it's every supporter's nightmare, and we lived through it. To quote Alan Hansen, "absolutely shocking defending Des." Too true!

More changes were made and results continued to rollercoaster. Three goals were scored against Exeter but we still lost 4-3. More "shocking defending Des." Our play-off hopes now looked as secure as David James' gloves.

On transfer deadline day we signed Troy Bennett, who scored a magnificent last-day goal in our 2-0 win at Hull, and as the season petered out Mick Wadsworth gave the chairman's son Matthew Russell a full debut at Chester. He'd done well in a couple of substitute appearances and it must have been great for him to stick it up those who'd said he was just at the club because of his father.

Before I sign off, here's a little insight into Mick Wadsworth's approach to handling the media. In January I went with *Yorkshire Coast Radio's* commentator Andy Dorrie to cover Boro's game at Rochdale. When we reached Dale's ground it was cloaked by a huge fog cloud and the game was off. In search of some journalistic compensation, Andy went to record Mick's reaction. What he got was Fred Flintstone impressions and some views on European Monetary Union! You had to be there to believe it. Then in March, for the Friday night sport round-up, Andy asked Mick for any team news. The gaffer replied by saying, "We'll start with eleven on the pitch I think, and probably three subs on the bench!" Couple this with the numerous times he's pulled his false teeth out during live interviews, and you've got one mad football manager!

Mad he may be, but Mick Wadsworth has done wonders for this club so far. We finished 12th in his first season and three players scored over ten goals (unheard of in recent times). The boss is also currently in the process of signing the five or six players he needs for next year's Championship winning team. Rumours abound that a French defender called Alexandre Mariacove, Andy Saville of Wigan, Rod Thomas of Carlisle, and Alan Shearer of Newcastle will be joining the remaining squad of '96-97 for the assault. I must stress that these are only rumours, although I think someone has just made up the last one.

SEASIDE SAGA

Brighton And Hove Albion

What a season, surely one unparalleled in modern times. At the beginning there was no question about it, the chants on the terraces made it clear: "We are going up, say we are going up!" Oh no we weren't; anything but in fact. Our cover for issue four read: 'Smile, things could be worse!' We were wrong. At the end things were worse than even the most rabid pessimist could have imagined.

During the summer, behind closed doors, talks started between the leaders of the seven main supporters' groups and the club's board. They didn't last. It was clear that there was to be little co-opera-

tion or mutual understanding; they didn't trust us and we didn't trust them. Some agreements were made; very few were enforced. It was a time for the fans to take joint action... the protests started!

For the first time in many years the club had invested several hundred thousand pounds in new blood, but early indications were that it hadn't helped. By October any optimism had passed away, and we found ourselves firmly rooted to the bottom of the Football League. The protests against the board also moved up a gear with the first signs of a boycott. It started with a successful walkout, supported by 90% of the crowd, 15 minutes from the end of a game. Fireworks were the cue to move and it was clear that the fans were united.

However, people soon became restless as we were cast further and further adrift at the bottom of the table. Soon there were cries for Jimmy Case to quit, and after losing 3-2 at home to Darlington, a result that left us 12 adrift at the bottom of the table, he was duly sacked.

Off the pitch, regular meetings were taking place and several fresh ideas were vetted on how to get rid of the club's board. The consortium who were hoping to take over the club, led by Dick Knight, made it clear that they felt any official and prolonged boycott should only be started if it was endorsed by all fans. That didn't happen, but it was agreed to stage a one-match boycott. Once again about 90% of regulars observed the 'stay-away' as did, quite amazingly, a few Mansfield supporters. The only ones who did cross the lines were season ticket holders who reckoned that the regime already had their money so why not go in... missed the point there I think!

Steve Gritt was soon confirmed as the club's new manager, beating names such as Dave Merrington to the job. And the crowd's reaction to Gritt? A chorus of boos greeted his entrance and I reckon he knew that life was going to be tough. We were soon won over though. 'Gritty' proved his worth by transforming a set of players who had earlier been branded 'the worst ever bunch to wear Albion shirts' into a stylish and effective team capable of starting a 12 game unbeaten run at home. The fans at last had something to cheer about on the pitch, and despite our wretched away form, as well a sudden improvement in teams such as Hereford, Hartlepool, Doncaster and Darlington (strange that), we started to make up ground at the bottom.

The fans decided that they would be foolish to hinder the revival, and it was agreed that any protests should not affect the team. So several new ideas were put forward: boycotting Focus DIY (the chain owned by our chairman), marches up in Mellor near Crewe (home of chairman Bill Archer), marches through London to Lancaster gate, whistle-blowing at matches, jamming the phone lines at the FA on the day of the Italy game and destroying the credibility and political career of David Bellotti (our much-hated chief executive) were just some of the campaigns that were instigated. And finally there was the *coup de gras*: 'Fans United' day.

The idea came from a 15-year-old Plymouth fan and the organising soon started, culminating in an unrivalled day in Football League history. Supporters from rival clubs all over the country and internationally converged on the ground arm-in-arm: Brighton-Palace, Spurs-Arsenal, Rangers-Celtic, all stood together against corruption and the unscrupulous money-men looking to make a killing from the game. Sod Girl Power, this was Fan Power. Those who attended were treated to the spectacle of the team rooted to the bottom of the Football League winning 5-0. Mind you, the fans couldn't have been further from the truth when they sung "It's just like watching Brazil," but for a team in our situation it was at least a good as watching Wales! The success of the day led to the declaration that it should become a yearly event, and indeed I believe it should.

Despite all this, our aim still hadn't been achieved; the club was still in the hands of Archer and Bellotti and it was clear that further action was still needed. Ideas such as getting a Wimbledon Premiership game abandoned were all put forward, but it was decided that the last thing we needed was to upset or anger other fans, so plan B was put into action: pressure the FA.

We soon reaped some rewards from our efforts. The FA brokered a meeting between the board and the Dick Knight consortium. With the aid of some experienced mediators, and after several months of talks, it was announced that an agreement had been reached. What the agreement was, we didn't know; only that we would be informed in a few days. Several weeks followed, and there still hadn't been an announcement. Our last-ever game at the Gold-

stone was only days away and a sequel to the York City riot was widely tipped
to occur, when the FA - miracle of miracles - finally took some proactive steps
and told the parties to make a statement. And while it wasn't exactly what we
wanted to hear, Archer and Stanley retained a 49~% shareholding and Bellotti
kept his job, we all knew that it would have to do for now.

As the final curtain was set to fall at the Goldstone, we still had to beat
Doncaster to keep alive any small faint hopes of staying up. On a great day we
were treated to a tense-scrappy-bloody awful-wonderful-brilliant game of football, as well as an excellent lucky goal by the much-(ex)maligned bloody-won-
derful-bloke Stuart Storer. To add to this ecstasy, the word came in that Hereford had lost 2-1, meaning that we would only need a draw against them at
their place in the last game of the season to stay up.

The war for tickets started and 3,300 were snapped up by Albion fans
within hours. The day soon came and we were in for a real bloody treat. We
had to suffer in silence as we were outplayed by Hereford, even being treated to
Kerry Mayo's first goal for the club; sadly it was a great shot into his own net.
Stick and taunting followed at half-time from the Hereford fans, but we weren't
finished yet. An inspired substitution from Steve Gritt followed, as our newish
signing Robbie Reinelt, who had joined us from Colchester two months earlier, ran out onto the pitch and changed the game. He made great runs, held the
ball up well and showed more of the never-say-die attitude that we'd been
treated to since he arrived at the club. And it was he who was first to react to
the rebound off the post from Craig Maskell's terrific Le Tissier style flick-up
and volley. Suddenly it was us crying tears of relief, screaming and cuddling
each other, while the Hereford supporters went deathly quiet.

Ultimately, it was the three goals more that we'd scored that kept us up,
the exact amount Reinelt had netted since joining the club. Hereford who had
a better goal difference were relegated, and we were all treated to a parody of
what a police state may look like.

I'm writing this a month on from the Hereford game and sadly the dark
clouds are once again gathering. We have no plans or even a site on which to
build a new stadium, and at the moment we don't even know where we will be
playing next season. The deafening silence is now being broken by the fans;
once again they're becoming impatient, and the threat now looms that if action isn't taken by the board, it will once again be taken by the fans. There is
a light however. The performances of the team towards the end of the season
indicate that they are more than capable of winning promotion, and after all,
we do have our man on the board.

THE SHEEPING GIANT

Wrexham

It's a funny old world, eh? Before last season I, Dai Shovett, was a mere football journalist, carving out a meagre living writing about Wrexham in a local paper, with a lucrative sideline writing copy for the back of Swedish porn videos. But now I've been asked to write in this book again! This is the most surprising piece of news I've had since I heard that Cubby Broccoli was dead - after all, aren't vegetables supposed to be good for you? The only previous recognition I've achieved was in a police line-up. I don't usually write in books, although I have been known to do a bit of colouring in.

The life of a journo is terrifically strenuous - let me give you a taste of a typical working day for a conscientious football correspondent like myself: arrive at match at about 2.50; park in free space; enter free of charge; pick up free programme; go to press bar; enjoy free buffet; have a few beers with my mates on the account; send a YTS lad to the bookies at half time (the wingers are usually quickest). Sometimes I pop out to take in some of the second half . On Monday I ask one of the staff writers to do my report for me (look for a young enthusiastic one who went to the match).

But enough about me (as if that were possible!) - what about Wrexham? Well, they had a funny sort of season. Like a Fantasy Postman, they promised much but delivered nothing. It could have been us as play-off glory beckoned, but Lady Luck's fickle finger of fate delivered the thumbs down and turned its back as we were handed the cold shoulder. League success was built around a solid defence, with Reliable Andy Marriott commanding in goal. He has a natural control of angles previously known only by William the Conqueror! Indeed, his form only dipped when he broke his jaw against battling Bury, a minor injury which he insisted on using as an excuse to miss a whole three weeks of the season! Honestly, Britain didn't become the great nation it is today through such shirking. No! It became great by invading the Third World and robbing foreigners!

This solid defence led to some dull matches, though - at Wycombe I kept myself awake by recalling classic episodes of *The Munsters Today*. Frustratingly, we also set off on long, unbeaten runs throughout the season. God, what's a journalist supposed to write about? At least we played on Good Friday again, against Millwall. I decided to take advantage and throw in all the clichés I could think of. I'll give you a taste of it - I reckon this report could win me the Booker, or at least its rhyming slang equivalent.

FANS CRUCIFY FLYNN'S FALLEN ANGELS
NEWMAN THE SAVIOUR AS LIONS DEVOUR ROBINS

It was hardly a Good Friday for Wrexham as Millwall rose from the dead to gain a share of the hot cross bun of league points. After suffering a private march up Golgotha in the first half, the crafty cockneys resurrected their hopes of promotion with a couple of deadly crosses. Humes netted, then Bennett scored from the spot after Carter had denied him three times. Millwall pulled one back, but it seemed Phillips had driven in the final nail with an Easter eggcelent goal. Neill saw red and betrayed his team mates, but this Judas nearly gained thirty pieces of win bonus as the Lions roared back. The crowd had sighed, Newman had risen, and Millwall came again. The ball brushed Carey, and the referee gave a penalty, although he claimed it merely kissed him on the cheek. Will this match be a last supper for Wrexham's hopes of rising again? If so, Brian Flynn could find himself leaving town on a donkey.

Of course, it was the cup run which brought us the most publicity and fulfilment. Who would have thought a second round dismissal from the Sherpa Van Basten AutoGlass Cup at the hands of Crewe could make such an indelible mark on the nation's consciousness? We did well in the FA Cup too. It all started against someone called Colin Bay, then went on to Scunthorpe. I must admit, when I first heard the draw I thought it was a joke - surely there's not really a place called Scunthorpe! Isn't it a town in a Charles Dickens book? I've got lots of books at home, but I still can't stop the draught under my kitchen door. Maybe I should cut it down from the ceiling. Anyway, a lengthy correspondence with *Watchdog*'s own feisty Ginger Spice, Anne Robinson established that there really is a team called Scunthorpe! I looked into the matter and found out that they are known as the Irons, thus offering me the opportunity to do what all sports writers do best - make up puns. Indeed, the Rockin' Robins had to steel themselves as the Irons steamed into town. They knew they had to show their mettle ore face the consequences of alloying the hard men of Yorkshire the sweet smelt of victory.

Having triumphed in a replay, the reward was a West Ham tie (interestingly, the NUJ have ruled that a cup game against Chelsea is now officially to be called a cravat). West Ham've got piles of foreigners in their team: they really are the United Nations of Football (^{TM} J. Motson 1986 - this phrase patented when Liverpool bought Craig Johnston). After our 1-1 draw, three-jowled Harry Redknapp said on-loan Hugo Porfirio had never seen snow before, but I took that with a pinch of salt - after we beat Arsenal, George Graham had said the same about Paul Merson. The replay was postponed; the official reason was fog, although I can exclusively reveal that the real reason was that when appropriately-named Julian Dicks arrived at the ground at 5.45 the bar wasn't open so he destroyed a stand in a sober frenzy. (By the way, did you know that the gut-lord full-back was the inspiration for the TV character Father Jack?)

The funniest thing happened in the replay - we won! I believe Ravanelli-lookalike bald eagle Kevin 'Kojak of the Kop' Russell scored the goal, but these days I can't really tell the difference between all these players - they all look the same to me. Anyway, I was half way out of the press box when he scored - if I didn't leave early I'd get caught in traffic! I decided to return to celebrate our famous victory, jumped to my feet and, in my best Norwegian accent, started shouting across Upton Park: "Alf Garnet! Wendy Richard! The Queen Mother! Can you hear me? Can you hear me? Your boys took one helllllllll of a beating!"

Then a funny thing happened. Hundreds of angry West Ham fans jumped out of the stand and ran across the pitch towards me. I decided to get out of there pretty sharpish.

The cup run had its down side, however. It meant we played Peterborough twice in a week, which was awful as I do my best to avoid Poxy Barry Fry these days after the disaster that was my appearance as him in *Stars in Their Eyes*. I performed *Money Money Money* in a cockney accent, pausing half-way through to buy Paul Peschisolido on a two-week contract. If silence is golden, the audience's response to my performance was pure 24 carat, and Barry's lawyers sent me a lovely letter too!

Then it was on to somewhere called Birmingham. What an awful draw! What could I write about? They haven't even got a funny nick-name! Is Jasper Carrott still alive? Someone told he was doing *Question of Sport* now. Actually, I was a bit worried about the possibility of going there after my **"SOFT PORN LEGG, HORNE"** story. However, it all went really well - we beat them and I got into the Guinness Book of Records for the most puns in a newspaper report. Here's just a flavour of it :

The Blues' dreams of the Twin Towers were Bruced and battered when their Swedish star Limpared off after an hour, and they were soon down to ten men after Paul showed the Devlin him. Despite his industry, Holland was soon facing up to the Nether Netherlands of FA Cup elimination. Rather than a Horne of plenty, the Brummies were not in the cup Furlong.

Norris McWhirter said he hadn't been so excited since Cheryl Baker produced the longest sentence without a consonant.

Then came the quarter final draw, the highlight of which was when Gordon Banks swapped his glass eye for Portsmouth's ball. We drew cup-fighters Chesterfield, who always have a good cup run when a vast comet is visible in the Northern skies. Also, we were finally playing at a ground I can find! Sadly our hopes of a red landslide died as Tony Benn's blue and white army scored the majority of goals. Wrexham's left wingers could hardly hit a black rod from ten paces, and I hadn't brought my banjo.

With our FA Cup run ended our hopes of recording a Cup Final song were dashed. A studio had already been booked (Yolanda's Curl Power Salon and Video Hire) and we were due to collaborate with Wales' top rock group, Funky Blodwen and the Caergwrle Five (Who could forget their seminal ROCK-IN' ALL OVER GWYNEDD (AND SOME OF THE LESS REMOTE PARTS OF POWYS) '87 tour?). Maybe next year...

On the transfer market, Wrexham were the victims of a remarkable con. Two years ago they sold top striker Gary 'Hundred Goal' Bennett. This season they bought him back, but rather craftily Preston sold us an older version of the Bennett we once owned! I must admit, when I first heard that Mr Bennett was back I immediately went round to the ground to get my *Tony Hart 1981 Annual* signed, but I soon realised my mistake. Typically, Wrexham's fans welcomed him back with open hearts, as Christian Barnard once said. After all, there can be no substitute for class, not even if it goes off at half time with a groin strain. Expect more signings by the Reds in the summer, when they are likely to strengthen their squad by taking advantage of the Bosman ruling and buying cheap players from foreign clubs like Shrewsbury.

I'm quick to pick up exclusives at the club, which is surprising, as there are always hundreds of journos from around the world hanging around the ground. (The Croatian press is full of leader pieces considering Wrexham's season as a metaphor for the Balkan conflict.) However, I'm the one with the ear of the men who matter, as Don Corleone once said, and have broken a number of sensation stories this season. The biggest one was undoubtedly the revelation that the Red Red Robins will be bob-bob-moving to a new, 175,000 all-seater stadium - the Abermorddu Megadome - next season. Little Brian Flynn was laughing his head off as he told me - he loves to see me! The stadium will be opened in August by a prestigious friendly between Llansantffraid and Botafogo, but ironically enough, building work has yet to start as a scruffy man was found sleeping rough in a home-made tunnel beneath the site. At first it was thought to be a Swampy-style protest, but it turned out to be Booby Gould, in my humble opinion the most popular manager Wales has had this year. Despite being English, he has been accepted by the Welsh people; clearly he has achieved a great deal in building bridges between races.

I must admit, I've not been able to pay as much attention as usual to the football this season. Inspired by the election campaign of Martin Bell who, before he joined Erasure, was a journo, apparently, I stood at the election as party leader of the Wrexham Independence Front (WIF). I must admit, we didn't win as many seats in Wales as Labour, but we did manage a 0-0 draw with the Conservatives. With my trademark white suits, complemented by a red away suit with green sleeves which I changed slightly every week, my public profile was high, although it was my pubic profile which got me into the papers. I felt my policies won a lot of people over. Sadly, most of them were under ten, which hardly boosted my vote. It seems I didn't help my cause by following Kevin Ratcliffe around in a chicken suit. The basic planks of my manifesto were:

- To make football matches shorter, but wider
- All footballers called Ronaldo must serve three years' national service for Wrexham FC (after extensive bargaining this was revised to all players named Ron, although I had been hanging out for a compromise of all players called Aldo)
- Irrational victimisation of Crewe Alexandra.

I must admit that I've got Crewe under my skin. I had hoped to completely remove them from all Wrexham fans' existence by way of a small thermo-nuclear device, although their promotion seems to have done a similar job (**"LAURELS FOR GRADI"** as I reported).

So, Wrexham look forward to next season with anticipation. There has been talk of their being floated on the stock market, although they'll never be able to compete with the big boys, like Bisto. As for myself, I'm excited to reveal that my boss has offered me a chance in a lifetime - over the summer I'm reporting on a top European sporting event so select that we have the exclusive rights to cover it - a tournament so prestigious that I'm to pay my own expenses for the right to be there! I can't say I've heard of it before, but I'm sure I'm going to love covering the Intertoto Cup!

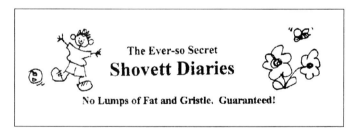

The Ever-so Secret
Shovett Diaries

No Lumps of Fat and Gristle, Guaranteed!

THE SILENCE OF THE LAMB

Preston North End

It would have been nice to have likened Preston's season back in Division Two as a rollercoaster ride but unfortunately we spent most, or should I say all, of the campaign firmly at the bottom end of the table. In fact we started to think that our brush with Second Division football was coming to an end, but fortunately lady luck decided to smile on the boys from Deepdale over our last three games.

So there were plenty of on-field disappointments, but even worse were the excuses from the chairman, Gary Peters and the players about why the season hadn't gone to plan. Some of what they came out with was more feeble than

27th August 1996

ISSUE 1 40p

The Silence of the Lamb...

"Division 3 Champions - But will they make it in Division 2?"

the things we used to say to our teachers when we couldn't be arsed to do our homework. Yes, it's been a long season, so I'll tell you about it in the A to Z of Preston North End '96-97:

AutoWindscreens — the Mickey Mouse shield saw us beat Chesterfield 2-0 (a) and lose to York 1-0 (a). Couldn't complain though because we fielded our reserve team who didn't give a monkey's about the competition.

Brentford — after a fighting 0-0 at Griffin Park we turned the league leaders over 1-0 at fortress Deepdale thanks to Ian Bryson who must have had his zimmer on supercharge; it's always brilliant to beat a team 19 places above you.

Cards — some of the bookings our players got were pathetic. The best, a real cracker, was when the almost mute Ryan Kidd got the yellow for foul language at Crewe. Red ones were dished out to Mark Rankine for a Cantona kung fu style tackle at Dean Court and to poor David Reeves, making it the first in his career, for two bookable offences at Deepdale - ahhh...

Coca Cola Cup — after getting to the third round of the fizzy pop for the first time, Spurs played party poopers at White Hart Lane... Cheers lads!

Donkeys	-	we beat them 3-0 live on *Sky* in front of a crowd of 14,000 at Deepdale and just to prove that B******l are crap, Gary Bennett managed to put two past Banks in a 'Baxi' shirt. We lost 2-1 at the Garden Shed (bow heads in shame) in front of only 8,000, but we would've won if the pitch was flat, honest!
Embarrassments	-	Losing 5-1 to Luton was awful but the 1-2 reverse against B*******l was far worse. Oh, the shame.
FA Cup	-	non-league outfit Altrincham were despatched 4-1 but losing 3-2 to York ended our interest. Still, there was much hilarity when the FA Cup produced B*******l 0, Hednesford Town 1.
Gregan, Sean	-	God in disguise. If it wasn't for this outstanding player we would have been making the trip to Spotland next season.
Headlines	-	nearly a full page in the *Sun* and *Star* after our 1-1 with Spurs. They also enjoyed rubbing the salt into our wounds when we lost the second leg - sods!
Injuries	-	we almost had to resort to the YTS lads, such was the injury crisis in the first four months of the campaign.
Jackson, Michael	-	not the crotch grabbing crooner, but a brilliant defender brought in from Bury. What a great buy he turned out to be, one of the few players at Preston who can run *and* pass the ball.
Kick Offs	-	surprise, surprise, a certain Mr Davey and 'Mr Temperamental' Ashcroft have been trying their great Muhammad Ali acts on the field this season. Well, I suppose it's something to brag about.
Linesmen	-	if I see any more of these favouring the opposition at Deepdale next season, believe me, I'll stick their flags were the sun doesn't shine.
Moaners	-	yes it's our friends from Burnley who whinge and whine, win, lose or draw. They sold us a reject by the name of Nogan and we beat them 2-1 at Turf Moan.
Nogoals Nogan, Kurt	-	bought from the moaners a few months back and I'm not surprised they wanted to get rid of him, arrogant git! He hasn't done much but irritate and annoy me since he signed. He'll be top scorer next season!
Open goals (misses)	-	Nogan and Bennett were the main culprits.

Peters, Gary	-	PNE's saviour. He's done well as boss and I think this guy will take us places we've never been before.
Ref	-	every bloody ref we've had has made cock-ups galore which have usually cost us three points.
Streakers	-	none so far, but we have had strippers on at home to Argyle. I am seriously willing to pay £50 to anyone who fancies running on the Deepdale turf naked for a laugh and a night in a police cell. Any offers?
Top teams	-	we were well able to beat teams above us in the table but always made mountains out of molehills when it came to the division's strugglers. It's a mystery to me.
Useless	-	a flattering description for a few Preston players who need shooting.
Vermin	-	a polite word to describe a certain Tony 'Judas' Ellis who is afraid of a blue and white Baxi shirt and will never score against Preston.
Wycombe	-	the boo-boys got stuck into the team at this home fixture. Peters threatened to quit and the tears welled up in Kevin Kilbane's eyes. For the record we won 2-1.
YTS lads	-	they walk around like they're God's gift to football, reckon they're good looking and watch games for free. Gits. But don't we all wish we were in their shoes...
ZZZ	-	some of the games were the ultimate cure for insomnia.

So there you have it; not much to shout about really. Still, if it had gone on much longer we'd all have been in an asylum. Special thanks have to go to Bury for Michael Jackson, Darlington for Sean Gregan and West Brom for the return of crowd favourite Lee Ashcroft. If it wasn't for these players I think we'd be dusting the maps off for some return trips to Lincoln and the like.

Up with the whites, down the 'Pool!

SING WHEN WE'RE FISHING

Grimsby Town

"Next year, we fully expect to be relegated."

So reads the account of Town's '95-96 season in SOTF2. And so it proved.

From the opening day of the season, when we were comprehensively beaten by Wolves despite outplaying them for long periods, it looked to be an uphill task. That first game, which saw Steve Bull in imperious mood and Iwan Roberts more useful off the pitch injured than most of ours on it, told us so. Manager Brian Laws had an absolute nightmare, being completely humiliated by Wolves' Steve Froggatt, and afterwards he swore he would hang up his boots.

So something good came out of the game, after all...

That day, the hatred of Laws which had been simmering since the initial outburst following the Bonetti incident found new expression, and he was bayed off the pitch. That one game proved to be a microcosm of our season; despite some good football, we couldn't put the ball away, and were then let down by defensive fallibility.

"Was Laws still there?" I hear you asking. Yes, his reward for hitting our best player, exposing the club to national ridicule and High Court litigation, and nearly getting us relegated was a three-year renewal of his contract. This is the way they act at Grimsby Town!

"What does that say for the judgement of the board; especially the chairman?" I also hear you say. Well, I'll tell you: it said volumes. They haven't got a clue, and as the season wore on, more and more people came out and said it. No matter; a group called 'Action 2000', led by former chairman Dudley Ramsden, and fronted by legendary Grimbarian (although not Grimsby Town) footballer Duncan Mackenzie, amongst others, looked set to oust them in an extraordinary general meeting in November.

Meanwhile, results were dreadful, and the season-long problem of goals conceded late in either half became a plague. Laws took refuge in a series of sound-bytes which no one believed any more, as he was now widely recognised as clueless, incapable of halting the slide into obscurity. I mean, when a bloke says things like "I'm a winner!" and "This will stop!" after it's become obvious that he's a loser and it won't, you just laugh, don't you?

Hostility towards the manager was matched by hatred of the board, now widely seen as incompetent and dithering, although strangely not when it came to fighting off take-over attempts by people who might have saved the day. Bidders for shares were shut out, and chairman Carr said he would sell out for £6 million, as the club "was on a sound financial basis" and didn't need an injection of cash from the feared Deadly Dudley.

So bad did things get that stewards at Barnsley were forewarned of aggressive action to be taken against Town directors by angry fans, and the result was one of those SA-type pre-war brawls between said stewards and Town fans celebrating a rare win. Yes, we won at Barnsley!! Three chances and we put them all away! In retrospect, these odd famous victories were dangerous delays on the road to getting rid of Old Sound-Byte, whose dismissal was postponed by wins nicked against the odds against QPR and the Reds. The height of anti-Laws feeling was demonstrated in one issue of SWWF, which comprised 64 pages of relentless piss-taking and abuse.

When Laws did eventually go, just after buying a house in the borough for himself and his family, the board turned to former caretaker boss John Cockerill in an obvious attempt to deflect the constant criticism they were by now receiving. We thought things were on the up... until Cockers turned the job down. As we later discovered, this was because he was refused £800k which he needed for two players to help put things right.

Who else could we get? After a few wild rumours and months of dithering, they gave the job to Laws' assistant Kenny Swain until the end of the season, with the injunction to keep us up. Characteristically, the board confirmed Kenny's appointment on the Monday after a humiliating 7-1 cup thrashing by Sheffield Wednesday!

Meanwhile, Town fans' hearts were gladdened as West Brom sacked our former manager Alan Buckley for failing to do any good and being unpleasant to everyone who didn't agree with him. At SWWF, we had been receiving regular updates on Buckley from Si Wright of Grorty Dick, who had rechristened Buckley 'the Obnoxious One'. Baggies fans were glad to see him go, muttering as he went that not a one of them knew anything about football. Boy, were we lucky to be rid of him! After all, he had insulted and betrayed us by decamping with the staff and poaching players, and was roundly abused until his little head went red at Blundell Park. Little did we know what the future held...

Kenny Swain quickly gained the reputation of being a really nice guy. Too nice! From hopeless failures and cast-iron certainties for relegation, we became in Kenny's words "the best of the bottom four," although he was never blamed by the fans for poor performances. By now, "Sack the board!" and "Carr out!" became the most regular chants, as Swain's team proved incapable of stringing a decent set of results together, and the Evening Telegraph bulged with letters calling for the board's heads. Kenny failed to sign the players he needed to get us out of the mire, but it was widely known that he had had a £250k ceiling placed on transfer fees. No-one wanted to come to Grimsby anyway, and the Telegraph pinpointed the reason: "a perceived lack of ambition at the club."

Mr Moneybags chose the eve of the final game of the season to announce that the club was losing £8,000 a week. This clashed somewhat with his earlier claim that the club was on a sound financial footing. Still, we took no notice, believing by now that he just made things up to suit his own purposes. More annoying was the fact that he blamed us, the fans, for not going in sufficient numbers.

Well, despite winning, we went down, and the mutant mascot took his horrible head off and cried; but I didn't, because with many others, I had known that this pitiful farce was inevitable before the season had even started. Angry 'sack the board' protests took place outside the main office and even on the pitch, when Town's Tommy Widdrington ripped the offending banner from the perpetrators, and was roundly booed from the stand.

Kenny then moved his family into the borough, thinned out the staff, and prepared for the tough job of returning us to the First at the first attempt. He might have saved himself the trouble. As contracts were exchanged, he was sacked; saddled with the blame for the disaster the season had become, and the unthinkable happened - they re-appointed the Poison Dwarf himself, the hated Buckley, with Cockers as his assistant to mollify the fans.

But we are not placated so easily as that! The Telegraph is bulging once again with protests from people who can neither forget nor forgive his previous betrayal; though widely predicted, this is seen as a desperate, dirty deed - to stab in the back the man who no-one outside the boardroom blamed.

But typically, they took no notice of popular feeling, and, oblivious to the hatred with which Buckley is widely regarded, paraded his picture across the Telegraph and predicted a return to the glory days. A campaign is now afoot to boycott season ticket and merchandise sales, in an attempt to bring the club to its knees and get rid of the despised and derided board. As the paper's sports editor wrote: "Town clearly have a tough task on their hands to bring the fans back into the fold. I'm not sure whether the board realise the depth of ill feeling which exists."

"They didn't listen, they won't listen still - perhaps they never will..."

Reasons to be cheerful: the discovery of John 'Oysterboy' Oster; the form of Jack Lester. But SuperClive has gone, to Charlton for £700k! Who will score goals for us now?

SON OF A REF

Scunthorpe United

The majority of Scunthorpe United's supporters accept that their destiny is pre-determined. Every year we finish in roughly the same spot, somewhere between eighth (just missing out on the play-offs) and 18th (after flirting with the nightmare that is the Conference trap door). We have probably been the most consistently mediocre team in the Football League over the past five years or so, and generally this can be attributed to the usual factors of: too many points dropped by conceding stupid goals right at the beginning/end of matches, too small a squad to cover for injuries, the sale of our better players due to financial necessity (and consequent lack of investment), and just sheer frustrating inconsistency.

"Son of a Ref"

Issue Two

a scunthorpe united fanzine £1.00
limited edition away strip coloured cover

OK, all those factors came into play again, but our lack of success this season can be pinned down to one particular match and placed, whether fairly or not, directly upon the shoulders (or more accurately the boot) of one player. Step forward Mr Mark Samways, goalkeeper extraordinaire with the shot-stopping ability of (let's be fair) a decent First Division 'keeper; the secure-handling of a rather mediocre semi-pro goalie and the kicking prowess of Arthur Askey (post operation). Unfortunately for Samways and us, it was this last skill which was found out to be so lacking that it is now the basis for a comedy series showing to great critical acclaim on Finnish television.

Let me take you back to the fateful day in question: December 17th 1996 and the FA Cup second round replay with Wrexham. Planned as a bit of a birthday treat for my son Joseph's ninth birthday, there's nothing like a midweek cup tie in winter for a bit of atmosphere, and as we left the car and walked on with (yes!) hope in our hearts, the floodlights seemed to act like a magnet to the teeming crowds as they flocked towards the ground in their thousands. Oh, all right, 3,976 to be precise, but the fact that we actually had to queue up for ten minutes to get into the ground added to the sense of excitement and anticipation. I can remember the build up to the match much more clearly than the game itself; selective memory I suppose, but I have been unable to obliterate the blunder. To put things in perspective, at this stage

Scunthorpe were on a real high, having won their previous four games and risen to fifth. They actually looked as if they could score at one end and defend at the other. Manager Mick Buxton had put together a decent mix of younger players and a few old troopers, who, although lacking somewhat in style, at least seemed confident and willing to fight for each other.

And they needed to because Wrexham made it tough. A Match of the Day live game with West Ham awaited the winners, and at 2-1 up with 90+ minutes on the clock we were praying for the ref to blow for full time. Three minutes into injury time and Wrexham mounted what was surely their last attack, but we had it under control and all Samways had to do was despatch a back-pass into the night air and preferably out of the ground. OK, so it wasn't the greatest back-pass and it did leave the 'keeper with little time to compose himself, but trying to kick the ball with your right boot when you're left-footed was always a dodgy recipe... Swoosh - the merest kiss of leather on leather - the ball spun gently away and behind our custodian for the gleeful striker to tap in. Defender gawped at 'keeper, who stared at the ball nestling in the back of the net, as the crowd looked at each other in numbed disbelief, then after a momentary silence screamed with one voice: "You stupid wanker!" When Wrexham scored the winner in extra time no-one expected anything different.

It's funny how depression doesn't set in until a few days later. We trudged off home trying to convince each other that at least we could now concentrate on a real push for promotion. But of course we were kidding ourselves. The belief had gone out of the team and with it the inevitable realisation that whatever we did, however hard we tried, there was always someone ready to piss on our strawberries. To all those who weren't there and tried to console me by saying "I saw the highlights - what a joke their second goal was," I'd like to say, yes it was a joke, but only in the sense it was the Hale & Pace of goals - so unfunny as to be virtually criminal.

And so it goes; seven defeats out of the next ten games sent us plummeting down to 17th spot in the division and heralded the departure of manager Buxton in mid-February. Samways was sent out on loan to York for the remainder of the season in exchange for their second-string 'keeper Jim Clarke who proved to be a much more dominant and confident player. Brian 'useful with his left' Laws was eventually installed as the new manager even though he still had an FA enquiry pending, following the infamous Bonetti-cheekbone-plate of sandwiches incident whilst manager of Grimsby. However, Laws proved to be a popular choice with players and supporters alike and even rekindled vague hopes of making the play-offs before the team slipped at the final few hurdles to finish (surprise!) mid-table.

Laws has recently had a clear-out and released eight out of contract players while purchasing a number of promising replacements. Another few signings to strengthen the squad and the future could be bright. Automatic promotion next year? Of course! There again we could drop too many points by conceding stupid goals right at the beginning/end of matches, might have too small a squad to cover for injuries, be forced to sell our best...

SOUR GRAPES

Wimbledon

"We're on course for the quadruple!" I announced to my colleagues.

I was flushed with success after the Dons defeated Wednesday in the Cup. I was convinced we wouldn't win and that our truly amazing season would collapse from then on. But no, the team had produced an amazing performance, despite, or perhaps because of, that terrible band and droning chorus; I do hope this was just this season's fad and not a permanent feature of Hillsboro' as it is an awful assault on the ears! I think I read somewhere that the band wasn't allowed in Selhurst - for once our happy group of traffic-warden reject stewards showed some sense!

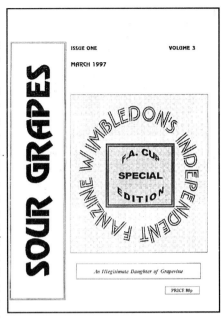

The quadruple? Yes, at that point of the season, the Crazy Gang was giving the "Up yours and go and stuff your crisps where the sun doesn't shine" message to Gary Lineker; the Dons were in the semi-final of both Cups, heading for a place in Europe and in danger of winning the Fair Play League (honest!). Of course, it proved to be the impossible dream for a team which didn't have one posh Latin or unpronounceable Eastern European with a bad haircut in its midst, and was relying at times on some very home-grown stock. Stewart Castledene, whose main claim to fame is appearing in Top Man's window; may have the looks to rival Ravanelli but these aren't - um - quite matched when it comes to footballing skills. I don't think Dons fans would want pampered, preening, collar-turning-up types playing in the team anyway. However, I think we can take pride in our own produce; Chris Perry, for instance, had a magnificent season and Leonhardsen, who was a tremendous buy, deserved his chance to go to Liverpool; he was a team man and obviously had a sense of humour - no one associated with WFC can be without one!

My favourite Crazy Gang story of the season concerns the awarding of the Man of the Match prize to a Portsmouth Player after the second leg in the Coca Cola Cup, which the Dons won on aggregate. The lucky man was given a rather smart bike which was wheeled onto the pitch. Later, apparently, the player decided to ride it home, and proudly mounted it, only to discover the tyres had been let down! Now, I wonder who did that?

It's not the sort of prank one imagines the foreign stars of other teams would even understand, let alone take part in. Nor would they go shopping before a match in BHS in Leeds, where my husband and I had a lively conversation with Vinny, Mick Harford and several others on the escalator down to the lighting section! I can't imagine Ronaldo saying to his colleagues, "There's a special offer on string vests at M&S, see you later" or doing the same as Peter Fear, purchasing several 'three for the price of two' offers including shampoo and shower gel in Boots at Sutton. I suppose that says much about the Dons' pay structure; I expect George Weah gets his Hugo Boss smellies delivered by taxi.

For Dons fans, the genuine ones I mean, (yes we had glory hunters - wow, we've arrived, ha ha!) it was a wonderful but long and expensive season. We had to dig deep into our pockets, although it was money well spent going to Old Trafford for the fourth round of the Cup. The Dons' performance was breathtaking, as a packed but muted Old Trafford watched the two sides seemingly heading for a draw. The Old Trafford 'faithful' really do only sing when they're winning. Not so Wimbledon fans, who were behind the team even when Man U scored seconds from the end. Only then did the United fans wake up.

I wasn't the only one with a tear in my eye, as all of us were on our feet, getting behind the team with no time to go. I couldn't see the pitch because of the tall guy in front of me but I suddenly realised the ball was in the back of the net - we'd scored. I allowed the tears to fall and realised I wasn't alone, even the toughest blokes were blubbing. For me it was the best performance I'd ever seen from the Dons in my 13 years of support, and even longer serving-fans agreed with me. Old Trafford emptied quickly as we savoured the moment. Marcus Gayle kept our feet firmly off the ground with his brilliant goal in the replay.

Of course, we had some stunning wins and it did seem as if we'd joined the Big Boys. Failing to score at Filbert Street allowed us to go out of the Coca Cola on the away goal rule, although I was delighted that Leicester, another small club and one without a mighty foreign contingent, won. Putting out a second team for the Villa match in the week before the cup semi-final killed off Europe and a lot of us were disgusted with Joe for resting our 'stars' before such a big match.

The sight of a tearful fan in his Womble outfit, his 'head' tucked under his arm, told the story at Highbury in that semi-final. I was appalled at the sight of empty seats around us. The club had only allowed season ticket holders and members two tickets each (in 1988 we got four for the Cup Final) and because of the inadequacies and intransigence of the box office at Selhurst, many people failed to get tickets. Worse still, we were surrounded by Chelsea fans openly wearing colours - not one or two but blocks of a dozen or so. How had they got tickets? And why were they allowed to sit with us when there was supposed to be segregation?

The answer was forcefully given to us by a Highbury steward who said that it was all the fault of our f****** club and why didn't we all f*** off! Nice to know our safety is in such compassionate hands. So I wrote to my f****** club and, at the time of writing, NINE weeks after the event, I have not had the courtesy of a reply. This is the major trouble with Wimbledon. Our much-loved Sam may talk about the 'family' but we're all soon disinherited when it comes to bums on seats. Every big match, especially against Man U, we are surrounded by alien fans, even in so-called 'members only' areas. Why? They tell me that these people are Crazy Gang members or have got their tickets from members of convenience. So why not tighten up and police membership? I haven't had an answer but obviously that's too much like hard work and it might mean a small cut in profits. Bugger the true fans who part with their precious money in June; come on in glory hunters and anyone in a Man U strip. Feeling bitter? Moi?

I have to report that the Chelsea fans were far from gracious in success. In fact a large section behaved like cretins. We were at Stamford Bridge earlier in the season on the day they decided to have an emergency evacuation. It took 25 minutes before I got out, my little 5ft 2ins frame having been carried along in the crowd, gasping for air. When a Chelsea steward was asked why we couldn't go onto the pitch, he replied that in a real emergency we could so what was the point of doing it? I bet they wouldn't have acted in such a way if we'd been Man U, Newcastle or another London club.

Two other off-pitch matters dominated Dons fans' conversations: a certain trial and Dublin. I obviously can't say too much about the former, except if guilt is proved then we will feel very let down. I was at the matches involving Segers, and after the Everton one in 1994 Sour Grapes did make some tongue-in-cheek observations about how we'd let a two goal lead slip. If it turns out we were right I'll be livid - we paid good money to see those matches and Segers and Fash are such important figures in Wimbledon's history. I just hope they are innocent.

Dublin. Glasgow, Milton Keynes, Neasden, Basingstoke (yes, Basingstoke!): I think they all got a mention as possible stadium sites for Wimbledon Wanderers. For most genuine fans the thought of leaving Selhust is orgasmic. It will never be home and as Palace are back up we'll be second class again. I think Sam enjoys flirting with all these businessmen and apparently a marriage has been arranged. Whether this has anything to do with Millwall sporting 'The weather in Norwegian' on their chests as part of their sponsorship deal with L!ve TV I don't know, but I gather he's done a deal with some Norwegians. We get a lot of them sitting around us at Selhust. They look as if they are day-trippers and have large rucksacks full of sandwiches which fill up the rows and make it impossible to get to and from your seats. We'd always assumed they were there to cheer on Leonhardsen and they're no trouble, and have rather jolly chants which may or may not be rude as we can't understand them. Are they part of a fraternisation programme started by Sam, so he can ship us off to Oslo or somewhere else in Scandinavia for the weekend?

No Dons fan ever feels secure but at least we didn't have to face relegation, and I'd like to end by paying tribute to Sunderland fans. Every year at Selhurst on our last home match the away supporters have run on the park and spoiled the atmosphere. Well no-one would have blamed them if their frustration spilled over on to the pitch. I didn't want them to go down and did my best to console the young man next to me. The dignity shown was tremendous and applauded by our fans. I just hope you bounce back. Of course clubs like Sunderland have real fans - unlike some others! Dons fans are cheerful souls and will be quite content when they get back to Merton - will it always be a dream?

Source: Spitting Feathers

SOUTH RIDING

Barnsley

In one respect at least the '97-98 season will kick off for Barnsley FC in the same way as all the recent others: we will be made favourites for relegation (unfairly, as it is now a quarter of a century since we dropped a division) by all those paid to predict these things.

In another way though, we Barnsley fans will now have the confidence to shove our arses in the face of God, and you know why? Man may have been on the moon and discovered alleged evidence of life on Mars, but the club representing the 'grimmest of northern towns' (© Private Eye) has gone several hemispheres the far side of credulity in making it to the Premiership. At a stroke we have transformed the image of Yorkshire's football from the lasting reputations of Bradford, Hillsborough, Leeds fans and innumerable Hovis clubs (ourselves included) by an act of unlikely romance that even Barbara Cartland wouldn't have dreamt up, even if she'd heard of us. And we did it from an insubstantial base, only fairish crowds and little income. It's on a par with Albania making the World Cup Final, and it was met with near unanimous praise as Wilson was voted Managers' Manager of the Year in succession to Peter Reid (ominously), and various national newspapers bought road maps that didn't just cover cities of over a million inhabitants. Only Mark McGhee, with enough sour grapes to run a market stall for a year, begged to differ, on the basis that Wolverhampton is a larger place than Barnsley and therefore has more right to footballing success. Let's hope he never becomes responsible for US foreign policy or he could make Kissinger look like Ghandi.

As seasons go it has never been bettered, even when we won the Cup, and it will always be the moment for the club unless we keep going and get into Europe (but let's take things one step at a time). The town has reacted as though Yorkshire Water has been giving away ecstasy tabs as compensation for the leakages. The home capacity will be sold out by advance season ticket sales alone for every league game, as people seek the sophistication and affluence of the Premier League in a town where the average person would mainly associate 'Hornby' with toy trains and 'job' with the Bible. The image of the town, as battered as its economy, could be transformed. The only regret is that we didn't get a gong to put in the trophy room which has been more than under-used since its last occupation as an air-raid shelter.

At the start, prospects were unclear. Danny Wilson, beginning his third season as manager, had brought in new players to replace those bought during the dour reigns of Clarke, Machin and Anderson, players who never would have taken us up (although they wouldn't have taken us down either). Machin's reign in particular had hit morale at the club probably harder than the miners' strike, as he packed the defence and opted for the long-ball game. He was the kind of bloke who'd instruct the players to play for a 0-0 draw in a penalty shoot-out, and his criteria for buying players would have made Brian Close look like Ruud Gullit. On top of that he wasted more money than any other Barnsley manager before him, making Sarah Ferguson look a model of thrift and sound investment. Anderson replaced him briefly and dismally be-fore buggering off to join Bryan Robson at Middlesbrough (at least he'll be spared the embarrassment of coming back to Oakwell next season) and Wilson was promoted from the No.2 job (the board couldn't afford anyone else).

In his first season alone he had to put up with the ignominy of having no sponsors for a time. This was after the DTI had closed down the new sponsors' dodgy pyramid-scheme outfit. Their appointment, by the way, was made by the present board who are currently being heralded as visionary genii but who readily admit that their preferred tactic in fighting racist abuse was by ignoring it and hoping it would go away. The ground might have been back up to three sides by August 1994 but crowds were falling to around 3,000. From such tiny acorns...

Two years on and still lacking money, Wilson was looking abroad for players, having already brought in the excellent Dutchman De Zeeuw and add-ing a Serb and a Trinidadian, neither of whom would have brought with them the "Barnsley? Has it come to this?" attitude common among the usual jour-neymen, even though they obviously knew we were no Man Utd. Machin would've been pushed to buy a Chinese take-away. Such multi-culturalism was the first sign of New Barnsley. Better still though was the departure of Andy Payton to Huddersfield for the largest pay-rise he could get. If he'd stayed he could have topped that next season by more than a bit.

The football last season was of course sublime, despite starting with a defeat at Rochdale and ending with a celebratory 5-1 stuffing at Oxford on the last Sunday. In-between we never fell below fifth position and the fans re-sponded with chants of "It's just like watching Brazil," sung to the tune of Blue Moon. This might have been an overstatement, but it was our song, even though other fans have already nicked it. (Slight embarrassment followed when the chant's originator turned out to have been involved in illegal sexual indis-cretions involving under-age girls, but let's gloss over that one and leave it to the authorities.) Perhaps the nearest the chant got to the truth was the drib-bling of Clint Marcelle, so fast and skilful was he that besides scoring his own fair share, he won us a ton of free kicks and penalties, hitting the deck so often that he's probably had more contact with the soil than Swampy.

De Zeeuw again won Player of the Year, John Hendrie scored often enough to keep us on track and the young Adie Moses matured rapidly when asked to step in after Steve Davis had his leg broken. Only the other ex-Boro forward Paul Wilkinson needs an immediate replacement. Neil Redfearn, one of the few who've already played at the highest level, had what was probably his best season for us, finishing top scorer despite giving up taking penalties. If anyone tips this team to go straight back down they have not seen us play and are basing their prejudice purely on the image of the club and the town. Arseholes.

Highlights of the season obviously included the double over the Blunts of Sheffield 2, thereby consigning them to the play-offs where they fell at the last hurdle, and the unforgettable last home match against Bradford where just about everyone was in tears at the end, the bloke sat to the right of the bloke to my left included. Before the kick-off a PA-led rendition of You'll Never Walk Alone which could easily have been trite was genuinely moving. Strangely the crowd for this match was smaller than those for the two previous promotion-clinchers at home to Grimsby in 1979 and Rotherham in 1981 (no glamour spared, eh?), thanks to our now all-seater stadium. Still, it topped both for romance and glory and as I doubt that there's anyone left alive who saw the 1912 Cup win it will remain the game to have seen for sometime (no doubt at least 100,000 already claim to have been there). The actions of some Bradford fans in staying behind at the end to congratulate us was acknowledged, and in the aftermath of all this, Danny Wilson's honest integrity and all-round good-blokeness finally got national recognition. Some people praise the board for their role but I remain cynical. They never did more than just enough and if and when Wilson leaves it'll be interesting to see how they'll cope with keeping us in the Premiership.

Now I'm not a betting man but I don't think we'll go down, and I speak as someone who would never have forecast us to go up. We're lucky in that our 15 minutes of fame will last at least nine months, but I've got a feeling it'll last longer, if only because at least half the Premiership will be fellow relegation possibilities too. We may even become fashionable and storm to the top, we may become the team everyone hopes to beat because we're so omnipotent. Christ, people from Barnsley not only using words like that, but about themselves! Who'd have thought it?

The only dangers I foresee is when we hit a bad patch and the crowd turns abusive. We've had a recent history of very bad racist abuse and this could resurface if things start to go wrong. The club has never dealt with this and all the praise we've received recently could evaporate just as quickly. The achievement in getting promoted has been recognised as extraordinary because Barnsley is such an under-privileged place with a lot of poverty and frustration. People want an outlet and if this is stifled, things could rapidly change for the worse. We will have the cheapest season tickets in the Premiership but quite a few people will still have made some real sacrifices, even with a maximum price of £250, and they will want a return. The flip-side to this negativity is the enlightenment that being in the Premiership will bring; the chance to experience a higher level of existence, to be in the spotlight for once and widen our horizons. That may sound pretentious, but Barnsley is a very insular place that few people from outside move to, or many who are born there ever leave. It will (hopefully) be a learning process for many.

Of course there will also be self-induced gaffes. An inordinate amount of effort is spent pushing the club personality Toby Tyke, a mutt that seems to appear on owt connected with Barnsley FC. Is there no knackers yard for such mascots? Ironically he did get Oakwell some bad publicity when he showed his arse to Man City fans, who complained in writing. Firstly, have they no sense of humour beyond watching the type of football their team produces? Secondly, is the social deprivation of Moss Side not a good enough context in which to place a furry anus? And thirdly, after about 25 years haven't they got used to arseholes on a football pitch? That leaves us with the real-life celebs. You are probably already sick of Michael Parkinson and Dicky Bird, a man who could burst into tears at the sight of us winning a throw-in, but be grateful. You have so far been spared Geoff Boycott, who if he appeared on Match of the Day would make Jimmy Hill look withdrawn, and Roy Mason whose bodyguards (yes, as in 20 years on) must for once be grateful he goes to Oakwell so often. Darren Gough also seems to have converted to supporting Barnsley after declaring himself to be a devoted Forest fan some years ago (supporting a scab club - I just don't know), but Scargill apparently doesn't appear to be interested in football (although I seem to remember him expressing an infinity with Leeds United some years ago - or maybe it was Dynamo Moscow).

As for us fanzine celebs though, I'm afraid it's the end of the road. After seven years and 30-odd issues we're calling it a day as we've nothing left to moan about. But our mantle will be taken up by a new fanzine Better Red Then Dead which will take over where we left off. No more selling in the rain for us then and we wish the bandwagon-jumpers - sorry committed supporters - who are taking over from us all the best. Normal consultancy rates will apply of course.

SPEKE FROM THE HARBOUR

Everton

When the highlight of your season turns out to be the very first game, it is difficult to look back on the proceedings with much affection.

There was a feeling that a top six place was attainable if our best players performed to their peak and some of the youngsters matured. Things were quiet on the transfer front with only two arrivals in the shape of boyhood Evertonian Gary Speed and Oldham's England U21 goalkeeper Paul Gerrard. Speed was brought in to add some goalscoring potential to a midfield that had been too reliant on Andrei Kanchelskis during the previous season. Gerrard on the other hand

SPEKE FROM THE HARBOUR

Issue No. 15

GREAT PASS, JAMIE. GREAT GOAL, STEVIE.

an Everton fanzine   **80p**

was expected to learn from the master before being given his chance. There was a down-side to the Speed signing though, because it meant almost certain banishment to the periphery of crowd darling Anders Limpar, who had often been made the scapegoat for Blues' poor performances. Criticising Limpar for his lack of tackling is a bit like criticising Alan Shearer for his lack of goalkeeping skills; that's not why he's there. Anyway, the outgoing transfers proved a lot more to Evertonians' liking as deadwood such as the woefully overrated Amokachi, the workmanlike Horne and the just plain shit Ablett all waved their fond goodbyes and turned their collective gaze to pastures new.

Many other eyes were on Goodison Park for the first game of the new Premiership campaign. Not, I have to add, to see anyone in a blue shirt, but rather to witness the introduction of a certain Mr Alan Shearer. Fortunately his thunder was stolen by a debut goal for Gary Speed and another from David Unsworth. The Gwladys Street end struck up a chord of "What a waste of money" (but not until it was 2-0 with two minutes of injury time on the clock).

A trip to Old Trafford followed four days later, where we were found ourselves 2-0 up courtesy of goals from the irresistible Duncan Ferguson. In a thrilling climax we were pegged back to 2-2, but we were liking what we had seen so far. Two points from the next five games sobered us up a bit, as did our by now ritual humiliation by a lower league team in the Coca Cola Cup, York doing the honours this time, beating us 3-2 at home.

Off the pitch the rumour mill started to whirl concerning Fiorentina's interest in Andrei Kanchelskis, our previous season's top scorer. Kanchelskis himself was out of form having scored only twice in ten appearances, and his obvious frustration in playing in a poor side only served to signal the beginning of the end of his all too short Goodison career. And with Duncan Ferguson on the treatment table again the familiar issue of who was going to put the ball in the back of the net reared its head. If you'd have cornered any Evertonian over the last two seasons they'd have told you that the side lacked an out-and-out goalscorer; a Shearer, a Wright or a Tony Cottee. Whether Joe Royle understood this or not, he didn't appear to do anything about it, and throwing in the raw 17-year-old talent of Michael Branch was not the answer. Nick Barmby probably wasn't either, but he was a current England international, and he was available, so for the fourth time in two years Everton broke their transfer record and handed over a cool £5.75 million.

While we're on the subject of strikers, let's remember that Tommy Lawton, second only in the legend stakes to W.R. Dean and one of the greatest ever to wear any shirt, let alone the blue of Everton, died at the start of November aged 77. A minute's silence was held before the Southampton home game and the eleven boys in blue did not let him down, turning in a virtuoso 7-1 performance.

The first Merseyside derby was washed out due to a drop of rain on the Anfield pitch; either that or some of the Liverpool boys had a photo shoot that day. When it did get under way a few weeks later Liverpool were happy (and lucky) to get away with a point, thus preserving (for ever in all likelihood) Joe Royle's managerial record of never having been beaten in a derby game. Around this time things weren't too bad; we even got as high as sixth which prompted those less pessimistic souls to dream of a European place. They were in for a rude awakening as we started a ten week spell without a win.

On the personnel side, Andy Hinchcliffe's season came to a premature end at Christmas when he came off second best in a clash with some advertising hoardings. This paved the way for the rather controversial signing of out-of-favour Terry Phelan. Andrei Kanchelskis swapped the chippie for tagliatelle en route to his £5.5 million transfer to Fiorentina, but not before he'd gifted a soft goal to Bradford in our humiliating 3-2 cup defeat. A world-beater the year before, one can only assume that his alleged gambling habit had shagged his form and forced his agent to engineer another big signing-on fee.

Christmas also saw the first broadcast of TV Everton. Conveniently situated monitors were placed around the ground to ensure that nobody would miss a kick, even when queuing for Bovrils or taking a leak. And let's face it, when 'seventies starlet' Duncan McKenzie was our chosen front man you couldn't help but be glued to the screens. Liverpool? Showbiz? We'll show them a thing or two!

The new year proved to be a mixed bag for veteran 'keeper Neville Southall. It got off to a good start with a visit to the Palace to receive his M.B.E. but hit an all-time low when he was dropped at the end of January. It got worse when naughty Nev was caught with some slip of a girl from the valleys, proving that there's hope for us all yet. The News of the World was only too happy to wheel out all the old 'playing away from home' clichés.

The next big issue to raise its head was the possibility of building a new purpose-built stadium to replace 'old lady Goodison'. Undoubtedly one of the best grounds in the country in the sixties when it saw World Cup action, she was now beginning to show her age. Peter Johnson promised a last game ballot on any move, and despite pressure from the 'Goodison for Everton' faction, 84% of respondents voted for a new stadium which should be ready around the millennium.

One thing's for sure: big Joe won't be warming his arse on the new home bench. He finally lost the last of his ever-diminishing bag of marbles when he decided that the press were to blame for Everton's poor results. Actually the local media hadn't been writing anything that wasn't true. Everton were playing poorly, and Joe had sold Limpar, Ebbrell, Jackson, Samways, Kanchelskis and Kearton without replacing them and there wasn't any sign of things getting any better. Finally, on transfer deadline day, club and manager parted company 'by mutual agreement' after three big-name (!) signings had been vetoed by chairman Peter Johnson. The superstar trio were in fact Barry Horne and a couple of Norwegians that nobody had ever heard of.

This was the cue for wild speculation about Joe's successor. While Dave Watson was temporarily entrusted with the job of killing off any lingering possibilities of relegation, Bobby Robson's name was the most frequently mentioned. The Liverpool Echo had Barca Bobby's ruddy features on the back page five out of every six nights for the next two months with the headline 'ROBSON D-DAY' being used on no less than four occasions.

Meanwhile, Joe Parkinson was ruled out for the season and we were forced to put all our faith in Joe's final signing, midfielder Claus Thomsen. Yikes! Now Thomsen is one of those amazing footballers, and when I say amazing I mean shit. No, what I actually mean is that I'm amazed that he makes a living at the game: he can't pass, he can't shoot, he can't tackle, he's got no stamina, he's about 6'3" and he can't even head the bloody ball! As if that wasn't bad enough, the rumour mill reckoned that he was the second biggest earner at the club after Barmby!

The playing staff was now so depleted that Paul Rideout was recalled from his trial spell in China to play against Spurs in midfield! It proved to be a masterstroke by Watson as Everton picked up the three points. So now we were safe... or were we? With Liverpool still in with a good chance of winning the Premiership or at least a back door route into the (almost) Champions League they came to Goodison needing a win. They left with a point and their best player sent off and banned for the rest of the season, haaaa! I'm not sure what was funnier, their sad little faces when Duncan twisted on a sixpence and slotted it past Bobo James, or horse's arse-face Fowler getting his knickers in a twist as he disappeared down the tunnel along with Liverpool's title hopes.

Everton's final point was gained with a last minute equaliser at Upton Park courtesy of Duncan Ferguson, who had, unnoticed by most people, played in all but five games this season. The final game at home to Cup Finalists Chelsea was memorable only for a female streaker turning cartwheels in her pink thong.

So that was it. No hold on, I almost forgot to mention our new away kit: a black and yellow striped affair with blue bits sort of thrown in. We didn't particularly like it (preferring a traditional amber kit) but Umbro did. Enough said really! Roll on '97-98.

Jamie Redknapp - Hairdryer, perfume, mirror and a string of completely redundant female admirers.

SPITTING FEATHERS

Sheffield Wednesday

It's official! If you want to climb the Premier League... get yourself a band!

The Wednesday 'band' had been in existence for some time, but this was the season where it came of age. That we were top of the Premiership and five points clear after four games was something of a surprise for the media. For your average Wednesdayite, it was beyond belief! For those who'd travelled to Upton Park for the final game of the previous season, where relegation was narrowly missed, the imminent replacement of David Pleat with Chrissie Waddle was top of the agenda. The fight to avoid joining city rivals in the Nationwide

AN INDEPENDENT VIEW OF SHEFFIELD WEDNESDAY

RUSH TO JOIN WEDNESDAY BAND REACHES MAMMOTH PROPORTIONS!

BOOTH!

NUMBER 14 - ISSUED 12th March v SUNDERLAND

In this Issue... Spitting Blood at Spitting Feathers... Share and Share Alike (part 2)... Bandwagon Boys... I have a Dream... Waddle's Exquisite Chip (on his shoulder)... and much much more....

WRITTEN BY WEDNESDAY FANS FOR WEDNESDAY FANS

was going to be a difficult one. Pleato (a philosopher who speaks Greek) was under some considerable pressure; in fact the inmates at the local turkey farm were probably looking forward to Christmas with considerably more relish than was our manager.

In a radical plan of action, he first got rid of his backroom staff and appointed the influential Peter Shreeves. He then set about changing some of the playing staff by moving in younger players from the lower divisions: Wayne Collins from Crewe, Scott Oakes from Luton, Matt Clarke from Rotherham and Andy Booth from Huddersfield. The future looked bleak. It also looked orange as Wednesday unveiled their latest away kit. Whether this was a tribute to Dutchmen Regi Blinker and new signing Orlando Trustfull or just a means of saving Tango from taking his shirt off in midwinter, we'll never know.

And then it happened. Four straight wins. These saved Pleato's job and put a huge smile back on the Wednesday fans' faces - not because we were hoping for a title shot; rather, it was 12 points towards the 40 or so predicted to be needed for survival. People cut the league table out of the nationals and pasted it into scrapbooks; some even had their photo taken caressing a television showing the top half of the table on teletext (OK, guilty as charged m'lud)... Yes, it was that good, and yes, it had been that long (October 1967 actually). We were top of the league and everywhere we went we let them know it.

It wasn't to last. Just as we were doing our Icarus impersonation (you know, the guy whose sister uses Natrel Plus), we were brought back down to earth with all the certainty of a Richard Branson world record attempt. Remember that scene in Indiana Jones where the guy shows off, twirling the big sword, and then Indy just pulls out a gun and shoots him? Well, we were that swordsman and Chelsea played a mean Harrison Ford.

Thus began our free-fall down the Premier League, with Pleato desperately trying to remember where he packed the parachute. A series of home draws against opposition we expected to beat, sandwiched by four goal hammerings at both Wimbledon and Arsenal (robbed again... I really don't know why we bother playing Arsenal; we should just ring up and tell them we aren't coming - you know, like Middlesbrough did - it never did them any harm, did it?). A little Italian guy arrived from Inter Milan, and although most of us had heard of him (sort of), none of us really knew what he looked like. Benito Carbone's introduction amid a fanfare of Siennese flag-waving and a group of Pavarotti look-a-likes (don't ask - it's what we're good at) was embarrassing to say the least. The poor little sod must have wondered where the hell he'd landed up. There were further red faces in the Coca Cola Cup at the hands of Oxford, Nigel Jemson scoring the winner. Now that's humiliating!

The band played on despite the arrival of the Utrecht virus. Even if you think you've never heard of it, you've definitely heard it - and it's contagious! This is no computer ailment that makes your hard drive go all floppy, neither is it an unspeakable disease that alienates you from other people (then again...). After a 25 minute rendition at Coventry which annoyed the hell out of the Sky Blues fans - the 'Utrecht song' had arrived! First heard in a pre-season friendly in Holland, Tango had pestered the band to perform it and the rest is... driving every other club up the wall. Meanwhile it was driving Wednesday up the Premiership.

It was the Sky match at home to Forest that set the season alight; in a game that the commentators described as the most one-sided they had ever covered, we hammered Forest. Well, only 2-0 actually. Carbone was inspirational, but even more than that, the pitifully low 16,390 crowd was awesome. Drums and trumpets helped produce a wall of sound that would have impressed Phil Spector. The Hillsborough atmosphere, the demise of which has long been the subject of nostalgic letters to Wednesday fanzines, had returned. The song seemed to inspire the players and a run of 23 League games with only one defeat set Wednesday up for a tilt at a European place.

An accompanying cup run started with a 7-1 trouncing of Grimsby, whose fans did their club proud, arriving with a virtual shoal of inflatable haddock. Carlisle were the next to succumb, then Bradford as the much-hyped (by Chris Kamara, who must suffer from the sourest grapes since Napoleon mistakenly applied lemon juice to his piles) shoot-out between Pleato and Waddle failed to materialise. The march to Wembley seemed to be running hand-in-hand with the rise up the table, just as it had in 1993.

As the 'big' clubs fell by the wayside, we started thinking that this could be our year, but two unfortunate incidents in our quarter-final with Wimbledon did for us. Jon Newsome's awkward fall left him with an ankle that resembled one of those Sam Torrance putters and a bad tackle from Earle also put the tenacious Graham Hyde out for the season. The loss of both players for the game (and the run-in) was insurmountable. The hasty rearrangement of the team left us devoid of height at the back (a major problem against Wimbledon) and the midfield minus Hyde and Atherton (now playing in defence) left us more wanting in the tackle department than John Wayne Bobbit after the unkindest cut of all.

The season just sort of tailed off, the loss of Newsome never more apparent than at Blackburn and West Ham, two games where a point at each might have made all the difference to our European aspirations. By the time our final game with Liverpool arrived, we needed a mathematical miracle beyond the wit of even Carol Vorderman. It was a strange game in which ever-present Kevin Pressman finally gave his understudy a chance of a game. Pressy's hamstring pulled and young Matt Clarke, a Wednesdayite since birth, took his chance and made a fine save in his first call to action. The momentum of his second save took him to the edge of his area with the ball. So to say we were gobsmacked is an understatement, after referee David Elleray sent Clarke off, ten minutes into his debut, for 'handling outside the area'. I would like to take this opportunity to say that David Elleray is a complete tosser! Andy Booth proved that one volunteer is better than ten pressed men (though not one Pressman, of course, ha ha), took the gloves and kept the cream of Premiership talent (!) at bay for the remaining ten minutes, using as many different body parts as he could. After we'd booed off Elleray, we showered our praises on a team that had defied all the odds.

Throughout the season, opposition teams (noticeably, the smaller clubs) were somewhat rattled by the 'extra player' our support provided. The band were banned from Wimbledon (where you'd think they'd be glad of any noise), Sunderland (due to safety concerns... Stand up! Cos we've got no seats!), Derby (we took along 2,000 party blowers for that one - what a hoot!), Southampton (let us in last year and we won, didn't this year and we still won... doesn't that tell you something, Saints?) and Forest (where despite being banned, our musicians nipped out for their instruments with ten minutes left and serenaded Wednesday's third goal while being ejected by the stewards).

Please take note, however: the rise of Wednesday was nothing to do with the tactical philosophy of Pleato and his sidekick Socrashreeves; nothing to do with the classy play of Italian import Beni Carbone (who is so talented, he can sometimes make you weep); nothing to do with the rebirth of Pembo - the finest ginger Welshman since Dai Torange (sorry about that one); nothing to do with the fact that in Pressy, we have England's No.16 (he's No.1 in our eyes, but apparently Glenn Hoddle suffers from Cockerel's Myopic Syndrome - he can't see further than White Hart Lane); nothing to do with Des Walker being the best (and the quickest) English defender in the country (that's Hoddle's myopic thing again); and definitely nothing to do with having a captain called Atherton (which is not usually a good move) who is the best man-marker England has seen since Olaf the Skull-Splitter invaded our shores during the Dark Ages. No, we won't be going to Europe this year... not unless there's a war (and if you need someone to play Who do you think you are kidding Mr Hitler, I know some guys who can!), but we didn't half do well!

It's been a wonderful season and the football's not been bad either. As for the Utrecht Song, it'll be appearing at a stadium near you next season. Sorry about that!

SUNDERLAND FANATIC

Sunderland

If a week's a long time in politics then a year in football can be an eternity. Just ask any Sunderland fan. The summer of 1996 saw jubilant supporters looking ahead to the Premiership challenge with confidence, having clinched promotion as First Division Champions. Peter Reid was a god and the club was going places. Come the summer of 1997 and those same fans are simultaneously dejected, angry, frustrated and wanting answers for yet another squandered opportunity in Sunderland's recent history. This was our sixth relegation in 27 years, but until 1958 the club had never played outside the old First Division!

Despite a recent history littered with struggle when returning to the top flight, fans were quietly confident that the mistakes of the past would not be repeated. And there were good grounds for this optimism. Reid and Bracewell seemed to be our best managerial partnership in a long, long time. They'd won the First Division Championship against all expectations, and seemed well able to meet the Premiership challenge, particularly as notoriously tight-fisted chairman Bob Murray had indicated there was £10m for Reid to spend. £10m? It seemed too good to be true!

Crucially, Sunderland had also won permission to build their new stadium at Monkwearmouth, on the site of the old colliery. It was a perfect location; in the heart of the city, high on the banks of the River Wear, and only a stone's throw from Roker Park, which was hosting its final season after 99 years. Gradually, the new stadium has become an impressive and imposing landmark on the city horizon, and it was hard not to get excited about it. However, if the stadium was to exploit to the full the corporate and public cash potentially available, it was vital that Sunderland stayed in the Premier League.

The first indication that events weren't quite going to plan was the conspicuous lack of transfer activity over the summer. In the wake of huge season ticket price rises, fans hoped the club would show some ambition in return, and go after some big names to justify the price hike. Ha! How naïve we Sunderland fans can be at times. The only signings Reid made were Tony Coton from Manchester United, Alex Rae from Millwall, Niall Quinn from Manchester City and Paul Stewart, who had been on loan from Liverpool and who we'd acquired on a free. To put it mildly, these were not what we had in mind.

Sunderland's opener in the Premier League saw a 0-0 draw at home to Leicester. This game would be a portent for the rest of the season; a lot of hard work and effort - the commitment of the players could never be questioned - but with no outstanding individuals in a team lacking skill, flair and goals. This methodical approach had worked well in Division 1, but now? Sunderland's cause certainly wasn't helped by career-threatening injuries to Niall Quinn and Tony Coton. Quinn's cruciate was finally strong enough for a return in April, but Coton's fractured leg could still mean a permanent hanging up of the green jersey.

The goalkeeping problem was at least solved with the purchase of little-known Bordeaux 'keeper Lionel Perez for £250,000. Adjectives for Perez include flamboyant (long golden locks, rolled up sleeves, strutting Cantonesque posture) and unorthodox (legs just as important as hands when it comes to shot-stopping and saving). Despite these eccentricities (or perhaps because of them) Perez won over the hearts of Sunderland fans with a string of consistent performances, culminating in being voted our Player of the Season. Perhaps his biggest success was to mollify, if not totally remove, calls for Peter Reid to sign Shay Given, the brilliant young Irish 'keeper who'd been so impressive at Sunderland while on loan the previous season, and who the club had typically failed to sign permanently. Incidentally, Perez was one of 17 (yes, 17) trialists who paraded their skills, or lack of them, at the club this term. Such foreign luminaries as Bogdon Stelea, Kgetil Nilsen, Alfonse Tchami and Monadou Diallo were put through their paces, and all bar Perez and Kim Heiselberg were rejected.

Much had been made of Sunderland's world-wide scouting network by the club, but impatient fans wanted tangible results, not a constant stream of have-a-go's who clearly weren't up to it. As the weeks and months went by, Reid's failure to land a top class striker in particular caused huge frustration. "I won't be rushed into spending," "I won't pay over the odds" and "there's no-one available better than what I've already got" were the excuses trotted out. And while the first two statements could possibly be applauded as honest and principled, the third was clearly ridiculous, and led to many fans questioning whether the money was actually there. If Reid did have the best part of £7m burning a hole in his pocket, why was he content with a squad that had Nationwide written all over it?

December saw Sunderland hop on the floatation bandwagon. Fans were welcome to buy shares as long as they had a spare £585 for the minimum 100 allocation. The club dropped a bombshell in the glossy prospectus by unveiling, totally without warning or consultation, a new club crest. The new design went down like a lead balloon with supporters, and the fact that it had been foisted on us without any say only made us more angry. The float may have been a financial success but it was a PR fiasco.

After a 1-0 home victory over Arsenal thanks to a Tony Adams own goal, Sunderland's slide began in earnest as we won only one of our next 12 games; a dismal run that included four consecutive defeats and a 4-0 hammering at Roker by Spurs. Strangely enough, and so typical of Sunderland, the solitary victory came over Man Utd. A 2-1 home victory, which in all honesty should have been 4-1, highlighted that while the team could raise themselves on the day, they were finding it increasingly difficult to repeat the act!

Reid's increasingly bizarre tactics - one man up front and five in midfield - were leading to growing discontent and anger on the terraces. This was OK away from Roker, but at home, when the fans wanted a more adventurous approach, it proved inappropriate and backfired too many times. As for Reid's team selections, it was the old pals act. Paul Bracewell, Gareth Hall, Paul Stewart and David Kelly were players who could do no wrong in his eyes, no matter how badly they played. To be fair to Bracewell, he'd done well but tired towards the end and should have been replaced by younger legs. Meanwhile, local favourite and leading scorer in the Championship season, Craig Russell started only ten league games, but still managed to be joint-leading scorer with four goals. That's right, four goals! Martin Smith, one of our brightest recent prospects, was totally ignored last season, and even more surprisingly, Reid's own signing, the impressive Alex Rae, also found himself out of favour. It simply didn't make any sense when the side cried out for creativity in those player's positions. In defence, the ever-popular Dariuz Kubicki lost his right back berth to Gareth Hall, to the consternation of everyone but the boss. If nothing else, this proved that Reid was very much his own man and would not be easily swayed.

With seven games remaining Reid finally made a couple of major signings (by our standards anyway): Chris Waddle from Bradford, and Alan Johnson - he of the hat-trick against Rangers at Ibrox - from French club Rennes for £500,000. By now Sunderland were in big relegation trouble and this was undoubtedly Reid's last throw of the dice. Waddle was making a sentimental return to the team he supported as a boy, and the fans took to him immediately.

Chris made a big impact in the remaining handful of games, having a hand in nearly every goal that was scored by us including a crucial 1-0 victory at Middlesbrough. For the final league match at Roker Park against Everton, an emotional home crowd saw Waddle provide another magical moment. With the score at 1-0 he rifled in a venomous free kick from the edge of the box into the top right hand corner of Neville Southall's goal, right in front of the packed Fulwell End. How we celebrated! Johnson scored a third to put the seal on a magnificent victory and 99 years of football at our famous old home. Who knows how things might have ended had Reid signed the pair at the start and not the end of the season? Unfortunately, this marvellous victory and the efforts of 15,000 travelling fans on the last day at Wimbledon couldn't save us from the drop.

So what should have been an enjoyable final season at Roker, instead turned into a complete disaster. Angry fans couldn't decide who to blame most: Bob Murray or Peter Reid. At TSF we believe that rather than casting blame, the club should decide on whether they really want to be part of the elite or whether they want to remain a second-rate club permanently. This is the third time in the last four promotions that Sunderland's stay in the top flight has lasted just one season. Mistakes haven't so much been ignored, but embraced and repeated with enthusiasm. Despite their relegation, at least Middlesbrough showed ambition (even if it was mis-placed at times), something Sunderland have never done. Steve Gibson is as ambitious as his fans and deserves applause for bringing world-class players to Teeside. John Hall, who deposed a similarly inept board to ours, has a clear path mapped out for Newcastle and you know that they will arrive at their destination. Sunderland, on the other hand, is the sleeping giant in danger of never waking up.

Source: Roots Hall Roar

SUPER DARIO LAND

Crewe Alexandra

Nick Hornby had it easy...

It was 2:15am and there'd been five hours' worth of thirst-quenching cider quoffed since our arrival back in Crewe, so the rose-tinted spectacles were understandably hazy. Not even the dreary slog that is the M1/M6 route back from our national stadium had dampened spirits or, for that matter, slowed their consumption.

Permit a little poetic licence, if you will: Nantwich Road and the approach to Gresty Road witnessed scenes reminiscent of '78 Buenos Aires, as the town of Crewe came to terms with the Alex's elevation to the First Division. Flags, banners, screaming, shouting,

chanting and car horns shattered an otherwise peaceful night; nobody too bothered that hundreds of drunken football nutters were intent on partying 'til dawn. And we did, with an essential late-evening Balti for ballast before usually unacceptable behaviour continued well into the best Sunday night of my life. Hanging out of a car sun-roof, joining the tail-end of a 300 yard conga along a busy main road, or doing your best Liam Gallagher impersonation (insert Freddy Mercury, Mick Jagger or Elvis, depending on your favoured era) on top of a BT pay-phone are none too clever, but rule books, convention and anything regarding sensible behaviour were off the menu as our promotion-fest gathered pace.

It started back at the ground as several ecstatic coach-loads swarmed about the car park soaking up the freely-available adulation as if we'd lifted the cup ourselves. We had, of course, in our own way, by pouring a lifetime's passion into every song, chant and heartfelt piece of criticism that you know many players quite simply don't appreciate. We couldn't knock our lads on this day, however; warriors everyone of them. The previous games had re-vealed their true colours - against Luton in the play-off semi-finals; epic battles both. They wanted it as much as we did, perhaps for different reasons, but they really wanted it. And walking away from a match believing that you've fought for the same cause really carries some weight, no matter how daft that may sound. Shackled to a piece of plastic often renders you helpless, but the knowledge that your support is valued means something special to anyone who has given their all for something that ultimately they can't control.

Crewe had seen nothing like it, although I can't comment upon Tom Bailey leading his Alex side to Welsh Cup glory in 1936 and 1937. Our modern day equivalent has already formed as images that have been consigned to memory, never to be forgotten, waiting to be recounted to mates across subsequent years. You see it's a select few who have actually won at Wembley, and whatever the competition, no matter how much you despise the over-priced concrete carbuncle, it leaves the victorious with a warm glow - like several pints of good ale, that perfect curry, hot chocolate and sex rolled into one. But you don't usually get that lot together.

There was no other place to savour that First Division feeling, something many fans for so long had viewed as an unobtainable dream which the club didn't want anyway. They, we, everyone who didn't keep the faith has been proved wrong. The sight of Neil Baker (Crewe's assistant manager) leaping around the Wembley turf like something deranged was testament to that. Heart-warming, awe-inspiring and frightening, with kids and pets best kept well out of the way. Even Dario let slip a cheeky grin, his otherwise sensible persona for once shaken by the moment. The chairman had his calculator out and our always pleasant ticket office staff prepared their lines ahead of the inevitable onslaught for First Division tickets - "one pair of hands," "rushed off my feet" and "bugger off, I'm busy" were early favourites with the bookies.

Putting it all into context, imagine having to explain to a level-headed, non-football mate why you were spotted on national television hugging and kissing a 22-stone Real Ale monster. You can't. You understand or you don't. But hug we did, all shapes and sizes, from the moment Shaun Smith converted and my typical over-confidence for once bore fruit. Nothing else mattered and a massive weight fell from our shoulders leaving us to enjoy the following months quite literally without a care in the world. June and July without the postmortems of failure, the prospect of returning to grounds you've visited a dozen times before and vow to give a miss the following season... but you don't. Not for us. Instead, new horizons and at last the renewal of local derbies against Stoke and Vale.

Describing the moment, several of our merry band delivered the "better than sex" line, although their wives and girlfriends were out of sight at the time! Come to think of it, giving the "better than football" line after a good session in bed probably wouldn't go down too well either, let alone carry any credibility. You can't win.

The fact that our triumph came via the back door of the play-offs is of no consequence. Pointing fingers at players, identifying single matches where we should have taken three points, and bemoaning 'dirty' teams for kicking our lads is, I've found, quite pointless. We were good enough, no doubt about it. However, this season, more so than the previous few, I've been driven to distraction, nearly walking out early (a cardinal sin and a matter for the football police, I know) on a couple of occasions because the bastards didn't want it as much as me, or so I thought at the time. Quite why I haven't taken up smoking is still a mystery to me.

We didn't go up automatically but victory at Wembley was incredibly satisfying, having fallen at the final hurdle just four years previously, when the prize then was a place in the Second Division. So Sunday May 25th 1997 was nothing short of amazing; an achievement to be celebrated for years; sex on a stick; that incredible high which can't be bought and certainly doesn't last.

As I see it, Nick Hornby had it easy. Having to wait 17, sorry, 18 years for your next League Championship doesn't sound too tough to me. How about a lifetime, several lifetimes, and we can't even buy Crewe Alex boxer shorts! The problem is expectation, and the Gunners have got it bad - we've had it and we'd like some more, thank you very much. The Alex, thankfully, are still refreshingly small, and should stay that way for ever and a day. We hope, dream and want to win of course, but we'll never buy high-profile stars, play in front of 40,000 home crowds, sell Gresty Road wine or make millions on the Stock Exchange. But who cares? The '96-97 season was nail-biting and emotionally draining, but special. Sure - competing against the big city teams won't be easy. But compete we will, with smiles etched across our faces that would put the Cheshire cat to shame. Just visiting stadia usually reserved for FA Cup round three days should sweeten any fall from grace, although we're not planning a swift return. Move over Arsenal...

TALK OF THE TYNE

Newcastle United

After seeing a 12 point lead eroded in the '95-96 season and eventually gifting the Premiership to Man Utd, '96-97 was always going to be a huge test of Keegan's bottle. The club was about to be floated on the stock exchange and chairman Sir John Hall wasn't prepared to take another season of empty promises. He coughed up £15m to land arguably the world's greatest striker and it was now time to reap some rewards.

The highlights of the season were many, and I'm sure the 5-0 defeat of Man Utd will be well documented elsewhere in this book, plus the seven goals against Spurs, Keegan finally cracking up, Dalglish signing

off the dole and our team's back-door entry into the Champions League. So we'll leave that to others to analyse and dissect and we'll offer you a little taste of what every fan should experience: the chance to follow your team into Europe.

SWEDEN

Copenhagen was our base for the two day trip, and a wise one at that considering the ridiculous price of beer in neighbouring Sweden. Having booked into the hotel, which was situated in one of the many red-light districts of the city, we went walk-about to socialise with our beautiful Scandinavian cousins. We didn't actually know it was a red-light district until the following day, although the pub opposite, 'The Spunk Bar', should have given us a clue.

The police kept a watchful eye although it was always from a distance. While the prospect of Newcastle, Aston Villa and FC Bruge supporters mixing in bars in the same city was no problem to the three groups of fans, it did worry the local plod.

We travelled by ferry to Sweden and it took us longer to board than the time it took for the 20 minute journey, then up by coach to the tiny holiday resort of Halmstads. Now I ask you, what would you expect to pay for a sandwich and a half bottle of beer? Yes, it is Sweden we are talking about here, but wouldn't you feel ripped off at a bill of £14? £9 for the sandwich and £5 for the beer!

The ground at Halmstads is probably a poor man's version of Hartlepool's Victoria Ground. Small, compact and tidy, but with some rather dodgy make-shift terracing for the Toon fans and wooden seats that were about as secure as Sunderland's chances of staying in the Premiership. Once inside, up went the TALK OF THE TYNE flag behind the goal and we settled down for the evening's entertainment - and what a contradiction in terms that was. The team as a whole... weren't. If you get my drift! Some may call it 'disjointed', some would call it 'inconsistent'... we'll just cut the bullshit and call it 'crap'!

We had to endure a last 30 minutes of absolute deplorable defending as the Abba fan club left our back-line in tatters. Two goals from the Swedes was the least they deserved, and although we were never in any danger of losing the tie, Newcastle looked the team full of part-timers rather than the opposition.

Back to Copenhagen for an evening to remember as we sang the night away until 7am. Villa fans visited the brothels (one paying £290 for 30 minutes with Suzy Wong) and the Toon fans downed the ale and taught the singer/ guitarist in one bar the words to 'Wonderwall'. Touring the city later in the day we came across the famous Little Mermaid, which is no larger than 5ft. We visited Brussels for the pre-season friendly against RSC Anderlecht in July and visited Belgium's national treasure, the Manneken-Pis, which is only 2ft in length, and as one lad put it: "It would only take a couple of drunk Geordies celebrating a win, and two of Europe's most famous treasures could end up at some car boot sale in Gateshead."

HUNGARY

Off we set for the two and three quarter hour flight to meet the mighty Magyars and their - how shall we put it - 'enthusiastic' fans.

Ferencvaros are without question the biggest club in Hungary, boasting what they like to call 'the most fanatical fans in Europe', and the welcome mat was certainly laid out for us. Graffiti on a bridge told its own story:

'Welcome to HELL English Jew boys!'

Budapest still has the scars of poverty and communism, seen in the old decaying buildings, but without doubt for the first time it now has money, and in certain quarters plenty of it. Beer is still 30p a pint down the back streets and £2 for the same bottle on the high street. They are learning, and learning quickly.

I have never witnessed anyone have a nervous breakdown. Not until this trip, that is. So let me introduce to you our Hungarian holiday rep, Granville. His trouble started when we were due to be taken to the match. Newcastle United devised a cunning plan to get us all inside the stadium two and a half hours before kick-off. All the buses had to meet up at Heroes' Square so there could be a convoy to the ground. Unfortunately NUFC and the supporters weren't quite on the same wavelength. We had to return to the hotel to pick up our passports but to Granville's frustration we hit the town once again. He pleaded with us to board his coach but we told him to go and take some tourists for a trip along the Danube. So the poor fellow joined the convoy without a single person on his bus.

The security for this fixture was probably the most intense I have seen in all of my years following football. Yet the guards were everywhere but the place they were most needed - outside the ground. Scuffles took place, with one report of 30 Hungarians attacking six Geordies, and the most serious case was an incident in a bar where two Union flags were hacked to bits by Magyars with machetes!

Inside the ground the greeting from the Ferencvaros fans was intimidating but expected. They charged to the fence screaming and shouting, but got the shock of their lives when the Geordies charged back at them. Some at the front had the expression of scared little rabbits caught in car headlights. To Newcastle's credit it takes a team rich in character to come back from 2-0 down in such a manner at such a place. Ferdinand shrugged off the ugly Nazi salutes and white hankies of Hungarian racism and gave his own reply.

So where was dear old Granville while all of this was going on? Sat in the coach park waiting for his customers to return.

Not all of the Toon fans travelled to Eastern Europe by plane. Some, like our friends, had made their way by train, so we offered them all a lift back to the city centre on our double-decker bus... and a few more stragglers we came across. Poor Granville had the arduous task of accounting for each individual on his list. He didn't quite know where to start, and he sure as hell didn't know where to finish, as people were hanging out of windows and out of the emergency exit at the back.

Someone tried to kidnap some poor Hungarian who wanted to swap shirts, and Granville tried desperately to stop people smoking because it is strictly forbidden to smoke on public transport. I don't know if this was the final straw that broke old Granville's back but I realised something was wrong when his eyes started to protrude from the sockets. He had a sort of Mongolian look on his face and his hands started to spasm, and this was the point when the man obviously needed hospital treatment.

We sincerely wish him a quick recovery.

FRANCE

And so to our trip to Metz on the French border with Luxembourg and Germany.

Now no-one can generalise about a race of people, but let's face it... the French bloody hate us, don't they? And they do everything at such a leisurely pace I'm surprised anything gets done at all.

The cafe/bars simply couldn't cope with the influx of custom and everywhere immediately ran out of glasses as soon as we walked in. We even came across chairman John Hall wetting his whistle in one establishment. He told us Newcastle's proposed ground move to a new site was under threat from campaigning students, birdwatchers and Morris dancers. Twitchers are out to protect the habitat of the Spotted Flycatcher and as one fan put it, "Give me a packet of bird seed and a .22 air rifle and I'll solve the problem!" And I'm sure he would.

Three hours to kick-off, the town square was like a scene from a Christmas card as the snow fell from the heavens. I cannot recall any match where my feet felt so numb.

Ginola suffered taunts from his countrymen as soon as he took to the field. Once a national hero, now the scapegoat for the French national side who failed to reach the 1994 World Cup finals. But that seems to be the French way... if something goes wrong, blame someone else. All in all a tremendous display by Newcastle to come away with a 1-1 draw considering we were without the most potent strike force in Europe - Shearer and Ferdinand.

As for celebrating the draw, Metz is the sort of place Judith Chalmers would take her granny. Slumbering, sedate and bloody boring. At 1:30am we'd had enough excitement (!) for one night and caught a taxi back to the hotel six miles away. £22 it cost!

MONACO

Monte Carlo, the playboy capital of the world. Having lost the first leg 1-0 it was very much a case of enjoying it to the full because not many of us expected us to get any further in this competition; and so it proved.

The scenery on the train journey from Nice to Monte Carlo was beyond belief. Put it this way; it even overshadowed our journey to Cleethorpes when we played Grimsby in our promotion season.

Monte Carlo, although small, makes use of every square yard, even if it means constructing a building on a crag of a mountain three quarters of the way up. The cliff face is like one huge complex of hotels and apartments. And the shopping centre isn't clean - it's immaculate.

We sat supping our beer on the corner of 'Las Rascalles', the hair-pin bend on the Grand Prix circuit, watching the motors flash by. Ferraris were ten-a-penny, but the star of the show was an immaculate black Lamborghini that nearly cleaned us all up as it flew past. We walked around the circuit two seconds faster than Damon Hill managed it in his Arrows.

The arena was like a palace. No turnstiles; we entered through this large smoked glass door then up some stairs to the stadium that is built on top of a multi-story car park! How they get the grass to grow at all is a miracle. The 4,000 Geordies were in good voice, despite the shocking performance of the team, and even though we took a hiding there was still humour on the terraces. The Geordies sang: "In your Monaco slums; you look in the dustbin for something to eat. You find a dead rat and you think it's a treat; in your Monaco slums!"

It wasn't the defeat that upset the fans so much as the way the team folded. Man for man Monaco had the better players, and I don't think there are many who would argue with that, but once again Shearer and Ferdinand weren't playing and that would have made a tremendous difference. But under the circumstances there is no excuse for lack of effort. Monaco had players with more heart, more determination and more pride. And that is why this defeat was so hurtful.

As for next season, it'll be the Champions League, and more travels to come. But let's be realistic and say this new format dilutes the whole competition. We are not the Champions, so we shouldn't be in it. But since we are, who's to say we won't do a better job than the Cockneys of Man Utd?

TALKING BULL

Hereford United

We'll meet again?

"With our appetites whetted, a return to anywhere near our traditional 17th place simply won't be tolerated." Such were the words that closed our entry in last year's Survival of the Fattest 2, after we had appeared in the play-offs for the first time ever. The following sorry tale will reveal that we didn't finish anywhere near our traditional place in the league. In fact nothing could have prepared us for the horror story that was about to unfold before our disbelieving eyes. As it turned out, 17th would have been a very fine placing indeed.

I think it was Bill Shankly who said that the secret of a strong team was strength down the middle, and in his day that meant goalkeeper, centre-half and centre-forward. For our purposes it meant goalkeeper, a big bugger at the back and a poor sod all on his tod up front. The previous season we were served in those areas mainly by Chris MacKenzie, a combination of Dean Smith, Stuart Watkiss and Tony James (back after 14 months out through injury), and Steve White. The only one of those five who played this season was Dean Smith, and he was on a week-to-week contract.

Our steady ship started to flounder early on. Stuart Watkiss was released by manager Graham Turner when Tony James returned to action. Unfortunately, James repaid the boss' misplaced loyalty by deserting for Plymouth to be nearer his Sheffield home! (Geography obviously isn't one of Tone's strong points). Steve White wanted a two-year contract, which at the age of 38 the club felt was a bit much, so he committed the ultimate treason and joined Cardiff. That left MacKenzie who was injured and didn't start a match all season.

We opened with a 1-0 defeat at Fulham, where 500 travelling fans were treated to a thoroughly insipid display from United. However, consecutive victories followed (something which was only to repeated twice more all season), one of which was the 3-0 over Cambridge in the first leg of the Coca Cola Cup, giving us an unbeatable leg-up to the second round and a plum tie against Middlesbrough. Away for the first leg, we were understandably apprehensive

TALKING BULL

THE INDEPENDENT VOICE OF HEREFORD UNITED SUPPORTERS

12 MONTHS AGO, THINGS WERE LOOKING UP FOR FREETOWN KUDOS AND HEREFORD UTD

NOW LOOK AT US!

HEREFORD

100% CORNED BEEF
INGREDIENTS
FREETOWN KUDOS

COOL THE CAN THOROUGHLY BEFORE OPENING

CORNED BEEF
PRODUCT OF BRAZIL

ISSUE 50   CHRISTMAS 1996   80p

about how our defence would cope with the likes of Juninho, Ravanelli, Emerson and Branco. We were right to be worried, as the team went down 7-0, the biggest defeat in our history. When Ravanelli completed his hat-trick, our response was, "So what? He managed three against Liverpool!" As usual, our support on the night was superb, leading the chant of "5-0 to the Boro" in the absence of any noise from the home fans. The second leg was predictably an anticlimax, especially when Bryan Robson left out his biggest names and only sent us Branco and Beck (!), saying that he didn't have any obligation to entertain the Hereford public. I'm afraid my admiration for Robson diminished markedly after that statement. Time will tell whether he sees it as his duty to entertain the likes of Bury and Stockport (clubs arguably the same size as ours), who are now Boro's equals.

Our league season continued to be the model of inconsistency, until October, with THREE successive wins (see SOTF 2 for the significance of that). One of these was at Brighton, coinciding with a protest by their fans, who had announced their intentions to leave the ground when the fireworks started (literally). Then followed a club record run of 15 matches without a win. This spell contained several matches of note, the first being a 1-0 defeat at Gillingham in the FA Cup, when we hit them with everything for the last few minutes and even had some Gills' fans admitting that they'd been lucky. The following week we went down to Cardiff and lost 2-0, accompanied by some unnecessarily provocative remarks by the PA announcer. On FAC2 day, we had the dubious compensation of a rescheduled home encounter with Millwall in the Tesco Trolley Trophy. Our 4-0 hammering left us in the unusual position of not having a single cup match or scheduled midweek match after Christmas; surely a first for the club, because even in the old, old days we usually had at least one Welsh Cup match in the second half of the season!

Of course this all meant that we could 'concentrate on the league'! But even then, our directors seemed reluctant to do this, especially when a major Nationwide League meeting took place in London to discuss life outside the Premiership. By all accounts we were one of only two clubs who didn't even send their apologies for absence. Perhaps our directors foresaw the fate that awaited us?

The win at Cambridge which finally ended our barren spell was the team's first appearance in a carbon copy of the Manchester United away kit (the one with the blue and white stripes). The likeness was no coincidence; the powers that be reckoned that if we could attract local kids to wear ours instead of theirs, we'd get more support. There was an element of logic in their thinking, but if they had bothered to consult the fans, they would have realised how much hatred there is around here for MU PLC. And it's not jealousy either; Liverpool were never disliked to this extent. Rather, it's anger at the way they and their commercial empire are indirectly destroying clubs like ours through gross over-exposure in the media, not to mention the glory-hunting tossers who have attached themselves to a club with which they have no natural or local affinity. As an aside, I was interested to read a comment in one of their fanzines (Red Issue, I think) who said that there is rarely an atmosphere worthy of the size of the crowds at Old Trafford because a lot of the people in the stadium do not know how to behave in a football ground. It is scandalous that they have had to appeal for more noise on European nights. The Taylor Report may have made our grounds more pleasant places to visit, but it has also got a lot to answer for.

A few weeks later our traditional early Sunday kick-off against Cardiff contained the usual cross-border passions, but more than ever on this occasion, since we now seem to be a nursery club for the Blueturds. Their squad that day contained five ex-United players - sorry, rejects. A month before, Gareth Stoker had been one of us, and we loved his attitude, but his transfer to them changed all that. Our opinion of him plummeted further when he took advantage of an horrendous howler by Trevor Wood to put them 1-0 up, sprinting over to their fans with a Klinsmann dive. That kind of turn-coat behaviour just makes you realise that players generally don't give a toss about the fans; they just see it as a job. Adrian Foster increased his previously fragile public image with a cracking equaliser, before we got as close to happiness as we are ever likely to against the 'turds at Edgar Street when Stoker was sent off for his second booking with a couple of minutes to go. Our last good run ended after a 3-3 draw at our ultimate bogey side Lincoln, when John Williams stunned the entire crowd with a goal from near the corner flag in the last minute. Was it a cross? Was it a shot? Who cared!

Still, with only one win in our final seven matches we were always going to struggle. Mind you, Adrian Foster attained near-sainthood with a hat-trick in a famous 3-2 win away at Carlisle, helped by a penalty save by Wood in the last minute, and the last away game at Leyton Orient was also notable, mainly for the cacophony of noise which the 800 travelling fans managed to sustain for 90 minutes, unfortunately with little effect.

But with Brighton predictably beating Doncaster in the last ever match at the Goldstone Ground, we were bottom of the table. The fixture computer had decreed that for the last game of the season Edgar Street would be host to the play-off to end all play-offs: we had to win to stay in the league, and Brighton only had to draw to avoid the same fate. It was that simple; that black and white.

Even now the whole match is a blur... despite our pressure and effort, it ended 1-1. All of you supporters of teams that have ever been relegated, let me tell you; you haven't come close to the feeling of desolation that comes with losing your place in the Football League. In truth, we had an abysmal season; for the first time ever I didn't even vote for a Player of the Year - I couldn't think of anyone who deserved it. Although I accept that we didn't deserve to stay up because we simply didn't win enough points, we do feel aggrieved that most of the country couldn't give a toss who went down as long as 'poor old' Brighton stayed up. The turning point for them was probably at the beginning of February when the Brighton Independent Supporters Association called off their series of protests against their board and started to give the team their wholehearted support instead. From then on they were unbeaten at home, although they should have lost against Leyton Orient before other factors conspired to save their skins that day, but I'm sure that that will be dealt with elsewhere in this book. We do sympathise with Brighton's supporters for what they've been through, but not for the wankers who chanted "You're going down to the Conference," in spite of the pleas for compassion from both sides before the match.

So what does the future hold for the two clubs that featured in this kill or be killed shoot-out? Well Brighton have to all intents and purposes, got rid of their evil regime and have everything to play for next season. We on the other hand have the same board that gave visiting fans over 30% of the tickets for the most important match in our history, presumably because they didn't consider that we were in danger of being relegated, and debts worryingly close to £1 million.

Much like for our last game, the equation is simple; if we don't get promoted then there's every chance that Hereford United will cease to exist. So this time, spare a thought for us as we navigate our way to Stevenage and Kidderminster, both of whom have their own grounds, unlike one particular club in the Third Division. Bitter? Me? Too bloody right!!

THE TEA PARTY

Stockport County

Veritably it was an odyssey: 259 days, 1 hour and 50 minutes; 7,984 miles; 34 grounds; a 67 game programme fit to reduce Ferguson to tears, from Carlisle to Gillingham, Plymouth to Middlesbrough and seemingly every point in between. We'd had the full vagaries of the English climate: sunstroke at Crewe; monsoons when the cameras showed at Edgeley; fog-bound at Mansfield and Stoke; icebound at Wrexham. Not to mention the complete gamut of emotions: ecstasy at the Dell; dumbstruck at Burnley; anger at Carlisle, but, most importantly, complete and utter joy at Saltergate. So there

it is; the County season summarised, and the honours board showed promotion to the First, semi-finalists in the Coke Cup and AutoWotsit, and a decent FA Cup outing. All in all, not a bad nine months' work.

But it wasn't unexpected. Fifteen months of Dave Jones' stewardship had suggested to those who could think further than the next five minutes that '96-97 could well produce the harvest from the seeds sown by himself and Danny Bergara. For those on the superstitious side, there was also the 30 year cycle to be completed - Division 3 North in '36-37, Division 4 in '66-67, so why not Division 2 in '96-97? Certainly the pre-season outings, with a trip to Portugal replacing our normal friendlies at Cheadle Town and Northwich Victoria, a four goal stuffing handed out to Birmingham (prompting Trevor Francis to claim that the grass was too long and thus setting the tone for his woeful season-long contributions on *Sky*!), and a win at Prenton Park added to pre-August 17th confidence.

Six games in and the mood had changed. Two points, and half as many goals, in nine hours of league football saw Plymouth arrive at EP as the Last Chance Saloon threw open its welcoming doors with the guest of honour one David Jones. Informed gossip suggested that anything less than three points and he would be yet another notch on chairman Elwood's Edgeley Park bedpost. But this was insanity to those who had suffered through the years, who realised that the drop in form was but a minor blip on what was clearly an onward and upward trip.

So it's worthwhile remembering that the journey didn't start last August, but in mid-November 1986, when a return of six points from 15 games was indisputably leading to a permanent one-way ticket out of the league. Colin Murphy, summoned back from the Middle East to replace dancing master Jimmy Melia, did the trick and saved our bacon. Then, and after a couple of years treading water under Asa Hartford, the appointment of Danny Bergara was the catalyst which led to what has been thus far an inexorable rise up the league. One promotion, four play-offs and two Auto finals later, Jones' appointment came courtesy of Bergara's inevitable dismissal following an alleged bout of fisticuffs with the chairman!

In preparing for the new campaign, DJ took a financial (and fans' loyalty-testing) gamble by replacing perennial favourite, Wales' No.1 Neil Edwards, with a Wolves reserve. Nine months later, this proved to have been a masterstroke - we still had Wales' No.1, but the name had changed to Paul Jones. His contribution was simply awe-inspiring, and effectively he was the final part in a defensive jigsaw which proved insoluble for attacks from the Premiership downwards. Quite simply, pound for pound, Jones was the best buy in the whole league - no argument invited or countenanced!

Plymouth it was, then, on September 14th - the pre-season dreams had dissipated and been replaced with a tense EP atmosphere. The Fat Lady, tucked away in the wings awaiting the call from the directors box, was sent packing without exercising her vocal chords, courtesy of a Jim Gannon double and Alun Armstrong's first of the season. The performance owed more to a belief which the team had instilled in themselves, supposedly over a pot of tea, than to the appearance of a Winchester Court-bound Grobelaar in goal. From that point on there was no stopping them. Seventy seven points from the remaining 39 games gave the just reward of a place in the upper reaches next season - the holy grail which had slipped by in three previous play-off attempts.

To most people, and certainly those outside of the SK postcode area, the campaign must have seemed to centre around triumphant cup exploits. Certainly those cannot be denigrated - they offered incredible highs, the like of which had never before been experienced. Undefeated in four outings on Premiership grounds, and victorious in three of them; the ecstasy of Mutch's late winner at The Dell captured for posterity by the *Sky* cameras; a win at Blackburn which saw off Harford; a battling performance at West Ham which afforded us the delights of Dowie's 'Classic Own Goal of All Time' in the replay; and the bittersweet victory at the Riverside. We dined with the elite and slummed it at Field Mill and Belle Vue; old, and bitter foes, Stoke and Burnley were drilled out on their own midden. In total, 21 cup games and only three defeats. The one at Birmingham was quite unbelievable, not for the loss itself but for the fact that a fourth Round FA Cup tie, a virtually unknown occasion for County, was treated with seeming nonchalance by the fans who appeared more interested in the forthcoming Coke Cup tie.

The cups represented a fantastic effort, appreciated by the fans and unlikely to be bettered in our lifetimes. They were assuredly welcomed by chairman Elwood, who scooped a clear bonus of well over a million quid into the EP vaults, from whence it has yet to reappear. More importantly, they introduced County to a national audience more accustomed to linking us with a Music Hall act.

Yet through all of this, there was a sneaking feeling that it could prove costly on the league front, and there were those who positively coveted an exit from the AWS. A day out at Wembley would have meant 13 games in the last four weeks; with the benefit of hindsight, it could (and probably would) have been a game too far. The latter stages of the season saw the players performing from memory. Not for us the luxury of the type of 24 man international squad enjoyed by that whinger over at the self-styled 'Theatre of Dreams'. The team remained virtually unchanged all season, eight of the lads playing in 55 games or more. It showed. The away form, so consistent all year, seemed to go AWOL as within the space of four days the team staggered to a single goal defeat at Gillingham and fell to a sucker punch at Preston, having dominated the game. At that point, with four games left and just hanging onto a play-off berth, things looked bleak. A season where success was richly deserved was going to end in tears, and as Tolson rolled in a real Mickey Mouse goal for York on April 22nd, the bleakness turned to an Arctic blast. No-one would have dared dream that a few days later we would be in heaven at Saltergate (surely a contradiction in terms!). In between, victory was salvaged from the Minstermen, and we endured the most nerve-racking 25 minutes ever as a comfortable two goal lead against Wycombe was almost squandered. All we needed was three points at Chesterfield and the play-offs were someone else's problem.

It was highly fitting that it should end there, just over the hill. Two sides which had captured the imagination of the country by their cup exploits had it all to play for. No animosity either, as the home fans acknowledged the support they'd been given by County fans on the way back from their semi-final at Old Trafford. It was also highly fitting for those of us who'd seen our first attempt at the play-offs, seven years previously, end in a debacle on the same field. As for the match itself, an Angell goal was a sub-editor's dream, ('Heaven Sent', 'Winging to Glory', etc), as promotion was secured amidst scenes of virtual delirium. Galley slaves a short decade ago, now invited to the captain's table.

But it was the Coke semi that summed up the season on and off the field, and the game itself was, sadly, almost incidental. The biggest game in the our history - national networked TV, the prospect of a Wembley final, and Europe beyond. Despite this, the so called 'Friendly Club' managed, as on many other occasions, to make a complete cock-up. Ticket prices were virtually doubled under the guise of a league ruling, which proved to be naught but nonsense when the Riverside tickets went on sale. Christmas came early for the touts, who had a free-for-all, and many regulars were left empty-handed and bitter. On the field, a below-par EP performance left a mountain to climb, which was all but scaled as the return leg victory on Teesside saw the homesters have the gall to do a lap of honour in celebration of a home defeat by "Second Division rubbish." To add insult to injury, their management were mightily relieved at not being left with a pile of redundant Coca Cola Cup Finalists shirts, which they had the sheer effrontery to sell before the game!

So after all that, to be honest, anything else will be a bonus. The *Tea Party* end of season soirée was unanimous in settling for survival this coming year - although some optimistic souls thought that we might actually do a bit better. Seeing Man City in anything other than a friendly will be a new experience, but the fixture we all look forward to is welcoming Boro and Captain Caliper back to EP. As they make the salutary trip, devoid of foreigners, perhaps their 'fans', the vast proportion of whom probably never even knew where Ayresome Park was, might like to reflect that money doesn't always buy success. Because, whatever happens, that will never be the case for us - Elwood's purse strings are far too tightly drawn. Success has had, and will have, to be earned, and what's more, whilst trips to the Shay and Hartlepool may now be distant memories, the fans will always remember those dark days, and recognise just how far we have come in ten short years.

THERE'S A GOOD TIME COMING (BE IT EVER SO FAR AWAY)

Exeter City

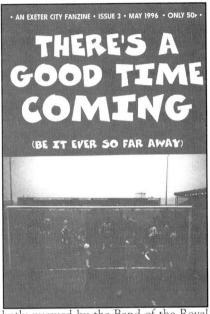

* AN EXETER CITY FANZINE * ISSUE 3 * MAY 1996 * ONLY 50p *

THERE'S A GOOD TIME COMING

(BE IT EVER SO FAR AWAY)

We peaked too soon; no doubt about it.

There was barely a minute gone on the opening day at Field Mill when an Exeter shot crashed against the Mansfield crossbar. The travelling Devonians scarcely had time to think "Crikey, it normally takes us until October to get that close to scoring," before Leon Braithwaite gleefully bundled the rebound onto the back of the net.

The away end went bonkers in the blazing August sunshine. Lines of leggy dancing girls in spangly red and white striped outfits high-kicked their way triumphantly across the pitch, hotly pursued by the Band of the Royal Marines and the White Helmets Motorcycle Display Team. A mighty 21 gun salute was sounded from the row of cannons atop the J W Twatwhistle & Sons (Central Heating & Plumbing) Family Stand, almost causing the stewards to drop the trays of ice cold Becks which they had been freely distributing amongst the joyous Exeter following. As the players prepared for the re-start, the perfect blue sky grew brighter and brighter, and brighter still, until a brilliant sapphire light shone with electric intensity over Field Mill, and lo, angels did appear in the East Midlands sky, and the angels floated wistfully between fluffy white cotton wool clouds, chorusing dreamily;

> "Drink up ye cider, drink up ye cider,
> For tonight will merry be,
> I'd rather have a scrubber, and roll her in the clover,
> But there's still more cider in the jar."

It took some time for the blinding blue light to subside and for the cannon-smoke to clear. Typically, the Becks-carrying stewards didn't hang around, although the Band of the Royal Marines and the dancing girls had to wait for the White Helmets to perform their famous 'jump through the hoop of fire' trick before they could follow them down the players' tunnel. This did at least provide the Exeter supporters with an opportunity to regale the shapely lasses with a chorus of "Get yer tits out for the lads" which everyone agreed was ever so amusing.

We didn't realise it at the time of course, but with only 60 seconds of the season gone, that really was about as good as our Division Three campaign was ever going to get. As dreary defeats and drab draws set in, the remaining 248,340 seconds were spent as follows:

98,203 seconds — **Frustrated** (including shouting abuse at own players, and various acts of self mutilation)

47,164 seconds — **Depressed** (not including crying, see below)

34,757 seconds — **Bored** (usually singing endless choruses of anti-Plymouth Argyle songs to keep spirits up in the huge gaps between noteworthy incidents on the field of play)

29,207 seconds — **Worried** (actually one of the more pleasant Exeter City-related emotions, this tends to set in approximately ten seconds after we've scored a goal. You've never seen the phrase 'hanging on by the skin of their teeth' brought to life quite so vividly as when City are 'sitting back on a lead')

22,304 seconds — **Furious** (ranging from silent rage to truly frenzied out-bursts of Ballyesque ferocity at anyone in the vicinity)

7,003 seconds — **Numb** (including those odd moments when you almost want the other team to score just so you can show how unconcerned you really are)

3,200 seconds — **Denial** (usually taking the form of listening out for Brighton or Hereford results, and insisting that Brighton must surely have further points deducted for pitch invasions, attacking Ray Wilkins, excessive sympathy-seeking in the media, etc)

2,108 seconds — **Sobbing hysterically**

1,602 seconds — **In pub** (having left early)

1,304 seconds — **In pub** (trying to pluck up the courage to leave for the ground)

986 seconds — **Queuing for pasties** (only to find they've sold out)

502 seconds — **Quite happy**

As you may have noticed (unless you were one of the millions droning on and on about 'Poor old Brighton' and how it would be such a shame if the side which gave the world Steve Foster and the Tesco carrier bag kit went out of the league at the expense of nobodies like us), Exeter City came quite close to waving a tearful cheerybye to league football in '96-97.

It wasn't until the penultimate Saturday that we secured survival with a 5-1 defeat at home to, er, Lincoln, I think (the opponents don't really matter down in Division Three; I have a theory that every visiting side is just Torquay in a different kit, so similarly skilled are they all at looking bloody hopeless and at scoring soft goals past the disorganised muddle that we call a defence).

We ended up relying on Orient's 2-0 win over Hereford to secure our safety, which was a bit disappointing when our final game had been billed as the climax of our 'fight for survival'. We even had Uri Geller, whose son is apparently an ardent City fan, doing his orange dot routine to ensure that the energy of positivity was on our side. As our heroes trooped off the field, a chorus of "Uri Geller is a wanker" echoed around St James' Park. An interesting reaction, which leads me to leave you, dear reader, to ponder two rather poignant questions;

a) Should the City supporters not have been seeking to cast the net of blame wider than a helpful mystic?, *and* b) in view of his special powers, if Uri really was a self-abuser, surely his todger would have bent in two and fallen off ages ago, were he to partake in such bishop-bashing activities?

Source: *King of the Kippax*

THERE'S ONLY ONE F IN FULHAM.

Fulham

Football survives on hope, whether your team is in the upper or lower spheres of the league. As the start of each campaign nears, fans everywhere offer the same silent prayer: "Please let this be our season... Maybe, just maybe, we can get it right this time." For the likes of Manchester United and Liverpool fans these prayers are directed at some grand aim such as yet another Championship triumph or success in Europe. In Third Division terms, the hopes are much more basic, like avoiding the dreaded, and possibly terminal, drop to the Conference. A money-making run in one of the cups

would be more than welcome, as would striking a decent vein of form in the league. Then, if you're ever the optimist, there's the 'p' word: Promotion!

Of course any dreams of a take-over by a mega-rich white (ish) knight prepared to sink tens of millions of pounds into your lowly outfit would of course be dismissed as wholly implausible. Get real!

When Micky Adams took over the Fulham hot-seat from Ian Branfoot in February 1996 the only way out of the basement division looked to be downwards. Then, only Torquay kept the Cottagers off bottom spot, but Adams was to lift the team to a relatively respectable 17th spot by the season's end. He rebuffed any congratulations at the time, saying he should be judged on what he would achieve during the following campaign. With *his* team.

So, season '96-97 began with quiet optimism. The air of doom and gloom, so obvious in recent times, was replaced by a cheerier mood. It helped that Adams had been busy in the transfer market, even if his purchases came from the Oxfam shop rather than Harrods (!). Pre-season friendlies gave little inkling of the tremendous few months ahead, possibly because the squad had suffered a spate of injuries. But it was clear that the tour to Ireland had engendered a wonderful team spirit.

Sun, shirtsleeves and balloons - and of course no end of hope - greeted the first match at home against Hereford. Balloons? Well, the club had just received the long overdue OK for the ground development plans seen as critical in its quest to regain the freehold (but more of that later). It meant there was a definite feel-good factor around Craven Cottage, which even the players acknowledged after the match. And even if the game itself was pretty crap, we managed a single goal win and put three points on the board.

The goalscorer against Hereford was born-again Mick Conroy. Used by the previous regime as a 'chase-that' merchant and, accordingly, voted a runaway winner of the Not the Player of the Year category by the fan-zine readership, a leaner, fitter Conroy (soon to be dubbed 'Super Micky') was now being played to his strengths, chiefly as penalty-box predator. Supported by the tireless Scott and Freeman, Fulham suddenly had a forward line capable of scoring!

It was 18 games into the campaign before we failed to score - ironically against struggling Brighton - while First Division Southend were knocked out of the Coca Cola Cup and only a couple of dodgy decisions (honest!) ensured Ipswich didn't go the same way in the following round. Conroy was for a while the country's leading scorer as he rattled up 18 goals by Christmas. Oh yes, and Fulham were top of the league. Things were certainly looking up.

It was really fun to be a Fulham supporter again. Away trips, which had always been a laugh as long as you discounted the games themselves, were now a hoot. Wins were almost guaranteed and several off-licences near the respective railway stations enjoyed bonanza sales when Fulham came to town. All in the cause of a celebratory tipple you understand!

Home form was never as assured. Points were stupidly dropped, particularly against Mansfield, Torquay and Lincoln, but we remained top and all of us fans were self-adopted members of the 'Adams family'. *Sky* came to Craven Cottage in late January for the visit of Cardiff. A formality, surely? But if ever there was a reminder that this was Fulham we're talking about, this was it. Here was a chance to strut our stuff, stamp our authority on the division and draw a few more punters in through the gates. Instead we were thumped 4-1, our only goal coming courtesy of a Cardiff defender. A further lacklustre performance at Lincoln the following week meant we were knocked off the top. Oh dear, an untimely wobble.

Adams later admitted that he thought the bubble had burst and, despite being pace-setters for much of the season, he feared we may have to resort to the play-offs to gain promotion. Some of the senior pro's seemed to have lost it and Adams even abandoned a training session because he felt that most players were simply going through the motions. But to their credit the players *were* bothered and had a few get-togethers in an attempt to cure the ills.

Meanwhile, even without being privy to these behind-the-scenes wran-glings, the murmurings on the terraces prior to the following evening's match were deafening. Had the tremendous turnaround in the club's fortunes been too good to be true after all? As it turned out Fulham's showing against in-form Swansea proved an eye-opener. Fulham tore into the visitors with their rediscovered blend of skill and determination, only to find themselves a goal down! Fulham were up for the challenge, however, and after Darren Freeman had levelled, a tremendous comeback was completed when Paul Brooker struck a late winner.

Although knocked off the top perch, we were back in the hunt with renewed confidence. Fellow high-fliers Wigan were held to a 1-1 draw and another unbeaten run was set in motion. Promotion was all but assured at Brisbane Road where our raucous supporters found another cheerleader - injured centre-back Terry Angus was up and chanting with the best of 'em!

The 2-0 win against Orient set us up for the final stretch - which included a trip to Carlisle, one of three teams now vying for the title. What a day (and night!) that was. Carlisle opening the scoring, Conroy - naturally - nodded home the equaliser before a scorcher from Rod McAree, out of the side since September, earned us the three points. Cue another off-licence bonanza! Engineering works meant a meandering magical mystery tour back to the Smoke (bloody railway operators) and numerous congas on platforms at unscheduled stops. Worth recording, too, that BT Police commented on our excellent, albeit boozy, behaviour. We eventually pulled into Euston well after midnight - tired and exhausted, and with no tubes to get us closer to home. Great... Thanks a bloody bunch!

One more point needed, which duly came at Mansfield three days later. "A dour draw" claimed the papers. Maybe so, but nothing dour about the emotions and celebrations. We were up! And farewell and good riddance to a dreadful basement division. Some decent clubs and supporters, it's true, but the pits as far as playing levels and most of the facilities goes. And as for the standard of officials...!

With that, we blew the chase for the Championship. Carlisle and Wigan were also faltering but we too hit a barren patch, including a 1-0 home defeat by Northampton, which saw Adams make two 'tactical' substitutions in the first 15 minutes, and a disappointing goalless draw at Doncaster.

But it was a great season, nevertheless - epitomised by Fulham's travelling supporters making up more than half the crowd at Cambridge on the last day. (One coach had a board on its back seat saying "Follow us to Colchester," a reference to the coach driver who in January insisted on taking his party of Fulham supporters to Cambridge instead of Colchester, despite the pleas - and later threats - from his entourage.)

Decorum went out of the window as many turned up in weird fancy dress and a host had daubed black and white paint all over their faces. The ticker-tape welcome for the team, meantime, was almost claustrophobic in its density. OK, so the title was Wigan's provided they didn't slip up at home to Mansfield. But we needed a win all the same, and miracles could happen, couldn't they?

They didn't. Freeman's strike ensured a club record 12th away success of the season but it was a strangely subdued Fulham crowd that trooped away from the Abbey Stadium. Wigan had duly taken the crown by the narrowest of margins; how ironic that it was Fulham's own chairman, dear old Jimmy Hill, who had been instrumental in changing the rules. With both clubs on 84 points, Wigan were Champions on goals scored; any other yardstick would have seen the title and the silverware coming south. But then, rules is rules!

The main shock to everyone's system was yet to come, however. It wasn't that the *London Evening Standard* (aka The North London Gazette or simply The Substandard) had suddenly woken up to Fulham's existence, neither was it the news of Jimmy Hill standing down as chairman after ten years. In a move that astounded the world of football, Harrods supremo Mohamed Al Fayed was announced as the club's new chairman and he promptly pledged £30-60m ("or whatever it takes") to get the club back to the big time. The sums were mind-boggling, particularly so for a club of Fulham's relatively lowly status. Al Fayed also immediately scuppered the previous hard-fought-for plans for a 15,000 all-seater stadium part-surrounded by flats. Instead his cash injection would re-secure the Craven Cottage freehold outright and he had grandiose plans for the site to be developed into a state-of-the-art arena with a capacity of 25,000+. And, naturally, a team to match.

Oo-er! Things are never going to be the same again down by the Thames.

THE THIN BLUE LINE

Cardiff City

When you consider that there are 92 league clubs, it's fairly easy to work out that not many are going to be celebrating success at the end of a season. Only so many teams can get promoted, and there's only so many cups to win. And we didn't do either. But despite the lack of trophies, we're not too down-hearted. At the end of a season that saw us go through more managers than the Midland, more loans than Lloyds, and more trials than Judge Jeffries, Cardiff City finished in seventh place, and took part in the Third Division play-offs. And are we happy? Yes, I suppose so. It could have been worse, after all...

THE
THIN BLUE LINE
A VERY AVERAGE CARDIFF CITY FANZINE

WEMBLEY BECKONS

When Joan said we had a new coach, I thought Osman was leaving.....

BUT DOES HIBBITT KNOW THE WAY?

ISSUE NINETEEN   FIFTY PENCE

Compared to recent history, '   .
The last three terms have seen near-relegation, relegation, and finishing two places off the bottom of the entire league (an all-time low). This time, had it not been for a few awful spells, when the side inexplicably reverted to the dire football of those lean years, we could have won automatic promotion. But instead of dwelling on what might have been, let's go back to the start of the season, and watch the events unfold...

At the start, we'd just finished in 22nd place, our lowest ever league spot, so fans could be forgiven for expecting heads to roll; manager Phil Neal's perhaps, or director of football Kenny Hibbitt's maybe. But no! Both of them not only held on to their posts, but somehow managed to come out of the whole thing smelling of roses, showered with praise from chairman Samesh Kumar. After all, these two heroes had kept us up! And as a reward for this 'success', they were allowed to continue with their rebuilding plans, trawling the free transfer lists looking for those elusive uncut gems.

This policy was not exactly conducive to great optimism on the part of the fans, and the queues for season tickets did not stretch down Sloper Road, despite the signing of the Third Division's highest scorer. Steve White may have grabbed a hatfull last time out, but he was 37, and on a free transfer from Hereford. Others arrived, some we actually paid good money for, plus a whole host of loanees and trialists. Over the season, we used 32 different players and only fielded the same team in consecutive games once. Now there's consistency for you!

Our worst fears were realised when with Neal in charge City started by playing dire, unattractive and defensive football. OK, keeping a clean sheet is a laudable objective, but you've got to score a few to actually win, haven't you? Strangely though, most fans were so pleased that the side wasn't re-enacting last season's disasters that they were prepared to put up with these atrocious displays.

Then, just as we were beginning to despair of ever seeing an attractive game of footie at Ninian Park ever again, we were released from the purgatory by an Act of God. Up in the heady heights of the First Division, crisis-torn Manchester City appointed Steve Coppell to pull them out of the mire. And guess who Coppell wanted as his assistant? You got it - our Phil. Oh, thank you God! It ended in tears at Maine Road - as we all knew it would - but there was jubilation on the terraces of Ninian Park. We'd got rid of him! And it didn't cost us a penny!

Neal's resignation caused a storm of protest from those few fans who hadn't twigged that he was taking us nowhere. But those with a brain celebrated, and prepared for the coming of the messiah; the man to lead us out of the darkness. Great names such as John Toshack (get real!), Kevin Ratcliffe or even Mike Walker were bandied about by an eager local press. But instead of appointing a big name, Kumar followed his ex-manager's example and scoured the free transfer list. Ironically (as it turned out) one of the many (and we mean *many*) that turned down the job was Northampton's Ian Atkins. It seemed that no-one wanted to manage the forever sleeping giant that is Cardiff City.

In the meantime, Kenny Hibbitt took up the reins, which was enough to start us on a surge up the table. The whole place started to buzz: players who hadn't kicked a ball in weeks turned up early, banging on the door to be let in for training (honestly!). With Neal out of the way, we looked a different side, and turned from goal-shy draw-merchants into free-scoring winners almost overnight. Sadly, Hibbitt had just eight games in charge before Kumar appointed fifth-choice Russell Osman as manager, but in that time the side had chalked up four wins and two draws, displaying some excellent football in the process.

Osman's reign was to be a short one. He presided over just ten dreadful games (albeit with a run of results not that different from the previous eight) before Kumar decided enough was enough, and bravely put Hibbitt back in charge. And you could see why: the football on show had been awful, in particular two defeats at home, first by arch-rivals Swansea, and then in a humiliating display against Gillingham in the FA Cup - all the worse for being shown live on *Sky*. Sit-in protests by disgruntled fans probably also swayed Kumar's thinking.

So 'King Kenny' was back in charge - our fourth manager in five months - and after a few minor hiccups, we were back on a roll. A fine run of wins took us into the play-off places, and there we stayed. On the way we'd beaten every side above us in the table, usually away, but our home form seemed to have some sort of hoodoo attached to it. A prime example of this 'Ninian Park phobia' was the week that saw us murder league leaders Fulham 4-1 away, only to perform dreadfully at home the following Saturday, losing 1-2 against lowly Colchester. As usual, the only consistent thing about Cardiff City was their inconsistency.

But the gradual acquisition of a player here and a player there, plus the return to form of some of our more talented youngsters, particularly teenage striker Simon Haworth, meant that as the end of the season drew near, we were playing some of our best football. Haworth had been out with a knee injury for nearly a year, but given a chance by Hibbitt, he proved himself to be a bit of a goal-machine, scoring nine times in 12 outings, and hitting the winner for the Wales U-21 side against Holland. It wasn't long before we had scouts from the top divisions watching him, and the talk grew of a big money move. After an on/off transfer to Norwich fell through on medical grounds, he was eventually 'sent to Coventry', who chose to believe the score-sheets rather than the doctors, for £500,000.

Feelings amongst fans were split about the lad's move; it seemed that the club had once again sold off a valuable player, just as we were about to go places. But in reality, we probably got a good deal. Haworth's contract was up at the end of the season, and the Bosman ruling meant that he could have taken his pick of the top clubs that wanted him. And be honest, if you were him, what would you have done? From the club's point of view, they were getting half a million quid for a youngster who had played barely 20 games. Since then, Haworth has picked up his first Welsh Cap, and with International appearances built into the deal, we could end up with even more money. Let's hope the club spend it wisely.

Darlington for our last 'proper' game saw wild celebrations despite a 2-1 defeat, because by beating Lincoln, Rochdale had gifted us our play-off place. The novelty of getting there was somewhat spoilt by having to play Northampton, who were a bogey side for us this season. And they were to do it again. A 1-0 home defeat in front of 11,500 fans showed the sort of support we could call upon, but it also underlined the lack of teeth in the side. With most of the possession, we were just unable to make it count. But still, there was another leg to come - could our famous away form get us through? Sadly not. We lost 3-2 at Sixfields after being reduced to ten men, and were left to rue the cost of all those dreadful home performances.

So we finished where we started, though some progress has been made, both on and off the pitch. The team is without a doubt stronger than it was, though further team-building is required if we are to mount a serious challenge next season. The club shop, once a joke, now stocks almost all you could want. There was also a largish cash boost mid-season via a link-up with the local all-conquering Ice Hockey side, the Cardiff Devils. Their owners put up £300,000 to join the board, although it's beginning to look as though this ties the club to moving in with the skaters at a new sports village planned for the rapidly developing Cardiff Bay area. Despite the somewhat ramshackle state of our home, most supporters would rather see Ninian Park restored to its former glory. Much like the side, really.

We'll close with a quick mention for defender Jason Perry, who earned a testimonial season after ten years with the club. Well done, Jason, we could do with a few more like you.

THOSE WERE THE DAYS

Ipswich Town

Defeat From the Jaws of Victory. As Bloody Usual.

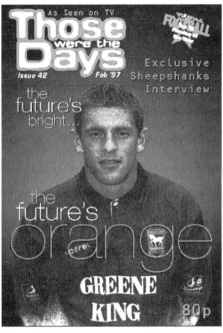

I'm still not over it completely. For a week I was in denial. I even bought a play-off final ticket and only just managed to get rid of it two days before Sh... Shef... She... oh, you know who, played Palace. How on earth did we lose the semi? I still find it painful to think about some aspects of the game; Katchouro's early give-away goal, Andy Walker's late give-away goal and Steve Sedgley's free kick hitting the post in the last minute. I was not pleased that evening. Not at all.

Getting away from our 'loss' (we drew on aggregate, only losing on the away goals rule) it was a strange old season. Early predictions from local media 'personalities' Alan Brazil and Mel Henderson suggested a difficult campaign with us finishing mid-table. What do they know anyway? They thought Birmingham would win the title. Mad! I mean Trevor Francis is their manager! *TWTD* of course was far more optimistic; easy progress to promotion positively foreseen. But there was controversy even prior to the season beginning. We signed Ian Crook from Norwich (controversial enough in itself) and a few days later he buggers off back up the A140 with not so much as an "I'll get my coat." The club were not pleased. And neither were we. Crook became our anti-hero for the season with plenty of amusing and unprintable songs flying around. As things turned out we had the last laugh; as a Norwich fan friend of mine (I say friend in the loosest sense, of course) told me, we were lucky not to sign him as he had a pitiful season. Norwich were also forced to pay us an undisclosed sum for him (apparently £200,000 which must be about 200,000 times his value) which cheered us up no end. However we did feel that the FA's fine of £250 on Crook was a bit pathetic considering a footballer's earnings *and* as he'd recently had a testimonial. Strange also that no action was taken against Mike Walker for an illegal approach...

Things didn't start well with a loss at Man City, although everyone took heart from the fact that we almost got a draw and Man City were 'going to walk away with the Division anyway'. Hmm - seems strange to remember that piece of folk wisdom now doesn't it? Next we beat Bournemouth in the Coca Cola and Reading 5-2 which included the unique spectacle of a Tony Vaughan goal (which became less than unique as the game went on when he scored a second). On a more sombre note the Reading game was Ian Marshall's last game. Now you out there in Not-Supporting-Ipswich-Land may snigger at Ian Marshall and our affection for him. Despite the Billy Ray Cyrus (sorry for bringing back the memory of that song) haircut and the strange matelot-like gait, he was a well respected man in these parts. So what if he was always injured; so what if he looked lazy; so what that he is the only player in history to crock himself in a supermarket ("shopping for the wife" apparently. Footballers are not new men, not even slightly); in Ipswich he was a hero. And still is apparently if the tale regarding a fan running into a local restaurant to sing his chant at him is anything to go by. Suffice to say it was a sad day when he left, although there was no great outcry as we all knew someone would have to go, and it was better that it was an older player rather than one of our up-and-coming youngsters. I'm tempted to explain that during our Premiership years the manager and chairman of the time allowed us to get into a dodgy financial position, but I won't as the former manager gets terribly litigious these days. So one of our two 19 goal strikers from the previous year had gone but we still had Alex Mathie. Well, we did for a month more before he took to his hospital bed for the season to allow surgeons to rebuild both his shoulders. Bugger!

By November my promotion prediction, so confident in August, was looking a bit far-fetched with us nearer going down than up and dissenting voices heard on the North Stand terraces. "Burley - sort it out!," chanted a group sitting directly behind the goal. "There's only one George Burley" chanted the rest and a Tory-style split developed which went on for a month or so, with punches even being thrown. Things were not good. Up front youngsters James Scowcroft (not Jamie, his mummy doesn't like it and apparently complained to a local radio station for referring to him by this crass diminutive) and Richard Naylor we doing OK but the goals were not going in. We were also falling into last season's trap of losing and drawing to the likes of Grimsby. No insult but we are better than that aren't we? Two years ago we beat Man U for Christ's sake. *Not* happy.

Christmas came and we were looking a little better and were doing quite well in the Coca Cola Cup. We'd lost a derby, which was sad, and the 'physical' tactics of the Norfolk Police made it all the worse for some people. We were, however, injury-hit and there was always the derby at Portman Road. These days the Carrow Road derby is of secondary importance because at home we not only usually win but one of their players normally humiliates himself by scoring our last-minute winner. Gary Megson and Bryan Gunn (although Robert Ullathorne officially scored that goal and Town fans will always remember Gunny's contribution with greatest fondness) have already entered the hall of fame and we were all hoping that Ian Crook would join them. By the way have you noticed how I have got 976 words through this article and not made a Crook by name crook by nature gag? Well there it was.

After Christmas we decided we quite fancied promotion after all and started winning left, right and on occasion even centre. We buggered up the FA Cup, losing to Nottingham Forest 3-0 but in the league few beat us between Christmas and the end of the season. With about six weeks to go some Statto or other pointed out that if there were a league based on the results of the matches between those teams in the top six we would be well clear. That was rather spoiled by us losing at home to Bolton but we really deserved to win that one. The fact that we'd beaten them away helped sugar the pill, but by the end of March we were considering away draws as bad results. Then things went a bit mad, Ted. We won five games in a row. We hadn't managed three on the trot since George Burley became manager. Things were becoming too much to take; we were getting carried away. Annoying people kept saying "So, how are you getting to Wembley then?" People you'd never seen before started turning up to Portman Road and hiding their Man United scarves. It was all going too well, wasn't it?

Well, yes it was. We did our usual trick of snatching defeat from the jaws of victory and are now doomed to another year in this most irritating (although I grudgingly admit entertaining) of leagues. Was it a good season? Yes, I suppose it was. We lost our top strikers, made the play-offs, discovered more good youngsters coming through and, most importantly, beat Norwich. Mauricio Taricco was a true hero loved by all (except Robert Fleck) and seems set to remain at Portman Road despite a £2 million bid from a Premiership club. He played brilliantly all season, capping things with the first goal in our derby victory over Norwich. No Crook own-goal sadly, but we totally out-played them and they had their usual seven men booked. Norwich, by the way, had the league's worst disciplinary record last season. Thought you might want to know.

And so what of next year? Well, we may lose one or two players: Tony Vaughan seems set to go to Manchester City, Sedgley to anywhere but here and all the big clubs seem to be sniffing around youngsters like Richard Wright, Jamie - oops, James - Scowcroft and Kieron Dyer (the new Gordon Strachan according to youth coach Paul Goddard, although to be fair to him he's is not Scottish, bad-tempered or ginger). We should however do fairly well again despite the presence of so many big clubs in Division One. Whoever leaves through the summer, we already have next season's Ian Crook sorted out: Jan Aage Fjortoft. His whining throughout our 3-0 (a highly irregular Neil Gregory hat-trick) victory over the Blades (spit) wound us up enough but his taunting of the new Ipswich God Mauricio Taricco has him down as public enemy number one. Sorry Ian, your time has passed.

TIGER RAG

Hull City

Read through the *Tommy Cook Report* (Brighton) in *SOFT2*, substitute '95-96 for '96-97, delete the last bit about the riot, and you have Hull City's last campaign in a nutshell.

This is a blow-by-blow account of what happened on the field last season: BUGGER ALL.

Hull City scored just 44 goals, finishing 17th in Division Three, the worst ever in our 93 year history. Quote of the year came from Radio 5 Live's Alan Green when he suggested if Leeds United were playing in his back garden he would close the curtains. Well, if Hull City ever found their way onto his back lawn he'd surely move house.

We were entertained only when Duane Darby got the ball, but the atrocious lack of service he received, courtesy of Terry Dolan's 'everybody behind the ball' system, ensured that our hero grabbed just 20 goals in all competitions. And most of them came against Northern League Whitby Town in the FA Cup first round. A torrential downpour thwarted Town's impressive attempt to play us off the park at a muddy Scarborough (where we had already been dumped out of the Coca Cola Cup at the first hurdle), allowing the Tigers to escape back home for a replay.

At fortress Boothferry the visitors led 4-3 in the final minute, but Darby's fourth goal of the game gave him the opportunity to grab two more in ET as City triumphed 8-4. Crewe emphatically ended our Wembley dreams in the next round.

That this was as exciting as it got was hardly surprising after Dolan's shopping spree, snapping up five more defenders to add to the four he'd signed towards the end of the previous term. He was already intensely disliked by the Tigers' faithful who had endured two relegations under his tedious five year stewardship. The rejection of two substantial take-over offers, together with Dolan's three year contract extension, led to the formation of Tigers 2000, which would rapidly become Hull City's largest official supporters' group.

The Tigers 2000 campaign literally took to the streets back in June when chairman Martin Fish's home was visited by an open top double-decker armed with a couple of extremely loud loud-hailers. In no uncertain terms he was told enough was enough; things had to change and Tigers 2000 would be around until our club was allowed to pass into the hands of someone who would attempt to realise its potential.

The majority of Hull folk chose to demonstrate in the same way they have done for the best part of the last 25 years, by staying at home. The record low home league crowd of 1,775 which watched us 'entertain' Torquay appeared mighty compared with the 553 who turned up, probably for curiosity value, for the WindowWipers Cup clash with Chester. But it wasn't always so. Back in the late '60s and early 70's, crowds at Boothferry often hit the 40,000 mark, largely to watch the goals of Ken Wagstaff and Chris Chilton, both of whom now found themselves banned from the ground as Fish frowned on their support for Tigers 2000.

The club has experienced a steady decline over the last 25 years, and its association with the no-ambition, no-spend Needler family (owners since the war) has seen local business turn its back on the club in the same way that the local population of 500,000+ has consistently failed to frequent the dilapidated Boothferry Park. And though the removal of Christopher Needler was Tigers 2000's main aim, he is an infrequent visitor and his puppet chairman was an easier target. Hull was soon adorned with the words 'Fish Out' by way of poster, sticker and T-shirt.

It wasn't long before yet another sizeable take-over bid was on the table. Again it matched the demands of a board adept at shifting the goalposts. Former chairman Don Robinson (who'd presided over two promotions on a shoe-string budget in the '80s, before disenchantment with all things Needler prompted his departure) offered to take on all the club's debts, build two new stands at Boothferry Park, and guaranteed £1m for "team and club improvements." The bid was rejected and instead Robinson was offered the playing side for £1m, and he'd have to build a new stadium. Needler wanted to keep Boothferry Park for himself, and the accusations of a systematic run-down of the club were ringing even more true than ever.

As we slipped into November the club's end of year accounts were released, revealing a debt of some £730,000. That had us all reaching for his programme notes from the final game of '95-96 where he clearly stated that the sales of Dean Windass and Alan Fettis had cleared the club's debts. Once again we were left asking, where has the money gone?

Needler's apparent desperation to separate Hull City from Boothferry Park was even more emphatically revealed at the club's AGM in December when he insisted that the only way to clear our debts was to sell the ground. In his words, "The alternative will be to close the gates of Boothferry Park without any football supporters." It was hard to believe he'd said this just a month after such a substantial take-over offer, but the even more obvious question as to where we would get the money to build a new ground - especially since the

Football Trust had run out of cash before we'd bothered to apply - remained unanswered.

Shareholders demanded the sacking of Dolan; the man who'd master-minded two relegations and who in six years has failed to give us even one decent cup run; the man who wrecked the club's successful youth policy and who has consistently allowed potential talent to stagnate; the man who em-ploys the most dull, unimaginative, naïve defensive tactics you could ever imag-ine and who refuses to let his players talk to the press; the man who is consid-ered a joke by the majority of Hull people.

The response? "We can't afford to sack him, he's got a three year con-tract." The place erupted! The only good news to come out of the AGM was that we were told we did not owe any tax and so would be spared our annual trek to the High Court to do battle with the Inland Revenue.

Into January, and as the Tigers slipped back into the bottom half of the basement, Martin Fish hatched a devious plot to ensure Terry Dolan would achieve his longest ever cup run with the Tigers. When Carlisle called off our second round Windscreens Cup clash at the eleventh hour, our opportunistic chairman called for their expulsion from the competition and an automatic place for us into round three. Of course, he failed and we eventually lost the tie 4-0.

After January had yielded just two goals, City fans were reaching the depths of despair as it was revealed that Needler had been negotiating with rugby league neighbours Hull (soon to be) Sharks to share their Boulevard ground. Soon after it was reported that Scarborough, York, Grimsby, Scunthor-pe and Doncaster had also been approached for ground-borrowing.

After a beating at the Abbey Stadium, *Radio Cambridgeshire* described us as "a poor and negative pub team." But it was our two-man 'board of directors' who were really taking the piss. The time was nigh for City die-hards to do the same.

A holiday in Torquay provided an unexpected opportunity. Plainmoor is a peaceful friendly place and their awfully nice stewards decided to let the 200 or so travelling fans freedom to roam between the terraces behind the goal and the seats behind our team's dugout. Hurrah! Guess where the majority of us headed?

A group of those who remained behind the goal unfurled a 20-yard long 'Fish and Dolan Out' banner. Other flags and banners had been evident at the majority of games, but this was by far the most impressive. Meanwhile, in the seats some Tigers 2000 types were handing out 'Sack Dolan' and 'Fish Out' stickers and posters to many willing takers as Messrs Dolan and Lee, as usual leaning against the dugout, endured endless taunts from fans enjoying the rare chance of giving advice from such close quarters.

In the second half our leaders introduced 16 year old Lee Ellington for his debut. Moments later, the youngster trotted back to the bench to ask which position he was supposed to be playing. If Dolan thought he could never be more embarrassed he was soon in for a rude awakening. In the face of constant shouts to sit down, the ever-arrogant Dolan held his pose, arms folded, only yards away. It was an opportunity one fan felt he couldn't miss. He crept out of his seat, down the steps and sprang onto the dugout roof launching his hand in one movement slap bang onto Terry's head. Dolan bellowed angrily at the stewards who remained unmoved as our hero quickly made himself scarce. The exasperated Dolan turned back round in despair, revealing to the crowd a bright orange 'Sack Dolan' sticker right in the middle of his bald pate.

The best thing was, he didn't even realise, thinking someone had simply tried to clobber him. Even better, nobody told him. For the best part of ten minutes Terry stood unwittingly displaying our message for all to see. The howls of derision eventually prompted him to sit down and when he emerged later, minus sticker, we responded with "Where's yer sticker gone?," *Chirpy-chirpy-cheep-cheep* style.

As shareholders called for an extraordinary general meeting in March, Terry Dolan signed another defender.

Of course, a year in the life of Hull City would never be complete without a trip to the High Court, and Martin Fish chose April Fool's Day to announce that this was exactly where we would be going the following week. But it was no joke, as the tax man had issued a winding up order in February for an unpaid bill of £250,000. Yet again, City were granted a 28 day adjournment by virtue of a letter from a mystery businessman, expressing an interest in taking over the club. Days later, £1 million-rated goalkeeper Roy Carroll was sold to Wigan for £350,000 and the bill was paid.

So where are we now? Talk of an impending take-over is rife and the rumours have to be heard to be believed: George Michael, Richard Branson and The Pet Shop Boys head the list of possible sugar-daddies, with Kevin Keegan, Peter Beardsley and Chris Waddle vying for the manager's job.

At the time of writing Hull City is still under the ownership of Christopher Needler and we are still waiting for the opportunity to support a club of which we can truly be proud.

TILL THE WORLD STOPS

Leeds United

In the summer of 1988 Leeds United staged a testimonial match for two of their greatest player, John Charles and Bobby Collins. Everton were the visitors to Elland Road and they took on a Leeds eleven which included such luminaries as Kenny Dalglish and Michel Platini. Also pulling on a Leeds shirt for the first time that evening was a certain Ian Rush, who had recently signed for Juventus. He scored three times against Neville Southall in this game, prompting the Everton 'keeper to tell him to "f**k off back to Italy." A hat-trick on his first appearance in United colours, and ironically that's as many times as

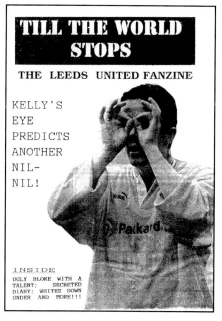

TILL THE WORLD STOPS

THE LEEDS UNITED FANZINE

KELLY'S
EYE
PREDICTS
ANOTHER
NIL-
NIL!

INSIDE

UGLY BLOKE WITH A
TALENT: SECRETED
DIARY: WHITES DOWN
UNDER AND MORE!!!

he scored for us during the '96-97 season. Conversely you could say that Leeds never lost a match in which he scored for them. This echoes an earlier proud boast made during his first spell with Liverpool, the only difference being that then the goals came in hatfuls, not handfuls.

If you must analyse it, I suppose that Ian Rush puffing, panting and pontificating in a vain attempt to regain some kind of form and consistency was a microcosm of United's season. We've heard all the cracks, thanks: "I found a blank video tape, but realised it was Leeds' goals of the season review!" So, in total we scored 28 times in 38 Premiership games. But, and it's a very big but, we only conceded 37. Nine of those came in the first five games, the extent of Howard Wilkinson's tenure at the club during '96-97. Not long, you may think, especially when you consider this opening spell consisted of two wins and a draw. But Howard had long since received the thumbs down both from Caspian, the new owners of the club, and the supporters. A disastrous run-in to the end of the previous season, following the debacle at Wembley in the Coca Cola Cup Final, had the 'Wilko, it's time to go' anthem primed and ready.

There was some form of masochistic irony in the fact that Wilkinson's final match should be a 4-0 home defeat at the hands of Manchester United. Bitter rivals since Noah was a lad, the club that Sgt. Wilko had outflanked to win the Championship four years previously hammered the last nail into his managerial coffin. And even more irony: Eric Cantona's final act at Elland Road was to score the humiliating fourth and stand, arms aloft, in the very spot in front of the Kop where we once acclaimed him. Ryan Giggles had the sense to man-handle him away, lest the front few rows attempted some form of French resistance.

So what of Wilko - had he really run out of ideas? I think so. Like any individual, in any job, the motivation to keep going has to wear a little thin after a while. I suppose that you can only cajole, bully or plead with players such as Gary Kelly, David Wetherall etc. to do the same thing so many times before everyone gets bored and the troops begin to break ranks. I suspect, judging by his record, that Wilko is not the greatest diplomat in the world, hence the 'sullen substitute syndrome' prevalent during his spell at Leeds, and this may have resulted in the player revolt hinted at by Alex Ferguson towards the end of the previous season. So, Howard had had his time - won two Championships, given us a great day out at Wembley in 1992, not to mention a couple of sorties into Europe - a far cry from what we had come to expect before he joined us. Thanks very much Wilko, but it really was time to go.

Only 24 hours after Wilkinson's dismissal, 'Stroller' George Graham did just that, and took charge at Elland Road. His ban from football due to financial misdeeds barely got a mention - George was back in the game and surely set to transform a team that was going nowhere. Naturally Leeds fans would have to endure another period of transition - an almost constant state since Don Revie left the club. It was obvious to all that our defence needed sorting out and the new manager seemed the ideal candidate for the task after years of success at 'Boring Arsenal FC'. A manager stamps his identity on a club, so we envisaged an era of success, accompanied by endless 1-0 victories and the closure of the Ladbrokes booths around Elland Road due to lack of business.

Up to the point that the new manager arrived, summer signing 'keeper Nigel Martyn had conceded the nine goals previously mentioned. Not an overly impressive record for someone who we recognised as our best custodian for years. Come the end of the season he had kept 20 clean sheets and had been voted Player of the Year - a sure sign that George had tightened things up at the back. The unoriginal chant "England's number one" even came true, as Nige became the first Leeds player for years to wear three lions on his shirt.

Our other two major summer signings, Lees Sharpe and Bowyer, had what might be classed as a very quiet opening season, football-wise. Sharpe naturally had more to prove to devout Leeds fans, coming from the land of the red. Unfortunately, as had proved the case during his final two years at Old Trafford, he spent much of the season struggling against injuries. The inbuilt distrust of anything from Lancashire led to a feeling that Wilko may well have bought yet another duck-egg. On a personal note, Sharpe had never endeared himself to me with those ridiculous goal celebrations (remember the League Cup semi final in 1991?) but even I would have put up with them on more than the six occasions necessary during '96-97.

Lee Bowyer's first season at Elland Road probably won't be remembered for his half dozen goals, tigerish tackling, which normally led to a booking, or his honour of captaining England's U21s. No, an early morning fracas in a MacDonald's restaurant led to a court appearance, a heavy fine and a ticking off from the club. The poor kid had obviously had too may alco-pops and got into a 'confused' state: "You promised me a Big Mac!" he may have cried - a resentful yearning for our dear departed Scottish captain.

George Graham was apparently handed a transfer kitty of anything between £15-20 million by Caspian. Well, it probably wasn't 'handed' to him, if you see what I mean. They probably pointed at it from a great distance, sort of: "There it is George, in that vault, behind those fifty foot thick walls, electric fencing and pack of dogs trained by Vinny Jones during his time at Leeds." And there's no truth in the rumour that puppet - I mean chairman - Bill Fotherby offered George a 'bun' on his first day and that the ex-Gooner needed to be revived with smelling salts.

With all that money burning a hole in his pocket (enough, already!) it was surprising that he didn't make his first signing until mid-December. Perhaps he was a little nervous of re-entering the transfer market for some reason. Maybe we shouldn't have been surprised that his first deal brought a Gunner (Halle of Oldham) to Elland Road - a player that Wilko had been on the verge of signing just as he was displaced.

Not that the tabloids haven't been full of stories linking us with anyone who ever expressed an interest in football. However, George didn't seem to be having a lot of luck on the transfer front. Perhaps the biggest slap in the face came from John Scales, who had virtually had his name painted on the side of a sponsored car, before changing his mind and joining Spurs. You can't blame him really as many years earlier he'd been rejected by Leeds, who'd off-loaded him on a free transfer to Wimbledon. He was merely returning the favour. Let's face it, if it was deliberate, then it must have felt so sweet!

George made his second signing at the turn of the year, and it was (surprise, surprise) another defender. Robert Molenaar is a colossus and seemed quite capable of attaining 'Blood on boots' cult status at Elland Road during his early days, but when the manager reshuffled his defensive pack as the season closed, he had to make do with a role as substitute. Two more new signings, Lilley and Laurent, which sounds like a haberdashery from the Thirties, made their debuts in early April, so it's too soon to pass judgement upon them.

So what of the other players that Mr Graham inherited? I'm very surprised that one of the independent TV companies hasn't taken up the option on the 'Foreign Leeds Star Wrangle' soap opera. Tomas Brolin and Tony Yeboah probably shared more column inches on the back pages than most of the other players put together. The script goes something like this:

Leeds pay a small fortune for big name foreign international; he is delighted to be given the opportunity to play in England; he will take time to 'adjust' to the pace of the Premiership; niggling injury curtails full fitness; still unfit six months later; declares himself fully fit; plays in one reserve game; tells tabloids that he should be back in first team; chosen as sub; papers reveal 'rift' with manager; rift denied; plays for ten minutes and is clearly unfit; player turns sulky. Etc., etc. It gets very boring at this stage as the contradictions and rumours continue. No doubt we'll end up paying someone to take Brolin off our hands - if we're lucky.

What I found even more disappointing is the Yeboah situation. When he settled down at Elland Road he was scoring goals for fun, and spectacular ones at that. He was the hero that we'd been waiting for, but after his injury arrogance and petulance took over, culminating in him throwing down his shirt after being substituted at Spurs. Now there are a lot of things that players can get away with before incurring the wrath of their supporters. Drug-taking, pocketing bribes, even wife-beating can seemingly be overlooked, but irrational as it may seem, when you insult the shirt, you insult the fans. I think that it probably has something to do with the fact that the team colours are one of the few constants in the game. Players, managers and chairmen (thank God) may come and go, but the colours and crest, in one variety or another, remain. The team shirt has become more of an emblem of support than anything else in recent years and fans have invested (in more ways that one) in this expression of loyalty in a big way. Okay, that's the deep and meaningful bit over.

Whilst we're on the subject of the supporters, what a great season it's been for being a Leeds fan. Forget the football, and the nature of this article underlines that it's been very forgettable; this year Leeds fans have brought back a little bit of magic attached to watching a game live. And that's live - in the flesh - not some sanitised TV version! Every fan likes to believe that the devoted who follow his/her club are the wittiest, loudest, proudest, looniest and loyalist bunch in the business, but Leeds fans really are unique - and we've proved it once again. Up and down the country this past season we've performed a half-time cabaret that has simply gob-smacked the home fans. Bare-chested, even in sub-zero temperatures, we've launched into our all-time favourite ditty, "Champions of Europe!" People simply don't know what to make of this phenomenon - and isn't that great?! If you can't beat 'em, baffle 'em - that's what I say. We don't need silly bands playing *Ilkley Moor* Mr Fotherby, we're Leeds and we're proud of it! The final game of the season was a case in point. Okay, so it's always special, but it was a great carnival atmosphere. I reckon we all stood up for the final quarter, there was loads of passion and noise, the sun shone, the ground was packed, the Kop bar even ran out of beer! All this for a team that finished in the bottom half. That word 'potential' that everyone keeps spouting - this paragraph can serve as its definition.

So what of the future? I think that this coming season is either going to be a rip-roarer, or a relegation rollercoaster. No middle ground this time I feel. We've added Hasselbaink and Haaland (*they* sound like a firm of boilermakers) and more are likely to have arrived and certainly departed by the time you read this. Beyond '97-98, the juniors are reigning League and FA Youth Cup winners, so that looks promising, although it should be noted that not one of the Youth Cup winners from four years ago remain at Elland Road. Early season optimism will no doubt have gripped me by the beginning of August and we'll all be shouting for United and St George!

THE TOMMY COOK REPORT

Brighton and Hove Albion

Dick Knight In, Dickhead Out!

Phew! So you expect a review of the '96-97 season in 2,000 words or less? To be honest I'm not sure that's possible! No amount of adjectives or hyperbole could go half way to describing the range of emotions Albion supporters felt in this, the season from hell. We can confidently say that no club has *ever* witnessed the kind of season we did - experiencing the kind of things we have. As ever, ladies and gents, Brighton and Hove Albion lead, others can merely follow....

Saturday May 3rd 1997 is a day that will live forever in our hearts and minds. Indeed, it is a day that we never ever dreamt (should that read 'nightmared'?) would happen. The scenario: Albion, *our* Albion - not West Bromwich or Witton, but Brighton & Hove - the team we followed to Wembley, to Old Trafford, to Highbury, to St. James' Park (er, that's both Newcastle and Exeter!), needing a draw on the last day of the season to avoid relegation... to the bloody Vauxhall Conference! If Doncaster, Darlington, Scunthorpe, and, er, Exeter, weren't bad enough on cold Tuesdays in March, what about Dover, Stalybridge, Gateshead and heaven forbid, Hereford! (Below the belt, that last one). As nightmare scenarios go, this one was on par with Crystal Palace winning the European Cup. Yeah, *that* bad.

Fate being fate meant that I missed out on the delights of Edgar Street, a honeymoon in Cuba when the tickets went on sale saw to that. So instead I sat, paced, squatted, paced again, jumped around, held head in my hands, etc, alone in my front room with just *South Coast Radio* and Tony 'excitable' Millard for company (ten minutes remained when he uttered the immortal words "Pass the bloody thing for Christ's sake" - impartial reporting at its best). It was absolutely the worst 90 minutes I have ever had to endure; quite how it felt to be one of the travelling three and a half thousand, I don't know.

Anyway, you all know the score - literally. Suffice to say, when the final whistle blew I jumped for joy and felt a totally unbelievable sense of relief.

As the result was relayed around the nation I switched from TV to radio, from channel to channel, catching all the sports round-ups, just to ensure it was true. It was. Commentators everywhere were offering sympathy to the Hereford fans. I must say I felt nothing for them - and if I'm honest, I still don't. That probably sounds selfish, but the truth is this: someone has to drop out of the league; every team knew that when the season kicked off. Hereford went down mainly because of their on-field inadequacies; we were only in our precarious position because of a pair of tyrants, about whom the words 'mis' and 'management' would be the very kindest ones you'd use. They tried to destroy our club and we didn't let them get away with it.

If the final weekend of the season saw tears of relief shed wholesale, then the previous one saw tears of sadness as we said farewell to our home, the Goldstone Ground, for the last time. Alas, too much was at stake to go out in carnival fashion, but as the final whistle blew and the pitch became a sea of singing, dancing and crying blue and white, only then did the thought that this place, this spiritual home of mine for more than 20 years, was to be demolished and replaced by Toy's 'R' Us. I took my turf and left.

Albion, of course, began the season with a three point suspended sentence over their heads, imposed by the FA for *that* game against York. Talk amongst the supporters was not, 'if we lose the points', but 'when'. Sure enough, with the team struggling on the pitch, and chief executive Bellotti and chairman Archer seemingly as entrenched as ever, it took until the visit of Lincoln City for a few hundred supporters to say 'enough is enough' and invade the pitch.

The FA, as they had been doing since the saga began, missed the point completely and instead of bringing a disrepute charge against the directors, plumped for the easy option and docked us two points. Hey, but what's two points when you're 11 adrift at the arse-end of the Football League? (And how come the only two sides to have points deducted this season were at the time bottom of their respective divisions?)

The laughable and contemptible way in which the FA treated our club galvanised the already growing protest movement. Throughout the season event after event took place: marches (in both London and Hove), match boycotts, mass walkouts, numerous stormings of the directors box (seeing Bellotti running for his life always 'Brightoned' up our games), picketing of Focus DIY and Bill Archer's home, throwing snowballs at Bellotti's windows (see, you don't want to mess with Albion fans!) and countless petitions/letter writing campaigns, etc. I suppose the protests culminated in the events of Saturday February 8th with 'Fans United'. Followers of most British sides, and a number of European ones too, were there to offer their support in our struggle - although I don't think anybody saw Man U fans in attendance; strange that, considering so many of them live in Sussex. It was at this point that we knew the world and his wife were aware of our problems. Such a pity then, Geoff Clarke and his colleagues at *Meridian TV* stitched us up when in their *Goodbye Goldstone Special* they shamefully let Archer (who appeared via a video link dressed as Captain Pugwash - eyepatch and all, I kid you not) and Bellotti (who closely resembled Master Bates) off the hook. Cheers, lads!

By now though, things had improved on the pitch. Jimmy Case had departed and Steve Gritt had been installed by the dictatorship, a fact that most Albion fans deeply resented; 'GRIT BELEIVES BELLOTTI BULLSHIT' was the heartfelt, if incorrectly spelt, slogan which appeared on the main stand wall in letters 3ft high to welcome our new manager. Steve soon won us over though by instilling belief, desire and most importantly, discipline to the team (at home anyway). On the road we were still shite - anyone who witnessed Peter Shilton's 1000th and easiest ever league game on *Sky* for Leyton Orient will testify to this. Still, at home we were unbeatable, the crowds picked up as a result and we went from having a ground in which you could easily swing a Bellotti to one where we were getting the highest gates in Divisions 2 *and* 3. The North Stand was seemingly packed each game and those in it gave nothing but 100% unerring support. Even a Palace source was moved to quote in the *Guardian* that if they'd had our beautiful but crumbling North Stand instead of their flash new all-seater, they'd have won automatic promotion. Praise indeed.

If Fans Utd was the pinnacle of the protest campaign, it also marked the start of a backlash against the club by supporters of some smaller sides. Gillingham's labelled us 'arrogant' and Hereford's fanzine said ours was a 'trendy' cause, jumped on because Brighton is a "wealthy, South East, London commuter town." Now Brighton has been described as many things, but this is a first! There were mumourings that we were getting too much attention and not enough was being given to the problems facing lower league football as a whole. To an extent this was true, but you have to realise that our club was not simply being mis-managed, or for that matter just being shafted by the big boys, it was being systematically destroyed by a wealthy absentee businessman and his odious sidekick. Brighton fans, in standing up so valiantly to the enemy and tirelessly campaigning and badgering, got the press on their side and garnered support from fans of other clubs. If Hereford and Gillingham fans are so concerned about the future of the game then there is nothing to stop them campaigning for what they believe in. Hereford United's fanzine editor posed the question in that last fateful game's match programme: "If Hereford were in the same position as Brighton, would Brighton fans help out?" To which there is only one answer: Yes, of course we would.

On the subject of Gillingham, or more to the point their chairman Paul Scally, he sensed the chance of making some cash at our expense and he let Bellotti tie us into a legally binding ground-share even though the FA, Football League and every Brighton fan on the face of the planet didn't want it to happen. He now wants us to fork out a quarter of a million quid whether we share or not. Yes Gills fans, it ain't only the big boys who try to screw you, eh? As they say, Scally by name...

And so to the present. We survived the dreaded drop, lost our ground and as I type, we still do not know exactly where we will be playing next season.

Dick Knight's consortium are now on board so things look rosier, albeit with Archer holding on to a 49~% stake. Oh yeah, and just for good measure, the toe rag Bellotti is still around too, but not for much longer we understand.

There is no real need to panic though, because the season doesn't start for ten weeks. The Greyhound Stadium, just 400 yards up the road from the Goldstone, is still the favoured option for next season, but quite whether it will be ready in time for an August kick-off remains to be seen. A temporary ground-share with Crawley Town is now definitely off; apparently they prefer to let the Crystal Palace Reserve team use it for their Capitol League games instead. A word of warning, Crawley folk: if you jump into bed with the devil, don't expect us to come running when you give birth to the hoofed bastard offspring of Ron Noades! The Albion theme tune, *Sussex By The Sea*, now officially contains the following line: "Good Old Sussex by the Sea, Good old Sussex by the Sea, apart from the bit where the Palace scum play, it's Sussex by the Sea..."

What of the prospects on the pitch? Well, there's supposedly nigh on two million quid in the transfer kitty. If spent wisely, and decent additions are made to the current squad, then promotion is the very least we'll be expecting. However, given the devastating blows we've received year on year since about 1991, anything could happen.

Source: *The Abbey Rabbit*

THE TRICKY TREE

Nottingham Forest

Up the Down Escalator

A Kevin Campbell hat-trick on the opening day of the season?

It happened, it *really* happened. I was there at Highfield Road on August 17th 1996 and I witnessed it. With my own eyes. I wouldn't have believed it otherwise. Unfortunately - and somewhat worryingly - I found what happened at the City Ground over the remaining nine months far easier to accept. Our fall from grace was surrounded by an air of depressing inevitability, as the name of Nottingham Forest became a laughing stock in football hotbeds up and down the country. Even Derby and Leicester got in on the act. We could sink no lower.

We only have the best interests of the club at heart!

We're not exactly short of people to blame for the fiasco that was the '96-97 season either. The club's 209 (now ex-) shareholders top many people's lists, for reasons that I could never hope to explain in sufficient detail within the number of words I'm allowed here. Suffice to say that many of them were blinded by pound signs and power (in that order), and forgot their obligation to the many thousands of supporters whose interests they laughingly claimed to hold so dear. September 27th was the day that then chairman Fred Reacher officially announced that the club was, in effect, for sale. It should have been a day of celebration, a day when Nottingham Forest finally shed itself of the antiquarian constitution that had become increasingly outdated as the big money men seized upon the idea of football as a sound financial investment. Instead, hindsight sadly marks it as the date on which the take-over fiasco began in earnest, as the club stumbled from one embarrassing attempt to sell itself to another. Despite assurances from the board of a pre-Christmas sale it was not until February 24th that the self-monikered 'Bradford Consortium' emerged victorious, and by then relegation was already a certainty in the minds of all but the most optimistic.

So what happened in the months between these two dates of destiny? Well, supporters' scapegoat no.2, Frank Clark, mumbled through increasingly incoherently post-match explanations for yet another appalling performance and painful defeat, until he was literally reduced to shrugging his shoulders and admitting he had run out of ideas. "There's so much wrong, I just don't know where to start..." was his now infamous and succinct summing-up of the situation at the time. Shit doesn't smell much worse than that! In fairness he did the decent thing and resigned, two days after the annual humiliation at Anfield. If ever there was an indication of the sheer desperation of our situation then that was surely it.

December 19th and only one man could save us now - his name: Stuart Pearce. Rothmans may tell the tale that Mr S Pearce was the man who took us down, but you won't find a single Forest fan who'd point the finger at Psycho. After all, he did enough to delay the inevitable until the penultimate Saturday of the season, and that alone must put him in the running for the England job when Hoddle decides to call it a day. Not only that but he ensured that we had accumulated enough points to avoid what many supporters had secretly feared as the final and most painful ignominy imaginable: relegation at Derby. Instead we went down the game after, at home to Wimbledon.

Had Clark remained in charge Ceefax would have been highlighting our name in red and following it with the tell-tale (R) long before May 3rd. So why the sudden fall from grace of a man who just twelve months previously was being touted as a successor to Terry Venables? Basically, Clark was given little money to spend while all about him were throwing millions around (away?) as though it was going out of fashion. The lack of financial backing was clearly not his fault. However, and this is the crucial point, when he did spend, he did so with startling ill-judgement, a far cry from his honeymoon period signings of Stan Collymore, Colin Cooper and Lars Bohinen. Campbell was the first and most expensive of the bunch, but you would be hard pressed to find any other Premiership club who would have even looked at the likes of Chris Allen, Alan Fettis, Andrea Silenzi and Nikola Jerkan, never mind actually bought them. Clark, however, spent the best part of six and a half million pounds on the five-a-side team from hell, despite his knowledge that the club had to count every penny in the spiralling transfer market.

They added nothing to a squad already threadbare by the standards of the Premiership's elite, and in the end they probably cost Clark his job. However, there were other mitigating circumstances. The loss of Steve Stone just five games in cannot be underestimated, especially as there was no-one anywhere near capable of filling his boots. Paul McGregor was a possible, but the 'first Britpop footballer' (how he must now hate that tag) seemed far more interested in pushing the merits of his band Merc than for a first team spot, and the right hand side of midfield offered no further threat for the remainder of the campaign as the likes of Dean Saunders, David Phillips and Alfie Haaland took it in turns to prove what we already knew - that Stoney is irreplaceable. Not that he can in any way be blamed for the shambles that passed for football over the ensuing months. In fact, his efforts to fight back from yet another career-threatening injury saw him shed a great deal more sweat than many of his colleagues, who, we were continually assured, were battling to keep Forest in the top flight.

While our prehistoric constitution clearly led to the cash-flow crisis and ultimately all but tied the manager's hands in the transfer market, turning us from UEFA Cup quarter-finalists to Premiership whipping boys in the space of twelve painful months, by far the biggest buck has to stop fairly and squarely at the doors of the changing room. It would be easier to pick out those players who emerged from the whole sorry shambles with reputations intact - step forward Messrs. Crossley (although a late season back injury prompted a return to bad old ways), Pearce, Cooper, Haaland (the only one to actually enhance his), Stone (despite taking part in less than 360 minutes of football), Chris Bart-Williams (at a hefty push) and Pierre Van Hooijdonk (signed far too late to prevent our relegation but showing all the signs of being able to 'do a Collymore' and take us straight back up). The rest weren't worth the paper their huge pay cheques were written on. Some, like Des Lyttle, Steve Chettle, Jerkan, Phillips, Scot Gemmill and Allen (I could go on) simply lost the plot and performed for the most part like badly-coached schoolboys, while others like Ian Woan and Bryan Roy clearly retained the necessary ability but simply couldn't be bothered to use it.

The threat of a Psycho left-footer up where the sun doesn't shine at least prompted a mini-revival around Christmas (funnily enough the only time all season Woan looked even half-interested), but even the re-introduction of a Clough into the City Ground plot wasn't enough and Nigel's departure coincided with the introduction of Dave Bassett as general manager. The irony was not lost on those of us who had watched helplessly as Forest's reputation for free-flowing play had disappeared almost as quickly as a safe Tory seat: a player who was living up to a family name synonymous with the beautiful game was run out of town by a man who gave the world route one football. The joke was on us but we weren't - and still aren't - laughing. Both at least avoided the ignominy of playing any part in the proceedings at Saltergate on February 15th (Clough was cup-tied and Bassett still 12 days away from walking out on Crystal Palace), when a season of countless lows reached its absolute nadir with the most inept and spineless of displays at Chesterfield as the 'giant killers' (some giant!) deservedly dumped us unceremoniously out of the FA Cup with humiliating ease. And that just about summed it up: a Forest side apparently devoid of all interest, confidence and cohesion being beaten by an honest and workmanlike performance.

So, what of the future? Well, let's just say we're a long way from putting on the shades. Our new owners, led by newly-installed chief executive and 'lifelong Forest fan' Phil Soar (don't worry, we'd never heard of him either until the club came up for sale - apparently he's big in the publishing world and has written a few books about football, though curiously never one about his 'beloved' Forest) promised to keep things "on the up" despite relegation, and to be fair they have stayed more or less true to their word. Mr Bassett is far from a universally popular choice as the man to lead us out of the nether regions of the Nationwide - supporters at Forest want to see the ball played on the ground, not in the air. (Nigel's dad had it about right: if God had meant us to play football in the clouds he would have put grass in the sky.)

But the ball is not the only thing 'on the up' at the City Ground - season ticket prices have followed suit. By almost 25%. Interesting, I'm sure you will agree. We are being asked to pay considerably more to watch the likes of Bury, Crewe and Stockport (no offence intended; I'm sure supporters of those clubs will get my point) than we were to see Manchester United, Liverpool and Chelsea. I suppose that's what happens when you have a 'lifelong fan' running the club, somebody who knows what it's like to have to scrimp and save every penny to follow their team through thick and thin. Still, not everything's bad news. Kevin Campbell is now halfway through his contract, which means he's got just two seasons left. Two seasons? Come back Fashanu, (almost) all is forgiven!

Sheepshaggers in the Premiership
No. 2 : Igor Stimac

Injured again, Igor receives treatment from the Derby physio Tom Jacks and Bob B

TRIPE 'N' TROTTERS

Bolton Wanderers

That's Entertainment

Issue 20 - Apr/May 1997
60 PAGES FOR 99p

BURNDEN

Sometimes you just know when a season's going to be good. But it was more in hope than expectation that loyal supporters of Bolton Wanderers set about the last nine months at Burnden Park.

After all, we'd just been relegated and coach Ian Porterfield had resigned in connection with a drink-driving charge. Many had attributed our vast improvement (honest!) in the latter stages of the Premiership campaign to Porterfield. Who could we get to replace him? Phil Brown, that's who. A folk hero in these parts, Browny was at the heart of all the good things during the '92-95 two promotion-gaining, cup-running, rootin'-tootin' Rioch era.

The expected and welcomed sale of Alan Stubbs was off-set by the signing of two hard-working Danish midfielders. But how were we going to fit Sasa Curcic into the 4-4-2 system that Colin Todd had pledged to use? Looking back now, it was obvious that we couldn't. But the mood of shock and anger upon his £4 million sale to Aston Villa three days before the Big Kick-Off (© *Shoot!*) could easily have turned against Todd and the club. What would the atmosphere be like for our opening match at exotic ol' Port Vale?

Luckily, it was great. Let Sasa go if he wants. Let people laugh at us. We don't care. From here on in, we wouldn't give a toss about anyone else. Balls to 'em. And at a stroke, that which could have divided Bolton Wanderers unified it.

First victims of this newly-forged fans' and team spirit were three of the favourites for the title. QPR, Norwich and (best of all) local rivals Man City were brushed aside by a club possessed. The wingers winged, the attackers attacked and the defence... erm, they attacked as well. In short, we grabbed the division by the balls. Even if some people attributed our success to our new 'teal' green away kit which was remarkably similar to a referee's.

Central figures in the Wanderers resurgence were players reborn: Alan Thompson, Nathan Blake and Gerry Taggart had wildly disappointing Premiership seasons, yet each took his department by the scruff of the neck and wrung out the winning habit. Blakey remembered how to score, Tommo remembered how to pass and Big Ged remembered how to growl at opposing forwards. With the stylish and guileful Danes Per Frandsen and Michael Johansen slotting freely into an already capable team, we effortlessly moved into first place, playing a fast-flowing, incisive passing and running game which the pride of the poor old Nationwide couldn't cope with.

Oh, we had our blip. The next time the issue of bungs to goalkeepers rolls around, one or two people might raise an eye at the scoreline Southend 5 Bolton 2, given the finishing positions of the two teams. But you can't complain really, when two months' worth of bad luck and performances comes at once. Especially when you go out three days later and twonk Grimsby 6-1.

By that time of year when people put effigies of leading Catholic dissidents on top of bonfires, we were six points clear and had put Chelsea out of the cup (no, the other one). Thus, it seemed like a slump when new promotion rivals (pah!) Crystal Palace, Sheffield United and Barnsley held us to draws. So we hammered somebody else 6-1; this time, Spurs.

Off the field, the club announced it was to sell off the name of our new £40 million stadium. Now this provoked a storm of mild ire. Several even wrote in to the local newspaper. *Tripe 'n' Trotters*, whilst against the decision, sold off some paperclips and tendered a bid of £284. The chief executive of the new stadium didn't accept our business proposal, but he did take out a subscription, so never mind. Dismayed at *TnT*'s sponsorship rebuttal, the team took four points from 21, giving Barnsley fans the highly improbable Christmas present of being top. Not for long though. Seven straight wins showed the rest of the division exactly who was top of the flat cap brigade.

During that run, Wolves came to Burnden baring their teeth. Four minutes had gone when new midfield string-puller John Sheridan had a disagreement with Geoff Thomas. New midfield wirecutter Jamie Pollock dived in to have his say, and 18 others did likewise; Taggart ran 20 yards into the middle of it at full pelt, goalie Gavin Ward raced 80 yards to kick somebody and Bryan Small stood aloof from it all with hands on hips.

Wolves were as rattled as they'd intended us to be, and were crushed 3-0 in an awesome Bolton display which some Wolves fans took simian revenge for, by throwing pies and threats at our six foot furry mascot. The FA found *Lofty the Lion* not guilty of any wrongdoing; the teams were eventually fined and warned as to their future conduct. By the end of the season, Bolton could put their £10,000 Fair Play prize money towards the fine. Within a month, Wolves were scrapping again at Bradford.

However, it soon became obvious that the only points decision affecting Bolton was the margin by which we'd win the league. While the team continued to find fascinating new ways to concede goals, simply no-one could live with our orchestrated attacking force. Lead violinist in this beautiful symphony was left winger Scott Sellars, who twinkled like a little star. The moaners did make a return after Chesterfield put us out of the cup (Burnden Park had to deliver one last cup upset), and Sheffield United left town with a point in the long ball bag. Moan, moan, moan!

More, more, more, said the Wanderers, as they picked up 28 points out of the next 30. The *Radio Wiltshire* commentator sobbed on air after seeing his beloved Swindon Town annihilated 7-0. But now the flair was welded to a pragmatism that led to a vastly improved defensive record. Quite simply, Bolton were a goal better than every team they came across.

With the league a formality, the target became 100 points and 100 league goals. The last five league games at Burnden saw the Trotters score 21 times. QPR were beaten 2-1 (again) to seal promotion in the first game after the Easter break, and suitably, it was club captain John McGinlay who clinched this elevation. The Championship was won, oh irony of ironies, at Maine Road. Mighty Mixu 'Moose' Patelaainen scored only his third goal in two seasons to equalise an early City goal; the *TnT* editors, through the selling of fanzines and the late arrival it sometimes caused, hadn't seen Moose score since we last clinched promotion at Wembley in 1995. Scott Sellars won the Championship with a marvellous slaloming run from the half-way line, thus confirming that you don't have to be Georgian to dribble.

A fun 4-0 at home to Oxford was followed by a frustrating 0-0 at Oldham which left us needing two wins and six goals from the last two games to become the first team in history to complete the double century. In our way were Charlton at home and a trip to former rivals Tranmere. The curtain came down on 102 years at Burnden Park on a Friday night of high emotion. Charlton, no strangers to leaving home, kindly agreed to take just 250 seats. So 22,000 Bolton fans saw BP close its doors for the last time and the Trotters come back from 1-0 down (it's that spirit again). John McGinlay made sure that the old lady had excitement right to the end by scoring the last ever goal at Burnden Park in the 89th minute.

And so, the last significant act at Burnden Park was the presentation of the Football League Championship Trophy. We all wanted that night to go on forever, but we had to leave eventually. Not before standing in silence, gazing misty-eyed at the place that had become a home. As an elegy, you can't beat a valedictory Championship, but it made it no easier to turn your back on the pitch and walk down that tunnel for the last time.

The fairytale ending needed two goals and a win to achieve the double hundred in the last game. Golden Boot winner McGinlay's 30th goal of the season set the stage, and Trampmere's equaliser mattered none when new terrace icon Jamie Pollock smashed home the ton. The players, those brave, brilliant men who'd brought us so much pleasure and thoroughly deserved credit, beamed with joy in front of the ecstatic fans. The season was complete. But hang on a minute. This is Bolton, not Broadway. That sort of scriptwriting might go down a bomb in Hollywood but it just ain't proper in Lancashire. If anyone looks less like Tom Cruise than our Jamie, he should stay indoors. The referee's whistle was in his mouth when Tranmere's Lee Jones smacked a quite brilliant equaliser past substitute goalie Ward (only on the pitch for the last five minutes to complete enough appearances for a Championship medal).

It was a crap ending to a brilliant story. Bolton had walked it by 17 points. History beckoned. Chelsea's record of 99 points was there to be deservedly broken by a supremely-controlled domination of the division, generally accepted to be the hardest to get out of; ask Wolves. (Sigh)

Bolton's success this season has been built on a special togetherness that can't be bought (ask Middlesbrough). The only player to be linked with a move to a 'big' club was Alan Thompson, a member of the midfield department stuffed full of match-winners: Thompson, Pollock, Sheridan, Sellars, Frandsen and Johansen. Not that one department won the league. John McGinlay and Nathan Blake, totally incompatible in the Premiership, became best buddies, Bonnie (Prince Charlie) and Clyde, shooting 54 goals and making enemies in grounds the country over. Keith Branagan between the sticks gained in confidence and won *Sky*'s Save of the Season award. A Ward named Gavin pushed him all the way and is totally trustworthy when guitar-toting Branny's injured. In front of the men in green, Gerry 'Beast' Taggart and Chris 'Consistency' Fairclough were a wall of class... eventually! And left-back Jimmy Phillips was born in Bolton.

So a season that began more in hope than expectation ended with exactly the same feelings. No-one in Bolton, not even the team itself, expects to win the Premiership in 1998. But even the most cynical of Bolton fans can now harbour hopes of setting up two new homes: The Reebok Stadium and the Premiership. Perhaps it's an indication of how far the team has come that many fans expect it.

TWO TOGETHER

Barnet

So there we were; after a fine finish to last season, we'd avoided having to unload any star players and now everything was set fair for a promotion push. Clemence had finally got things right and as long as we maintained a bit of stability this was going to be our year... Oh dear!

Just a few weeks after signing a new contract with Barnet, Clemence upped and left us to join Glenn Hoddle's England crusade (stop laughing). In response the club installed coaches Terry Bullivant and Terry Gibson as a managerial duo two days before the start of the season. Never mind, we thought, we could still do it.

TWO TOGETHER

A **Barnet** F.C.
Supporters Magazine

Issue Number
Seventeen
£1

"MAY THE FOUR-FOUR-TWO BE WITH YOU"

I won't dwell too much on what happened from then until October. Suffice to say that our respectable ninth position was a whole lot better than the bottom spot we'd occupied at the same stage last season. But then Terry Bullivant upped and resigned (spot a theme yet?) saying that the chairman had differing views on the direction of the club. Shortly afterwards Alan Mullery was appointed as 'Director of Football'. I challenge anyone to define exactly what this job was meant to involve. Mullery certainly didn't know.

It would be very easy for me to stop now, because our season effectively ended the day that Mullery was appointed. His joining was nothing short of a catastrophe for the club; he'd not worked in football for nine years, and boy did it show! For the next six months we were treated to some of the most inept football management and tactics ever seen at Underhill. The man obviously didn't have a clue.

The writing was writ large on the wall when Terry Gibson also upped and resigned shortly after Mullery's appointment. Gibbo was under the impression that day-to-day team affairs were his concern, so when Mullery entered the dressing room during half time at Colchester and announced that he was taking over, Gibbo understandably got the hump and bailed out.

Nevertheless, our director of football did enjoy a brief honeymoon period of six games unbeaten. Mullers was quick to lavish praise on himself, claiming that we hadn't lost since his arrival. Yet when someone pointed out that we had in fact lost at Colchester, he was mighty quick to remind all and sundry that Gibson was in charge for that one… well, for half of it anyway.

Divorce proceedings started with the defeat at that ever-so-friendly family club, Fulham. By all accounts Mullers had been quoted (out of context he later bellowed) that Barnet would be able to turn the Cottagers over at Craven Cottage. Their manager Mickey Adams had alluded to this in his programme notes and reckoned that the Fulham players would need no further motivation come three o'clock. Then, allegedly, Fulham defender Terry Angus decided to get a bit 'catty' and started to take the piss out of the ex-Fulham captain after the game. To which the raging Mullers insisted on an apology. Ooh the bitchiness!

Two comfortable wins followed over Doncaster and Farnborough. However, the Farnborough win on November 26th was to be our last victory until February 25th - a 15 match spell that saw us plummet from 6th to 23rd in the table. Be under no illusion; but for our half decent start, we'd have given Brighton and Hereford a run for their money. Needless to say the faithful started to get restless and "Mullery Out!" was regularly heard. He had to go.

This didn't stop the bloke blaming anyone within earshot: players were slagged off on a regular basis, fans were criticised for not supporting the team, but there was never a hint of self-admonishment. Oh no, *he* was doing a *great* job. After the 13th game without collecting three points he announced that the team had played "his way" for those first six winning matches, but they hadn't liked his style so he let them revert to "their way" for the next 13 and this was the return. Ah - so it was their fault, not his. Oh please!

Wins over Lincoln and Orient proved to be a false dawn as the next four games produced a draw at Exeter and defeats against Chester, Swansea, and Wigan. A 'Mullery Out' banner, unfurled at the Swansea game, also contained the statement 'The players were good enough before you arrived'. And an indication of the feelings in the dressing room became clear when Alan Pardew (yes, that Alan Pardew) offered to help put the same banner up at Wigan.

The news that we'd all been waiting for came on March 21st. After 158 days of incompetence, Mullery's tenure at the helm was ended as he simultaneously announced that he was only supposed to be the chief scout anyway (?). Terry Bullivant was reinstated as manager and the players duly responded with a win at home to promotion hopefuls Cambridge. At the end of the game it was great to see the whole team make a point of applauding the fans. Happy days were here again.

The rest of the campaign was played out in semi-contentment and we eventually finished 15th. But there can be no hiding the fact that '96-97 was a huge disappointment for Barnet fans, especially when last season's finish had given us realistic expectations of a play-off place at least. More worrying is what long term damage has been done to the club by the

Mullery interlude. While we're the first to admit that we didn't see eye-to-eye with Ray Clemence on many occasions, he did at least make some progress.

Off the field, the club is attempting to relocate to a nice new all-seater stadium, although where a club that can't afford to stock its club shop is going to get £15-20m from is anyone's guess. Still, something's got to be done. At the end of next season the Football League will introduce new and tougher minimum facility rules, and if they're enforced rigorously then Underhill will just not be able to stage professional football.

Last season my article ended with a moan about Fulham and their racist fans. Well just to let you all know, they were even worse this year!

THE LOCAL DRAMATIC SOCIETY'S 'RENT A CROWD'
CERTAINLY HELPED THE ATMOSPHERE...

Source: White Love

THE UGLY INSIDE

Southampton

"I'll just sit there and wait for the grass to grow"

Survival and the euphoria that went with it now seems like ancient history. Southampton Football Club has been thrown into the hands of people whose loyalty is to themselves and acquiring as much wealth as quickly as possible. They have demonstrated their total lack of football knowledge with a couple of absolute classic quotes which I will divulge later.

The future looks bleak unless we can dust them quickly. This is not a load of lefties going off on one because the capitalists have taken over the asylum, it is a concerted opinion shared by supporters and various high levels of authority.

"What the hell is happening at Southampton?," you may be asking. Well, let me try to explain. Over the years we have been duped into believing that the old board of directors were nice caring gentlemen acting in the best interests of the club, albeit at a snail's pace. Wrong!! Guy Askham, the old chairman who we described in *SOTF 2* as 'the vicar of bumble' has turned into the biggest wolf in sheep's clothing you will ever find.

Askham who joined the board in 1980 and became chairman in the mid-80's has spent a vast period of his involvement with the club greedily hoovering up shares at the ludicrously undervalued price of £1 each. Askham, an accountant, has been ruthless in his objectives. Relatives of deceased shareholders have been continuously blocked from inheriting both small and large holdings. Mr Askham has on several occasions only allowed share transfers when threatened by families with legal action. Concerted attempts to question the undervaluing of shares have been met with blunt reactions from the chairman who has always claimed he was worried about so called hostile take-overs.

Grave suspicion surrounds the legality of certain practices Askham has used in order to accumulate his share-hoarding. The use of nominee companies based in the same building as his former employers have aroused the suspicions of supporters, the media and official authorities alike. And yet when questioned, Mr Askham has remained tight-lipped, claiming to the BBC that these nominee companies were just like Lloyds Bank.

Askham also appears mainly responsibly for conducting a bizarre and disastrous reverse take-over Plc flotation, which has seen the arrival of Rupert Lowe, head of a relatively impoverished retirement home business, as new chairman. Lowe's total lack of football acumen combined with insufficient financial clout has so far seen the departures of both Graeme Souness and Lawrie McMenemy from the Dell.

This lack of finance was never more clearly illustrated than when supporters met with the board in June. Mr Lowe was asked five times what financial commitment had been put aside for the new stadium. Five times he replied with a complete load of waffle. He started preaching to us that we should be making representations to all the local councils to push for the stadium but not once did he give us a figure!

Arsenal and Coventry. I'm sure that Everton, Liverpool and Man Utd would have something to say about that!!

Then Andrew Dowder of Financial Dynamics, speaking to one of our colleagues regarding a *Daily Mirror* article exposing past share dealings of SFC, came out with this little gem: "Rupert and Andrew (another new director) can't be held responsible for any of this, in the same way we can't take credit for the *Jim McCalliog* goal that won the Cup Final." !!! (For anyone who can't remember that far back, it was the late Bobby Stokes, bless him, who scored.)

When David Jones was appointed manager we were outside the ground. Dear old Andrew of the Jim McCalliog fan club came out beaming and presented us with the official press statement. He was seeking approval and praise for the new appointment but was instead bombarded with questions regarding financing the new stadium, and was asked why the start date had been put back another year. He came up with the usual waffle about planning applications, then came the *pièce de résistance*: "Of course when it's finally built you then have to wait for the grass to grow!!" Mr Dowder, I've been waiting 37 years for the grass to grow on our new stadium and with you lot in charge I reckon I'll be waiting another 37...

These clowns have to go, but now we are a Plc it's not that easy. We have asked Rupert Lowe to sell up to a more realistic consortium who can fulfil our dreams. However it's up to the shareholders to make that move. By the time you read this we hope to have a new regime in place. If so, we have a future to look forward to! It will be mighty hard work but if everybody pulls in the same direction it can be done. If Rupert Lowe stays, it spells disaster for the long term future of the club. Our new club song, written by our team manager Davy Jones and the Monkees is:

> *Sell up Rupert Lowe*
> *Now it's time to go.*
> *For a underachiever,*
> *and a piss poor cash flow-oh-oh!*

I cannot finish without paying tribute to the efforts of the players, Graeme Souness and most importantly the fans at the back end of the season when another great escape was achieved. Coventry's may have been the most dramatic on the last day but our rise from the ashes in April surpassed all our recent brushes with disaster. There were so many pressure games against teams around us and we ended up winning three and drawing the other to turn the relegation fight on its head.

April 5th, Forest away was just one of those last chance games. Everything felt right and everything went right. The team spirit was there for all to see and the supporters responded. Then Derby midweek, where a battling display looked like ending in what would have been an unjust result, until Daryl Powell (ex-Pompey) scored an own-goal in the last minute. (What must he have felt like??)

April 12th, West Ham at home. Another shit or bust match and another win, marred slightly by Jason Dodd getting sent off. We had a great laugh playing a West Ham supporters' side connected with *Over Land & Sea*; they beat us narrowly but were a great bunch. See you next season lads.

Safety was firmly in our sights, but being a Saints fan you get used to being shot in the foot, and that was exactly what happened as we surrendered a 2-0 lead and were lucky to hang out for a point against Coventry at home.

A mammoth task now faced us. Sunderland away midweek; the last ever competitive night game at Roker. They were nervous as hell early on and we took advantage through Egil Ostnstad. It wasn't till Niall Quinn came on that their crowd got going, but when they did, boy was it noisy. That lifted their team and it was backs to the wall stuff as we held out for a vital win. I really felt for Sunderland fans when they went down and we'll miss them. Although it is a long old trip for us, they do respect you for making the effort.

May 3rd and daylight opened between us and Coventry and Forest as we did our annual stuffing of Blackburn at home. Middlesbrough could still overtake us but it was unlikely. And so it proved, in a massive anti-climax of a game at Villa Park on the last day. The match was awful but results elsewhere brought mass celebrations. Our triumph over adversity couldn't disguise an otherwise dreadful season, though. Our league struggles were only compounded by exits in the cups to Stockport and Reading Iceskaters FC, although there were a couple of dazzling performances, notably the ones when we hammered Man Utd 6-3 and beat Newcastle 1-0 away.

On staying up, Graeme Souness said "It's just like winning the FA Cup." What happened next?

UNITED WE STAND

Manchester United

There are definitely inflated expectations watching United these days. For so long the underachievers, now, due to 'public demand', only victories seem to do. Our support may seem to put out a 'United' front, particularly in the media where public hysteria follows any defeat, but Old Trafford is far from a happy place. Us and them. Out with the old and in with the new - the new with their carrier bags of souvenirs, their TV pundit analysis and their sit down, don't swear, "do you mind not drinking, smoking or appearing to have a good time please, after all I am as much a fan as you, and have been coming at least three years." Yep,

and not always in a Manc accent either. Do I sound bitter? You bet.

On a happier note, for the fourth time in five years we achieved greatness. Well, relative greatness. Europe is still the final frontier, the ultimate challenge, and also the ultimate reward for the fan. At least Euro aways are still done properly at United. Trips often involve four or five-day breaks with several stop-overs on the way, many finding the most bizarre routes to their destinations. So this season, with a minimum of five excursions on offer, was the best in years for the experienced traveller.

First up was Juventus, and as if the pre-season in Milan had been a rehearsal it was off to Nice for a week in the sun, broken up only by the return train trip to Turin. Nice is a millionaires' paradise and can be expensive, but if you head for any red light district you'll always find a nice little hotel that doesn't cost the earth. On the beach, prince and pauper look alike clad only in shorts, and as Reds seldom let you down on the dress front, the nightlife was sampled with gusto. The train trip, was if nothing else bereft of barmcake, beer and ticket collectors. However on arriving in Turin we were given a taste of things to come - a heavy presence of police dressed in riot gear which insisted on steering everybody away from any central meeting area. By mid-afternoon it had become apparent that this policy had failed and when most eventually made their way to the Stadio Del Alpi the armed guard had given up. The game told a tale of inadequacy, but the reception afterwards for the exiting fans was a timely reminder that in Europe memories are long; the batons and tear gas was perhaps only unreported in the media because of the lack of a celebrity victim.

Rapid Vienna at home brought some cheer and a 2-0 scoreline that reflected a competent United first half and more magic from Beckham and Solksjaer. After Euro '96 'The Wizard' had strengthened our squad with Poborsky and Cruyff. Karel (as he's definitely not known) and Jordi (who can't possibly be related to his dad surely) were deemed to be the final pieces in the European jigsaw. Mmmm... From the opening day Beckham decided to burden himself with superstar status by way of a ridiculous chip, and Solksjaer who was everything Cole had promised to be, decided otherwise. Right side of midfield was David's property and he would continue to prove this all season. As for Olly, well Alan Shearer may be dearer but few would swap him. £1.5m from a part-time Norwegian club, and he's only 12.

Next up was Fenerbahce. Just great - Istanbul for the third year running. To say the Turks are complete nutters would be unfair and Xenophobic. 1994 saw hundreds locked out, locked up and deported. 1995 saw us return and be treated like royalty. So this year saw us take more of a look at the 'bul, with the 'Pudding Shop' made famous by the film 'Midnight Express' being of particular interest. Unfortunately there are about 17 of them claiming to be the original one. Golden temples, beautiful palaces, ornate mosques. What more could you want? Well beer and women actually, so Istanbul isn't ideal, just hot and sunny, and as it turned out it was the calm before the storm.

The storm: by the time Fenerbahce returned to Old Trafford our league visits to Newcastle and Southampton had made national news headlines, PM's question time and a *Radio 5* 'crisis' phone-in; *Radio One* DJs garnered popularity with their rapier wit: "and the time's coming up to five past - five passed Schmeichel of course. Ha Ha!" And for his favourite meal? "Anything with chips." And you think we're paranoid? The country held a public holiday. Cheers for the invite, but we'll have ours in May thanks.

Fenerbahce at home was the disappointment of the year. Forty years of invincibility at OT was destroyed by one of its poorest visitors. Our 2-0 scoreline over there was made to look useless. We may have expected defeat at the hands of Juventus three weeks later, but this was ridiculous! Subjected to a cacophony of sound at home, the Turks folded, but met with the silent disbelief they encountered here they were able to take away the most impressive and proudest record in Europe without a struggle. To rub salt in the now gaping wounds, Juventus did prove as tough as we thought and a 0-1 scoreline despite a much more impressive performance left us with an uphill struggle to qualify.

I've never watched football in minus 11 degree temperatures before, but that was what was in store for our visit to Vienna. In line with our usual habit of making a holiday out if it, many made their way out of Manchester airport as early as Sunday (which I suppose is strange seeing as we are supposed to be nearer to Gatwick or Heathrow). Munich was the favoured destination for some, others preferred Prague or Bratislava. None seemed disappointed with their choice, although parties that had gone via the Czech borders found the beer prices much increased. Vienna is stunningly beautiful, and apart from the ones with guns who shot the two lads from North Manchester, most of the people were friendly, which is a change when you watch United. We needed a result and by the time Cantona bagged our second, the score from Turin confirmed our fate. Nine points was enough to take us through to the QF stage. Mission accomplished, and it was time to play catch-up in the league. The Wizard promised that by the time of Porto's visit in the spring we'd be top. And we were.

T-shirt and shorts weather would be a nice change to the winter cold, and Porto greeted us with a heatwave, cold beer and overspilling bars and cafes. For some the Algarve seemed the natural choice, others chose Lisbon and a few Madrid. Ferries booked months in advance were full, as were the roads through France and every available flight. This was our biggest game in years, and Manchester had been alive with travel talk for months. The game as a spectacle was dead; the Portuguese Champions were destroyed at home 4-0, with Giggs' finest performance. It was now time to party and there were 11,000 guests. Unfortunately the stadium was of Heysel quality and the police decided to shoot their way out of trouble. It was again a sad hangover from what we hope are the dark ages of football. To dwell on these events would be to ignore a proud achievement - as a European force, we were learning quickly.

Two legs against Borussia Dortmund would give us the chance to emulate the heroes from '68, but it wasn't to be. Many that travelled had used every excuse in the book to get time off. Dead relatives, dodgy wisdom teeth, bad backs and sick children coincided frequently with a change to Coronation Street's programming time. Unfortunately these excuses were put away for another year as two 1-0 defeats left us regretting missed chances. We may have been top Premiership scorers, but Europe was a different matter!

As for the rest of the season, the League Championship was landed on Merseyside, and Liverpool eventually finished fourth in a two-horse race. Newcastle learned that he who laughs last certainly laughs longest, and of course Eric retired - a pity because one more crack at Europe would have been fitting for our King. He brought us the Holy Grail after 26 years and gave us back our dignity. He was a god on and off the pitch and for him to leave at the top was the only way to go. His legacy? For the pubs around Manchester to be once again next year filled with the inevitable, "What ya doin' for Charin/V-N-orr/Part-o/ Dort-mond?" Cheers Eric.

VOICE OF THE BEEHIVE

Brentford

Bloody Brentford. Bloody, *bloody* Brentford. I'm sorry, but it needed to be said. Bloody, bloody, *bloody* Brentford.

For more years than I care to remember there has been the conspiracy theory around Griffin Park that Brentford don't actually *want* to get promoted. In fact the phrase 'you don't want to go up Brentford' has become, like the first cuckoo of spring, a call to listen out for. Sometimes we hear it as early as the first game, but it's most commonly heard around transfer deadline day as another decent player goes

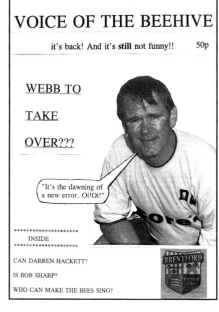

through the door marked 'Exit' never to return. Brentford are a cruel club who haven't even got the dignity to be crap all season. They lead us on like bewildered tourists in a Soho clip joint. We're shown flashes of talent, we're tantalised as the team go on a record unbeaten run, we're teased with a long spell topping the table. But just when we think it really might be our season the whole house of cards comes tumbling down, leaving us with egg on our faces and too many cooks spoiling the broth (I know that last bit doesn't make any sense, but I've got a cliché quota to fill).

To be fair the Bees had an excellent start to the '96-97 campaign, losing only two out of the first 15 matches, and *those* were against Blackburn in the Coca Cola Cup. What's more we weren't just not losing, we were winning! Our front line of Nicky Forster, Bob Taylor and Carl Asaba were rattling in the goals, the midfield were tigerish and the defence were playing as though they actually knew what they were doing. Total Football! Things were going really well and like flies, we had been lured into Dave Webb's, er, web. The sun was shining, goals were being scored and the Bees were sitting proudly at the top of the league; even our pre-pubescent cheerleaders, The Babettes, had won the European Championship (that's the European Cheerleading Championship you understand, not the football one. That would be silly). Yep, we had been suckered once again.

Brentford could have, and should have, easily achieved automatic promotion to Division 1. We were even in the position where we could afford to lose games and still stay top. Come January the Bees were four points clear and looking unstoppable. So, if *you* were running the club, which of the following options would you choose at this point?

a) Keep faith with the squad you've got?

b) Spend a few bob to strengthen the team in preparation for the run-in?

c) Piss on your chips by selling your best player?

I'm sure you can guess which option Brentford took. Nicky Forster packed his bags, went through that door market 'Exit' and vanished off to Birmingham. If Nicky was as good as he should be, then he'd be very good; sadly he's only as good as he can be bothered to be on the day. That aside there was always the chance he would do something special and he certainly had an eye for goal. Also he was the only Brentford player with the ability to unlock, as opposed to batter down, opposing defences. After his departure the Bees won the next couple of games, lulling us into thinking we could survive without him after all. Then the inevitable happened and the goals dried up. Partly it was general incompetence, partly it was bad luck, mostly it was a lack of confidence. Tireless workhorse Bob Taylor suffered the most; game after game he was hitting every part of the goal apart from that big netty bit in the middle.

Not surprisingly the Brentford faithful were getting just the slightest bit pissed off, especially when the transfer deadline came and went without anybody being bought to replace Forster. We started to see our lead slip and only managed to keep up with the promotion race thanks to the other challengers having equally poor runs. Things came to a head after a lame 1-0 defeat at Preston, when a few supporters started to tell Mr Webb exactly what they thought of him and his decision to let Forster go without a replacement. Dave Webb showed what a tough fighter he was by mincing back to Griffin Park and slapping down a letter of resignation on the chairman's desk (who'd have thought that big jaw of his would be made of glass?). Webb's tantrum turned into farce when his letter remained unread for a couple of weeks as chairman Martin Lange was, as usual, in America. Upon his return we had the obligatory statement of support for Webb and condemnation of "a handful of disloyal fans." Yeah, lots of casual, part-time supporters make the trip to Preston just to slag off the manager. Doesn't it piss you off when you get called 'disloyal' just because you dare suggest that things are less than perfect at the club you spend so much time, money and effort supporting?

He even went as far as to threaten to ban from Griffin Park any supporters who criticised the players and management. This led to the worrying sight of PC Plod filming Bees supporters in the club's last home match against Peterborough, no doubt on the look-out for dissenters. (Must be fun in the police viewing room watching a video tape of five and a half thousand Brentford supporters giving them the finger.)

The Bees' last four games were dire and saw the team lose to high-flying Crewe, and not-so-high-flying Blackpool, Walsall and Peterborough in succession without scoring a single goal in reply - in fact we only managed six in the last 14 matches. Ouch! But, thanks to nuts gathered during the winter, we were assured a play-off place and were to face Bristol City in the semi-finals. Dave Webb, in a typically Del Boy-esque manner, said he'd rather be sitting on a beach drinking a Pina Colada than going through the agonies of the play-offs. Had he managed to hold on to, or at least replace, Nicky Forster then we *all* could have been on beaches drinking Pina-bloody-Coladas and planning our trips to Nottingham Forest, Sunderland and QPR but instead we had to face a two-legged semi-final.

After the Bees' poor end to the season (winning only four times in their last 15 matches, Aaaaaah!) and their unerring ability to fall to pieces on the big occasion (to Brentford, playing against a team whose stadium has a tea bar is a big occasion), I didn't fancy our chances of making it to Wembley for the final. I'm ashamed to say I didn't even go to Ashton Gate for the first leg game, electing to watch it on the box instead. I thought the disappointment of losing wouldn't seem so bad in the comfort of a friend's house with a couple of beers to drown my sorrows. Bloody, bloody, *bloody* Brentford. We only went and won 2-1, didn't we! Goals from Paul Smith and (gasp) Bob Taylor put us in the driving seat for the second leg match at Griffin Park the following Wednesday. I still had the sickening feeling that we'd blow it as playing in front of a home crowd seemed to turn the players into gibbering wrecks of ineptitude. But no, we won 2-1 with goals from Marcus Bent and another from Bob Taylor (who certainly picked the right time to remember what his job was; "Oh *now* I get it, you want me to put the ball in the back of the net!").

So, much to our surprise we had a Wembley final to look forward to. More importantly, we had another chance to secure the promotion we should've had stitched up months beforehand. Of course I started telling anyone who would listen that the result wasn't important just as long as Brentford played well. Of course I was talking bollocks. Despite having been let down on so many previous occasions I still walked up Wembley Way on that sunny May afternoon thinking, nay believing, that Brentford would win. Fool! I even shelled out £1.50 for a crappy rosette (well, you do don't you?). Having taken my seat, made the usual nervous jokes with friends and 'enjoyed' the pre-match entertainment (some gospel singers and kids waving flags around) the game kicked off.

Brentford were magnificent! Well, they were OK for the first seven minutes. After that we were already regretting the money wasted on silly hats and wigs and were wondering if we should leave early to beat the rush. (Rush? The game only attracted 34,000 punters - the Northampton v Swansea game the previous day got more than that!) The Railwaymen looked like a team who knew where they were going and weren't going to let a pile of damp leaves like Brentford knock them off track. We on the other hand looked like a team who didn't want to make the journey in the first place and couldn't go anyway because we'd left our *Supersavers* at home. Crewe won 1-0 and should have scored several more. They played well and good luck to them; they'll certainly grace the First Division more than Brentford's leaden up-and-under game would have. I couldn't even take comfort in our lads' commitment and fighting spirit - they didn't show any. It's a sad day when your team gets to Wembley and plays so badly that you can't even be bothered to clap them off at the end.

The Brentford spin doctors (or spin quacks in the Bees' case) will no doubt try to package the '96-97 campaign as a wonderfully successful 'almost' season. We supporters know better. Not for the first time we'd been let down by the inability of the manager and chairman to see beyond the chance of making a quick buck at the expense of promotion (it woz selling Nicky Forster wot lost it) - and they still wonder why morale is low and attendances are falling... But yes, I'll be back next season.

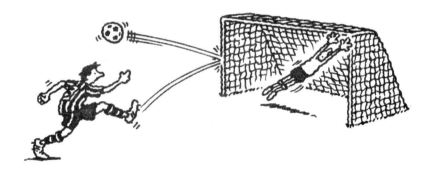

VOICE OF THE VALLEY

Charlton Athletic

It's tough being a fanzine editor at Charlton.

Times are comparitively calm, although it wasn't always this way, as *Voice of The Valley's* title pointedly reminds us. But it would be churlish to deny that things in the SE7 garden are relatively rosy these days. The summer of 1997 sees a magnificent new main stand taking shape on the west side of the pitch, paid for entirely by money raised in the City at no apparent detriment to the supporters.

The directors - who at 13-strong have a bigger squad than manager Alan Curbishley had to

Voice of The Valley
The INDEPENDENT Addicks mag

| No 65 | March 1996 | £1 |

Club splashes out in bid to revive promotion hopes

Addicks sign foreign player

☐ Did MI5 use Charlton to spy? The full incredible tale after 50 years

Are you sure it's not just Colin Walsh in drag?

☐ And we open the book on betting at The Valley — are you being ripped off?

choose from at times during the season - have proven and strengthened their commitment to open government, with an elected fan on the board, and are remarkably accessible. Gates held steady despite a poorer season on the field and there are encouraging signs that we've already outgrown the 15,000 capacity and need the new seats. Even the miniscule club shop, bane of the matchday visitor since the club returned home in 1992, is being demolished and replaced with one six times its size.

OK, so there's the team, which finished 15th in the First Division and flirted with doing worse. But even they held Liverpool and Newcastle to draws in cup competition (the Geordies requiring a Shearer special to eliminate them in replay extra time at St James' Park). Actually, it's Curbishley's misfortune that there is so much to smile about, because Charlton fans do like a moan so he's really the only available target.

Take Carl Leaburn. Please! Charlton's perennial big man up front was once more a fixture in the side, scoring a distinctly average nine goals. But he spent the entire season out of contract, hoping for a move to the Premiership. At the time of writing, he's still waiting, to no-one's great surprise but his own. I've always defended Carl, along the lines that he contributes much more to the team than his goals, which is just as well. It's also true that the Addicks look lost without him, although I tend to think this is because he looms too large in their plans in the first place. But his time is up. He needed to move on last summer and so did Charlton. What we got from him was a season of uncertainty, which almost undermined the best transfer deal of the year.

Midfielder Mark Kinsella arrived on trial from Colchester at the beginning of pre-season training. It was obvious from the outset that he was a star and that the £150,000 asking price was a steal. On Tuesday August 6th the deal looked signed and sealed. Twenty-four hours later it unwound alarmingly, apparently because of a bizarre dispute over when the money would be paid. By that weekend, Curbishley had decided that his priority was now a forward as cover for Leaburn and Kinsella was left in limbo (Essex actually, but it's the same thing).

So Charlton duly kicked off with a demoralising 1-0 defeat at Huddersfield, which set a miserable trend. They went on to lose all of their opening seven away games, the nadir coming with a 4-0 midweek defeat at Tranmere during which we are given to understand that voices were raised, to put it politely, in the dressing room at half-time.

Despite five wins and two draws in the first seven home games, significant damage had been done to the team's always slim chance of emulating the previous year's play-off place. In fact the Addicks did not win away in the league until they visited Norwich on November 2nd. And guess who scored the winning goal? Yes, Mark Kinsella with a sublime shot from 25 yards. More of the same later. Charlton had eventually gone back for their man at the end of September, paying the same fee as previously agreed, when he seemed on the brink of joining Gillingham. It was vindication of managing director Richard Murray's claim that they had always retained first refusal on him. But it was difficult to see what had been achieved by the delay.

Here, finally, was a man to fill the departed Lee Bowyer's boots. But it was too late.

Kinsella's debut against Oldham, fittingly, was marked by a visit from famous Dutch band Kleintje Pils, who serenaded the bemused players throughout the game. David Whyte gave the crowd more to sing about by coming off the bench to grab a last-gasp winner. But here, too, were the seeds of disappointment.

The Addicks' leading scorer of '94-95, with 21 goals, was trailed to be on the comeback. And as he hit a purple patch of five goals in six games, the claim seemed justified. But the maverick Whyte, never a strenuous competitor, began to believe his own publicity too. At Tranmere he was withdrawn at half-time amid complaints from team mates about his attitude. At Norwich four days later he was dropped. And on the Monday, he was transfer-listed. Unbelievably, the club at first announced that this was at his own request. This was hastily amended to 'mutual consent' by wiser heads.

That might have been the end of him, especially as replacement Bradley Allen responded with three goals in five games. But Allen got injured. Back came Whyte with three in four and we thought we were in business. But the goals dried up and so increasingly did the fans' patience.

On January 11th at Reading, Whyte scored a goal of breathtaking arrogance that was to prove his final strike for the club. The other Charlton goal in the game was a scuffed shot from teenage substitute Kevin Lisbie. As one door closed, another opened. The match, incidentally, was the first away draw of the season. By now, there had been four away wins, but since they were matched the following week by a fourth home defeat, progress was limited. Still, at least the FA Cup provided a glorious and lucrative interlude. In front of *Sky's* cameras, Mark Kinsella (of course) guaranteed us another crack at King Kenny's outfit with a glorious long-range strike.

Having already re-signed Anthony Barness from Chelsea, Brendan O'Connell from Barnsley and more recently taken Gary Poole from Birmingham, Curbishley moved into the transfer market yet again. First, one-time Charlton youngster Jason Lee returned on loan and a week later the £400,000 signing of another striker, Steve Jones from West Ham, was sealed.

Lee and Leaburn looked an unlikely combo, but Tranmere were duly battered into submission on its debut and at home it worked a treat. Steve Jones, meanwhile, immediately aggravated a knee injury and was never seen again.

Just when a relegation struggle looked on the cards, however, the Addicks put their collective foot down and pulled away. A scruffy home win over QPR and a delicious one over Palace - the first such victory in nearly 12 years - were swiftly followed by three points at WBA and the danger had passed.

By now Andy Petterson had taken over in goal from an injured Mike Salmon and no review of this season would be complete without mentioning his breathtakingly awesome save from a Neil Shipperley header. Not only did it prevent Palace taking a first half lead but it also helped the Australian to become the least likely supporters' Player of the Year ever. Other than that it's best to tactfully draw a veil over what remained, although a nice warm blanket and a pillow would have made it more comfortable at the time.

Why so little cause for complaint, then? Largely because the relative failure of the Charlton players to set the pulse racing during '96-97 was substantially offset by events off the field which produced their own diversionary momentum. Nevertheless, Curbishley will have to do better in '97-98, but he knows that. The well-worn excuses of refereeing incompetence and freak injuries won't suffice again. Fans' expectations will rise with the new stand, as they have at every stage of The Valley's rebirth.

Who knows - there could even be something to write about in the *Voice*.

WAKE UP BLUE

Birmingham City

"He's coming home, he's coming home, he's coming..." roared the fans, as the hero strode out into the sunshine of St Andrews to take his place as the 27th manager of Birmingham City. The return of the messiah. Trevor. The Son of God. Granted, the name doesn't have the same impact as Jesus, but for the Blue half of the second city this indeed was the second coming. If TF couldn't rouse the sleeping giant and kick him into England's footballing elite, nobody could. QPR and Sheffield Wednesday fans may at this point wonder whether the euphoria of Euro '96 had mutated into a severe form of madness within the walls

WAKE UP BLUE-"FULL OF MORE SHITE THAN MARK McGHEE"

of Brum, but what they will fail to understand is that TF, the man about whom thousands in the seventies sang "Walked on water," is the only truly great thing to have happened to Blues in recent times. And it has always been written in Brummie footballing folklore that when he returned to the club which launched him to stardom, Birmingham City would finally rid themselves of the tag 'unluckiest team in world football' and assume their rightful place amongst soccer's elite.

Forget the fact that he may be a crap manager; cometh the hour, cometh the man. And the '96-97 season would be our hour and Trevor would be our man. He quickly got to work. The captain of Manchester United was signed with David Sullivan proudly boasting he would easily be the highest paid player in the First Division at a reputed salary of £17,000 a week. And it didn't even bother us that he was 34 and could soon be past it; this was genuine excitement. Further big-name signings were rumoured, then those rumours became reality. Boom! Barry Horne, 33. Boom! Garry Ablett, 32. Boom! Mike Newell, 31. Was there some sort of pattern emerging?

Yet the icing on what had to be this promotion cake of a team was still to come: the top class striker that Trevor needed, the fans wanted and the chairman was going to buy. Who was going to wear the Royal Blue No.9 shirt? We screamed, we partied, drank champagne and celebrated big-time as it emerged that we were in talks with Jean Pierre Papin, ex-European footballer of the year, formerly of Marseilles, A C Milan and Bayern Munich. We sighed, sat down, slurped a four-pack of Skol and watched Coronation Street when we signed Paul Furlong, formerly of Coventry, Watford and Chelsea. Even now I can still hear Ken Bates laughing.

The first game of our season came with a *Sky* appearance and big media coverage; it was obvious that the extraterrestrial ones wanted to kick-off the live Nationwide matches with a team full of known faces. And Steve Bruce was an even bigger draw, though if we'd known then that most of his appearances on *Sky* from then on would be from a studio with the caption 'ex-Manchester United' under him rather than in a Blue shirt captaining Birmingham City, we might have told them to bugger off...

We won 1-0, after being outplayed by Crystal Palace, with a goal from Paul Devlin. Six points from the next six games, and failing to score in four of them, proved to be an early warning sign of trouble ahead. It was also becoming clear that the goals promised by Messrs. Newell and Furlong were not coming.

A riot at Man City by the travelling Zulu Army successfully managed to redesign Maine Road's seating and more importantly direct attention away from our poor start, as did Gary Poole's sending off after we conceded a last-minute penalty. The referee, Richard Poulain, claimed he suffered whiplash after Pooley pushed him, trying to grab his attention. Fair enough it wasn't the cleverest move by our right back, but *whiplash*! If ever the ditty "the referee's a wanker" applied, it was to this geezer! Three months later Mr Poulain was injured after being hit by a blown kiss from his wife on their 25th wedding anniversary.

Two weeks on and only into October, a press release from St Andrews was released stating that our owners, the unholy trinity of porn, David Sullivan and the Gold Brothers, might be leaving, due to an impending court case brought by Birmingham City Council. This was absolutely fantastic. I raced around work with the news. It was great saying "Have you heard?" to people when you know they hadn't. I've not had so much fun since Robbie left Take That.

Days later it was confirmed as a big publicity stunt. For what reason nobody knows, but we suspect that it was probably a temper tantrum in the boardroom about fans who had reported the club to the Council's Trading Standards department. It was probably also a reaction to the impending court case over the away travel scheme set up by the innovative Karren Brady, which was eventually proved in court to have ripped-off the fans. This rocked the world of football; surely it can't be so?!

During all of this nonsense, new signing Mike Newell announced that he wanted to leave the club because the commuting was getting him and his family down. Just ten games into the season and Francis agreed to let him go. The lad was clearly not fit; it was probably carrying his wages every week that did his back in. It was also around this time that we realised that we were not going to feature on *Match of the Day* next season, and that the club had been more stable under Barry Fry; a statement that I don't make lightly.

A hum-drum set of results which saw us hovering just above mid-table was punctuated by one of the two highlights of the season: an away win at

Wolves. The pleasure at beating the scruffy yam yams wasn't purely because it was our first away victory, four months into the season, but rather because it enabled us to stick it up Arsehole McGhoo - a character ranked up there with Adolf, Fred West and Jeremy Beadle in the popularity stakes. The other highlight was Paul Devlin and his increasingly confident and superb displays; why did they continue the constant comparisons between him and those of his so-called superior strike partners Newell and Furlong who'd managed only eight goals between them?

After a second away win at Norwich we'd reached a mighty seventh in the table, and promotion hopes were rekindled further when a home win over Barnsley three days later gave us a place in the hallowed ground of the top six.

We didn't realise it then, but that was about as close as we were going to get to a promotion place. A run of six losses destroyed our season and the cynics had a field-day. They cited the £2.5m transfer of Garry Breen, our international central defender, to Coventry as one of the main causes of our malaise. Yet watching his performances for Cov over the next few weeks on *Match of the Day*, we reckoned a new theory was needed on why the defence that had been the best in the First Division was now suddenly shit!

Amongst this painful run of losses was the season's low point. Low point... what an understatement! After knocking out Stevenage Borough and Stockport County in the FA Cup we were presented with a home draw against the Welsh tinkers from Wrexham, and our best chance to go forward in the cup for over a decade. Shit, shit, *shit*. In the most gutless and shameful performance of the season we lost 3-1. Finding out that Chesterfield would have awaited us in the quarter finals only heightened the furious response from the Blues; it's just not every day that you get such a comparatively easy path to the final of the world's greatest club competition. The only tiny consolation was that at least we got further to the twin towers than the Villa.

Two months before the end of the season we became BCFC plc. The prospectus told us that the squad has been valued at just under £8m by a footballing expert: Howard Wilkinson. Yes, that's right, the bloke who valued Tomas Brolin at £4m.

The last part of a disappointing season saw us go on a bizarre ten match unbeaten run including away beatings of ultimately promoted Barnsley and Crystal Palace. Sickening. In tenth place we finished, and we'd hammered all the division's biggies. So to round up: Devlin won Player of the Season, Furlong failed to score enough goals, Newell - not even able to interest a shite team like Bradford who he was on loan with - is still with us, Horne has been dropped after failing to have a shot all season, and TF is rumoured to be leaving after not getting the millions promised to him for a summer spending spree.

Have we got the Blues? You bet.

WE ARE LEEDS

Leeds United

How can I review something that I've already forgotten, even though it only finished two weeks ago? It's true! The '96-97 Leeds season was *so* dull and *so* boring right the way through that all the games seemed to merge into one. I'll give you an example. We were originally due to play Derby County at home on March 29th, but for some reason the game was brought forward a couple of months. On March 29th proper, I swear to God, nearly 30,000 turned up for the original fixture. Nobody could remember playing the first game!

Anyway, here goes. We kicked off at the Baseball Ground and our ever-consistent defence played so badly they made it look like we had a midfield and attack - oh, how we were fooled. Elland Road's first action was the curiously over-hyped derby match against Sheffield Wednesday. In reality the simple truth is that we care very little about them, and I'm sure the feeling is mutual. We lost 2-0.

Early in September we were treated to the annual visit of our friends from anywhere but Manchester. Now, never in my life have I been anything but contemptuous towards them. Thirty seven years of bitterness cannot be easily forgotten. However, for once in my sad life I have to swallow my pride and offer a tiny amount of begrudging acknowledgement (still falling short of gratitude, though) for the part they and their fans played in the eventual downfall of Howard Wilkinson. We'd been trying to shift him for years, but all it took on the day was one 4-0 defeat and a couple of 'Wilko for City' chants, and that was it. They got him sacked before Monday lunchtime. Which brings me nicely to the Wilkinson-Graham affair. Now this fine club of ours usually takes months of negotiations with incoming players, before the guy concerned goes and signs for someone else. Yet we are asked to believe that the same body of men, without the benefit of prior knowledge, pulled off the sacking of Howard Wilkinson, had a couple of board meetings, interviewed and installed George Graham in what amounted to just about 24 hours. Hmmm... But don't get me wrong, the whole affair couldn't have made me happier.

Did you ever meet the girl of your dreams? She can understand football like any you have ever met, she drinks like a fish, cooks like a master chef, looks like a star, and much, much more. Well I met mine, just as the campaign entered its second half. Unfortunately by the time it ended she was gone, back to her world of black Porsches and Armani suits. I should have guessed, because that's the way the whole season went. We had the much published take-over, then found out they intended keeping the same old chairman. We were promised millions of pounds for the transfer market; during the first eight months of George's reign we signed four players for just two million between them. We got a used Ian Rush, who promised us that he'd share 50 goals with Tony Yeboah, he scored three and Yeboah was abused out of the club. We got a new manager, and thought things must get better. They got worse. 'If we can stop teams scoring, the goals we score will win us a place in Europe', we dreamed. We stopped scoring. We won at Arsenal in the fourth round of the cup when all the big clubs were dropping like flies. A home draw against First Division Portsmouth conjured up thoughts of cup glory. Pompey put three past us. Oh yes, the season was one big failed love affair!

Considering my famous prowess with the opposite sex (or lack of it, more like) it seems hard to believe but during '96-97 even *I* scored more times than Ian Rush. All that said there were three or four points of amusement. Oh all right, two or three.

Since being robbed in Paris all those years ago, as a show of defiance, our fans have chanted "We are the Champions... Champions of Europe" at every opportunity. This season with the cold weather, while all the foreigners (and John Barnes) togged-up in their tights and gloves (especially at Rio de Riverside where mid-winter sunshine is a pre-requisite for some) the lads started braving the arctic conditions and doing it topless. As the weather warmed up a bit towards the end of the season, some of the girls even joined in. And why not? Equality for all - that's what I preach; why should the girls have all the fun? This generally went down very well with the opposition, who took it for what it was: a bit of fun. I did say generally, didn't I? The exception was that jolly First Division place they call Sunderland (they of the eternal 'We won the Cup' chant) where the natives took exception to it. Those trendies in their platform shoes and three star jumpers spat, threatened and threw their pies at us. To this the local stewards reacted by jumping in and ejecting Leeds fans for daring to smile in Wearside.

Other high points? Well, relegating Bryan Robson's Middlesbrough was a laugh. It's nothing personal against Boro but we do enjoy sending teams down. This is purely out of spite you understand because nobody cried for us when we went down. Also memorable was the stick Alan Shearer got for whining and moaning until he got Carlton Palmer sent off. The press that man gets, you'd think he was some kind of deity. Some of us fans see a different side to him.

The chants of the season had to be "We'll score again, don't know where, don't know when," and at Forest, remembering union allegiances during the miners' strike "Barnsley up, Forest down, hallelujah." Anything else? No, that's about it really.

WHAT A LOAD OF COBBLERS

Northampton Town

The date: March 22nd, the place: Field Mill, Mansfield, the time: 4.50 pm. It was all over. The season that had started with hopes of reaching the play-offs had surely just ended. We had just been subjected to the most abject display of the season against a poor Mansfield side. We'd even had the chance of snatching a win when we were awarded a penalty. With regular spot-kicker Roy Hunter suspended, there was confusion when both Jason White and David Rennie grappled for the ball. Eventually Rennie took the penalty, but hit it so incredibly slowly that the 'keeper had time

How many more times, boy, You must ALL get back in the box at corners.
After all, if its good enough for Ian Atkins then....

to nip home for his slippers before catching the ball one-handed. Mansfield won 1-0. A thousand travelling Cobblers trudged away disconsolately; a season that had started poorly but by New Year had seen us in prime position for the play-offs had to be over. How could we even consider a top seven place after that? A few people vented their anger vocally at the players and the manager. We felt let down; cheated.

At that moment I thought, bugger it, if they can't be bothered to perform I can't be arsed travelling to Torquay on Easter Monday. Meantime we had to play league leaders Wigan at Sixfields. A much better performance, but a late Wigan goal gave them a double over us. Why did we concede so many late efforts? Why couldn't we score just one last minute goal ourselves to cheer us fans up a bit?

True to my word, I boycotted the English Riviera and tuned in mid-afternoon to listen to Radio Northampton's match report, not expecting anything. We were 2-0 up! Torquay pulled one back and by all accounts should have equalised well into injury time, but for once we didn't concede that late goal. OK it was three points, but that Mansfield game had illustrated how inconsistent we were, so I didn't get over-excited; we still had to play Cambridge and in-form Fulham and Colchester away from home.

Scarborough were also in the play-off frame when they came to Sixfields, and in a scrappy game a Roy Hunter goal from a penalty gave us three points -

we were well and truly back in the picture now. Cambridge away, and another 1,300 Cobblers fans saw a backs-to-the-wall display for a 0-0 draw. If we could just get the same at Fulham we'd really be in with a chance. The best part of 2,000 travelled to London for this one. Having won promotion the previous Tuesday, Fulham were in party mood, despite the best efforts of Ian Atkins to dampen their spirits by insisting that our lot warmed up at the Fulham end. Not that I witnessed that bit - I was still in the queue to get in and desperate for a pee, after a few beers in the Pharaoh & Firkin (recommended if you go to Fulham). By the time I made it into the ground, I headed straight for the loo. You can guess what happened next... we scored! By all accounts it was a great goal by last season's leading scorer Jason White, which brought his tally for this year up to the dizzy heights of TWO.

The public of Northampton by now had woken up to the idea that the club had a good chance of reaching the play-offs, and 6,400 turned up against Exeter to watch us tear them apart, their last-minute penalty being the only goal we were to concede in April. (As an aside, isn't it funny how things change? Two seasons ago Exeter fans had come to Sixfields facing extinction, and on an emotional day both sets of supporters swapped scarves and shirts in a spirit of empathy and goodwill; all Exeter fans were interesting in exchanging this time was blows!)

We went into the last Saturday in sixth place, behind Chester and Swansea. Scunthorpe were the opposition, and despite a complete sell-out in the home seats, the club refused to re-seat the visitors in a smaller area, even though everyone knew Scunny wouldn't bring more than 250 fans with them. Inevitably a few Cobblers got in the away enclosure, but fortunately there was no trouble. A first half goal by Sean Parrish eased the tension - we'd made the play-offs! The news got even better: Swansea and Chester had both lost, so we finished fourth, thus gaining home advantage in the second leg. Cardiff were to be our opponents and since we'd won five of our last seven games, we were the form side.

The queues for tickets, especially for the home leg, were horrendous. Many regulars had a tough job getting any, as part-timers crawled out of the woodwork. What really angered me was to see the number of people in the queue wearing Man United and Liverpool shirts - some were even wearing Saints jerseys (the local Rugby Union team). Funny, I don't remember seeing them on a cold windy night in Hartlepool!

Our record against Cardiff this season had been good, including a good 4-0 stuffing at home on New Year's Day. So a very hostile atmosphere greeted us as we walked to Ninian Park, and I didn't fancy bumping into some of their neanderthals after the match, whatever the result. On entering the ground I was informed that the referee was Mr J Kirby, who'd previously sent off Mark Cooper in the CCC against Cardiff. Surprise, surprise, in the second half Mr Kirby reached for his red card and the recipient was... Mark Cooper! But just like in the cup game, this seemed to spur Cobblers on, and a brilliant solo goal from Sean Parrish sent me and 2,000 others into ecstasy. We had a few narrow escapes, but when the final whistle went we had won. Only 90 minutes from Wembley. We had to keep a low profile back to the car as gangs of Cardiff youths were on the prowl for trouble.

For the second leg, the police were out in force: riot squads, police horses, dogs and a helicopter, but this didn't stop all sorts of fights breaking out near the ground, and at one stage 30-40 Cardiff 'fans' charged down the bank right towards me wearing my Cobblers shirt selling fanzines. They just ran round me and engaged a group of locals just waiting in the queue to get in. Phew!

Although officially the gate was not a record, you could have fooled me as there appeared to be several hundred too many Cardiff fans in the away end. I guess they'd travelled without tickets and to contain them the police had let them in anyway, but if that was the case, then why did they open the gates ten minutes from the end? It just allowed the hooligan element to promptly head round to the home sections to cause more mayhem.

The game? The atmosphere was incredible; the whole ground was singing, and when we scored, it was bedlam. But then our two goal cushion became just one when Cardiff scored, and the nerves really started. We couldn't possibly blow it... could we? Then Uriah Rennie, always a hate-figure at Northampton, for once became a hero as he sent Jeff Eckhardt off for a vicious backhander on Neil Grayson. Talk about symmetry! Like Cooper, Eckhardt had also been sent off in an earlier fixture between us. In the end we ran out 4-2 winners on aggregate, prompting joyous celebrations on our part and wanton rampaging on theirs. Why do Cardiff City attract such morons?

In the final it was to be Swansea. Uh-oh, we'd played them twice, lost twice (one of the games had seen new signing John Frain's debut and the inevitable last-minute goal for the oppo).

Wembley. A devalued dream? Not so for an incredible 32,500 Cobblers who bought tickets. No problems for the regulars this time, so the others were more than welcome, especially if it meant some of them might come back next season. Wembley Way was a sea of claret; no Man Utd or Liverpool shirts on display today, and it was no surprise - the club shop had been devastated; you couldn't get a Cobblers shirt anywhere, they'd even sold out of replica goalkeeper's jerseys! Claret flags flew everywhere. And unlike their Welsh compatriots, the Swansea fans also seemed to be out for a good day. It has to be said that they out-sang us, even though they were outnumbered three to one. I put that down to the fact that their hard-core of 4,000 were grouped together amongst 12,000, whereas our 5,000 regulars were scattered amongst the 32,500.

To see my team come out onto the Wembley turf in the club's centenary year brought a huge lump to my throat. OK, to those fans used to FA Cup Finals and European glory it may not mean a lot. But to me, and those of us at Shrewsbury four years ago when we so nearly got relegated to the Conference, it was heaven.

It was a crap game, heading for extra time. Swansea had held the territorial edge, but apart from one good save from Andy Woodman, they'd never really threatened. The stadium clock had been showing 90 minutes for ages, when Christian Lee, looking for an opening, was fouled on the edge of the D. John Frain stepped up to take it, and when his shot hit an onrushing Swansea defender, we figured "Oh well, extra time for sure." But hang on... The ref booked the Swansea player for encroaching and ordered the kick to be retaken. Frain stepped up a second time. He hit it oh, so sweetly; wrong-footing the 'keeper who dived in vain as the ball nestled in the bottom corner. YYEESSSSS! The feeling was incredible; we'd scored, at Wembley, in our end, in the last minute. Swansea restarted, but the final whistle blew immediately.

Last minute goals, why don't we ever score them?

Source: *Spitting Feathers*

WHAT'S THE STORY SOUTHEND GLORY

Southend United

We beat the Champions 5-2!

Question: Who has the hardest job in football? Millwall's accountant? Chris Waddle's Hairdresser? Man Utd's kit designer? No, the real answer is the poor guy who has to compile Southend United's season '96-97 highlights video.

We've all learnt the hard way that when following a team such as Southend we shouldn't expect the world, or even a small African continent, or for that matter not even a tiny Welsh village, we must simply be happy with keeping our First Division status. A task which, for the last

six seasons, the team and its many, and I do mean many, managers has succeeded in doing. During that period I have been happy to witness the team sacrifice so-called 'total football' in return for survival; I've put up with a simple 4-4-2 formation, long balls and sloppy goals, and let's face it with this style of football you know exactly where you stood: no thrills, no bullshit!

This season promised to be different however. We had Republic of Ireland International, League Championship winner with Liverpool and all-round football genius Ronnie Whelan in charge; Mike Marsh, ex-Premier and Turkish veteran in midfield, and in goal England's No.1 'keeper Simon Royce. And just for good measure, let's not forget our very own male model Phil Gridelet. How could we possibly fail in our goal of Premier League football?

With Tranmere offering the first test of our credentials we felt sure that three points were already in the bag. Then came the first surprise of the season - where had our trusty 4-4-2 formation gone? Looking out across the sacred Roots Hall turf, unless my pint-laden eyes were deceiving me, we were playing three at the back, wingbacks and a three man midfield. The stands were a buzz with talk of Brazilian-style football systems being introduced over the close season, but no matter how hard and long I closed my eyes I couldn't conjure the image of Roots Hall as the Maracana Stadium, the samba drums just didn't seem at home.

Barely one minute into the game and Southend were 1-0 up through Andy Rammell. "Say we are second in the league, say we are second in the league." Short-lived however, as later on we conceded a weak equaliser, the first of many, and had to settle for mid-table mediocrity. Still, looking back now, what wouldn't I give for a piece of 13th placed limbo. The rest of the season rolled by with very little to excite; on the pitch the team failed to live up to even the *Sun's* predicted table positions, and behind the scenes there were rumours aplenty of players not being paid, security guards taking bungs and of chairman Vic Jobson looking to sell his interests in the club.

But looking on the bright side, we at least gained two new mascots: out went Sammy the Shrimp and in his place we had two blokes dressed up as garden peas courtesy of our sponsors Telewest Communications! One of our games was witness to, in the words of the *Sun*, "the worst refereeing decision ever!" The official somehow mistaking and sending off a black teenage defender in the place of a white thirtysomething striker. And, oh yeah, I nearly forgot "We beat the champions 5-2, we beat the champions 5-2, we beat the champions 5-2."

We've made it! Yes! After six years of trying, we've finally made it to Division 2. Six seasons of blood, sweat and fans' tears and they've finally got their just rewards! Let's thank a few of the people who have made this possible:

The players - whose consistent performances have been a key ingredient in our success. Our home record goes without saying, and our away form has been incomparable!

The manager - whose psittacine comments after each impuissant performance have brought smiles to many faces!

The directors - whose own companies have helped produce a programme unique of its type - and reacted to other clubs' free travel for away fans with immediate pusillanimous obmutescence! (*Go on, reader - look 'em up! - Ed*)

The marketing manager – who, despite the handicap of us being the only club within 30 miles of one of the most densely populated areas of the country, has helped build a following which is the talking point of visitors to Roots Hall!

The chairman - panjandrum whose Second Division ambitions, Third Division team and Vauxhall Conference playing kit have made Southend United what it is today!

So to everyone involved in our promotion to Division 2, look in the mirror and say with pride:
WE DESERVE IT!

WHEN SKIES ARE GREY

Everton

Ball of Confusion

It's that time of year again when those good people from Red Card Publishing get on the phone requesting 1,500 words on Everton's '96-97 season. It's a task about as enjoyable as sticking pins in ones eyes. Well, reader, stick on that Leonard Cohen album, pour yourself a stiff drink, sit down and prepare yourself for a tale of few bright spots and plenty of doom and gloom.

It wasn't always like this though. Back in August, a packed-to-the-rafters Goodison roared the Toffees to a more than convincing eclipse of title-

when skies are grey
55 £1.00

pretenders Newcastle. Then three days later we shared four goals with Man Utd at Old Trafford on a veritable rollercoaster of spills and thrills. Prospects were indeed bright. With Gary Speed adding balance, guile and purpose to a previously one-dimensional midfield and Duncan Ferguson at his most frightening, Blues fans flocked to the bookies to snap up the generous odds-on offer. However, as the saying goes, you never see a skint turf accountant, and unbeknown to us the first cracks were already appearing. After finishing the previous season with the best run of performances that I've ever witnessed by any Everton player in 20 years, Andrei Kanchelskis started the season slowly as results tailed off. Rumours began to circulate that the Ukranian had been tapped by his eventual employers Fiorentina, and the team suffered as a result.

September brought the latest in a long line of cup humiliations with York dumping us out of the Coca Cola. I was in America with work at the time, and forgot the second leg was being played. My girlfriend casually broke the news, in between telling me about the weather and how the washing machine was playing up (Nickie - I still love you).

Immediately afterwards, form did pick up and by Christmas things were again looking rosy. Nicky Barmby had been bought for £5m and Tony Grant and Michael Branch were starting to fulfil their immeasurable potential. Southampton were washed away 7-1 and a trio of East Midland teams had been beaten in their own backyards.

It was then that things went horribly wrong. The entire defence and midfield was wiped out by injury, illness and suspension over the holiday period and inevitably results suffered as a result. The manager was feeling the pressure and the previous genial, jovial media figure began to mutate into a paranoid misery, as Joe lost the plot big-time. He began to wage war with the local and national media and this caused untold damage to our already pathetic public profile.

NB: Glossy football magazine editors: there's a club in the North West of England who attract 35,000 every home game, despite an inconsistent team. They're called Everton, you pretentious, middle-class 90's pricks. Give us some coverage! Instead of your beloved Chelsea, Spurs and Liverpool.

Ahem, getting back to the story...

This was not perhaps the best time for megalomaniac chairman Peter Johnson to start sounding out the fans about moving to a new 60,000 seater stadium. However despite a brave campaign by the traditionalists among us, 85% opted for a new arena at an unknown site with only a dodgy artist's impression to go on. They're a funny lot them Blue-noses!

With the ground debate raging, Joe Royle rucking with the press and Andrei finally buggering off to Italy... (another digression I'm afraid, but I could never understand why Man United fans got so het up about Kanchelskis leaving them. Fact: Andrei is Ukranian, he is a mercenary and had probably never heard of either Everton or United before he came over here. Fact: United fans: the world is a big place). *(Get on with it, Redmond - Ed.)* Where was I? Oh yes, another cup humiliation. Bradford this time. We were indescribable but to be fair Bradford were inspired with Rob Steiner running us all over the place. Despite what the media would have you believe, this was not the Chris Waddle show.

League results were still hideous and Everton fell down the table like a stone. Royle, hampered by long-term injuries to key players like Hinchcliffe, Parkinson and Grant, did himself no favours by selling off the majority of his squad. He brought in Terry Phelan who quickly became a crowd favourite and Claus Thomsen who did not. Indeed Claus is making a good attempt at becoming the most vilified Everton player since Brett Angell. However with the media row still continuing the writing was on the wall for Joe Royle and it all came to a head on transfer deadline day when Johnson blocked a move for two Scandinavians. Joe resigned on principle. Many fans were pleased to see him go, claiming he wasn't big enough for the job. I wasn't one of them. It should never be forgotten that Joy Royle saved Everton from certain relegation and took us to cup triumph in 1995, a feat that should have had him beatified instead of vilified. How short some people's memories are in trendy, success-demanding, unforgiving Premier League land 1997.

In the short term Johnson turned to big Dave Watson to save us from the drop and the tough defender, forced to play numerous spotty 17-year-olds, managed to keep us up by the skin of our teeth. Make no mistake though, if the season had lasted a further fortnight then Blues fans would have been checking the routes to Crewe and Bury.

And so we have it; as I write (mid-June) Everton remain managerless, sponsorless and - even more seriously - playerless. It's now ten weeks since Joe Royle went to that great dug-out in the sky and although Peter Johnson claims a lot is going on behind the scenes, fans are not convinced. And a new apparent abomination of a kit is being held back until we get a sponsor (Danka screeched away to back another loser in Damon Hill).

We have the smallest squad in the Premier League with a minimum of eight players needed before it all starts again. Pre-season training starts in three weeks *and* I had a burst water main the other day!

FIVE ALTERNATIVE SLOGANS FOR ROBBIE FOWLER'S VEST

1. Bluenose
2. Judas: Jobs a good'un. Where's me 30 pieces of silver?
3. I'm mad me. Zany la!
4. Not Guilty
5. Clueless Cunt

WHEN YOU'RE SMILING

Leicester City

How do you judge how successful your season has been? Is it by the number of referees you've seen stretchered off or injured before the end of 90 minutes? (Two by our reckoning.) Or is it by how many refs should have been stretchered off after 120 minutes? (As in Mike Reed.) Could it be by how many multi-million pound signings you made during the season? (None.) How about how many times your team has been shown live on TV? (Ten.)

The truth is that the acid test of your club's success (and pious Pontus 'Teetotal' Kaamark will be utterly disgusted by this) is not what the alleged 'experts' or pundits say. It is the fans' beer consumption. Measured in units sunk, the reasons behind this theory are clear: after a sound thumping (for example, by six goals at Middlesbrough, or 4-2 at Filbert St - oh sorry, that was Derby, wasn't it!) you drown your sorrows, but research has shown that victory is celebrated with up to *five times* the volume! For example, the average Leicester City fan would drink 17 units of alcohol per week during the season. But this rose to:-

* 26 units in the week following our 3-1 home defeat to Chelsea
* 34 units following our controversial FA Cup exit at the hands of the inept and partially-sighted Mike Reed
* 51 units after back-to-back wins against Leeds and Spurs
* 70 l' units following the BeLittleing of Villa away
* 207 units post-Coca Cola Cup final replay victory against the Salsa slumps from the North East of nowhere!
* And a staggering 323 L' units in the week following the Derby demolition job - completed 4-2 by a City reserve side!

Unfortunately our report lacks any data following our 4-2 crucifixion of Blackburn on the last day of the season, as all our researchers were subsequently admitted to hospital!

However, back in August, Leicester publicans had no reason to order in extra supplies for the forthcoming months. No-one outside The Towers hospital for the mentally ill would dare suggest Premiership survival, let alone silverware. Our expectations were so low that even last time's points tally of 29 seemed beyond our reach. Elsewhere, the multi-million pound foreign stars were flooding in faster then Ken Bates and Steve Gibson could write out their cheques. Yes, even the shit teams had continental 'stars'. How could the apparent panic signings of Kasey Keller and Spencer Prior compete with the might of Milli Vanilli - sorry, Ravanelli, Vialli and the others? The answer was BLOODY WELL! Yes, they felt studs in legs like any other mortal, but unlike some 'star players' drawing huge wages in the Premier League, they always got back up and got stuck in. We call this the 'Steve Walsh Effect'!

Our teenage sensation Emile Heskey was the first on the Leicester City roll of honour as his searing double killed off Southampton. Just two games to get our first win - it took six last time we were here! So we could see Emile was up for it; but what about the old man of the pack - super Stevie 'If anyone calls me journeyman again, I'll nut 'em!' Claridge? Could he cut the Premiership mustard? He did more then that - he cut open defences and scorched his way to the City top-scorer spot with 12 league goals... and one or two rather memorable cup strikes into the bargain! He dillied and dallied; he fumbled and tripped; but if Steve didn't know where the ball had gone - well, there were more then a few 'top-class' defenders who had even less of a clue!

Then there was our chart-topping troupe - The Spice Thugs. Led from the back by Spencer 'Receding Spice' Prior and then later by the all-dominating Matt 'Scary Spice' Elliott; 15˝ stone of finely honed muscle, a scoring touch to boot, and a head with no nerve-endings. Then it was up to Steve 'Old Spice' Walsh, Neil 'Ginger Spice' Lennon, Simon '(Not So) Posh Spice' Grayson, and the rest of the 'girls' to help crush all before them. Well, nearly. It was certainly a case of showing the world some serious 'Blooo Power'!

Our Premiership survival odds were in stark contrast to the sky-high expectations of virtually every other club. Those who succumbed to the might of Leicester City made embarassed excuses: "It's the injuries...," "the sheep-shagging orgies on Friday night...," "our goalie's a mate of Hans Segers..." They tried 'em all! Money can't guarantee success (or in Boro's case, even survival). It takes more then expensive and overpaid foreign internationals to do the biz and win silverware as well. Instead, our motley crew of assembled small clubs' supporters' favourites and outright battlers achieved just that.

Travelling to Aston Villa was like a carnival, despite the freezing weather. Judas managers have a 0% success rate against us, and that wasn't about to change. The pubs were packed, and so hoards of City fans could be found in the streets guzzling beer from cans acquired from local offies. Not even the fact that our Stella was freezing to ice as we drank it could detract from the samba feeling that afternoon. OK, maybe a bit of an exaggeration, but we certainly danced all the way out of the West Midlands after Muzzy Izzet slid our third in.

Yet suspensions and injuries were getting ridiculous. Pontus Kaamark had lasted just six games from his comeback from cruciate ligament surgery before breaking his arm. Emergency replacement Rob Ullathorne subsequently became the world's most expensive player, when 12 minutes into his debut he broke his leg, giving his price-tag of £600,000 a real value of £50,000 per minute. So it was a virtual reserve side that faced the Sheep Shaggers at Filbo. But we still had the mighty Ian Marshall up front. Ungainly and donkey-like he may be, but this cheap replacement for Iwan Roberts will go down in Blue Army mythology for his explosive first half hat-trick against Derby. Steve Claridge netted the fourth and our ecstasy was complete.

Matt Elliott, the mid-season wonder-buy from Oxford, single-handedly slaughtered the Dons (again), and then terrorised Bosnich's goal and set up Claridge for a back-to-back League double. Poor Brian Little - NOT! But not even Matt could prevent an alarming loss of form during the run-up to our fizzy drink success, and the collective hangovers after it. A string of draws and defeats saw us slump alarmingly. Now of course, Europe and Division 1 don't mix. But who cared, as we celebrated a night of titanic struggle at Selhurst Park by beating Wimbledon on the away goals rule after extra time.

As for Wembley, I didn't think the Final was all that bad - though in truth all I can remember is fighting with an inflatable whale and blinding sunlight worsening my already seriously dodgy condition. Emile provided the touch, and the trek to Hillsborough was always going to be fruitful. Emile nearly finished the job, but opted for extra time and another bit of history for Super Steve. I still can't recall anything that happened after 10:45 that night.

Back to the league and our worries were mounting - but Martin had it under control. Although it still took one Mr Elliott to do what our strikers couldn't - get a priceless goal against Sheffield Wednesday. He did; we'd done it. Safety was ours. Did the glory end there? NO. Having crushed Blackburn away on the final afternoon, we then climbed into NINTH place, and overtook Derby at the same time. Only Coventry's survival (predictable but disappointing) took the shine off a season's climax which saw Forest bottom of the table; Middlesboro' lose everything; Wolves getting beaten in the play-offs; and McJudas getting roundly slated. Hasn't it been a marvellous ten months to be alive?

The best season ever? Well, put it this way, we came top of the League of Alcohol Consumption - with an average supporter consuming a staggering 2,876 units in the season. And we know alcohol never lies. After all, even the quiet and reserved O'Neill has been "diabolically drunk" and "lambasted with wine" this season. Well, Martin, when I bump into you next time, the drinks are most definitely on me...

WHERE WERE YOU AT THE SHAY?

Bury

Division 2. Just passing through.

WHERE WERE YOU AT THE SHAY

MIDWINTER POSTPONEMENTS PILE UP !

Too much snow!

ISSUE 25

The ORIGINAL Bury F.C. Fanzine

60p

Where should I start? The wonderful day out to win promotion at Watford, Championship day at home against Millwall, winning at Brentford in the first v second match of the day? No, I'll start at the very beginning (which seems as good a place as any).

Stan Ternent had been his usual shrewd self in the summer, wheeling and dealing in the small-money transfer market, spotting bargains that teams like Bury thrive on. He bolstered the team, picking up Gordon Armstrong from Sunderland, signing Huddersfield cult hero 'Rocket' Ronnie Jepson and then, on the eve of the season, he made his most inspired signing yet as Shakers' supremo, acquiring York City's Dean Kiely and taking the matter to a transfer tribunal. More on this later.

The opening day saw Brentford at Gigg. Our first game back in Division 2, and by half time we were missing the safety of the Third Division as Brentford were murdering us 1-0. The second half was much better and we got off with a draw - phew. Unfortunately injuries plagued us early on, losing Chris Lucketti against Brentford, captain David Pugh in the Coke Cup at Notts with a broken arm, and countless other niggles, but we rode these out picking up results along the way, winning at Chesterfield, Wycombe and looking a very good home team.

We didn't lose until we got to Crewe in September; the combination of their disciplined side who'd done a bit of homework and the *WWYATS?* team not using our lucky pub at Great Budworth en route to this Tuesday night game meant the first disappointment of the season. Worries surfaced in the way that we exited the Coke Cup against Palace, losing both games and outclassed away, but they needn't have. We were being talked of as the surprise team of the first few weeks, and maintained a top ten position.

Peterborough was our first really memorable away day. The Shakers produced an organised performance before David Johnson banged in the winning goal with ten minutes to go. Jonno's 'pineapple' hairstyle had been ridiculed by the Posh fans, so when the goal went in he bounced down the touchline pointing at his head and telling them the score. When the Bury fans stopped celebrating the goal and looked back at the pitch, Jonno was heading down the tunnel, sent off for celebrating and taunting his persecutors.

This kind of thing started to happen regularly. Loan star John O'Kane's winner against Bristol Rovers lead to the police investigating Dean Kiely's celebration, but nothing came of it, of course. This game was also a sad day as it marked Phil Stant's last goal for the Shakers; soon he was off on loan to Northampton, then signed for Lincoln just before Christmas. Then came the potential flash-point: the long-running transfer tribunal saga was settled, with Bury paying just over a quarter of the £450,000 that York wanted for Kiely, and guess who was visiting Gigg on the following Saturday? Deano maintained his composure when the York fans lost theirs, and kept his usual playful gags with the crowd to himself on that day.

Interest in the FA Cup lasted as far as the first round, but we did go out to the team that would have made the final but for some bad reffing. What a shame that Chesterfield should have a decision go against them, it couldn't happen to a nicer team! As the weather began to close in around Christmas we were still holding a more than creditable position and the optimists began to talk of play-offs.

For a second year running the Shakers took part in the pilot scheme for shutting down the league in January, appearing only to put six past Mansfield in the Windscreens (but at what cost with David Pugh breaking his other arm?), and for our live and exclusive *Sky* debut, away at Burnley. All I wanted was for us not to be shown up for all the world to see, and my concerns seemed justified as they put three goals past us in 20 minutes. But fortunately we came back well and ended up unembarrassed with a 3-1 reverse.

Our games in hand started to tell now - we were picking up points at home with ease and an occasional swagger. Only us and Brentford remained unbeaten at home and we were moving up, slowly but steadily. Which is not how you could describe the most ridiculous moment of the season, when a very cross Bournemouth fan vaulted onto the pitch and sprinted towards the referee to give him a piece of his mind. He grabbed the man in black round the neck and aimed a punch before the stewards arrived like Dad's Army to save the day. Our hero has since been heavily fined, banned for life from Bournemouth and every ground in the country. I wonder if he thinks it was worth it.

By now we were hot on the trail of Luton for second spot, and Brentford who were starting to look dodgy were also glancing nervously over their shoulders. We increased the pressure in the run-up to Easter, eased past Luton and on March 25th won 1-0 at Notts County with just nine men by the end, to go top of the league.

The major turning point came the following Saturday. To celebrate our No.1 status the *WWYATS?* team held a champagne breakfast on the train to the first v second place game at Brentford. We should have saved the bubbly for the way home as the Shakers defended magnificently and hit them on the break to win 2-0.

A pattern was established: we would defend resolutely away and win at home. We entered the final three games needing two points for promotion, facing last year's three relegated teams: second-placed Luton, play-off chasing Watford and managerless Millwall. The Luton game was tense; 750 followers on a Tuesday night sang us to within a point of promotion with a 0-0 draw. Away at Watford the following Saturday was better with over 1,500 following the team in search of the point that would take us up. With only four minutes to go, the parties were already beginning. Then Armstrong gave away a penalty. Utter silence at our end (apart from a single wailing child), and the pressure was all on Deano. He saved it! I can't remember those last minutes except for the pandemonium which was going on all around. Tears flowed - we were up!

But there was one more act to perform; a win on the last day would see the Shakers crowned as Champions for only the third time in the club's history. The ground was a sell-out and we broke the fanzine sales record, selling 600 in 25 minutes. We then watched the Shakers nervously plod to the title. It was not until the 71st minute that we could relax after Jepson's bullet header gave us the lead. Soon after, Johnrose made it two and the biggest party Gigg Lane has had in years really began to rock. Pughie came on for his second comeback of the season and Stan the Man gave everybody a game in the last few minutes. Then it was over - we were the Champions!

Looking back the team was amazing. The defence was a brick wall: at home, only seven goals conceded all season and no league defeats. The midfield was tigerish and brave (Stanley claimed that Daws and Johnrose had three lungs at one point), and the strikers did their jobs. Praise should especially be given to Player of the Year Chris Lucketti, whose performances were inspirational, and for showing devotion to the cause by staying with the Shakers when he could have left for bigger teams and more money.

Next year it's City, Forest, Sunderland and Middlesbrough. We're probably the bookies' favourites to go down again, but then again, we were this time last year, so that shows what they know! All I know is that I can't wait.

WHERE'S THE MONEY GONE?

Darlington

"Ah!" I said to myself when asked to review Darlo's '96-97 season, "So many happy memories and highlights. I'll wait for a bit and let the dust settle before writing anything." Then I came to my senses, remembering that the '96-97 season had been a total shambles. Consider for a moment that the previous year we'd had the thrill of reaching the play-offs, and as such hoped for some more of the same. But alas no, there were to be only two high points to make Darlo fans scream with joy and excitement in the entire season. One was finishing above the monkey hanging people from Hartle-fool, and the other was the Coca Cola Cup second round tie against Leeds United.

You see, when we were drawn with Leeds, I and many other Darlo fans thought that the mighty Leeds United, who have such quality in the form of Yeboah, Martyn, Rush and Paul Beesley, would totally annihilate humble little Darlo. However, we came back from the first leg at Elland Road with a 2-2 draw, which set the pulse racing for our next few games.

We occupied a play-off place at that time, and had already recorded several fine wins over supposedly good teams (although our away form was awful and a million miles away from last season's when we only lost one game on our travels). Yippee! Then it all started to go wrong. First we lost the return leg of the Leeds cup tie. Next, all our players got injured in a bad-tempered home game with Fulham (but it wasn't their fault, Mr Fulham fanzine editor!) and Darlo proceeded to slip down the league grid faster than Damon Hill's Arrows.

Drastic action was needed, so WTMG swung into action and installed our erstwhile Ed as lucky mascot for the game. This would surely do the trick... The resulting draw ensured that never again could we despatch this man to the centre circle with any conviction. Personally, I blame our slump on him.

But everything came together in the next game, away to our hated rivals 'Fool. We won 2-1 and suddenly all was well again. After all, we could still make the play-offs. "We can't have this," said the evil Hartlepool fan in the sky, as he kindly made us lose all our other games that month.

What's more, the Feethams faithful held a demonstration against our genial general manager, Steve Morgon. I wouldn't have minded that, but the people who held the demonstration chanted "Where's the money gone?" without our permission! It turned out to be a reference to the disappearance of money raised from selling players such as Matty Appleby, Stevie Gaughan, Robbie Painter, Sean Gregan and Robbie Blake. Lucky that I forgot to make that call to our top copyright lawyer!

Our ambitious board showed just how committed they were to team strengthening by getting one of those fluffy mascot thingys. WTMG later came to the conclusion that the person inside the suit was the editor of the semi-official Darlo magazine, *Tin Shed*. We only won one league game that month. Now I blamed our slump on the fluffy one for not being lucky, while Steve Morgon blamed the fans for not turning out in large numbers. This despite the fact that the team were playing like a bunch of inebriated Hartle-fool players! *(Not that we've ever seen any drunken Hartle-fool players - WTMG libel lawyer).*

In the same month that our unlucky mascot arrived, manager Jim Platt was sacked. This came only months after chairman Bernard Lowery had promised Jim a job for life (although at the time we'd taken this to mean that Jim was going to be murdered in the near future). The board contrived loads of excuses to make the fans think that Platt deserved the sack, but frankly none of them held water. The whole business created a very unpleasant atmosphere at the club with arguments raging among fanzines, the board and the supporters club.

Then the ever-diplomatic Morgon announced his thoughts on Darlington becoming a feeder club (Premiership reserve side), despite a clear indication from 99% of Darlo fans that we were totally opposed to such an idea! What timing! What tact!

Platt's replacement was David Hodgson, who'd managed us before but had walked out because the board wouldn't let him throw paper aeroplanes in the chairman's office (or something like that). Many fans thought that he might resign again, but I was sure he would lead us to Division Two. The fact that he failed to do so was definitely the fault of Mr Q, our hairy mascot type thing.

We went through the Christmas period on a hot streak of losses, and just when we thought we'd never win again, we did, at home! The shock sent Darlo fans throughout the country scurrying for the best medical care and many were so traumatised they spent the rest of the season in hospital. And that's why our crowds were so low.

Now there was no stopping us: home win followed home win. Suddenly we were zooming up the league like... erm, well, we didn't really move up at all, because our away form was still awful. But Darlo fans could sleep at night, because we knew that once we started winning away, we'd arrive in the play-offs, get promotion and ram it right up Hartlepool's... sorry, got a bit carried away there.

The bad news was that Brighton were fast catching up with us. We needed to pick up points or we'd be sucked into the relegation battle and knowing us we'd probably go down, which would have the Fool's fans going mental. I was worried. Then suddenly it was upon us. No, not that daft comet, but the BIG encounter of the season: Darlo v Brighton. We won 2-0 (with the help of a 70mph gale - someone up there must like us after all), and suddenly everything clicked into place. We were getting results away from home, we were winning all our home games, Dave Hodgson won Manager of the Month for March, and it was still mathematically possible to make the play-offs.

We'd signed Finnish goalkeeper Teuvo Moilanen on loan from Preston North End, and he'd virtually kept us afloat single-handed, but the "We haven't paid a fee for a player for the last two years" board of directors refused to sign him permanently. And even when a bit of fan power (petitions and the like) forced them to meet Preston's £50,000 valuation, they were turned down as higher offers rolled in on the back of his brilliant form for us.

Fortunately, another typical bad run with only one win to show for the whole of April didn't suck us into the Conference dogfight, but it did scupper any chance of a play-off place. But hey, at least we were safe from relegation and we could rest easy knowing that next year would be OUR year.

The final game saw us rise to the big occasion once again as we dented Cardiff's own play-off hopes by beating them 2-1, but the Welshies still made the lottery thanks to Lincoln's inability to beat Rochdale on their own patch.

The prospects for next season look good: hooped shirts are coming back and a new sponsor is on the cards to replace the ill-fated Soccerdome, the leisure complex that ended up not being built, but you'll have to ask Morgon and Brealey about that. As long as the current team isn't broken up (and it's unlikely because we've already sold everyone who can be sold) and Hodgson can get a few new players, I might just be able to tell you about a successful season in next year's *SOTF*.

WHERE'S THE MONEY GONE?

Leicester City

OK, here goes: an A to Z of Leicester City's '96-97 'Cup-Winning, European-Qualifying, Two-Fingers-Up-To-Everybody-Who-Tipped-Us-To-Go-Down' season:

Away wins - Three points at White Hart Lane, Villa Park, Riverside Stadium, Anfield (nearly!), Selhurst Park and Ewood Park. Away wins counted for 15 of the total 47 Premiership points gained. Away wins kept us up, and City finished in ninth position. That's 11 places above Forest - a gap of 'Nationwide' proportions!

Boring, boring Leicester - so chanted the Middlesbrough fans during the Coca Cola Cup Final replay at Hillsborough. I guess the Boro fans, unable to see through the hype surrounding their side, were mistaking 'boring' for a few traditional English footballing virtues like teamwork and grafting hard for each other. The truth is, Leicester City played some neat stuff and the players ran their socks off week after week, and I can't remember any of them fucking off back to Brazil for weeks on end every time the missus got PMT either. There is more to football than some overpaid Italian running around with his shirt over his head or a pre-pubescent Brazilian ordering the ref to book anyone with the audacity to take the ball off him. Was it tears at the end of the season I saw running down the cheeks of those same fans who had chanted "Boring, boring Leicester" with such self-assured superiority at Hillsborough? Or had they simply been splattered with some of that disgusting 70's wet-look gel after a certain South American had been asked if he'd be staying on another season?

Cheat - Referee Mike Reed *twice* cheated us. The first time, away at Newcastle, City had led 3-1 before they pulled it back to 3-3. Fair enough, a win up there would have been great, but we'd settle for a draw. Physically drained, the City players were hanging on for the whistle. Reed, for reasons known only to himself, made Leicester endure three minutes and 48 seconds of injury time when there hadn't been a trainer on the pitch. Shearer got the fourth, Reed blew for full time and joined the Newcastle players in a lap of honour. For the second Mike Reed cheat, see 'P' for Penalty.

Drunks - Comments attributed to Pontus Kaamark in a Swedish newspaper, branding his team-mates a "bunch of boozers," found their way back to the British tabloids. Pontus denied it of course. As if... The following Saturday a City side missing nine regulars beat Derby 4-2. If Leicester were the boozers, I guess that made Derby the girlie barmaids.

Elliot - Matt Elliot looks like an alien and plays out of this world. This man is a class defender and a sharper finisher than Vanhoydonkey. Anybody that doesn't pick him in their Fantasy League team next season knows nothing about football. A quality signing by Martin O'Neill.

Flare - At the start of extra time at Hillsborough one of those European-style flares whizzed across the pitch, narrowly missing Steve Walsh. Walshie, in his testimonial year, ducked and smiled it off, jokingly patting his heart. Anybody else would have required a change of shorts. In the 11 'duck nothing, hard as fuck' years at Filbert Street, this was the first time we had seen the great man flinch. We're not worthy!

Goal of the Season - So many to choose from, with contenders from Izzet and a couple from Marshall. Claridge's volley against Man Utd after Heskey had flicked it up for him with his heel perhaps should have won it, however, the *WTMG* Goal of the Season goes to Emile Heskey for his late, late scrambled equaliser at Wembley. Not the prettiest of goals, but absolutely priceless nonetheless.

Hat-tricks - Just the one, from Ian Marshall of all people against Derby. Either he's a top class Premier striker or they're crap. Judge that one for yourselves.

International Goalkeeper - Kasey Keller, a Yank who's off his line a lot quicker than his country joined the Second World War (I thought better of using the analogy that Keller's a good-shot stopper just like some of his ex-Presidents). Another quality signing by Martin O'Neill.

Jesper Olson - Signed for AC Milan instead of Leicester. Here's a few of the many reasons why you chose wrong, twat face: John Merrick, aka the Elephant man, was born in Leicester. So too was Daniel Lambert, who at 52 stone was the fattest bastard in the Victorian world. Milan's famous sons are Gino Ginelli and the famous Italian revolutionary Luigi Biscuit. Big deal! Meanwhile, Mario's Chippy is 1,381 miles from the San Siro. It's only 600 yards from Filbert Street.

Kray Twins - Neil Lennon - hard-working, tough-tackling, ceaseless runner, owner of some deft creative touches. A young man at the peak of his game. Muzzi Izzet - the other half of Leicester's engine-room. Talent? This lad reeks of it. These boys look after each other on and off the pitch and will take on anyone. The Kray Twins can handle it. And if they can't... "WALSHIE!!"

Leicestershire - The capital of the sporting world: Leicester Tigers - European Cup finalists and Pilkington Cup winners. Leicestershire County Cricket Club - County Champions. Leicester City Football Club - Coca Cola Cup Winners. It is also rumoured that both Engelbert and Showaddywaddy are back in the recording studios.

Manager - Martin O'Neill. It came as a great relief when O'Neill signed a two-year extension to the twelve months he had left on his contract. For a while it looked as though it was going to be three managers in as many seasons as Everton and Celtic circled Filbert Street like a pair of vultures. Martin O'Neill is a top manager and the Leicester City board of directors have a unique opportunity, which is to back a manager who's proved he can deliver. In this day and age, contracts mean nothing so give the man some proper money to spend to make sure he stays, before he fucks off as well. If not the start of this season, maybe the start of next - and remember, Dave Bassett's only twelve months away from the sack...

Nottinghamshire - *Not* the capital of the sporting world. Forest relegated. County relegated. Some historians are also making a claim that Robin Hood could be from Sheffield.

Open Top Bus - The City of Leicester rewarded its team with an end of season tour around her streets. It is rumoured that the skinflint board of directors have approached the council with a view to borrowing the bus for the away legs of next season's UEFA Cup ties.

Penalty - Chelsea may have won the FA Cup but they shouldn't even have been in the hat for the quarter final draw. Egomaniac referee Mike Reed played a perfect one-two with Chelsea cheat Earland Johnson at Stamford Bridge. Johnson dived and Reed blew. Not since the days of 'Turnip Taylor' had the press been so united in justifiably calling someone crap.

Quiet - It took Steve Claridge just nine minutes to shut the Holte End up. The Villa fans were giving it to him because he used to be a Blue Nose, but he answered them back in some style. Six points off Villa last season - "Can we play you every week?"

Relegated - Saturday September 7th, at the City Ground, Mickey Whitlow tackled Steve Stone. Stone went down, and took Forest's season with him. So who could argue that Leicester City didn't effectively put Forest down?

Signings - Spencer Prior, Kasey Keller, Ian Marshall, Matt Elliot, Robert Ullathorne and Steve Guppy. When you balance it against what we sold, this represents an outlay of well under £3m; not bad considering how spread out it was throughout the season (if Walshie hadn't have got injured, Elliot would not have been signed). Still, it was pretty good spending by our usual standards, and even then, when the injuries hit and the suspensions cut in, O'Neill was at times struggling to get a decent side together. Ullathorne was signed just to bolster the side for the Coca Cola semi against Wimbledon, and lasted 12 minutes before breaking his leg. At six hundred grand that's 50 grand a minute. Still, a better return than Andy Cole then.

T raumatised Tommy - Get your writs out for the lads. That's what Leicester City fan Tommy Tyrell did (with a little help from a certain fanzine) after suffering Post Penalty Traumatic Disorder following Mike Reed's incompetent performance at Stamford Bridge. Tommy sued the FA for two days' wages after he was unable to work due to the trauma. The FA pulled out all the stops to defend their position and anybody who fancies taking up the man in the middle's job should look very carefully at what they stated in their defence: "Defence note 7 - The FA denies that it is the employer of the Referee. The Referee is self-employed and not employed by the FA." So basically the FA are saying "if you fuck up, you're on your own, mate!"

U nforgiven - Mark McGhee, you're still a greedy fat bastard.

V erruca - Rule 7, which insists that flip-flops are worn in and around the shower room, dressing room and treatment areas once again proved invaluable. The end of season medical report shows no sign of the nasty foot disorder that just 25 miles up the road at Coventry City reached near-epidemic proportions.

W embley - Five visits in six years. Are we good or what? There used to be a chant from opposing fans that went "You'll never win at Wembley," due to our four FA Cup Final defeats. These days, "We never lose at Wembley," and you should get some money on Martin O'Neill getting that FA Cup statistic sorted next season as well.

X tra Time - In the 100th minute, unmarked in the six yard box, Steve Claridge, his socks rolled down and legs so weary he could hardly walk, turned and shot in one movement to win the Coca Cola Cup for Leicester City.

Y ellow Cards - City finished third in the fair play league, picking up 51 bookings and just one red card - proof in itself that we can play a bit. This also belies a popular misconception that City only picked up points by kicking the opposition into touch.

Z ero - the amount of points everybody outside of Leicester thought we would get at the start of the season. European qualification, some silverware and 47 points later, you can all bollocks!

WHITE LOVE

Bolton Wanderers

"I've seen things that you people wouldn't believe. I've seen attack ships on fire off the shoulder of Orion... memories all lost forever, like tears in the rain." So said a soaked Rutger Hauer in the sci-fi classic, *Blade Runner*. Well, here at Bolton we're a bit sorry for old Rutger because we've seen things far more beautiful: a rejuvenated Wanderers team soundly thrash the rest of the Nationwide First Division, some of the best football ever played by a Wanderers squad and our team regain their place back in the Premier League of English football following our last season at Burnden Park. Truly, these are memories to cherish.

The season started in controversy - again - with more dissent among the ranks. This time our Serbian Messiah Sasa Curcic declared that he no longer wanted to play for the team. A summer trip back to his Balkan paradise for the wedding of his best mate, Villa's Savo Milosevic, had obviously given him food for thought. It came as no surprise then when Villa offered to stump up £4 million for 'Big-Nose', and Colin Todd snatched Brian Little's hand clean off.

All of which caused uproar among the Burnden faithful. You don't sell your best player only days before the start of the season, do you? In this case the answer was an emphatic yes. Apparently, Sasa's unrest was causing all sorts of problems with morale, and Toddy wasn't prepared to sacrifice team spirit because of one player. To placate the more vociferous supporters he released the details of the entire transfer saga to the local press. And this strategy seemed to work as the first match against Port Vale turned into one long Sasa side-show; the Bolton crowd openly questioning both his parentage and the state of his immune system in a game that saw Alan Thompson score in a 1-1 draw.

Manchester City were the first visitors to Burnden Park. They arrived as 3/1 favourites for promotion, but left in pieces after being soundly played (and kicked) off the park. Alan 'Squeaky' Ball hurriedly left his birthplace declaring that "The only person I'll be speaking to tonight will be my wife" after a 1-0 massacre. Danish International Per Frandsen's goal soon had the bookies revising their odds on the Super-Whites and Bolton claimed their first managerial scalp of the season as Bally resigned from the Maine Road hot-seat.

Norwich came next, and left on the wrong end of a sound 3-1 thrashing. A revitalised and much slimmed-down Nathan Blake bagged two goals while Michael 'Smurf' Johansen (the other half of our Danish double act) grabbed the third. With August barely over, the omens were looking decidedly good for the Whites.

September saw our first visit to the capital. At 1-1, and with injury time showing on the ref's watch, we were playing out a 1-1 draw with QPR in front of the cameras, until Alan Thompson took matters into his own hands and thundered a 25-yard shot past the helpless Jurgen Sommer. Cue our second managerial scalp as Ray Wilkins left Loftus Road on the wrong end of another Wanderers victory.

There were some hiccups; Southend gave us a 5-2 drubbing and that weekend saw Barnsley gain the top spot, but Grimsby Town paid the price for Wanderers' south coast mishap by ending up on the wrong end of a 6-1 pasting. With Brian Laws' position with the Mariners being decidedly shaky, after doing his bit for Anglo-Italian relations, we fully expected to claim our third scalp and a unique record, but the old bugger clung on to his job with all the tenacity of a barnacle on the hull of a North Sea trawler. The bastard!

October started with our biggest test of the season so far: a trip to Wolves. To set the scene, the last time the two teams met, Bolton had dumped Wolves out of the play-offs. To add injury to insult John McGinlay, who'd not only scored twice, added to his cult-hero status by dropping David Kelly with a cheeky right-hook and getting away with it! So when McGinlay was named in the starting line-up at Molineux, it was no surprise to find him the target of mass abuse from the home support, mainly concerning the state of his waist-line. After going a goal down, McGinlay struck twice to secure the points, and in tribute to the rapidly departing home crowd he flashed them a six-pack of Peter Andre proportions! The match nearly ended in controversy as the son of Satan (AKA Darren Ferguson) brought down Michael Johansen in the 89th minute to start a mass pitch brawl involving the players and both dug-outs.

As the league simmered nicely, particularly with a vital away draw against Charlton after being 3-1 down, Rudd Gullit's much-fancied Chelsea headed North for a Coca Cola showdown. Scott Minto fired the blues ahead, only for Blake and McGinlay to reply with two identikit headers. However, our 2-1 victory was overshadowed by the tragic news of the deaths of Matthew Harding and his party. One of those travelling back to London with him was John Bauldie, journalist for Q magazine, Bob Dylan fan and Wanderers fanatic. What a desperately sad time that was for all of us.

If a lift was needed then it arrived as we entertained Reading at home. Our previous meeting had been at Wembley in the play-off final, but now the prospects were somewhat different even if the match itself proved just as memorable. With Bolton leading 2-1, Keith 'The Cat' Branagan went for an early bath after deciding the Burnden air was a bit nippy for his liking. Who would replace him with no goalie on the bench? Step forward Super John McGinlay. In a 'Boys Own' performance he kept a clean sheet for 30 minutes before sealing his place in Bolton folklore with a stunning fingertip save.

As winter approached Bolton hit their traditional shit patch. Still, how many clubs would have settled for our return of five points from a possible 18 after the start we'd just made? Despite buggering up recent results, the feeling around the town was that the side was definitely promotion material even though we were only four months in.

The rigours of the league were forgotten for a night when Spurs visited us for another Coca Cola bash. The nation watched open-mouthed as the sophisticates from North London were dismantled by Wanderers. Even then they got off lightly with a 6-1 pasting after the myopic Paul Danson had failed to see England's No.1 (?) fumble a Scott Sellars shot over the line; even the Spurs supporters let the referee know that it had gone in.

Unhappily, our poor league run continued as Christmas approached with a freak home defeat to Ipswich. With barely a point separating Bolton from the pack, we scabbed a draw from Swindon and a win at Grimsby in two of the coldest matches I've ever known. The arctic chill at Blundell Park was fucking unbelievable, and so was the cock-up in ticket allocation that saw two thirds of the ground going mental as Blakey's solo screamer ripped into the net in the second half.

January brought fresh controversy when Wolves came to Burnden Park for a re-run of October's dust-up. We must say that John Sheridan has a lovely right-hook, and as for Chris Fairclough, well we are looking at a born pugilist here! Even club mascot Lofty The Lion jumped in on the act at half time with the away support. Johnny Mac, scourge of the Black Country, got his name on the scoresheet again as the Whites cruised to a cushy and justified 3-0 victory.

If on-pitch events became predictable as Bolton went stratospheric, the activity away from the green stuff began to take on an ever increasing significance as our new ground rose at the side of the M61. Horwich looked as if the alien mothership had descended on it in a blaze of publicity. What the club had failed to mention was the fact that the good folk of Horwich were doing their best to prevent a landfill site the size of the Arizona crater appearing next to the ground. For the moment, the plans for a Super Tip next to our Super Stadium have been shelved. Furthermore the Wanderers became the subject of a reverse take-over from the blokes who brought you those Kung-Fu Turtle thingies.

Ever-increasing success for the runaway leaders brought its own problems, namely scant attention in the press who were concentrating on the teams struggling for the second spot in our wake, and the hordes of Johnny-come-lately supporters making every away match a mad scramble for the scant tickets on offer. Cheers must go out to Man City principally, as the tight-arsed scrotes at Maine Road deemed the Super-Whites fit for 2000 tickets only.

Our only blip came with an FA Cup defeat at the hands of the mighty Chesterfield courtesy of a Kevin Davies hat-trick. At least it allowed us to trot out that oldest of clichés about concentrating on the league!

April, and the league was sewn up convincingly. A home win over QPR ensured promotion in a 2-1 thriller, and a midweek tanking of Man City bagged the Championship. The Bolton crowd, many resplendent in their Borussia Dortmund tops, did their part by reminding the home fans that Gigg Lane was only a bus ride away for the once touted promotion contenders. Champagne supplies were now getting dangerously low in Bolton as we homed in on the magic double of 100 points and 100 goals.

And so to the last ever game at Burnden Park. Charlton Athletic's visit brought the part-timers crawling out of the woodwork in even greater numbers to witness a 4-1 victory and not one but two streakers invade the Burnden turf. After saying our farewells to the old lady only Tranmere remained. Prenton Park was bursting with Bolton fans as Jamie Pollock grabbed the magic 100th goal, but Lee Jones' injury time equaliser denied us the magic double. The Merseysiders, somewhat pathetically, treated the whole match as their FA Cup Final; you'd have thought they'd won the league given their reaction to drawing level. Sorry to disappoint you lads, but I don't think we'll ever come to Prenton Park again.

So that was how the Division 1 title was won. Actually we pissed it in the end with Barnsley lagging some 18 points behind in second spot. In retrospect we could have lost our final seven games and still gone up as Champions. But the accolades don't finish here; oh no! If you care to cast an eye on the goalscoring charts you'll see that John McGinlay and his strike partner Nathan Blake sit proudly atop that table as well. The Premiership beckons and this time we're ready!

WOT NO QUARTERS?

Bristol Rovers

When we left our heroes last season they had just failed to make the play-offs, another change of manager was in the offing and the club was in the process of moving its headquarters from portakabins in the grounds of a chocolate factory to a ritzy upmarket mansion house. Oh, and we were also leaving Bath City's Twerton Park after ten years to return to play in Bristol.

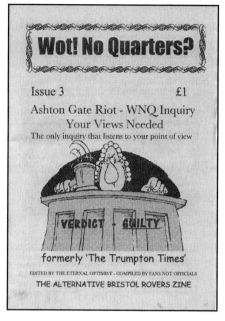

Meanwhile Aunty Doreen had joined the Jehovah's Witnesses as a direct reaction to the news that her daughter Mitzi had been convicted for prostitution, uncle Albert had just come out of hospital after an operation on his piles, the next door neighbours had moved into our living room after their house was petrol-bombed by the Hare Krishna Kamikaze Corps and sister Ellie was still insisting the family dog had been abducted by aliens even though father had admitted drowning it in the canal after another drunken binge. But back to the world of dreams...

With the close season events and off-field shenanigans proving far more interesting than anything that happened on the pitch it's been a fairly normal season for us.

We pick up our story where we left off, and the first news was that the directors had slung out manager John Ward, replacing him with former Rovers' favourite Ian Holloway. Olly's first action was to sack youth team coach Tony Gill only to reinstate him 24 hours later. You smooth talker, Mr Gill! Still, Olly got it right eventually when the following March, with a relegation battle staring us in the face, he sent both Gill and first team coach Terry Connor off in search of the nearest job-centre.

So, we had a new manager. Next, the directors announced they'd signed a lease with Bristol Rugby Club and we would be moving back to our home city to play at the Memorial Ground. "Oh no you're not!" shouted Bristol City Council. "Oh yes we are!" cried the board. "Oh no you're not!" yelled some of the residents. "OH YES WE ARE!" screamed the fans, especially those who lived near the ground.

Let battle commence!!

A couple of agitators whipped up local hysteria by spreading patently untrue tales about violence and no-go areas. It was enough for some residents to form a group calling itself RAGE with the object of preventing us returning to play in Bristol. The city council threatened to take out an injunction to prevent it too, until their own solicitor advised them that they didn't have a case. Thwarted in their attempt, they skulked off and plotted other ways to obstruct us. Huh! Just wait 'til our next trip to Wembley and you all come creeping round for tickets!

But we'd won and we were going back in Bristol! But wait, the city council hadn't finished with us yet: "You're not having a safety certificate for the Memorial Ground." So back it was to dear old Trumpton for the first home league game against Peterborough, where we were treated to the sight of sex-god Barry Fry topless sunbathing. It didn't put us off - we still won!

A safety certificate now issued, Saturday August 31st v Stockport County was to be the historic day when the Gas came home. Leaving nothing to chance, several Rovers supporters patrolled the Memorial Ground on the Friday night before the game, on 'RAGE watch'. Their vigilance was rewarded in the early hours when the leader of the protesters was apprehended attempting to clamber over the wall into the ground carrying several garden implements.

Saturday arrived; we'd made it! The pitch looked immaculate, and there were a few tears in the eyes of several Gasheads as the team made an emotional return to Bristol to play on a pitch about a mile from their old home at Eastville. A perfect day was spoiled a bit when Stockport grabbed a late equaliser, but what the hell!

At first the atmosphere in our new home was somewhat strange, as we only had access to two sides of the ground. A new stand was being built, giving rise to a new game: spot the workman, or (even more difficult), spot any work done since the last home game. I know Rome wasn't built in a day, but honestly, they could have built Rome, Paris and half of Milton Keynes in the time they took to build our new stand. Mind you, we can't complain about the catering, which is much improved. You can get just about the finest pasties on sale anywhere. If you visit the Memorial Ground, this culinary treat is a must! And if you can't eat it all, you can join in our latest game and throw the remains at the linesman.

Meanwhile on the pitch it was situation normal. Hoofed out of the Fizzy Pop Cup in the first round by Luton, we bettered this in the FA Cup by contriving to lose to Exeter. Oh well, at least we didn't lose to a non-league side this time. Add to this a defeat by Brentford in the "wash your windscreen for 50p guv" cup, a mid-table placing in the league and we were effectively out of all competitions before Xmas. Talking of Brentford, they did provide us with one highly amusing moment earlier in the season. Their goalie Kevin Dearden played as if he'd been at the Paul Merson nose-candy; his eccentric performance culminating in the award-winning *Sky TV* blooper of the year when he calmly placed the ball on the floor, walked away from it and stood and watched as Rovers midfielder Marcus Browning strolled up and plonked it into the net. Realising what he'd done, Dearden then tried to cover his mistake by galloping up to the ref and saying he heard a whistle. Oh, how we chortled!

But if that made everyone laugh, the local derby at Trashton was no joke. Those of us who'd heard the whispered rumours around the town of what was being planned by the neanderthal followers of City'82 decided it would be safer to watch it on *Sky*. And it proved a wise decision. Those that did go endured the frightening sight of the City'82 cavemen attacking not only the Rovers fans (we've got used to that - they do it EVERY time we go there), but also our players. Are there no depths to which they won't stoop? And all in full view of *Sky*'s cameras. Still, I suppose if you've got fans of the calibre of Baldrick (yes, Baldrick aka Tony Robinson is a shithead) swearing into the PA microphone at half time, what can you expect?

I'll tell you what you should expect - the League clamping down hard on City'82. Make no mistake, the trouble you saw on your screens had nothing whatever to do with Bristol Rovers or their supporters, unless you call scoring a last minute equaliser incitement to violence. It was City'82 followers alone who were responsible. So what did the Football League do? Heavy fine? No. Close the ground? No. Deduct points? Not exactly. They got a slapped botty and were told not to be naughty boys again, because if they were they *might* be docked two points. How about that for punishment then, Middlesbrough? Mind you, they were probably shown leniency because it was their centenary year. Hold on a minute, I thought a centenary meant you were 100 years old, not 15...

By the new year we'd gone two months without a win in any competition and we were starting to read newspapers upside down to make the league tables look better. Mid-February, and the new stand was ready at last! Rovers fans were invited to an open day to look around, and we all had a good laugh when we inspected the executive boxes and realised you couldn't see the pitch properly from inside. The poor loves who fork out £9,500 a season were going to have to join the rest of us oiks and brave the elements to watch the game!

But having fans on three sides of the ground helped the atmosphere, and it seemed to have an effect on the team too, as in the new stand's inaugural game we beat Luton 3-2. However, another clutch of poor results saw us back in danger of the drop before two events turned things around. First, we signed 'Madge' Allsop, the world's tallest centre-forward at 17ft 6ins, who won everything in the air (it's like having the Blackpool Tower on your side; no-one could out-jump him). Then came the aforementioned sacking of coaches Terry Connor and Tony Gill after - allegedly - the management team received complaints from parents about the pair using foul and abusive language at the trainees. Their places were taken by ex-Rovers players Phil Bater and Harold Jarman, and the first team showed their relief at getting shot of Connor and Gill by winning five of the next seven games to ensure survival.